P9-AOF-036

THE
MOVIE
MUSICAL
FROM
VITAPHONE
TO
42nd STREET

THE MOVIE MUSICAL FROM VITAPHONE TO 42nd STREET

As Reported in a Great Fan Magazine

EDITED BY
MILES KREUGER

DOVER PUBLICATIONS, INC., NEW YORK

THIS BOOK IS DEDICATED
TO MY BELOVED VIZSLA FRIEND SANDOR,
AND TO GRANDMA AND MOTHER.

Published in Canada by General Publishing Company, Ltd., 30 Lesmill Road, Don Mills, Toronto, Ontario.
Published in the United Kingdom by Constable and Company, Ltd., 10 Orange Street, London WC 2.

The Movie Musical from Vitaphone to "42nd Street" is a new work, first published by Dover Publications, Inc., in 1975, and is an anthology of selected articles and illustrations from PHOTOPLAY Magazine which appeared between 1926 and 1933. The selection, text and arrangement of this material are exclusively by Miles Kreuger and the editorial staff of Dover Publications, who are not connected in any way with the current publishers of PHOTOPLAY Magazine.
The Publisher would like to thank the Louisville Free Public Library for making available copies of some of the material reprinted in this edition.

International Standard Book Number: 0-486-23154-2
Library of Congress Catalog Card Number: 74-76739

Manufactured in the United States of America
Dover Publications, Inc.
180 Varick Street
New York, N.Y. 10014

FOREWORD

THE ERA OF TRANSITION from silents to talkies, and the subsequent birth of the screen musical, the only genre of motion pictures actually created by sound, have been chronicled in countless film histories. The subject is usually treated with the solemnity that such an important epoch in the development of an art form deserves. However, to audiences who lived through those days, it was not history, but rather a thrilling and adventurous and often heartbreaking day-to-day saga. Perhaps more exciting than any movie ever made about Hollywood were the actual events of this period.

It is this adventure that springs vividly to life in the volume you are holding, for this book is not history as re-created by scholars. It is a collection from the monthly issues of PHOTOPLAY magazine that were contemporary with the events discussed. All the latest news from Hollywood leaps from its pages with an immediacy and impudence that are characteristic of fan magazines at their best.

And PHOTOPLAY was, until the death in 1932 of its highly respected editor, James R. Quirk, the very finest periodical of its type. Unlike most of today's fan magazines, which have degenerated into sleazy rags with sensationalistic headlines, hideous cover and interior design, and language that seems to have been scrawled by illiterates, Quirk's PHOTOPLAY was a tasteful, soberly written, highly informative, and immensely attractive monthly.

Each issue featured exquisite full-page portraits of the stars, and virtually all motion pictures released in America (except for some "B" programmers) were reviewed, with lengthy cast and character listings provided as well. In a time when many outlying communities still lacked adequate radio communication, and newspapers had barely begun to publish news of Hollywood activities, PHOTOPLAY provided vivacious and copiously illustrated biographies of newcomers to the screen and fresh stories about established favorites. In addition, the magazine kept its readers up to date on all the latest production techniques. There were detailed articles about the introduction of talkies, wide film, and even an exposé of the method by which singers dubbed the voices for nonmusical stars, a practice that the studios tried vainly to keep secret. Full-page ads with interesting period design gave insight into the relative "pecking order" of players of the day.

When Hayward Cirker, president of Dover, invited me to prepare this book, I had no idea how satisfying the project would be. As a child in the late 1940's, I had read fan magazines that were, for the most part, little more than slickly packaged gossip columns, adorned with occasionally attractive color or black-and-white star portraits. Only *Screen Romances* (later retitled *Screen Stories*) held my interest, because it published (and continues to do so) complete synopses and cast lists of the latest pictures and therefore had some "redeeming social value." But no fan magazine I had ever seen prepared me for the happy discovery of Quirk's PHOTOPLAY, which proudly and accurately called itself "The National Guide to Motion Pictures."

This volume of excerpts deals with the development of one genre of motion pictures: the musical, as seen on the pages of PHOTOPLAY from the inception of Vitaphone through the moratorium years of 1931 and 1932, when production of musicals almost ceased, to the resurgence of the form with the release of *42nd Street* early in 1933.

Not only will this collection hold a nostalgic appeal for general readers, but it will also prove to be a valuable research tool for serious film scholars. For example, every musical released in the United States until *42nd Street* is reviewed with detailed cast and character information, with the single exception of Al Jolson's *Say It with Songs* (Warners, 1929), an obvious oversight. In addition, we have reprinted without exception all the full-page ads for musicals during this period and several for nonmusicals of particular interest to those doing research on musicals. Many biographies contain details that have escaped today's film histories, and of course the gossip tidbits of yesterday are often the film lore of today.

Many recent books of magazine reprints have been published, but this is the very first one to focus on one specific aspect of motion pictures. It has been a joy to prepare; and I am grateful to Mr. Cirker for enabling me to share this material with you, and to Dover's gifted editor, Stanley Appelbaum, who knew of my musical research and brought us together. My special thanks to film historians John Cocchi and Norman Miller, who helped with research, and to George Robinson for assistance in copy editing.

M. K.

CONTENTS

FROM THE BEGINNINGS THROUGH 1928

DESPITE A POPULAR MYTH to the contrary, *The Jazz Singer* (Warners, 1927) was neither the first talking picture nor the first feature to contain songs. In his earliest caveat on the motion picture, Thomas Alva Edison wrote in 1888 of his plan for "an instrument which does for the eye what the phonograph does for the ear, which is the recording and reproduction of things in motion. . . . This apparatus I call a Kinetoscope." He added that "by insertion of the listening tubes of the phonograph into the ear the illusion is complete and we may see and hear a whole opera as perfectly as if actually present although the actual performance may have taken place years before."

As early as 1894, Edison's Kinetograph camera recorded on film many performers then appearing in Broadway musicals. Although their routines were preserved without the benefit of sound recording, we may today marvel at brief songs and dances from *1492 Up to Date, The Passing Show, A Gaiety Girl, A Milk White Flag,* and other stage shows of the day. Quite properly, these excerpts may be regarded as the earliest movie versions of Broadway musicals.

These fifty-foot films, like all those shot by Edison's Kinetograph, were shown in Kinetoscope peepshow parlors all over the world. The first opened on April 14, 1894, in a modest storefront in downtown Manhattan. There were two rows of five peepshow machines each. A customer paid a cashier 25¢ and was permitted to view one row; for another quarter he could see the entire show.

Within a year, Edison equipped some of his Kinetoscopes with ear tubes to permit the customer to listen to an accompanying cylinder record. A machine so modified was known as a Kinetophone and must be regarded as the earliest form of talking picture.

Not long after projected films were introduced in 1895, inventors in various countries took out patents on systems for synchronizing projectors with cylinder or flat-disc records. The first great forum for talking pictures was the 1900 Paris Exposition Internationelle, where three different types of talking pictures were presented. In one theatre audiences could see and hear *Lolotte,* the first original, audible comedy written for the screen, directed by its author, Henri Joly. A French steamship company offered a second talkie program, while the most impressive presentation of all was an all-star bill featuring the immortal Sarah Bernhardt in the duel scene from *Hamlet,* Coquelin as Cyrano (a role he had created), the popular English comedian Little Tich, and excerpts from ballet and grand opera.

On November 21, 1904, Léon Gaumont, later a famed film producer, began a lengthy engagement of sound shorts with top music-hall artists as a regular feature of the variety program at the London Hippodrome. His Chronophone shorts featuring Harry Lauder, Vesta Tilley, and others preserve the talents of numerous turn-of-the-century artists at the height of their careers.

In the years preceding World War One, many other systems of sound-on-disc or cylinder were offered to the public, including a French system by the Pathé Frères, Oskar Messter's Kosmograph (1903, Germany), Cecil M. Hepworth's Vivaphone (1907, England), Jules Greenbaum's Synchroscope (1907, U.S.), Harold Jeapes' Cinephone (1908, England), and J. A. Whitman's Cameraphone (1908, U.S.).

Whitman's studio was located above the fashionable Daly's Theatre on Broadway, where the inventor had easy access to all the leading players in town. Just as Gaumont had captured on film and disc the great British and Continental stars, Whitman preserved the talents of Broadway favorites like Blanche Ring, Anna Held, Stella Mayhew, and the irrepressible Eva Tanguay, singing her famous "I Don't Care."

Inspired by the success of Whitman's Cameraphone, Edison decided to revive his Kinetophone, but newly redesigned for theatre projection. He continued to use cylinders to provide the sound, but instead of the small, conventional ones (four inches long and two inches in diameter) that he had used in the peepshow machines, his new records were a giant eight inches in length and 5½ inches in diameter. The increased size enabled the sound to be heard in a large auditorium in those days before electronic amplification. As in all disc and cylinder systems, the record player was located behind the screen. Most systems required two operators: one in the booth for the projector and another behind the screen with the record player; but Edison's Kinetophone was automatically synchronized by means of an arrangement of pulleys and shafts.

Because the sound and picture were not wedded on the same strip of film as they are today, retaining synchronization was a laborious and often exasperating task. A jump in the record or a splice on the film strip resulted in the hero's speaking with the heroine's voice or the remarkable phenomenon of performers able to sing with their mouths closed.

The development of modern sound-on-film dates to 1873 and the discovery by Willoughby Smith that an element called selenium was photoconductive. For the next two decades other inventors perfected the selenium cell and learned to transmit speech over a beam of light, using such a cell to receive the fluctuations.

Edmond Kuhn, an American, was the first to photograph sound onto standard motion-picture film in 1900, using an ordinary telephone receiver to pick up the music from a record. Others attempted to record and reproduce sound-on-film, but the father of today's techniques is Eugène Lauste, who, in 1904, devised a crude apparatus that demonstrated the practicality of his theories. Until World War One interrupted his work and left his funds depleted, Lauste continued to perfect both the variable-density and variable-area methods of photographing sound waves on what today is called a soundtrack. Lauste's patent of August 10, 1907, is regarded as the master patent in the field of film recording.

What Lauste lacked to make his methods fully practical was an electronic system to amplify his soundtracks loudly enough to fill a large theatre. It was the perfection of Dr. Lee De Forest's Audion tube that eventually made fully electronic playback possible.

By the late teens, several systems throughout the world were being developed to employ such electronic sound reproduction. In Germany, three inventors in 1919 patented the Tri-Ergon method of film recording. Professor Joseph T. Tykociner at the University of Illinois recorded sound-on-film in 1921, and the team of Theodore W. Case and Earl I. Sponable collaborated to develop the first widely exhibited sound-on-film system.

When Lee De Forest himself decided to concentrate on talking pictures in the early 1920's, he leased the Case-Sponable system and marketed it under his own name as the De Forest Phonofilm. This was a series of short subjects, usually shot with a single camera on one reel. They incorporated the talents of numerous operatic, vaudeville, theatre, and orchestral stars of the day: Sophie Tucker, Marie Rappold, Raymond Hitchcock, Lillian Roth, Harry Richman, George Jessel, Pat Rooney, Vincent Lopez, Eddie Cantor, Sissle and Blake, and many others.

The Phonofilm made its debut on April 15, 1923, at the Rivoli in a program featuring Pola Negri's first American picture, *Bella Donna.* As De Forest sent his only cameraman, Freeman H. Owens, around the country to wire theatres for sound, the Phonofilms became a popular part of silent movie programs, along with the indispensable organ concerts, silent shorts and newsreels, and live stage prologues. Legal entanglements and Case and Sponable's feeling that De Forest was not satisfactorily developing the Phonofilm beyond its novelty value led to the decline of this pioneering venture.

By the mid-1920's, hundreds of musical short subjects had been produced both in America and abroad by disc, cylinder, and sound-on-film methods. Yet only one feature-length movie had offered a song. This was D. W. Griffith's pretentious allegory *Dream Street,* which, as a standard silent film, had proved a swift failure when it opened on April 12, 1921.

A San Francisco inventor, Orlando E. Kellum, had organized a sound-on-disc system called Kellum Talking Pictures. Under the direction of Wendell McMahill, the Kellum process was to be showcased at New York's new cultural center, Town Hall, on May 1, 1921. McMahill decided to add a touch of prestige to his presentation of musical and dramatic short subjects by adding the magic name of D. W. Griffith to his program. Happily, Griffith proved quite willing to try an experiment to recoup some of the losses he had suffered by the disastrous reception of *Dream Street.* Because the film's star, Ralph Graves, portrays a singer, it was decided to have him perform a love song. This was recorded at the Kellum studios on April 27, just four days before the somewhat shortened "sound" version of *Dream Street* was to open. Except for this one song played on a record backstage, the entire accompaniment for *Dream Street* was performed by a live orchestra, a standard procedure for downtown engagements of silent films. Although the critical reception of the Kellum system was uniformly enthusiastic, the experiment lasted only two months, with only one other talkie engagement for *Dream Street,* in Brooklyn's Shubert-Crescent Theatre on May 29.

What Kellum Talking Pictures and the De Forest Phonofilm lacked was the professional polish, star appeal, and publicity ballyhoo that only the Hollywood dream factories could provide. However, for all the independent experimentation in talking pictures over the last quarter-century, the major studios had remained sternly aloof. Their investment was in the silent drama with its pantomimic acting, often performed by actors with little or no stage training. Production techniques, distribution, and theatre projection were geared to silents only. Shooting stages lacked soundproofing and were crammed next to each other with entirely different films being shot simultaneously under the same roof. Discussion about talking pictures was always greeted with disdainful cynicism and shrugged off as casually as a fly from the back of a horse.

Western Electric, which had purchased the rights to De Forest's Audion tube and had perfected it, had tried unsuccessfully for years to interest the studios in talkies. In 1925, Nathan Levinson of the company's West Coast division, showed Western Electric's new sound-on-disc system to Sam Warner, youngest of the Warner brothers.

The brothers had always felt that small-town audiences were being cheated of the live, opulent orchestral accompaniment provided by big-city movie palaces. The prerecording of an entire orchestral score seemed a perfect way to stabilize performance standards and also to focus attention to the studio's product. As an independent company with few theatres of its own in which to showcase its films, Warner Bros. decided that talking pictures might be just the attraction to excite the public and theatre managers as well.

A contract with Western Electric was signed; and on April 20, 1926, the Vitaphone Corporation was formed, with Warners holding 70% of the stock and an option on an additional 20%. In May, the studio leased Oscar Hammerstein's old Manhattan Opera House in New York and began, under the supervision of Sam Warner, to film the earliest Vitaphone shorts, many of which starred members of the Metropolitan Opera. To accompany the silent *Don Juan,* starring John Barrymore, a complete orchestral score was arranged by Major Edward Bowes, David Mendoza, and Dr. William Axt.

The historic debut of Vitaphone was a program comprising operatic, instrumental, and popular-music shorts and concluding after intermission with *Don Juan,* accompanied by the New York Philharmonic under the baton of Henry Hadley. The event took place at New York's Warners Theatre, on Friday evening, August 6, 1926, a turning point in motion-picture history.

Warners next "Vitaphoned" *The Better 'Ole,* a war comedy with Sydney Chaplin. The accompanying program of shorts included Al Jolson's debut in a program of his old favorites and George Jessel singing Irving Berlin's "At Peace with the World." As before, the public was wildly enthusiastic.

William Fox meanwhile had aligned himself with Theodore Case and had formed the Fox-Case Corporation to produce the sound-on-film Movietone, with Sponable its guiding technical genius. On January 5, 1927, Fox unveiled his new system at a press screening and announced a cross-licensing with Vitaphone to encourage the installation of Western Electric sound-on-disc and film equipment all over the country.

Throughout 1927, the public was treated to numerous Vitaphone and Movietone shorts, both dramatic and musical, on programs with silent feature films. The first Fox film with a completely orchestral score was *Sunrise,* which opened on September 23, 1927, at the Times Square Theatre. Music was added to *What Price Glory* and *Seventh Heaven,* two Fox hits already released as silents. The love song, "Diane," already popular, was heard on the soundtrack of *Seventh Heaven.*

Meanwhile, General Electric had developed its own sound-on-film system, which was acquired by RCA and named the Photophone. Paramount's popular aviation picture, *Wings,* which opened at the Criterion on August 12, 1927, was the first to use a variation of this system with the sound effects of motors whirring, propellers turning, and planes hurtling to the earth, all recorded on a separate film strip.

All these events were simply preludes to the debut of *The Jazz Singer,* which opened October 6, 1927, at the Warners Theatre. Although most of this sentimental tale of a search for identity by a cantor's son was silent (but synchronized with background music), the picture's galvanic star, Al Jolson, electrified audiences by belting out five showstopping popular tunes and also, for contrast, the Hebrew prayer "Kol Nidre." In addition, the film featured the celebrated cantor Josef Rosenblatt.

Delighted by the reception of *The Jazz Singer,* Warners swiftly began adding talking and singing sequences to many other silents already in production. On July 6, 1928, the first all-talkie feature, *Lights of New York,* was released and, despite its obvious banality as a cheap gangster story with a nightclub background, it proved still another hit for the audible screen.

On May 15, 1928, Paramount, MGM, and United Artists signed with Western Electric for the use of talkie equipment, with the other studios joining the parade soon after. Each followed Warners' pattern of producing a few part-talkies before attempting an all-dialogue picture.

Jolson's second part-talkie, *The Singing Fool,* gave sound films the greatest boost to date by becoming one of the top-grossing pictures of all times. Moreover, it proved that if the public was delighted to hear its movie stars speak, it would become hysterical with glee when those stars started to sing. At the same time, the studios were coming to the grim realization that many of their top silent stars were incapable of making the transition to talkies either because of thick foreign accents or inexperience at using the voice for dramatic expression.

The obvious solution was to turn to the theatre for a whole new roster of players. And thus began late in 1928 the start of a massive westward trek of hundreds of Broadway stars and unknowns alike, some of whom were to find permanent success in the movie Mecca.

January 29, 1973 MILES KREUGER

1926–1928

JUL. 1926

THE idea of talking pictures has come to life again. Warner Bros. have acquired the tenancy of the old Manhattan Opera House in New York City, and will remodel it as a studio for filming talking pictures. Warners have a new device called the Vitaphone, which is said to synchronize sound with action, and they will engage singers to take part in the making of pictures that will take the silence out of the silent drama. And so another old dream takes a new lease on life.

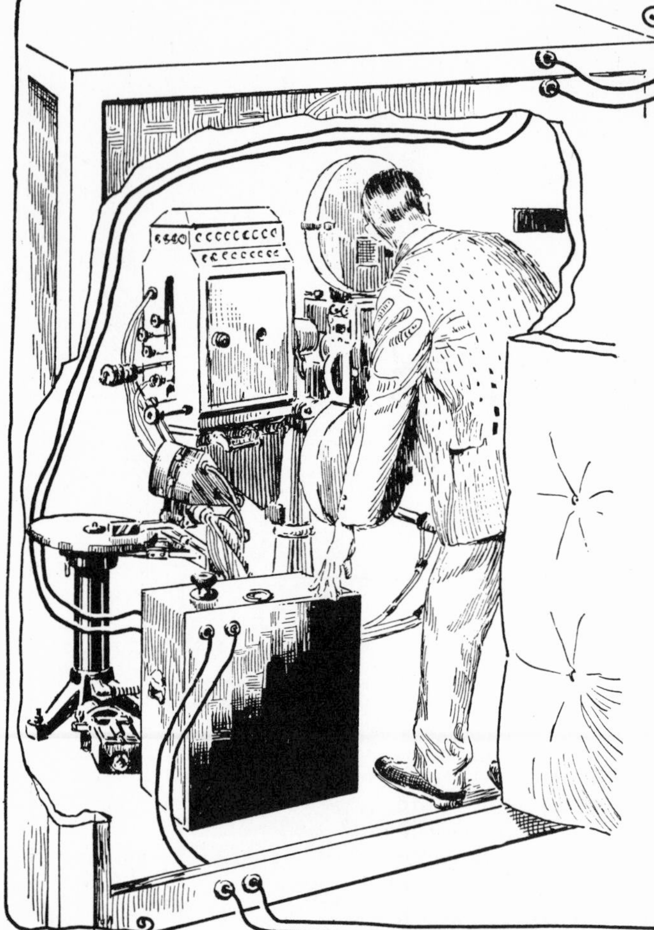

OCT.

Bringing Sound

THE presentation of the newly created Vitaphone in New York City has created a sensation in motion picture circles. The presentation was made by the Warner Brothers, in connection with the Western Electric Company and the Bell Telephone Laboratories, with the showing of the new John Barrymore picture, "Don Juan."

The Vitaphone is the newest application of sound to motion pictures. Since the beginning of films, various unsuccessful attempts have been made with so-called "talking pictures." The Vitaphone, however, is an unusual thing, miles ahead of the famous early Edison talking pictures. The invention has created a stir in the electric field, as well. Such an authority as Michael I. Pupin, Professor of Electro-Mechanics at Columbia and President of the American Institute of Electrical Engineers, says: "No closer approach to resurrection has ever been made by science."

Actually, the Vitaphone is not a new invention. It is a combination of old and new ideas, an application of telephone, phonograph and radio principles. The Vitaphone utilizes the system of producing photographic records with discs made in synchronization with the film. The discs are reproduced through a machine coupled to the motor which drives the projector. A high tension microphone transmits the sound into electric voltage through an amplifying reproducer and then retransmits it back into sound through loud speaking telephones and a loud speaker.

Former methods of "talking pictures" have generally consisted of photo-electric cells on the outer edge of the film, necessitating special projectors for theater presentation. The

OCT.

DON JUAN—Warner Bros.

HEY, Mr. Fairbanks, come home quick! John Barrymore is stealing your stuff. He climbs balconies, he rides horses, he fights duels and he makes hot, hot love. Here is a young feller who is determined to live down his dark past as a Shakespearean actor. And here is an actor who is more than just a star; for you cannot tell this reviewer that Barrymore didn't have an active hand in producing this film.

"Don Juan" is a lively burlesque of "The Great Lover" of legend. This boy is so mean with women that the girls won't let him alone. As soon as he sights a good girl, however, he reforms. You can't blame him; good girls were a novelty in Renaissance Italy. In the course of enacting the adventures of the wicked Spaniard, Barrymore gives us *Jekyll-and-Hyde, Don Q, Zorro, Hamlet* and *Beau Brummel.* His is such a boundless talent that he can afford to be profligate.

He acts with an abandon that will arouse the disapproval of the School of Eyebrow Lifters.

The whole production has a lavish beauty. Surely never were so many beautiful girls assembled in one cast. Estelle Taylor gives one of the great performances of the year as *Lucrezia Borgia.*

Montagu Love and Warner Oland are a couple of sinister heroes, while Mary Astor is the girl whose glance has the purifying effect.

Here is a picture that has great acting, thrilling melodrama and real beauty. Anyone taking a child to "Don Juan" is nothing but a silly.

With the Vitaphone, a real film event.

"DON JUAN"—WARNER BROTHERS.—From the poem by Lord Byron. Adapted to the screen by Bess Meredyth. Directed by Alan Crosland. Photography by Byron Haskins. The cast: *Don Juan*, John Barrymore; *Adriana Della Varnese*, Mary Astor; *Pedrillo*, Willard Louis; *Lucretia Borgia*, Estelle Taylor; *Rena, Adriana's maid*, Helene Costello; *Maia, Lucretia's maid*, Myrna Loy; *Beatrice*, Jane Winton; *Leandro*, John Roche; *Trusia*, June Marlowe; *Don Juan (5 years old)*, Yvonne Day; *Don Juan (10 years old)*, Phillipe de Lacy; *Hunchback*, John George; *Murdress of Jose*, Helene D'Algy; *Caesar Borgia*, Warner Oland; *Donati*, Montagu Love; *Duke Delle Varnese*, Josef Swickard; *Duke Margoni*, Lionel Brahm; *Imeria*, Phyllis Haver; *Marquis Rinaldo*, Nigel de Brulier; *Marquise Rinaldo*, Hedda Hopper.

to the Screen

Vitaphone is a separate mechanism, which may be attached to any projecting machine. In other words, the film is run off on one machine and the record on another. To assure synchronization they are coupled to the same motor. The speed of the motor is attuned by a vacuum tube regulator. Should the film break or the projection machine stop, the Vitaphone stops in accord with the projector.

At the New York premiere of the Vitaphone, films and records of the New York Philharmonic Orchestra, as well as of Martinelli, Elman, Zimbalist, Bauer, Anna Case and Marion Talley were presented with astonishing success. These reproductions have been worked out during the past few months by the Warner Brothers, together with Bell Telephone and Western Electric experts, at the old Vitagraph studios and in the Manhattan Opera House.

The method of making the Vitaphone records will be of much interest. In the case of Marion Talley a setting was built upon the stage of the Manhattan Opera House. Cameras were perched on stands built above the seats. A master camera, which controlled the sound registration apparatus for the making of the records, ground out the whole scene. The other cameras took the required close-ups.

Miss Talley sang just as if she were at a public performance. Microphones were placed at strategic points on the set, hidden from the cameras. These picked up Miss Talley's voice, together with the orchestral accompaniment. So sensitive is the registration apparatus for the making of the records that the master camera has to be enclosed in a sound-proof box to prevent its click from being recorded.

The registration apparatus gathers the sounds and transmits them into waves of electrical energy. A vacuum tube amplifier magnifies the fluctuations to a degree sufficient to operate a cutting machine. This machine, utilizing a needle, cuts its impressions into the wax disc.

It should be pointed out that the Vitaphone is not used in connection with "Don Juan," save to record the orchestral accompaniment. "Don Juan" is not a talking picture.

The executives of Warner Brothers, the Bell Telephone Company and the Western Electric Company believe that the Vitaphone will revolutionize the presentation of motion pictures. It will bring famous singers and orchestras to the smallest theaters. Exhibitors will be able to get an accompaniment to their feature pictures played by the most famous orchestras. The Vitaphone will not be sold to exhibitors. The Vitaphone mechanism, which can be attached to any projector, will be leased.

Perhaps, back in their minds, these experts believe that the Vitaphone eventually will make possible a genuine talking picture. However, no definite plans have been made along this line. So far they are confining their activities to an invention which bids fair to transform the exhibition of pictures.

OCT.

THE new Vitaphone was introduced to New York at the opening of "Don Juan" at the Warner Theater. If you have any prejudices against singing movies, Vitaphone will rob you of them. For this new process, which synchronizes music with the film, is a long jump from the old, hideous "talkies."

The program opened with the "Tannhaeuser" overture, played gloriously by the Philharmonic orchestra. It's a musical education for the novice, as close-ups of the various sections of the orchestra, judiciously cut into the film, give a casual idea of some of the intricacies of the Wagner orchestration. Certainly the closing section, with the brasses predominant, sounds immensely effective when you get a near view of the Big Boys in action.

OF the singers who have made Vitaphone records and posed for the films, Martinelli made the biggest hit. Martinelli sang the "Vesti la Giubba," from "Pagliacci," and proved that he is no mean pantomimist. Harold Bauer and Efrem Zimbalist, playing variations on Beethoven "Kreutzer Sonata," also made a hit. But the one frost of the evening was Marion Talley, the Kansas City canary. Miss Talley sang the "Caro Nome" from "Rigoletto" and her voice was far from attractive.

As for her face, the producers made the mistake of allowing the camera to come too close to Miss Talley. Long-shots—and good, long ones—were just invented for that girl.

MAMMY!

A GREAT, big, fervent moment in the Drama is transferred to the screen. Here you behold Al Jolson, piteously imploring the world in general to take him back down South to Georgia, Alabama or Virginny to the sunny cotton fields, the little old cabin or Mammy's knees. This moment is the climax of "The Jazz Singer," his first movie vehicle.

Preston Duncan

THIS photograph of May McAvoy is just one of the proofs of the beautiful manner in which the producers are treating Al Jolson. May, playing a ballet dancer, will lend perfect support to Al in "The Jazz Singer."

DEC. 1926

IN the second presentation of the Vitaphone stars, Al Jolson romped away with the honors of the evening at the Colony Theater. The funny part of Jolson's appearance was that, only a week before, he had been earnestly trying to convince a jury that he was a poor film subject. Several years ago, Griffith tried to anchor Jolson with a contract, but Jolson slipped away, claiming he had no camera possibilities.

But the Vitaphone proves that Jolson is, most decidedly, a film bet. Even with indifferent photography, the black-face comedian is very much there.

And when he sings—Mammy!

REINALD WERRENRATH made a little flop, which was a surprise to me. But the Vitaphone producers made the mistake of dressing up Reinald in an illustrated song costume and then having little birdies twitter in the background.

It was all wrong, *Gunga Din*.

GEORGE JESSEL made such a hit with his Vitaphone monologue that Warner Brothers have signed him up for another picture. He will appear in a film version of "The Jazz Singer," and the film will have several interpolated songs.

This is the first important break-away and it may mark the beginning of the end of silence in the silent drama.

The importance of the Vitaphone grows daily. Here is one branch of the movies that is really in its infancy. Famous Players-Lasky is acquiring the Vitaphone for its Public Theaters and I predict that it won't be long now before we are looking at entire musical comedies on the screen.

SEPT. 1928

LIGHTS OF NEW YORK—Warner Vitaphone

ANNOUNCED as the first all-talkie, this melodrama of Manhattan night life aroused a lot of attention from the New York critics. The Warners originally intended this to be a short talkie subject, then they got enthusiastic and enlarged it to seven feature reels. It's full of murder and attempted crime.

The cast, headed by Helene Costello, Wheeler Oakman, Cullen Landis and Gladys Brockwell, struggles hard with the pioneer problems of sound filming. None of the players emerge with particular glory. Sound films will have to work out a better technique to advance—and, of course, they will. This film, however, is a landmark of the sound movie.

"LIGHTS OF NEW YORK"—WARNERS.—From the story by Hugh Herbert and Murray Roth. Scenario by Hugh Herbert and Murray Roth. Directed by Bryan Foy. The cast: *Kitty Lewis*, Helene Costello; *Eddie Morgan*, Cullen Landis; *Molly Thompson*, Gladys Brockwell; *Mrs. Morgan*, Mary Carr; *Hawk Miller*, Wheeler Oakman; *Gene*, Eugene Pallette; *Detective Crosby*, Robert Elliott; *Sam*, Tom Dugan; *Collins*, Tom McGuire; *Tommy*, Guy D'Ennery; *Mr. Jackson*, Walter Percival; *Mr. Dickson*, Jere Delaney.

OCT. 1928

DOWN SOUTH—Warners

THE Three Brox Sisters, of vaudeville fame, make their Vitaphone bow under one big garden hat, humming harmonies from the South. Their opening number is "Back In Your Own Back Yard," which they render with several skillful variations. They follow with a crooner and a song called "Call Of The South." Low voices register most successfully on the Vitaphone, so the performance of the Brox Sisters, with their mezzo-soprano and contralto, is flawless.

NOV. 1927

WE are glad to report that Al Jolson has a splendid picture in "The Jazz Singer." One of our scouts who saw it at a secret preview given at a theater near Los Angeles reports that Jolson does some remarkable work in it, and that it ought to be a great box office attraction.

DEC. 1927

THE JAZZ SINGER—Warners

AL JOLSON with Vitaphone noises. Jolson is no movie actor. Without his Broadway reputation, he wouldn't rate as a minor player. The only interest in the picture is his six songs. The story is a fairly good tear-jerker about a Jewish boy who prefers jazz to the songs of his race. In the end, he returns to the fold and sings *Kol Nidre* on the Day of Atonement. It's the best scene in the film.

"JAZZ SINGER, THE"—WARNERS.—From the play by Samson Raphaelson. Scenario by Alfred A. Cohn. Directed by Alan Crosland. Photography by Hal Mohr. The cast: *Jakie Rabinowitz*, Al Jolson; *Mary Daly*, May McAvoy; *The Cantor*, Warner Oland; *Sara Rabinowitz*, Eugenie Besserer; *Moisha Yudelson*, Otto Lederer; *Jakie Rabinowitz (aged 13)*, Bobby Gordon; *Harry Lee*, Richard Tucker; *Levi*, Nat Carr; *Dillings*, Anders Randolf; *Buster Billings*, William Demarest; *Doctor*, Will Walling.

OCT. 1928

THE SINGING FOOL—Warners

"IF you have tears to shed, prepare to shed them now." Al Jolson surpasses himself. This is a better picture than "The Jazz Singer," and it is guaranteed to pull your heart strings when you *hear* Jolson singing "Sonny Boy."

"By occupation, a waiter; by desire, a song writer; by nature, a 'singing fool.'" That's the way he begins life, and his big inspiration is *Molly*, the beautiful girl who sings and dances at the Club Cliquot, where he is waiter and, for diversion, entertains the guests with songs of his own composition. A song goes over big, *Molly* marries him, "Sonny" is born, and success and happiness are his. *Molly* two-times him and he catapults to the bottom of the ladder faster than he went up.

Josephine Dunn plays the part of *Molly*, beautiful enough for any man to lose his heart over. Betty Bronson, as *Grace*, the cigarette girl, is perfect. But, the picture that lingers is of Jolson and Davey Lee, the three-year-old son. Don't miss it.

"SINGING FOOL, THE"—WARNERS.—From the story by Leslie Barrows. Scenario by Graham Baker. Directed by Lloyd Bacon. The cast: *Al Stone*, Al Jolson; *Grace*, Betty Bronson; *Molly Winton*, Josephine Dunn; *Blackie Joe*, Arthur Housman; *John Perry*, Reed Howes; *Sonny Boy*, Davey Lee; *Louis Marcus*, Edward Martindel; *Cafe Manager*, Robert Emmett Corrigan; *Maid*, Helen Lynch.

NOV. 1928

AL JOLSON secretly married Ruby Keeler, musical comedy dancer, in New York, September 21, and sailed the same day for Europe.

OCT.

It's a bear. And not just a plain bear, but an Australian species rare in this country. Fannie Brice caused a panic on the "My Man" set when she appeared with her new pet

MAY

Bessie Love is taking a vacation. She has gone on the stage. On the West Coast, Bessie played the leading rôle in "Burlesque," which gave her a chance to do some of her nifty hoofing. Also it gave audiences a glimpse of one of the best figures outside of an Art Museum

STORIES IN SONG—Warners OCT.

IN transferring from vaudeville to the Vitaphone the voice that made the waltz ballad "Alice Blue Gown" famous, Adele Rowland achieves a distinct triumph. Her rich contralto registers most effectively, due to the fact that sound films are gradually being perfected to allow the human voice complete naturalness. Also, she is one of the few Vitaphone performers who can be seen and heard with equal pleasure. She sings two charming crooners and a jazz epic in her first sketch for Warners.

TED DONER—Warners NOV.

THE smiling and affable Ted Doner, head man of countless musical shows, brings his debonair personality to the Vitaphone with success. Backed by what the varieties would call a "sparkling bevy of beautiful girls," Ted goes through some songs and dances.

THE SYNCO SYNCOPATORS—Warners NOV.

OTHER people are fast proving Paul Whiteman a great man by their increasing madness to imitate him. The jovial Dick Rich, he of the booming tenor, takes to the Vitaphone, carefully made up like Mr. Whiteman; he gives the famous Paul a couple of nonchalant digs and goes on his merry way.

NOV.

SHOW GIRL—First National

THIS is a "yes" and "no" picture. Like "Gentlemen Prefer Blondes," the production misses the piquant quality of the book. Stripped of its sharp humorous observation, the story is a melodrama of a night club dancer involved in a scandal for publicity. Alice White dances away with the honors in her first starring vehicle. If you haven't chuckled over the book, you'll scream with laughter over the picture.

"SHOW GIRL"—FIRST NATIONAL.—From the story by J. P. McEvoy. Directed by Alfred Santell. The cast: *Dixie Dugan*, Alice White; *Alverez Romano*, Donald Reed; *Denny*, Lee Moran; *Jimmy*, Charles Delaney; *Milton*, Richard Tucker; *Nita Dugan*, Gwen Lee; *Mr. Dugan*, James Finlayson; *Mrs. Dugan*, Kate Price; *Eppus*, Hugh Roman; *Kibbitzer*, Bernard Randall.

NOV.

A SPANISH SERENADE—Warners

XAVIER CUGAT, violinist, presents his gigolos in a musical sketch with a Spanish atmospheric setting. Constant improvement has advanced the Vitaphone to the stage where it can now record perfectly the intricacies and variations of Spanish music.

There are two general methods. The Vitaphone uses a disc. In the Movietone method sound is photographed on the film itself. Here you see a camera equipped for both. With the Vitaphone, sounds, picked up by microphones, are recorded on a disc of soft wax

How TALKIES

Do you want to know how sound is synchronized with film action? Here is a simple explanation of the best 1928 methods

You can thank any number of inventors for sound pictures. Into their creation has gone the best ideas of the screen, of radio, of the telephone and so on. For the simple presentation of the Vitaphone and Movietone methods shown on these pages, it has been necessary to eliminate many items. Many vital parts of the camera and projector are not shown and certain essentials of a sound film studio are omitted. But, if you look across these two pages, you will see, for the first time in condensed and easily understood style, exactly how the talkie comes to you

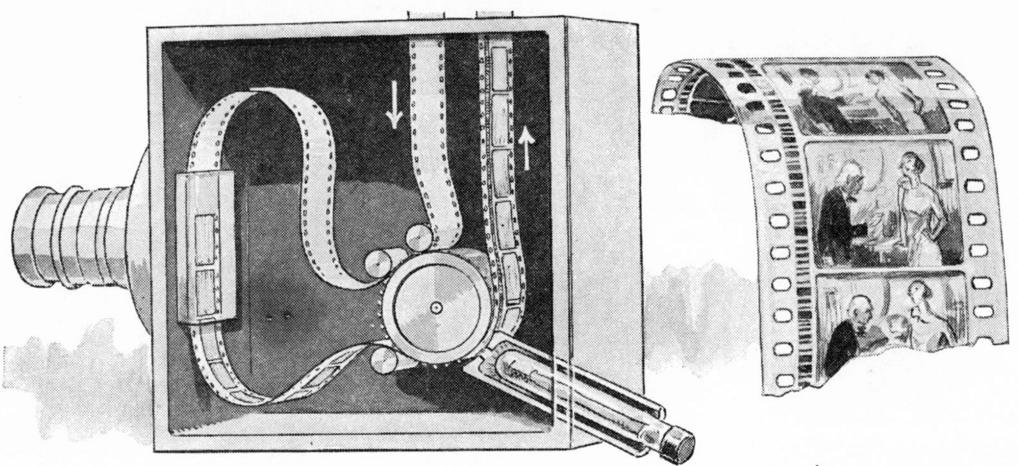

At the left you see a bit of Movietone film. The little margin just at the edge of the pictures is the sound track. Note that standard film is used for Movietone. When this film runs through the projection machine, shown directly below, the process is reversed. An ordinary projector is used, plus a sound reproducing unit

Above, a camera with the Movietone equipment simplified. The sounds are caught by microphones having the property of changing sound vibrations into electrical vibrations. These vibrations are amplified and, in turn, vary the intensity of the recording light. This recording light is contained in a glass tube inserted at the back of the camera in such a way that the variations in light fall directly upon a narrow strip of the negative film. This occurs at the exact moment the motion picture itself is being recorded. A light-tight barrier, not shown here, is between the narrow strip edge and the rest of the film

Are M*ade*

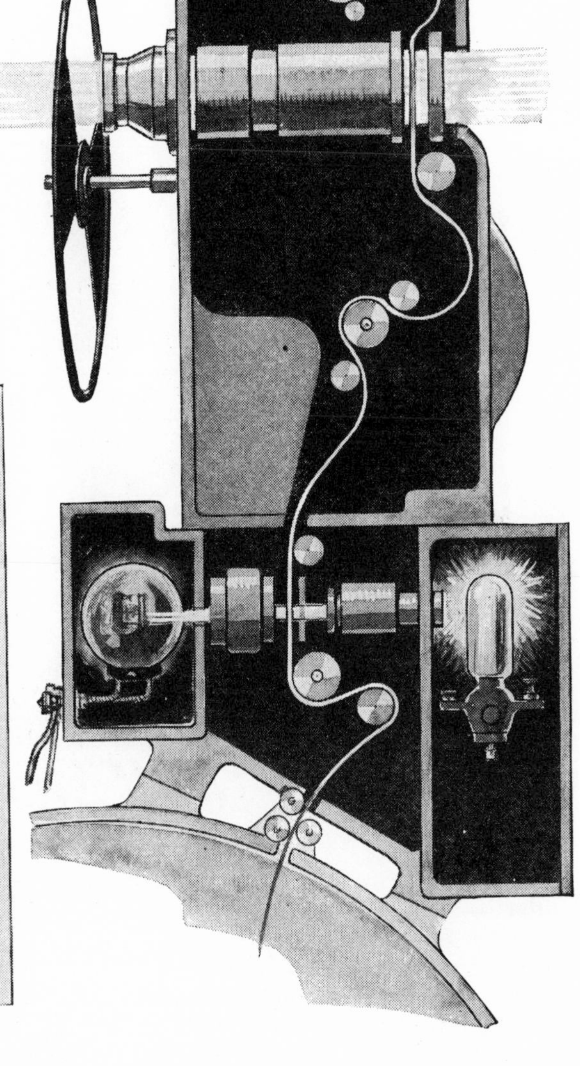

The Movietone sound reproducing unit, shown attached to projector at right above, has a light which is focused on the sound strip of film. This sound record passes before the rays, interrupting the constant light according to the photographed vibrations. The variations hit upon a photo-electric cell, are translated back into sound vibrations, amplified and carried to horns behind the screen. The projection booth, at left just above, is equipped for both Movietone and Vitaphone. Note the disc upon the Vitaphone turntable, operated by the same motor that runs the projector. Wires carry the sound vibrations from the disc to the loud speakers behind the screen. In either case the voices or sound effects are exactly synchronized with the action on the screen

HERE! HEAR!
the Modern Movie Miracle!
WILLIAM FOX presents
FOX
MOVIETONE

HEAR! and see the Orchestra play

HEAR! and see the Desert Sheik

HEAR! and see the Gondolier sing of Love

HEAR! and see the ORIENT

Best to HEAR!! Best to SEE!!

IT'S coming your way! Another Fox Masterpiece—FAZIL! A picture with an enthralling story dramatically narrated by Howard Hawks.

East loves West and West loves East..Greta Nissen and Charles Farrell. See these two daring lovers, who first find themselves through the song of a Venetian gondolier and then lose themselves in the maze of reckless romance. Follow them through the gay Western World—the mysterious East. See Her conquer over His harem. See Him undecided between breaking Her heart and breaking His laws! Then one of the greatest climaxes in moving picture history—the final scene beside a desert oasis—where Greta Nissen will make you forget Cleopatra!

FAZIL is indeed an amazing picture to see! And—it is also *an amazing picture to HEAR!* In FAZIL you will hear that astonishing movie miracle—FOX MOVIETONE. It puts SOUND into movies—realistic, true-to-life sound! In FAZIL you hear the gondolier sing his Venetian Song of Love. You hear the voices of the desert. You hear a full symphony orchestra, as though you were sitting in a great moving picture cathedral on Broadway. Fox Movietone doubles your movie fun. You won't believe your own ears! It's as true to your *ears* as it is to your *eyes*—because the SOUND, like the scene, is PHOTOGRAPHED. Watch for Fox Movietone in your town—See a Fox Movietone, you'll *hear* a great show!

FOX MOVIETONE-*The Sound and Sight Sensation*

1929

IN THE ENTIRE HISTORY OF MOTION PICTURES, there was never a year as exciting as 1929.

Although the industry had been forced to accept the coming of talkies in 1928, it was in 1929 that the full impact of sound was felt. Silent stars that were worshipped by the public at the year's outset found themselves out of work or even the objects of derision by Christmastime. Hordes of songwriters, conductors, arrangers, instrumentalists, dance bands, musical comedy stars and supporting players, dance directors, vocal coaches, vaudevillians, stage directors, prestigious playwrights, and anyone in fact associated with the speaking or singing stage descended on the film capital with a determination to immortalize his gifts on the silver screen.

MGM's first all-talkie, *The Broadway Melody,* which opened February 1, 1929, at Grauman's Chinese in Los Angeles, established the mood for the entire year. This was a brassy backstage fable of two sisters who arrive in New York, and, through the help of a songwriter friend, land chorus spots in a big Broadway revue. Their emotional and professional entanglements were so stereotypical that they became the prototypes for virtually every backstage musical made thereafter. But the combination of snappy quips, attractive songs by the team of Arthur Freed and Nacio Herb Brown, the insertion of a Technicolor production number ("The Wedding of the Painted Doll"), and the star appeal of Charles King (a Broadway favorite), beautiful Anita Page, and pert Bessie Love (both from silents) proved a magic combination. *The Broadway Melody* became the box-office hit of the year.

Technicolor arrived as an adjunct to sound, and four musicals *(On with the Show, Gold Diggers of Broadway, The Show of Shows, Sally)* were shot entirely in color, with over a dozen more containing color sequences. Unlike today's color film, which captures the full rainbow spectrum, this was two-color Technicolor and was largely incapable of capturing blue. Thus blue skies and oceans often had a characteristic greenish cast. Although this would seem like a limitation, early color when seen today often adds a charm and a fantasy quality particularly well suited to musicals.

As fast as the studios could retool to accommodate sound, they began to grind out one musical after another. Even dramatic pictures could not escape the insertion of one or two "theme songs" introduced either by a nightclub entertainer, by the dramatic star (often with a dubbed voice), or by an off-screen voice behind the opening or closing credits.

This was a year obsessed with musicals: light ones, farcical ones, operettas, tear-jerkers with songs, revues without a plot, all were fair game. As a reward for setting the trend that filled the coffers of the studios and helped to repay exhibitors for equipping their theatres with expensive sound equipment, *The Broadway Melody* was given the first best-picture Oscar ever awarded a talkie.

"All singing! All dancing! All talking!" screamed the marquees of the nation. Unfortunately, they screamed a bit too loudly. By the year's end, with numerous musicals already in production, the studios began to sense that the public had had enough. Overexposure had made them hypercritical. The uncertain singing voices of Janet Gaynor, Charles Farrell, and Buddy Rogers, for example, had seemed charming at first, but by the year's end the public demanded better-trained voices. The effect was not yet serious enough to cause havoc in the industry, but it began to cause concern.

M. K.

"Sounding" *a* Song

LOOK over these pictures revealing the inside of a sound film studio in action. They're the last you will see for some time. The producers have banned disclosures of the talkies.

Here you see "The Desert Song" in the making at the Warner Brothers Coast Studios, with the same scene from above and from behind the camera booth lines. The cameras are within glass windowed sound proof booths. They bear the numeral 2 in both pictures. Look close for the microphones hanging in lines and on stands just above and out of reach of the camera lens. Also behind the camera booths and fronting the orchestra. Thus you get the dialogue, the songs and the background music. A sound film set still is a pretty cramped place—but the talkies are in their infancy.

Incandescent lights are used for the talkies. Sound film photography still is handicapped by the fact that the cameras have to be out of sound range, so that the microphones do not pick up their whir.

JAN.

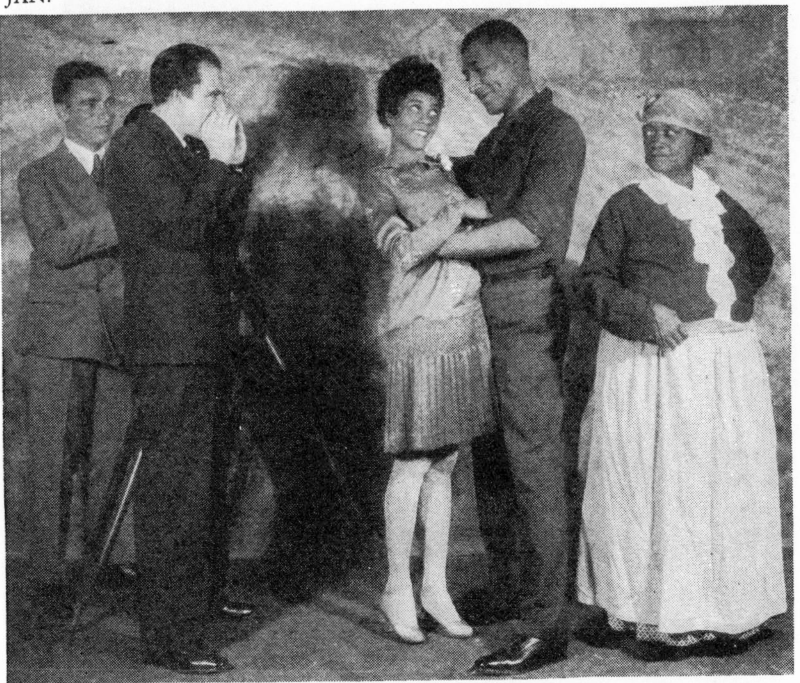

A brown study. King Vidor screen-testing some of the colored principals for "Hallelujah," his forthcoming Metro-Goldwyn-Mayer picture of American Negro life. The colored players are Honey Brown, of Harlem cabarets; Daniel Haynes of "Show Boat" and Mrs. Fannie Belle de Knight, a veteran colored actress. Vidor is the hand-cupper

FEB.

THERE is a very interesting rumor in Hollywood.

It seems that Warner Brothers wanted George Jessel to play the title rôle in "The Jazz Singer" but were unable to give him the money he demanded.

Al Jolson agreed to do it for a block of Warner stock. He was given the stock when it was selling at 20. Now it has gone up to 125 and Jolson, so "they" say, has made a neat little pile.

It will buy Ruby a couple of bracelets anyhow.

FEB.

Questions & Answers

M. A. H., Wilmington, Del.—Al Jolson has been married three times. His first wife, whom he married in 1906, was Henrietta Keller. They were divorced in 1919. In 1922, Mr. Jolson married Ethel Delmar and that marriage lasted until 1926, when they were divorced. Last September, Al married Ruby Keeler, the stage dancer.

FEB.

Director Richard Wallace is in a terrible jam. When the talkies came he threw away his megaphone and now his technicians are all locked up in a glass show case and can't hear a word he's saying. This is the filming of a scene for "The Shopworn Angel," new Paramount talking picture, and the leggy young lady getting a good horse laugh on poor Richard is Nancy Carroll, the leading woman

FEB.

THE SHOPWORN ANGEL—Paramount

WARTIME lovesong in ultra-modern jazz tempo. A blasé show girl plays inspiration to a dumb doughboy in a Jersey training camp. Nancy Carroll, as the merry magdalene, makes naughtiness so attractive that we're with her, right or wrong. Paul Lukas' suave sophistication and Gary Cooper's charming boyishness are effective foils for the scintillating Nancy. An unexpected and artistic ending saves this from the tawdriness of the usual city-girl, country-boy picture.

"SHOPWORN ANGEL, THE"—Paramount.—From the story by Dana Burnet. Adapted by Howard Estabrook and Albert Shelby LeVino. Directed by Richard Wallace. The cast: *Daisy Heath*, Nancy Carroll; *William Pettigrew*, Gary Cooper; *Bailey*, Paul Lukas.

MAR.

LUCKY BOY* —*Tiffany-Stahl

THIS is a direct but left-handed descendant of Jolson's "Jazz Singer." In it George Jessel plays the little singing boy who defies his sweet poppa and momma and becomes a mammy singer, winning fame, fortune and a pretty blonde in the last reel. It is a silent picture patched and vulcanized with sound and talk, and Jessel sings several songs, the theme number being a tear-oozer, "My Mother's Eyes."

"LUCKY BOY"—TIFFANY-STAHL.—From the story by Viola Brothers Shore. Directed by Norman Taurog and Charles C. Wilson. Photography by Harry Jackson and Frank Zukor. The cast: *Georgie Jessel*, George Jessel; *Momma Jessel*, Rosa Rosanova; *Poppa Jessel*, William K. Strauss; *Eleanor*, Margaret Quimby; *Mrs. Ellis*, Gwen Lee; *Mr. Ellis*, Richard Tucker; *Mr. Trent*, Gayne Whitman; *Becky*, Mary Doran.

FEB.

Rescued from vaudeville—Bessie Love. Bessie can dance, sing, talk and play the uke. Those who have seen her in "Broadway Melody" say that she is the Marilyn Miller of the talkies. Very nice for Bessie—and very nice for audiences

"Ole Man River—he don't plant 'taters, he don't plant cotton," but he sure do make a swell background for a movie. King Vidor, knee-deep in the yaller water, catches a beautiful and sinister view of the Mississippi for a scene in "Hallelujah." This is the picture that has an all-colored cast, plus sound effects of darky voices singing negro spirituals. All of which should make it something very much worth seeing and hearing

FEB.

THAT PARTY IN PERSON—Paramount

EDDIE CANTOR seems a real bet for the cinema. Indeed, he appears to be the only possible contender to Al Jolson anywhere on the horizon.

In "That Party in Person" he does a brisk turn, several nervous songs and gets neat assistance from a cute trick, one Bobbie Arnst.

Cantor is going to do more talkies, we hope. His style is exactly suited to the sound films.

"THAT PARTY IN PERSON"—PARAMOUNT.—The cast: Eddie Cantor, Bobbe Arnst.

MAR.

WOLF SONG—Paramount

MOUNTAINS and trees don't make a picture, even with sound effects, so "Wolf Song" won't keep the wolf away from Paramount's door. Gary Cooper, don't you ever, ever wear Davy Crockett clothes again! Trappers are good hunters but terrible tailors. And Lupe, you sing beautifully, but such placid and restrained acting! This time we'll blame the director, but don't do it again.

"WOLF SONG"—PARAMOUNT.—From the story by Harvey Fergusson. Adapted by John Farrow. Directed by Victor Fleming. The cast: *Sam Lash,* Gary Cooper; *Lola Salazar,* Lupe Velez; *Gullion,* Louis Wolheim; *Rube Thatcher,* Constantine Romanoff; *Don Solomon Salazar,* Michael Vavitch; *Duenna,* Ann Brody; *Ambrosia Guiterrez,* Russell Columbo; *Louisa,* Augustina Lopez; *Black Wolf,* George Rigas.

You don't know the HALF of him-

You always knew he was the screen's greatest fighting lover . . .
You always knew he was the greatest male star in pictures . . .
. . . . . . but YOU DON'T KNOW NOTHIN' YET.

Wait till you get ALL of him-

VITAPHONE

Makes the Greatest Male Screen Star TWICE as Great!

All these years the wealth of Richard Barthelmess' rich voice has been concealed. Now, VITAPHONE unearths this hidden treasure for you to enjoy. VITAPHONE brings you a Barthelmess so much greater it's like discovering a NEW STAR. A voice so sensationally fine he could have won stardom on it alone. You and millions of others have gone just to see him act. Now you can HEAR him TALK and play the piano.

You'll enjoy TWO GREAT STARS IN ONE when you see and HEAR

RICHARD BARTHELMESS

TALKING and PLAYING in

"WEARY RIVER"

An epic of a down-and-outer whose plaintive music reaches through prison's bars to find love and a new life a thousand miles away! Weary River reminds you of the story "The Noose"—it's every bit as big.

With Betty Compson.
A Frank Lloyd production.
Screen version by Bradley King.
Presented by Richard A. Rowland.

FIRST NATIONAL VITAPHONE PICTURES

Here's one to watch for—
CORINNE GRIFFITH in "THE DIVINE LADY"

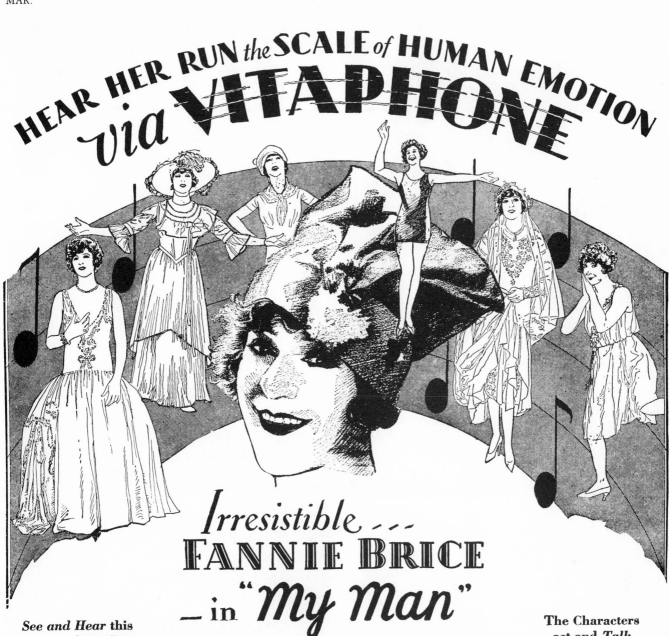

HEAR HER RUN the SCALE of HUMAN EMOTION via VITAPHONE

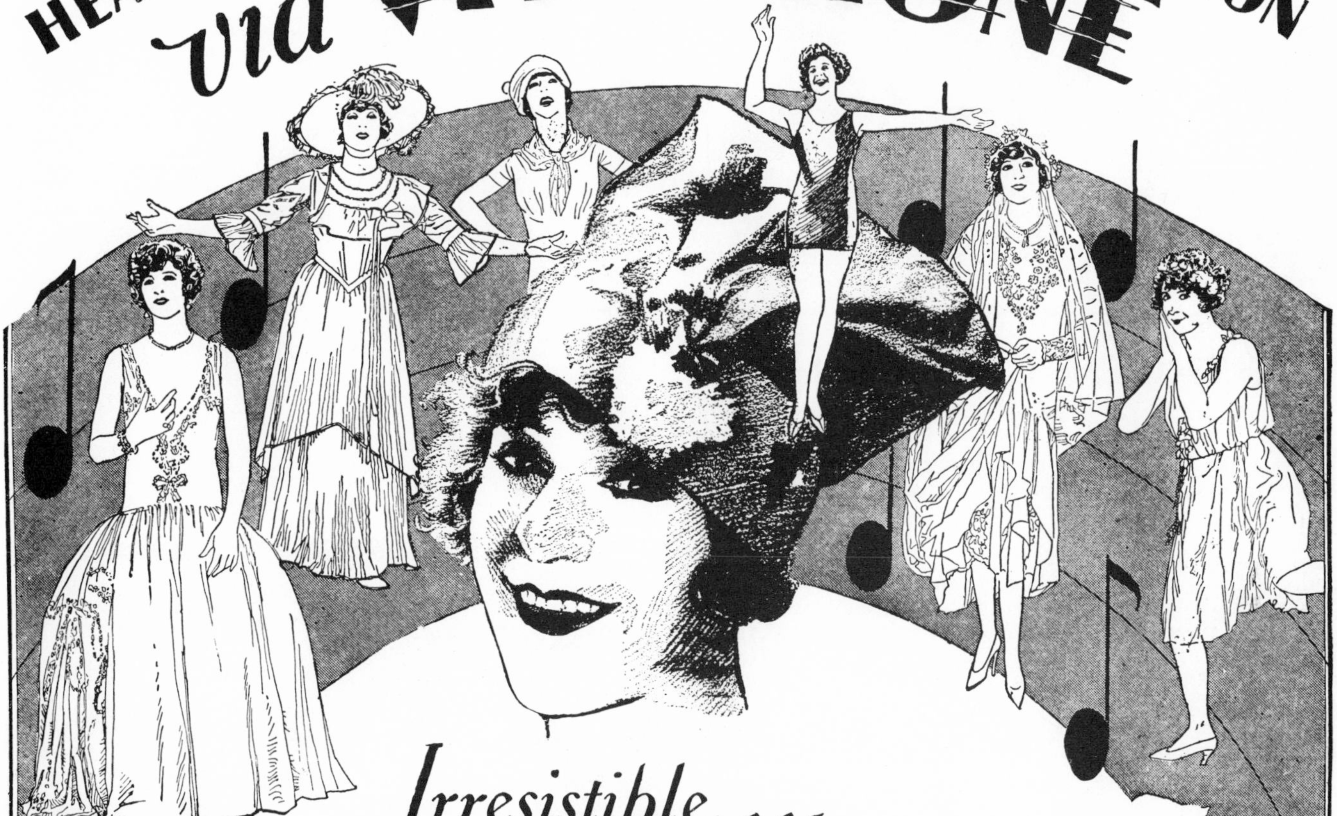

Irresistible . . .
FANNIE BRICE
— in "My Man"

See and Hear this charming Comedienne in her varying moods

Hear Fannie Brice sing "*My Man*"—"*I'd rather be Blue over You*"—"*I'm an Indian*"—"*Second-hand Rose*"—"*If you want the Rainbow, You must have the Rain*"—songs that run the entire scale of human emotion—that strike responsive chords in every heart.

"My Man" is a tense drama, full of tragedy and comedy. It will bring tears—laughter—love—to every audience.

Again Vitaphone makes history—brings to you America's premiere comedienne—*Fannie Brice in "My Man."*

See and hear this famous star sing the songs that have thrilled audiences the world over. You will be captivated with her inimitable humor. Moved by her tender pathos. Lifted to soul-stirring emotional climaxes, as she triumphs over lost love and gains the love of millions.

The world today acknowledges the leadership of Warner Brothers Vitaphone Talking Pictures. Vitaphone success has swept this country. It has aroused unprecedented demonstrations of approval in the capitals of Europe. It has enkindled a degree of public enthusiasm never even approached in any other form of entertainment. *Decide now* you will see and hear *Fannie Brice in "My Man."*

The Characters act and *Talk* like *living people*

"My Man" is a 100% Vitaphone Talking Picture — every character in the play *alive* with voice and action!

Remember—that Vitaphone is an exclusive product of Warner Bros.—that you can see and hear Vitaphone *only* in Warner Bros. and First National Pictures.

Make no mistake. Be sure it's either a Warner Bros. or a First National Picture — then you'll KNOW it's VITAPHONE.

IF THERE IS NOT A THEATRE IN YOUR COMMUNITY EQUIPPED AS YET TO SHOW "MY MAN" AS A TALKING PICTURE—BE SURE TO SEE IT AS A SILENT PICTURE

APR.

WEARY RIVER—First National

REMEMBER "The Prisoner's Song"? Remember how it was written in prison and how it swept the radio loud speakers of the land? Courtney Riley Cooper seems to have based his "Weary River" upon the incident. The brash young gangster of "Weary River" is sent to prison, reforms, writes a song, sings it over the radio and wins a pardon. His golden voice redeems his blonde lady love.

The chief interest of "Weary River" lies in the fact that Richard Barthelmess talks and sings the chief rôle. He really talks, but the vocalism is a neat piece of song doubling. Barthelmess does splendidly in his first talking appearance.

Betty Compson is the blonde who shares the gangster's joys and sorrows. A strong hit is contributed by William Holden as the prison warden.

"WEARY RIVER"—FIRST NATIONAL.—From the story by Courtney Ryley Cooper. Adapted by Bradley King. Directed by Frank Lloyd. The cast: *Jerry*, Richard Barthelmess; *Alice*, Betty Compson; *Warden*, Wm. Holden; *Spadoni*, Louis Natheaux; *Blackie*, George Stone; *Elevator Boy*, Raymond Turner; *Manager*, Gordon James.

MAR.

MY MAN—Warners

IF you have liked Fannie Brice in musical revues and in vaudeville, you will like her in her first Vitaphone film, "My Man." It isn't strong on story, just the yarn of a kindly East Side girl who mothers a wayward sister and a little brother and gets treated terribly by circumstances and relatives. In the end, she gets her man and becomes a Broadway star, but the real interest centers in Fannie's songs. She does her entire repertoire of favorites.

Miss Brice is not another Al Jolson. Her acting and personality—when she isn't making a paste song into a diamond—isn't very compelling. The real acting honors go to Edna Murphy. Miss Murphy is excellent as the selfish little sister. Guinn Williams is the awkward window demonstrator who is *my man*. This is a three-quarters talkie.

"MY MAN"—WARNERS.—From the story by Mary Canfield. Scenario by Robert Lord. Directed by Archie L. Mayo. Photography by Frank Kesson. The cast: *Fannie Brand*, Fannie Brice; *Joe Halsey*, Guinn Williams; *Edna Brand*, Edna Murphy; *Landau*, Andreas De Segurola; *Waldo*, Richard Tucker; *Thorne*, Arthur Hoyt; *Sammy*, Billy Seay; *Mrs. Schultz*, Ann Brody; *Forelady*, Clarissa Selwynne.

The South's Very Soul
Speaking to you from Down in Dixie
"HEARTS in DIXIE"
is the first authentic screen record of the Old South ever produced. It is a singing, dancing comedy with music — all the actors speaking their parts in a 100% Dialog Dramatization of Dixieland and its people.
200
native entertainers, including the famous Billbrew Chorus of 60 Voices, re-live the vivid romance of Ante-Bellum Days below the Mason and Dixon Line. All the happy-go-lucky joy of living, laughter and all-embracing gusto of plantation life has been re-created with thrilling realism . . . .
Forty negro spirituals are sung by a magnificent chorus—a plantation orchestra struts its stuff—folk songs are hummed by roustabouts and stevedores as the "Nellie Bly" pulls into the wharf. Cake-walks, folk dances—breathlessly beautiful, crowd the action of this greatest of all
FOX MOVIETONE productions
Watch for it at your favorite theatre
Presented by WILLIAM FOX
Story and Dialog by Walter Weems
PAUL SLOANE Production
OLD DIX-IE — LAND
HEAR THOSE HEARTS BEAT THE CADENCES OF THEIR RACE..
.. along the levees and in the cotton fields...strummin' banjos...chanting spirituals...where life is infused with an ageless melody — throbbing with emotion — epic in its simplicity.
MOVIETONE
More than Sound—Life itself!

APR.

THE BROADWAY MELODY—M.-G.-M.

"THE Broadway Melody" is going to sing merrily across the screens of the country, entertaining millions and making new friends for the talking pictures.

For "The Broadway Melody" is sparkling, smart and entertaining—a credit to its makers and a joy to the fans.

In it Bessie Love, as half a little sister team who loves and loses, gives the most astounding emotional performance in many months. In it the screen finds a first-rate singing actor in Charles King, from the musical comedy stage. And in it the blonde beauty of Anita Page blooms anew.

The picture is most notable, however, because in it the talkies find new speed and freedom.

The microphone and its twin camera poke themselves into backstage corners, into dressing rooms, into rich parties, and hotel bedrooms.

Smart Broadway dialogue by James Gleason is expertly and naturally spoken.

There is one colored sequence with a new song, "The Wedding of the Painted Doll," that will start you dancing.

The story is an odd twist of the love triangle—a little sister team from the vaudeville honky-tonks of the Middle West in love with the successful song and dance man of a great New York girl show.

The crafty directorial hand of Harry Beaumont has tickled, teased and whipped it into a fast, funny, sad little story, alive in turn with titters and tears.

Don't dare to miss "The Broadway Melody." It is Double A, triple-distilled picture entertainment.

Why, Bessie Love alone is worth the tariff at the wicket!

"BROADWAY MELODY, THE"—M.-G.-M.—From the story by Edmund Goulding. Continuity by Sarah Y. Mason. Directed by Harry Beaumont. The cast: *Queenie*, Anita Page; *Hank*, Bessie Love; *Eddie*, Charles King; *Uncle Bernie*, Jed Prouty; *Jock*, Kenneth Thomson; *Stage Manager*, Edward Dillon; *Blonde*, Mary Doran; *Zanfield*, Eddie Kane; *Babe Hatrick*, J. Emmett Beck; *Stew*, Marshall Ruth; *Turpe*, Drew Demarest.

APR.

THE PAGAN—M.-G.-M.

FOR the first time since "Where the Pavement Ends," his outstanding success, Ramon Novarro plays a native boy, a rôle to which he is eminently suited. He gives profound understanding and pagan grace to his characterization of a half-caste youth whose "only god is nature, and whose only law is love." Dorothy Janis, a new screen find, plays her first big rôle as Ramon's native sweetheart, combining the warmth of the tropics with irresistible appeal.

This tropical idyl establishes W. S. Van Dyke as an unusual artist and director. In "White Shadows" he shared honors with Robert Flaherty; here he stands alone. To him and to John Russell, the author, a coral reef is a halo and the South Seas are heaven.

The story unfolds the romance of two natives. If left alone, they would have mated as naturally as birds. Enter the white man, with his superior knowledge of good and evil. He tries to make the girl Christian, and cheats the trusting boy of his birthright. Back of this apparently simple tale lies the terrific tragedy of the South Seas. It is a tremendous indictment against the Anglo-Saxons, who arrogantly entered these magic islands to "save," and remained to betray and pollute. Under the delicate story surges the powerful undercurrent of Polynesian history, portrayed with heartfelt sympathy by the perfectly-chosen cast.

Both Renee Adoree and Donald Crisp are splendid—Renee as the generous-hearted French adventuress, and Crisp as the white trader whose greed and lust are a deadly menace to the lovers.

The entire production was made in Papeete, Tahiti.

"PAGAN, THE"—M.G.-M.—From the story by John Russell. Scenario by Dorothy Farnum. Directed by W. S. Van Dyke. Photography by Clyde De Vinna. The cast: *Henry Shoesmith, Jr.*, Ramon Novarro; *Madge*, Renee Adoree; *Tito*, Dorothy Janis; *Joranson*, Donald Crisp.

MAY

DOROTHY PARKER, the Broadway poet and wit, can always be counted on for a stinger.

Metro-Goldwyn imported her to Hollywood to write talkie dialogue. Mrs. Parker specializes in ultra-smart sophistication, with a rash of cynicism, so of course the studio gave her the old tear-squeezing melodrama, "Madame X," to play with. It would.

A day or two after her assignment Dotty met James Gleason.

"Got a swell idea, Jimmy," she said.

"So what?" answered the actor-writer.

"Going to jazz up the story, stick in a few hot numbers, and call it 'Mammy X'!"

MAY

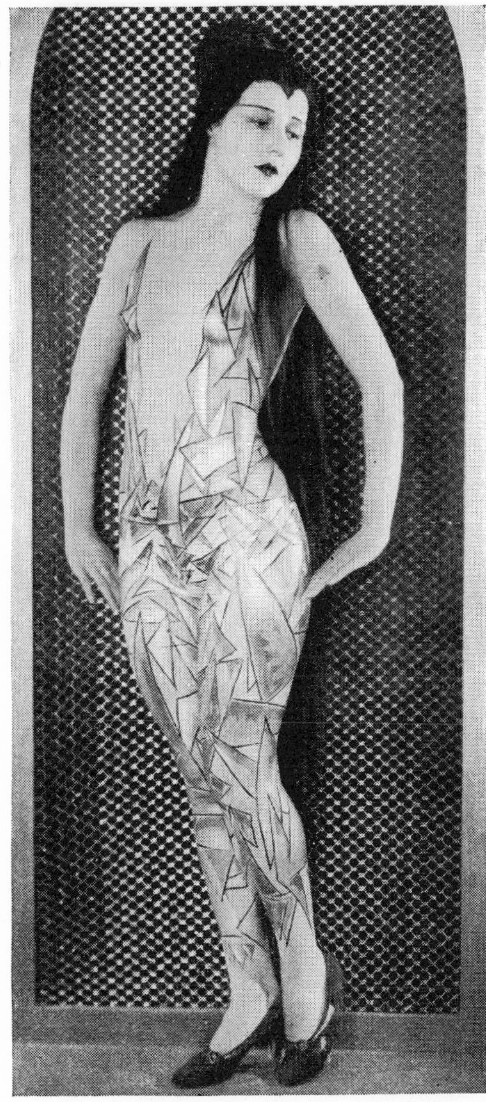

Join the Painters' Union and see the girls. Iris Ashton, one of the Fox Movietone Follies beauties, has merely slipped on a coat of paint and is ready for the camera. But Iris doesn't look very happy about it, somehow. Perhaps she is thinking of the fatal moment when she will have to scrub it off!

MAY

Sweet rest for the tired business man! The first picture of Nancy Carroll as *Bonnie* in the Paramount picture version of the brilliant drama of life backstage "Burlesque." This is the big chance of Nancy's fair young life. And when it comes to filling tights, La Carroll certainly has what it takes!

MAY

DARK work was done by Slickum, the colored bootblack at M.-G.-M., when he made a valiant effort to crash the dress circle at the opening of the Fox negro opus, "Hearts in Dixie," at the United Artists Theater in Los Angeles.

Slickum has just been elevated from bootblack to assistant director on King Vidor's colored folk classic, "Hallelujah," and he was anxious to see just how much better "Hallelujah" is going to be than "Hearts in Dixie." Also he wanted seven of his dusky friends to bear witness to this triumph.

Knowing that he might experience some difficulty in crashing into the orchestra section for the opening night, Slickum conceived the bright thought of asking for the tickets in King Vidor's name. He put through his phone call from the Vidor office and not until some time after the reservations were made was the ruse discovered. Naturally consternation reigned, for Slickum and his party of fellow darkies had been seated next to Cecil De Mille's elegant and aristocratic party.

The difficulty was met, however, by transferring Slickum's party to the balcony. Slickum was probably just as happy, for he appeared with a broad smile, his dusky friends, a tuxedo and a green fedora hat.

MAY

KING VIDOR is heaving a fine, rich sigh of relief, now that his all-Negro production, "Hallelujah," is finished.

Not that the colored boys and girls were hard to direct.

Two things, however, made Vidor gray over the ears.

One was getting them to work. The other was getting them on the set once they were in the studio.

In Memphis he signed two colored dancers. But when the company assembled at the depot they had faded, and couldn't be found.

At last King signed up "Slickum," the Metro-Goldwyn bootblack, to ride herd on the cast. Even this blew.

For "Slickum" was so cocked up with his new power that he made the younger players dance for every visitor that came near the set, with the result that they were too worn down to hoof for the camera!

MAY

HOLLYWOOD is going gaga thinking up titles for new theme songs.

Here's one waggishly suggested for Norma Shearer's new picture—

"Mary Dugan, you're a trial to me!"

BROADWAY'S DAZZLE
BROUGHT TO YOU
FOX MOVIETONE FOLLIES
Now through the Magic of
FOX MOVIETONE— Broadway's greatest song and dance entertainment, dazzling with beautiful girls, comes to the screen of your nearest theatre.
WILLIAM FOX presents
this gorgeous extravaganza with a conviction that you will await it each year with expectancy. No theatre anywhere can duplicate this unrivalled revue with a brilliant cast of 200 including:
LOIS MORAN, SUE CAROL, DAVID ROLLINS, SYLVIA FIELD, DAVID PERCY, SHARON LYNN, DOROTHY JORDAN, DIXIE LEE, TILLER GIRLS.
Music and Lyrics by Dave Stamper Con Conrad Sid Mitchell and Archie Gottler
Story by Harlan Thompson
Produced by Marcel Silver
Staged by Edward Royce

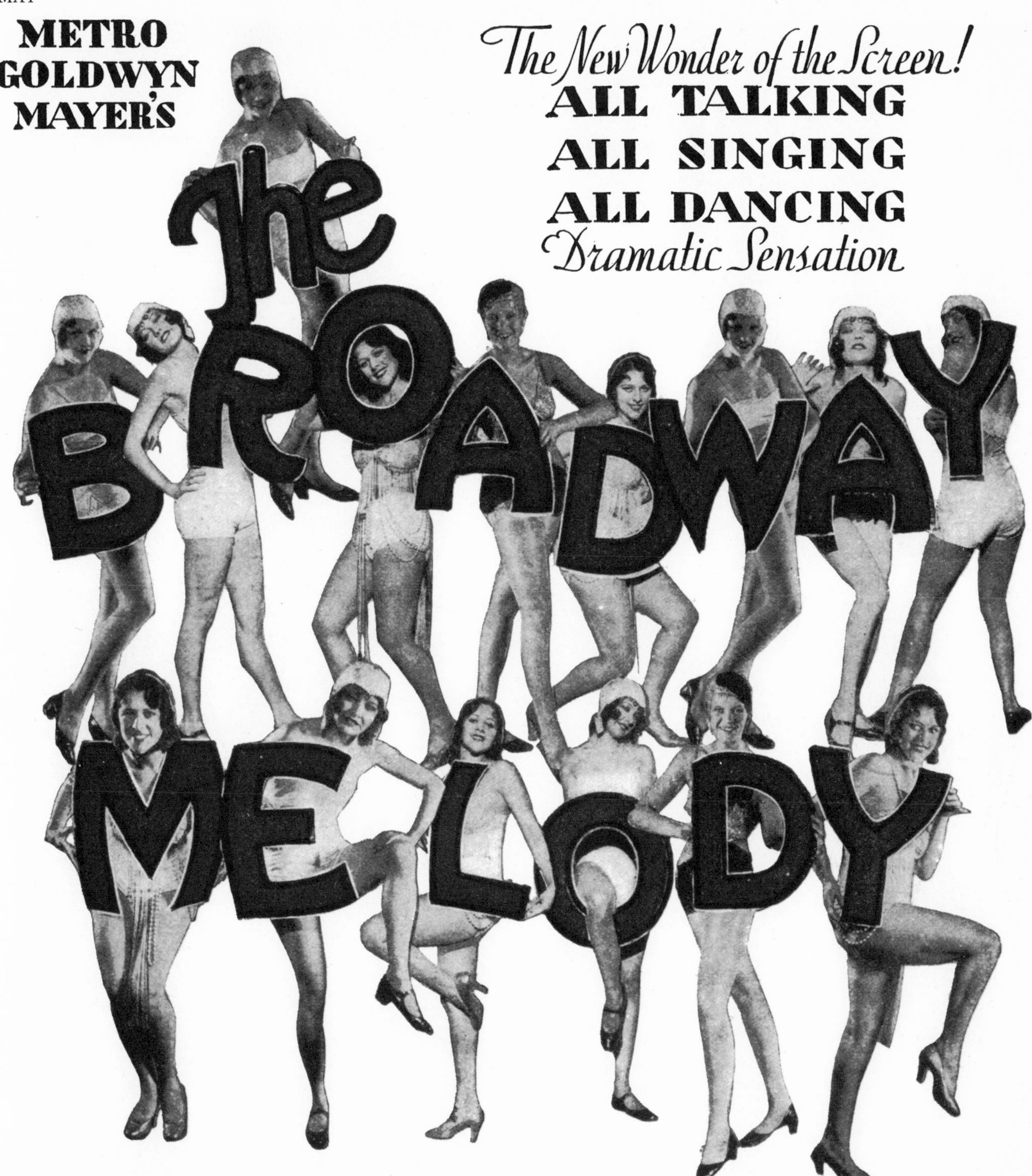
METRO GOLDWYN MAYER'S
The New Wonder of the Screen!
ALL TALKING
ALL SINGING
ALL DANCING
Dramatic Sensation
The BROADWAY MELODY

with
CHARLES KING
ANITA PAGE
BESSIE LOVE
Directed by
HARRY BEAUMONT

Story by Edmund Goulding
Continuity by Sarah Y. Mason
Music by Nacio Herb Brown
Lyrics by Arthur Freed
Dialogue by Norman Houston and James Gleason, author of "Is Zat So?"

FROM COAST TO COAST has swept the fame of the newest miracle of the films. All the magic of Broadway's stageland, stars, song hits, choruses of sensuous beauty, thrilling drama are woven into the Greatest Entertainment of our time. Metro-Goldwyn-Mayer, the leader in production of silent pictures, now achieves supremacy of the Talking Screen as well. See "The Broadway Melody" simultaneous with its sensational $2 showings in New York, Los Angeles and elsewhere.

METRO-GOLDWYN-MA

THE METRO GOLDWYN MAYER LION
THE GREATEST STAR ON THE SCREEN

"More Stars than there are in Heaven"

Louise

WHEN you see "The Broadway Melody," the new film hit, you will be amazed at little Bessie Love's performance. Bessie talks, sings and dances perfectly. Back of this hit, which has captured a fine contract for Miss Love, lay years of inferior rôles. The silent screen never did right by our Bessie. It passed her by—but the talkies have brought her back with a crash

Bessie Love, otherwise Juanita Horton, at the ripe age of five. Bessie came to Hollywood from Texas. Her parents were pioneer folk—and Bessie knows all the old songs of the range

The GIRL who Walked Back

They shoved Bessie out of the Old Star Buggy—but, all the same, D. W. was right when he named her Love

By Herbert Howe

ALL Hollywood clapped hands the other night. Bessie Love came back.

Shakespeare asked, "What's in a name?" The answer in the case of Love is—love. When Hollywood unanimously says, "I'm glad" over anyone's success, without adding, "But of course—" you may be sure that that one is closely related to God. In fact, the only names I can think of that are above invidious cavil are the Lord's and Bessie's.

IT was in the Black Cat in Greenwich Village that I first met Bessie Love, when I was very young, many years ago. Bessie looked as young as she does today and so, for all I know, was an old lady then.

There's Magic on her. Father Time nicks all of us as he makes his rounds, but when he tries to touch Bessie some one gives him a gallant kick in the knickers.

Every now and then old souls are born into the world who for recompense are given eternally young faces. So I was told when a child by a toothless aunt who nearly got hung for witchcraft. Are you getting creepy?—just hold onto my hand and follow me; I feel a bit sh-shaky myself. Let's get back to the Black Cat. . . .

AN angel face shining mistily in the tobacco smoke of the cabaret, Bessie thrummed her uke and sang "Willie the Weeper," in a thin nasal voice.

The effect was evangelical. At the table next a cargoed lady, so powdered and warm she resembled a melting marshmallow, beamed over at Bessie and tried to stop hiccupping, even going so far as to drink water. A whoopee lad lurched to his feet in a sudden miracle of mind over matter and made an almost straight line to Bessie's table to present a bunch of violets.

It was Bessie's first trip to New York and her first moonflowering into night life, yet she sang as sweetly unconcerned as on the home beach at Santa Monica.

Beside her sat her mother, a woman with pale gaunt face and the burning eyes of the mystic, about her that strange remoteness of one who lives in spirit more than flesh. Speaking of her daughter she uses the full name, Bessie Love, a curious detachment, yet between them there's an affinity beyond the mother-daughter bond. Though Mrs. Love has never been a managing mother, I'm convinced that through her there's a mystic power over Bessie, giving her the quaint, the unearthly *spirituelle* of a Peter Pan.

WHEN I first went to California I made an almost straight line to the bungalow of Love in Laurel Canyon. I was received with that Oh-Gee-Look-Who's-Here glee that friends of Bessie know full well.

That night Bessie gave one of her famous wiener roasts on the beach of Santa Monica. After a swim in the moon warm sea we sat around the fire listening to Bessie as with her solemn, far-seeing eyes she

(continued on next page)

Bessie in the old Triangle Fine Arts days of twelve years ago. Despite the glamorous predictions of Griffith, little Bessie slipped to minor pictures, because Hollywood said she had no IT. She was Cute, but Unawakened

(continued from preceding page)

chanted her songs in a small haunting voice.

Bessie then was a Vitagraph star. D. W. Griffith had discovered her, as ginghamed and pigtailed she played extra during school vacation.

They tell how the Master summoned her, saying, "What's your name, little girl?"

"Juanita Horton," piped Little Girl.

"From henceforth you are Bessie Love," intoned the Master—and a few months later, "Bessie Love you are going farther than any of my stars."

Maybe that prediction held back the tear when many times it tried to shove ahead of the smile.

BESSIE'S eyes were so big there wasn't much room for her face, and it looked cheated. She played starved orphans in a way to attract Near East Relief. But before the Armenians could sue for infringement of patent, Bessie would turn around and play the betrayed mother.

The land was washed with tears for her and strong men wept like babes; indeed, it looked for a time as though she'd make Willie the Weeper the national anthem. Then suddenly she turned to comedy, there were rainbows o'er our shoulders, and Bessie Love was discovered all over again.

B*UT she had no sex appeal*—so producers said ominously, and to say that was to breathe damnation, for Madame Glyn had made IT as sacred in Hollywood as the dollar sign.

Bessie was thin and big-eyed and without taste for clothes. A fine actress, they agreed, but no IT.

Cute, but Unawakened.

In all the world there never was such wisdom as lodges in the turrets of Hollywood film producers.

Thus little Bessie who had started early and travelled far was shoved out of her starry vehicle and told to walk back.

"Oh Gee," I can hear her say as she stood forlorn in the road. She didn't weep. Willie could do that. She picked up her uke and started back through the road that is called Poverty Row.

As she walked she sang and her toes took to wriggling. Somewhere *en route* she saw the Charleston, and when at length she emerged into the brighter kleigs of Hollywood, where she was half-forgotten, it was no longer the starved orphan but the flexuous cup-taking Charleston dancer.

The big eyes sparkled as before but the tiny feet twinkled and Bessie's legs were discovered to be the sightliest and sprightliest in all our great leg land.

Her glorious past was forgotten, the actress was no more; directors only gave her dancing parts, sometimes bits. Socially she was in a leading rôle.

She was the life of the party. At Mable Normand's I heard Pola Negri beseeching her for Charleston lessons.

At another party I heard a sobering gent ask her what she drank to give her such a lasting kick.

"I take mine straight," laughed Bessie, pointing at a White Rock bottle.

If licker is nourishment she's still the starved child.

She has never taken a drink, never smoked a cigarette nor even endorsed one, but if you go to her home you are given your favorite brand.

IN New York last summer I heard that Bessie had slipped away into vaudeville. The old eyes dimmed; I felt like Willie as I recalled the child whom I thought the greatest of all our young actresses: her death scene in "Human Wreckage," devoid of theatric agony and like a foretaste of eternal beauty, a passing into the ultimate dream; her genius in scenes of "The Eternal Three" and in tawdry pictures which held nothing else.

Returning to Hollywood I stopped at the Roosevelt Hotel. As I passed down the corridor to my room I heard a woman's oath. I stopped dead still.

Only one woman in Hollywood uses that oath: "Oh Gee!" I rapped on the door and Bessie opened.

After the gaiety of greeting, and only under question, she told me reluctantly of her vaudeville tour.

It hadn't delighted her, though of course everyone was marvelous—they always are, according to Bessie.

Now she was going to New York, she said, to try musical comedy.

As a farewell to Hollywood she was doing one picture, a talkie.

It would be sort of nice, she thought, to have a picture released while she was in New York, so that people wouldn't think she wasn't wanted any more.

TWO months later "The Broadway Melody" came to Graumann's Chinese theater, and *Hank* was made immortal because *Hank* is Bessie. Heaven itself was apprized by searchlights that dusted Mars. All the stars of the local firmament arrived in diamonds that dimmed the searchlights and ermine that queens once could afford. They were filmed and radioed throughout the world. Carmel Myers, school girl chum of Bessie, stepped to the microphone and said, "I'm grateful for this night because Bessie Love is triumphing, and, if ever anyone deserved success, Bessie Love does."

Carmel said what all Hollywood felt as that night the Love of our town was given our greatest hand. And every night since there has been a hush—then a storm of applause for that great scene in which *Hank* sobs alone in her dressing room.

I REPEAT what I wrote two years ago in PHOTOPLAY: "There's no finer actress or sweeter character on the screen than Bessie Love."

D. W. was inspired when he named her Love.

MAY

Talking Pictures have to do the craziest things! Here's a sound-proof camera booth raised on stilts to get smart camera angles for "The Cocoanuts," the Marx Brothers talkie being filmed at the Paramount eastern studio. If anyone says this dialogue will sound stilted he will get a hand-grenade, C. O. D., by the next mail

MAY

CLOSE HARMONY—Paramount

THIS vaudeville backstage hit is the last word in talking pictures. First, Buddy Rogers encounters the "mike" with the most pleasing results. He has a gorgeous speaking voice. His poise and facility prove his phenomenal success due to honest ability, not lucky breaks. Also, it's Nancy Carroll's first all-talkie. Her voice is clear and resonant—her songs the latest from Ziegfeld's. Likewise Skeets Gallagher and Jack Oakie, a comedy team that'll panic the world. Harry Green is a knockout as the harassed producer.

There's no attempt at epic. A sophisticated chorine helps a shy but clever boy sell his act to Broadway. To this modern story and the cast's excellent work is brought brilliant handling and faultless synchronization.

"CLOSE HARMONY"—PARAMOUNT.—From the story by Elsie Janis and Gene Markey. Screen Play by Percy Heath. Directed by John Cromwell and Eddie Sutherland. The cast: *Al West,* Charles Rogers; *Marjorie Merwin,* Nancy Carroll; *Ben Barney,* Jack Oakie; *Johnny Bay,* Richard "Skeets" Gallagher; *Max Mindil,* Harry Green.

MAY

Bull

This is Joyce Murray, the adorable mite who led the beautiful "Wedding of the Painted Doll" number in that great talkie, "The Broadway Melody." "Always on her toes, this baby!" say her studio bosses

Recall "The Wedding of the Painted Doll" in "The Broadway Melody"? Then you remember Joyce Murray, who is the new type of talkie extra girl. She can do all sorts of acrobatic dances—and do them well

AUG.

MAY

A STUNNING view of the enormous night club set used by Director Paul Fejos in making the Universal film version of the famous play, "Broadway." Fejos, megaphone in hand, is perched on the summit of the camera crane, built especially for this picture at a cost of $75,000. It is capable of every possible motion, and can travel 600 feet a minute on a horizontal plane. Three hundred extras and a chorus of 30 were on this mighty set at one time. It is 70 feet high, and a city block wide and deep. The night club sequences are being filmed in natural color. Glenn Tryon is starred, and Evelyn Brent and Merna Kennedy are featured. Uncle Carl Laemmle's $1,000,000 beauty!

MAY

★ ***HEARTS IN DIXIE—Fox***

AT the risk of giving that colored boy, who glories in the classic monicker of Stepin Fetchit, a bigger opinion of himself than he now possesses—if possible, we are going to say that you ought to see that boy throw his flat feet around in "Hearts in Dixie," Fox's all-negro picture. This is the lad who has usurped the leadership of colored society in cinema circles. He stands outside the theaters in Hollywood and when one of his race goes by he points to himself on the posters and yells: "Look ahere, big boy, that's me!"

This is the first really all-colored cast (we were going to say "all-colored picture") and it gives you on the screen a grand exposition of plantation life with its joys and sorrows, its ignorance, its superstition and religious frenzy. It's all very real and understandable.

"HEARTS IN DIXIE"—Fox.—From the story by Walter Weems. Directed by Paul Sloane. Photography by Glen McWilliams. The cast: *Nappus*, Clarence Muse; *Chinquapin*, Eugene Jackson; *Gummy*, Stepin Fetchit; *Chloe*, Bernice Pilot; *Rammey*, Clifford Ingram; *Trailia*, Mildred Washington; *Deacon*, Zach Williams; *Emmy*, Gertrude Howard; *Melia*, Dorothy Morrison; *Violet*, Vivian Smith; *Hoodoo Woman*, A. C. H. Billbrew; *White Doctor*, Richard Carlysle.

JUL.

Glenn Tryon is showing Merna Kennedy one of those gay night clubs. The little toy is a model of the big night club set used in "Broadway." The set is all wired for electricity, it has miniature chairs and tables and, probably, miniature prohibition agents

JUN.

This dear little schoolgirl, with the big bow and the pink sash, is our Bessie Love, made up for her rôle in one of the skits in the forthcoming M.-G.-M. "Revue of Revues." What can be wrong with the gay blades of Hollywood? Not a single one has turned up to carry her books home from class!

FEB.

International Newsreel

The snooping camera platform—it looks right into your windows. This monster was invented by Dr. Paul Fejos to catch difficult scenes at every possible angle. It can go 600 feet a minute horizontally and 400 feet a minute vertically

JUN.

All handshakers, but not quite able to make it. The Marx Brothers, four of Broadway's favorite clowns, make their talkie debut soon in Paramount's "The Cocoanuts." Their names? Oh, Zeppo, Groucho, Chico and Harpo, if you really care

JUN.

QUEEN OF THE NIGHT CLUBS—Warners

WARNER BROTHERS made this to exploit Texas Guinan, the big blonde who is the self-elected and publicity-made head girl of New York's night club life. A trite story of skullduggery in cabaret land gives her a chance to lead the silly revels with her bass voice, and to give all the little girls big and audible hands. Tex does what she has to do, but three stunning performances are turned in, in this all talkie, by Eddie Foy, Jr., Jack Norworth and Lila Lee. A stirring comeback for Lila. A film as phoney as the life it portrays.

"QUEEN OF THE NIGHT CLUBS"—WARNERS.—From the story by Murray Roth and Addison Burkhart. Adapted by Murray Roth and Addison Burkhart. Directed by Bryan Foy. The cast: *Tex Malone,* Texas Guinan; *Don Holland,* John Davidson; *Bee Walters,* Lila Lee; *Andy Quinland,* Arthur Housman; *Eddie Parr,* Eddie Foy, Jr.; *Phil Parr,* Jack Northworth; *Gigola,* George Raft; *Nick,* Jimmie Phillips; *Asst. District Attorney,* William Davidson; *Lawyer Grant,* John Miljan; *Crandall,* Lee Shumway.

JUN.

Herb Howe wants to know who's talking for who in Hollywood. Feats of daring have been performed for the $5,000-a-week star by extras getting ten bucks. Acting has been supplied by directors, wit by sub-title writers and beauty by make-up experts. Now the robust baritones and glowing tenors belong to others

Illustration by
Ken Chamberlain

JUN.

THE DESERT SONG—Warners

"THE DESERT SONG" is the first all-singing and talking operetta to reach the screen and our only criticism is that the screen has not been fully utilized. Most of this picture was made six months ago and much talkie progress has been made since then. The real joy of the picture is John Boles, with his new screen personality and delightful baritone voice. Pictorially beautiful and interesting to music lovers.

"DESERT SONG, THE"—WARNERS.—From the story by Otto Harbach, Laurence Schwab, Oscar Hammerstein 2nd, Sigmund Romberg and Frank Mandel. Scenario by Harvey Gates. Directed by Roy Del Ruth. The cast: *The Red Shadow*, John Boles; *Margot*, Carlotta King; *Susan*, Louise Fazenda; *Benny Kid, a reporter*, Johnny Arthur; *General Birbeau*, Edward Martindel; *Pasha*, Jack Pratt; *Sid El Kar*, Robert E. Guzman; *Hasse*, Otto Hoffman; *Clementina*, Marie Wells; *Capt. Fontaine*, John Miljan; *Rebel*, Del Elliott; *Azuri*, Myrna Loy.

JUN.

SYNCOPATION—RKO

THE Talkie-Singie-Dancie pictures are still in the night clubs of New York and "Syncopation" follows along the golden trail blazed by "The Broadway Melody." But this is a good, entertaining picture on its own. That brilliant band, Waring's Pennsylvanians, plays; Morton Downey sings, and there are fine performances by Bobby Watson, Barbara Bennett and Verree Teasdale.

"SYNCOPATION"—RKO.—From the novel "Stepping High" by Gene Markey. Adapted by Frances Agnew. Directed by Bert Glennon. The cast: *Flo*, Barbara Bennett; *Benny*, Bobby Watson; *Winston*, Ian Hunter; *Lew*, Morton Downey; *Hummel*, Osgood Perkins; *Henry*, Mackenzie Ward; *Rita*, Verree Teasdale; *Peggy*, Dorothy Lee.

JUN.

 *SHOW BOAT—Universal*

WHEN you say that Universal's version of Edna Ferber's episodic and sentimental novel is a lavish production, you say nearly everything possible about it. The weakness of the film "Show Boat" lies in the obvious direction of Harry Pollard.

Miss Ferber wrote a colorful novel that swept from a Mississippi river show boat to Chicago in the days of the World's Fair and on to New York. It had verve, spirit and fine atmospheric detail. Some of this comes through to the screen.

Laura La Plante is the best of the cast as *Magnolia* but Joseph Schildkraut overacts the rôle of *Gaylord Ravenal*. So does Emily Fitzroy in the rôle of *Parthenia Ann Hawks*, who rules her show boat with an iron hand.

"SHOW BOAT"—UNIVERSAL.—From the story by Edna Ferber, Continuity by Charles Kenyon. Directed by Harry Pollard. The cast: *Magnolia*, Laura La Plante; *Gaylord Ravenal*, Joseph Schildkraut; *Capt. Andy Hawks*, Otis Harlan; *Parthenia Ann Hawks*, Emily Fitzroy; *Julie*, Alma Rubens; *Windy*, Jack McDonald; *Magnolia, (as a child)* Jane La Verne; *Kim*, Jane La Verne; *Schultzy*, Neely Edwards; *Joe*, Stepin Fetchit; *Queenie*, Gertrude Howard. *Prologue:* Helen Morgan, Jules Bledsoe, Aunt Jemima and The Plantation Singers.

JUL.

SAYS Groucho Marx, one of the famous Four Marx Brothers, in an article in a New York daily in which he comments on his return to the vaudeville stage:

"And the vaudeville actors talk differently. In the old days they'd grab you and tell you what a riot they were in Findlay, Ohio, and how they wowed them in Des Moines. Now, all you hear is, 'We don't know what to do—Vitaphone wants us to make a short, but Movietone is after us to do a full length.'"

Making a Sound Picture
—with Western Electric Equipment

SILENCE in the studio! The director discards his megaphone, cameras whir in soundproof booths.

In the sound-proof "monitor room" a man at the control board regulates the volume and quality of sound recorded by Western Electric apparatus on a film or disc.

Hear Sound Pictures at their best—*go to a Western Electric equipped theatre*

Sound Pictures, made by the eleven great producers who have adopted the Western Electric system, are naturally best when reproduced in theatres with equipment from the same source.

That is why exhibitors everywhere, mindful of their patrons' satisfaction, either have installed or are now installing the Western Electric system—the sound equipment that assures clear and natural tone, that reflects a half century's experience in making telephones and other apparatus for reproducing sound.

(Photographs courtesy of Paramount)

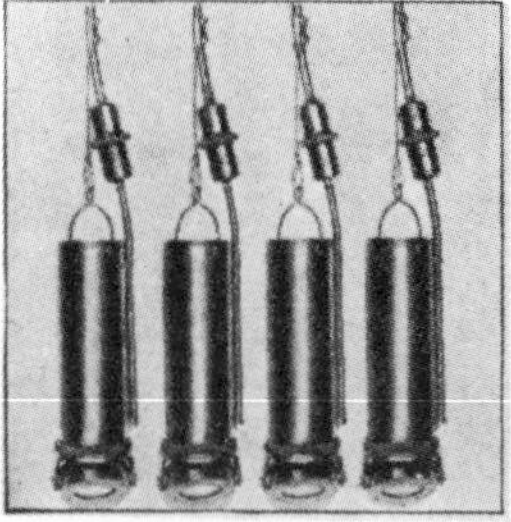

Western Electric builds special microphones for studio requirements.

The "monitor" controls quality and volume of all sound recorded.

Western Electric-made apparatus insures true-tone reproduction.

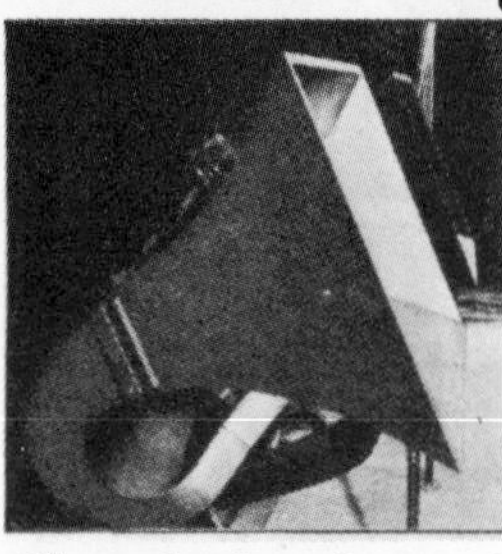

Theatre loud speakers, product of acoustical experts and craftsmen.

The projector which plays the sound picture in the theatre.

Western Electric

SOUND SYSTEM

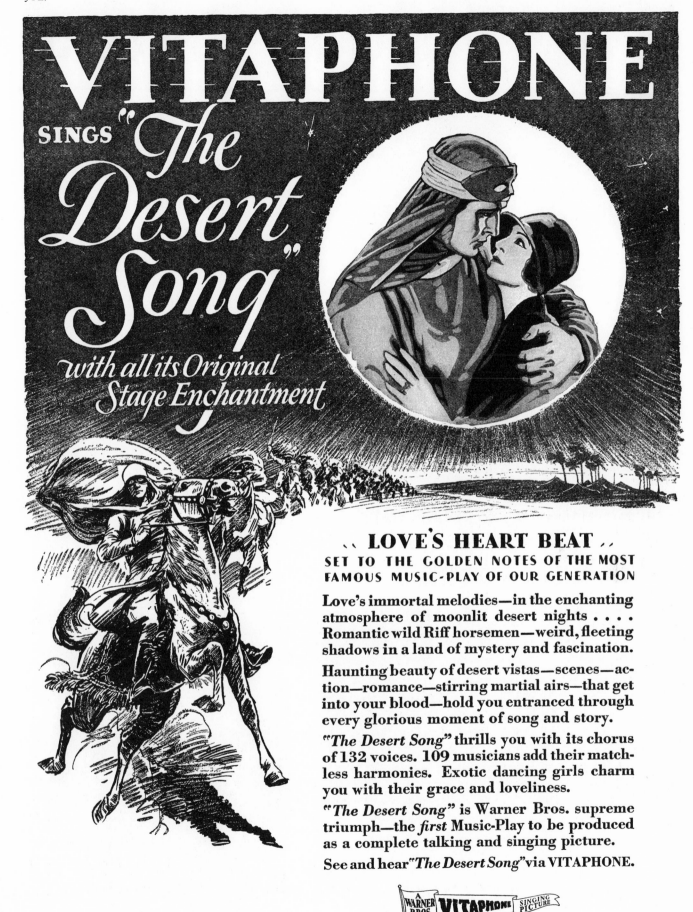

VITAPHONE

SINGS "The Desert Song"

with all its Original Stage Enchantment

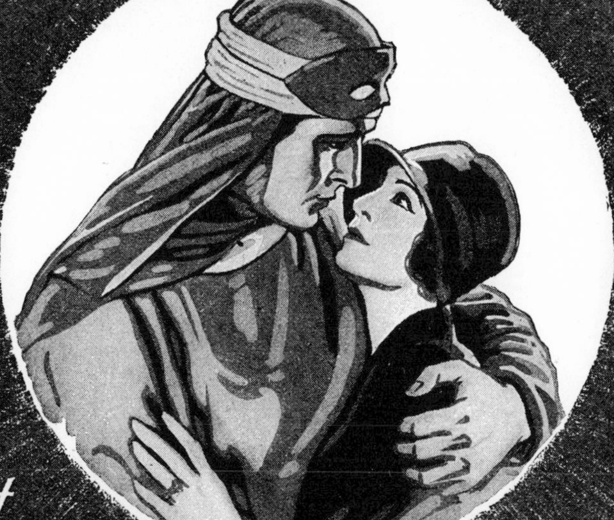

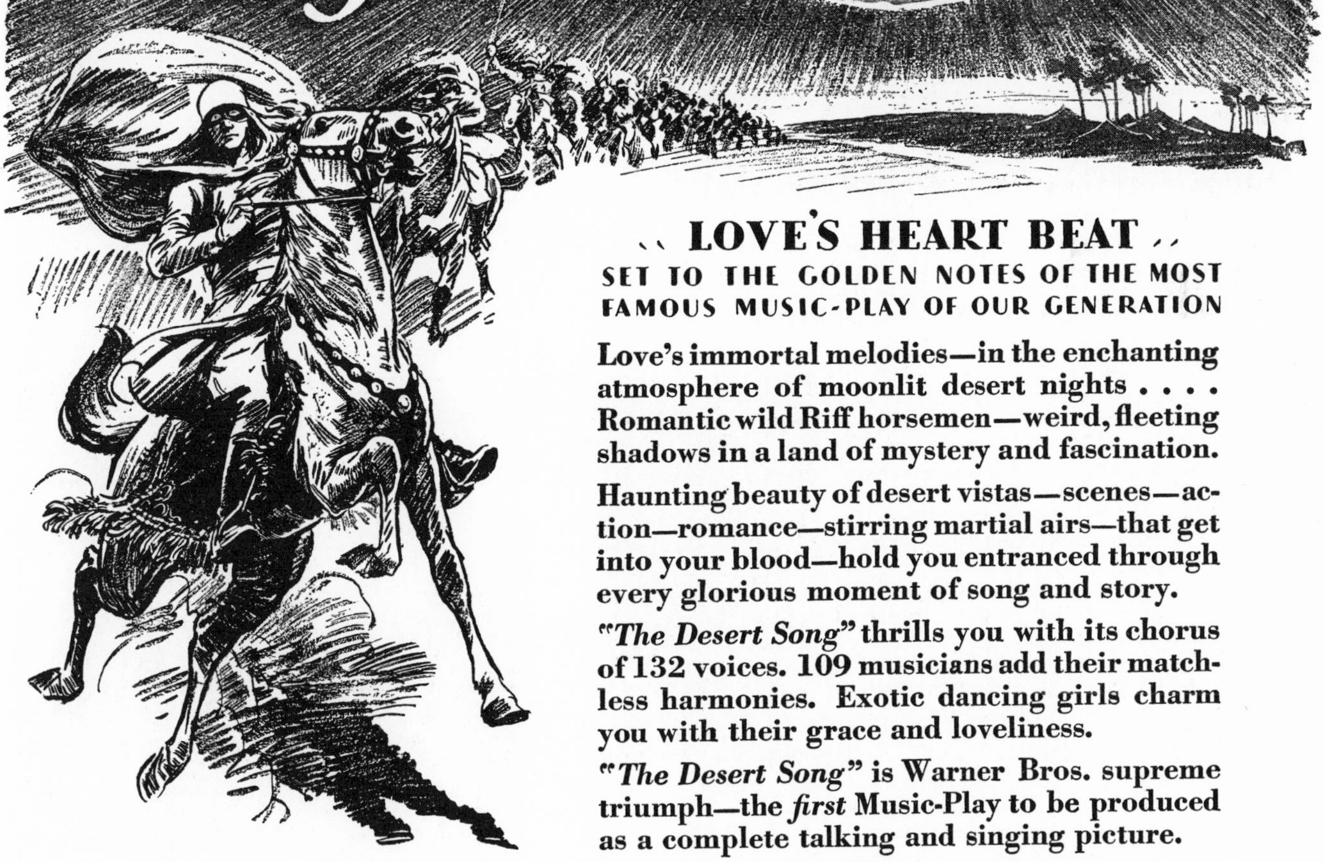

LOVE'S HEART BEAT

SET TO THE GOLDEN NOTES OF THE MOST FAMOUS MUSIC-PLAY OF OUR GENERATION

Love's immortal melodies—in the enchanting atmosphere of moonlit desert nights . . . . Romantic wild Riff horsemen—weird, fleeting shadows in a land of mystery and fascination.

Haunting beauty of desert vistas—scenes—action—romance—stirring martial airs—that get into your blood—hold you entranced through every glorious moment of song and story.

"The Desert Song" thrills you with its chorus of 132 voices. 109 musicians add their matchless harmonies. Exotic dancing girls charm you with their grace and loveliness.

"The Desert Song" is Warner Bros. supreme triumph—the *first* Music-Play to be produced as a complete talking and singing picture.

See and hear *"The Desert Song"* via VITAPHONE.

You *See and Hear* **VITAPHONE** *only in* Warner Bros. *and* First National *Pictures*

The TRUTH About

Laura La Plante did not really sing or play the banjo in "Show Boat." Doubling in another voice was easy, but Miss La Plante had to study banjo strumming so that her work would look right

When you hear your favorite star sing in the talkies, don't be too sure about it. Here are all the facts about sound doubling, and how it is done

LIGHT travels 186,000 miles per second, but nobody cares. Sound pokes along at approximately a thousand feet per second, and still nobody cares.

But when Richard Barthelmess, who is famed as a film star and not as a singer, bursts into song in "Weary River," playing his own accompaniment, folks begin to prick up their ears.

And when Corinne Griffith plays a harp in "The Divine Lady" and acquits herself vocally, with the grace of an opera singer, people commence asking pointed questions.

And when Barry Norton does a popular number to his own accompaniment in "Mother Knows Best," a quizzical light appears in the public's eye.

Then, too, when Laura La Plante strums the banjo in "Show Boat" and renders negro spirituals in below the Mason and Dixon line style, the public breaks out in an acute rash of curiosity which can be cured only by disclosing state secrets of the cinema.

Richard Barthelmess did not sing and play the piano in "Weary River." A double did it.

Corinne Griffith did not sing or play the harp in "The Divine Lady." A double did it.

Barry Norton did not sing in "Mother Knows Best." A double did it. He did, however, play the piano.

Laura La Plante did not sing and play the banjo in "Show Boat"—at least not for all of the songs. Two doubles helped her. One played the banjo, the other sang.

And so it goes, *ad infinitum.*

THERE are voice doubles in Hollywood today just as there are stunt doubles. One is not so romantic as the other, perhaps, but certainly just as necessary.

Those who create movies will probably not cheer as we make this announcement. In fact, they may resent our frankness. They may even have the Academy of Motion Picture Arts and Sciences write letters to PHOTOPLAY about it.

Richard Barthelmess received what he considered rather embarrassing publicity in connection with the song he did not sing in "Weary River." And, as a result of that, persons who undoubtedly know say that he is effecting a change of policy regarding future pictures. I was told on good authority that he informed Al Rockett, who heads First National's studios in Burbank, that he did not choose to

Everybody knows now that Richard Barthelmess did not sing in "Weary River." And, of course, he didn't play the piano. Johnny Murray sang "Weary River" into a "mike" out of range of the camera while Frank Churchill played the accompaniment. It was done very neatly

Voice Doubling

By

Mark Larkin

Lawford Davidson, who gets $500 a week as Paul Lukas' voice double. Lukas has a heavy accent

Eva Olivotti, who did Laura La Plante's singing in "Show Boat" and did it very well, indeed

Johnny Murray, Dick Barthelmess' voice double. He's under contract to be Dick's voice for all 1929

sing in forthcoming photoplays. "I am not a song and dance man," he explained, "and I don't want any pictures that feature me as such."

Nevertheless, Richard will sing — or rather someone will sing for him—in his forthcoming feature, titled at present, "Drag." That is, he will have a voice double unless they change the story. One never knows, you know, until the picture is released. There's many a slip between the screen and the cutting-room floor!

But Dick will not be seen actually in the act of singing as was the case in "Weary River." Probably there will be only his shadow, and the expression of the man for whom he is singing, this man—in the rôle of a song producer—registering reactions to the song.

If you saw "Weary River," you will remember that Dick sat at a piano and played and also sang. The means by which this was accomplished was ingenious, to say the least.

YOU will remember that it was a grand piano. Mr. Barthelmess faced the audience. You did not see his hands upon the keys, yet you saw him go through the motions of playing and singing. And you heard what you thought was his voice. But it was not his voice.

Many persons have said that it was the voice of Frank Withers. But it was not. It was the voice of Johnny Murray, former cornetist at the Cocoanut Grove, and now under contract to First National to sing for Richard Barthelmess. He is a real, dyed-in-the-wool voice double, Johnny is.

There was much enthusiasm on the set the day Johnny Murray put over the song, "Weary River." Dick threw his arm around Johnny's shoulder and said something like this: "Don't you ever die, young fella, or go East, or get run over, or anything!" And they both laughed.

Dick faced the audience during the filming of the scenes at the piano so as to conceal his hands. It has been said that a dummy keyboard was built on the side of the piano at which Dick sat, but that is not so. But the strings of the instrument were deadened with felt so that when Dick struck the keys the strings would give forth no sound. And Frank Churchill, pianist in a Hollywood theater orchestra, sat at a real piano off stage and played the accompaniment while Johnny Murray sang. The recording microphone was close to them and nowhere near Barthelmess. Dick merely faked the singing and playing, but he did it so beautifully that the results were convincing beyond doubt.

Probably the highest paid voice double in pictures is Lawford Davidson, who doubles *(continued on next page)*

It may surprise film fans who saw "The Divine Lady" to realize that Corinne Griffith neither sang nor played the harp. Miss Griffith did study the fingering of harp strings to get the correct illusion

(continued from preceding page)

for Paul Lukas. Mr. Lukas, an exceptionally fine actor, is handicapped for American pictures by a foreign accent. For that reason, therefore, it is necessary for someone else to speak his lines. And Davidson is said to receive five hundred dollars a week for this service.

Many individuals in Hollywood are wondering why Davidson has seen fit to submerge his own personality for this sort of work, for he is regarded as fully as gifted an actor in his own right as Paul Lukas. He is listed in all casting offices as a five-hundred-dollar-a-week man. It may be, of course, that he has an arrangement to appear in other pictures, too.

There are a number of ways of doubling the voice on the screen. Usually it is done through a method known as "dubbing." This means that it is done after the picture is shot. "Dubbing" is a term handed down to the movies by the makers of phonograph records. When portions were taken off several phonograph records to make one record, the process was referred to as "dubbing." So "dubbing" it is these days in pictures.

Most of the doubling that Margaret Livingston did for Louise Brooks in "The Canary Murder Case" was accomplished by "dubbing." Miss Livingston took up a position before the "mike" and watched the picture being run on the screen. If Miss Brooks came in a door and said, "Hello, everybody, how are you this evening?" Miss Livingston watched her lips and spoke Miss Brooks' words into the microphone.

Thus a sound-track was made and inserted in the film. And that operation is called "dubbing."

All synchronizations are dubbed in after the picture is finished. The production is edited and cut to exact running length, then the orchestra is assembled in the monitor room (a room usually the size of the average theater) and the score is played as the picture is run. The sound-track thus obtained is "dubbed" into the sound film or on to the record, depending upon which system is used.

If foreign sounds stray into the film, such as scratches and pin-pricks, they are "bloped" out. Some call it "blooping." This means that they are eliminated with a paintbrush and India ink. The method is not unlike that applied to the retouching of photographic negatives.

Voice doubling is sometimes forced upon the producers as an emergency measure. Such was the case with Paramount in connection with "The Canary Murder Case."

THEY called Miss Livingston to the studio one day and said, "Miss Livingston, we are up against it and we think you can help us out. We want to turn 'The Canary Murder Case' into a talkie and Miss Brooks is not available. We think you can double for her. Will you do it?"

She thought it over. Well, why not? It meant experience in the talkies, *and double her usual salary*. So she wore clothes that duplicated Miss Brooks', "dubbed" some of the stuff and played some of it straight, her profile always to the camera.

A few times she missed the timing, and as a result her words did not come out even with Miss Brooks' lip movements.

After it was all over a very amusing incident occurred. Miss Livingston was sitting in a restaurant in New York and the friend with whom she was having dinner remarked, "So you have been talking for Louise Brooks, have you?"

From a nearby table came a strange voice. "Yes," quoth the voice, "and it had better be good!"

They looked around in astonishment and there sat Louise Brooks!

Of course, they all laughed and immediately went into a huddle about Hollywood.

A surprisingly large number of players in the film capital are now training their voices, in diction as well as singing, for the express purpose of avoiding the necessity of voice doubling. Vilma Banky, for instance, spends two hours a day perfecting her English. And James Burroughs, Bessie Love, Carmel Myers, Billie Dove, Gwen Lee, Jacqueline Logan, Frances Lee, Leatrice Joy, Armand Kaliz and innumerable others are all taking vocal lessons. Most of these have sung professionally at some time in their career.

In that worthy picture, "Alibi," Virginia Flohri, a widely-known radio singer, doubled for Irma Harrison who, you remember, sang a song in the cafe as *Toots*, the chorus girl. Miss Harrison simulated singing while Miss Flohri actually sang into the microphone off stage. In this instance their timing was not perfect.

MISS FLOHRI also sang for Jeanne Morgan in the Romeo and Juliet vaudeville number, if you remember it, and Edward Jordan sang for Robert Cauterio.

Obtaining suitable voice doubles is often a difficult task. The voice must not only fit the player, it must suit the characterization as well. And good singing voices are not always easily found. One reason for this is that persons of marked vocal accomplishments are frequently reluctant to double. They are afraid their voices will be recognized, that it will cheapen them. A notable case in point was that of Marion Harris, the vaudeville headliner, who turned down an offer of $10,000 from Universal, according to one of her representatives, to substitute her voice for a film player, presumably in "Broadway."

No end of problems develop, of course, in connection with registering the voice. When Douglas Fairbanks did his bit of talking for "The Iron Mask" his stentorian tones all but wrecked the recording apparatus.

BEFORE beginning, he was cautioned by the sound engineers to speak softly. However, for Doug this was impossible. He could not get dramatic effect with his conversation thus cramped. As a result the first uproarious line of his speech brought the sound men pouring out of the mixing chamber like a swarm of mad hornets. Much argument ensued. Finally Earle Browne, director of dialogue, hit upon the bright idea of moving the microphone thirty feet away and turning it so that it faced *away* from Fairbanks.

Laura La Plante's problem in "Show Boat" was quite the opposite of Doug's. The most difficult thing she had to learn in working with a double was, not to sing silently, but to finger a banjo perfectly. She realized, naturally, that the eyes of countless trained musicians would be upon her in audiences the world over. In consequence, she could not fake. She had to be convincing. So she spent several weeks learning the correct fingering of a banjo.

Some of the stars, of course, actually play musical instruments, though few have done so professionally. There's Bessie Love and her ukulele, and a few others. In "Mother Knows Best," Barry Norton actually played the piano while Sherry Hall sang his song. Sherry stood before the "mike" just outside the camera lines and Barry played his accompaniment and at the same time spoke the words of the song inaudibly, putting into them the proper timing, a thing possible to him because of his knowledge of music.

Of course, every effort is made on the part of producers to guard the secret of doubling. Picture-makers feel that it spoils the illusion, that it hurts a production's box office appeal. In this respect, however, they are wrong. I know this from my own personal experience in exploitation work. In nearly twelve years of steering the box office destinies of photoplays—especially film roadshows, some of the largest of which I have handled personally—I have yet to encounter a single set-back or loss because the public had knowledge of a double's work. On the other hand, I found that it often stimulated business to let the public in on a secret or two.

Eva Olivotti, one of Hollywood's most promising voices, assured a friend that, if it became known that she doubled for Laura La Plante in the singing numbers of "Show Boat," she would never be able to obtain another job. That is an example of the fear instilled into the hearts of the doubles by the companies for which they work. They are afraid even to breathe the nature of their employment.

THE fact remains, however, that Miss Olivotti *did* sing Miss La Plante's songs, and sang them very well, indeed.

Songs for "The Divine Lady" were "dubbed" in after Miss Griffith completed the picture. An odd complication developed when it came to doubling the harp. It had been arranged for Zhay Clark to play this instrument for Miss Griffith, but when that portion of the picture was viewed it was discovered that Miss Griffith's fingernails were longer than Miss Clark's, and that her hands, therefore, could not substitute effectively for Miss Griffith's.

So Miss Clark spent two days teaching Miss Griffith the fingering of the harp, and how to come in with the orchestra. Then the star did the scene herself. The music and songs, according to those acquainted with the facts, were "dubbed" in the East—a feat easily accomplished merely by watching the picture on the screen and getting from doubles a sound-track that would fit properly.

Voice doubling is often done in the monitor room after the production is complete, the double playing the designated instrument or reading the lips of the player and timing his words to fit these lip movements.

But voice doubling seems to be on the wane. As time goes on, there will be less need for it. In rare instances, of course, it will be done where stars can't sing or play the instruments called for in the script. But stars are rapidly learning to sing and play. It won't be long now until a majority of players can boast of these accomplishments.

Then, too, microphone miracles are becoming more prevalent every day. This is due primarily to rapid improvement in equipment. Josef Cherniavsky, the musical director for one company, says: "Give me a person who is not tone deaf and I will make him ninety-five percent perfect in talking pictures." Perhaps Mr. Cherniavsky is a wee bit enthusiastic, but at least his outlook indicates the present Hollywood trend.

Bearing out his statement, it is interesting to note that if a voice has tone quality, but lacks volume, the fault can be easily corrected by the amplifier. Take Alice White. Alice sang her own songs (unless I have been terribly fooled, and I suspect I have!) in "Broadway Babies," sang them sweetly, but in a piping little voice that couldn't be heard off the set. Yet when the "play-back" gave evidence of surprising volume in her tones, loud cheers went up from company officials. The "play-back," by the way, is a device which plays back the voices of the cast from a wax record shortly after the scene is filmed. It's an invaluable check-up.

The problem of the foreign player is, of course, difficult to solve. At first it was regarded as an insurmountable obstacle. It is being discovered by producers, however, that what they thought a hopeless liability in the beginning has actually become an asset. In the case of feminine players in particular, accent is a decided charm. Such foreign players as Baclanova, Goudal, *et al*, are giving up the thought of perfecting their English. Nils Asther is studying English religiously. Care will always have to be exercised, nevertheless, in casting these players.

Another instance of piano doubling occurred in "Speakeasy," that splendid underworld picture about the prize-fighter and the girl reporter. Fred Warren, an exceptionally capable pianist, doubled at the piano for

(continued on next page)

(continued from preceding page)

Henry B. Walthall. This was accomplished by tying down the keyboard of the real piano at which Walthall sat, so that when he struck the keys, nothing happened. You will remember, of course, that he sat facing the audience in such a position as to conceal his hands. Warren sat off stage at a real piano, about fifteen or twenty feet away, in a spot where he and Walthall could see each other. The recording "mike" was near Warren. As he played, Walthall imitated his motions. They had rehearsed the thing to perfection.

Although voice doubling is to the public the most interesting phase of sound work—because it is hidden from public view, no doubt—it is one of the comparatively simple things which confront producers. Problems much more subtle really vex them. For instance: New caste has grown up with the advent of conversing pictures; sound engineers are competing with directors for prestige and dominance; there is often open warfare between directors and monitor men; the new terminology of the business—"dubbing," "bloping," the invention of "split sets"; the mere fact that light travels faster than sound—a circumstance frequently baffling to engineers, and one that gives them grey hairs.

Just recently sound engineers found out that perfect synchronization in a big theater is virtually inpossible—all because light travels faster than sound. If you are sitting comparatively close to the screen, all is well. If you are sitting in the back of the house, or in the balcony, it's another matter. Sound vibrations reach you after you have seen the image speak. The speed with which light vibrations exceed sound vibrations will depend of course upon where you sit. And this is a problem that sound engineers are trying to solve.

So you see producers have other troubles than doubles!

You thought Irma Harrison sang as the cabaret darling of "Alibi," didn't you? She didn't. The voice you heard belonged to Virginia Flohri, a well-known radio singer

APR. When you heard Richard Barthelmess sing in "Weary River," that was a young gentleman named Frank Withers. . . . And Belle Mann sang so prettily for Alice White in "Show Girl" that the Victor platter people have given her a recording contract. . . . Alice opened her mouth in Hollywood, but Belle sang in Camden.

JUL.

★ *FOX MOVIETONE FOLLIES—Fox*

WHEN the "Follies" were being filmed, visitors at Fox Studio had to put on dark glasses and false moustaches to get within calling distance of the set. All activities were shrouded in mystery. But the revue is finished at last. Glorified gals! Legs! Abbreviated costumes! Everything!

Other studios have already followed suit with this type of entirely new entertainment. Song writers are as numerous as microphones in Hollywood, but the "Fox Follies" is first—and, as such, is important. As this is to be an annual event it is likely to improve with age and experience.

The music is the best part of it. "Break Away" and "Big City Blues" should be instantaneous hits. The big dance acts are breath-taking, but there is not enough variety.

Sharon Lynn and Sue Carol are the two picture players with leading rôles. Most of the rest are from the stage. Sharon is surprisingly good, revealing, as she does, a hot blues voice. Sue is full of pep and particularly cute in "Break Away." Stepin Fetchit furnishes his usual brand of unexcelled comedy. Dixie Lee and David Rollins distinguish themselves.

The slight story (which is only an excuse for the presentation of the acts) weakens rather than aids the revue. Legitimate plays are often better in talkies, but synthetic follies are not quite like the real thing. Revues depend upon personality. The baldheaded row can't send mash notes to a shadow on the screen.

However, don't miss the "Follies." You'll find yourself absorbed by the spectacle and, if you don't go away humming those good tunes, we'll be surprised. *All Talkie.*

"FOX MOVIETONE FOLLIES"—Fox.—From the story by David Butler. Dialogue by William K. Wells. Directed by David Butler. The cast: *George Shelby*, John Breeden; *Lila Beaumont*, Lola Lane; *Jay Darrell*, DeWitt Jennings; *Ann Foster*, Sharon Lynn; *Al Leaton*, Arthur Stone; *Swifty*, Stepin Fetchit; *Martin*, Warren Hymer; *Stage Manager*, Archie Gottler; *Orchestra Leader*, Arthur Kay; *Le Maire*, Mario Dominici. *Principals in Song and Dance Numbers:* Sue Carol, Lola Lane, Sharon Lynn, Dixie Lee, Melva Cornell, Paula Langlen, Carolynne Snowden, Jeannette Dancey, David Percy, David Rollins, Bobby Burns, Frank Richardson, Henry M. Mollandin, Frank La Mont, Stepin Fetchit. *Adagio Dancers:* Vina Gale and Arthur Springer, Helen Hunt and Charles Huff, Harriet and John Griffith. *Specialty Dancers:* Stepin Fetchit, Carolynne Snowden, Jeannette Dancey, Evans and Weaver, Mitchell and Redman, Four Covans, Sam and Sam, Brown and Stevens.

JUL.

Princeton Goes Talkie

By Jay O'Gee

"CHANGE the needle!" That's the new cry of the picture audiences in Princeton, for talking pictures have "come to college."

This venture of the Vitaphone and Movietone into the lair of the Princeton tiger is a hazardous one. The boys have been accustomed to furnishing their own dialogue and sound effects. In the era of the mum movie, some leather-lunged undergraduate provided deep bass wise cracks for the lip action of modest heroines; a sophomore soprano would put sweet words into the lips of villains; and one student considered it a duty to bring his alarm clock to every performance so that the ringing of a telephone on the screen might be made realistic.

The first talking picture was "The Singing Fool," with Al Jolson. All the seats were filled by show time. Many sat in the aisles. Not only was this to be the first talking picture for Princeton—it was the first for a good many Princetonians.

When Al Jolson and "The Singing Fool" reached Princeton, something went wrong with the reproducing apparatus. This resulted in Al losing his voice and in little Davey Lee singing "Sonny Boy" to himself

Seemingly resentful that they were no longer to provide necessary sound effects, part of the audience had armed themselves with whistles, cow-bells, inflated paper bags, and every noise-making device within their resources. The lights went out; the audience became hushed in anticipation. A girl appeared on the screen and began to sing. With the first note, bedlam broke loose — bells, whistles, bicycle sirens, bursting bags, and the rhythmic clap-clap-clap of disapproval of the short subject. No one knew what song she sang. They had come to scoff and were scoffing. Not a note was heard above the confusion.

The feature followed and the audience quieted itself in appreciation of a promising story. For the first few reels all was well, but by the time Al Jolson had married Josephine Dunn the inexperience of the local hired help contributed an amusing situation. Al Jolson sang an entire song without a sound issuing forth from the Vitaphone! When the sound finally came, it was way behind the action on the screen. In the course of the next five minutes, Josephine Dunn spoke Jolson's lines, Jolson talked nothing but baby-talk, and Davey Lee sang "Sonny Boy."

"Fix it!" cried the audience, but it was not fixed until the beginning of the next reel. The noise-makers had gained their end.

Subsequent showing of talking pictures has shown that the Princeton students will have nothing else. They pack the theater for "talkies" as they formerly did only to see Greta Garbo. And they no longer bring bells and whistles, or alarm clocks. They are loud in their approval and their criticism. That makes it easy for the manager when booking future programs. And he doesn't need to proclaim talking pictures a success—he just points to the line at the box office.

JUL.

 ***INNOCENTS OF PARIS—Paramount***

THIS picture is Maurice Chevalier's (pronounced Sheval-yay) first screen appearance and, because of his great popularity in Paris, his screen debut has been awaited with unusual expectancy.

Dispel your doubts, he can stay as long as he likes. He sings with joy. He plays with abandon and his personality gets you. He renders half his songs in French and half in English, but it is not just his pleasing voice, nor even his perfect pantomime, that makes him a success.

The plot is inconsequential and much of the dialogue is stilted and unnatural, but the sparkling, lovable personality of Chevalier lifts the story out of the commonplace—and makes it delightful entertainment. Fans will love Chevalier. *All Talkie.*

"INNOCENTS OF PARIS"—PARAMOUNT.—From the story by C. E. Andrews. Dialogue by Ernest Vajda. Directed by Richard Wallace. The cast: *Maurice Marny,* Maurice Chevalier; *Louise Leval,* Sylvia Beecher; *Emile Leval,* Russell Simpson; *Mons. Marny,* George Fawcett; *Mme. Marny,* Mrs. George Fawcett; *Mons. Renard,* John Miljan; *Mme. Renard,* Margaret Livingston; *Jo-Jo,* David Durand; *Jules,* Jack Luden; *Musician,* Johnnie Morris.

JUL.

THE TIME, THE PLACE AND THE GIRL—Warners

All Talkie

THE experiences of a jaunty bond salesman, fresh from the gridiron, with an unbreakable bump of ego. Lively college atmosphere, with Grant Withers playing football, singing, whistling, and using his sex appeal . . . all to good advantage. Betty Compson and Gertrude Olmstead are nicely contrasted. John Davidson gives an excellent performance. You will want to see this all-talking comedy drama.

"TIME, THE PLACE AND THE GIRL, THE"—WARNERS.—From the play by Frank R. Adams and Will Hough. Continuity by Robert Lord. Directed by Herbert Bretherton. The cast: *Jim Crane*, Grant Withers; *Doris Ward*, Betty Compson; *Pete Ward*, John Davidson; *Mae Ellis*, Gertrude Olmstead; *The Professor*, James R. Kirkwood; *Bert Holmes*, Bert Roach; *Mrs. Davis*, Vivian Oakland; *Mrs. Winters*, Gretchen Hartman; *Mrs. Parks*, Irene Haisman; *Radio Announcer*, Gerald King.

JUL.

MOTHER'S BOY—Pathe

All Talkie

ANOTHER lad makes good in a night club and then becomes a great big star on Broadway. Al Jolson discovered this plot. Here Morton Downey is the singer who makes good triumphs. Exactly like all the other talkie plots except that Mort plays an Irish boy. Downey is a little hefty for screen popularity but, with a bit of reducing, a new plot and better recording, he has his chance.

"MOTHER'S BOY"—PATHE.—From the story by Gene Markey. Dialogue by Gene Markey. Directed by Bradley Barker. The cast: *Tommy O'Day*, Morton Downey; *Mrs. O'Day*, Beryl Mercer; *Mr. O'Day*, John T. Doyle; *Harry O'Day*, Brian Donlevy; *Rose Lyndon*, Helen Chandler; *Jake Sturmberg*, Osgood Perkins; *Joe Bush*, Lorin Raker; *Beatrix Townleigh*, Barbara Bennett; *Mrs. Apfelbaum*, Jennie Moskowitz; *Mr. Apfelbaum*, Jacob Frank; *Mr. Bumble*, Louis Sorin; *Gus LeGrand*, Robert Gleckler; *Duke of Pomplum*, Tyrrell Davis; *Dinslow*, Allan Vincent; *Evangelist*, Leslie Stowe.

JUL.

NOT QUITE DECENT—Fox

Part Talkie

ANOTHER version of "The Singin' Fool," with Louise Dresser as Al Jolson and June Collyer as an idealized Sonny Boy. Louise sings the theme song, "Empty Arms," with tears in her eyes and a choke in her larynx because her daughter (who doesn't know she's a daughter, mind you) has left her. And, to make the idea even more identical, she does it in black face! *Mammy!* We ask you, can you cope with it?

"NOT QUITE DECENT"—FOX.—From the story by Wallace Smith. Scenario by Marion Orth. Directed by Irving Cummings. The cast: *Linda Cunningham*, June Collyer; *Mame Jarrow*, Louise Dresser; *Jerry Connor*, Allan Lane; *Canfield*, Oscar Apfel; *Al Bergon*, Paul Nicholson; *Margie*, Marjorie Beebe; *A Crook*, Ben Hewlett; *Another Crook*, Jack Kenney.

JUL.

HONKY-TONK—Warners

All Talkie

SOPHIE TUCKER is on the Vitaphone. Her first feature is a night club comedy drama with a synthetic plot that is a medley of "Singin' Fool," "My Man," and "The Little Snob," but Sophie keeps it afloat with song. A cabaret hostess, educating her daughter abroad, has always kept her whoopee life secret. The kid breezes in, gets wise, and snooty, and walks out. Lila Lee is gorgeous as the upstage daughter. A hit.

"HONKY-TONK"—WARNERS.—From the story by Leslie S. Barrows. Adapted by C. Graham Baker. Directed by Lloyd Bacon. The cast: *Sophie Leonard*, Sophie Tucker; *Freddie Gilmore*, George Duryea; *Beth*, Lila Lee; *Jean Gilmore*, Audrey Ferris; *Jim Blake*, Mahlon Hamilton; *Cafe Manager*, John T. Murray.

JUL.

NOTHING BUT THE TRUTH—Paramount

All Talkie

SOME fifteen years ago Max Figman created the principal rôle in this famous farce on the stage. Time has been kind to the drama. The situation, which concerns a gentleman who bets ten thousand dollars he can tell the absolute truth for twenty-four hours, is still hilarious. Try it over on your vocal chords and see what happens. Richard Dix is at his best in this light comedy. Helen Kane is a hit.

"NOTHING BUT THE TRUTH"—PARAMOUNT.—From the play by James Montgomery. Adapted by John McGowan. Directed by Victor Schertzinger. The cast: *Robert Bennett*, Richard Dix; *E. M. Burke*, Burton Churchill; *Frank Connelly*, Louis John Bartels; *Clarence Van Dyke*, Ned Sparks; *Sabel Jackson*, Wynne Gibson; *Mabel Jackson*, Helen Kane; *Gwen Burke*, Dorothy Hall; *Mrs. E. M. Burke*, Madeline Grey; *Ethel Clark*, Nancy Ryan.

JUL.

THE RAINBOW MAN—Sono-Art—Paramount

All Talkie

SOMETHING will have to be done about the one singie-talkie plot now in vogue. Al Jolson started it with "The Singing Fool." Here it is, with variations, with Eddie Dowling as a minstrel man with a breaking heart. Frankie Darro is the current Sonny Boy. Real talkie honors are won by Marion Nixon. The hokum is liberal in this film, but Dowling *has* a personality.

"RAINBOW MAN, THE"—SONO-ART-PARAMOUNT.—From the story by Eddie Dowling. Adapted by Frances Agnew. Directed by Fred Newmeyer. The cast: *Rainbow Ryan*, Eddie Dowling; *Mary Lane*, Marion Nixon; *Billy*, Frankie Darro; *"Doc" Hardy*, Sam Hardy; *Colonel Lane*, Lloyd Ingraham; *Daredevil Bill*, George Hayes; *The Dog*, Beans; *Minstrel Men*, The Rounders Quintet.

AUG.

LAURA LA PLANTE, Universal's captivating blonde star, has no fear of the glare from the huge incandescent "sun-spot" lights used for a close-up—for she keeps her skin flawlessly smooth with Lux Toilet Soap. She says: "I've used the famous French soaps and know that Lux Toilet Soap is made the same way—it gives my skin the same marvelous smoothness."

AUG.

Laura La Plante is a clever cook who knows the value of presenting healthful foods in attractive and palatable form. The star of Universal's "Show Boat" includes bran in many of her recipes

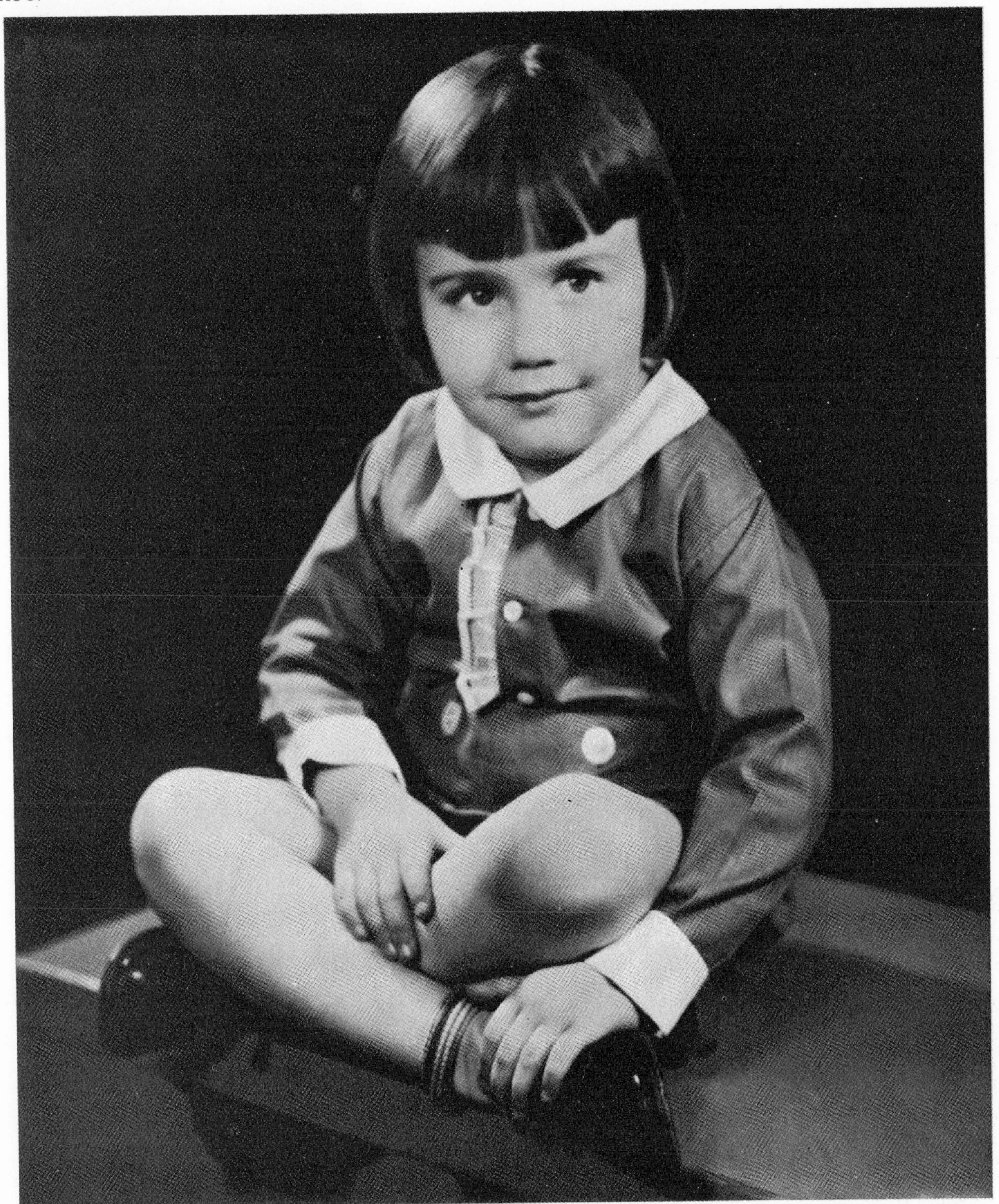

NEW PICTURES

THE little boy who started an avalanche of mammy and daddy pictures in the talkies—Davey Lee. Davey is the only star actually born in Hollywood. He is four years old—going on five. And you'll see him next with Al Jolson in "Little Pal"

Hal Phyfe

THIS is the American Girl who will be glorified in Paramount's sound revue inspired by the Ziegfeld slogan. Although new to the screen, Mary Eaton has been singing and dancing on the stage since she was nine years old. Miss Eaton made such a good impression in her first talkie, "The Cocoanuts," that she was placed under contract for "Glorifying the American Girl"

Bachrach

BEBE DANIELS swears that she will make no more tomboy comedies; she is going to change her whole style of acting when she makes her debut as a talkie star. She'll go in for singing and dancing instead of stunts. In "Rio Rita," produced by RKO, you'll discover a new and glamorous Bebe. The picture, of course, is a talkie version of the Ziegfeld stage production

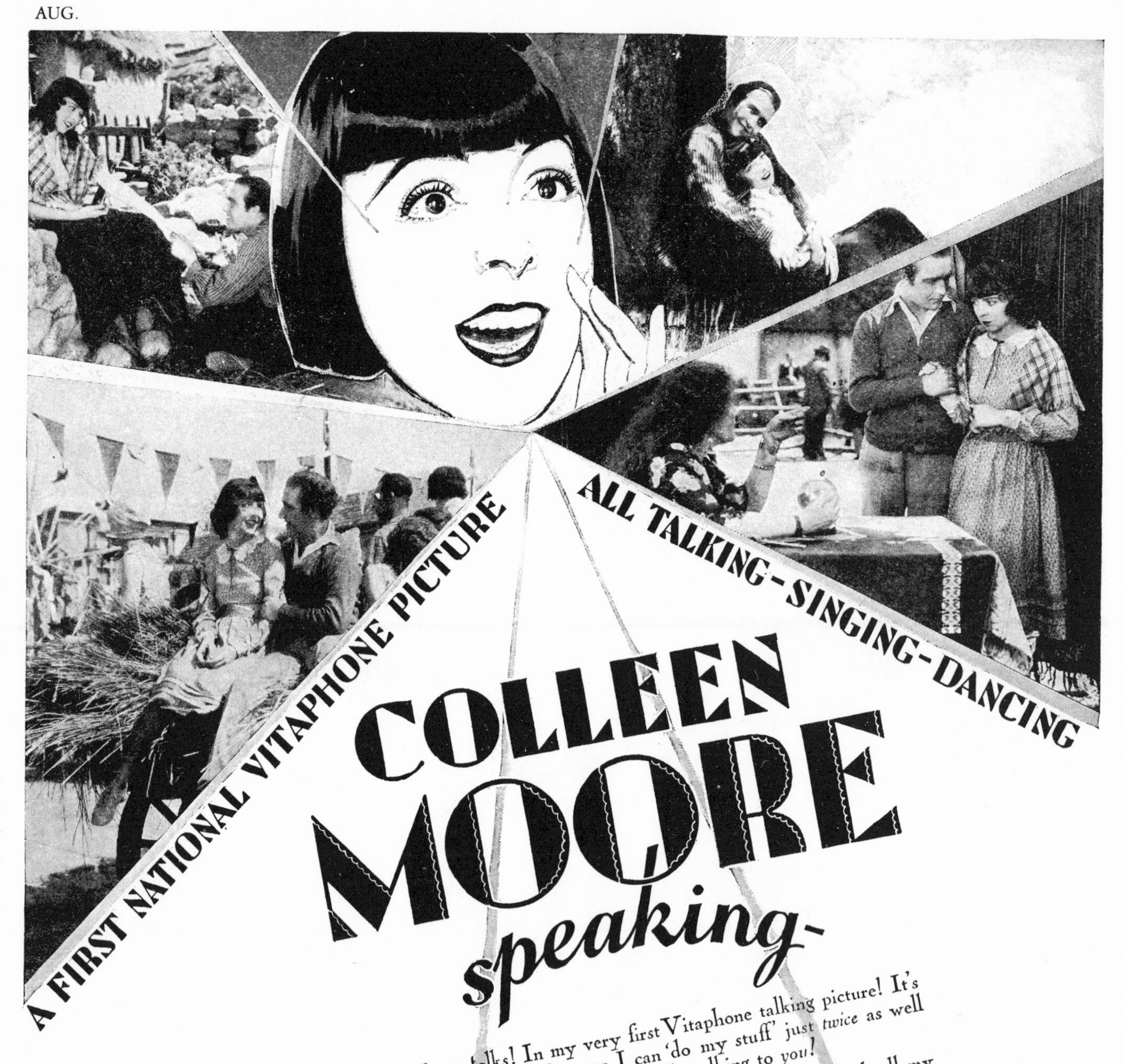

"Here I am, folks! In my very first Vitaphone talking picture! It's great.—I love it.—Because I can 'do my stuff' just *twice* as well ....And when I talk, I feel I'm really talking to *you!*

"Acting on the Vitaphone seems just like shaking hands with all my friends. And I'll certainly be 'pleased to meet you' when 'Smiling Irish Eyes' comes around your way!"

▲ ▲ ▲

"Smiling Irish Eyes" is a standing-room-only invitation to "come back to Erin." It will take you on a condensed excursion through the carefree land of playboys and poets—then bring you back to Broadway for a behind-the-scenes surprise. And Colleen's Talking Picture debut will make it *the* event of the cinema season. Find out the date today at the box-office of your favorite theatre.

In Her First Talking Picture

"SMILING IRISH EYES"

Tune up your vocal cords! You'll want to join with Colleen in the chorus of these 3 catchy, new song hits—"Smiling Irish Eyes," "A Wee Bit o' Love," and "Then I Can Ride Home With You."

Presented by **JOHN McCORMICK**

A WILLIAM A. SEITER *Production*

First National
VITAPHONE Pictures

AUG.

THE COCOA-NUTS—Paramount

All Talkie

THE Marx Brothers are photographed and sounded in their Broadway musical comedy of this title. The thing has been screened *in toto*, painted back drops and all. This shows signs of hurried production, but Groucho Marx is funny in his rapid fire wise-cracking and there are hilarious moments. His brothers lend assistance. Mary Eaton and Oscar Shaw are present but buried beneath the Marx antics. Fairly good.

"COCOANUTS, THE"—PARAMOUNT.—From the stage play by George S. Kaufman. Directed by Joseph Santley and Robert Florey. The cast: *Hammer*, Groucho Marx; *Harpo*, Harpo Marx; *Chico*, Chico Marx; *Jamison;* Zeppo Marx; *Polly*, Mary Eaton; *Bob*, Oscar Shaw; *Penelope*, Katherine Francis; *Mrs. Potter*, Margaret Dumont; *Yates*, Cyril Ring; *Hennessy*, Basil Ruysdael; *Bell Captain*, Sylvan Lee; *Dancers*, Gamby-Hale Girls and Allan K. Foster Girls.

AUG.

 ***FASHIONS IN LOVE—Paramount***

ADOLPHE MENJOU breaks out with a voice, a French accent and the best performance he has given in many a movie moon. Disguised by a ridiculous title, this is "The Concert," played so successfully by Leo Ditrichstein. It's an old school farce of a concert pianist whose spirit to be a Lothario is willing, but whose flesh is weak. Its glaring fault is that a great musician should compose such inferior melodies. Fay Compton and Miriam Seegar, both from the English stage (the former a native of Britain, the latter an American girl) give their first film performances in this country. Both are capable actresses.

But the honors go to the star. His French accent is excellent, although he was born in Pennsylvania. Not a great picture but big entertainment. *All Talkie.*

"FASHIONS IN LOVE"—PARAMOUNT.—From the stage play "The Concert," by Hermann Bahr. Adapted by Louise Long. Directed by Victor Schertzinger. The cast: *Paul De Remy*, Adolphe Menjou; *Marie De Remy*, Fay Compton; *Delphine Martin*, Miriam Seegar; *Frank Martin*, John Miljan; *Miss Weller*, Joan Standing; *Levisohn*, Robert Wayne; *Joe*, Russ Powell; *Jane*, Billie Bennett; *Valet*, Jacques Vanaire.

AUG.

 ***BROADWAY—Universal***

THE original of all the night club and underworld dramas —and still the most effective. You may quarrel with the too lavish settings given the Dunning-Abbott play, but you'll have no complaint against Director Paul Fejos' direct and sharp handling of the story.

Here you will find no hodgepodge talkie, trying to get by on the strength of its novelty, but an expert drama, with concise dialogue, tense melodrama and, for the most part, good acting.

Glenn Tryon plays the rôle of the innocent hoofer embroiled in a bootlegging murder.

Tryon is surprisingly good in a difficult part. But he has keen competition in Thomas E. Jackson, a member of the stage cast, and Evelyn Brent, as the vengeful chorus girl, who steal the show. Mr. Jackson is decidedly a talkie find. What a voice! Paul Porcasi, as the proprietor of the night club, also duplicates the hit he made on the stage. Merna Kennedy is not so good and is swamped by superior performances.

"Broadway" is tricked out with theme songs, with special dancing acts and with a mammoth cabaret scene, three times as large as any New York night club.

But these bits of over-elaboration are immediately forgotten in the rush of the melodrama back-stage in the night club.

And so you will not be disappointed in Universal's version of one of the most entertaining plays presented in several seasons. *All Talkie.*

"BROADWAY"—UNIVERSAL.—From the play by Philip Dunning and George Abbott. Scenario by Edward T. Lowe, Jr. Directed by Paul Fejos. Photography by Hal Mohr. The cast: *Roy Lane*, Glenn Tryon; *Pearl*, Evelyn Brent; *Billie Moore*, Merna Kennedy; *Dan McCorn*, Thomas E. Jackson; *Steve Crandall*, Robert Ellis; *Nick Verdis*, Paul Porcasi; *Porky*, Otis Harlan; *Lil*, Marion Lord; *Mose Levett*, Fritz Feld; *Dolph*, Arthur Hausman; *Joe*, George Davis; *"Scar" Edwards*, Leslie Fenton; *Maizie*, Betty Francisco; *Ruby*, Edythe Flynn; *Ann*, Florence Dudley; *Grace*, Ruby McCoy.

AUG.

★ *ON WITH THE SHOW—Warners*

ONE hundred per cent everything—singing, dancing, talking and technicolor. The color photography makes it unique.

The situations have whiskers, but the transitions from back stage drama to footlight hey-hey are well done. There is a large chorus with lively dance routines, and tuneful music. The conversation consists of snappy comebacks, 1910 variety.

Performances from the large cast are almost uniformly good, with Joe E. Brown standing out with sparkling comedy interpolations. Sam Hardy scores as the harassed producer, and Betty Compson is optically entertaining. The Blues singing of Ethel Waters is a highlight. Alan Crosland's direction is competent. *All Talkie.*

"ON WITH THE SHOW"—WARNERS.—From the story by Humphrey Pearson. Scenario by Robert Lord. Directed by Alan Crosland. The cast: *Nita,* Betty Compson; *Sarah,* Louise Fazenda; *Kitty,* Sally O'Neil; *Ike,* Joe E. Brown; *Sam Bloom,* Purnell B. Pratt; *Jimmy,* William Bakewell; *Twins,* Fairbanks Twins; *Durant,* Wheeler Oakman; *Jerry,* Sam Hardy; *Dad,* Thomas Jefferson; *Pete,* Lee Moran; *Joe,* Harry Gribbon; *Harold,* Arthur Lake; *Harold's Fiancee,* Josephine Houston; *Father,* Henry Fink; *Bert,* Otto Hoffman; *Ethel Waters,* Ethel Waters; *Harmony Four Quartette,* Harmony Four Quartette; *Four Covans,* Four Covans; *Angelus Babe,* Angelus Babe.

AUG.

COLLEGE LOVE—Universal

THIS post-graduate edition of "The Collegians" is one of the first two all-talking collegiate pictures to be made. Different college, different names, but they cut all the cute Calford capers. Fickle frat pins jump from one sweater to another—there's football, its subsequent flag-waving, croony jazz, and moonlight necking. Dorothy Gulliver is the college yell. The regular series stuff, much elaborated on and well directed and synchronized. You'll like it. *All Talkie.*

"COLLEGE LOVE"—UNIVERSAL.—From the story by Leonard Fields. Adapted by John B. Clymer and Pierre Couderc. Directed by Nat Ross. The cast: *Robert Wilson,* George Lewis; *Eddie "Flash" Thomas,* Eddie Phillips; *Dorothy May,* Dorothy Gulliver; *Jimmy Reed,* Churchill Ross; *Coach Jones,* Hayden Stevenson.

AUG.

THE FLYING FOOL—Pathe

BILL BOYD and Marie Prevost hit the sky in this comedy drama of a high-flyer with planes and janes. Bill's a self-styled tough egg who "finds 'em, fools 'em, and forgets 'em." Marie is one he almost didn't find, didn't fool, and couldn't forget. So—high drama, roaring planes, then—well, see it! And the way Marie croons "If I Had My Way"! It's no down-payment voice, either. It's all hers. *All Talkie.*

"FLYING FOOL, THE"—PATHE.—From the story by Elliott Clawson. Dialogue by James Gleason. Directed by Taylor Garnett. The cast: *The Flying Fool,* William Boyd; *Pat,* Marie Prevost; *Jimmy Taylor,* Russell Gleason; *Tom Dugan,* Tom O'Brien.

AUG.

ARTHUR CAESAR, Broadway wit now writing for moompitchers and who runs a sort of Hollywood embassy for lonely Manhattanites in our midst, comes forth with this month's smart crack:

"If there's a theme song in heaven it must be 'All God's Chilluns Got Options.'"

AUG.

WHEN "Burlesque" makes its appearance on the screen, with Hal Skelly in the rôle he made famous during the long New York run of the stage play, it will have the prepossessing title of "The Dance of Life."

There is a reason why Paramount changed the title. Outside of New York the play, "Burlesque," confused the natives. They expected to see Irish and Hebrew comedians and a lot of snappy stouts in tights.

In one town in which the play was presented a clubwoman saw the sign, "Burlesque," in front of a theater, and went in to view the show. She was horrified at the risque jokes and scantily clad dames. It was reported to the police. When the coppers viewed the play they found nothing wrong with it. A meeting was called and the prominent clubwoman discovered she had made a mistake in the theater and had actually seen a third-rate burlesque show in a down-at-the-heel playhouse.

Paramount isn't taking any chances.

JUN.

The dashing, uniformed figure at the right, partly hidden by that high privet hedge, is Marion Davies, made up for her rôle in "Marianne," her next picture for Metro-Goldwyn-Mayer. She is shown here at moustache drill with her director, Mr. Bob Leonard. "Twirl-WHISKERS!" orders Bob, and Marion twirls smartly. Miss Davies, as a French chasseur, should prove an apt pupil, while Bob has won several prizes as a moustache-twirler

AUG.

Hollywood goes Broadway and Joan Crawford practices up on her old chorus steps under the tutelage of Sammy Lee, the dance director. Joan will dance in M.-G.-M.'s Revue of Revues

AUG.

WRITING of theme songs is becoming one of Hollywood's greatest industries. Every picture has its theme melody, and songs are turned out at the various studios about as rapidly as new-born flivvers. Tunes are growing scarce, with about everything in use from Handel's "Messiah" to "London Bridge Is Falling Down."

A good title was suggested for a theme song to the new John Barrymore picture, "General Crack," in production at Warner Brothers:

"You may show your whole face to some other girl but you're only a profile to me."

AUG.

THERE is something darned insidious about this theme song business. Even Pauline Frederick, now at work on "Evidence" at Warner Brothers, will warble two numbers for the picture.

Fans will undoubtedly be surprised at the richness of Miss Frederick's contralto voice. Unless Cal is mistaken it will be the first time this emotional star has used her voice in public since she sang "Towsee Mongolay" in "Innocent," fifteen years ago.

AUG.

COME to your local theater and take left-overs. That's what a new Fox opus, "Words and Music," will be. The phrase is used without attempt to belittle.

When "Fox Movietone Follies" was made, Lois Moran had an important role. There were many numbers where she did excellent work. And there were several catchy tunes for her to sing. But when the picture was completed it was much too long. Certain sequences had to be cut out. Lois was removed bodily by a film editor's shears. But the stuff was all good. The numbers were elaborate. Lois proved herself clever. The tunes were catchy.

Therefore James Tingling was given the job of directing a half-finished picture. The left-overs or cut-outs are the basis for "Words and Music."

AUG.

Introducing the Gold-diggers of Broadway, all of whom will take part in the Warners' talkie revival of the stage hit. The girls on the ladder are Gertrude Short, Ann Pennington and Nancy Welford. The girl on the left is Lilyan Tashman and on your right is Winnie Lightner

AUG.

Al Jolson's "Mammy" troupe, assembled for his production of "Little Pal." The sweaters were Al's gift to his co-workers. In the center, of course, you recognize Jolson and Davy Lee. Marian Nixon is the girl in the picture and the others are Lloyd Bacon, director, Lee Garmes, cinematographer, George Gross, Vitaphone expert, and Frank Shaw, assistant director

SEPT.

THERE'S weeping and wailing and gnashing of teeth out at Universal City.

Last fall when Paul Whiteman was placed under contract by that studio he was given a good will offering or free booty of $50,000.

During the long winter months when there wasn't much to do but plan super-productions, a story was prepared for the monarch of jazz.

Last June it was decided that the story wasn't any good, and another one would have to be written. Not an easy matter, for Whiteman is willing to conduct his orchestra, but he's durned if he'll do one iota of emoting.

His contract says just that, and try and get out of it.

SO, a new story was written with Paul Whiteman and his band on the lot, drawing salaries. If the band leader isn't through the picture in eight weeks he has the right to demand any salary he wishes.

That, too, is in the contract.

Whiteman gets $8,000 a week for eight weeks. The band gets $4,500 a week for eight weeks. Counting in the original $50,000 that makes an initial investment of $150,000 for Universal before a set is built or a camera is turned. And there's no story.

How's that for one of these real life sob stories?

AUG.

More hard work for the new type of Hollywood extra. Rehearsing the girls in the "Say It With a Big Brass Band" number of Metro-Goldwyn-Mayer's "Hollywood Revue of 1929"

SEPT.

HERE'S the ultimate. There can't be anything more to add to pictures. M.-G.-M. has now introduced the smell-a-tone.

At the opening of "The Hollywood Revue of 1929" at Grauman's Chinese Theater the audience thought the orange blossom finale was so realistic that they could actually smell orange blossoms. Well, they could. A gallon or so of perfume was put in the ventilators when the finale flashed on the screen.

ALL THE BRIGHTEST LIGHTS OF BROADWAY MERGED IN ONE!

INCANDESCENT with "IT" . . . One million watts of what millions have come miles to see . . . Every film-foot flaming with the Spirit of 46 — and Broadway . . . NO WONDER "BROADWAY BABIES" HAS MADE THE MAIN STEM JEALOUS!

All Broadway's best stuff stolen for the Talking Screen. The Street of Streets transferred to celluloid and Vitaphone as it's never been before! Girls and guns and glare and glamor . . . Honest-to-Ziegfeld songs and dances and stunning stage effects . . . Then back to the dressing-rooms of glorified beauties — off to their parties after the show.

Wait for "Broadway Babies" before you decide how perfectly the screen can mirror the wonders of world-famed revues. Tell the folks right now that the night "Broadway Babies" comes to town is going to be your night out!

A First National Vitaphone Picture

Vitaphone is the registered trade-mark of the Vitaphone Corporation

"Authentic"—"moving"—"beautiful"—"stirring"—"sure-fire"—"will show the way to high-priced stage musical comedies"—said New York newspaper critics.

The success of the season in New York, at $2.00 per seat! Stunning dancing chorus and great comedy cast. Directed by Mervyn Leroy. Presented by Richard A. Rowland.

Introduces 3 new song-hits "Broadway Baby Dolls," "Wishing and Waiting For Love," and "Jig, Jig, Jigaloo." "They will be hummed and played in every household all summer."
—N. Y. Journal

The Treat of Treats in MUSIC - BEAUTY - DRAMA

RADIO PICTURES

PRESENT

FLORENZ ZIEGFELD'S
Outstanding Success

"RIO RITA"

Glorifier of beauty . . . king of extravaganza . . . whose radiant success, "Rio Rita" has now been glorified for the screen by Radio Pictures.

Featuring Bebe Daniels as "Rio Rita," Dorothy Lee, as "Dolly,"... John Boles, as Jim, the Ranger Captain . . . and Bert Wheeler and Robert Woolsey.

Produced in the original settings of the play with exquisite color sequences . . . gorgeous costumes . . . "Rio Rita's" scintillating music, and new interpolated numbers.

VINCENT YOUMAN'S
Nautical Musical Comedy

"HIT the DECK"

The play that gave the public "Hallelujah" and "Sometimes I'm Happy."

A lavish Radio Pictures' musical extravaganza, in which flashes of sheer humor mingle with stirring drama. Glamorous scenes of Chinese revolution. Swinging choruses of gorgeous girls and gallant gobs. The rattle of distant gun-fire blends with lilting melodies.

Master of melody . . . monarch of comedy . . . producer of "Hit the Deck," the charm and glamor of which have been translated to the screen by Radio Pictures.

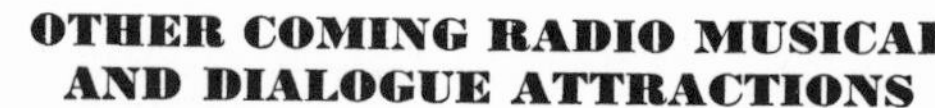

OTHER COMING RADIO MUSICAL AND DIALOGUE ATTRACTIONS

"Radio Revels of 1929"—The first annual screen review released by Radio Pictures . . . A song and musical spectacle comparable to anything on stage or screen.

"Street Girl"—An eye-filling, heart-stirring musical drama. Cast includes Betty Compson, Gus Arnheim's Cocoanut Grove Band, Jack Oakie, Joseph Cawthorne.

"The Vagabond Lover"—Starring the inimitable Rudy Vallee and his Connecticut Yankees . . . A romantic musical comedy, full of color and action.

"High River"—A Herbert Brenon production . . . A majestic story of conflicting wills and passions in the river-threatened levee country of the Mississippi.

RKO DISTRIBUTING CORPORATION
A subsidiary of the Radio Corporation of America

For pictures that forecast the screen of tomorrow—see Radio Pictures of today

Carl Laemmle
presents

THE ONE AND ONLY BROADWAY

YOU'LL see things you never saw before in "Broadway." You'll be plunged deep into the blazing heart of New York's mad night life! You'll see people you wouldn't believe existed doing things you wouldn't believe possible! You'll hear songs you'll never forget—songs like "Hittin' The Ceiling," "Sing a Little Love Song," and others! You'll be amazed at the biggest set ever built, as you're entertained by the most extravagant girlie revue numbers ever staged! You'll be charmed and thrilled by the color scenes in Technicolor.

As a stage play "Broadway" was the outstanding success of two seasons; as a talking picture it swept blase New York off its feet when it ran at the Globe Theatre at $2.00. Now you can see it at your favorite theatre exactly as shown on Broadway.

The cast includes Glenn Tryon, Evelyn Brent, Merna Kennedy, Otis Harlan, Robert Ellis; two members of the original stage cast —Thomas E. Jackson and Paul Porcasi, and many others.

100%

TALKING
SINGING
DANCING
THRILLING

With the original play dialog from the Jed Harris stage success by Philip Dunning and George Abbott.

A CARL LAEMMLE, JR., PRODUCTION
Directed by PAUL FEJOS

SHOW BOAT

"SHOW BOAT" keeps rolling up new records everywhere. It is truly a talking and singing triumph. The receipts at box offices in every part of the world are almost unbelievable. Never was there a picture with such Universal appeal for grown folks and youngsters of every nationality. You simply MUST see "Show Boat."

The cast includes Laura La Plante, as "Magnolia"; Joseph Schildkraut, as "Ravenal;" Otis Harlan, Alma Rubens, Emily Fitzroy, Jane La Verne. Music from the Florenz Ziegfeld stage production of EDNA FERBER'S great novel, with the singing hits of Helen Morgan, Jules Bledsoe and Aunt Jemima.

A HARRY POLLARD PRODUCTION

UNIVERSAL PICTURES
730 FIFTH AVENUE, NEW YORK

NOW COLOR TAKES THE SCREEN!

TALKING

SINGING

Warner Bros. present
The first 100% Natural Color
ALL SINGING PRODUCTION
IN TECHNICOLOR

Vitaphone is the registered trademark of the Vitaphone Corporation.

"ON WITH THE SHOW"

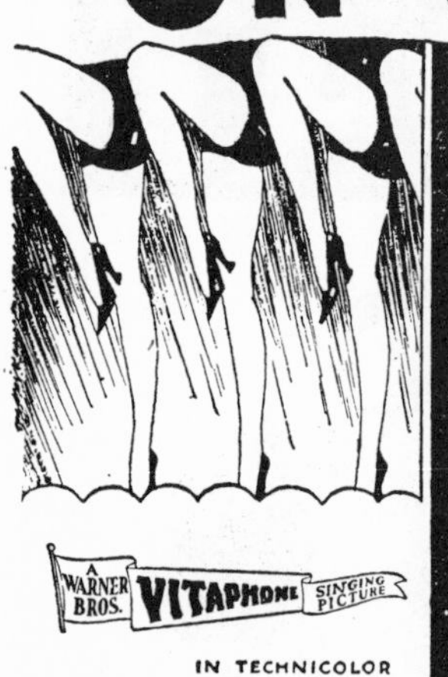

Now Warner Bros. pioneer again with another radical development in motion picture production—COLOR! Full colors—natural colors—real colors, reproduced direct from life!

Color breaks the last barrier between you and Broadway at its best. Now the Screen can give you *everything* the Stage can offer—and more...

For at "On With The Show" you can sit "out front" and revel in all the color and rhythm of the spectacular singing and dancing numbers of a Broadway revue—than step behind the curtain to listen in on the strange drama and romance that wings and dressing-rooms hold secret... see heart-break hiding behind hilarity because—*"the show must go on!"*

A $2 Broadway Hit Direct to YOU at POPULAR Prices

With 100 per cent Talking and Singing, an all-star cast of 14 famous names, a glorified beauty chorus of 100, and 3 brand-new hit songs—"Am I Blue?", "Let Me Have My Dreams", and "In The Land of Let's Pretend"—"ON WITH THE SHOW" would be superb picture entertainment, even in black and white... But the added thrill of Technicolor makes it an artistic event of commanding importance in entertainment history. Make—or break—a date to see it!

You *See and Hear* VITAPHONE *only in* Warner Bros. *and* First National *Pictures*

Help John McCormack Select His Movietone Songs

Vote for your ten favorites on the ballot below

WHAT songs do you want to hear John McCormack sing in his Fox Movietone production?

That is a question uppermost in the minds of Fox Films executives. The beloved Irish tenor has become so thoroughly established as an American institution that all music lovers are familiar with his repertoire.

McCormack will sing ten songs in the Movietone production about to begin shooting and microphoning in Ireland, with Frank Borzage directing.

In the ballot below, you will find a list of McCormack's best loved songs. Check your ten favorites. In the blank spaces you may write in any of McCormack's songs which may have been omitted from the list.

Mail your ballot to John McCormack Picture Director, Fox Studio, Los Angeles, Calif.

John McCormack

To John McCormack Picture Director
Fox Studio
Los Angeles, Calif.

I suggest that John McCormack sing the ten songs designated:

☐ Believe Me If All Those Endearing Young Charms	☐ At Dawning	☐ Beneath the Moon of Lombardy
☐ The Harp That Once Through Tara's Halls	☐ Macushla	☐ Little Mother of Mine
☐ Silver Threads Among the Gold	☐ The Rosary	☐ Wearing of the Green
☐ When Irish Eyes Are Smiling	☐ Ave Maria	☐ Kathleen Mavourneen
☐ When You and I Were Young, Maggie	☐ Mother Machree	☐ Dear Love, Remember Me
☐ That Tumble-down Shack in Athlone	☐ Roses of Picardy	☐ I Hear You Calling Me
☐ Somewhere a Voice Is Calling	☐ Moonlight and Roses	☐ My Wild Irish Rose
☐ Serenade (Softly Through the Night)	☐ Dear Old Pal of Mine	☐ A Little Bit of Heaven
☐	☐	☐

Name______________________________

Street Address__________________ Town and State__________________

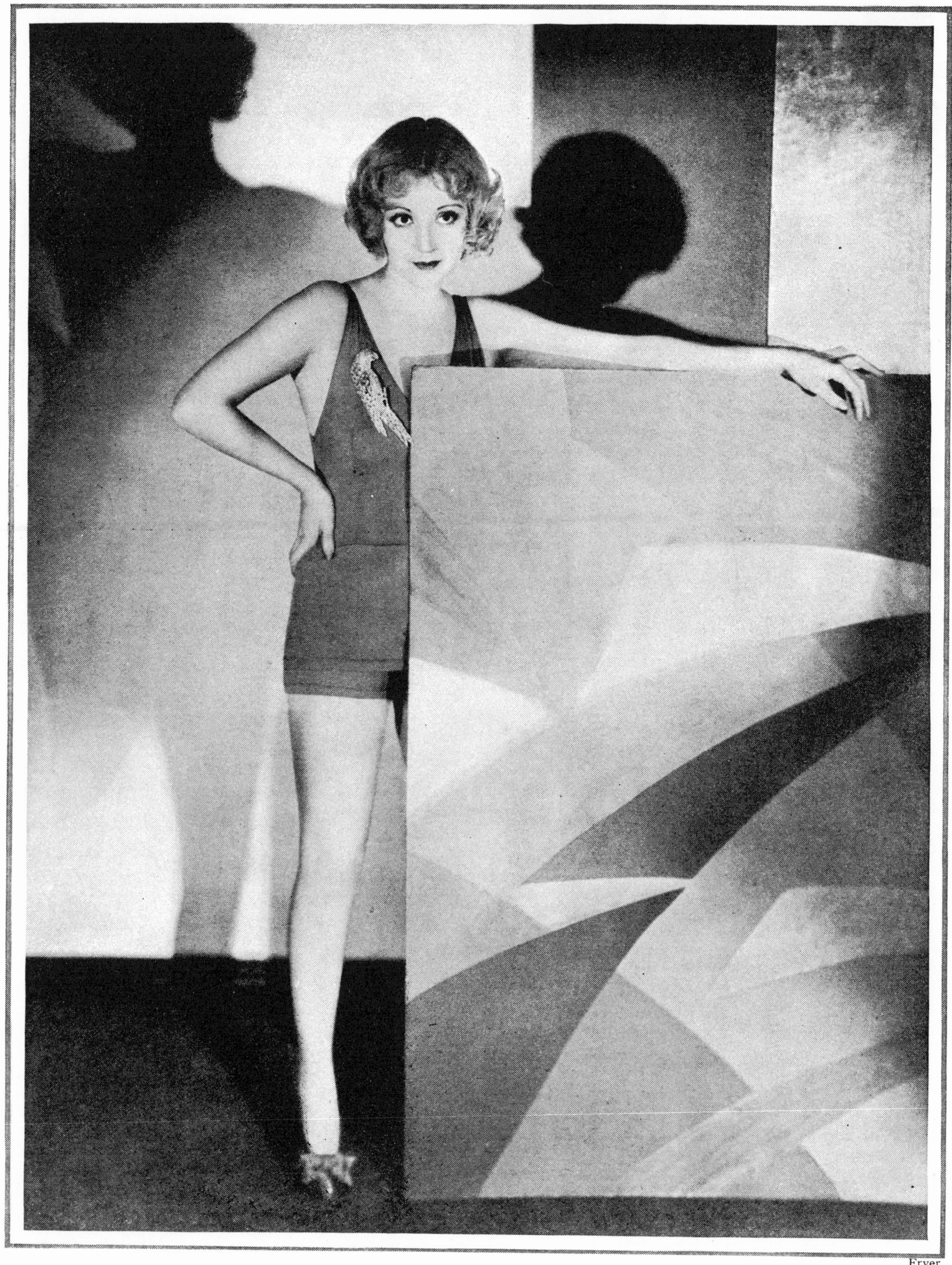

Fryer

ALICE WHITE, in a futuristic setting, is a girl followed by two shadows. One is a talkie shadow and the other is silent. First National is surrounding Alice with plenty of singing and dancing in her musical film, "Broadway Babies"

Talbot

MARILYN MILLER snubbed all movie contracts until the talkies came along. When First National offered her $100,000 to make a film version of "Sally," Marilyn deserted musical comedy and took her dancing shoes to Hollywood. Little incidents like that make things look black for the new theatrical season and explain why so many New York managers are having their theaters wired to accommodate the triumphant talkies

Irving Berlin

He wrote the words and music of "Coquette" and "Marie"

L. Wolfe Gilbert

You sang his lyrics of "Ramona" and "Lilac Time"

Con Conrad

He collects royalties on "Breakaway" and "That's You, Baby"

Dave Dreyer

Think of him when you dance to "Rainbow 'Round My Shoulder"

Westward *the* Course

Why Mammy's Boys—the song-writers—are shouting "California, Here I Come!"

THAT little gray home in the West is no longer for rent. The bird who first glorified it from a piano on West 46th Street has moved in—with his Mammy.

The home-cooked bacon, the sugared yams which his Mammy was scheduled to turn out, are also in the picture. Mammy, however, isn't doing the cooking, but daily you can find those who write the nation's songs gathered around tables in Wilson Mizner's Brown Derby, Henry's, and Eddie Brandstatter's Montmartre.

For ten years they've been singing the warning: "California—Here I Come."

They've come,—and how! That yearned-for Golden Gate has sprung a hinge in opening wide to let 'em in. And they'll never ask for more.

It is now a question as to which has absorbed which. Is the motion picture industry a subsidiary of the music publishing business,—or have film producers gone into the business of making songs?

TO the song-writer himself, the question means nothing. All that matters is that he has never been so happy in his life. Never before were things as easy for a composer or lyricist as the present. That goes, financially, artistically and comfortably. Named in the order of importance to the song-writer.

During the so-called "good old days," the song-writer sweat agonies before an idea came for a song. There were comparatively few production writers who were given situations on which to build themes.

Henderson, Brown and DeSylva

The fathers of "Sonny Boy." It was first sung over a long distance telephone from Atlantic City to Hollywood

After writing it, the trouble of getting the song marketed began. If the composer or lyricist was under contract to a music publisher, that difficulty was easily removed. Even then, his work was just starting. A staff of "pluggers" were assigned to get the song placed. This meant personal interviews with vaudeville actors, band leaders, radio entertainers, cabaret performers and even circus troupers. The function of the "plugger" was to convince such persons of the tremendous merits contained in the new song, in order to warrant their learning it and placing it in their routines or repertoires.

INDIVIDUALS in all branches of the amusement industry were showered with courtesies by the representatives of the publisher or by the song-writers. These attentions varied in size, according to the artist's importance.

Many rated only a lunch. Others were given theater tickets, or admissions to baseball or football games or fights. The very highest of the high were "cut in." In this fashion many of the better known orchestra leaders, black-face comedians, revue stars and vaudeville headliners obtained a percentage of royalty on a song featured by them. Such methods were (and still are) supposedly forbidden by members of the Music Publishers Protective Association.

The taboo was (and still is) overcome by the simple expedient of naming the singer or musician as one of the song's writers.

Some hits of the past have had as many as eight writers named responsible for a lyric or a melody.

The more bands or

Louis Silvers

Mammy theme song daddy. He wrote "Mother I Still Have You"

Nacio Herb Brown

Not getting poor on "The Wedding of the Painted Doll"

Harry Akst

Who wrote the music of "Am I Blue?" for "On With the Show"

Fred Fischer

He contributed "Strike Up the Band" to the "Hollywood Revue"

of Tin-Pan Alley

By Jerry Hoffman

acts using a song, the better became its commercial value, for it reached the ears of so many more music-buyers. If a song was a "natural," the work was easier, for many performers would voluntarily use it. A "natural" in songwriterese is a number that clicks with the public the first time it is heard. It doesn't require constant plugging, for its melody is whistled and learned easily.

AFTER he had his song with hundreds of acts, the song-writer's worries were far from ended. There was the job of keeping that song in the routine or repertoire of the performer as long as possible. Personal jealousies among actors or orchestra leaders; a sore throat or laryngitis suffered by a singer; peeves at the song-writer or his firm often resulted in a song being taken out of an act after one or two weeks.

There is a big difference in writing songs for motion pictures. To a song-writer there is no greater comfort than the knowledge that once a number is set in a movie—it *stays* in.

The song *stays* in. To a layman, the big thing in motion picture exploitation of songs would appear the increased financial returns resulting from a greater appeal. That is a minor consideration to the professional writer. The star who sang it originally may have paralyzed vocal chords a week later; the song-writer may say the nastiest things about the star's mother or wife. But regardless of what happens—once that picture is released, the song is *IN*.

WITHIN a month of a film's release, the average motion picture song with commercial possibilities will sell from 100,000 to 500,000 copies, plus an equal number of records. Formerly, the average good number, with very rare instances, would be fortunate to sell 30,000 copies in three months.

For example: Last June, the "Fox Follies" opened in fifty-seven cities over the entire country on the same date. Within three weeks, "Breakaway," "That's You, Baby" and "Walking With Susie" had sold over 100,000 copies and records. Had Con Conrad, Archie Cottler and Sydney Mitchell written those songs for a theatrical production or just as popular numbers, it would take the time for the show to play over the entire country or the acts using them to appear in the same territories to produce results probably not as good.

THE first song written for a motion picture, to be sung as part of the film's action, was "Mother I Still Have You," in "The Jazz Singer." It was written by Louis Silvers and Al Jolson, who sang it. Had the number or the picture been released a year later, its sheet music sale would have been from 300,000 to 500,000 copies instead of 30,000. The reason for this small number of sales, even with Jolson singing it, was the few theaters equipped for sound at the time of the picture's release. Incidentally, Louis Silvers may be termed the advance guard of the song-writers now flooding Hollywood. He was the first to establish permanent residence in the film colony under the new era. He came with Jolson, with whom he has been associated for seventeen years in the theater, conducting the orchestras for all Jolson shows.

However, the possibilities shown by "Mother I Still Have You" caused motion picture producers to realize that here was an element worth considering. It was further impressed a year later when "Sonny Boy" swept the country as one of the greatest selling hits in the history of popular music.

"SONNY BOY" may or may not have been a "natural." It was played and sung often enough during the course of "The Singing Fool" to stamp it indelibly on the minds of its hearers. Incidentally, the method of its creation is one of those freak tales which eventually will come to be regarded as a choice bit of fiction. But it's true.

(continued on next page)

BECAUSE of the tremendous interest of its readers in theme songs of motion pictures, PHOTOPLAY will inaugurate a new service department. Beginning in the October issue, PHOTOPLAY will review phonograph and piano records of the music used in screen productions, so that you may know where to obtain recordings of your favorite songs.

PHOTOPLAY is the first national publication to give its readers a specialized music service, and its music reviews will be up to the high standard maintained by its Shadow Stage.

(The record reviews will be found on pages 337–352 of this volume.)

(continued from preceding page)

Irving Berlin, whose music business hadn't been any too good in recent years, found new life for it via the motion picture field. Originally he was intended to write the score for "The Singing Fool." It was almost a year between the time that plan was made until the film went into production. Meanwhile, Berlin tied up with United Artists, but had written one number for the new Jolson picture. Al wanted one to sing to Davey Lee. Berlin's melody was pleasant enough, but the idea didn't quite suit Jolson's needs.

A LONG distance call from Hollywood, Jolson speaking, to De Sylva, Brown and Henderson in New York revealed that those three publisher-writers were in Atlantic City, preparing a show. Jolson explained his wants to Bobby Crawford, general manager for D. B. & H. Crawford told Jolson he'd call him back.

Again via telephone, Crawford relayed Jolson's wants to De Sylva, Brown and Henderson in Atlantic City. Four hours after the Mammy-glorifier had put in his first call, his 'phone in Hollywood rang. (Service was awfully good that day.) It was De Sylva, Brown and Henderson, in Atlantic City.

Buddy De Sylva sang the lyric and melody of "Sonny Boy" over the wire.

"Great," yelled Al. "Send me a lead-sheet and lyrics by air-mail!"

By July, "Sonny Boy" had sold one and a quarter million copies of sheet music. Two million records had been disposed of—for cash.

A music publisher's gross return on a copy of music is twenty cents. From this are subtracted royalties and all other expenses. The writer's royalty on sheet music ranges from three to six cents on a copy. The publisher gets two cents on every record sold. Two-thirds of that he keeps, the other third goes to the writers. De Sylva, Brown and Henderson were both writers and publishers of "Sonny Boy." Al Jolson added to the lyrics, made some changes and collected one-fourth of writers' royalty. Try that on your comptometer.

IS it any wonder then, that motion picture producers began to look upon the music publishing business as more than an incidental? Warner Brothers received nothing of the monies made by "Sonny Boy" the song. Having sponsored the industry's best-seller, they decided not to overlook any future possibilities and made the most expensive gesture of all producers. This was the purchase, lock, stock and barrel of Witmarks, Inc., one of the oldest music publishing firms in existence. That firm's catalogue of past hits and classics alone brings a revenue of several hundred thousand yearly to the firm. The deal involved over five million dollars for Warners, but all future song profits will go to them.

Since then, almost all the major producers have either merged or made working agreements with various publishers. De Sylva, Brown and Henderson supply the writers and own all copyrights to songs used in pictures made by William Fox. Metro-Goldwyn-Mayer and the Jack Robbins Music Company have a similar agreement.

Paramount has made an exceptionally wide arrangement. It formed the Famous Music Company as a subsidiary of the established firm of T. B. Harms, Inc., and its allied group. Old firms such as Remick's, and Chappell-Harms, which is responsible for the Harms' music popularity in England and Europe, are included. There is the younger concern of Spier and Coslow in the deal. This arrangement gives Paramount call on any of the contracted writers with these music publishers, and publication of the numbers through the Famous Music Company. Hence, "Louise," which sold almost to the million mark in copies, made money for Paramount as well as the publishers. Leo Robbins and Dick Whiting collected the royalty profits due the writers.

SEPT.

You can see by the expression on Director Millard Webb's face that he doesn't care for brunettes—even of the glorified variety. Now if that were blonde Mary Eaton in the polka-dotted bathing suit—! Incidentally, Director Webb's opus, "Glorifying the American Girl," is going to be something new—a backstage drammer, no less, showing us how the chorus girls really talk. Why not begin numbering 'em? For instance "Broadway Melody" could be X1394, "Broadway" X1993, etc.

Song writing for pictures has made every person engaged in Hollywood now a "production writer." This is different from old conditions, when one had to grope for an idea before turning out a number. The writer is given situations. The film's director and the scenarist can tell in advance what they want the lyrics to convey.

In this respect, the writers of songs have one difficulty to overcome, which seems slight, but is annoying. They have to contend with the popular impression shared by producers, scenarists and directors—that a song's lyric is written first. It isn't. In fact, it is well-nigh impossible to set a tune to a lyric. A song-writer may build a melody on a title, but never on a complete lyric. The tune is always composed first, and then the lyric set to it. If a line runs short or long one or two notes—the melody is altered.

Definite ideas are not always available—or else the producer cannot express 'em. One example, in an incident at Paramount, is typical. The producer simply told the song-writing team:

"WE'VE got a picture called 'Wolf-Song.' It's all about a man on a mountain. Write a song for it."

From such premise came "Yo Te Amo," warbled by Lupe Velez and "Wolf-Song" roared by Gary Cooper and the mountaineers.

There are quite a few producers, on the other hand, who have a very definite idea of what they want and know it when they hear it. The numbers in Harry Rapf's production of "The Hollywood Revue of 1929" for Metro-Goldwyn-Mayer are an exceptionally fine illustration. In this picture, the songs were not written for situations. The scenes and the numbers were built and staged for the numbers.

Seven teams of song-writers were used by M.-G.-M. in getting numbers for the revue. Rapf wanted a military finale to the first half, and assigned all fourteen writers to the task, the intention being to select the best of all submitted. For a month, various ideas and finished compositions were turned in—none of them suiting Rapf.

Many were original and novel, but didn't convey just what Rapf wanted to get over.

One day the entire group were assembled in the rehearsal hall discussing ideas. Fred Fisher finally burst out with:

"Well, Mr. Rapf. I don't know what you want. If it were twenty years ago—I'd give you something like this—" sat down at the piano and improvised a strain of six-eight rhythm (march style).

"THAT'S it!" shouted Rapf, "that's it!!"

Thus was born "Strike Up the Band," one of the most effective military finales seen in any revue. The style of composition may have been twenty years old, but the production gives it all the essence of sensational novelty. Here it is showmanship that makes the song effective.

A number such as "Strike Up the Band" will sell very few copies. It has no commercial value in royalties to either its writer or publisher and comes under the heading of special material. In direct contrast is another song in the "Hollywood Revue" called "Singing in the Rain." This is the "plug" song of the show, meaning the one selected as having best possibilities for popular appeal. Therefore it is rendered *(continued on next page)*

(continued from preceding page)

throughout the production more than any other song. This is to thoroughly familiarize fans with it and create a demand.

"Singing in the Rain" will sell over a million copies and easily as many records. "Strike Up the Band" probably won't go to 10,000, if it goes to any fraction of that. To balance things, studios have made an unique arrangement in financial matters with song-writers.

Unique in the history of song-writing, although obvious to members of other businesses. Prior to the Hollywood era of song-exploitation, song writers were paid strictly on a royalty basis. Every dollar they were handed was charged against the financial earnings of their songs published by the firm. If the final accounting showed they had drawn more than they were entitled, such sums were charged against future possible royalties. The writer was in debt for whatever amount was overdrawn.

THE new arrangement has made Hollywood brighter than any blue heaven for the composer and lyricist. He is paid a salary plus drawing account against royalties. *The total amount paid the writer is guaranteed to the music publisher by the motion picture producer.*

No matter how much money a writer has drawn, or has been paid—and whether his songs have earned a single penny or not—he does not owe the publisher or producer a cent in the final statement!

He may draw $10,000 against royalties in one year and his total earnings in that respect be no more than $2,500. The following year, he may still be drawing $10,000 and his royalty earnings total $40,000.

The music publisher still owes him $30,000! And he gets it! The balance, supposedly due the publisher from the preceding year's statement, *is not deducted.*

All such sums are guaranteed, as I have said, by the motion picture producer. The film man still feels himself ahead and he is, for he does not have to pay royalty on theater box-office receipts to song-writers as do producers of legitimate shows. All standard composers and lyricists are paid a percentage of the show's gross earnings during its entire run. Jerome Kern, for example, gets three percent of the total intake at the box-office of any operetta, revue or musical comedy for which he has written the music. Vincent Youmans and George Gershwin get similar percentages. Box-office royalties on legitimate attractions to music and lyric writers range from two to seven percent. The seven is usually set aside by theatrical producers for division between composer, lyricist and librettist.

Hence the savings to motion picture producers can easily be seen. The average weekly envelope for a song-writer attached to a studio contains $350. In such cases, half is charged to future royalties and the other half considered salary. Total weekly checks vary from $200 weekly to $750.

THIS system is now undergoing slight changes —even to the still greater benefit of the song-writer. De Sylva, Brown and Henderson, mentioned several times heretofore simply because they have been most active in film-song business, were paid $150,000 in advance by Fox for the score, book and lyrics of a musical comedy called "Sunnyside Up," which is to star Janet Gaynor. This sum was paid because the boys gave up several offers for legitimate musicals in New York to remain in Hollywood. Meanwhile, they will also collect profits in royalties on all songs written for Fox productions. This trio had the publication of the music written by Conrad, Gottler and Mitchell for Universal's "Broadway."

At the present writing, the music publishing business is in a better position financially since the advent of radio, when receipts started on the down-grade. Not in eight years or more have there been as many songs selling over the million copy mark.

The first to hit six figures was "Charmaine," written as a thematic score song to "What Price Glory?" by Lew Pollock and Erno Rappe. Both these gentlemen repeated with "Diane" for "Seventh Heaven." The first sensation in theme songs since "Mickey," written for Mabel Normand ten years ago, was "Ramona" for Dolores del Rio's picture. L. Wolfe Gilbert, who has been batting out lyrics as far back as "The Robert E. Lee" and "My Little Dream Girl," was responsible for "Ramona," with Mabel Wayne.

These earlier songs were written in New York, before the music business was made a collaborator of motion picture production. Gilbert is now ensconced in Hollywood with Abel Baer as his partner. Baer wrote "Lilac Time" with Gilbert for Colleen Moore's picture and has teamed with him since.

They are also scheduled to write the special numbers for Paul Whiteman's first movie at Universal.

NONE of these "best-sellers" were used vocally in the pictures for which they were written. Even the master Irving Berlin melodies are as yet to be heard from the voice of a screen actor. Probably the first will be Harry Richman, whose picture for United Artists will have an entire score written by Berlin. Berlin, however, has also found new inspiration, financially and idealistically via the screen. Both songs sponsored by him have topped the million mark in sales. His first was "Marie," for Vilma Banky in "The Awakening." The other was "Coquette," for Mary Pickford.

Warner Brothers have been most fortunate with vocal hits. Although "Sonny Boy" didn't bring his song pennies to them, "Am I Blue?", by Harry Akst and Grant Clarke from "On With the Show," is rapidly mounting the lists of numbers called for most in music shops. Metro-Goldwyn-Mayer cleaned up for Jack Robbins and themselves with "The Broadway Melody" by having three big sellers in the one show. This is very unusual, even for the best written Broadway revues. "The Broadway Melody," "You Were Meant for Me" and "The Wedding of the Painted Doll" are all from the score by the same writers, Arthur Freed and Nacio Herb Brown.

Oddly enough, the writers of "The Broadway Melody" are probably the only composer-lyricist team not brought to Hollywood by producers. Arthur Freed spent ten years in Los Angeles, producing musical comedies and straight dramas which somehow never clicked. Nacio Brown composed melodies for the spasmodically produced musical shows on the West Coast, and attained prominence finally with the "Doll Dance," written for Carter De Haven's Music Box Revue in Hollywood.

WITH the hits from "The Broadway Melody," "Singing in the Rain" from the "Hollywood Revue" and "The Pagan Love Song" bringing royalties, the boys have gained sufficient confidence to embark on a music publishing business of their own.

The free-lance song-writer has little or no market in motion pictures. In fact there are but three known successful ones, and their connections in the past have made the road easy. Billy Rose, otherwise famous as Fanny Brice's husband, is one. Fred Fisher ceases to be by signing a contract at this writing with M.-G.-M., and John Milt Hagen is the third. Hagen was an established vaudeville and revue writer in New York prior to coming to Hollywood, and since has been very successful in writing the themes for independent firms and for short subjects.

IT is also a fact that the very topmost of Those Who Rate are still in New York and evince little desire to join their brothers in A Paradise for Two—Or More. George Gershwin has turned down $100,000 to do a picture. Jerome Kern also remains aloof. Rudolf Friml, probably the most prolific of living composers, has succumbed to the wiles of Sam Goldwyn and will write an operetta for him.

The field for production writers seems a set-up for newcomers in New York. That is for the theater—not for pictures. Harry Ruby and Bert Kalmar, who have been banging out book lyrics and scores of shows for years, were captured by RKO and will write "Radio Revels" which is to star all the important names of the National Broadcast System. Kalmar and Ruby will be placed in an adjoining cage to Oscar Levant and Sidney Clare, who have been holding down the entire RKO lot by themselves and have turned out songs for three pictures "Street Girl," "Side-Street," and "Half-Marriage."

IN connection with the song-writers are a few unheard of individuals known professionally as "arrangers." Their modesty is not assumed, neither need they worry about publicity. The average salary of an established arranger is more than the weekly pay check issued to most of the song-writers. Arthur Lange, at Metro-Goldwyn-Mayer; Victor Barravalle at RKO, Louis Silvers at Warners, Leo Forbstein at First National, and Arthur Kay at Fox are said to be paid $1,000 weekly.

However, they have no accrued royalties coming, unless a composition be one of their own.

It is these people who are responsible for the orchestrations of a song. Their arrangements can make a poor number sound great and a great one—rotten.

There is still another feature of the new song era that is lovely for the Hollywood Chamber of Commerce and the members of the Motion Picture Producers Association. They are relieved of any possible rush to Hollywood by film-struck song writers. Simply because the song-writers are not engaged by studios in Hollywood—but by publishers in New York.

It is just as well. Right now it is impossible to cross the lobby of the Roosevelt Hotel without wading waist-deep through song-writers. In Hollywood's cafes they get into your hair.

And that is the solution of why Sid Grauman finally got his famous locks sheared. He knew what was coming.

Songs across the Sea

Put on your smoked glasses, for here is that million dollar Maurice Chevalier smile, which made that French singing comedian the Pet of Paris and the Honey of Hollywood

Meet Maurice Chevalier, Unofficial Envoy of France

By Dorothy Spensley

MADAME Chevalier walked across the room with Adolphe tugging on leash.

M. Chevalier watched her reflectively.

Adolphe is as proud a wire-haired terrier as ever thrust his nose aristocratically aloft, and has to be taken out for air occasionally.

"Adolphe Menjou gives us Adolphe," Chevalier beams. On the wall of the dressing room is a thumbtacked picture of Charles Chaplin. "To Maurice from Charlie," it says, and an autographed photograph of Jesse Lasky, to whom Chevalier is contracted. On the desk are leather-framed pictures of Mary and Douglas Fairbanks, Joan and Douglas, Jr., and a small drawing of Madame Chevalier.

Over all, though, is Jesse Lasky. Some consider this a mark of diplomacy. But they do not know Chevalier. It is a gesture of devotion. It was Jesse Lasky who discovered him and in twenty-four hours signed him to American pictures.

In France they call him the Idol of Paris. In America they call him the Idol of Seattle or Louisville or Hoboken or Jersey City or wherever "Innocents of Paris," a really bad picture, is playing.

Monsieur and Madame Chevalier in a pretty domestic scene in their Hollywood hut. The beautiful dark eyed missus is a prominent French musical comedy actress in her own right

The publicity department is responsible for that. Responsible for sending out copy that is easily transferable from theater manager to small or large town paper.

IT is all very confusing, this thing of fame. It is all very confusing, this thing that makes idols. That makes people shriek and yell and scream and stamp when one slim man with full lower lip and tight upper, with glistening teeth and flashing smile, with snapping fingers and syncopated limbs, with a blue-eyed wink and brown hair, comes strutting out.

It is all very confusing until you meet Maurice Chevalier, and then you understand everything. You understand personal magnetism, mob adoration, gloves split from applause, fan worship, the supreme ability—the genius—that lifted itself above a worthless first picture and made him an ascending American idol.

You understand Chevalier as he sits groping for modest words to explain just how the French public feels about him; just how he cannot desert them permanently for perhaps greater glory on the American screen.

His wish is to make three pictures a year, one in Hollywood, one in New

(continued on next page)

(continued from preceding page)

York and one in Paris. His eyes, pleasant, kindly eyes; twinkling, devilish eyes, at will, grow fond as he speaks of France. His France.

"In Paris, you see," he paused for a moment to find the right words in the jumble of English that he has picked up, "I am what Carpentier is to the ring. They like me very well." The last word is left suspended, a poor little English "well," in French mid-air. "I could not leave them—no. That is why I should like to go back once a year, say, and make a picture there, eh?"

ADOLPHE, well-aired, saunters across the room, pulling Madame Chevalier, black-haired and black-eyed, a Frenchwoman such as the American pictures her; a musical comedy actress carrying her own name of Suzanne Vallee to personal fame, with him.

Reflectively, as before, Chevalier watched her, and undoubtedly thought of many things, including the voice, the costume and the camera tests he must make before "The Love Parade," his second picture, goes into production. Thought of the lines in French and English that he must learn. Of the songs by Clifford Gray and Victor Schertzinger that he must master. Thought of the five days of rehearsals with Ernst Lubitsch, who directs him, that he must negotiate. Thought of this and that, and the offer that Mary Pickford made him six years ago in Paris when she asked him to come to America and be her leading man.

"What I want to do is this," said Chevalier. "I want to try and blend the liveliness, the sprightly tempo of the French songs—you notice how different they are from yours?—with the rhythm of the American jazz. That is what the modern Parisian is doing today. That is what I want to do."

In doing that Chevalier is becoming international. And the greatest artists are international, with an art that transcends language.

"RAQUEL MELLER is international. A marvelous artist. And yet she sings in Spanish to a French audience and she is a great success, eh? Also Bernhardt, Sarah Bernhardt, when she comes to thees country, she spoke in French, and they understand. Al Jolson is a great artist. Eef he ever went to Paris he would be a sensation. He, too, is international."

But what is it that makes for international success? What in France do you call that thing that Americans call It?

"Eet is person-al-ity, eh? I don't know. Maybe more than that. Yes. In Paris we would say 'heart.' Eef you put your heart into anything, into your songs or your dancing, your audience feels eet, of course, yes? Look at girls like Clara Bow. You know that she wants to please, that from her heart she is trying very hard. And you love her because you know she is doing that. Is that not so?

"I want to blend the two song tempos as I have say. Make what you call a Paris, New York cocktail, yes?"

And cement the *entente cordiale*. But, better still, mix a Chevalier Cocktail?

He grinned, a grin that was boyish and pleased. He is amazingly modest, this man who has two continents at his feet; this man who says "fled," interrogatively, for the past tense of "fly"; who received an ovation during his month's appearance on the Ziegfeld Roof recently such as Gotham has rarely, if ever, seen. Who sang his "Valentina" song ("what beautiful eyes and lips and chin and . . ." ah! with appropriate gestures) to a clamorous throng who paid eleven dollars cover charge to buy ginger ale and white rock. But mostly to hear Chevalier.

"I want to remain Parisian. I think a foreigner make a meestake to Americanize himself too much. Rather that they stay themselves than to try to be converted into something else."

Hobnobbing with interned English soldiers during a twenty-six months' sojourn at Altem Grabow, a German prison, where he was carried, suffering from shrapnel wounds, after one of the first battles of memorable 1914, was what taught him his first English.

"Always before, and sometimes after the war, I was too poor to learn English," Chevalier says, frankly. There is a nice lack of pretense, a simplicity, a basic modesty about him. And now that he has means to learn English, he is not to perfect it, by order of Jesse Lasky; a portion, so it is reasoned, and perhaps rightly, of the Chevalier charm being in his accent.

Chevalier was born in Menilmontant, a suburb of that city called the Capital of the World, where pink lights gleam and chestnut trees bloom in the spring. "And I know less about eet, maybe, than I do New York, as is the way of provincials, for in New York as soon as I arrive this last time—I have been there before, but not professionally—they say, 'Come, we will make a feelm to send back to Paris showing what Chevalier is doing in America.' So we go to the Statue of Liberty and along the Avenue and I am photographed; also I am photographed mounting a bus, and I know more about that city than the person who lives there all his life."

Chevalier has been, in turn, from the fatherless age of eleven, an apprentice carpenter, electrician, printer, doll factory employe, painting waxen faces until discharged for making Harlequin spots of vermilion on dolls destined for domesticity, paint shop salesman, nail maker, always with the vision of stage or circus before him. In his first American picture (he has made several unspectacular French pictures) the plot followed the general pattern of his life.

"But eet is not the thing I should like to do, that sentimental love making," says Chevalier with a deprecatory shrug of shoulders well-fitted in darkish stuff with a light stripe running through. On his little finger, right hand, gleamed a three-diamond ring set in platinum. His white polka-dotted tie was chastely held by a single pearl stickpin. His cuff links, in a shirt of fine white fabric, were round and flat and paved with small diamonds. There was nothing of the flashy, volatile Frenchman, dear to American minds, in the quiet perfection of his attire. On the third finger of his left hand was a slender platinum wedding ring. Madame Chevalier, heard moving in the other room, had been monsieur's dancing partner; that was after he parted from Mistinguett of the million dollar legs.

"THE love making which I like is that with the light touch of humor, the smile, but yet sincere. None of this romantic stuff, with everything so serious. I do not feel comfortable in that kind of rôle. Eet is not my type. Love, with a bit of humor, is what they like in Paris."

Chevalier was in his middle teens, drunk with theatrical ambitions, when he approached the manager of the Concert of the Three Lions and demanded an audition on the grounds that he was an accomplished singer. The truth was that Chevalier was an accomplished charlatan as far as vocal experience was concerned. And as that, he was soon found out.

At the Casino des Tourelles, some time later, he did his first singing turn. He also gave impersonations of local favorites. It was not long before he was presented to Mistinguett, the musical comedy sensation. It was scarcely longer before he found himself her dancing partner at the Folies Bergere, which no tourist can conscientiously miss.

1913 found Chevalier doing his compulsory military service, a part of every French lad's life, and September, 1914, found him a part of the wedge of blue that was stopping the flood of grey that poured into his beloved country. He awoke to find himself prisoner and after over two years' internment, escaped, by the simple expedient of walking out of camp with his pal, Joe Bridge, an actor who had assisted him in impromptu entertainment at the encampment. They passed themselves off as Red Cross workers, and for it Chevalier received a Military Cross.

"In Paris, Mary and Douglas Fairbanks are present at one of my performances," continued Chevalier, blotting out the war hurriedly. "I send them a card asking them to come backstage; I should like to meet them. But Douglas, he does not wait until the show is over. He comes back between the acts."

IT was the beginning, six years ago, of a strong friendship. The Chevaliers are frequent visitors at Pickfair. In fact, it is said that the songs of "The Love Parade" are to be given a try-out before the distinguished audience that gathers there, before they are movietoned.

Again, after the war, Chevalier danced with Mistinguett. He became a star. He appeared in London with Elsie Janis in "Hello, America." He went to the Argentine, Buenos Aires. He crossed to America for a week to see New York. He accepted the Fairbanks' invitation to come to Hollywood, thinking it was a ride of several hours, and discovered it was not. "I am sur-prised, eh?" he says, shrugging his shoulders, a movement unconsciously French; the only Gallic gesture in what appears to be a typical Englishman or American of poise and discernment.

Vocal Boy *Makes* Good

John Boles is lucky in having a voice and face that synchronize

By Janet French

Go tell Aunt Rhodie
Go tell Aunt Rhodie
Go tell Aunt Rhodie that her old grey goose is dead.

AND that was John Boles' first singing lesson. If you were born in the "yes, ma'am" and "no, suh" belt you can go on from there and repeat the other forty-eight verses. There are forty-eight more verses, done to a tune about as gay as the Congressional Record.

John Boles could sing them all when he sat on the wide front porch (called a gallery in the South) of his grandparents' home in a little town not far from his birthplace, Greenville, Texas.

The last census reports do not, I'm afraid, give Greenville a very high rating. Maybe you'd need a few extra fingers to count the inhabitants on your hand, but you can certainly list the streets in that fashion. Would you call them streets? There is no paving at all and the sidewalks are made of planks set up above the mud of the road. If a wagon got stuck during the rainy season, it had to remain there until the rainy season was over. *Kismet.*

GREENVILLE, being a loyal Southern hamlet, had remembered its heroes by naming these muddy thoroughfares after them. There was a village well at the corner of Lee and Stonewall avenues.

In another little town, not far away, lived John's grandparents, and it was with them he spent the summers. It was they who encouraged him to sing. He used to lead all the other children when they gathered on the gallery during those long summer evenings.

His mother had a dear friend who had ventured past the so-called city limits of the town. Romance clung to her like a gag man to Joe Miller's joke book. It was bruited about that she had once danced with Sam Houston.

She had lived in Paris. Actually lived there for several years and it was from her that John learned of the world to which the muddy roads of Greenville led. She taught him to speak French and he, seated at her feet on the wide porch, deftly swinging a palm leaf fan, resolved to see the great world some day for himself.

He went through grammar school and high school and was, in both of these institutions, the leading singer. He always appeared as the headliner in the Friday afternoon "entertainments."

Mr. Boles was wasting his voice in the dumb drama until the talkies came along and made him a singing star

It was his ambition to become a doctor and so he went to the University of Texas, at Austin, and took his degree just in time to join the army.

WITH his knowledge of French as a background he was immediately put in the intelligence department in France. He was overseas eighteen months, but when he returned the threads of his existence were too raveled to be woven into a pattern again. He felt he had lost too much to return to school, so he gave up the idea of medicine and turned, as every good Texan should, to the raising of cotton.

All during this time he was singing and when Oscar Seagle came to Austin on a concert tour Boles determined to see him. The day he sang for the star, he had dragged himself out of a sick bed. His fever was as high as the notes of his songs.

But Seagle was entranced at the beautiful quality of his voice and persuaded him to come to New York to study. John phoned

(continued on next page)

(continued from preceding page)

his father, asked him to go bond on a thousand dollar note, which he willingly did, and appeared in New York to conquer the world.

Seagle taught the lad when he was not on concert tour, and John lived near his home in upper New York. But he couldn't continue indefinitely on the original thousand dollars.

He took a position as French and music teacher in a nearby high school. But it wasn't enough. He wasn't receiving enough hard musical work, so he organized a band of students and, with Seagle's help, took them abroad where, for a year, he and they studied under the best masters.

UPON his return he walked up Broadway feeling fully equipped to meet the career that was bound to come his way. Walking up Broadway and living on Broadway are two different matters. His funds had run low again, but kind Providence, disguised as his one time army buddy, Ray Monroe, stepped in. Monroe offered him the use of his home until he found a job.

For three months he tramped the White Way, as so many have done before him. Every day or so he refused an offer to go on the road.

"It's ridiculous," said Monroe, who had a second or third cousin in the show business, "it's ridiculous for you to think you can get work in New York right away. Why, you've got to go on the road and get experience before you'll ever amount to anything."

But John felt that if he left the big city he was cutting himself off from what contacts he had. He was determined to stay on.

He at last obtained an interview with Lawrence Weber's assistant, Friedlander, and sang for him. The musical director wrote down his name in a book and scribbled something under it. Boles, consumed with curiosity, risked one eye on the page when Friedlander turned to answer the telephone. He had written, "John Boles—a find!"

"Come to rehearsal tomorrow morning," Friedlander said. "I've a part for you in 'Moonlight.'"

Strangely enough, the musical comedy was the composition of William Le Baron, head of RKO.

Boles went to rehearsal the next day and every day thereafter for weeks. But he never rehearsed. Others were singing the leading rôles. He simply appeared every morning as he had been told to do.

One morning early, he and Friedlander were alone in the dingy rehearsal hall. Suddenly the director turned to John.

"Look here," he said, "you're going to open in the lead in 'Little Jesse James' in two weeks."

The show had been playing at the Longacre Theater for several months. The leading man was leaving.

For many days John stood in the wings and watched the performance of "Little Jesse James." He knew every stage cue and every song, but he had no rehearsal with the cast until two days before he opened.

And then he was not allowed to rehearse in the theater, but in the dingy hall, with only chairs as props. In the next room a Russian hussar band was working fiendishly. Above the din John's clear, true voice rang out.

And when he stepped on the stage two nights later, to sing the leading rôle in a musical comedy hit, it was the first time he had ever acted in his life.

Other opportunities presented themselves after that, and it was while he was playing in "Kitty's Kisses" in New York that Gloria Swanson saw him and insisted that he come to California to play the lead in "Sunya."

You might think that this was a marvelous break, but it wasn't. "Sunya" was not a very good picture and Boles, although a handsome enough leading man, did not distinguish himself particularly as an actor.

Gloria Swanson's choice became just another Hollywood trouper. Yet he felt as if he couldn't go back to the stage. He had made the break. He had allied himself with the films.

FOR many months he remained in Hollywood, getting a part when he could. He at last managed to get a contract with Universal. But the odds were against his ever being anything but just a leading man had it not been for a little mechanical contrivance that made a noise on film.

The microphone changed John's career completely. Here he was on the ground, with screen experience and a voice.

He heard the Warners were to film "The Desert Song," and he knew he could do it.

He learned the score from beginning to end, had a test made and then, fearful lest he would not get the part, went away from Hollywood, hoping that fate would take a hand in his absence.

He drove hectically up north, past San Francisco. His mind raced as fast as his motor. The motor went too fast and he found himself telling it to the judge. The judge threatened him with a jail sentence, but finally let him go with a severe fine and a severer admonition.

Considerably humbled in spirit, he found his way to a little garage and called Los Angeles long distance. Above the noise of the mechanic's hammer in the back room of the garage he could hear these words, "Come back at once. You've got the part in 'The Desert Song.'"

From there on it's history. Universal loaned him to Warners for "The Desert Song" and "Song of the West," and then to RKO for "Rio Rita" with Bebe Daniels.

After that they plan to star him in three pictures.

Although slightly bewildered by his sudden success, Boles takes it as more or less his due. Certainly his was the proper background. Certainly he has worked hard enough and studied long enough hours.

Unlike so many men with good voices he has good looks as well. He is handsome, tall and medium dark, with blue eyes. His fan mail jumped from a few scattered letters into the thousands after "The Desert Song."

And the fans ain't heard nothing yet. Just wait for his next and his next and his next.

And a few months ago he was a second rate leading man!

Although his life has been devoted to his work, sentiment has not been lacking. The day before he was graduated from the University of Texas he married a pretty Southern girl, and he has been married ever since!

SEPT.

Alice White leading the dancing ensemble in the First National-Vitaphone *production "Broadway Babies"*

SEPT.

"THERE is nothing the matter with the talkies. They are mechanically perfect. The trouble is with the dumb stars who are making them.

"Someone has got to teach Hollywood how to use the instrument. I don't believe there is anyone out there who knows anything about it. There are others out there beside Al Jolson, but you have to get them from the stage."

NO, Auntie, this is not the squawk of a soreheaded ham actor knocked into oblivion by the microphone. It is a broadside fired by no less a personage than Florenz Ziegfeld from his "Follies" fortress in New York.

It is just another perfect instance of a man talking through his hat about a medium concerning which he knows practically nothing.

FLO ZIEGFELD is the man who, after twenty years of musical show producing, allows his productions to run until one o'clock in the morning on opening nights and then cuts them to fit an evening by throwing out bodily expensive scenery, costumes and actors.

In twenty years, for all his brilliant talents, he has never learned any smarter way to produce an air-tight show than to cut it in two and throw away half. In his "Follies" days it was nothing for him to heave out a $20,000 scene after the *première*. Certainly he can hardly give the wasteful photoplay any pointers on the conservation of talent and money.

When Flo Ziegfeld, master of the American revue, learns his own trade well enough to judge the entertainment value of a scene before he unveils it on opening night, we shall be willing to listen patiently to his criticisms of the "dumb stars" who are laboring in the new field of the talking picture.

SEPT.

The screen is outdoing the stage in eye-catching spectacles, as witness this Garden of Love scene from "Glorifying the American Girl." It is typical of the new trend in pictures, which is to out-Broadway Broadway

Ruth Harriet Louise

AN ornament to any home—Bessie Love. The boulevards of Hollywood are crowded these days with friends who always knew that Bessie would make good and be one of the great stars. But only two years ago Hollywood was just as crowded with people who thought that Bessie was an awfully clever kid but "not the type" for big time productions

SEPT.

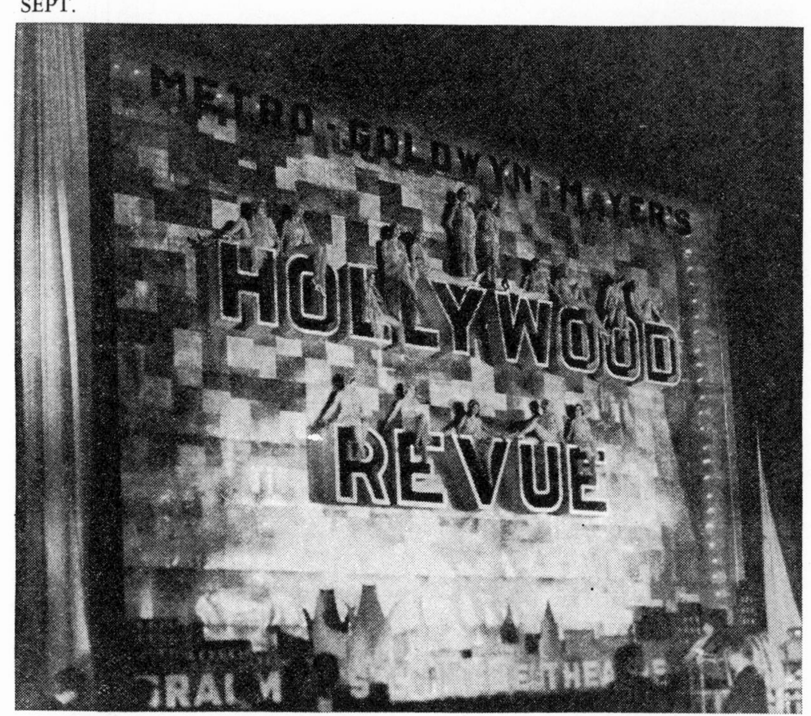

How do you like your alphabet—blonde or brunette? The living signboard is the very latest thing in Los Angeles advertising methods. It is the *ne plus ultra,* the *vox populi*—in short, the nuts. It looks to us as if the gal sitting in the nice comfortable V is getting all the breaks

NOV. M-G-M's latest acquisition is the New York Weather Man! It was the night of the Broadway opening of "The Hollywood Revue of 1929," and Times Square was jammed with thousands gaping up at the famous Living Billboard above the Astor Theater.

On it stood a score of pretty chorus girls in tights. Spotlights played on them, and cameras ground. Traffic was at a standstill. Led by a loudspeaker, the young ladies began singing the hit song, "Singing in the Rain."

And they hadn't finished one chorus before, upon the girls and the billboard and the great crowd, a gentle downpour began falling!

NOV.

A month or two ago PHOTOPLAY printed a picture of the living billboard, the sensational advertising stunt which was used to call attention to the "Hollywood Revue" when it opened in Hollywood. Here you see the New York version which tied up traffic on Times Square and caused policemen to fall fainting to the ground

SEPT.

 *THE DANCE OF LIFE—Paramount*

YOU should hang your head in shame if you're not able to answer the most technical questions concerning backstage life. How educational the pictures are!

If you're not already tired of hoofers and troupers, you'll enjoy this. In many ways it has more than the play, "Burlesque," from which it was adapted. The characters achieve a definite background. And you can see Hal Skelly's expressive face and putty nose in close-ups.

The story, as you know, concerns a clown who can't refuse a drink. It has tremendous heart appeal and looks deeply into the shallow, but lovable, soul of a comic. In spite of the fact that he is drunk on his wedding night and leaves his wife to take a big job without even writing to her, she goes on loving him indefinitely.

Skelly, who created the rôle on the stage, gives an excellent performance, doing his best work in the hysterical climax where he leaves his wife, as he thinks, forever.

Nancy Carroll comes in for a big share of the laurel wreath. She is natural and charming and uses her head for something besides her permanent wave. Equipped with stage experience, this little girl has climbed to the top of the sound film successes.

The backstage atmosphere is well done and, if you're Turkish in your tastes, you'll care for the beef trust chorus in a large way. There is a big dance number and some bright music (no picture is without them these days) but the story is the thing. And that survives all the intricacies of the talking apparatus. *All Talkie.*

"DANCE OF LIFE, THE"—PARAMOUNT.—From the play, "Burlesque," by George Manker Watters and Arthur Hopkins. Adapted by George Manker Watters. Directed by John Cromwell and Edward Sutherland. The cast: *Bonny Lee King,* Nancy Carroll; *Ralph "Skid" Johnson,* Hal Skelly; *Sylvia Marco,* Dorothy Revier; *Harvey Howell,* Ralph Theadore; *Lefty,* Charles D. Brown; *Bozo,* Al. St. John; *Gussie,* May Boley; *Jerry,* Oscar Levant; *Miss Sherman,* Gladys DuBois; *Jimmy,* James T. Quinn; *Champ Melvin,* James Farley; *Minister,* George Irving.

SEPT.

 *HOLLYWOOD REVUE OF 1929—M.-G.-M.*

THIS is a great show for the money. And there's something in it for everybody.

Like Shakespeare? Well, you'll find Jack Gilbert and Norma Shearer as *Romeo* and *Juliet.* Like low-brow slapstick? Well, there are Laurel and Hardy in a comedy act as low as they come. Like big musical numbers with glorified gals singing and dancing? All right, there's the hit, "Singing in the Rain," and many breath-taking girl numbers.

Besides all this there are your favorite screen stars who do their bits expertly. Marion Davies is remarkably good in "Tommy Atkins on Parade." And can that girl tap dance? Watch her! Marie Dressler, Polly Moran, Bessie Love, Ukulele Ike, Charlie King and Gus Edwards are howlingly funny in a Gay Nineties number. Gus, by the way, does more than his share by appearing in the show, writing most of the numbers and directing some of the dancing acts, although Sammy Lee, of Ziegfeld Follies, directed many of them.

Conrad Nagel and Jack Benny deserve especial praise for their work as masters of ceremonies. Besides those mentioned there are Joan Crawford (photographed rather badly), William Haines, Anita Page, Nils Asther, Buster Keaton, Karl Dane, George K. Arthur, Gwen Lee, the Brox Sisters, Natacha Natova and June Purcell.

Whether picture revues will ever be as good as the real thing is still conjecture. This is strictly a revue with no semblance of a story, for which Producer Harry Rapf deserves credit. There are bad spots, but it is, to date, the best of its kind and great entertainment. *All Talkie.*

"HOLLYWOOD REVUE OF 1929"—M.-G.-M.—Directed by Charles F. Riesner. Dialogue by Al Boasberg and Robert Hopkins. Music by Gus Edwards. Lyrics by Joe Goodwin. Orchestra and musical arrangement by Arthur Lange. Dances and ensembles by Sammy Lee. Photography by John Arnold, Irving G. Reis and Maximilian Fabian. The cast: Conrad Nagel, Bessie Love, Joan Crawford, William Haines, Buster Keaton, Anita Page, Karl Dane, George K. Arthur, Gwen Lee, Ernest Belcher's Dancing Tots, Marie Dressler, Cliff Edwards, Charles King, Polly Moran, Gus Edwards, Lionel Barrymore, Jack Benny, Brox Sisters, Albertina Rasch Ballet, Natacha Natova and Company, The Rounders, Norma Shearer, John Gilbert, Marion Davies, Laurel and Hardy.

SEPT.

BROADWAY BABIES—First National

All Talkie

ALICE WHITE'S newest portrayal of a cabaret cutie—and better than anything she has done thus far. But Fred Kohler steals the film as a great big Detroit bootlegger who is the soul of honor and adulteration. The Detroit gentleman loves our *Nell*, but he gives her up to our hero, finally, along with a big wad to star her. Phoney story—but a lively melodrama, thanks to Kohler.

"BROADWAY BABIES"—FIRST NATIONAL.—From the story by Jay Gelzer. Screen story by Monte Katterjohn. Directed by Mervyn LeRoy. Dialogue by Monte Katterjohn and Humphrey Pearson. The cast: *Delight Foster*, Alice White; *Billy Buvanny*, Charles Delaney; *Perce Gessant*, Fred Kohler; *Scotty*, Tom Dugan; *Sarah Durgen*, Bodil Rosing; *Navarre King*, Sally Eilers; *Florine Chandler*, Marion Byron; *Blossom Royale*, Jocelyn Lee; *Gus Brand*, Louis Natheaux; *Nick*, Maurice Black.

SEPT.

Helen Morgan, the girl who made the piano famous, makes her first full length talkie. It is called "Applause." Before she became a night club star, Miss Morgan played in "Six Cylinder Love," and fled from the silent studios to make a reputation as a sob singer

SEPT.

★ **DRAG—First National**

NOT a splashy feature as was Richard Barthelmess' "Weary River." A simple, domestic story, it has a genuine dramatic hold, due to Mr. Barthelmess' acting and Frank Lloyd's direct handling. And to the sparkling work of Lila Lee. *David Carroll* buys the Paris (Vermont) *Courier* and then marries the wrong girl. His bride and her family attach themselves to *Davey* and the *Courier* sinks under the weight. So *Davey* runs away to New York, where he scores a success as a writer of songs. At the end there is a Paris divorce in the offing, with the right girl waiting.

Miss Lee is the right girl and Alice Day is the bride. You'll be amazed at Lila's performance of a flip villager who later makes good in New York as a revue designer. Barthelmess gives a delightful performance. *All Talkie.*

"DRAG"—FIRST NATIONAL.—From the novel by William Dudley Pelley. Adapted by Bradley King. Directed by Frank Lloyd. The cast: *David Carroll*, Richard Barthelmess; *Pa Parker*, Lucien Littlefield; *Ma Parker*, Katherine Ward; *Allie Parker*, Alice Day; *Charlie Parker*, Tom Dugan; *Dot*, Lila Lee; *Clara*, Margaret Fielding.

OCT.

WONDER OF WOMEN—M.-G.-M.

Part Talkie

PEGGY WOOD, late of the legitimate, makes her bow as a dramatic actress of rare ability with a *Hedda Gabler* type of personality. She plays the dutiful wife of the concert pianist, admirably done by Lewis Stone. Leila Hyams is the decorative "other woman." A Sudermann theme of misunderstood genius. Beautiful direction, delightful acting, remarkable emotional undercurrent. Go prepared to think.

"WONDER OF WOMEN"—M.-G.-M.—From the novel "The Wife of Stephen Tromholt" by Hermann Sudermann. Continuity by Bess Meredyth. Directed by Clarence Brown. The cast: *Stephen Trombolt*, Lewis Stone; *Karen*, Leila Hyams; *Brigitte*, Peggy Wood; *Bruno Heim*, Harry Myers; *Anna*, Sarah Padden; *Doctor*, George Fawcett; *Stephen Tromboll's Housekeeper*, Blanche Frederici; *Wulle-Wulle*, Wally Albright, Jr.; *Lotti*, Carmencita Johnson, Anita Louise Fremault; *Kurt*, Dietrich Haupt, Ullrich Haupt, Jr.

SEPT.

International Newsreel

And still the stage stars descend on Hollywood. Mary Eaton arrived with her dog, her parrot and her director, Millard Webb. Mr. Webb is also her fiancé. Miss Eaton will be the première blonde in "Glorifying the American Girl." Miss Eaton and Mr. Webb first met while they were filming "The Cocoanuts"

SEPT.

A new "best dressed woman" for Hollywood. Irene Bordoni arrived with scores of trunks and a half-dozen servants, to give the natives something to talk about. With her are Robert North, Galen Bogue and Clarence Badger—all of her production staff. The clothes are French, so is the accent, and so—oddly enough—is Miss Bordoni

OCT.

WHY BRING THAT UP?—Paramount

All Talkie

GEORGE MORAN and Charles Mack, the famous Black Crows, are black only part of the time in "Why Bring That Up?" their flicker debut. The two idols of the phonograph records are at their best in burnt cork. Without the shellac it is evident that they aren't such a much at heavy emoting. When they get going about the early bird and the worm and other comedy skits they are superb.

"WHY BRING THAT UP?"—PARAMOUNT.—From the story by Octavus Roy Cohen. Directed by George Abbott. The cast: *Moran*, George Moran; *Mack*, Charles Mack; *Betty*, Evelyn Brent; *Irving*, Harry Green; *Powell*, Freeman S. Wood; *Casey*, Lawrence Leslie; *Marie*, Helen Lynch; *Eddie*, Selmer Jackson; *Treasurer*, Jack Luden; *Skeets*, Monte Collins, Jr.; *Doorman*, George Thompson; *Manager*, Eddie Kane; *Tough*, Charles Hall.

OCT.

STREET GIRL—RKO

All Talkie

WESLEY RUGGLES has established a reputation for making consistently good pictures at minimum cost. He keeps the present picture well up to his fine standard. Story hinges around a girl violinist and a group of musicians who befriend her. Betty Compson, Jack Oakie, John Harron and others appear to advantage. Incidentally, Miss Compson, who used to be a vaudeville violinist, really plays.

"STREET GIRL"—RKO.—From the story "The Viennese Charmer" by W. Carey Wonderly. Adapted by Jane Murfin. Directed by Wesley Ruggles. The cast: *"Freddie" Joyzelle*, Betty Compson; *Mike*, John Harron; *Happy*, Ned Sparks; *Joe*, Jack Oakie; *Pete*, Guy Buccola; *Keppel*, Joseph Cawthorn; *Prince Nicholaus*, Ivan Lebedeff; *Club Manager*, Eddie Kane.

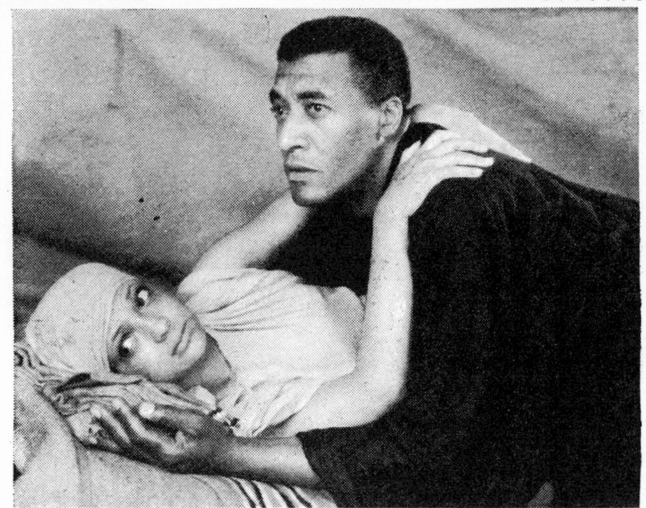

OCT.

★ HALLELUJAH—M.-G.-M.

KING VIDOR has a number of notable motion pictures to his credit. "The Big Parade," for instance. That interesting experiment of last year, "The Crowd." And, back of those two films, were many pictures revealing a fine understanding of humanity, along with a superb sympathy.

His new photoplay, "Hallelujah," is another experiment—and a striking one. His hero is a harum-scarum negro lad who gets involved in a gambling house brawl. His younger brother is killed in the fight and the boy, his world turned upside down by the tragedy, becomes an evangelist. But he can not stand up against all temptation. He backslides, serves a year on a chain gang—and then comes back to the little plantation of his father.

The story is told with a fine appreciation of the negro race. Indeed, the picture is something of a racial epic. Vidor's camera wanders into the little cabin after the boy's death and records the lamentations of the lad's family with startling emotional effect. Later, Vidor shows the negro evangelist upon his mission, and he pictures a great revival and a river baptism. Behind the simply written dialogue, is a colorful background of negro spirituals.

Every member of Vidor's cast is excellent. Although none of them ever worked before a camera or a microphone before, they give unstudied and remarkably spontaneous performances. That speaks a lot for Vidor's direction. A word for the excellence of Daniel Haynes' *Zeke*, Nina Mae McKinney's *Chick* and Fannie Belle DeKnight's *Mammy*. All three are great. *All Talkie.*

"HALLELUJAH"—M.-G.-M.—From the scenario by Wanda Tuchock. Dialogue by Ransom Rideout. Directed by King Vidor. The cast: *Zeke,* Daniel L. Haynes; *Chick,* Nina Mae McKenney; *Hot Shot,* William Fountaine; *Parson,* Harry Gray; *Mammy,* Fannie Belle DeKnight; *Spunk,* Everett McGarrity; *Missy Rose,* Victoria Spivey; *Johnson Kids,* Milton Dickerson, Robert Couch, Walter Tait; and the Dixie Jubilee Singers.

OCT.

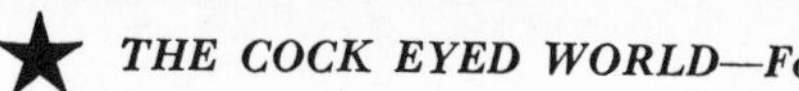

★ THE COCK EYED WORLD—Fox

THOSE two hard-boiled marines, *Sergeants Flagg* and *Quirt*, are back again. Remember them in "What Price Glory"? *Flagg* was a captain then, but peace times demote him back to the post of top sergeant.

"The Cock Eyed World" takes up the further adventures of the two leathernecks: in Russia, in Central America, in and about the Brooklyn Navy Yard and at that playground of civilian and soldier, Coney Island. The immortal quarrel of *Flagg* and *Quirt* goes on endlessly whether the cause is the sweetie of a tough Russian or the sweetheart of a timid Spanish-American. Between policing the world, *Flagg* and *Quirt* are eternally plotting to outwit the other.

There is less of war in "The Cock Eyed World" than in its predecessor, although the sequel carries the marines through a campaign against rebels in Central America. Victor McLaglen, it seems to us, has a shade the best of it as *Flagg* in "What Price Glory." In "The Cock Eyed World" the edge goes to Edmund Lowe as the crafty *Quirt*. And Lily Damita stands out brightly as a peppy Central American jungle belle.

Bear in mind that "The Cock Eyed World" is not a family picture. It is a little rough and profane. Remember that the microphone records everything—and the repartee between the two marines is not Sunday School conversation.

Raoul Walsh's direction has a fine gusto. "The Cock Eyed World" was written by Laurence Stallings and Maxwell Anderson, authors, as you know, of "What Price Glory." It lacks none of the flavor of that war epic. *All Talkie.*

"COCK EYED WORLD, THE"—Fox.—From the story by Laurence Stallings and Maxwell Anderson. Scenario by Raoul Walsh. Directed by Raoul Walsh. The cast: *Top Sergeant Flagg,* Victor McLaglen; *Sergeant Harry Quirt,* Edmund Lowe; *Elenita,* Lily Damita; *Olga,* Lelia Karnelly; *Olson,* El Brendel; *Connors,* Bobby Burns; *Katinka,* Jeanette Dagna; *Brownie,* Joe Brown; *Buckley,* Stuart Erwin; *Sanovich,* Ivan Linow; *Fanny,* Jean Bary; *Inn Keeper,* Solidad Jiminez; *O'Sullivan,* Albert Dresden; *Jacobs,* Joe Rochay.

SMILING IRISH EYES—First National

OCT.

ANOTHER boy makes good as a Broadway song writer! This time he comes from old Ireland, aided by money won by his fair colleen who captures a greased pig at the fair. The girl is Colleen Moore and the boy is James Hall, having a little difficulty with a brogue. Mediocre story—but Miss Moore gains personality and charm in the talkies. And she sings pleasantly. *All Talkie.*

"SMILING IRISH EYES"—FIRST NATIONAL.—From the scenario by Tom J. Geraghty. Directed by William A. Seiter. Photography by Sid Hickox and Henry Freulich. The cast: *Kathleen O'Connor,* Colleen Moore; *Rory O'More,* James Hall; *Michael O'Connor,* Claude Gillingwater; *Shamus O'Connor,* Robert Homans; *Granny O'More,* Aggie Herring; *Frankie West,* Betty Francisco; *Goldie Devore,* Julanne Johnston; *Sir Timothy,* Robert Emmett O'Connor; *Sir Timothy's Butler,* John Beck; *Ralph Prescott,* Edward Earl; *Black Barney,* Tom O'Brien; *Max North,* Oscar Apfel; *County Fair Manager,* Fred Kelsy; *His Assistants,* Barney Gimore, Charles McHugh; *Izzy Levi,* Otto Lederer; *Moe Levi,* William Strauss; *Scotch Barker,* Dave Thursby; *The Trouble-Maker,* Dan Crimmins; *Fortune Teller,* Madam Bosocki; *Taxi Driver,* George Hayes; *Landlady,* Ann Schaefer.

THE WAGON MASTER—Universal

OCT.

NOW the Westerns grow up. "The Wagon Master" is synchronized throughout with songs and dialogue sequences. The first of the kind. Ken Maynard is the stalwart hero who brings the caravan across the perilous desert. Ken scores with his cowboy songs and although a bit embarrassed about it, possesses an excellent voice. Tom Santschi is the bad man. The picture is magnificently photographed and there is rugged grandeur in scenes of the tugging wagon-train. *All Talkie.*

"WAGON MASTER, THE"—UNIVERSAL.—From the story by Marion Jackson. Directed by Harry J. Brown. The cast: *The Rambler,* Ken Maynard; *Sue,* Edith Roberts; *Bill Hollister,* Frederick Dana; *Jake Lynch,* Tom Santschi; *Jacques Frazelle,* Al Ferguson; *Billie Hollister,* Jack Hanlon; *Buckeye Pete,* Bobby Dunn; *Stuttering Sam,* White Horse; *Grasshopper Jim,* Frank Rice; *Tarzan,* Tarzan.

MELODY LANE—Universal

OCT.

BEING Eddie Leonard's first organized attack against the microphone, this picture is expected to cut a lot of ice. It will, but not the kind the studio thinks. Diversion-seekers, fed to the teeth with "Singin' Fool" themes, will turn a cold shoulder, and Eddie's lyrics and hoofing will undoubtedly be received in frigid disdain. The maudlin Pagliacci yarn is about as dramatic and sophisticated as a monosyllabic nursery rhyme. *All Talkie.*

"MELODY LANE"—UNIVERSAL.—From the story by Joe Swirling. Adapted by J. G. Hawks, Directed by Robert Hill. The cast: *Des Dupree,* Eddie Leonard; *Dolores Dupree,* Josephine Dunn; *Danny,* George Stone; *Rinaldi,* Huntly Gordon; *Nurse,* Blanche Carter; *Orchestra Leader,* Jake Kern; *Stage Manager,* Monte Carter; *Constance Dupree,* Jane LaVerne, Rose Coe.

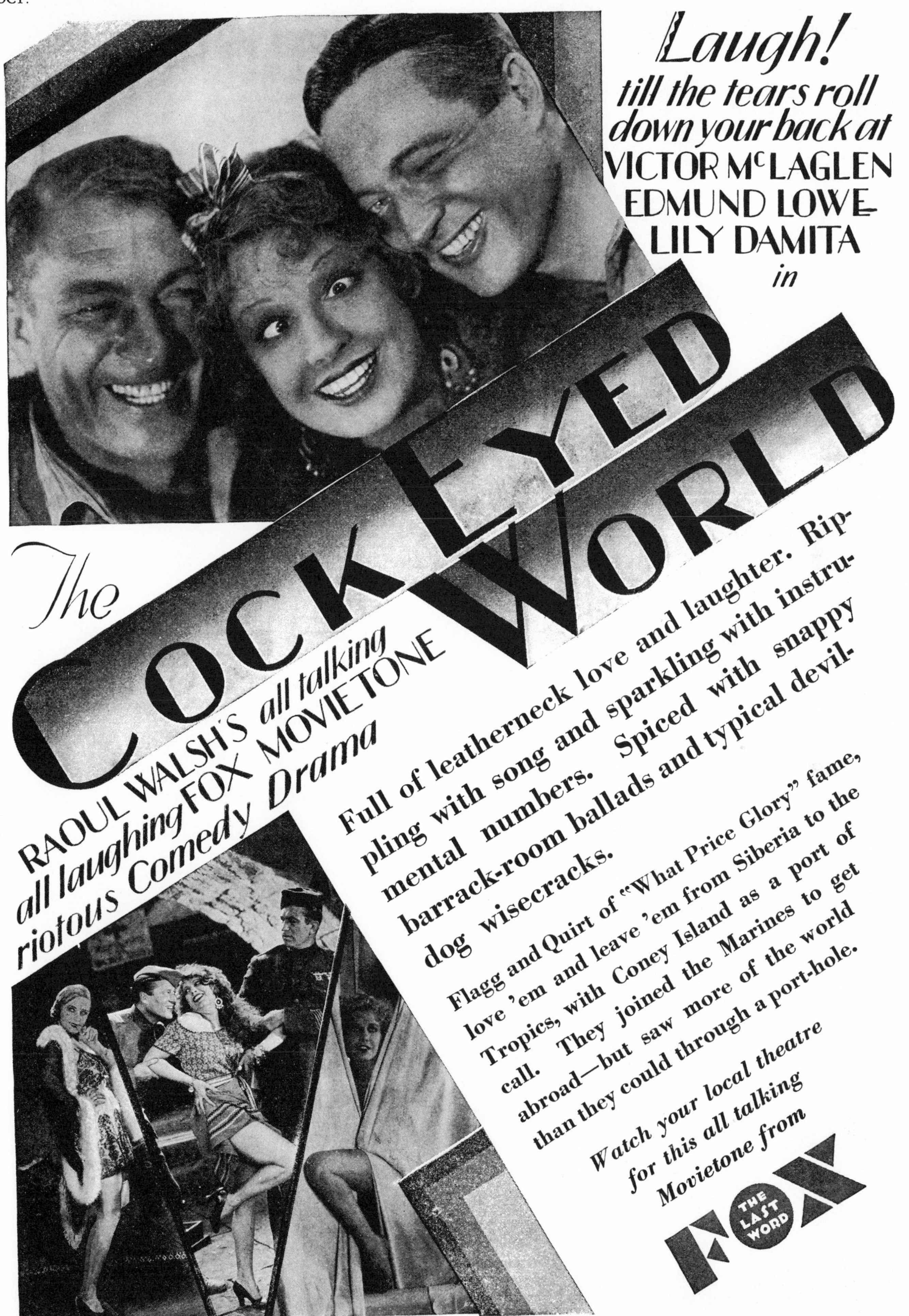
Laugh!
till the tears roll down your back at
VICTOR McLAGLEN
EDMUND LOWE
LILY DAMITA
in
The COCK EYED WORLD
RAOUL WALSH'S all talking
all laughing FOX MOVIETONE
riotous Comedy Drama
Full of leatherneck love and laughter. Rippling with song and sparkling with instrumental numbers. Spiced with snappy barrack-room ballads and typical devil-dog wisecracks.
Flagg and Quirt of "What Price Glory" fame, love 'em and leave 'em from Siberia to the Tropics, with Coney Island as a port of call. They joined the Marines to get abroad—but saw more of the world than they could through a port-hole.
Watch your local theatre for this all talking Movietone from
FOX
THE LAST WORD

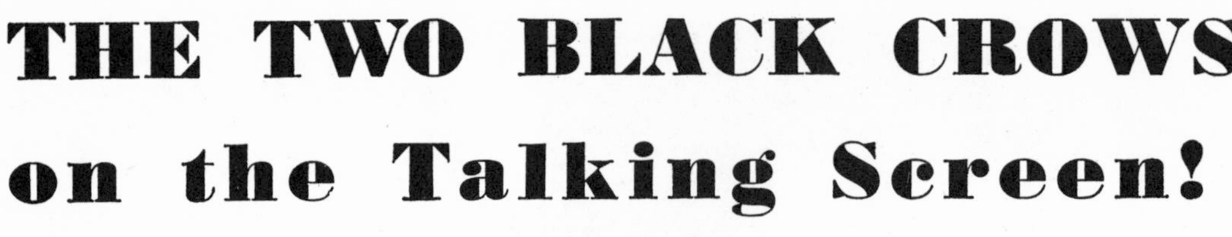

THE TWO BLACK CROWS
on the Talking Screen!

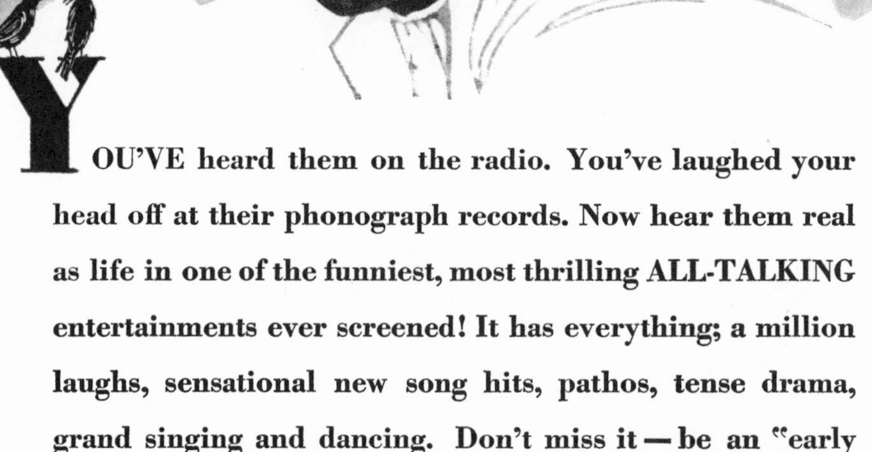

YOU'VE heard them on the radio. You've laughed your head off at their phonograph records. Now hear them real as life in one of the funniest, most thrilling ALL-TALKING entertainments ever screened! It has everything; a million laughs, sensational new song hits, pathos, tense drama, grand singing and dancing. Don't miss it—be an "early bird" yourself and make a date now to see and hear

MORAN & MACK

IN

"WHY BRING THAT UP?"

A Paramount All-Talking, Dancing, Singing Hit of The New Show World. Directed by George Abbott. Story by Octavus Roy Cohen. With Evelyn Brent and Harry Green.
"If it's a Paramount Picture it's the best show in town!"

METRO-GOLDWYN-MAYER'S
HOLLYWOOD
REVUE
Marion DAVIES
Norma SHEARER
Joan CRAWFORD
Conrad NAGEL
Jack BENNY
Ukelele IKE
Polly MORAN
John GILBERT
William HAINES
Buster KEATON
Gwen LEE
DANE and ARTHUR
Bessie LOVE and Charles KING
Marie DRESSLER
Anita PAGE
LAUREL and HARDY
Gus EDWARDS
BROX SISTERS
25 of the Screen's Greatest Stars—Chorus of 200—Amazingly Revolutionary Motion Picture!
SURPASSING the dreams of the most optimistic, attaining a goal that was deemed impossible only a few months ago, Metro-Goldwyn-Mayer has created in its gigantic "Hollywood Revue" an entertainment that will stand as a landmark in the annals of the talking screen. Every important resource and talent of show business contributed to its making. It is star-studded with names, its choruses are picked beauties, its voices represent the choice of experts, its songs are from the genius of the country's most famed, its dialogue was conceived by the leaders of their craft, its settings and costumes, its recording, each element of this mighty entertainment is the product of the top-notchers! Now playing at Grauman's Chinese Theatre, Los Angeles, and the Astor Theatre, New York.
"The Hollywood Revue" with
MARION DAVIES
JOHN GILBERT
NORMA SHEARER
WILLIAM HAINES
JOAN CRAWFORD
BUSTER KEATON
Bessie Love
Charles King
Conrad Nagel
Marie Dressler
Jack Benny
Gus Edwards
Dane and Arthur
Laurel and Hardy
Ukelele Ike
Anita Page
Polly Moran
Gwen Lee
Brox Sisters
Albertina Rasch Ballet
Natacha Nattova and Company
The Rounders
Dances & Ensembles by Sammy Lee
Directed by Charles F. Riesner
A METRO-GOLDWYN-MAYER Singing-Talking-Dancing Picture
Metro-Goldwyn-Mayer
"More Stars than there are in Heaven"
THE METRO-GOLDWYN-MAYER LION THE GREATEST STAR ON THE SCREEN

OCT.

(Presented by Carl Laemmle)

The last word in Motion Picture Entertainment comes from Universal!

The ONE and ONLY

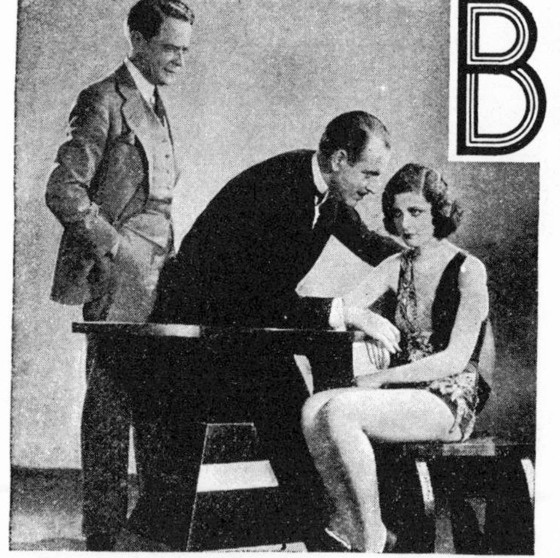

BROADWAY

If ever there was DRAMATIC DYNAMITE this is it—with a glorious musical background. For two years the stage play stood out as the greatest of the era . . . and NOW all the thunderous drama, the graceful romance, the thrilling situations, the magnetic climaxes of this wonderful stage play have been transferred to the screen with the original play dialog. With Glenn Tryon—Evelyn Brent—Merna Kennedy—T. E. Jackson—Otis Harlan—Robert Ellis—Paul Porcasi—Leslie Fenton—Betty Francisco—Arthur Housman. A Paul Fejos Production. Associate Producer, Carl Laemmle, Jr.

100% TALKING—SINGING—DANCING

College Love

RED-HOT youth aflame on the campus! A football game that will thrill you to the core! Moaning melodies put over by the University of California Glee Club! College chatter that will surprise you! Sorority parties, fraternity dances, roadhouse affairs that will amaze you. SEE and HEAR George Lewis, Dorothy Gulliver, Eddie Phillips, Churchill Ross, Hayden Stevenson and others of the original Collegians cast in the hottest film that ever sizzled on the screen. Directed by Nat Ross. THE FIRST 100% TALKING, SINGING COLLEGE PICTURE. Associate producer, Carl Laemmle, Jr.

100% TALKING and SINGING

THE GREATEST LOVE STORY EVER TOLD

Pictured with all the movement, beauty, thrills and grandeur of the colorful floating theatres on the Mississippi River. That is Edna Ferber's romance of the ages transferred to the screen. SEE and HEAR Laura La Plante, Joseph Schildkraut, Otis Harlan, Alma Rubens, Emily Fitzroy, Jane La Verne. Including the musical hits from the Florenz Ziegfeld stage production. Directed, silent and in movietone, by Harry Pollard.

UNIVERSAL'S TALKING AND SINGING TRIUMPH!

FORWARD MARCH *with* UNIVERSAL!

Universal Pictures Corporation . . . . 730 Fifth Ave., New York

RED LETTER EVENTS IN NEW DAY SCREEN ENTERTAINMENT

RADIO PICTURES

PRESENT

RIO RITA

Florenz Ziegfeld's Most Glorious Musical Comedy, Now Glorified for the Screen

STREET GIRL

A Star-Sprayed Romance of Life and Love Beneath the Glitter of Broadway's Night Clubs

At last the screen does justice to the name of Ziegfeld . . . The master producer's greatest musical comedy success, staged on a scale that dwarfs all other screen musical attractions in beauty and magnificence... Exquisite color sequences, gorgeous girls, glittering costumes, Rio Rita's lilting melodies, and new, interpolated numbers, and the superb singing and playing of the title role by Bebe Daniels, make this production even greater than the original.

Betty Compson, as the cabaret violin girl, scores the greatest triumph of her career in "Street Girl."

The story of a Broadway Cinderella and a Prince, who was *not* her Prince Charming . . . Music that creeps into your heart and sets your feet atapping . . . Sentiment, comedy, action, drama form the background for a characterization of unusual appeal by Betty Compson, aided and abetted by a Radio beauty chorus, Gus Arnheim's Cocoanut Grove Band, John Harron, and a fast-cracking comedy trio, Jack Oakie, Ned Sparks and Joseph Cawthorn.

COMING RADIO PICTURES THAT FORECAST THE SCREEN OF TOMORROW

"HIT THE DECK"—A lavish Radio Pictures presentation of Vincent Youman's round-the-world nautical musical drama, with the popular song hits, "Sometimes I'm Happy," and "Hallelujah."

"HIGH RIVER"—A Herbert Brenon production from the play, "High River House." . . . A majestic story of conflicting wills and passions in the river-threatened levee country of the Mississippi.

Elaborate production plans await the arrival of Rudy Vallee in Hollywood where he will make "The Vagabond Lover" for Radio Pictures.

RKO DISTRIBUTING CORPORATION

Subsidiary of the Radio Corporation of America

Richard Dix, newest Radio star, who is now completing the first of his three starring vehicles for this organization.

"RADIO REVELS OF 1930"—An all-dancing, all-singing, all-star, all-novelty extravaganza. The first annual screen revue, to be presented yearly by Radio Pictures.

"THE VAGABOND LOVER"—Starring the inimitable Rudy Vallee and his "Connecticut Yankees" . . . A romantic musical comedy, with color, action, comedy and Rudy's "come hither" voice.

NEW PICTURES

NO, this is not a bellhop scolding you for asking too much ice in 211. Nor is it a chorus boy tricked out for a musical comedy bit. It is Marion Davies, blonde hair craftily hidden, ready for a song and dance in the "Hollywood Revue of 1929"

Richee

THE smile that won America! The first French actor since Max Linder to win gobs of love and glory in American pictures—the one and only Maurice Chevalier, fascinating artist and charming man of the world. The Parisian revue star won a large and growing public with Paramount's "Innocents of Paris." His admirers are hungrily awaiting his forthcoming talkie

Ruth Harriett Louise

THIS girl will go singing down the ages as the first operetta star of the audible screen, so you had better save this picture as an exhibit in phonoplay history. Carlotta King came from the stage to make "The Desert Song" for Warners—a film that was also to bring fame to one John Boles. Now Carlotta, much in demand, hits high C's for M.-G.-M.

OCT.

These New Faces

Watch for This Each Month

IRENE BORDONI ("Paris," First National) has been for years the leading oo-la-la French girl on the American stage, and successor to Anna Held as owner of misbehaving eyes. She sings naughty little songs. Her husband, at present, is E. Ray Goetz, stage producer. It is reported that there's a divorce on.

HELEN KANE ("Pointed Heels," Paramount) is the most imitated baby-talk singer in America just now. Paul Ash discovered her in New York, and she scored at the Paramount Theater. In the musical comedy, "Good Boy," she was a tremendous hit singing "I Want to Be Loved by You," and founded the "poo-poo-poo-doo" school. Pretty, plump, big-eyed.

EDDIE LEONARD ("Melody Lane," Universal) is about the last of the great minstrel men, though for the last ten years he has been headlining in vaudeville. Still sings his famous hits, "Ida" and "Roly Boly Eyes."

FRANK FAY ("Under the Texas Moon," Warners) is one of the greatest vaudeville favorites in New York, often playing one theater for three and four weeks at a stretch. Has a mop of reddish hair, blue eyes, affects a drawling style. His greatest achievement was marrying Barbara Stanwyck.

HELEN MORGAN ("Applause," Paramount) was first noticed as prima donna of one of George White's "Scandals." She became famous singing "Bill" and other hits in Ziegfeld's musical comedy smash, "Show Boat." She has also headed the entertainment in her own New York night club.

SOPHIE TUCKER ("Honky Tonk," Warners) has been well known for a great many years as a vaudeville headliner singing hot songs. She is one of the survivors of the royal line of Nora Bayes, Belle Baker and others. Now billed as "The Last of the Red Hot Mammas."

GERTRUDE LAWRENCE ("The Battle of Paris," Paramount) came to America with a "Charlot's Revue" a few years ago, and since has starred in several musical comedies as a singer and comedienne. English, tall, slender, very pretty and packed with plenty of charm.

OCT.

Nancy Carroll, as usual with few clothes and plenty of charm, the way she looks in "Illusion," her next picture with Buddy Rogers. Watch for a fascinating life story of Nancy in the next PHOTOPLAY

OCT.

HOW can Irene Bordoni, the oo-la-la lady of the stage, peg along on the $10,000 she is said to rate from Warners each week she works in "The Show of Shows"?

That's a mere bag o' shells! Safety-pin money! John McCormack, the silver tongued tenor who hits High K with ease, is to get $500,000 for ten weeks' work in a Fox picture.

OCT.

HAL SKELLY ("The Dance of Life," Paramount) will be seen in the same rôle he made famous on Broadway in "Burlesque," the name having been changed. Nancy Carroll has the Stanwyck rôle. This was his first dramatic rôle, and a sensational success. For many years Hal has been in musical comedy.

OCT.

SALLY STARR ("Happy Days," M.-G.-M.) was first noted in a "Scandals" revue. All she did was come out, announce scenes and say "Thank you!" Little, plumpish, pretty and cute, and seems to have gone up in the world via talkies.

OCT.

A THOUSAND dollars an hour! Do you suppose you could stand off the installment collector with a fee like that?

That's what Marilyn Miller collected for her camera labors in "Sally." The queen of the Ziegfeld girls received $100,000 for the picture, and she put in an even hundred working hours. Truly, Heaven has protected the working girl!

OCT.

Who's the pretty little dark-eyed blonde? Three guesses, and you're still wrong. It's Colleen Moore, wearing a yellow wig in "Footlights and Fools," her next and last First National talkie-singie. With her is Max Scheck, a famous director of musical numbers

NOV.

Lionel Barrymore deserted the grease paint to become a director. But Director Robert Z. Leonard picked up the discarded make-up box and went back to acting. Only temporarily, of course. Leonard plays a doughboy bit in "Marianne," Marion Davies' new starring picture for M-G-M which he also directed

NOV.

LUCKY IN LOVE—Pathe

A GRAND opportunity was missed somewhere. This might have been a good picture, hokum and all. As it is, you'll laugh at it, not with it. Morton Downey is the buxom lad who gets back to Ireland in time to pay off the mortgage on a castle which looks like the Parliament Building. Most of it is silly, and badly directed. The Downey hush-a-by tenor helps considerably, and there's a "foine" performance by J. M. Kerrigan. *All Talkie.*

"LUCKY IN LOVE"—PATHE.—From the story by Gene Markey. Dialogue by Gene Markey. Directed by Kenneth Webb. The cast: *Michael O'More*, Morton Downey; *Lady Mary Cardigan*, Betty Lawford; *Capt. Brian Fitzroy*, Colin Keith-Johnston; *Earl of Balkerry*, Halliwell Hobbes; *Connors*, J. M. Kerrigan; *Tim O'More*, Edward McNamara; *Paddy*, Richard Taber; *Rafferty*, Edward O'Connor; *Kate*, Mary Murray; *Cyril*, Mackenzie Ward; *Abe Feinberg*, Louis Sorin; *Lulu Bellew*, Sonia Karlov; *Potts*, Tyrrell Davis; *Landlady*, Elizabeth Murray.

NOV.

WHY LEAVE HOME?—Fox

A COUPLE of years ago Fox made the silent version of the stage play "Cradle Snatchers." This is part of the same story. Strangely enough the other picture was Nick Stuart's first juvenile lead and this is his first talking picture. The story is about three married women whose husbands go duck hunting and the wives go fun hunting. Walter Catlett is somewhat disappointing, but Sue Carol, Nick Stuart and David Rollins are delightful. Lots of fun. *All Talkie.*

"WHY LEAVE HOME?"—FOX.—From the play "Cradle Snatchers" by Russell Medcraft and Norman Mitchell. Adapted by Robert S. Carr. Music by Conrad, Mitchell and Gottler. Directed by Raymond Cannon. The cast: The girls: *Mary*, Sue Carol; *Billie*, Dixie Lee; *Jackie*, Jean Bary. The boys: *Dick*, Nick Stuart; *Jose*, Richard Keene; *Oscar*, David Rollins. The husbands: *Elmer*, Walter Catlett; *George*, Jed Prouty; *Roy*, Gordon De Main. The wives: *Ethel*, Ilka Chase; *Susan*, Dot Farley; *Maude*, Laura Hamilton.

NOV.

When a beginner is admired by the leading feminine stars of her own lot it means something—especially if the novice happens to look like Virginia Bruce. This young lady, still two years on the sunny side of twenty, appears in Maurice Chevalier's "The Love Parade." She is said to have a lovely singing voice, and her eyes—well, look at them!

NOV.

When Jeanette MacDonald appears in "The Love Parade" in a gorgeous court gown with a sweeping train of white satin, audiences will gasp at the effectiveness of the costume as a whole, but they will not notice the detail. Yet ten bead workers labored with infinite patience for two weeks, taking the millions of tiny stitches necessary to snare the sequins, rhinestone brilliants and pearls to this costly fabric. The workers here are shown at their frame in the wardrobe department of the Paramount studios in Hollywood

NOV.

NIGHT CLUB—Paramount

"NIGHT CLUB" was made a long time ago at the Paramount Eastern studio, and really is little but a series of face and voice tests for many Broadway celebrities, including Fannie Brice, Pat Rooney, Ann Pennington, June Walker and others. Little song and dance specialties are tied to a fine short story by Katharine Brush. A companion feature to "Night Club" is a short comedy called "Pusher-in-the-Face," with Lester Allen and Estelle Taylor. The double bill can be labeled an early talkie experiment. *All Talkie.*

"NIGHT CLUB"—PARAMOUNT.—From the story by Katherine Brush. Directed by Robert Florey. The cast: Fannie Brice, Ann Pennington, Tamara Geva, Bobbe Arnst, Minnie Dupree, Pat Rooney, Pat Rooney, Jr., Jimmy Carr, Donald Ogden Stewart.

NOV.

THE BIG REVUE—All-Star

ONE wonders just where modernism is taking us when ten-year-old kids sing "Moonlight Madness" and other such rot into the microphone. But, at that, the youngsters are good. It's straight revue (thank goodness they didn't bring in Papa Boy) and gives the Ethel Meglin Wonder aggregation a chance to see the world without joining the navy. It's an all-talking, singing, toddling juvenile extravaganza, and ought, somewhere, to please someone. *All Talkie.*

"BIG REVUE, THE"—ALL-STAR.—Written by Ethel Meglin. Dialogue by Barney Williams. Directed by Dallas Fitzgerald. The cast: The Meglin Wonder Kiddies.

NOV.

Completing a successful Technicolor test for Paramount's flashy musical romance, "The Vagabond King." The big wheel behind the camera is a gelatin light filter, which gives the required Technicolor hues to the background

Herr Lubitsch, Der Old Master from Ger-

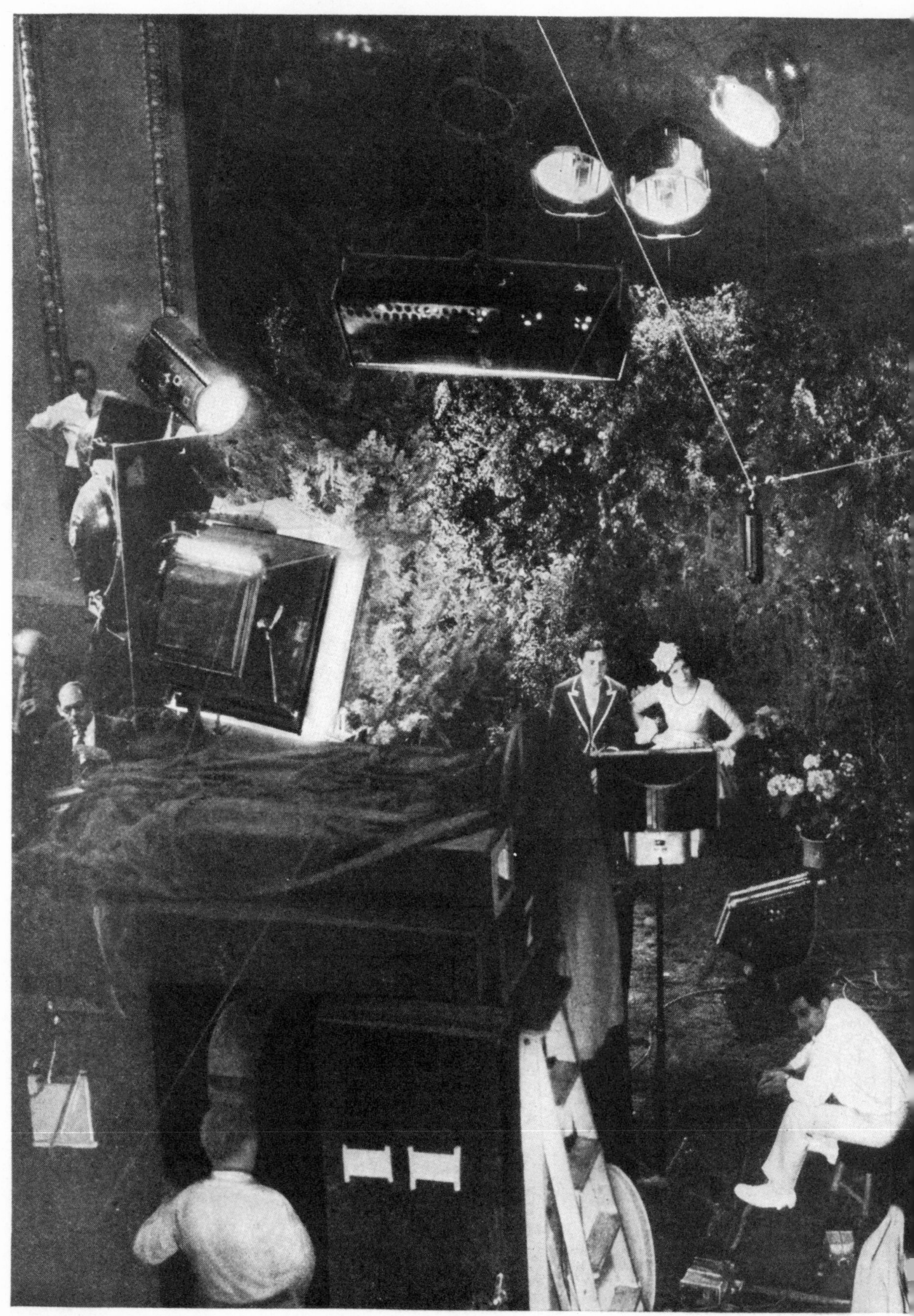

THE most striking photograph, friends, to be smuggled from the sound stages since the silent drama found its larynx. It shows Ernst Lubitsch, the great German director, doing something unheard of in the history of pictures—staging two scenes at one and the same time, and without the aid of a plug hat full of rabbits. Herr Lubitsch sits on the milking stool between the two camera booths. In the secluded garden nook on the left are Lupino Lane and Lillian Roth. Before the screen on the right, and seated on a sofa, are Maurice Chevalier and Jeanette MacDonald, star and leading lady of the new Paramount singie-talkie, "The Love Parade." The script and score of the production called for a double duet by these four principals, and Herr Lubitsch was forced to devise ways and means for directing

many, Directs Two Talkie Scenes at Once

two sets of actors with one wave of the wand. So he had his hirelings erect the two sets cheek to cheek, arranged his people, and went at it. In the foreground are the two camera booths, each with its crew of camera and sound geniuses. At the left, out of the picture except for one bold fiddler, is the orchestra which accompanies the singers. Over the heads of the actors you can see the malicious microphones, suspended on cords. And this gives you a good idea of the enormous number of lights necessary to shine up a talking picture scene. Our hard-working directors may soon be expected to direct three scenes, juggle four pool balls, eat a bacon and tomato sandwich and sing "Mammy" simultaneously. Just out of camera range old Cal York, PHOTOPLAY'S studio nuisance, is being strangled by four assistant directors.

YOU can try from now until Clara Bow marries Harry Richman, and probably still go wrong on guessing who this flashing, flaming child is. Sparkling with the old zip and ginger, displaying undreamed of curves—Colleen Moore, not so long ago the coy little flapper who toyed with dangerous cocktails and had harmless dates with high school boys. Colleen will look something like this in her new one, "Footlights and Fools"

Vandamm

YOU'RE going to admire and envy, simultaneously, this extremely blonde and atrociously pretty newcomer to pictures. First, she's really a raving beauty. Second, she's zat fascinating Maurice Chevalier's leading woman in his second American picture, "The Love Parade." Jeanette MacDonald is her name, and she came to the studios from a line of Broadway musical comedy successes, including "Yes, Yes, Yvette" and "Sunny Days"

International

JUST a pretty little New York girl, all peaches and cream, whose path led from the Bronx to Broadway to Hollywood and glory. Nancy Carroll, in her new party dress of pointed tulle—no doubt earned by her remarkable work opposite Hal Skelly in "The Dance of Life." On the opposite page you will find the smile-compelling, tear-teasing story of Nancy's rise, starting with the days before she was a little dancer at all!

The Littlest Rebel in Hollywood

The Story of Irish Nancy Carroll, Who Battled Her Way to Film Glory

By
Elinor Corbin

That wise little redhead, Nancy Carroll, has learned how to get all the joy out of life—and put more in

"MY life didn't begin until I married," says Nancy Carroll. "Before that it was just nothing. I was but half a person. Now we are together. We hold the fort for each other."

But it was that life before her marriage that gave Nancy that wonderful courage of hers. It was when she was a little two-fisted Irish girl on Tenth Avenue, New York, that she began to wonder. What did she want? What did she want of life? She didn't really know. She didn't actually realize what she was seeking. But she had taken the first step. She knew what life wasn't.

It wasn't bending over a typewriter in a big factory under a dead blue light in a room with a hundred other girls trying to answer a letter from a lady in South America who seemed to want a pair of pink slippers. It wasn't going from one firm to another, getting fired as quickly as she got a job because she was only thirteen and didn't have her working papers.

And, although she liked her employers, Urchs and Hegemer, it wasn't being private secretary in their lace company. Life was something more gallant; Life had more spirit.

She was, like every other red-headed Irish girl her age, stage struck. Her family were all talented.

There were, in all, fourteen children. Nancy was the seventh child of a seventh child. Only eight are now living, Martin, Elizabeth, Sarah, Teresa, Tommy, Nancy, Johnnie, Elsie. It was a bright, laughing, Irish Catholic family, with big Thomas Lahiff, their father, at the head of it. Tom Lahiff played the concertina. Their mother told the children that's why she married him. All the kids inherited laughter from him and played the piano and sang and danced.

But Nancy's hopes of entertainment went beyond family gatherings.

It all began in an amateur way.

NANCY and Teresa worked up a little sister act. They crooned and harmonized popular melodies and, unknown to their mother, tried out at one of the vaudeville houses. They heard of a theater on the East Side, sufficiently far away from the disapproving parental roof. They were from the West Side and had no right to be there, but a friend, Buddy Carroll, told them to say they were his sisters and to give his address as theirs. And so they became Nancy and Terry Carroll.

They became sort of professional amateurs, and went from one local theater to another until various musical comedy impresarios began to call them. George White asked for an interview. And J. J. Shubert. It was the latter who offered them a specialty number in his "Passing Show of 1923."

The two sisters huddled in a family conference. Would their mother ever be reconciled to their going on the stage? Would their father allow them another night's rest under his roof if he knew?

But Nancy was willing to take a chance. As she always is.

Because both girls had jobs as secretaries, Shubert was good enough to let them rehearse at night and they didn't tell their mother until after dress rehearsal.

WHEN they got to the house on Tenth Avenue their mother was in tears and a fury. She had called the police. She had searched every hospital. They had to tell her that they were on the stage. Dark looks accompanied them to bed.

But publicity won Irish Ann Lahiff. The next day was Sunday and there—right in the rotogravure section of the paper, was a large and beautiful photograph of Nancy.

It was several weeks before she would go to see the show and when she did she sat high in the balcony to watch her daughters. Her only comment was, "Oh, you were very good, very good, but I thought you tossed your limbs a bit too high."

Still she groped for life. The stage was better than the factory. It was better than being a private secretary, but it was a full, important life she wanted.

She found what was important when she met a young reporter on the *New York News* named Jack Kirkland. And, when she married him a few months later, she knew that her life had just begun.

She gave up the stage for a while, but went back to it in "The Passing Show of 1924."

She danced until four months before her baby was born!

The enforced inactivity bored her. Nancy, who had never been idle in her life, could not be idle, so she talked to Jack's managing editor, Phil Payne, who went down with "Old Glory." He let her interview all the actors she knew because she could get past the imposing ogres who guard stage doors. *(continued on next page)*

(continued from preceding page)

She interviewed Hal Skelly and Fay Bainter and a number of others and, with Jack's help, wrote pieces about them for the paper.

Then, quite suddenly, the great idea was born.

They would go to Paris! Nancy would have the baby and Jack would write the Great American Novel.

A baby and a novel in Paris!

They looked at their bank balance. By some mysterious process a thousand dollars had gotten there.

Plenty of money for vagabonds.

Jack told his managing editor that he was going to resign and go to live for awhile in Paris.

"Well, as long as you're going," said Payne, "you might as well have a job."

So the amazing vagabondage was denied them for awhile. Jack was literally handed a position as Tom Mix's press agent at $350 a week and all expenses paid for himself and his wife.

THEY lived like kings in Paris.

They entertained all the newspaper men royally at the Ritz bar and then fled to a little restaurant on a side street and pretended that they were poor.

Nancy had thought it thrilling to have her baby born in Paris.

She had even made reservations at the French Hospital, but something American took hold of her and she wanted to be in New York when the great event occurred. They booked passage at once.

Nancy had not thought of a doctor. She went to a fine specialist just a few weeks before the baby was born and he took one look at her, said she was perfect and dismissed her at once.

Patsy was a very expensive baby. After she was born there was no money. So Nancy went back on the stage and Jack took his old job on the *News*.

JACK worked the graveyard shift. He finished at three A. M. At that time it was the fad for the big musical shows to send acts to the night clubs. Nancy completed the day at three, also.

And they met and found new adventure together.

But Jack, having once touched movie gold, was sick of newspaper salaries. He wanted to go to California.

They adventured to California. Jack found movie gold scarce, so Nancy went on the stage.

She worked in a little musical comedy called "Nancy."

Macloon saw her and signed her for three years.

During this time she had dozens of picture tests made. M-G-M, First National, Warner Brothers, Universal—all had her face recorded, but nothing ever came of it. Jack took a place writing for Paramount.

At last a test amounted to something and she did a picture for Fox called "Ladies Must Live."

But she was tied up on her contract with Macloon and that had to be straightened out before she did "Abie's Irish Rose" for Paramount and signed a long term contract.

In the meantime she held the fort for Jack. When he went back to New York to do his play, "Frankie and Johnnie," she stayed on with Patsy and worked to give him the chance to do it, and when he came back she was happy again.

Nothing really matters as long as the three of them are together.

"FUNDAMENTALLY," she said, "I'm an Irish Catholic girl like my mother and if Jack wanted me to stop work and be just a wife and have ten children like Patsy, I'd do it."

But fundamentally she is a rebel. She gets what she wants by fighting for it. Years ago, when she was a kid she fought with her two fists.

She fought to go on the stage. Now she fights with her mind. Her brisk, humorous, keen mind.

Studio politics worry her not at all.

She knows what she wants. She knows when and how she can do her best work. And she does it.

She is a rebel with her tongue in her cheek. She's a red-headed, fighting Irish kid with gypsy blood in her veins!

NOV.

Three lovely ladies of the cinema? No, only one. Marilyn Miller, as radiant a maiden as ever drew cheers instead of sneers from a Broadway first night audience, is shown here with her two sisters, Mrs. John Sweeney, of Glencoe, Ill., and Mrs. Robert Montgomery, of Boston. Marilyn has just finished recreating her famous rôle in "Sally" for the talking screen

VITAPHONE recreates The GOLD DIGGERS of BROADWAY

in 100% NATURAL COLOR

IN TECHNICOLOR

Hear these sparkling song hits: "Tip Toe Through the Tulips," "Painting the Clouds with Sunshine," "In a Kitchenette" and "Go to Bed."

Picture a profuse procession of revue spectacle scenes in amazing settings . . . superbly staged chorus dancing numbers . . . the flashing wit of Winnie Lightner . . . the charm of Nancy Welford . . . the astounding dancing of Ann Pennington . . . the crooning of Nick Lucas . . . love scenes as only Conway Tearle can play them . . . a story that had New York gasping and giggling for one solid year . . . and you have only begun to imagine the treat that is in store for you.

One hundred per cent Color, an additional feature of *Vitaphone* all-talking pictures, doubles the "life-likeness" of this most vivid and enjoyable of all talking pictures.

Look for the thrill of a lifetime the day you see "Gold Diggers of Broadway" . . . And look for the Vitaphone sign when you want talking picture entertainment—always!

Vitaphone is the registered trademark of the Vitaphone Corporation

You see and hear Vitaphone only in Warner Bros. and First National Pictures

Vandamm

ANNA HELD, you remember, had trouble making her eyes behave, according to her famous song. But Irene Bordoni's eyes are absolutely uncontrollable. This noted singing actress of the stage has made such a hit in her first phonoplay, "Paris," that she seems to be ready for as brilliant a career in Hollywood as her theatrical engagements permit. And believe us, zis Bordoni is certain death as far back in the house as Row Z!

YOU'LL SEE "PARIS" IN COLOR
—Breath-taking Broadway revue spectacles—glorified beauty ensembles—superbly extravagant gowns and settings—in all the glory of their full natural color, reproduced by the amazing new Technicolor process . . . setting the 1930 style for motion pictures!
YOU'LL SEE A FAMOUS STAGE STAR IN "PARIS"
—Irene Bordoni—Paris' present to America. For years her name has helped light Broadway . . . Now for the first time you'll see it on your home-town theatre! Dazzling, sparkling, inimitable—to see and hear her is to understand all the lure of playful Paree.
"PARIS" BRINGS YOU A GREAT BROADWAY HIT
—Last season's reigning New York stage hit transplanted to the screen, with all the color, songs and comedy that captivated critical Manhattan. See for yourself why thousands paid $4.40 per seat to see this hilarious story of the frantic loves of a great French actress and her "misleading" man!
3
Irene BORDONI in "PARIS" with JACK BUCHANAN
First National Pictures
With Jason Robards, Zasu Pitts, and Louise Closser Hale. A Clarence Badger production. Based on the play by Martin Brown.
VITAPHONE Picture
REG. TRADE MARK
"Vitaphone" is the registered trademark of the Vitaphone Corporation
A FIRST NATIONAL and VITAPHONE PICTURE
REASONS why you'll call this the greatest singing-dancing picture ever!

A Metro-Goldwyn-Mayer

ALL-TALKING ALL-SINGING PRODUCTION

DIRECTED by KING VIDOR

Who Made "The BIG PARADE"

"Like little children that ain't growed up"

"Soon forgotten were the fields of cotton"

CLAP yo' hands! Slap yo' thigh! "Hallelujah" is here! "Hallelujah" the great! "Hallelujah" the first truly epic picture portraying the soul of the colored race. Destined to take its place in filmdom's Hall of Fame along with "The Big Parade," "The Broadway Melody" and "The Hollywood Revue." ¶ King Vidor wrote and directed this stirring all-negro drama, this absorbing story of the colored boy, indirectly responsible for his young brother's death in a gaming house brawl, who becomes a negro revivalist; of his devotion to his ideals; and of his craving for a seductive "yaller girl." ¶ The soul of the colored race is immortalized in "Hallelujah." Every phase of their picturesque lives—their fierce loves, their joyous, carefree pursuit of happiness, their hates and passions—finds dramatic expression against vivid backgrounds of cabarets, cotton fields, gaming houses, and humble shacks called home. ¶ Daniel Haynes, noted Negro singer, plays the central character. Nina Mae McKinney, a beauty discovered in the night clubs of Harlem, has the leading feminine role. In addition, the celebrated Dixie Jubilee Singers and other noted performers sing the songs of the negro as they have never been sung before. Don't miss this tremendous event in the history of the screen!

Now playing simultaneously at the Embassy and the Lafayette Theatre, N. Y. Twice Daily

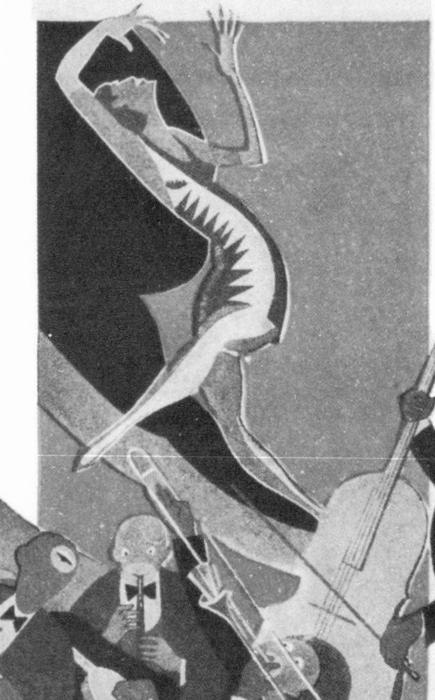

THE METRO-GOLDWYN-MAYER LION · THE GREATEST STAR ON THE SCREEN

METRO-GOLDWYN-MAYER

"More Stars Than There Are in Heaven"

NOV.

 ***MARIANNE—M-G-M***

THERE may be some limit to the versatility and cleverness of this Davies girl, but you won't find it in this musical cinema. Marion carries a difficult French accent through ten reels without a relapse, sings, gives imitations, dances, glides smoothly from delicious comedy to superb pathos, and for good measure registers one of the most poignantly beautiful parting scenes ever filmed.

Right on top of that comes Lawrence Gray, erstwhile indifferent screen actor, as her doughboy sweetheart, and knocks the audience for a row of sound sequences by his acting and singing. Ukulele Ike and Benny Rubin go into a frenzy of comedy lines and songs and dances.

Story? Well, would you ask Charlie Chaplin to play Shakespeare? *All Talkie.*

"MARIANNE"—M-G-M.—(Talkie Version) From the story by Dale Van Every. Dialogue by Gladys Unger and Laurence Stallings. Directed by Robert Z. Leonard. The cast: *Marianne,* Marion Davies; *Andre,* George Baxter; *Stagg,* Lawrence Gray; *Soapy,* Cliff Edwards; *Sam,* Benny Rubin; *Lieut. Frane,* Scott Kolk; *The General,* Robert Edeson; *Pere Joseph,* Emil Chautard.

"MARIANNE"—M-G-M.—(Silent Version) From the story by Dale Van Every. Directed by Robert Z. Leonard. The cast: *Marianne,* Marion Davies; *Stagg,* Oscar Shaw; *Andre,* Robert Castle; *Soapy,* Robert Ames; *Lieut. Frane,* Scott Kolk; *The General,* Mack Swain; *Major,* Oscar Apfel.

NOV.

HAPPY DAYS—M-G-M

All Talkie

BUT for the first half this would be the best college film ever produced. The U. S. C.-Stanford football game is done in sound and if it isn't one of the biggest thrills you've ever had, consult your doctor. The rest is just another farce that will make real collegians commit hara-kiri. But maybe they can bear it for Elliott Nugent and Robert Montgomery are perfect, as is Sally Starr.

"HAPPY DAYS"—M-G-M.—Directed by Sam Wood. The cast: Sally Starr, Elliott Nugent, Robert Montgomery, Phyllis Crane, Cliff Edwards.

NOV.

 ***RIO RITA—RKO***

FOR the wiseacres who said that a musical comedy could not be transplanted successfully to the screen, "Rio Rita," Ziegfeld's great hit, comes as a bolt from the blue.

In practically every respect it is the finest of the screen musicals, and yet it is more like the stage than the cinema, from the overture to the opera bouffe finalé. The plot is an evasive sort of thing, yet it ties the situations satisfactorily. Comedy, singing, dancing and romance are interwoven.

The "Rio Rita" music is ingratiating, warm and vivid. There are numerous examples of Ziegfeld pageantry in the Mexican fiesta scene, and again on the pirate's barge. Joseph Urban never conceived more fabulously lavish settings. Technicolor is glorious at times.

Despite very strong competition Bebe Daniels, in the name rôle, is the most glowing personality. Her voice, untrained as it is, has a rich quality which an experienced prima donna might well envy. Her performance is colorful and she appears lovelier than she has for years. "Rio Rita" will revive Bebe's one-time great popularity. John Boles' glorious tenor voice is heard to advantage; he is a romantic, dashing Texas ranger. Comedy is of the sure-fire, riotous type. Robert Woolsey and Bert Wheeler are principal funmakers. Wheeler's inebriate characterization is a classic. George Renavent, Don Alvarado and Dorothy Lee are also outstanding. The entire cast performs with tremendous pep.

Luther Reed's direction of a difficult assignment is most commendable. "Rio Rita" is elaborate extravaganza and well worth your while. *All Talkie.*

"RIO RITA"—RKO.—From the Ziegfeld musical play by Guy Bolton and Fred Thompson. Directed by Luther Reed. Stage direction by Russell Mack. The cast: *Rita Ferguson,* Bebe Daniels; *Capt. Jim Stewart,* John Boles; *Roberto Ferguson,* Don Alvarado; *Dolly,* Dorothy Lee; *Chick,* Bert Wheeler; *Lovett,* Robert Woolsey; *Ravinoff,* Georges Renevant; *Mrs. Bean,* Helen Kaiser; *Davalos,* Tiny Sandford; *Parone,* Nick de Ruiz; *McGinn,* Sam Nelson; *Wilkins,* Fred Burns; *Carmen,* Eva Rosita; *Cafe Proprietor,* Sam Blum.

NOV.

GOLD DIGGERS OF BROADWAY —Warners

All Talkie

TWO things stand out about this gay picture. One is the startling beauty of its all-Technicolor treatment. The other is the fact that it has two catchy tunes. The picture people are Conway Tearle and Lilyan Tashman, while Ann Pennington, Winnie Lightner and Nancy Welford, from the stage, have the fattest parts. A lavish story of life among the chorus girls of Broadway.

"GOLD DIGGERS OF BROADWAY"—WARNERS.—From the story by Avery Hopwood. Scenario by Robert Lord. Directed by Roy Del Ruth. The cast: *Jerry*, Nancy Welford; *Stephen Lee*, Conway Tearle; *Mable*, Winnie Lightner; *Ann Collins*, Ann Pennington; *Eleanor*, Lilyan Tashman; *Wally*, William Bakewell; *Nick*, Nick Lucas; *Violet*, Helen Foster; *Blake*, Albert Gran; *Topsy*, Gertrude Short; *Stage Manager*, Neely Edwards; *Cissy Gray*, Julia Swayne Gordon; *Dance Director*, Lee Moran; *Barney Barnett*, Armand Kaliz.

NOV.

International

Give these little boys a hand. Leonard and Bernard West, who sing and dance in the First National-Vitaphone picture "The Forward Pass." Don't know the gal's name, but "Cutie" will do

NOV.

"See?" says Ramon Novarro to Dorothy Jordan. "High C," comes back Miss Jordan snappily. Ramon is illustrating to Miss Jordan a high note of one of the several songs they will sing in "The Battle of the Ladies," the star's newest M-G-M picture. Miss Jordan, dainty musical comedy star, plays opposite Novarro in the production

NOV.

Alexander Gray

HE lives on one of Hollywood's most exclusive hills and if you didn't know that he had just rented the house you might suppose he'd been living in it all his life, so settled he seems to be.

But that's the sort of person Alexander Gray is. His mother and father and baby live with him and, although he still feels that the cinema is just a long rehearsal and he's still amazed that people do as good work as they do when the grand finalé of a moom pitcher is often shot before the introduction, he's signed a long term contract with First National and has completed the lead opposite Marilyn Miller in "Sally."

With that out of the way, he is now busy on "No, No, Nanette."

There have been several steps—somewhat unrelated perhaps—in his career.

He started out to be a business man. He had always sung, but concerts didn't pay.

A job as advertising manager for a motor truck company brought in a good-sized weekly salary. Yet that didn't make him entirely happy.

Alexander couldn't forget his sharps and flats and he suddenly found himself in a Ziegfeld show where he warbled about pretty American girls and lovely Hawaiian girls and elegant Chinese girls.

Unlike most young men who do this sort of work, Alexander could hit a grace note as well as look handsome.

So he left the revues and tried his luck on the musical comedy and operetta stage.

HIS first speaking and singing rôle was in "Sally" and that was followed by other successes, including "The Desert Song," which really made him famous.

Then Warners got Marilyn Miller's name on the dotted line for "Sally" and then came her request that Gray be her leading man.

He's a good looking lad of medium height, with blue eyes and light hair.

The eyes are grave, for tragedy came into his life when his wife was killed in an accident in January.

His charming mother keeps the home together and makes him happy.

NOV.

Vivienne Segal

"THIS," said Vivienne Segal to an important New York producer, "will be your last chance to hear me sing!" Some ultimatum!

She was all of sixteen years old and had sung only in amateur operettas in Philadelphia.

The manager, who was anxious to get away to an important engagement, had asked her to return the next day.

But Vivienne wouldn't listen to any such thing. No sir! She'd sing—or else.

It's just that attitude that brought about her success in "Blue Paradise," "Three Musketeers" and "The Desert Song" on the stage and has now prompted Warners to sign her to a long term contract after "Song of the West" and "Golden Dawn."

Vivienne's mother had wanted to be an actress. But her family was shocked, so she determined that Vivienne should choose a theatrical career. They went to New York for a week-end.

Nobody told them how hard it was to see managers, so they saw them all in one day.

And Vivienne sang.

What could the managers do?

There was no stopping her.

When the producers told her that she'd hear from them shortly she was frightfully downcast and quite sure that she was a failure.

Two weeks later a wire from Lee Shubert brought her back to New York.

She was told to watch three performances of "Blue Paradise" and to learn the lines and the songs in it.

Four days later she opened in the musical comedy in New York, and was a sensation.

"If I hadn't been so young and foolish I couldn't have done it," she said.

SHE was what Broadwayites call "a natural." She stepped into her first leading rôle at sixteen and she's been stepping into them ever since.

The camera shows her as a lovely graceful girl with a beautiful figure, but misses the transparency of her skin and the radiance of her light red hair.

These New Faces

Watch for This Each Month

NOV.

CARLOTTA KING ("The Desert Song," Warner Brothers) is a graduate of stage operettas and comic operas, with a beautiful soprano voice. Her first big part in "The Desert Song," opposite John Boles, brought her instant success, and Metro-Goldwyn signed her to a five year contract. She will next be heard in the sound version of "Rose-Marie."

CHARLES KING ("The Broadway Melody," M-G-M.) Charlie King has long been one of Broadway's musical comedy favorites. In vaudeville for many years, he became popular as leading man of such George M. Cohan shows as "Little Nellie Kelly." His last big stage hit was in "Hit the Deck." He's in the big "Hollywood Revue of 1929."

MORTON DOWNEY ("Mother's Boy," Pathe) first came to light as tenor soloist on a concert tour with Paul Whiteman's band. A success, he then became a popular and high-priced entertainer in New York night clubs. His first successful picture appearance was in Radio's "Syncopation." So he ups and marries his leading lady, Barbara Bennett.

MARILYN MILLER ("Sally," First National), it seems hardly necessary to say, is Flo Ziegfeld's leading musical comedy star, her last stage appearance for him being in "Rosalie." She began in show business as a specialty toe dancer, rapidly graduating to leading rôles. She is the former Mrs. Jack Pickford, and was later courted by Ben Lyon.

JEANETTE MacDONALD ("The Love Parade," Paramount) will be popular as Chevalier's leading woman in his second American picture. She is a beautiful blonde girl with a nice voice, and was a musical comedy lead in many Broadway shows, including "Yes, Yes, Yvette" and "Sunny Days." A Hollywood success, she will do some more pictures.

DEC.

LILLIAN ROTH ("The Vagabond King," Paramount) has been before the eyes of the amusement world a comparatively brief time. She came to New York's attention in the summer of 1928 as leading singing and dancing soubrette in Earl Carroll's "Vanities," the famous revue. A short term in vaudeville, and she went West to catch on nicely in pictures.

ANN PENNINGTON ("Gold Diggers of Broadway," Warners) became nationally famous years ago as a dancing sprite in Ziegfeld's "Follies." She then appeared in George White's "Scandals" as featured dancer for several years. Her press agents sold her to the public as the possessor of the prettiest dimpled knees in the world. And they still are.

WILLIAM FOX

presents

the first Viennese Operetta

A Song Romance with music by

OSCAR STRAUS

composer of

THE CHOCOLATE SOLDIER

Married in Hollywood

ALL SINGING - ALL DANCING - ALL TALKING

with

J. HAROLD MURRAY
BROADWAY STAR OF RIO RITA

and NORMA TERRIS
BROADWAY STAR OF SHOW BOAT

Walter CATLETT **Tom PATRICOLA**
Lenox PAWLE **Irene PALASTY**
John GARRICK

WHAT THE NEW YORK PAPERS SAY:

"...One of the loveliest of all the melody films, the most exalted score yet to be sung in the audible pictures... Audiences are going to find it a thing of joy."
—QUINN MARTIN, *World*

"...An especially fine example of vocal recording...adroitly interspersed with joviality and extremely clever photographic embellishments. The principal songs are charmingly rendered."
—MORDAUNT HALL, *Times*

"...it recalls sweet and pleasant theatrical memories...it is of such stuff as dreams are made of...glorious music."
—IRENE THIRER, *News*

"...boasts big sets, mob scenes, elaborate color sequences ...has been produced on a very lavish scale."
—ROSE PELSWICK, *Journal*

"...the most mellowing stuff that has made its way into the movies since Von Stroheim lifted the Merry Widow's face... principal waltz is pure delight."
—JOHN S. COHEN, *Sun*

Broadway contributes the stars, Hollywood the lavish and splendid settings, and Vienna the enchanting melodies of her greatest living composer, Oscar Straus—to make "MARRIED IN HOLLYWOOD" the most glamorous song romance ever conceived for stage or screen!

Here is $6.60 Broadway entertainment—plus! Leading stars of song and comedy, bevies of Hollywood beauties, settings that stun the vision with their magnificence, a plot that would have delighted George Barr McCutcheon himself and surrounding it all, a haunting, enchanting musical score by the world famous composer of the Chocolate Soldier!

"MARRIED IN HOLLYWOOD" will be at your favorite theatre soon. Don't miss this musical Movietone!

Directed by
MARCEL SILVER

All Set for THE BIG GAME of the Season
Get your winning colors and join the throngs who are surging to one of the greatest gridiron events ever!
"The Forward Pass" will give you Harvard-Yale football thrills for the price of a motion picture ticket—the roar of the stands, the snap of signals, the thud of flying feet racing to the most dramatic touchdown ever filmed... And every seat's on the 50-yard line!
Famous critics have led the cheers for this amazing college-life-like hit. It's a man's picture that women will love. Watch for it!
Story by Harvey Gates. Directed by Eddie Cline. With 4 new song hits—"One Minute of Heaven," "H'Lo Baby," "I've Gotta Have You," and "Huddlin'."
The FORWARD PASS
100% TALKING
with
Douglas Fairbanks, Jr.
and
Loretta Young
The lovers you loved in "Fast Life"
IT'S A LIBERAL CO-EDUCATION
First National Pictures
A FIRST NATIONAL & VITAPHONE PICTURE
"Vitaphone" is the registered trademark of the Vitaphone Corporation
VITAPHONE Picture
REG. TRADE MARK

DEC.

OF all the meteors that have flashed across the Hollywood sky, none in history has ever scooted brighter and faster than John Boles. It took him a long time to get started, but when the mike turned loose his splendid voice in "The Desert Song" our Answer Man began to spend sleepless nights answering questions about his hair, eyes and heart condition

Cornering

Six Famous Pairs Who Sing (Tra la!) and Dance (Hey! Hey!) in a New Revue

IN "The Show of Shows," Warner Brothers' Mammoth Aggregation of Cinematic Marvels and Motion Picture Mastodons, the famous sister acts of the screen warble their prettiest and point their toes—one! two!

Here are pictures of six of the fifteen or thirty star-spangled sister teams who will make the fans forget the old crack about good things coming singly. Each pair will wear the native costume of a different nation, and taken all together they will spell "Hollywood" in a great, big international way.

Glorifying Old Glory's little girls. Dolores and Helene Costello, who glorified the photoplay 'way back when screen silence was considered golden, add their scintillating bit to this singie-dancie-talkie

"The top of the mornin' to you, sister." Molly O'Day and Sally O'Neil, a couple of captivatin' colleens who do a sisterly turn in this big revue. They jig, they sing, and they smile with those Irish eyes

Two cute Dutch dolls—sisters Shirley Mason and Viola Dana. We can't be certain, but they probably sing a song of windmills, tulip time in Holland, and the course of true love in the land of the Zuyder Zee

the Sister Market

Over this colossal collection of native and foreign beauty Mr. Richard Barthelmess, accompanied by his best boyish blush, will preside as screen master of ceremonies.

This is undoubtedly one of the ace numbers of the revue, which contains everybody from John "Profile" Barrymore to the littlest and most freckled bat boy on the lot. Now if they could guarantee us Lillian and Dorothy Gish doing a hot black bottom, the world would be a better place to live and love in!

The prettiest girl in Hollywood (some say) and her pretty sister. Loretta Young (right) and Sister Sally Blane, as the French sisters. Loretta and Grant Withers are reported on the verge of marriage. What verge!

Just two little Bohemian girls, trying to get along. You know the Days, Alice (left) and Marceline. As representatives of the land of Pilsner beer and beautiful skies, they'll do their bit in the big show

And now for Rule Britannia! As representatives of the Mother Country we have Adamae and Alberta Vaughn, reading from left to right. You know Alberta. And Sister Adamae is an up and coming young player!

Billie Dove, the Ziegfeld girl of days of old, with sweeping lines and classic features, meets Maxine Cantway, the Ziegfeld model of 1929—the modern hey! hey! chorus girl of stage and talkies

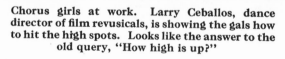

Chorus girls at work. Larry Ceballos, dance director of film revusicals, is showing the gals how to hit the high spots. Looks like the answer to the old query, "How high is up?"

The New Extra Girl

By Roland Francis

SHE goes to work at 8:30, and she's on time. She toils all day, and sometimes far into the night. She lives with the old folks at home, and when she isn't toiling she goes to bed long before midnight. She is a hard worker, and isn't too frivolous in spite of the fact that she is just high school age.

Now guess who?

Not Pollyanna.

Not Elsie Dinsmore.

You'd never guess.

She is the movie chorus girl, and she is as different from her sisters who gladden the eyes of the t. b. m. as is Peggy Hopkins Joyce from Mabel Walker Willebrandt.

One of the pleasanter features of talking pictures is the arrival of the 1929 model lady of the ensemble. There are more than two thousand of them living in stucco bungalows and apartment houses in Hollywood. None of them dwell in the familiar theatrical boarding house, so common in New York.

You can find in Hollywood a Hindu Yogi, a white elephant, and a boulevard where apparently your car rolls uphill, but durned if you can find a theatrical boarding house.

The chorus miss has taken the place of the more improvident, and, by the same token, more colorful extra girl of years past—the type of extra girl you met in "Merton of the Movies." At that, these young strangers in our midst are a self-reliant bunch, even if they wouldn't know a stage-door Johnny from Peter the Hermit.

Where are her "extra" sisters of the old silent days? Now they belong to history. Their beauty and ability to wear clothes with the necessary dash were not sufficient requisites for the talking screen. They couldn't dance, and they couldn't sing "Mammy." They had to find work in other fields. Some of them are waitresses now, others are manicurists. A few of

Chorus girls at play. Talkies have brought a new era for these chorines. No more backstage waits in a stuffy theater. Sun-baths, instead, on the green grass of "the lot"

She Must Dance! She Must Sing! She's Pretty and Pert, and So's Her Old Adagio!

the more fortunate are successful secretaries, salesladies, and buyers for stores. You may meet the old extra girl anywhere in Hollywood. Most of them are just "waiting around" for a return of the silent picture.

There is nothing wrong with the pay of the new extra girl. It assuredly beats typing and clerking. The old extra girl, if she had drawn such a salary, would have had illusions of grandeur and snubbed Gloria Swanson. The girls who display the epidermis in the screen all-talking, singing, dancing and what-have-you productions make, on the average, $75 weekly. During rehearsals they make $40. Not bad money for any miss in her 'teens. And not bad money for the highest paid chorus girls in New York.

The studio chorines have to work and work hard. They must keep in training like athletes. Quite likely they will be working in one picture and rehearsing dance routines for another. Champagne and lobster after midnight produce headaches the next morning, and a chorus girl who came to the studio all fagged would meet herself going out the gate.

Not many of them come from New York. Most of them have lived in and around (continued on next page)

Seven little tonics from the chorus of M-G-M's "Hollywood Revue." The talkies are universal in their appeal. Even the tired business man is not forgotten!

(continued from preceding page)

Hollywood. Some of them have attended dancing schools, and others have had experience in Los Angeles musical comedy productions. Every dance instructor will tell you that he prefers the local talent to Broadway importations.

The Broadway eyeful is too used to the old routine—toast and coffee at noon. And she's too hard-boiled.

THE Hollywood girl is younger—she must be youthful to stand the gaff—and she is smaller. The glamorous showgirl of the Broadway revues, the stately dame who looks like Salome should have and didn't in a string of synthetic pearls, is an unknown quantity around the studios. The movies want action.

No chorus girl in the world is in the hands of more capable dance directors. Larry Ceballos, Sammy Lee, Pearl Eaton, Albertina Rasch, Danny Dare and Seymour Felix, all in Hollywood, know their buck and wings when it comes to coaching.

First National and Warners, producing a long string of musical comedies and revues, have gone in the heaviest for beauty-on-the-hoof.

Five hundred girls were used in "The Show of Shows." First National keeps a great many busy. "Rio Rita," "The Love Parade," and the M-G-M musicals provide frequent work for many others. Perhaps there are four hundred girls with term contracts.

First National went very seriously into this chorus girl business. Out of the hundred-odd girls on the lot they took an average, and found little Maxine Cantway to be the ideal movie chorine. Maxine's measurements include a 32½-inch bust; a 23-inch waist; hips, 34 inches; calf, 12½ inches; ankle, 7½ inches. Venus De Milo, with her 28½-inch waistline, couldn't get a job as script girl on Poverty Row. Anna Held and Lillian Russell, with their hour-glass figures, wouldn't get to first base.

One studio issued a questionnaire to its chorus talent. The questions asked were varied: What is your ambition? Hobbies? Favorite books? Favorite screen actor and actress? Do you diet? How do you spend your evenings?

SOME of the girls took the questions seriously and made serious answers. Others took it as a grand joke, and answered accordingly.

The questions on how they spent their evenings brought back some of the following answers:

"None of your business."
"Working at the studio."
"I don't spend. The boy friend does."
"At home with the folks."
"When the fleet's in, you'd be surprised."
"Looking for excitement."

The favorite movie stars were set down as Billie Dove and Dorothy Mackaill, both originally from the chorus; Greta Garbo and Nils Asther, and a goodly number of votes for Clara Bow, John Gilbert and Ramon Novarro.

You can't make that old crack about the chorus girl not wanting a book, as she already has one. They all profess a liking for literature of one kind or another. Mystery novels got the most votes. One weighty miss named "Thus Spake Zarathustra." Another selected "The American Tragedy." At least they've heard of them.

They don't diet. As one girl expressed it—"When we're working, we dance it off. When we aren't, we worry it off."

NOT all of them wish to become stars by any means. Some of them are content to go right on dancing into eternity. One or two confess to a hankering for a husband. Most of them admit being able to cook, but they are dashed if they want to do it.

There are no Rolls-Royces. They're too busy to go about being corespondents in fashionable divorce suits. Quite a number of them drive their own, or the family flivvers. And quite a number of them hitch-hike to the studios, as did their extra girl sisters of the past.

In case there is a moment of rest between dances, most of them will go right on dancing. They dance for the sheer joy of doing it. Others scan magazines, or start a bridge game "for fun," or at a tenth of a cent.

The chorus girls one sees at First National, Warners, Paramount, and Radio Pictures are pretty much the same type—small, active and pretty.

The Albertina Rasch girls at M-G-M are a bit different. Madame Rasch was trained in the exacting schools of the ballet in Europe, and was a famous *premiere* ballerina at the Metropolitan Opera House. Her girls are larger and apparently stronger than the others. They must be. When they train for dance numbers there is no music. Only the rhythmical hand-clapping of Madame Rasch. She has a system of rigorous exercises which the girls take daily. No college athlete is more carefully trained. They have little time for flippancy. Madame Rasch would undoubtedly "fire" one of her girls if a smart-crack answer were given to a question. Like most Europeans she is a believer in discipline.

UNDOUBTEDLY among these two thousand movie chorus girls there are a few embryonic Doves and Bows, Shearers and Daniels. No Ziegfeld chorus surpasses them for looks. They must be pretty. Grease paint and footlights work miracles in hiding wrinkles and facial flaws. The camera is less charitable. Certain New York chorus girls are still in demand at thirty. You wouldn't find a girl past twenty-five among the entire two thousand in Hollywood. But if you believe what you are told, there are no women in pictures past twenty-five.

DEC.

Another Fairbanks

By Phillip Merton

DENNIS KING makes you think of Fairbanks. King is not tall, yet he is so active that you never notice his height. His carriage is erect, and he has Doug's slim grace.

He can do Fairbanks' "stuff," too, sword play and all. Even his voice has that same dramatic quality. Doug has always been a romantic figure. So has King.

There is a glamor to King that I have felt in few people. That is why I believe he is destined for greatness on the screen. He was a tremendous success in New York in "Rose Marie," "The Vagabond King," and "The Three Musketeers."

His first screen appearance will be in Paramount's Technicolor production of "The Vagabond King," which brings Rudolph Friml's glowing music to the screen. It has been in production for many weeks.

DENNIS KING

If Dennis King is like Fairbanks, there are times, too, when his resemblance to John Barrymore is startling. And like Barrymore and Fairbanks, Dennis King will always be at his best in costume pictures.

King's boyhood explains that, for he was born in Coventry, England. In the shadows of the spires of Coventry he heard of the good lady Godiva who took a little jaunt through the streets, garbed only in her long hair.

For a romantic boy there is no future but the stage, or writing, or wandering. When Dennis was fourteen he ran away and became a call-boy in John Drinkwater's repertory theater in Birmingham.

THE war delayed his career four years. He lied about his age and joined the conflict. He served for four years and was wounded.

He was beginning to make a small success in England when he came to America with "Monsieur Beaucaire."

One of his early American successes was as *Mercutio* in Jane Cowl's "Romeo and Juliet." He came to Los Angeles, but none of the producers were interested in his camera possibilities.

During the long New York run of "Romeo and Juliet" he took up the study of voice. His singing teacher discovered that he had a splendid voice. Hammerstein sent for him for the male rôle in "Rose Marie." His success was instantaneous. The rest is Broadway history.

His voice is beautiful, a baritone with the lyric quality of a tenor.

Dennis married a young English girl before he came to America. Mrs. King joined him in Hollywood before the picture was completed. Just before he left New York she presented him with a son, their second. Dennis is a great man with a rapier. He'll cut his way to film fame.

A CAMERA'S eye view of a group of very leggy young ladies from the chorus of "Painted Angel" in what looks to our unskilled eye like an extremely uncomfortable pose. Luckily for fans, people just will go on suffering for their art—or somebody else's art

The Microphone—*The Terror Of The Studios*

By Harry Carr

Mike, the demon, who sends the vocally unfit screaming or lisping from the lots

THIS is a story of Terrible Mike, the capricious genie of Hollywood, who is a Pain in the Larynx to half of filmdom, and a Tin Santa Claus to the other half!—who gives a Yoo-Hoo-There Leading Man a Voice like a Bull, and makes a Cauliflower-Eared Heavy talk like Elfin Elbert, the Library Lizard!—and who has raised more hell in movieland than a clara bow in a theological seminary.

Why, you can't even begin to write the half of the story of Terrible Mike and what he's done. You can only take a heap of ha-ha's here, and boo-hoo's there—laughs and sobs, heart-leaps and heart-aches, sudden wealth and sudden ruin, funny things and tragic things and howcum things—and try to string 'em together into some semblance of yarn.

And even then, every Hector and Hectorine that struts the streets of Hollywood will read it and say: "This guy ain't said NAW-thin' yet. . . ." And they'll be right—but here goes.

* * *

IN the first place—or is it? but let's put it there—young John W. Microphone, to give Terrible Mike his family name, has made the leading lady of the screen a LADY in fact as well as in name. Not that she wasn't ALWAYS a lady—no one'd EVER go so far as to say that. But look—

Before Mike crashed the studio gate and brought in his lady friends, what was little Miss Starlet like? You know. Ya-da-da-DA-poo-POO;—let's GO!!!—THAT'S what she was.

Little and hot, like a red pepper—and the Mexes were the hottest. She thought poise was just the label they put on imported canned peas, and *savoir faire*, she'd guess, was just the French name for a chocolate cruller, huh? She was a cute kid or a jumping bean from over the border, and Sex-Appeal and "It"—whatever THAT was—were her everything.

AND so Clara Bow says she's planning to take a year's trip abroad when her present contract with Paramount ends, and Ruth Chatterton is knocking 'em dead in the talkies. Mona Rico, for whom they had to fireproof the films, is God-knows-where, and Pauline Frederick flares into first-magnitude stardom.

Alice White is thanking Allah that she can sing, besides being cute, while Winifred Mrs. Bill-Hart Westover comes out of obscurity and wows it in "Lummox"!

Terrible Mike has cooled down the incandescent flapper—he's giving her an awful kick, and is putting Poor Old Lady Has-Been back on the throne.

Miss Humpty-Dumpty sat on a wall;
Miss Humpty-Dumpty had a great fall—
For all of her "S. A." and all of her "It"
Just couldn't make her in talkies a hit!
—from "Mother Goose in Hollywood"

Consider Bebe Daniels and Clara Bow. Envision for yourselves a see-saw. One end goes up; the other end goes down. Bebe is on the end that's going up, and Clara is—well, er, let's confine ourselves to her own admission that she's going to take a European trip by and by because she's tired.

"I've been working hard for years," she told a Hollywood friend the other day, "and I need a rest. So I'm figuring on going to Europe for a year or more, when my contract expires." It expires in about thirteen or fourteen months, and not a soul at Paramount has said it'll be renewed.

And at the same time, Mr. Paramount is kicking himself all over the lot because of Bebe Daniels. Bebe, you see, bought up her own contract with Paramount not so long ago because they didn't think she was worth two toots in talkies. They were paying her a fat salary, and using her in ordinary pictures. They couldn't afford to spend much on her productions, was the excuse, because her salary under contract was so big that they had to skimp on her pictures to make money. When they wouldn't give her a talkie chance, Bebe slapped down $175,000 and bought back the contract that called for her to make three more pictures.

And now what?

WHY, just this: Bebe Daniels, as this is written, has just finished the lead in "Rio Rita" for Radio Pictures. And there isn't a doubt in the world, say the wiseacres of Hollywood, that that talkie will be one of The Big Shots of the talkie year. Bebe's work is one of the biggest sensations of the millions of sensations Terrible Mike has pulled.

Strange, too. Bebe has a voice that you wouldn't think twice about, ordinarily. Nice voice, and all that, but no power—no force. Now that's just where Mike does his stuff. He took all the nice things in Bebe's voice—and there were plenty of 'em—and added the thing she didn't have—POWER. And boy, what a voice it gives her on the screen!—you'd even fall in love with a strabismic wart-hog if it had a voice like that.

On the other hand, Clara Bow's voice certainly didn't lack power. Her first all-talkie—"The Wild Party"—proved that. Her first scene called for her to dash into a dormitory full of girls and greet them with, "Hello, everybody. . . .!" Well, the sound-mixing gentleman in the monitor-room above the stage, not being familiar with the—ah—er—vibrations of Clara's voice, didn't properly tune down his dials for Clara's words.

She burst in, told them "HELLO, EVERYBODY!!!"—and every light valve in the recording room was broken!

Little Miss Starlet, in ermine and scarlet,
Getting a thousand a day,
Along came the talkies, revealing her squawkies—
And put poor Miss Starlet away!
—from "Mother Goose in Hollywood"

How'd you like another contrast—even more startling than the case of Clara and Bebe? *(continued on next page)*

DEC.

The Film *of the* Future

Standard Movietone film of Premier Ramsay MacDonald. Note the sound track at left

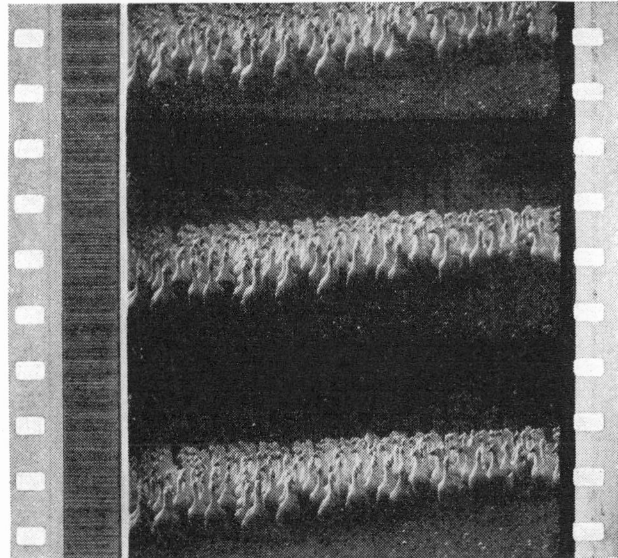

The new Fox Grandeur Movietone film. It is seventy millimetres wide, or twice the width of standard film. Hear the geese honk

Old fashioned standard width film, still used when sound is recorded on a disc

NOT long ago an astonished audience in New York saw the first showing of a new film which is going to revolutionize the making and showing of motion pictures—Grandeur Film.

The new film, with its wide sound track, is twice the width of the old-fashioned film, and requires a wide camera lens and a new type of projector. It is thrown on a screen forty feet wide and twenty feet high, or one about twice as wide as the sheet we know. It was perfected, after three years, by the Fox-Case Corporation and General Theatres Equipment, Inc.

Astounding effects are possible with Grandeur. Fox showed a Movietone News and a version of the "Movietone Follies," and thrilled a hardboiled audience. Grandeur's possibilities are limitless. It is the film of the future.

(continued from preceding page)

Well, then, here are Mona Rico and Joan Bennett—

Joan, you know, is one of the three daughters of the interesting Richard, which really doesn't matter.

Anyway, she, like thousands of others, sought fame in pictures—and sought and sought and sought, also like thousands of others. She got a bit here, and a bit there, but she never burned them up. She just looked sweet and pretty and nice and mary-ann-ish and so on.

And then she married herself out of the pictures, and that seemed the end of Joan. Married a chap named Fox, whose father had a lot of timberland.

ONE day a reporter called on her and chronicled the birth of a Foxlet. He found Joan and her hubby and baby living in a walkup flat in the south-of-the-tracks part of Beverly Hills, which is you know. Joan was just a nice little *hausfrau* who didn't look any happier than any other little *hausfrau*. And it turned out she wasn't even that happy—for she soon got a divorce.

And everybody in filmdom that cared said "Poor Joan" and "Life is like that," and forgot her.

But along came Terrible Mike, and Ronald Colman needed a leading lady for "Bulldog Drummond." Star after star was tested for the part—and somehow, poor Joan Bennett got a test. Maybe somebody felt sorry for her.

And Terrible Mike did his stuff—the stuff for which everybody that tried out, except Joan, calls him "Terrible." He set Joan out so far ahead of every other tryer-out that they gave her the part. And "Poor Joan" was such a success in the part that she's on her way to the top—she's played opposite George Arliss in "Disraeli," opposite Harry Richman in "Playboy," is signed for the lead with Joseph Schildkraut in "The Mississippi Gambler."

And from her walkup flat south of the tracks in Beverly, she's moved into one of those lemme-see-your-bankbook apartments in a house called the *Chateau Elysée*.

That's the story of Joan. Turn the picture, and see Mona Rico and what Terrible Mike has done to her—

Once upon a time, a little Mexican extra girl was standing around the United Artists lot, waiting to be called for the next scene so she could earn her day's $7.50. Director Ernst Lubitsch was giving a man a screen test. He needed somebody to work the test scene with the fellow.

"Hey, you!" he yelled at the first girl he saw. "Come over here and do so-and-so. . . .!"

The girl who called herself Mona Rico did. And when they ran off the "rush" of the test footage, Lubitsch forgot all about the man in the take and dashed wildly out to find Mona. She had stolen the scene.

It was one of those things that little extra girls dream about. And before she knew it, Mona Rico was playing lead opposite John Barrymore.

She put on all the stuff that went with it—apartment, maids, autos, chauffeurs, clothes. Lupe Velez must have lain awake worrying o' nights.

BUT Terrible Mike has a Nordic superiority complex or something. He stepped right into Mona Rico's life, planted himself before her, and said:

"You!—how do you speak English? . . ."

Poor Mona Rico! Gone is the dream. . . .

And gone or going with it are that swarm of duco-haired Don Tabascos who were cluttering up Hollywood.

O, Don Ro-dreek was a movie Sheik,
Knocking down a grand a week;
He gave the frails an awful kick—
But now he's OUT? He "no can spik. . . .!"
—from "Mother Goose in Hollywood"

The superheated senoritas and their male companions in arson aren't the only ones to suffer from Terrible Mike's linguistic demands. It's tough on other outlanders—even, as the passports say, "including the Scandinavian!" There are, for instance, Nils Asther and Greta Garbo.

A year ago, Nils was getting enough fan mail from heaving-bosomed damsels in the midlands to paper a ballroom with. And even yet.

But Nils, he bane got Swedish accent, and Terrible Mike is laying for him.

Ditto goes for the Garbo. So far, they've dodged Mike by sticking to the silents—they just made a valiant stand together in that picture ballyhooed by the billboard showing Greta in that bathing suit with Nils bending over her—quick, boys, the pyrene ! ! ! "Actions speak louder than words" is their motto—and their hope.

And a German beauty, as lovely a *fraulein* as ever was "Made in Germany," ran afoul of Terrible Mike in Hollywood and has returned to Deutschland to do her klang-filming.

TRUE, some of the importations have so far survived the terror of the mike. But only by a sort of artificial respiration—they've confined themselves to stories that call for an accent!

They can't talk English straight.

They can talk it, though, with a twist here and a twist there. And so they play the rôles of foreign princesses and things like that—leetle Fr-r-r-ranch *m'mselles, hein?* And manage to live.

Interesting, here, is the fact that Sessue Hayakawa, the Japanese star of how-long-ago, crashed back into celluloid BECAUSE of—not in spite of—the mike! As this is written, Hayakawa has just finished a short talkie back east for Warners, called "The Man Who Laughed Last."

It's Hayakawa's vaudeville skit, done for the silver screen—and probably ninety per cent of the people who see and hear him will be amazed to find out how well he speaks English!

Hayakawa died in the silent pictures many years ago because he could only do ONE kind of story—the Japanese prince or something who married the white girl and paid for it.

Or didn't, and paid anyway!

And so it's a funny thing, isn't it?—how Terrible Mike makes 'em or breaks 'em. . . . Old-timers come back through his ministrations, and the big shots go boom. . . .

Eenie, Meenie, Minie, Mo—
Stars, they face the mike with woe;
If they holler, watch 'em go. . . .!
Eenie, Meenie, Minie, Mo!!!
—from "Mother Goose in Hollywood"

The demon mike didn't frighten Gloria Swanson. Coached in speaking lines by the famous Laura Hope Crews, and with a high-priced singing teacher putting her through the eighth-notes, Gloria gave the performance of her life in "The Trespasser," and will undoubtedly find the greatest and most productive period of her long career in talking pictures.

But there's Vilma Banky. She had her Hungarian accent to lick.

Jane Manner, the New York voice coach, had Vilma in hand for six months, and now Sam Goldwyn is paying the Hungarian Rhapsody her $2,000 a week while the camera crank isn't turning, until the girl can clip her "darlinks" and speak better English into the ear of the choosy microphone.

THERE'S Lila "Cuddles" Lee, who has miked a comeback.

Starred by Paramount at fifteen, she grew up—and out of it.

Then she married James Kirkwood, disappeared from the screen, and finally, when he went abroad, she managed to get by, doing quickies here and there.

And now, suddenly, she's found the pot of gold hidden in the microphone.

No big smash, you know—just a good actress with a lovely mike voice. Maybe she'll never be a star, but with what she's got, she'll always be in the money.

And there's H. B. Warner. Of H. B., they used to say:

"Oh, yes, he's the fellow that played *Jesus* in that DeMille thing. What's he doing now?"

The answer is that he's got a great talkie voice and a First National contract.

Look at Louise Fazenda—good old Louise. She was always a good actress. But Terrible Mike has made her better. He's taken that fazendish giggle of hers and let the citizenry hear it.

Results?—Louise played in "No, No, Nanette," "Loose Ankles," "The Desert Song" and plenty more to come.

TERRIBLE MIKE has boosted Betty Compson to the top—for the third time in her career.

Young Douglas Fairbanks, Jr., who had the misfortune to be only his papa's son for a long time in the stillies, has been going fine in the talkies since Terrible Mike was good to him in "The Barker."

These are some that have been given a helping hand by Mike the Erratic. But look what happened to Dolores Costello, the sex-quisite.

Magnificent thing that she is, this Mrs. Jack Barrymore, she's got something in her voice that Terrible Mike simply snarls out loud about.

Headed for the heights she was, until she played in "Glorious Betsy."

Poor Dolores—there are two opinions in Hollywood as to what her mike voice sounded like.

One clique says it sounded like the barkings of a lonesome puppy; the others claim it reminded them of the time they sang "In the Shade of the Old Apple Tree" through tissue paper folded over a comb.

It's not Dolores' fault; it's just one of the Terrible Mike's dirty tricks.

And anyway, Dolores should worry—she and hubby Jack have gone back East to prepare for a new addition to the Barrymore family.

If it's a boy, it's certain they won't name him Michael.

But what Terrible Mike did to Dolores in "Glorious Betsy," he did just the opposite in the same opus for Conrad Nagel.

Conrad was just a nice blond leading man before that.

But suddenly the world discovered he had a marvelous voice.

And now the name of Conrad Nagel in Hollywood is as the name of Abou ben Adhem in that thing you had to learn when you were a kid.

And now we'll move on to the peculiar situation of Dick Barthelmess! . . . Dick, who has been helped and hurt at one and the same time because of Terrible Mike.

Dick has always turned out darned good pictures.

More than that, he has turned out a good talkie.

The word is used advisedly— for while Dick talks well, Dick is *not* a singer. And yet, in his talkie, Dick is seen to sing! . . .

And as he is seen to sing, there emerges from the screen a lovely voice. It synchronizes perfectly with Dick's mouthings on the screen—and if you didn't know better you'd say: Ah, how he can sing! . . .

But you know better. From East coast to West, and from border to border, there was printed in the public prints the news that a "voice double" had sung the song while Dick Barthelmess made his mouth go.

LIKE the golden idol with the clay feet, Dick Barthelmess was not perfection—his feet were all right, but his vocal cords needed tuning!

(continued on next page)

(continued from preceding page)

And it didn't help a bit when the 24-sheet billboards tried to kid the public with:

"See AND HEAR Richard Barthelmess in So-and-So. . . ."

The public, being a number of years older and wiser than in the days of Phineas T. Barnum, read the billboards, made a sound like a moribund raspberry and wanted to know how they got that way.

But see and hear him in "The Drag." He's our old Barthelmess again.

But don't draw the conclusion from that that voice-doubling is rare. Ah—no—Terrible Mike has brought a bag of money to a group of people who have heretofore had no chance whatever in the movies . . . people who can sing.

You who see and hear these talkie extravaganzas with the dazzling chorus girls, and wonder how they could find so many beautiful girls who could sing, too—cease your wondering. They DON'T SING! It's like this—

THE cameras are trained on the beautiful chorus girls, who dance and move their lips just like Dick Barthelmess did. But they are as silent as a bill collector isn't. And down below the camera-range, or at one side, are the microphones—in front of a dozen or so lovely-voiced creatures whose loveliness often ends there.

"Yes, dearie; I've got a job in the pictures."

"You! With that pan?"

"No, dearie—do-re-mi-fa-sol! . . . With this VOICE!"

And in just the same way as these chorus songs are "doubled," so, with a little rehearsing, can individual songs be doubled for such stars as can act and talk for Terrible Mike but who sing like a $198 piano six months after you have it paid for. But voice doubling will soon go out of style.

The one sad Barthelmess experience taught the movie makers a valuable lesson. In the future, the stars who can't sing will dance, or tell riddles.

One could go on and on and on about the big-timers to whom Terrible Mike has done so-and-so and this-and-that—Norma Shearer, who has been definitely located, thanks to her success in "The Trial of Mary Dugan" and "The Last of Mrs. Cheyney"; Bessie Love, who was just drifting and had gotten down to ukuleleing it in personal appearance stuff with a Fanchon-Marco road show, and who suddenly jumped through the microphone back into the starry realms in "Broadway Melody"; the Duncan Sisters, who left Hollywood rapidly after making a silent "Topsy and Eva" for United Artists, and whom Terrible Mike beckoned back because they CAN sing, to make "Cotton and Silk."

And so on, and on, and on.

But let's forget, for a bit, the actors and actresses.

Terrible Mike's machinations have had effect elsewhere.

HE has brought coffers full of golden shekels—or aren't shekels gold?—to others than these.

He has fattened the exchequers of the Building Trades unionists, since every studio has begun building sound stages on the subdivision plan.

He has made clinky the pockets of all sorts of ham-and-eggers who got on his band-wagon by opening schools of dramatic expression and elocution, even though they themselves talked of "erl" wells and "moiders."

He gave rise to a lot of funny stories about the people who didn't know the mike was turned on, and expressed their opinion of the director or supervisor as a bad ancestored person of amazing habits.

He gave the studio press agents a lot of things to write that never got into the papers or magazines.

And he's—he's—well, one more excerpt from "Mother Goose in Hollywood"—

Hey, diddle, diddle
Mike is a riddle,
He makes 'em both poor and rich!
The joke may be good,
But to Hollywood,
He's a—
gosh-darned mean old thing!

DEC.

SWEETIE—Paramount

COLLEGIATE capers provide lively entertainment, although "Sweetie" will not cause the lighting of bonfires. It scores chiefly through its pleasant youthfulness. That li'l "boop-a-doop" person, Helen Kane, romps off with the show. Her songs are grand. Jack Oakie wows 'em with his Alma Mammy college song. This will not mean much to Nancy Carroll, although she is effective in an unsympathetic rôle. *All Talkie.*

"SWEETIE"—PARAMOUNT.—From the story by George Marion, Jr., and Lloyd Corrigan. Dialogue by George Marion, Jr., and Lloyd Corrigan. Directed by Frank Tuttle. The cast: *Barbara Pell*, Nancy Carroll; *Biff Bently*, Stanley Smith; *Helen Fry*, Helen Kane; *Freddie Fry*, Joseph Depew; *Tap-Tap Thompson*, Jack Oakie; *Percy (Pussy) Willow*, William Austin; *Axel Bronstrup*, Stuart Erwin; *Bill Barrington*, Wallace MacDonald; *Dr. Oglethorpe*, Charles Sellon; *Miss Twill*, Aileen Manning.

DEC.

MARRIED IN HOLLYWOOD—Fox

BY far the finest thing about this—the first Viennese operetta to hit the screen via sound—is the exquisite music by Oscar Strauss. The story jumps from Vienna to Hollywood to Cinderella to Heaven knows what and where. An all-stage cast performs. J. Harold (Rio Rita) Murray and Norma (Show Boat) Terris sing the leads, and Walter Catlett and Tom Patricola handle the laughs. Good—but somehow it should have been better. *All Talkie.*

"MARRIED IN HOLLYWOOD"—Fox.—From the operetta by Oscar Strause. Dialogue by Harlan Thompson. Directed by Marcel Silver. The cast: *Prince Nicholai*, J. Harold Murray; *Mary Lou Hopkins*, Norma Terris; *Mitzi Hofman*, Norma Terris; *Joe Glitner*, Walter Catlett; *Annushka*, Irene Palasty; *King Alexander*, Lennox Pawle; *Mahai*, Tom Patricola; *Queen Louise*, Evelyn Hall; *Stage Prince*, John Garrick; *Adjutant Octavian*, Douglas Gilmore; *Charlotte*, Gloria Grey; *Captain Jacobi*, Jack Stambaugh; *Herr Von Herzen*, Bert Sprotte; *Mrs. Von Herzen*, Lelia Karnelly; *Herr Director*, Herman Bing; *Namari*, Paul Ralli.

DEC.

Hollywood did everything but call out the militia when Rudy Vallée crooned into town to make his first talkie, "The Vagabond Lover." Here's the band leader at the station, with his papa and mamma, Mr. and Mrs. Charles Vallée, and a few loitering chorus maids

DEC.

The eleven Technicolor cameras in Hollywood are so precious that they are carried from lot to lot in armored cars. They never did that for Pola Negri!

IRENE BORDONI

NORMA TERRIS

IRENE BORDONI is the hot sauce of the movie menu. She is small and "Fr-ranch," volatile and vivacious. Her naughty eyes have delighted audiences from Bangor to the Golden Gate. She has just made a talking picture version of her recent stage success, "Paris," for First National. This winter she will return to the stage, and, according to present plans, be back in the spring for further pictures.

The Bordoni's arrival in Hollywood was nothing if not impressive. She came quietly into town, accompanied only by a secretary, a chauffeur, a chef and two maids. Bordoni was going to be comfortable. In addition to her ménage in Beverly Hills, she maintains a home just off Park Avenue in New York, another in Paris, and a villa on the French Riviera.

This interesting singing comedienne was born on the Island of Corsica, in Ajaccio. She is not the only Corsican to sail from her native shores and conquer the world. Napoleon first saw the light of day on that island. Her great grandmother was the sister of Millet, the famous artist.

AFTER stardom in the music halls of the Continent, La Bordoni scored instant success in America in "Miss Information," a revue starring Elsie Janis. Her name soon appeared in electric lights on Broadway. Her particular forte has been versions of spicy French farces, in which she sings both in French and English.

In this day when many foreign stars have been compelled to leave the screen on account of accents, the greatest charm of the Bordoni is in her quaint handling of English. She has no desire to lose it. Bordoni without an accent would be applesauce without apples.

She is one of the most distinctively unusual women to enter pictures. Her presence at a première is noted with interest. She dresses with individuality and sometimes with startling effect. Yet, she is not an extremist.

The oo-la-la Bordoni's domestic affairs have been in one of those trying states of flux for the past year or so.

She was for a good many years the wife of E. Ray Goetz, theatrical producer and promoter. Then harsh words began to be spoken, which rose to near-screams when Goetz produced a play starring that hardy perennial, Peggy Hopkins Joyce. At last reports an armed truce prevailed.

Bordoni has been, throughout her American career, a good every-season bet at the box-office. She has capably furnished our Gallic spice in the place of the lamented Anna Held, bowling over sophomores of seventeen and seventy, year after year.

So be prepared for something glittering and alluring when you go to "Paris."

Irene will get you, even if you watch out.

THOSE hard-boiled cynics who'll tell you that Tom Mix's horse uses a double, thought it was a studio publicity gag when Norma Terris married Dr. Jerome Wagner just as she warbled the last high C in "Married in Hollywood."

"So," said Norma, "we took the stigma off it by having the ceremony performed in Beverly Hills."

And right after the wedding the presidents of the transcontinental airplane companies rubbed their hands together and called it a big day. For Norma, one of the latest recruits from Broadway, and Dr. Wagner will commute between Hollywood and New York.

Norma is different from most of the film gals. She's quite tall and, although her hair is dark brown and her eyes are black, hers is not the conventional type of brunette beauty. But you're so used to beauty in Hollywood.

There is something else, you know—mostly a voice, and Norma Terris has that.

For two years she was *Magnolia* in Ziegfeld's "Show Boat."

Because she had not been long in Hollywood her marriage didn't cause a ripple on the sound wave, yet it was one of the most spectacular that has yet been recorded in the annals of film romances.

TWO years ago she met Dr. Wagner. In June she came to Hollywood. He followed, begging her to marry him. She refused. He returned to his stethoscopes and sphygmomanometers, but he spent most of this time on the long distance telephone. And then Norma said "yes" so, in case she'd change her mind, he hopped a plane and married her right away at the home of Mr. and Mrs. Charles Mack, dignified for the tired member of the "Two Black Crows," and his little woman.

Because there were arteries hardening in New York, the couple jumped on a plane again and winged their way to the Eastern city. But there's a contract waiting for Norma in Hollywood that has to be fulfilled.

The doctor can't give up his practice. And that's how airplane companies get rich.

Norma had a glamorous rise in the show world, topping it off with this slam-bang marriage.

It was "Show Boat" that made her famous, and it is "Show Boat" that will mark her as long as she trills on stage or screen. "Oh, yes," our youngsters will say, "Daddy took me to see her play *Magnolia*." Up to the moment that magnificent Ziegfeldian bolt struck her for fame and fortune, she was just another young leading woman, forever on the make for jobs on Broadway. Now she's a personage.

Yup—it's forever just like the old song says—

"Mix the lot—what have you got?—MAGNOLIA!"

DEC.

 **FOOTLIGHTS AND FOOLS—First National**

UNQUESTIONABLY this is Colleen Moore's best picture since "We Moderns." Talkies have given her a curious break which she's taken big.

Her voice is pleasant and versatile, and the story standards raised by talking films permit her to chuck the synthetic program stuff and turn to something bigger. This is it. The story, by Katherine Brush, is a skilful combination of sophisticated humor and poignant emotional drama.

New York's musical comedy sensation, *Mlle. Fifi d'Auray*, is a temperamental French whirlwind before the footlights. Offstage, she's little *Betty Murphy*, who loves a boy who's a rotter. As *Fifi*, Colleen wears a hundred mad gowns and wigs, and sings French songs with a naughty lilt. As *Betty*, her piquant self. Both ways, gorgeous! *All Talkie.*

"FOOTLIGHTS AND FOOLS"—FIRST NATIONAL.—From the story by Katharine Brush. Continuity by Carey Wilson. Directed by William Seiter. The cast: *Mlle. Fifi d'Auray*, Colleen Moore; *Gregory Pyne*, Frederic March; *Jimmy Willet*, Raymond Hackett; *Chandler Cunningham*, Edward Martindel; *Claire*, Virginia Lee Corbin; *Jo, the maid*, Adrienne d'Ambricourt; *Stage Manager*, Sidney Jarvis; *Call Boy*, Mickey Bennett.

DEC.

 **THE LOVE PARADE—Paramount**

SPARKLING as Burgundy, and almost as intoxicating, "The Love Parade" is one of the outstanding pictures of the year. It is Lubitsch's most brilliant effort since "The Marriage Circle." The little director here conquers light opera!

After the dashing nobleman marries the *Queen of Sylvania*, he gets durned tired of constantly obeying. So he bludgeons the queen into letting him be head man.

Maurice Chevalier, a great favorite after his first American picture, despite a weak story, is grand as the prince. His songs are triumphs. Jeanette MacDonald is an eye-feast as the queen, and sings well. Lupino Lane amuses.

The music is relatively unimportant, although "Dream Lover" and "Nobody's Using It Now" may be popular. Don't miss "The Love Parade." *All Talkie.*

"LOVE PARADE, THE"—PARAMOUNT.—From the play "The Prince Consort" by Jules Chancel and Leon Zanrof. Story by Ernest Vajda and Guy Bolton. Directed by Ernst Lubitsch. The cast: *Count Alfred, Military Attache*, Maurice Chevalier; *Louise, Queen of Sylvania*, Jeanette MacDonald; *Jacques, Alfred's Valet*, Lupino Lane; *Lulu, Queen's Personal Maid*, Lillian Roth; *Master of Ceremonies*, Edgar Norton; *Prime Minister*, Lionel Belmore; *Foreign Minister*, Albert Roccardi; *Admiral*, Carleton Stockdale; *Minister of War*, Eugene Pallette; *Afghan Ambassador*, Russell Powell; *First Lady in Waiting*, Margaret Fealy; *Second Lady in Waiting*, Virginia Bruce.

DEC. **RED HOT RHYTHM—Pathe**

TECHNICOLOR sequences and cleverly staged dance numbers lift "Red Hot Rhythm" into an importance it could not otherwise attain. The story is a weak sister despite occasional flashes of brilliance. It is about a philandering song-writer. Alan Hale is the star, and he has quite a difficult time choosing between Kathryn Crawford and Josephine Dunn. Golly, wouldn't we all? *All Talkie.*

"RED HOT RHYTHM"—PATHE.—From the story by William Conselman. Adapted by Earl Baldwin and Walter De Leon. Directed by Leo McCarey. The cast: *Walter*, Alan Hale; *Sam*, Walter O'Keefe; *Mary*, Kathryn Crawford; *Claire*, Josephine Dunn; *Mabel*, Anita Garvin; *Mrs. Fioretta*, Ilka Chase; *Singe*, James Clemmons.

DEC. **A SONG OF KENTUCKY—Fox**

YOU just can't tell about pictures these days. Now here's one where the favorite pony, "Dixie," doesn't win the race. But don't let that get you all upset. The singing hero wins the gal. They can't be too radical, after all. You may not like Joseph Wagstaff's looks, but you'll care for his crooning in a large way. Lois Moran is the decorative heroine. And the music is nice and sentimental. *All Talkie.*

"SONG OF KENTUCKY, A"—FOX.—From the story by Frederick H. Brennan. Adapted by Frederick H. Brennan. Directed by Lew Seiler. The cast: *Jerry Reavis*, Joseph Wagstaff; *Lee Coleman*, Lois Moran; *Nancy Morgan*, Dorothy Burgess; *Kane Pitcairn*, Douglas Gilmore; *Jake Kleinschmidt*, Herman Bing; *Mrs. Coleman*, Hedda Hopper; *Mr. Coleman*, Edwards Davis; *Steve*, Bert Woodruff.

DEC.

THE GREAT GABBO—James Cruze Prod.

All Talkie

THIS is a bitter disappointment. Director James Cruze tried to cross a fine Ben Hecht story of an insanely egotistical vaudeville ventriloquist with one of these Hollywood musical revues, and both suffer. Only a fine performance by the bullet-headed Eric von Stroheim and a good one by Betty Compson save the pieces. Cruze seems to have lost his sense of humor, and the lighting and scenario are terrible.

"GREAT GABBO, THE"—JAMES CRUZE PROD.—From the story by Ben Hecht. Continuity by Hugh Herbert. Directed by James Cruze. The cast: *The Great Gabbo*, Eric Von Stroheim; *Mary*, Betty Compson; *Frank*, Don Douglas; *Babe*, Margie (Babe) Kane; *Otto Gabbo*, Otto.

DEC.

TANNED LEGS—Radio Pictures

THOUGH the story is what happens when a summer fad becomes a movie title, this frothy musical comedy will thrill the Tiredest Business Man. Not only are there Ann Pennington's knees—with Miss Pennington attached—but June Clyde's legs—the prettiest in Hollywood—with eyes and voice to match. Stranger still, she can act. Arthur Lake whoops gaily through the picture in his usual loose-limbed fashion. Exhilarating music. *All Talkie.*

"TANNED LEGS"—RADIO PICTURES.—From the story by George Hull. Adapted by Tom Geraghty. Directed by Marshall Neilan. The cast: *Peggy Reynolds,* June Clyde; *Bill,* Arthur Lake; *Janet Reynolds,* Sally Blane; *Roger,* Allen Kearns; *Mrs. Reynolds,* Nella Walker; *Mr. Reynolds,* Albert Gran; *Clinton Darrow,* Edmund Burns; *Mrs. Lyons King,* Dorothy Revier; *Tootie,* Ann Pennington; *Pudgy,* Lincoln Stedman; *Hosiery Model,* Helen Kaiser; *Hosiery Model,* Kay English.

DEC.

★ SUNNY SIDE UP—Fox

YOU'LL eat this one up, and it furnishes its own cream and sugar. Janet Gaynor turns loose her cute little singing and speaking voices in a story of high life and low in New York, and Charles Farrell is on hand to woo her with more than gestures.

"Sunny Side Up" is another Cinderella yarn, with the rich young Farrell finding the poor young Gaynor at a block party on the New York East Side. This will never do, thinks Charlie. Before you know it, Janet has cut out the rich girl friend, played by Sharon Lynn, and the Gaynor-Farrell love team scores a thumping old touchdown in the last minute of play.

El Brendel, Fox favorite, furnishes a lot of laughs, as does Marjorie White, a pert little piece from the musical comedy stage. The De Sylva, Brown and Henderson music is particularly gay. Janet pipes the theme song, and nearly everybody has a tune or two in his system.

Something new for Janet and Charlie, after their royal line of sobby little love stories. But they came through like good troupers, and you'll care for the result.

The bright little picture shows that we can have our songs, dances and loves without going backstage for them. And don't forget to keep your eye on the White girl. She should go far. *All Talkie.*

"SUNNY SIDE UP"—Fox.—From the story by B. G. De Sylva, Lew Brown and Ray Henderson. Adapted by David Butler. Directed by David Butler. The cast: *Molly Carr,* Janet Gaynor; *Jack Cromwell,* Charles Farrell; *Jane Worth,* Sharon Lynn; *Eddie Rafferty,* Frank Richardson; *Eric Swenson,* El Brendel; *Bee Nichols,* Marjorie White; *Joe Vitto,* Joe Brown; *Mrs. Cromwell,* Mary Forbes; *Raoul,* Alan Paull; *Lake,* Peter Gawthorne.

DEC.

FIVE real Ziegfeld gals have been collected to work in one picture, "Tanned Legs," at Radio Pictures.

Kay English, Ann Pennington, Anna Karina, Helen Kaiser and Pearl Eaton are among the cast, but the leading rôle is being played by June Clyde, who was never with Ziegfeld, but who was picked for the part because of her beautiful legs.

DEC.

It wouldn't baffle Freud a bit if this gown (right) haunted your dreams. Any good psycho-analyst would tell you your suppressed desire was to look like Dorothy Mackaill. The ensemble? Oh, yeah, it's of blue velvet with a double fox collar in white and silver. Howard Greer created it

DEC.

As We Go *to* PRESS

Last Minute NEWS *from* East *and* West

AFTER sitting around the M-G-M lot for five months waiting for a suitable rôle, Carlotta King has returned temporarily to vaudeville. Her contract has seven more months to run.

FLORENZ ZIEGFELD'S first picture for Samuel Goldwyn will probably be a version of his successful "Whoopee."

ERNST LUBITSCH scored a big success with "The Love Parade" and will make at least one more picture for Paramount.

AS a nice sugar plum for being a good girl in "The Devil May Care," Dorothy Jordan draws the feminine lead in Novarro's next phonoplay. It's to be an original by Josephine Lovett, titled "Song of India."

NOAH BEERY emerges in a new rôle. Warner Brothers have placed him under a two years' contract because of his remarkable singing voice.

PATHE'S "International Television Revue" is being done in five languages. A platoon of directors and a regiment of stars are working on and in it.

THE last word in titles is "Vagabond"—no really chic title is complete without it. Harry Richman's picture for United Artists has been definitely monikered "Broadway Vagabond" (a hangover from last season's "Broadway" rage); Rudy Vallée is making "The Vagabond Lover" for Radio; and Dennis King has just completed "The Vagabond King" for Paramount.

WARNERS have signed Alice Gentle, the grand opera star, for a series of rôles in 1930, due to her outstanding work in "Golden Dawn." The singer, contrary to all operatic traditions, is now svelte as a co-ed.

DEC.

Ethelind Terry is a stage star who came to Hollywood to wear rose velvet and lace pajamas, like the above, designed by David Cox.

DEC.

Meet the merry-makers of "Rio Rita." Seated in front are Hiram S. Brown, president of Radio Pictures, Bebe Daniels and William Le Baron, producer. Harry Tierney, composer, is standing. Others: Luther Reed, some swell director; Victor Baravalle, music, and Max Ree

1930

BY 1930, HOLLYWOOD'S ADJUSTMENT TO SOUND was quite complete. A handful of silents and part-talkies were released, but these were largely regarded as anachronisms. The industry and public alike had become so involved with sound that even pro-industry publications like PHOTOPLAY referred to the recent silent era as if it were a prehistoric age.

Towering silent favorites like Pola Negri, Jetta Goudal, Mae Murray, the Talmadge sisters, John Gilbert, Vilma Banky, Corinne Griffith, and countless others struggled for career survival or graciously retired, sensing that their professional days were numbered. They had been replaced by John Boles, Charles King, Jeanette MacDonald, Maurice Chevalier, Vivienne Segal, Nancy Carroll, Marilyn Miller, Helen Kane, Al Jolson, Eddie Cantor, and others with footlight experience.

Many of 1929's technical limitations in shooting with sound were solved by 1930. Because camera noise had been picked up by the sensitive microphones, cameras had to be placed inside thickly quilted soundproof huts ironically called "ice boxes." The heat inside often caused the cameramen to faint, and the restriction of camera movement resulted in the static appearance of many 1929 films. By 1930, the industry began to use "blimps," small housings that covered the camera only, thus restoring freedom of movement to the camera and comfort to the cinematographer.

This was also the year in which RCA Noiseless Recording vastly improved the signal-to-noise ratio of soundtracks, previously plagued with noticeable hiss level. No fewer than sixteen features, most of them musicals, were shot entirely in Technicolor, with color sequences inserted liberally into almost twenty other pictures. Several films, including the musical *Happy Days,* were released in wide-screen format.

Many of the year's musicals were screen adaptations of Broadway shows, both lavish operettas and light musical comedies, often featuring prominent stage personalities. Metropolitan Opera stars John McCormack, Lawrence Tibbett, and Grace Moore all made prestigious screen debuts, though Miss Moore had to wait until her 1934 comeback before attaining movie popularity. One of the year's happiest musicals was *Whoopee,* in which Eddie Cantor and many members of Florenz Ziegfeld's stage cast re-created their roles for the screen. This Technicolor picture also marked the film debut of Broadway dance director Busby Berkeley.

But the public was rapidly becoming restless toward the flood of musicals that had not abated since the release of *The Broadway Melody* over a year earlier. The studios began to delete numbers from already-completed musicals, and songs were dropped from many pictures still in preproduction stages. Many musicals that had been announced were cancelled before the cameras began to roll.

The greatest curiosity was MGM's *The March of Time,* a part-color all-star revue that combined current headliners with turn-of-the-century footlight favorites from the Weber and Fields Music Hall. Numerous stills and publicity items were published about this movie in PHOTOPLAY and elsewhere, but the completed film was shelved. Several excerpts were later used in *Broadway to Hollywood,* an unusually intelligent backstage musical of 1933.

By the year's end, a moratorium on musical production was in full swing. Theme songs were no longer being inserted into dramatic films, and the few musicals in production were released with only two or three songs at most. Only a handful of lavish operettas, for which expensive sets and costumes had already been made, were still being rushed through.

The first sweeping wave of musical films had subsided. The Broadway expatriates leased their Beverly Hills mansions and submissively returned to the Gay White Way. It had been a grand year for musicals, but it was to be the last one for quite a while.

M. K.

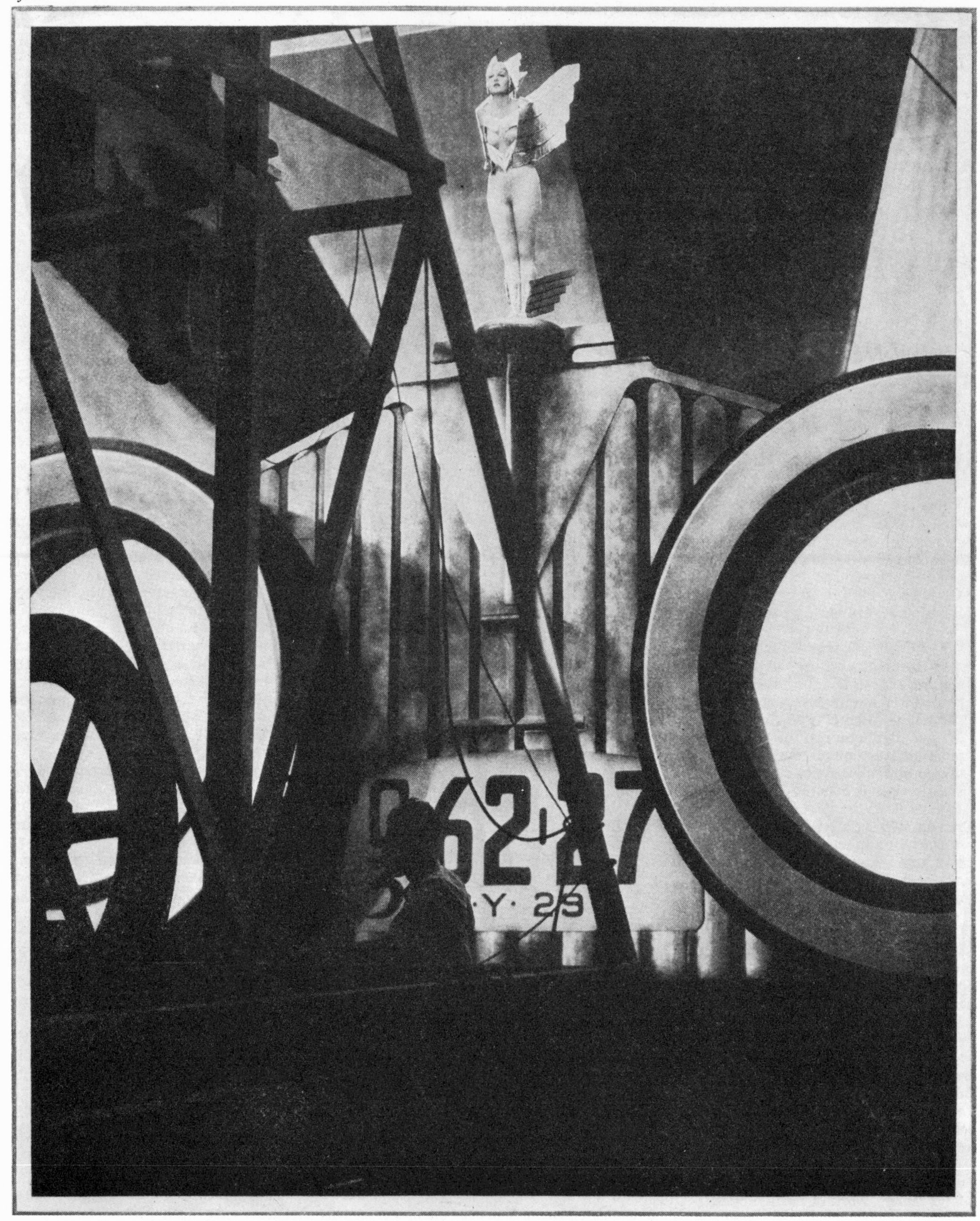

IN her rôle of show girl in "Lilies of the Field," Corinne Griffith takes part in a modernistic ballet-mechanique. She represents the figure of speed on the radiator cap of a gigantic automobile. The part calls for tights, and dignified Corinne wears 'em! Stunning picture, isn't it?

Hal Phyfe

HELEN MORGAN, the New York stage star and night club queen, whose first talking picture, "Applause," was an overnight sensation on Broadway. So brilliant was her screen debut that Paramount immediately put her to work in another film at its Eastern studio. How Helen can sing those sad songs about the man she loves!

Watch *this* Hombre!

Steady, girls! Our star-wise interviewer says that Don Jose Mojica has the lure of Rudy, the sweetness and musical genius of Ramon, the *everything* that makes for screen greatness

Is he the new Valentino, who will sing his way into millions of hearts?

By

Katherine Albert

His still pictures don't begin to do right by him. He is far from handsome in the Hollywood sense of the word. Nose is too flat. Jaw is too square. But a couple of flat noses and a whole school of square jaws don't matter when he starts to talk. Remember that Rudy Vallée kid that the gals were so mad about? Yeah, he had a sex appeal voice, too.

Jose has everything—the refinement and sweetness of Ramon Novarro and Buddy Rogers, and that old-fashioned lure copyrighted by Jack Gilbert and Rudolph Valentino. I've got that off my typewriter. I feel better about it.

HUSBANDS—lock up your wives!

Mothers—send away your daughters!

Jose Mojica is in the movies!

Stop the presses and chain me to my desk. Take the dictionary and find a complete set of brand-new adjectives.

It isn't as if I were just a little gal from the Junction. Why, I've sat in Jack Gilbert's dressing room and listened to him talk about art for hours. And I've heard Ramon Novarro sing away an entire afternoon. And then, of course, there was that luncheon over at Charlie Farrell's house that I'm always going on about. Once Dick Arlen took me to the theater. (Well, of course, his wife was in the play, but anyhow—)

Now there's Jose Mojica, and if he isn't the sensation of the season then I'll eat a box of sound effects.

WHO is and from whence comes the Lothario of all these raves?

The vital statistics sound tame. . . Born in San Gabriel, Mexico. . . Studied to be an engineer. . . Revolution. . . University closed. . . Amateur opera . . . To New York to study. . . A meeting with a musician who got him a part. . . . A contract with the Chicago Civic Opera Company. . . Leads opposite Mary Garden, Galli-Curci and Caruso. . . Talking pictures. . . Contract with Fox.

But vital statistics are the least vital of all gestures. The "Who's Who in Music" gives just such a bare outline. It neglects the color and dash and Latin naïveté of a lad who is destined (unless the entire public loses its collective mind) to be a sensation.

"I am no saint," said Jose, in the liquid, flowing tones of all Latins. "Ramon Novarro, whom I admire and respect, is a good boy. But I—I am not so good.

"My mother—bless her, she is a wonderful woman, living with me now and advising and helping me—gave me $500 to go to New York to study. It was all she had then. And I thought that $500 was all the money in the world. I thought it would last forever.

"So instead of going to a good teacher and studying, I took my friends to hear Caruso every night and spent what was left on those bea-u-tiful blonde girls. I had never seen girls with such fair skin before. They were so lovely. And one morning I find I have no $500 at all."

This confession left him breathless, so he went into a eulogy of his mother. "Oh, always she is so good to me. My father died when I was a baby. I am the only child.

"The minute I got a chance with a little opera company and put on a costume and smeared my (*continued on next page*)

(continued from preceding page)

face with grease paint, I knew that I had found my work.

"I realized, absolutely, that I was where I belonged.

"So when the university opened again I didn't go back.

"I told my mother. She was sorry because she had wanted me to be a business man, but she said that it was my life and if I were going to be an artist I should be a good artist and give everything to it.

"SO here I am—what luck I've had! What chances! I hope I am worthy of all the things people have done for me."

Putting his words on paper is like eating caviar without chopped onion.

Secretaries came and went through his bungalow. Phones rang. He gave to each silly message his rare quality of Latin charm.

I knew, somehow, even then, that he had the stuff.

Later I sat in a dark projection room and listened to his first singing test.

The bit of film had been shot on a plain stage without background. He wore a gray business suit. A rather ordinary looking young Mexican boy with a broad nose. And then he sang! And the gray suit became a toreador's costume with a black velvet jacket and a scarlet sash.

"I always overact. I always do too much," he had told me.

He did. He overacted. He threw himself too completely into the mood of the little Spanish songs he sang. But it was such perfect abandon, such charming Latin intensity. He did one number in English. The familiar words sounded stupid and inconsequential and unworthy of the fire he gave them.

He is almost six feet, but is a little too stocky to impress you as being tall. He is twenty-nine and seems about twenty-three or four. His eyes, I imagine, do the trick, and his voice (low and lovely and accented like Novarro's).

He is still under contract to the Chicago Opera Company and is also booked for a concert tour. (He sings his native number in costume.) In the meantime he will make original musical dramas for Fox.

No lazy Mexican—he! His energy is limitless. Once he dislocated his elbow (jumping through a window to save a fair maiden from a cruel husband, maybe) and was forced to stay at home for seven weeks. The servants gave notice. One can't live in the house with a volcano.

HE bought an enormous canvas and managed to hold a palette in the crippled arm. His mornings were given to painting, and in the afternoon he composed songs. He did five songs in seven weeks and chafed at the enforced inactivity!

He is all romance, all fire, all charm, all appeal—but virile enough to please the husbands of the women who rave about him.

A new luminary on the film horizon, as we laughingly say in Hollywood. Jose Mojica (it's pronounced Moheeka), but you'll be calling him just Jose.

JAN.

NOBODY ever went to Hollywood with more publicity hullabaloo than did Rudy, sax player and song crooner. And nobody got much less attention, and created less excitement, than this same curly-haired boy with the come-hither voice.

He arrived, made his picture, "The Vagabond Lover," and left after five weeks, with everybody feeling sort of let down about it all.

It isn't hard to understand. Nobody has known or cared an awful lot about Vallée except a few hundred thousand fans in the East.

Within a couple of months he became a high-salaried band leader on the strength of his radio crooning, and everybody expected a little too much of him.

The truth is, that he is a rather colorless, rather shy sort of kid—no outstanding personality, no lady-killer, no attention-getter. He hero-worshipped a good deal in Hollywood, and got very little. The picture people have a way of looking down the nose at nice looking boys from the East who go to Hollywood with a little too much publicity. And they gave young Mr. Vallée the gentle and polite bird.

Rudy's answer can be a good picture that will make money. Hollywood hasn't any smart answer for that. Only respect.

JAN.

THE old stagers are bowing, at this moment, to a newer comic sensation. That's Mr. Jack Oakie, the rubber-faced vaudeville graduate who leaps from film to film like a bounding gazelle.

A rapid fire succession of good comic parts have built Mr. Oakie to his present eminence. His work in "Fast Company" was elegant, and other such fast-cracking rôles have added to his rep.

So that when Oakie made his first appearance in the Nancy Carroll picture, "Sweetie," at the Paramount in New York, he was greeted by tremendous applause, and his singing of "Alma Mammy" could have taken ten encores if the film had been run over and over to satisfy the mob of Oakieites.

His vaudeville training made Jack perfect talkie-meat. He'll be famous if he gets good parts—as he will. The Old Oakie Bucket! May it ever be full!

SOME years ago Eddie Cantor made a silent version of his famous Ziegfeld stage success, "Kid Boots," for Paramount. Now it's to be redone properly, as a talkie-singie, and those two sudden and enormous hits, Jack Oakie and Helen "Baby Talk" Kane, will play the leading rôles.

Oakie will have the Cantor rôle. Helen will play the one originally done for the screen by a red-headed girl named Bow.

JAN.

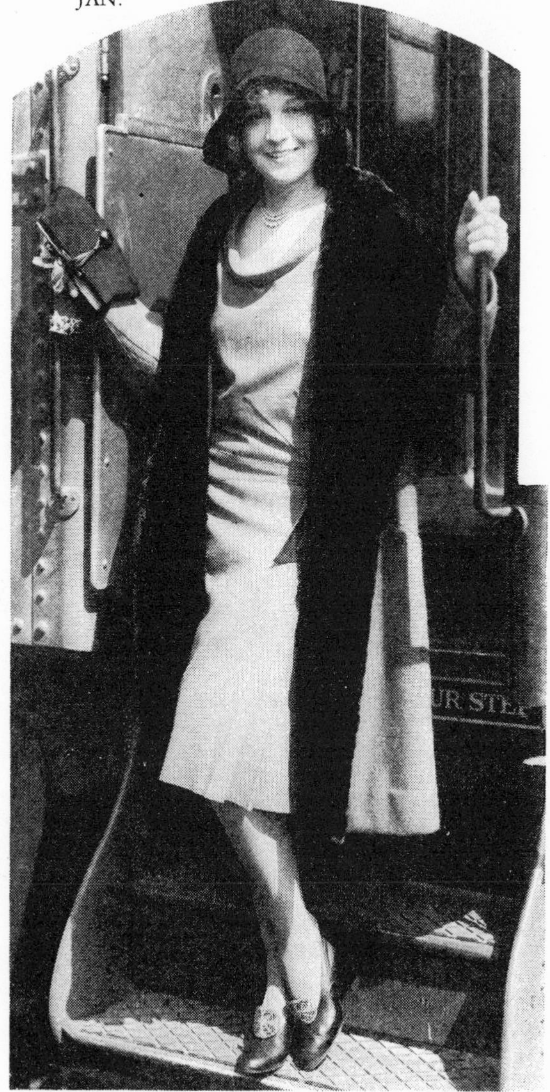

More youth and beauty for the films, and so for us. Fans, step up and make your party bows to Polly Walker, discovery of George M. Cohan for musical comedy. She will appear in new Radio Pictures.

INTRODUCING Miss Bernice Claire to you PHOTOPLAY fans. You'll want to keep your eye on this girl from the musical comedy stage. First National is betting all its blue chips on her, as a result of her work in "No, No, Nanette," her first musical film. She is a keen and sparkling comer!

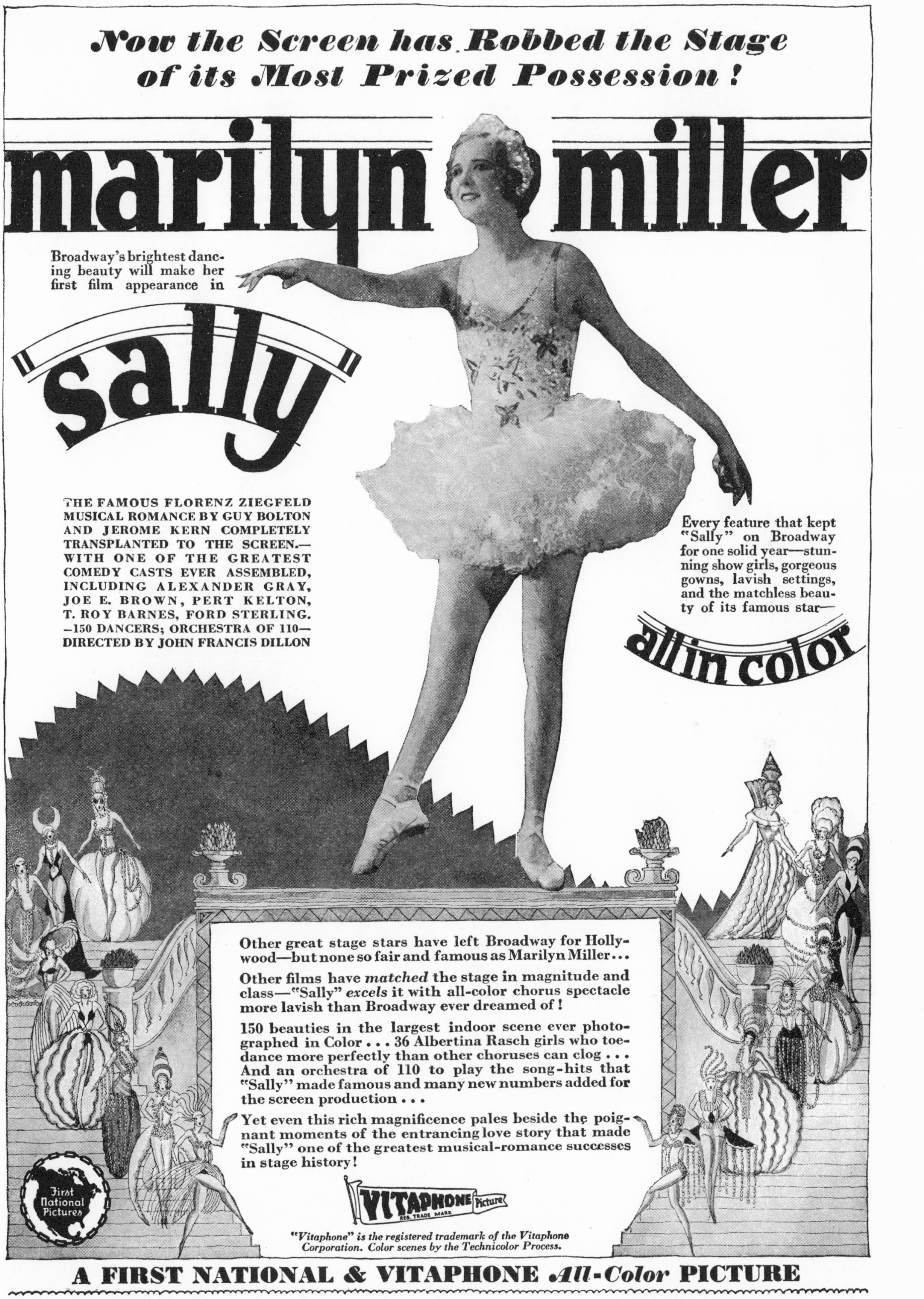

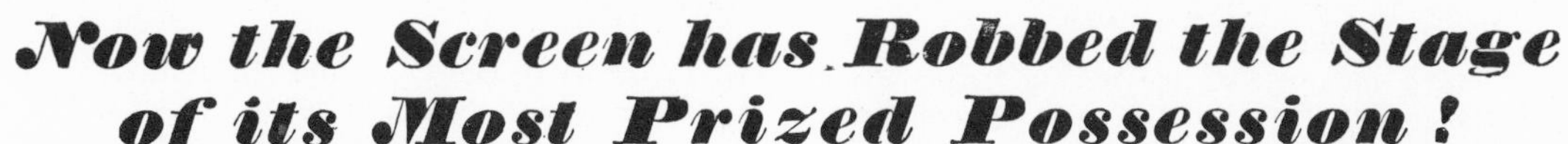

Now the Screen has Robbed the Stage of its Most Prized Possession!
marilyn miller
Broadway's brightest dancing beauty will make her first film appearance in
sally
THE FAMOUS FLORENZ ZIEGFELD MUSICAL ROMANCE BY GUY BOLTON AND JEROME KERN COMPLETELY TRANSPLANTED TO THE SCREEN.—WITH ONE OF THE GREATEST COMEDY CASTS EVER ASSEMBLED, INCLUDING ALEXANDER GRAY, JOE E. BROWN, PERT KELTON, T. ROY BARNES, FORD STERLING. —150 DANCERS; ORCHESTRA OF 110—DIRECTED BY JOHN FRANCIS DILLON
Every feature that kept "Sally" on Broadway for one solid year—stunning show girls, gorgeous gowns, lavish settings, and the matchless beauty of its famous star—
all in color
Other great stage stars have left Broadway for Hollywood—but none so fair and famous as Marilyn Miller...
Other films have matched the stage in magnitude and class—"Sally" excels it with all-color chorus spectacle more lavish than Broadway ever dreamed of!
150 beauties in the largest indoor scene ever photographed in Color . . . 36 Albertina Rasch girls who toe-dance more perfectly than other choruses can clog . . . And an orchestra of 110 to play the song-hits that "Sally" made famous and many new numbers added for the screen production . . .
Yet even this rich magnificence pales beside the poignant moments of the entrancing love story that made "Sally" one of the greatest musical-romance successes in stage history!
First National Pictures
VITAPHONE Picture
REG. TRADE MARK
"Vitaphone" is the registered trademark of the Vitaphone Corporation. Color scenes by the Technicolor Process.
A FIRST NATIONAL & VITAPHONE All-Color PICTURE

LOCAL boys seldom make good on the old "stamping grounds," so Stanley Smith carved out a career on the stage far from Hollywood.

Several years later, when he returned in "The Royal Family," he was given a long-term motion picture contract. He supported Eddie Quillan in "The Sophomore," and was Nancy Carroll's leading man in "Sweetie." He will probably do another picture at Paramount before he returns to his home studio, Pathe. Paramount thought so much of him they tried to buy his contract, according to report.

Stanley went on the stage after overcoming more than the usual amount of family objection. For several generations his father's family had been bankers. His mother's family dealt with lumber in forest quantities. It was a natural thing for Stanley to choose one or the other. But he says he considers acting just like any other business. If he can't make money in it, back to the bank or the tall timber, so to speak.

Stanley Smith

LENORE ULRIC gave him his first acting opportunity in "Kiki." Before that he had made an appearance in the Hollywood Bowl, during his high school days, as *Robin Hood*. After "Kiki," he played in stock for several seasons, and now he is getting friendly fan letters from people who remembered him as the "juvenile" in their home town stock company.

His alma mater was Hollywood High School, and most students of this institution, being at the doorstep of the industry, nurse ideas of picture careers. Many of them have put their dreams into actuality. Stanley brings youth, rugged good looks and a splendid speaking as well as singing, voice to the "soundies."

EDDIE DOWLING is about as familiar to New Yorkers as Times Square. In fact, he is so successful as author, actor and producer of Broadway shows that he has seldom gone on tour. "The Rainbow Man" introduced him to the world of films. Now he is making a second picture, "Blaze o' Glory."

Almost all of the authors who have written plays about New York have been farm boys. Eddie is not an exception. He was born on a farm in Rhode Island—just a few miles from Plymouth Rock. The land had been deeded originally to his great, great grandfather. There were seventeen children in the family and one hundred rocky acres yield a slim living for so many mouths. Eddie went to sea. A famous manager heard the boy sing at a ship's concert, and he persuaded him to give up the high seas for other kind of C's. With the first money he made, Eddie bought the old homestead. He has a regular village there now. Homes for all the family, and it can not be sold as long as there is a Dowling above the sod.

Eddie Dowling

FOR nearly four years Eddie played in "Sally, Irene and Mary." He never missed a performance in that time, although once he had a badly ulcerated tooth and had to play the show in profile. He also played for several nights with his arm in a splint at his side. But he says song and dance men are pretty hardy, all reports to the contrary. His own show, "Honeymoon Lane," broke the long-standing record of Fred Stone in "The Red Mill" at the Knickerbocker Theater.

Of all his achievements he is proudest of the fact that he is married to Ray Dooley. They were married when he was eighteen and she sixteen. He thinks Ray is the greatest comedienne on the stage.

JAN.

Sally Starr

BELIEVE it or not—but Sally Starr, the little gal who romped through "Happy Days" and looks like a vest pocket edition of Clara Bow, rides to the studio every morning on the bus and leaves the same way.

Sally used to be a chorus girl. She's a post graduate of George White's "Scandals," the same young ladies' finishing school that turned out Dorothy Sebastian and Dorothy Mackaill. Sally knows a gay party when she sees one and how to behave at a banquet for visiting firemen, but the bright lights are dim bulbs now. Mrs. Starr's little girl is out to make good in the movies.

"I've got plenty of time for whoopee after I'm a big success," said Sally. "But, believe me, while I'm trying to get along and preserve my microphone voice it's that downy couch at ten p. m. I'm keeping the sparkle in the eyes."

Proof that she means what she says lies in the fact that Sally has been in Hollywood for several months and her engagement hasn't even been rumored.

She was singing and dancing in a Los Angeles revue when Gus Edwards saw her and brought her to the studio to introduce her to Sam Wood who was, at the time, looking for youthful types for a college picture. When I look over the list of "discoveries" that Gus Edwards has sponsored, I can forgive him for writing "Your Mother and Mine."

SALLY was born in Pittsburgh. Her mother and father have come to Hollywood now to watch Sally grow up and be a big star. The best film predictors go about nodding their heads in her direction.

She has a dash of Clara Bow "IT," but she is only five feet tall, and she weighs 104 pounds. Hair and eyes are dark brown. She belongs to the modern pep and personality school.

JAN.

This eight-year-old youngster may soon be as famous as her name. She's called Mitzi and she was headlining in vaudeville when Paramount signed her for talkies. The first kid so contracted for

JAN.

The critics raved about her, the public is doing likewise—and all in all you'll probably see a good deal more of Marjorie White who arrived in "Sunny Side Up." Her next is "New Orleans Frolic"

An Original Movietone Sunny Side Up

IT was Jane's own fault, right from the start. If she hadn't quarreled with Jack Cromwell that Fourth of July morning, he would have stayed at Southampton with the "four hundred" instead of rushing off in a huff to New York to mix in with the "four million."

If he had stayed where he belonged, he probably would never have set eyes upon sweet Molly Carr. He'd never have been watching that block party up in Yorkville, or fallen under the spell of Molly's magic voice and twinkling feet during her song and dance number.

But that number started Jack thinking. Molly had looks, grace, manners, and remarkable versatility. What was the matter with inviting her down to Southampton as a special guest entertainer for his mother's Charity Bazaar?

Molly liked the idea, too, when Jack put it up to her. Like many another shop girl, she had had her day dreams of life among the idle rich. More than once she had envisioned herself the bride of a Park Avenue millionaire, with a summer home at Newport, and all the maids, butlers, Rolls-Royces and pleasure yachts in the world at her beck and call. It would be fun to play the part of a society bud, even for a little while. And then—she liked this particular young man. Even now, his picture, clipped from a Sunday paper, had the place of honor on her dressing table. All in all, it was too good to miss. Molly would go and she'd even do more. . . .

In order to help Jack bring his light-hearted sweetheart to her senses, she would pretend there was an affair between them. She'd make Jane jealous, for Jack's sake.

THE Charity Bazaar is on. Molly and her friends have been living in a rented home on the estate adjoining the Cromwell's and are all ready to take part in the entertainment. Between Jack and Molly, everything has been working out as they planned. Jane is a bit suspicious, and more than a little jealous of Molly. It seems to her that Jack pays more attention to this little outsider than her presence in his mother's Charity entertainment really necessitates. It is hardly likely that he would forget his social position and fall in love with a nobody — and yet, men do strange things. She'd better watch her man before he does something foolish! Perhaps a word to Jack's mother . . .?

Charles Farrell and Janet Gaynor

IT is Molly's turn to go on. The stage is set for her number. By now she is actually in love with Jack, and her emotions run riot as she hums to herself the duet which they are about to sing. She doesn't know that just a few moments before, Jane has managed to patch up her quarrel with Jack and that they are to be married soon.

Advertisement

Talking Romance

Suddenly she is confronted by Jack's mother. What is there between her and Jack? Is it true that Jack is paying the rent for the home she and her friends are occupying? Does she not know that Jack is engaged to a young lady of his own set and that an affair with a girl of no social antecedents is unthinkable? She must leave at once, the moment her number is finished. That is the best thing for her own happiness and Jack's!

Of course Molly leaves. She has tasted life as Society lives it. She has had her day—and she has helped Jack recover his sweetheart. Molly leaves and Jack doesn't know why—until . . . .

BUT we mustn't tell the whole story here, otherwise you would miss much of the enjoyment of the great surprise climax of "Sunny Side Up" when you see it at your favorite theater.

It's the first original all talking, singing, dancing musical comedy written especially for the screen. Words and music are by DeSylva, Brown and Henderson, authors of such stage musical comedy successes as "Good News," "Manhattan Mary," "Three Cheers," "Hold Everything," and "Follow Through," so you know what kind of music to expect when you hear "Sunny Side Up"!

David Butler never directed a better picture. Leading the cast are Janet Gaynor, who plays the part of Molly Carr, and Charles Farrell as Jack Cromwell. Farrell has a splendid baritone voice which will certainly add thousands of new friends to his long list of enthusiastic admirers. And you simply must hear Janet Gaynor sing to appreciate the remarkable scope of this young artist's talents.

Then too, there are Sharon Lynn, Marjorie White, Frank Richardson and El Brendel, and about 100 of the loveliest girls you've ever seen in a musical comedy anywhere! The scenes are laid in upper New York City and at Southampton, society's fashionable Long Island summer resort.

All things considered, "Sunny Side Up" is far and away the most entertaining talking, singing, dancing picture yet produced. Six dollars and sixty cents would hardly buy a ticket for it on the New York stage—but you'll be able to hear and see this great William Fox Movietone soon, right in your own favorite local motion picture theatre, at a fraction of that price.

Advertisement

JAN.

PARIS—First National

All Talkie

ZE fans are going to like zis Irene Bordoni. Her first picture, "Paris," has all the earmarks of a hit. La Bordoni sings in French and English in her famous oo-la-la manner, and wears ravishing gowns. She scintillates in the picture in the face of stiff competition from Jack Buchanan, another footlighter. And what a performance by Louise Closser Hale, the stage actress!

"PARIS"—FIRST NATIONAL.—From the play by Martin Brown. Screen version by Hope Loring. Directed by Clarence Badger. The cast: *Vivienne Rolland*, Irene Bordoni; *Guy Pennell*, Jack Buchanan; *Cora Sabbot*, Louise Closser Hale; *Andrew Sabbot*, Jason Robards; *Brenda Kaley*, Margaret Fielding; *Harriet*, ZaSu Pitts.

JAN.

THE VAGABOND LOVER—Radio Pictures

All Talkie

MR. VALLÉE'S boy, Rudy, is right there with the sentimental ballads. His voice makes you think of moonlight and roses. "The Vagabond Lover" will please Vallée fans. Rudy warbles with telling effect. But it makes us think of the man who said "for gosh sakes sing, Annie." The king of song has one facial expression. Marie Dressler is superb as a *nouveau riche* society leader.

"VAGABOND LOVER, THE"—RADIO PICTURES.—From the story by James A. Creelman, Jr. Dialogue by James A. Creelman, Jr. Directed by Marshall Neilan. The cast: *Rudy*, Rudy Vallée; *Jean*, Sally Blane; *Mrs. Whitehall*, Marie Dressler; *Officer Tuttle*, Charles Sellon; *Swiftie*, Norman Peck; *Sam*, Danny O'Shea; *Sport*, Eddie Nugent; *Mrs. Tod Hunter*, Nella Walker; *Ted Grant*, Malcolm Waite; *Manager*, Alan Roscoe; and Rudy Vallée's Connecticut Yankees.

JAN.

IT'S A GREAT LIFE—M-G-M

All Talkie

VIVIAN and Rosetta Duncan have made a snappy, hilarious comedy of the life of a vaudeville sister team in this elaborate picture. It is crammed to the gunwales with Duncan comedy, and they do a lot of the vocalizing that made them famous. Listen for "Following You"—you'll care for it. Lawrence Gray clicks again in the male lead, and there is lots to praise beside the cute Duncans.

"IT'S A GREAT LIFE"—M-G-M.—From the story by Leonard Praskins. Adapted by Byron Morgan and Al Block. Directed by Sam Wood. The cast: *Babe Hogan*, Vivian Duncan; *Casey Hogan*, Rosetta Duncan; *Mr. Parker*, Jed Prouty; *Benny Friedman*, Benny Rubin; *Jimmy Dean*, Lawrence Gray.

JAN.

THERE is, in "The Song of the Flame," a snappy chorine from the Folies Bergère—Countess Janina Smolinska, homeland Poland, and chief claim to fame so far the fact she advocates nudes for the screen.

JAN.

If this doesn't stop the press, nothing will. It is Rudy's first film kiss—Rudy Vallée smacking Sally Blane in his Radio Pictures talkie, "The Vagabond Lover"

JAN.

APPLAUSE—Paramount

THIS is a curious one. Helen Morgan is a beautiful girl famous as a singer of love songs, so they have her play, for most of the picture, a middle-aged and frowsy burlesque queen who emotes about her daughter instead of singing ballads. None the less, some brilliant acting by Morgan and by Joan Peers, a pretty ingénue, and some nice camera work, help save a confusing job. *All Talkie.*

"APPLAUSE"—PARAMOUNT.—From the novel by Beth Brown. Adapted by Garrett Fort. Directed by Rouben Mamoulian. The cast: *Kitty Darling*, Helen Morgan; *April Darling*, Joan Peers; *Hitch Nelson*, Fuller Mellish, Jr.; *Joe King*, Jack Cameron; *Tony*, Henry Wadsworth.

JAN.

BROADWAY SCANDALS—Columbia

IF this picture appeared six months ago, it would have looked better, for it is a late entrant in the line of love stories back of the theater curtain. It turns up a boy named Jack Egan, who looks like Buddy Rogers and sings well. And Carmel Myers glitters as a vamp with a French accent and a lot of come-hither. Sally O'Neil tries hard. *All Talkie.*

"BROADWAY SCANDALS" — COLUMBIA. — From the story by Howard Green. Continuity by Gladys Lehman. Directed by George Archainbaud. The cast: *Mary*, Sally O'Neil; *Ted Howard*, Jack Egan; *Valeska*, Carmel Myers; *Bill Gray*, Tom O'Brien; *Le Maire*, J. Barney Sherry; *Pringle*, John Hyams; *Jack, Radio Announcer*, Charles Wilson; *Bobby*, Doris Dawson; *George Halloway*, Gordon Elliott.

JAN.

GLORIFYING THE AMERICAN GIRL—Paramount

PARAMOUNT has been fussing with this idea for many months. As a result, this backstage trifle as a peg on which to hang big, girly scenes is stone-cold turkey, for all it has the use of the Ziegfeld name and stars. The coldly beautiful Mary Eaton, as the girl who breaks into the "Follies" to get glorified, is merely cold and beautiful. The fragile story is left hanging before the picture is half over.

"GLORIFYING THE AMERICAN GIRL"—PARAMOUNT.—From the story by J. P. McEvoy. Directed by Millard Webb. The cast: *Gloria Hughes*, Mary Eaton; *Buddy*, Edward Crandall; *Barbara*, Olive Shea; *Miller*, Dan Healy; *Mooney*, Kaye Renard; *Gloria's Mother*, Sarah Edwards; also Rudy Vallée and his orchestra; Helen Morgan, and Eddie Cantor.

JAN.

IS EVERYBODY HAPPY?—Warners

WELL, Jolson did it in "The Singing Fool"—then Texas Guinan did it and Sophie Tucker did it, and now Ted Lewis has done it. Only instead of saying "Sonny Boy!" Ted asks "Is Everybody Happy?" The answer is "No!" Ted is not the romantic type—nor is he an actor. As Ted Lewis, entertainer, he is the same old Ted and wields a mean saxophone. Alice Day plays the girl who gets him and Ann Pennington the girl who doesn't. *All Talkie*

"IS EVERYBODY HAPPY?"—WARNERS.—From the story by Joseph Jackson and James A. Starr. Scenario by Joseph Jackson. Directed by Archie L. Mayo. The cast: *Ted Todd*, Ted Lewis; *Gail Wilson*, Alice Day; *Lena Schmidt*, Ann Pennington; *Victor Molnar*, Lawrence Grant; *Mrs. Molnar*, Julia Swayne Gordon; *Stage Manager*, Purnell Pratt; *Landlord*, Otto Hoffman.

JAN.

These New Faces

Watch for These Each Month

WINNIE LIGHTNER ("Gold Diggers of Broadway," Warners). Winnie stole this picture from the rest of a high-powered cast by her speedy clowning, rough but funny. For five years she was featured comedienne of George White's annual "Scandals," and before that a member of the vaudeville act called "The Lightner Sisters and Alexander." She'll do more films.

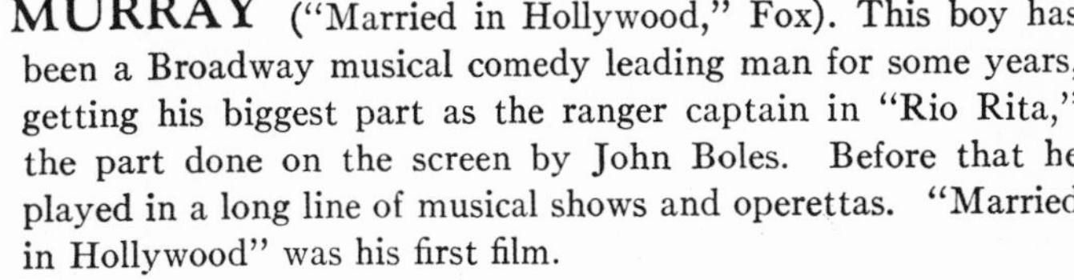

J. HAROLD MURRAY ("Married in Hollywood," Fox). This boy has been a Broadway musical comedy leading man for some years, getting his biggest part as the ranger captain in "Rio Rita," the part done on the screen by John Boles. Before that he played in a long line of musical shows and operettas. "Married in Hollywood" was his first film.

MARJORIE WHITE ("Sunny Side Up," Fox) made a whale of a hit in this, her first picture, as the little East Side girl friend of Janet Gaynor. She's to be watched. Still very young, she began her stage career as one of the White Sisters, vaudeville act which began when they were children. Last stage appearance—"Lady Fingers," with Eddie Buzzell.

CLIFF EDWARDS ("Hollywood Revue of 1929," M-G-M) is even better known as "Ukulele Ike." He's been a vaudeville feature for a long time—he and his little uke. And his records have been very popular, often becoming best sellers. His work in "Revue" was so good that M-G-M immediately slapped Ike into another big musical film, "Road Show."

NANCY WELFORD ("Gold Diggers of Broadway," Warners) was very sweet in the leading rôle of this bright picture. She's the daughter of Dallas Welford, veteran comedian who was in Edison pictures many years ago. Nancy has been in musical comedy for some years, singing leading rôles. Just another of Broadway's gifts to the baby phonoplay.

LAWRENCE TIBBETT ("The Rogue's Song," M-G-M) is one of the few real grand opera stars to take a regular picture job. He is without doubt the greatest living American baritone, and a feature of every season at the Metropolitan. He created the male lead in the American opera, "The King's Henchman," by Edna St. Vincent Millay and Deems Taylor.

ARMIDA ("General Crack," Warners) is a real baby discovery of the screen. Gus Edwards, the star-maker, found this little tamale, and she was a feature of his big vaudeville revue. When he went to M-G-M to write and direct, little Armida went along. Her first big part is with John Barrymore in "General Crack." Now she has others, too.

JOSEPH WAGSTAFF ("A Song of Kentucky," Fox) is another musical comedy song and dance man who seems to be making good on the big sound stages. As a juvenile in many musical shows, he was well liked but not conspicuous on Broadway. Then he attracted attention in George M. Cohan's show, "Billie," and Mr. Fox's sleuths snapped him up for films.

JAN.

NIX ON DAMES—Fox

THE life of the vaudevillian, like the life of the polyp, has been scandalously bared to a palpitating public by the talkies. The scene of this picture is a theatrical boarding house, and if you like watching acrobats, ventriloquists and dog trainers eat, sleep, shave, bathe and love, don't miss it. The players are mostly from the legitimate stage and the two-a-day. They're all real troupers and the film is good entertainment. *All Talkie.*

"NIX ON DAMES"—Fox.—From the story by Maude Fulton. Screen play by Maude Fulton and Frank Gay. Directed by Donald Gallaher. The cast: *Jackie Lee*, Mae Clarke; *Bert Wills*, Robert Ames; *Johnny Brown*, William Harrigan; *Stella Foster*, Maude Fulton; *Ed Foster*, George MacFarlane; *Baring*, Frederick Graham; *Miss Woods*, Camille Rovelle; *Bonnie Tucker*, Grace Wallace; *Jim Tucker*, Hugh McCormack; *Cliff*, Benny Hall; *Billy*, Marshall Ruth; *Hoffman*, Billy Colvin; *Magnolia*, Louise Beaver.

JAN.

LOVE, LIVE AND LAUGH—Fox

IT is a tender story about a little Italian and it moves from New York to the battlefields. It is tearful but never maudlin, for which Director Wm. K. Howard should be praised. George Jessel gives a splendid performance as the Italian, and scores with his songs. "Two Little Arms" will be popular. There are such fine Italian types as Lila Lee and David Rollins—but convincing. *All Talkie.*

"LOVE, LIVE AND LAUGH"—Fox.—From the story by LeRoy Clemens and John B. Hymer. Adapted by Dana Burnet. Directed by William K. Howard. The cast: *Luigi*, George Jessel; *Margharita*, Lila Lee; *Pasquale Gallupi*, David Rollins; *Enrico*, Henry Kolker; *Dr. Price*, Kenneth McKenna; *Mario*, John Reinhart; *Mike*, Dick Winslow Johnson; *Tony*, Henry Armetta; *Sylvia*, Marcia Manon; *Barber*, Jerry Mandy.

FEB.

From Ireland *to* Hollywood

Two little Celts arrive to act with McCormack

Maureen O'Sullivan

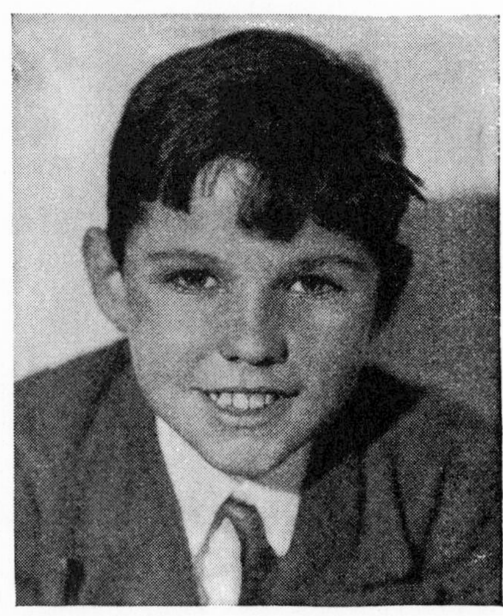

Tommy Clifford

TWO strange, Irish children are parked in Hollywood. They are Maureen O'Sullivan, not yet nineteen, and Tommy Clifford, aged eleven. Both have big parts in John McCormack's first starring vehicle.

If you've heard that all the Irish are gay, prone to enthusiasms and bubbling with pep, give your mind a thorough vacuum cleaning. Maureen has never worked in pictures before. She has never been on the stage. In fact, she had never done anything in Dublin but be a nice little girl who minded her mother and read PHOTOPLAY and admired Clara Bow and thought Charlie Farrell a perfectly adorable boy.

John McCormack went to Ireland and word sort of got around—as word has a habit of doing—that the Fox Company was looking for a leading woman with a real Irish accent.

Maureen told several of her friends to apply.

They did and were rejected and then, one day, Maureen was dining in a Dublin restaurant when Director Borzage saw her and sent the assistant director's first assistant, or somebody equally important, to ask her to have a test.

Her entire life was changed. She is in glamorous Hollywood, has become a picture actress, but she takes it all as casually as if she were on an excursion—summer rates.

She was but mildly curious about John Garrick, the juvenile who is to whisper sweet nothings into her ear before the camera, but when she looked at his picture, she calmly announced:

"Oh, I shan't mind his making love to me."

Most girls would be "thurilled" and excited. Not Maureen! She is apparently unimpressed by Hollywood and she talks mechanically about "dreams come true," etc.

She seemed to be more excited about having her picture in PHOTOPLAY than in appearing opposite John McCormack in a picture.

As for Tommy (snatched from a schoolroom to act)—well, he sat in the Munchers Club and placidly ate his way through a fruit cocktail, a kidney stew and an enormous piece of pie without batting a single eye.

Maureen's blue eyes, shadowed by dark lashes, were riveted on her plate. She ate salad.

She must diet, she says, to be as slim as the other girls on the lot. And her will power in this matter indicates, perhaps, the will for further success.

So there are Maureen and Tommy, two quiet, Irish children—to whom Hollywood, Mecca of the world's youth, is just another place to be!

Richee

HOT from Broadway came little Helen Kane—dimples, contours, pouts, baby voice and great big, begging eyes. So successful were her dimples, etc., that in four months she had worked in three talking and singing pictures for Paramount, the latest being "Pointed Heels." Now she "boopa-doops" for joy!

Helen Kane was born in the Bronx, New York City, on August 4, ??? She is five feet, two inches tall; weighs 119 pounds and has brown hair and brown eyes. Helen's real name is Schroeder

SUNNY SIDE UP
HAPPY DAYS
FOX MOVIETONE
FOX NEWS
WILLIAM FOX presents
Janet Gaynor
Charles Farrell
Warner Baxter
Victor McLaglen
Edmund Lowe
Will Rogers
Frank Albertson
El Brendel
Walter Catlett
William Collier
James J. Corbett
Richard Keene
Dixie Lee
Sharon Lynn
George MacFarlane
J. Harold Murray
George Olsen
Paul Page
Tom Patricola
Ann Pennington
Frank Richardson
David Rollins
"Whispering" Jack Smith
Marjorie White
and 76 other outstanding stage and screen stars in this all talking, singing, dancing MUSICAL EXTRAVAGANZA.
FOX
HOLLYWOOD
The Brightest Stars of Broadway & Hollywood Entertain You IN
HAPPY DAYS
Story by Sidney Lanfield Dialog by Edwin Burke
Staged by Walter Catlett
Directed by BENJAMIN STOLOFF
One hundred of the most scintillating personalities of stage and screen contribute their talents to this all-star, all-talking, singing, dancing musical extravaganza! The most colorful, tuneful, tantalizing show the stage or screen has ever known!
Coming soon to your favorite theater—don't miss this
FOX MOVIETONE

WITH 77 OF THE BRIGHTEST STARS IN HOLLYWOOD'S HEAVEN

Since their first startling introduction of *Vitaphone* Warner Bros. have gradually massed wonder upon wonder until it seemed that talking picture progress had surely reached its peak.

But now suddenly at a single stride *Vitaphone* comes forward with an achievement so immeasurably superior to any that have gone before, that the history of screen development must be completely rewritten and revised.

"THE SHOW OF SHOWS" is a connoisseur's collection of the supreme examples of almost every form of stage and screen entertainment.

Only *Vitaphone* could assemble the names of John Barrymore, Richard Barthelmess, Beatrice Lillie, Ted Lewis, Georges Carpentier, Irene Bordoni, Dolores Costello, and enough more for 20 average pictures, all on one prodigious program.

A WARNER BROS. & VITAPHONE NATURAL COLOR PICTURE IN TECHNICOLOR

"Vitaphone" is the registered trade mark of the Vitaphone Corporation. Color scenes by the Technicolor Process

And you'll remember as long as you live such sensational features as the Florodora Sextet composed of headline screen stars — the Sister Number with eight sets of celebrated screen-star sisters—the stupendous Lady Luck finale with a chorus of 300 and fifteen specialty "acts."

If you could see only one motion picture this season, that picture should be "The Show of Shows." Don't dare miss it—for you may never look upon its like again!

A SWEEPING DEMONSTRATION OF THE SUPREMACY OF VITAPHONE PICTURES, PRODUCED EXCLUSIVELY BY WARNER BROS. AND FIRST NATIONAL

HEAR HER *Again!*
You'll HEAR an entirely new and different Corinne Griffith in "Lilies of the Field," with a mellow, lilting voice that will win you from the first word....
You'll SEE a new Corinne Griffith in "Lilies of the Field"—a fast-stepping girl of today doing daring things in daring costumes.
"Lilies of the Field," made from a famous Broadway hit, rips through forbidden walls to lay bare the lives of worthless women and faithless men.
It probes the secret places of a mother's heart to find a love far greater than that which lovers know.
Its powerful dialogue, its catchy new songs, its striking chorus numbers, its lovely star, make "Lilies of the Field" one of the most satisfying talking pictures yet produced. Watch for it!
Corinne Griffith
in
LILIES OF THE FIELD
All-Talking-Singing
With Ralph Forbes, Jean Bary directed by Alexander Korda
A FIRST NATIONAL & VITAPHONE PICTURE
JANUARY IS FIRST NATIONAL MONTH!
VITAPHONE
"Vitaphone" is the registered trademark of The Vitaphone Corporation
First National Pictures

THAT HAPPY PAIR!

Here's Bessie Love and Charles King of "Broadway Melody" fame.

No wonder they're laughing and singing!

They've made a picture that's even greater than "The Broadway Melody."

THE ROAD SHOW

Marie DRESSLER

Polly MORAN

Gwen LEE

Jack BENNY

Eddie PHILLIPS

Geo. K. ARTHUR

Join the chorus with the hit songs:
"Love Ain't Nothin' But the Blues"
"Lucky Me and Lovable You"

Yes, it is even greater than "The Broadway Melody." Watch this absorbing drama unfold with its tantalizing tunes and its screamingly funny situations. Charles F. Riesner, the "Hollywood Revue" genius, directed it. Take a tip. All roads lead to "The Road Show."

THE METRO-GOLDWYN-MAYER LION
THE GREATEST STAR ON THE SCREEN

METRO-GOLDWYN-MAYER

"MORE STARS THAN THERE ARE IN HEAVEN"

Longworth

JUST when we thought all the possible poses had been exhausted along comes Mlle. Janina Smolinska and goes into reverse. She comes to pictures fresh from a beauty contest in which she carried on for old Poland, and will do a specialty dance in First National's operetta, "Song of the Flame"

Abbe, Paris

M. ABBE snapped these delightful lassies in Paris—the famous Sisters G, who will sing and prance in the Paul Whiteman talkie, "The King of Jazz Revue." But Universal advertises only TWO Sisters G! *Mon Dieu!* We are puzzled! Did one fall overboard, or elope with a Big *Beurre et Oeuf Homme?*

FEB.

DOROTHY JORDAN

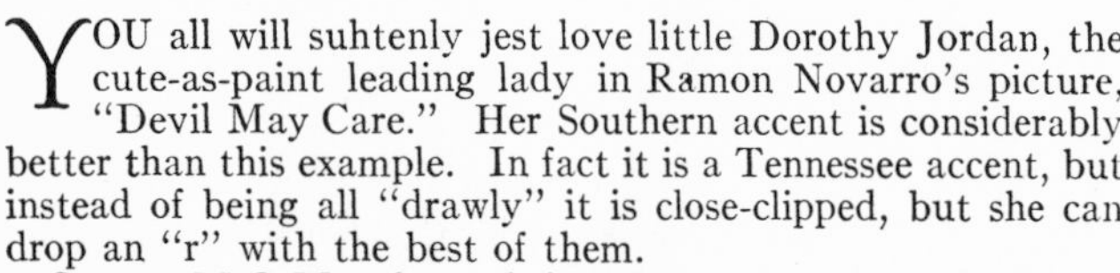

YOU all will suhtenly jest love little Dorothy Jordan, the cute-as-paint leading lady in Ramon Novarro's picture, "Devil May Care." Her Southern accent is considerably better than this example. In fact it is a Tennessee accent, but instead of being all "drawly" it is close-clipped, but she can drop an "r" with the best of them.

Out at M-G-M, where she's going to get an awful lot of fan mail when the news gets around, they think Dorothy Jordan is the find of the year, and maybe she is. At least Ramon thought so much of her that she will be his leading lady again in his next picture. Down in Clarksville, Tennessee, where papa Jordan is a merchant, Dorothy took an early interest in the stage, although Fritz Leiber in Shakespearean repertoire was about all she ever saw. She won her parents' consent to study in Sargent's School of Dramatic Art in New York.

While she expected to be a Jane Cowl, at least, she was not above taking the first job that happened along. She became a chorus girl at the Capitol Theater. From there she went to the "Garrick Gaieties" and became very indignant when a stage manager *shushed* her for talking back stage. Featured billing came in "Funny Face," and "The Treasure Girl."

HER advent in motion pictures was made in an inconspicuous and not-too-good thriller, "Black Magic." Her second rôle in Hollywood was *Bianca* in the Pickford-Fairbanks production of "The Taming of the Shrew." Dorothy thinks she should have been billed as "The Face on the Cutting Room Floor."

Dorothy is very fond of music, and knows a great deal about negro spirituals of her native South. She has brown hair, and blue eyes, and is about five feet in height—just as high as a fellow's heart. But this can't go on.

So much for M-G-M's offering as "The Discovery of 1929." Certainly the Novarro lead will put Dotty from Dixie well up in the affections of the fans. She's adohable!

FEB.

FRANK FAY

WHEN Barbara Stanwyck, the stage and screen actress, first saw Frank Fay, her husband, upon arriving in Hollywood, she burst into tears.

"Frank," she sobbed, "you're ruined."

Fay had been compelled to dye his red hair a jet black for Technicolor purposes in Warner Brothers' "The Texas Moon." His rôle of *Don Carlos*, the heart-breaking adventurer in this story of old Mexico, certainly did not call for red hair.

Now the red is again showing through the black.

Talking pictures take Frank Fay back to his native Golden State. He was born in San Francisco, and he was born to the theater, growing up behind the footlights. His first professional appearance was in "Babes in Toyland," when he was seven years old. For twenty-five years he has been entertaining the show-going public. He was in several Winter Garden shows.

His greatest success, however, was in vaudeville, and as master of ceremonies in leading picture theaters. He is, consequently, well known to the fans of Chicago, Boston, Philadelphia, St. Louis and Kansas City. His success as master of ceremonies was also demonstrated at the midnight shows at Warner Brothers' Theater in Hollywood.

PERHAPS his greatest charm is his ready wit. He is an entertainer par excellence in the theater and at the dinner table.

Along Vaudeville Gulch, in New York, they call Frankie "Broadway's Favorite Son." That's his billing on board and program—that's what they say when he plays the Palace Theater five weeks in a row, changing his act every week with the astonishing fluency that is peculiarly a Fay possession. As an "ad libber," or extemporaneous jokesmith, he stands alone.

If Frankie finally conquers Hollywood, it will be his third great triumph. First was his successful siege of Broadway; second, the winning of lovely Barbara Stanwyck.

By the time you read this, his work as master of ceremonies of "The Show of Shows" will be famous everywhere.

FEB

ARMIDA

A VERY short time ago, as the fly crows, a tiny Mexican ball of fire was singing and dancing, torridly for one of her tender years, in a Los Angeles restaurant.

Her body was slim and willowy, her eyes were black and snapping, and it wasn't long before Armida (for that was her name) was applauded, noticed and signed to contracts.

Her theatrical destiny came under the control of Gus Edwards, the star-maker—discoverer and developer of Georgie Jessel, Lila Lee, Georgie Price, Lola and Leota Lane and dozens of other beautiful or talented (or both) youngsters. After a whirl in vaudeville, little Armida came into pictures in her manager's train, and appeared in one of his Technicolor musical comedies for M-G-M.

You probably saw her in "Mexicana," a nice little Mexican musical comedy filled with all manner of song and dance in the tamale manner. Armida, as young and pretty a girl-child as ever crossed the Rio Grande, did a nice number or two in the picture, and people noticed "that sparkling little Mexican girl"—before they knew her name.

THEN, it wasn't long. Managers saw her and were conquered by her youth and verve. Suddenly we heard, with cocked ears, that the little Armida was to appear in "General Crack" with the redoubtable John "Profile" Barrymore.

She also flashed into "The Show of Shows" for a few moments of footage in that colossal revue wherein even great stars only rated a few smiles and a bow or two.

A swift shift of scene, and we are in the courtroom of Superior Judge Keetch. Appears one Señor Joaquin Vendrell, who deposes and says that he is the father of one Armida Vendrell, aged eighteen. She has been offered a five-year contract by Warner Brothers, and the señor prays the court to ratify and confirm the contract of one so young.

So there's the story of snappy little Armida—young, beautiful, full of the old Nick, and demanded by the makers of motion pictures. The prayer of Señor Vendrell was heard and favorably answered by the learned judge, and Armida, aged eighteen, is now safely enrolled in the great Warner army that marches daily to war down Wilshire Boulevard.

And over on the M-G-M lot, one Gus Edwards sits in his office and chortles a good chortle. For the old master's eye and showmanly sense are still keen.

FEB.

Two high-priced babes tucked away among the scented pillows and lace quilts of wealth-stricken Hollywood. In short, Charlie Farrell (a thumb-sucker) and Janet Gaynor. This is one of the novel scenes in the new Fox Revue, "Happy Days"

FEB.

WHAT are you going to do when a double won't double?

Vivienne Segal, Warner Brothers' singing star, would like to know.

One of the sequences of "Golden Dawn" called for a healthy rain storm. Since there was to be no singin' in the rain, the valuable Segal larynx was to be spared. Another girl was to take the drenching for the star.

The only hitch was that the double looked over the scene, and decided she wouldn't get wet after all.

Vivienne Segal doubled for herself.

FEB.

FIRST NATIONAL studio seems to have gone foreign. The place is overrun with extras in fancy costumes; Russians, Italians, and English soldiers on duty in India predominate, with smatterings of girls in Gypsy, Hindu, and Oriental costumes.

"Song of the Flame" is using over five thousand Russian extras; "Bride of the Regiment" something like one hundred Italians; and "Green Stockings" a troop of British soldiers stationed in India. While "Show Girl in Hollywood" is using the different costumes to illustrate how extras look on a studio lot in informal attire.

Incidentally, "Show Girl" company is using all these different extras, picking out the most picturesque for certain scenes.

FEB.

These New Faces

Watch for This Each Month

BELLE BAKER ("Song of Love," Columbia) is a vaudeville veteran of many years' standing, famous for her character songs and much beloved by two-a-day audiences. She is also noted for her rendition of "Eli, Eli," Jewish religious song, as an encore. "Song of Love" is her first picture experience. She has appeared in musical comedy.

BERT WHEELER ("Rio Rita," Radio Pictures) is a noted graduate of vaudeville, first to revue and musical comedy, and now to the talkies. After a long laugh-making career in the theater, he played the same part in "Rio Rita" for the screen that he played on the stage for Ziegfeld. A great hit, he has been signed for more films by Radio Pictures.

POLLY WALKER (Radio Pictures) is a discovery of the silver-haired George M. Cohan, who featured her in "Billie," a musical comedy he produced in the fall of 1928. Before that she had played in several shows without kicking up much dust. In "Billie" she scored a personal triumph, and Radio, busy with musical films, signed Polly right on the dotted line.

JACK BUCHANAN ("Paris," First National) has long been a luminary of the London musical comedy stage, and a great favorite of the silk-hatted song and dance man school. America saw him in the famous "Charlot's Revue," with Gertrude Lawrence and Beatrice Lillie. His spot in the English theater compares with Clifton Webb's in ours.

TED LEWIS ("Is Everybody Happy?" Warners) is a young-old veteran of vaudeville, musical comedy and revue—a Circleville, Ohio, boy who made good in all the big cities. The noted bandsman and singer of laugh, clown, laugh songs appeared in the first edition of the famous revue series, "The Greenwich Village Follies," and in several others.

FEB.

They rehearse for weeks just for one scene. Sammy Lee, noted Broadway dance director, puts the maidens of the merry-merry through the preliminary paces of a new Metro phonoplay

FEB.

A famous star of other days comes back to Hollywood and pictures! Dorothy Dalton, glamorous girl of the Ince days, and her noted husband, Arthur Hammerstein, who will produce a musical spectacle, "Bride 66," for the audible screen

FEB.

International

A couple of young fellers Hollywood and the talkies bound! Joe Weber and Lew Fields, one of the most famous comedy teams in American stage history, off to take part in Metro-Goldwyn-Mayer's old-timer revue, "Just Kids"

FEB.

LOVE COMES ALONG—Radio Pictures

IT was no cinch to pick a follow-up story for Bebe Daniels. Almost anything would suffer by contrast with brilliant "Rio Rita." "Love Comes Along" is just one of those things. It all happens in a Mexican port village. There are bad men, dance hall girls, fiestas, and young love—that's where Bebe comes in. A hackneyed yarn is enlivened by Bebe's rich, vibrant singing. Lloyd Hughes, Montagu Love and Ned Sparks help considerably. *All Talkie.*

"LOVE COMES ALONG"—RADIO PICTURES.—From the play "Conchita" by Edward Knoblock. Adapted by Wallace Smith. Directed by Rupert Julian. The cast: *Peggy*, Bebe Daniels; *Johnny*, Lloyd Hughes; *Sangredo*, Montague Love; *Happy*, Ned Sparks; *Brownie*, Lionel Belmore; *Carlotta*, Alma Tell; *Bianca*, Evelyn Selbie; *Gomez*, Sam Appel.

FEB.

THE GRAND PARADE—Pathe

A PATHETIC little yarn about a boarding house slavey who loved a minstrel man who loved a burlesque queen. If you're fond of Gishesque heroines you'll care for Helen Twelvetrees in a big, weepy way. She, by the way, got a five-year contract on the strength of her performance, as did Fred Scott, who isn't much for looks but who knows his sharps and flats. Lots of songs. *All Talkie.*

"GRAND PARADE, THE" — PATHE. — From the story by Edmund Goulding. Directed by Fred Newmeyer. The cast: *Molly*, Helen Twelvetrees; *Kelly*, Fred Scott; *Rand*, Richard Carle; *Polly*, Marie Astaire; *Calamity*, Russell Powell; *Sullivan*, Bud Jamieson; *Jones*, Jimmy Adams; *Madam Stitch*, Lillian Leighton; *Call Boy*, Spec O'Donnell; *Sam*, Sam Blum; *Dougherty*, Tom Malone; *The Drunk*, Jimmy Aubrey.

FEB.

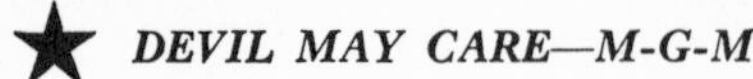

★ *DEVIL MAY CARE—M-G-M*

NOW comes another of the old guard to score a sensational success in the audibles. Ramon Novarro, in "Devil May Care," gives one of the finest performances of his career.

The picture itself is bang-up entertainment. The locale is France at the time of Napoleon's banishment to Elba, and Novarro appears as a loyal young Bonapartist officer who falls in love with a royalistic lady.

It is a swashbuckling affair with the star climbing walls, escaping from a firing squad, and kidnapping the heroine. Doug himself would have to get up early to do a better job.

A notable feature is the fact that dialogue does not slow up the action. "Devil May Care" is a *moving picture* first, and an all-talking picture second. It is romance punctured with subtle comedy.

From a pictorial standpoint the film is lavish. There is France of the chateau country, and a garden fête in honor of Napoleon at Grenoble, done in Technicolor.

Little Dorothy Jordan, as *Leonie*, the royalist, will be hailed as one of the discoveries of the year. She has vivid beauty and a sparkling personality. The singing end of the production is more than excellently taken care of by Novarro and Marion Harris, revue star. Miss Harris gives a beautiful performance as the countess who gives shelter to the Bonapartist.

Outstanding songs are "Charming," sung by Novarro, and "If He Cared," sung by Miss Harris. *All Talkie.*

"DEVIL MAY CARE"—M-G-M.—From the French drama "La Bataille Des Dames" by Eugene Scribe and Ernest Legouve. Adapted by Richard Schayer. Directed by Sidney Franklin. The cast: *Armand*, Ramon Novarro; *Leonie*, Dorothy Jordan; *Louise*, Marion Harris; *Degrignon*, John Miljan; *Napoleon*, William Humphrey; *Groom*, George Davis; *Gaston*, Clifford Bruce.

FEB.

★ *SHOW OF SHOWS—Warners*

THIS is the Warners' answer to every revue fan's prayer—the very last glittering word in girl and music entertainment.

No less than seventy-seven count-'em stars and near-stars lead the revels in this great display of talent and flash. If some appear only for a split second, and do little more than bow and smirk, you must remember that even the biggest and best pictures have to come to an end by breakfast-time.

Everybody will talk about John Barrymore and his impressive reading of a Shakespearean soliloquy. Frank Fay will make a million friends through his droll work as master of ceremonies. Frenchy Irene Bordoni warbles a warm ballad with much Technicolor eye-rolling. Winnie Lightner and Bull Montana sing a duet that is one of the picture's most terrific riots. Other yeoman service is done by Beatrice Lillie, Ted Lewis, Louise Fazenda, Nick Lucas, Myrna Loy and dozens more—including an enormous and perfectly trained chorus. In fact, if the picture has one especially grand thing, it is the succession of novel and beautiful stage pictures and routines devised by Larry Ceballos and Jack Haskell.

None of the songs is outstanding. The Technicolor work is extraordinarily beautiful. But best of all, "Show of Shows" is packed with storms of laughter from start to finish. That alone should send you scurrying in to see the richest and fastest screen revue yet produced. *All Talkie.*

"SHOW OF SHOWS"—WARNERS.—Directed by John Adolfi. Dances directed by Larry Ceballos and Jack Haskell. The cast: John Barrymore, Frank Fay, Richard Barthelmess, Beatrice Lillie, Ted Lewis, Alice White, Nick Lucas, Georges Carpentier, Winnie Lightner, Irene Bordoni, Dolores Costello, Grant Withers, Loretta Young, Ben Turpin, Lupino Lane, Jack Mulhall, Betty Compson, Lila Lee, Patsy Ruth Miller, Douglas Fairbanks, Jr., Louise Fazenda, Myrna Loy, Marian Nixon, Sally O'Neil, Chester Morris, Monte Blue, Noah Beery, Lloyd Hamilton, Alice Day, Viola Dana, Bert Roach, H. B. Warner, William Courtenay, Rin Tin Tin, Lois Wilson, Alexander Gray, Chester Conklin, Hobart Bosworth, Lee Moran, Tully Marshall, Bull Montana, Helene Costello, Molly O'Day, Marceline Day, William Collier, Jr., Jacqueline Logan, Edna Murphy, William Bakewell, Pauline Garon, Sally Eilers, Sally Blane, Alberta Vaughan, Armida, Shirley Mason, Carmel Myers, Marion Byron, Johnny Arthur, Sojin, Ruth Clifford, Heinie Conklin, Ethlyn Clair, Albert Gran, Frances Lee, Gertrude Olmsted, Anthony Bushell, Adamae Vaughan, Anders Randolf, Wheeler Oakman, Otto Matiesen, Philo McCullough, Kalla Pasha, Jimmy Clemons, E. J. Ratcliffe, Sid Silvers, Lola Vendrill, Hariette Lake, Williams Adagio Dancers.

FEB.

CAMEO KIRBY—Fox

All Talkie

HERE we are again, the South of crinolines and gallantry, and a famous old veteran of a story. "Cameo Kirby," romance of a river gambler, was one of John Gilbert's earliest successes. It has been re-tailored for J. Harold Murray, with theme songs thrown in. Even Stepin Fetchit sings. Too bad, too. Despite graceful charm, it isn't exciting, but Murray's voice is swell.

"CAMEO KIRBY"—Fox.—From the play by Booth Tarkington and Harry Leon Wilson. Adapted by Marion Orth. Directed by Irving Cummings. The cast: *Cameo Kirby,* J. Harold Murray; *Adele Randall,* Norma Terris; *Jack Moreau,* Douglas Gilmore; *Col. Randall,* Robert Edeson; *Anatole,* Charles Morton; *Croup,* Stepin Fetchit; *Larkin Bunce,* John Hyams; *Claire Devezac,* Mme. Daumery; *Lea,* Myrna Loy; *Poulette,* Beulah Hall Jones; *George,* George MacFarlane.

FEB.

HIT THE DECK—Radio Pictures

★

All Talkie

SOME very routine performances keep this from being one of the outstanding screen musical comedies of all time. Only Jack Oakie, as the sailor lover, stands out. He's a panic. Polly Walker, the leading woman, and the rest, are conventional. But it's a magnificent production, with some grand Technicolor work and brilliant dancing. And "Hallelujah," punch song, is the best yet.

"HIT THE DECK"—RADIO PICTURES—From the story by Vincent Youmans. Adapted by Luther Reed. Directed by Luther Reed. The cast: *Looloo,* Polly Walker; *Bilge,* Jack Oakie; *Mat,* Roger Gray; *Bat,* Franker Wood; *Bunny,* Harry Sweet; *Lavinia,* Marguerite Padula; *Toddy,* June Clyde; *Clarence,* George Obey; *Mrs. Payne,* Ethel Clayton; *Lieutenant Allen,* Wallace MacDonald; *Dan,* Nate Slott; *Dinty* Andy Clark; *The Admiral,* Dell Henderson; *Lieutenant Jim Smith,* Charles Sullivan.

FEB.

THE SONG OF LOVE—Columbia

All Talkie

BELLE BAKER makes the most successful début in talkies of any vaudevillian to date. The comedienne triumphs over the moth-eaten plot of the singer and the drunken husband who are brought together again by the little cheeild. And that's a feat! Ralph Graves keeps up his good work, and little David Durand is only occasionally too cute. Belle sings not-so-hot songs.

"SONG OF LOVE, THE"—COLUMBIA.—From the story by Howard Green, Henry McCarthy and Dorothy Howell. Directed by Eric C. Kenton. The cast: *Anna Gibson,* Belle Baker; *Tom Gibson,* Ralph Graves; *Buddy Gibson,* David Durand; *Mazie,* Eunice Quedens; *Acrobat,* Arthur Houseman; *Traveling Salesman,* Charles Wilson.

FEB.

THE FORWARD PASS—First National

All Talkie

DOUG FAIRBANKS, Jr., looks like a real college football hero, and that's a lot to say for the film boys. This is a bright, entertaining picture, unusually well acted by young Doug, Loretta Young, Guinn Williams and "Peanuts" Byron—the last-named little girl sneaking a song or two across the goal line. You will find this a nice, peppy film, notable for its youthful charm.

"FORWARD PASS, THE"—FIRST NATIONAL.—From the story by Harvey Gates. Directed by Eddie Cline. The cast: *Marty Reid,* Douglas Fairbanks, Jr.; *Patsy Carlyle,* Loretta Young; *Coach Wilson,* Bert Rome; *Asst. Coach Kane,* Lane Chandler; *"Honey" Smith,* Guinn Williams; *Ed Kirby,* Allan Lane; *Maizie,* Marion Byron; *Dot,* Phyllis Crane.

FEB

HOT FOR PARIS—Fox

All Talkie

RAOUL WALSH'S directorial genius for red-blooded incident is trotted out again in "Hot for Paris." A sailor falls in love with a "Fr-ranch" mam'selle, and wins a million in a lottery. It lacks the pretensions of "The Cock Eyed World," but it is good, rough fun. Victor McLaglen and El Brendel are amusing team-mates. As for Fifi Dorsay, she's simply elegant, that's all.

"HOT FOR PARIS"—Fox.—From the story by Raoul Walsh. Adapted by Charles J. McGuirk. Directed by Raoul Walsh. The cast: *John Patrick Duke*, Victor McLaglen; *Fifi Dupre*, Fifi Dorsay; *Axel Olson*, El Brendel; *Polly*, Polly Moran; *Mr. Pratt*, Lennox Pawle; *Papa Gouset*, August Tollaire; *Ship Captain*, George Fawcett; *Charlot Gouset*, Charles Judels; *Ship's Cook*, Eddie Dillon; *Fifi's Mother*, Rosita Marstini; *Fifi's Father*, Agostino Borgato; *Babette Dupre*, Yola D'Avril; *Mimi*, Anita Murray; *Monsieur Furrier*, Dave Valles.

FEB.

POINTED HEELS—Paramount

All Talkie

YOU can't keep a good plot down. "Pointed Heels" is another story of theatrical people, and it offers a show within a show. An elaborate production with Helen Kane, William Powell, Fay Wray, Phillips Holmes, "Skeets" Gallagher and Eugene Pallette. There's a swell Technicolor ballet, and an elegant performance from Powell. "Sinfonette," the theme melody, is fine.

"POINTED HEELS"—Paramount.—From the story by Charles Brackett. Adapted by Florence Ryerson and John V. A. Weaver. Directed by Edward Sutherland. The cast: *Robert Courtland*, William Powell; *Lora Nixon*, Fay Wray; *Dot Nixon*, Helen Kane; *Dash Nixon*, Richard "Skeets" Gallagher; *Donald Ogden*, Phillips Holmes; *Kay Wilcox*, Adrienne Dore; *Joe Clark*, Eugene Pallette.

FEB.

★ ***LILIES OF THE FIELD—First National***

CORINNE GRIFFITH in tights should be good news for the fans! As if that weren't enough, the Orchid Lady turns out a neat tap dance on top of the grand pianny.

"Lilies of the Field" deals in sophisticated manner with the girls who toil not—but, gosh, how they sin. It is the sprightliest Corinne Griffith film since "Classified." The major portion is comedy, but there is a note of pathos. A society woman is framed into a scandal, and is separated from her baby. She turns to revues for a living, and drifts into the easiest way.

Corinne's voice shows amazing improvement. And you should see those smart frocks! Ralph Forbes and John Loder are the leading men. There is a good *Ballet Mechanique*, accompanied by fine modern music. *All Talkie.*

"LILIES OF THE FIELD"—First National.—From the story by William James Hurbut. Adapted by John Goodrich. Directed by Alexander Corda. The cast: *Mildred Harker*, Corinne Griffith; *Ted Willing*, Ralph Forbes; *Walter Harker*, John Loder; *"Pink,"* Eve Southern; *Florette*, Rita LeRoy; *Gertie*, Jean Bary; *Joyce*, Betty Boyd; *Maizie*, May Boley; *Pearl*, Virginia Bruce; *Judge*, Charles Mailes; *Lewis Conroy*, Freeman Wood; *Lawyer for Harker*, Ray Largay; *Lawyer for Mildred*, Joe Bernard; *1st Maid*, Anne Schaeffer; *2nd Maid*, Clarissa Selwynne; *Baby*, Patsy Page; *Barber*, Andre Beranger; *Head Waiter*, Douglas Gerard; *Paymaster*, Tenen Holtz; *Butler*, Wilfred Noy; *Bert Miller*, Tyler Brooke; *Maid*, Alice Moe.

MAR.

A break for Larry. Tibbett and Catherine Dale Owen in a scene from "The Rogue's Song"

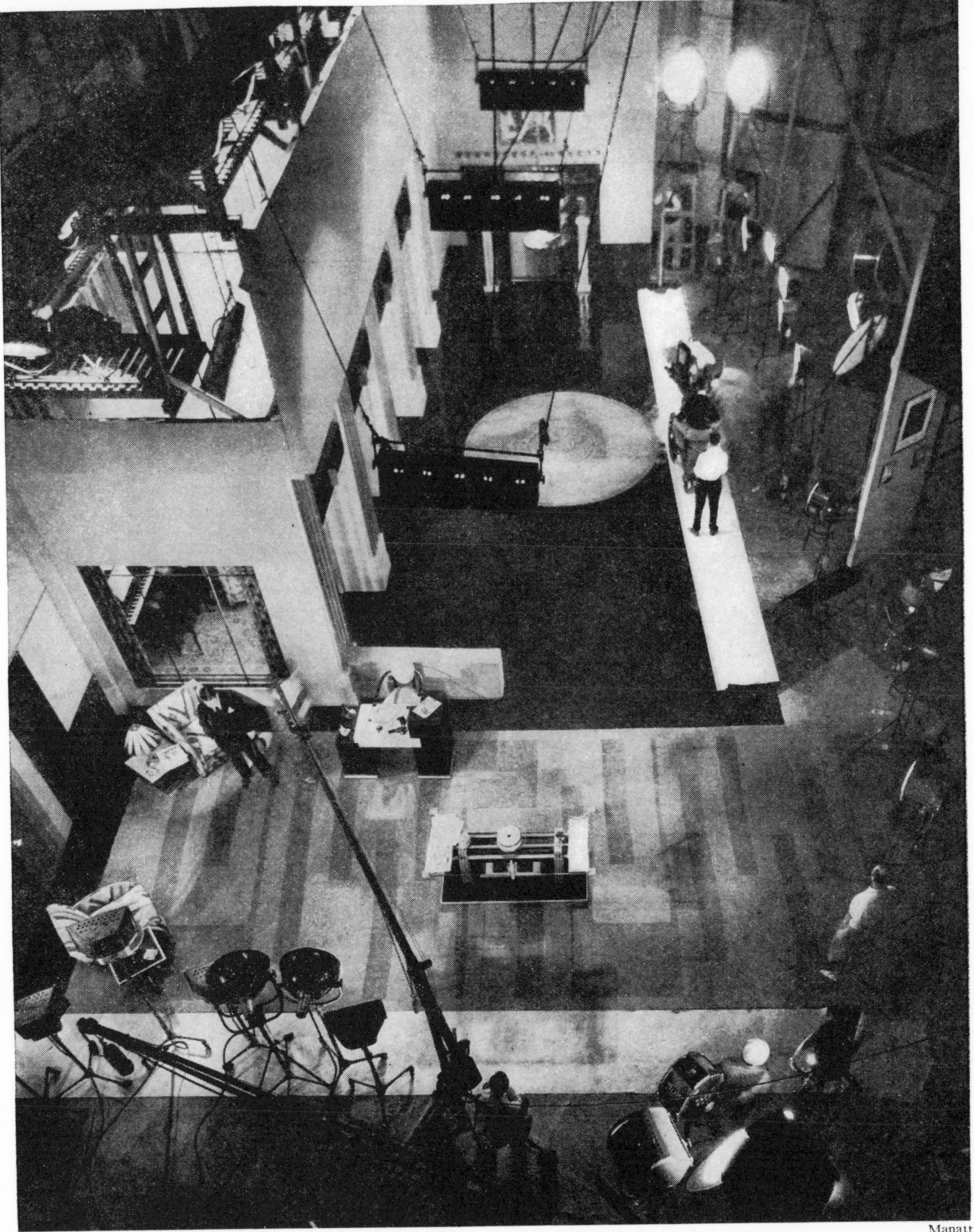

Manatt

THIS is what the Man in the Monitor Room sees as he sits perched high in his coop and fiddles with the fateful doo-dads that make voices come out sweet or sour. A great talkie set at the Metro studios, being a scene for "The Song Writer." At the left you can see Lawrence Gray, leading man, standing under the long boom which holds the microphone

MAR.

"Onward, onward swords against the foe! Forward, forward the lily banners go!"

IT lives again!—the thundering throb of "Song of the Vagabonds," in the glorious golden voice of Dennis King, star of Paramount's all-color musical romance, "The Vagabond King"! Once the greatest triumph of the Broadway stage, now the supreme triumph of the talking, singing screen—Paramount's New Show World. ¶ Blazing with gorgeous Technicolor throughout . . . vibrant with stirring melodies . . . packed with thrills and adventure, excitement, romance! ¶ With Broadway's favorite romantic stars, Dennis King and Jeanette MacDonald in the leading roles, and a great cast. The New Show World of Paramount at its most brilliant height! ¶ And only Paramount, with matchless resources and unrivaled man-power, could unfold before your eyes this glittering panorama of song, color and romance in all the blazing glory of the original, the greatest of all musical romances! ¶ Don't miss the outstanding eye-and-ear treat of the year. Ask your Theatre Manager now when he is planning to show "The Vagabond King". *"If it's a Paramount Picture it's the best show in town!"*

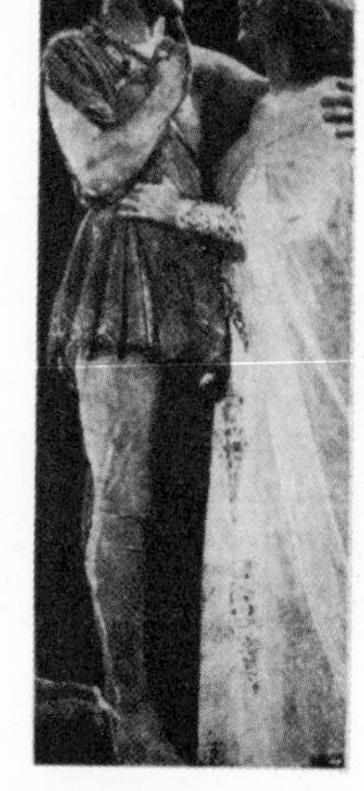

DENNIS KING

"THE VAGABOND KING"

WITH

JEANETTE MacDONALD

Warner Oland and O. P. Heggie and cast of 1000. Ludwig Berger Production. From "If I Were King" by Justin Huntley McCarthy and "The Vagabond King" by William H. Post, Brian Hooker and Rudolph Friml.

Pictures

PARAMOUNT FAMOUS LASKY CORP., ADOLPH ZUKOR, PRES., PARAMOUNT BLDG., NEW YORK CITY

The Great Voice of the Metropolitan Opera Now Yours

Lawrence TIBBETT

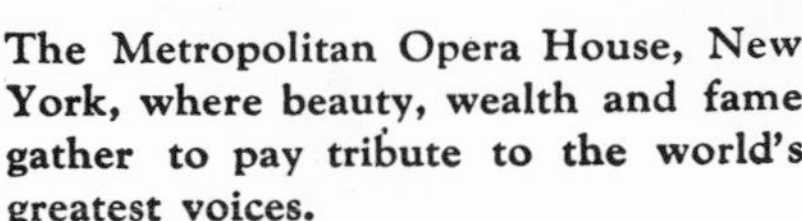

The Metropolitan Opera House, New York, where beauty, wealth and fame gather to pay tribute to the world's greatest voices.

THE ROGUE SONG

with

Catherine Dale Owen
Stan Laurel
Oliver Hardy

Directed by

Lionel Barrymore

Music by

Herbert Stothart

and

Franz Lehar

The Greatest Operetta Ever Produced

AGAIN Metro-Goldwyn-Mayer proves its leadership by being the first to present an operatic genius of such outstanding reputation as Lawrence Tibbett in a full length motion picture production. Now you can hear in your favorite theatre the same glorious baritone that has thrilled thousands at the Metropolitan Opera House—that has carried his fame around the world!

And what a magnificent picture Lionel Barrymore, the director, has built around Tibbett as the singing, fighting, carousing Bandit Chief! Follow this fascinating story of wild, barbaric passion that knows no restraint—that defies convention—that gets what it wants whether it be revenge, loot or love!

See also Laurel & Hardy, the funniest team on the screen today, as a couple of singing bandits! And what a help to the Chief *they* turn out to be!

ENTIRE PRODUCTION IN TECHNICOLOR

METRO-GOLDWYN-MAYER

"More Stars Than There Are in Heaven"

Here it comes!—The hit that made "Tea for Two" a national anthem . . . The smash that shattered all musical romance records in its one-year run on Broadway . . . Brought to you on the screen in all its glory—and more!—More girls—more song-hits—more stars — more stupendous settings than the stage production! . . . .

A unique round-the-world romance with Bernice Claire and Alexander Gray—convulsing comedy by Louise Fazenda, Lilyan Tashman, and Lucien Littlefield—studded with the most sumptuous song-and-dance scenes ever filmed, in full COLOR! . . .

Directed by Clarence Badger. From the musical comedy by Frank Mandel, Otto Harbach, Vincent Youmans, Emil Nyitray. . .

"NO, NO, NANETTE"

A FIRST NATIONAL & VITAPHONE PICTURE

First National Pictures

VITAPHONE Picture

"Vitaphone" is the registered trade mark of The Vitaphone Corporation
Color scenes by Technicolor

She wanted to write Christmas plays for children

BERNICE CLAIRE made her first motion picture test merely as a courtesy to Alexander Gray. The test was Gray's. He needed a girl to appear with him and Bernice expected to hear nothing further of it. She went home to Oakland for a vacation and found a telegram from Jack Warner, offering her the rôle of *Nanette* in "No, No, Nanette." And she was to sing opposite Alexander Gray.

This was the beginning of the new and talented co-starring duo at First National. Recently, Hollywood, the old gossip, has been saying that Bernice and Alexander are "That way" about each other. At least they are very old friends. When Bernice sang "The Desert Song" in New York, Alexander was the dashing "Red Shadow" in the same company.

It has been Bernice's fondest hope to write Christmas plays for children, but she has been too busy with singing and dancing to get around to it. That was her first great ambition. Now her wish is to be an opera star, a celluloid opera star, if you please.

This five feet-two prima donna with the blue eyes is one of the few native Californians in pictures. She was born in Oakland, and when she was fourteen months old—no more—she surprised her mother by singing. Right then it was decided that Bernice should be a singer.

AFTER singing leads in the operettas at Oakland High School, Bernice went to New York to do a little twinkling on Broadway. Jeritza, the opera star, was among the first to be captivated by the young coloratura. She immediately began studying with Emil Polak, the diva's accompanist.

On the New York stage, Bernice has appeared in "Babes in Toyland," "The Chocolate Soldier," and as *Margot* in "The Desert Song."

Her new pictures at First National, with Alexander Gray, are "Spring Is Here," and "Song of the Flame."

Little Bernice, of all the musical comedy singers who have come twinkling and trilling to Hollywood on the singie tide, came in perhaps the most roundabout fashion. A California girl who had won her spurs three thousand miles to the east, only to be called to pictures from her native heath!

Small wonder that Fate seems to have her ear-marked for fame and glory!

THE night "The Sky Hawk" opened, a new face struck the American screen—a nice, English face, modelled very closely on that of the Prince of Wales.

John Garrick not only talked in "The Sky Hawk," he sang and acted as well, and everybody in the theater kept asking, "Who is that new kid?"

The new kid is as repressed off screen as on.

"There isn't anything to tell, really, about me," he said. "I began in rather the usual way. Amateur theatricals and all that sort of thing. And when I came out of college I went to work in a bank in Brighton, but I kept on singing. Oh now, I don't mean I sang when people came in to put money away. I did confine that to the privacy of my home and to one theatrical agent who booked me out in a vaudeville sketch.

"There isn't anything to tell, really, about me"

"This got me a chance in the featured rôle in a revue which played the Queen's Theater in London.

"Then I was frightfully lucky and found work in 'Rose Marie.' I did that for two years, with one run right in Sydney of forty-six weeks. I did 'The Desert Song,' too. But one of the shows went broke again.

"I CAME to America. 'The Wishing Well,' in which I played in Los Angeles, managed to last just three nights. But one of the Fox officials had seen me in it and told me to come out for a test. I was right on hand when they decided to make 'The Sky Hawk' and it was just luck I got it."

John doesn't claim the famous David Garrick as his ancestor. His real name is Reginald Dandy, but Fox officials thought it sounded too much like Reginald Denny.

His is an attractive face with blue, blue eyes, very light brown hair and that ruddy British complexion.

You'll never hear of him making spectacular gestures, nor getting himself involved in private scandals. He isn't that kind of a lad. But you will hear about his excellent screen work and his reputation as a first calibre actor.

MAR.

Charles "Buddy" Rogers was born in Olathe, Kans., Aug. 13, 1904. He is six feet tall, weighs 165 pounds, and has black hair and black eyes. A Kansas University boy

WELL—America's Boy Friend! Does he need fuller mention? Buddy Rogers goes from hit to hit as a young Paramount star. He was the one very successful graduate of the almost forgotten Paramount School which graduated a class—the only class—in 1925. Buddy is a sensation in "Half Way to Heaven"

LILLIAN ROTH came to pictures in Chevalier's "The Love Parade," but behind that first picture appearance was a brilliant, though brief, career on the revue stage in New York. She was a sensation in Earl Carroll's "Vanities," and was so gay and so pretty that motion pictures were a certain bet

Lillian Roth, being a newcomer from the New York stage, has left few footprints, so far, on the sands of filmland. She made her big début in "Vanities," and was immediately snapped up for pictures

WINNIE Wows 'Em!

That Lightner girl lights in Hollywood, and she's there to stay

By Eugene Earle

Here's one newcomer to the phonoplay who won't broad A 'em to death. You won't confuse her with Ruth Chatterton. It's Winnie Lightner, the girl with the asbestos vocal cords and the million-watt grin

WINNIE LIGHTNER was on the terrace of her Beverly Hills *maison de luxe* as soon as I had parked my car at the curb—a very dashing Winnie in brown *lounjamas,* topped with a brilliant mop of red hair.

"Mr. Earle?" she carolled. "Harya? Welcome to the old manor." From that moment on I was ready to make over my life insurance policy to Winnie.

When Winnie whispers she blows out the tubes. Here she is putting a song over in the old Lightner zip-zowie-up-and-at-'em style. Put 'em over Winnie—we like 'em

Winnie is Irish and friendly and as natural as the air she breathes. Perhaps not quite as rough and rowdy as her characterization of *Mabel* in "Gold-Diggers of Broadway," but certainly just as lively and witty.

I'd like to see Bill Haines and Winnie sit down to a little wisecracking fest. I have a healthy respect for Bill's talents, but Winnie would give him a run for the money.

After Warners had seen the rushes of "Gold-Diggers" they realized that in Winnie Lightner they had a personality that would sweep across the screen, as it had conquered in vaudeville and in the Broadway revues.

They lost no time in casting her for "She Couldn't Say No," and then right into "Hold Everything."

In fact, Winnie had been so busy that we had to break interview dates one right after the other.

"I've looked the house over for cigarettes," she wailed, "and I can't find anything but Chinese punk. How's to borrow some?"

From that time on we smoked ourselves black in the face.

"I may not be at my best," she said, "I was up at four this morning looking for the pooch. I trailed all over Beverly Hills in a bathrobe. I didn't find the dog but a stray kitten attached itself to me and now I can't get rid of it. The dog came home at eight o'clock, and brought his girl friend with him. He looked like he had been in every mud puddle in the State of California.

"I'VE got a police dog and a bull terrier, but I thought I wanted a big dog. So I bought one of Harold Lloyd's St. Bernards. They're the breed that trot around the Alps with a flask of gin tied onto them. He's only nine months old now, but he eats six pounds of meat at a sitting and drinks a gallon of water.

"I brought him home in a taxi, and he sat on me. The driver couldn't find me when we got back. All he could see was dog. He had to excavate for Winnie.

"Didn't I have a swell break in 'Gold-Diggers'? I hope the others will be as good. You know that line I have about 'the spirit of the ages.' I was supposed to keep saying it wrong. And I got it right every time. I used to get up in the middle of the night to rehearse it. And me in those red tights! Just wait till the gang in New York sees me in those. They look like firemen's underwear.

"I didn't have the heart to go to the première of the picture. I'd probably have burst into tears when they introduced me I would have been so nervous. I'm funny that way. Everybody would say 'huh, just another actress taking it big.' I went the second day and sat in the back row of the theater. The man next to me roared at the picture and kept poking me in the ribs with his elbow. I roared, too, and poked right back. We had a swell time, and he didn't know who I was.

"I always laugh at myself. I can't help it, but I'm not conceited. I think I have the funniest voice. It's so loud. When I whisper they hear me four blocks away. One day during the picture Roy Del Ruth, the director, said 'not so loud, Winnie.' I said 'Roy, I'm whispering.' And he told me not to talk at all and it would probably be all right. *(continued on next page)*

(continued from preceding page)

"Some of the critics thought I was too rough and rowdy as *Mabel*. Gosh, I know girls just like her—the life of the party. When they get going at the party they start tearing the furniture apart and rip buttons off your clothes. I've never thought I was too good to be above criticism. A good critic knows his business. If he gives me some constructive criticism I analyse it, and if I think he's right, I change my act.

"What do you think? I'm getting fan mail. Couldn't you die? The letters are from kids and the old fellows. I can tell. Why doesn't Winnie get a break from the young bloods? They tell me that I will get baskets-full pretty soon. I wanted to know what kind of baskets. There are little ones and big ones."

ALMOST everybody in the Warner Brothers organization claims to have been the one to pick Winnie for a winner. She says that Roy Del Ruth is the correct Columbus.

When they were casting for "Gold-Diggers of Broadway" everyone was selected but *Mabel*. Somehow they couldn't find just the person to do the hard-boiled and good-hearted chorus girl. On one of the coldest and most disagreeable days of the California winter, Del Ruth went into a projection room and requested to see all the short subjects on hand. Reel after reel was run off to no avail. At last he got up to leave.

"Wait a minute," called the man in the projection booth. "Here's a can that says 'Winnie Lightner.' "

The reel was run. It was a short subject Winnie had made two years ago, called "A Song a Minute."

Del Ruth knew that he had found his *Mabel*.

The wires were kept hot. Winnie was tied up with a vaudeville contract, but difficulties were straightened and she was on her way to the Coast.

Only one thing happened to mar her happiness in Hollywood. Her mother died during the making of the picture, and when Winnie returned from the funeral her first line was "I feel like a dish of frog-legs." From that line she went into a comedy song. Del Ruth offered to postpone the song for a week, but Winnie was too good a trouper to hear of it. But she cried when the picture opened in New York. Her mother could not see it, and she had seen every show that Winnie had done, and had read everything ever written about her.

Winnie is absolutely sold on Hollywood. After years in vaudeville, and living in hotel rooms, it seems perfect to have a big house with lots of closet-space, and with clothes in every closet. It costs her $685 a month and she is paying $350 for an apartment in New York, but she thinks it's worth it.

California climate agrees with her fifteen-months-old son who is beginning to say "da-da" and "ma-ma."

To prove that she is an inveterate movie fan herself, the baby's name is Richard Barthelmess Georgine Holtry. Dick is her favorite actor.

Winnie wants to stay in pictures. Vaudeville has palled on her.

"It isn't like it used to be," she explained. "I've played on bills with the Duncan Sisters, Valeska Suratt, T. Roy Barnes, and wonderful dance acts. But now vaudeville is just the same. It opens with acrobats. The second spot is a couple of hoofers. Third is a guy with a violin. Fourth, a skit. And so on. The scenery is fierce. An old rag hung up with a few rhinestones on it, and they think it's swell. And a few trick lamps which the girls in the act made in a Cincinnati hotel."

Her rule in vaudeville was always to leave her audience wanting more. She didn't give encores. What she did on the stage she did fast. Some headliners stay on until they have to be wheeled off. Not Winnie. The same philosophy prompts her to be wary about signing a long-term contract with one studio. She doesn't want to be taken for granted.

WINNIE was quite hurt about a recent interview in one of the Los Angeles papers. It seemed that the writer had made Winnie out to be too tough and rowdy.

"I may not be a Vassar graduate," she complained, "but I don't talk out of the side of my mouth and say 'dese, dem and dose.' "

So, please don't think Winnie is hard-boiled. She isn't. She's one of the most genuine good sports in Hollywood. But, I'm telling you, Winnie, if you ever try to be a lady (Hollywood version of the word) I'm going to go out to your house with a shotgun.

MAR.

One of the reasons we're so anxiously awaiting John McCormack's first Fox picture is because our queenly Alice Joyce has a big part in it. Far too long between Alices these days

MAR.

The object in the foreground is a mere cameraman, pulling dinguses and twisting gadgets for a close-up of twinkling toes. They're the Sisters G from Gay Paree and thereabouts. And gee, how they dance and sing in Universal's "King of Jazz Revue"

MAR.

☆ NO, NO, NANETTE—*First National*

FIRST NATIONAL has learned a stupendous secret, and so has made a rip-roaring good picture out of this musical comedy. It has discovered that these girl-and-music things need laughs!

For all the beautiful Technicolor stuff—the finest to date; for all the songs, dances and love interest, "Nanette" is notable for its loud, continuous haw-haws. Led by ZaSu Pitts, Lilyan Tashman, Lucien Littlefield and Bert Roach, the picture has howl after howl. Littlefield plays an amiable Bible-publisher who gets into all sorts of grief by harmlessly helping pretty girls and producing a musical comedy.

Alexander Gray and Bernice Claire do the loving and sing the songs. The little Claire girl is pretty, and sings like a birdie. Entertainment plus. *All Talkie.*

"NO, NO, NANETTE"—FIRST NATIONAL.—From the musical comedy by Otto Harbach and Frank Mandel. Adapted by Howard E. Rogers. Directed by Clarence Badger. The cast: *Nanette,* Bernice Claire; *Tom Trainor,* Alexander Gray; *Jim Smith,* Lucien Littlefield; *Sue Smith,* Louise Fazenda; *Lucille,* Lilyan Tashman; *Bill Early,* Bert Roach; *Pauline,* ZaSu Pitts; *Betty,* Mildred Harris; *Brady,* Henry Stockbridge; *Flora,* Jocelyn Lee.

MAR.

☆ ROADHOUSE NIGHTS—*Paramount*

CHICAGO gangland and its merry running of the rum form the basis of what turns out to be a perfect pippin of a melodrama, written by Ben Hecht and produced on the murky shores of Long Island Sound.

Two scorching hits are scored—by men. Charles Ruggles crashes through again as the pi-eyed reporter who runs down the rum-runners, and a New York night club pet, Jimmy Durante, is immense in the roadhouse sequence.

Helen Morgan sings, and Fred Kohler is a grand king of the liquor smugglers. We think you will like this punchful mélange of melodrama and button-busting comedy. Score another smash for Hobart Henley, director, whose last excellent job was "The Lady Lies." Paramount has a polished jewel in Henley. And—watch this Durante! *All Talkie.*

"ROADHOUSE NIGHTS"—PARAMOUNT.—From the story by Ben Hecht. Directed by Hobart Henley. The cast: *Lola Fagan,* Helen Morgan; *Willie Bindbugel,* Charles Ruggles; *Sam Horner,* Fred Kohler; *Daffy,* Jimmy Durante; *Moe,* Lou Clayton; *Joe,* Eddie Jackson; *John Hanson,* Joe King; *Hogan,* Fuller Mellish, Jr.; *Keeley,* Leo Donnelly; *Jerry,* Tammany Young; and The Durante Orchestra.

MAR.

THE PAINTED ANGEL—*First National*

All Talkie

BILLIE DOVE sings and dances! Billie Dove puts on tights and performs as she did in the old Ziegfeld days, when Bill was second girl from the left. The lovely Dove plays a New Orleans entertainer who becomes Queen of the New York Night Clubs, and Edmund Lowe is her sweetheart. If you like them gay and giddy, then Bill's night club début is going to please you.

"PAINTED ANGEL, THE"—FIRST NATIONAL.—From the story "Give This Little Girl a Hand" by Fannie Hurst. Directed by Millard Webb. The cast: *Rodeo West,* Billie Dove; *Brood,* Edmund Lowe; *Oldfield,* George MacFarlane; *Pa Hudler,* Farrell MacDonald; *Ma Hudler,* Cissy Fitzgerald; *Sippie,* Nellie Bly Baker; *Joe,* Will Stanton; *Jule,* Norman Selby; *Sir Harry,* Douglas Gerrard; *Mac,* Shep Camp; *Singer,* Peter Higgins; *Dancer,* Red Stanley.

MAR.

SALLY—*First National*

All Talkie

THE amazing dancing of Marilyn Miller, lovely veteran of Ziegfeld shows, is about all that saves "Sally" from dullness. The old musical comedy, closely followed, just hasn't the laughs, in spite of frenzied efforts by Joe E. Brown, Ford Sterling and Sam Hardy. Alexander Gray, the leading man, sings pretty well, and there's nice Technicolor. But oh, the glorious dancing of the beautiful Miller!

"SALLY"—FIRST NATIONAL.—From the musical comedy by Guy Bolton and Jerome Kern. Screen version by Waldemar Young. Directed by John Francis Dillon. The cast: *Sally,* Marilyn Miller; *Blair Farquar,* Alexander Gray; *Connie (The Grand Duke),* Joe E. Brown; *Otis Hooper,* T. Roy Barnes; *Rosie, his girl friend,* Pert Kelton; *"Pops" Shendorff,* Ford Sterling; *Mrs. Ten Brock,* Maude Turner Gordon; *Marcia, her daughter,* Nora Lane; *John Farquar, Blair's father,* E. J. Ratcliffe; *The Old Roué,* Jack Duffy.

MAR.

☆ THE ROGUE'S SONG—M-G-M

HERE is a picture. Lusty as a north wind, wild as a virgin forest. Lawrence Tibbett, grand opera star, is a personality like none other that has flashed across the screen. His complete abandon, his lavish, mad acting and his glorious voice put him in a unique spot. He has no competition.

The operetta is an adaptation of Franz Lehar's "Gypsy Love" and much of the music is familiar, but it is more stupendous—all in Technicolor—than anything musical that has been filmed. A roistering, flashing drama of a group of singing bandits and a cold Russian princess. Catherine Dale Owen furnishes the beauty, Laurel and Hardy the comedy, but it's Tibbett's voice and smile that make this a picture you simply must not miss. *All Talkie.*

"ROGUE'S SONG, THE"—M-G-M.—Based on the operetta "Gypsy Love" by Franz Lehar, A. M. Willner and Robert Bodansky. Story by Frances Marion and John Colton. Directed by Lionel Barrymore. The cast: *Yegor,* Lawrence Tibbett; *Princess Vera,* Catherine Dale Owen; *Princess Alexandra,* Nance O'Neil; *Countess Tatiana,* Judith Vosselli; *Prince Serge,* Ullrich Haupt; *Yegor's Mother,* Elsa Alsen; *Nadja,* Florence Lake; *Ossman,* Lionel Belmore; *Hassan,* Wallace MacDonald; *Petrovna,* Kate Price; *Frolov,* H. A. Morgan; *Count Peter,* Burr MacIntosh; *Azamat,* James Bradbury, Jr.; *Ali-Bek,* Stan Laurel; *Murza-Bek,* Oliver Hardy.

MAR.

THEY LEARNED ABOUT WOMEN—M-G-M

All Talkie

VAN and Schenck, big rhythm and harmony boys, make melodious whoopee in their first talkie. The story, which concerns the trials of baseball and vaudeville, is slight and the stars sing better than they act. "He's That Kind of a Pal" is the hit of the show. A dance number led by that yaller gal, Nina May, is dragged in, and Bessie Love gets self-sacrificing again.

"THEY LEARNED ABOUT WOMEN"—M-G-M.—From the story by A. P. Younger. Scenario by Sarah Y. Mason. Directed by Jack Conway and Sam Wood. The cast: *Jack,* Joe Schenck; *Jerry,* Gus Van; *Mary,* Bessie Love; *Daisy,* Mary Doran; *Stafford,* J. C. Nugent; *Sam,* Benny Rubin; *Tim,* Tom Dugan; *Brennan,* Eddie Gribbon; *Haskins,* Francis X. Bushman, Jr.

MAR.

THE BROADWAY HOOFER—Columbia

THE national hoofer epidemic passes lightly over Columbia, leaving a stimulating backstage comedy. Marie Saxon's dancing and singing, combined with her personal charm and a story tailored to measure, make this New York musical comedy star's first talking picture a success. She's cast as a Broadway musical comedy queen vacationing incog, who falls for the hoofer-manager of a fourth-rate burlesque. *All Talkie.*

"BROADWAY HOOFER, THE"—COLUMBIA.—From the story by Gladys Lehman. Continuity by Gladys Lehman. Directed by George Archainbaud. The cast: *Adele,* Marie Saxon; *Bobby,* Jack Egan; *Jane,* Louise Fazenda; *Larry,* Howard Hickman; *Morton,* Ernest Hilliard; *Annabelle,* Gertrude Short; *Dolly,* Eileen Percy; *Mazie,* Charlotte Merriam; *Billy,* Fred MacKaye; *Baggage Man,* Billy Franey.

MAR.

THE GIRL FROM WOOLWORTHS—First National

ALICE WHITE goes on turning out snappy, entertaining little talkies, and this is one of the brightest. Bright and merry fare for the young folks, with Alice singing and dancing, Charles Delaney scoring as the boy friend, and a rich new comedy find in the sparkling person of Rita Flynn. *All Talkie.*

"GIRL FROM WOOLWORTHS, THE"—FIRST NATIONAL.—From the story by Adele Comandini. Directed by William Beaudine. The cast: *Pat King,* Alice White; *Bill Harrigan,* Charles Delaney; *Lawrence Mayfield,* Wheeler Oakman; *Jerry Donnelly,* Ben Hall; *Tillie Hart,* Rita Flynn; *Dowling,* Gladden James; *Dave,* Bert Moorehouse; *Cleo,* Patricia Caron; *Pa Donnelly,* William Orlamond; *Ma Donnelly,* Milla Davenport.

MAR.

THE BATTLE OF PARIS—Paramount

SOMEONE spoke French in the Ritz Bar, *et voila!* "The Battle of Paris." Gene Markey sold the story for a song, but Gertrude Lawrence overdoes it. Now that she's had her little joke, perhaps she'll throw a real picture. The songs in this banal musical comedy—it just missed being a floperetta—won't knock anyone cold. *All Talkie.*

"BATTLE OF PARIS, THE"—PARAMOUNT.—From the story by Gene Markey. Directed by Robert Florey. The cast: *Georgie,* Gertrude Lawrence; *Zizi,* Charles Ruggles; *Anthony Trent,* Walter Petrie; *Suzanne,* Gladys Du Bois; *Harry,* Arthur Treacher; *Tony,* Joe King.

MAR.

Paramount has found that George Bancroft sings. He was once half of the vaudeville team of Bancroft and Brosky. If he turns out to be another of these barrel-chested canaries I'll double for a Chicago cop.

MAR.

BLAZE O' GLORY—Sono Art-World Wide

EDDIE DOWLING goes melodramatic in this rehash of the war and talks with a tremolo, but the picture is swell in spots. A man's life passes in review while he stands trial for murder. The long arm of coincidence has a pretty far reach for strictest probability, but "Blaze O' Glory" will touch the tender-hearted. Dowling has a winning personality and a good singing voice, but the honors are taken by Henry B. Walthall and little Frankie Darro. *All Talkie.*

"BLAZE O'GLORY"—SONO ART—WORLD WIDE.—From the story by Thomas Boyd. Adapted by Renaud Hoffman. Directed by Renaud Hoffman and George J. Crone. The cast: *Eddie Williams,* Eddie Dowling; *Helen,* Betty Compson; *Burke,* Henry B. Walthall; *Jean,* Frankie Darro; *District Attorney,* William Davidson; *Hummel,* Ferdinand Schumann-Heink; *Abie,* Eddie Conrad; *Tony,* Frank Sabini; *The Rounders,* Themselves.

MAR.

THE TALK OF HOLLYWOOD—Sono Art-World Wide

WHY confine it to Hollywood? Everyone who sees it will talk about it, and what they'll say will be plenty. It doesn't quite seem possible that anything could be quite so bad, but here it is. It's all about the making of a talking picture, supposed to be awfully funny. Probably you've never heard of the players, and you probably won't again. Nat Carr is the star. *All Talkie.*

"TALK OF HOLLYWOOD, THE"—SONO ART-WORLD WIDE.—From the story by Mark Sandrich. Directed by Mark Sandrich. The cast: *J. Pierpont Ginsburg,* Nat Carr; *Adore Renee,* Fay Marbe; *Ruth,* Hope Sutherland; *John Applegate,* Sherline Oliver; *Edward Hamilton,* Ed LeSaint; *Reginald Whitlock,* Gilbert Marbe; *The Butler,* John Troughton.

MAR.

A TIP!

A comedian named Jimmy Durante—a droll nut—is the current comedy panic of New York. People lie down, roll over and say uncle when he appears.

You'll find him in a new Paramount picture called "Roadhouse Nights," and they say he steals the film from Helen Morgan and Charles Ruggles.

So watch for him. Remember the Four Marx Brothers in "The Cocoanuts," a real surprise hit, and don't say that old Uncle Cal didn't warn you.

Remember—"Roadhouse Nights"—Jimmy Durante.

You'll DIE!

MAR.

These New Faces

Watch for This Each Month

DOROTHY JORDAN ("Devil May Care," M-G-M) will stir up a lot of dust after you all see her as Novarro's lead in this. She is a Clarksville, Tenn., girl who came to Hollywood via Broadway musical shows. Her first part was *Bianca* in "The Taming of the Shrew," and Metro snapped her up. She will be seen in more films from the big Roaring Lion lot.

BERNICE CLAIRE ("No, No, Nanette," First National) is called, in Hollywood, "the youngest prima donna on the American stage." For one of her years, she has a considerable stage background. First National is highly delighted with the youngster's work in "Nanette," and they are going to have her make several more singies at Burbank.

TOM PATRICOLA ("Frozen Justice," Fox) is working in about as many pictures at Fox as El Brendel, and that's plenty. A young veteran of vaudeville and revue, Tom, for five years, was a featured comic in George White's "Scandals," where he won great fame. He is a brother of Miss Patricola, famous vaudeville singer and violinist.

VIRGINIA BRUCE ("The Love Parade," Paramount) is a new Paramount find who bowed in in this Chevalier gem. She came from Fargo, N. D., to enroll in the University of California, but her blonde beauty was sighted, and she enrolled at Paramount instead. She has played several bits, is under a long term contract, and will get bigger jobs soon.

JACK BENNY ("Road Show," M-G-M) came from vaudeville to Metro to act as master of ceremonies in "The Hollywood Revue," where his drolleries won public acclaim everywhere. Jack is a veteran comic and M-C of the two-a-day, his rambling monologue, with the aid of a property fiddle, having been known and liked for years. Jack's always good.

MAR.

Do you remember how people used to kid about the bossy director of the dear old silent pictures?

You should hear Hollywood now! Such language!

Because there are now, in these talkie times, no less than seven separate—and maybe distinct—directors on each photoplay. Here is what they do.

1. Pictorial Director, who guides the action. 2. Dialogue Director, who coaches the speeches. 3. Photographic Director, in charge of cameras, cameramen, and lights. 4. Sound Director, in charge of recording. 5. Dance Director, who rehearses the chorus girls in their intricate routines. 6. Musical Director, in charge of the orchestra and vocalists. 7. Color Director, responsible for all color photoplay.

So, as you can well understand, picture actors are learning new and lurid words for seven people, in most films. In the old days, one director and his puttees used to take them all.

MAR.

YOU'VE probably suffered with the poor, down-trodden, underpaid chorus girl of the stage—in the fiction stories you have read about her.

But that was A. T.—Ante Talkie.

Now the chorus girl is one of Hollywood's queens, and those lucky enough to be employed on the big sound stages are living on the fat of the land and hoping they aren't getting to look like the land.

In the old days scores of pretty little dancing girls were glad to get $35 a week for a few weeks from one of the leading producers, and when the show closed it was go out and hunt for another job.

Not long ago William Fox hired a hundred chorus girls for his musical pictures, and he put them under six months' contract—work, rehearse or loaf—at $50 a week.

And, next to a big-hearted millionaire with a bad heart, that is a chorus girl's idea of Heaven.

MAR.

YOU probably know by this time that The Great Little Guy is in pictures, but PHOTOPLAY would be less than on the dot if it did not record the coming of George M. Cohan to the screen. For George occupies a peculiar and wonderful place in the affections of American theater-goers. For many years his plays, and his acting, and his singing, and his dancing, have been our possession. "The Yankee Doodle Boy" holds precious memories for all with sentiments of which they are not ashamed.

And George M. is in pictures, signed to write Jolson's first picture for United Artists.

"I haven't left the theater," Cohan says, "but its golden days are over."

And it was those days of which George M. Cohan—historic figure of the stage—was a part. We remember The Little Gray Fox with joy and gladness, and we welcome him to the talking picture screen, which entertains more millions than he ever dreamed of reaching by way of his beloved theater.

MAR.

A couple of gay old dogs learning new tricks. Joe Weber and Lew Fields, for fifty years famous on the American stage, limbering up with a couple of chorus girls on the Metro lot, where they are playing in that company's old-timers' revue. Try this on your sixties!

MAR.

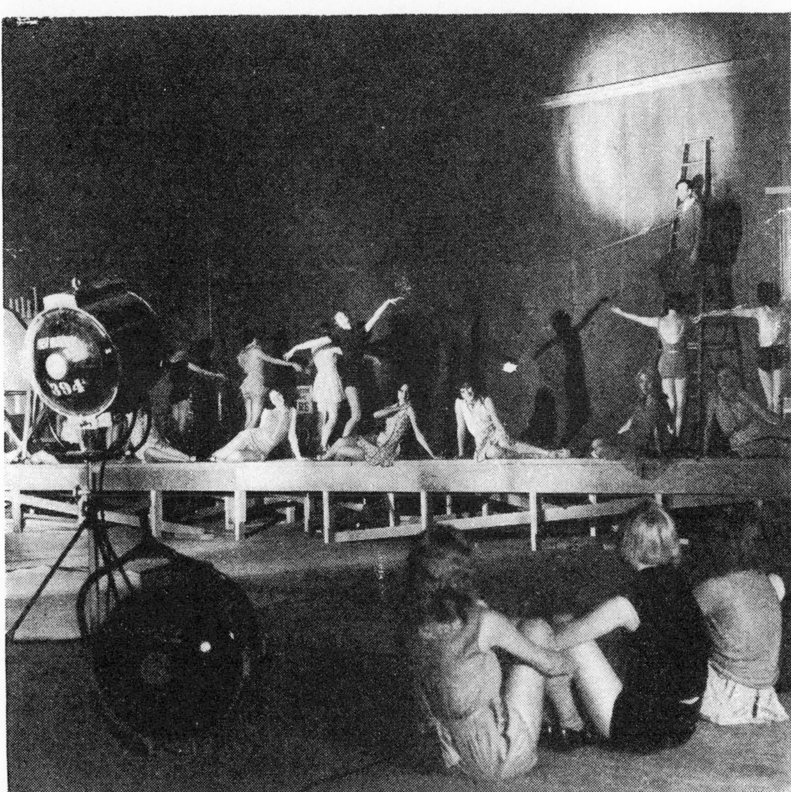

Jack Haskell (on ladder), famous stager of dance numbers for the theater and screen, puts the chorines through a rehearsal on one of the sound stages at First National. The three in the foreground have taken time out, and are watching their sisters labor

Hurrell

YOU wouldn't know him for the gay, spirited blade who sang, dueled and loved his way through "Devil May Care," now would you? The watchful camera catches Ramon Novarro in one of his thoughtful moods, when he is less the dashing actor and more the thoughtful boy. His new picture is "The House of Troy"

Richee

AFTER all, friends, why write a caption for this? Need we announce, with valuable ink, that this is the latest picture of that so *charmant*, that so *piquant*, that so *adorable* Maurice Chevalier, Pet of Paris and Honey of Hollywood and points East? He looks like this in the new "Paramount on Parade"

APR.

These New Faces

Watch for This Each Month

JUNE CLYDE ("Hit the Deck," Radio Pictures) has been in the show business since she was a small child. At ten she appeared on the screen in "The Sea Wolf," but during her 'teens she played in vaudeville and musical comedy with success. It was her excellent work in "Tanned Legs" that made Radio Pictures give her an excellent part in "Hit the Deck."

ZELMA O'NEAL ("Follow Thru," Paramount) is a cute little product of the New York musical comedy stage. She became famous when she did her famous stomping for the "Varsity Drag" number in "Good News," and followed it with a hit in "Follow Thru," which she will do for the screen. A mad little minx, and for a year the wife of the young man just below. *(Anthony Bushell)*

WALTER WOOLF ("Golden Dawn," Warner Brothers) has been, for some years, one of the leading baritone operetta stars of Broadway. He sang and looked his handsome way to fame in "The Lady in Ermine," and has been a Shubert star ever since. "Golden Dawn," done on the stage by Arthur Hammerstein, is his first singie. Walter is married to a Richmond, Va., girl.

APR.

How Popular *is* Rudy Vallée?

JUST how popular IS Rudy Vallée, the blond, blue-eyed boy from Maine, whose first picture, "The Vagabond Lover," showed him to those who had known him only as a voice on the air?

You'd be bewildered!

Rudy is a phenomenon of the amusement world. Nothing quite like him ever happened before.

He began as a radio voice, with a certain come-hither quality that sent a tremolo up and down the spines of listening girls. In two years he has become a high-priced band-leader, radio ace, master of ceremonies, vaudeville actor and film star, with a weekly income now estimated at $8,000.

Not long ago our old Cal York did a simple, friendly reporting job. He said that Rudy was over-press-agented when he went to Hollywood, that he was a shy sort of laddy, and that "Hollywood looked down its nose" at him. Oh, fatal phrase!

Letters crashed in from Maine to Minnesota. "Just a Mother" said she loved Rudy because he loved HIS mother. Dozens dared Jack Gilbert to try to sing "A Little Kiss Each Morning." Horrors!

RUDY'S piping hot, right now. His fans will enjoy reading what Sidney Skolsky, columnist for the *New York Daily News*, says about Vallée, their favorite:

"Rudy was born in Westbrook, Me., July 21, 1901, and was christened Hubert Prior Vallée. He took the Rudy from Rudy Wiedoeft, ace saxophonist, and Rudy's idol on the sax. . . . Curses like a stoker, but screams shrilly when his hot temper is aroused. . . . Doesn't drink much, but takes an occasional rye highball. The taste of Scotch makes him sick. . . . Tried to enlist in the Navy at fifteen, and failed. . . . Smokes a few cigarettes of an English brand, but hates the smell of pipe smoke. . . . Girls didn't like him when he was at Yale. . . . Gilda Gray put him up to using a megaphone, because his voice was low. Now he plans to employ a glass one so his face can be seen when he is singing.

Girls Didn't Like Him When He Was at Yale

"HE plays two instruments—the saxophone and clarinet. . . . He likes the Lenore Ulric type of beauty . . . . His blond eyebrows are inconspicuous, so he pencils them on the stage. . . . He married Leonie McCoy in May, 1928, but the marriage was annulled the following August. He likes to read Western stories. . . . His current ambition is to make a million dollars. . . . His great fear is that some day he will be fat and bald."

There you are. Another reporting job by a Broadway expert.

The favorite New York anecdote about Vallée concerns the time two high school girls called to see him backstage at the Paramount Theater.

He shook hands with them. One fainted.

The other, after her chum was revived, left the theater swearing she would never wash the hand that had shaken the hand of Rudy Vallée.

And is he popular? Ask Cal York!

Oh, my gracious me!

William Fox
presents
JANET GAYNOR
and
CHARLES FARRELL
in the Musical Romance
HIGH SOCIETY BLUES
Janet Gaynor and Charles Farrell have a surprise for even their most faithful admirers in this tender musical romance bubbling with carefree youth, fun and melody and seasoned with the matchless wit of William Collier, Sr., king of high comedy.
A love story of great beauty is unfolded in words and music as Janet and Charlie, strumming softly on their ukuleles, provide their own accompaniments while singing "I'm in the Market For You"—"I Don't Know You Well Enough For That"—"Just Like a Story Book" and several other unusually tuneful melodies written especially for them.
WORDS and MUSIC by JOSEPH McCARTHY and JAMES HANLEY
Directed by DAVID BUTLER from the story of DANA BURNET
MOVIETONE

APR.

Doctor, nurse and anguished husband stood behind the camera for ten hours while Alma Rubens finished this sequence for "Show Boat." Her breakdown followed

APR.

Six little girls of the Gay Thirties in the garb of the Gay Nineties—proving that women are still Floradora babies at heart. Lenore Bushman, Patricia Caron, Ilka Chase, Marion Davies, Vivian Oakland and Ethel Sykes, modern maidens every one, catch the spirit of the famous Floradora Sextette in "The Gay '90's," Miss Davies' next for M-G-M

APR.

The Helen Morgan we see in "Applause." For this picture Miss Morgan bought cheap and inferior scents in keeping with her rôle

APR.

☆ *MONTANA MOON—M-G-M*

JOAN CRAWFORD, still untamed but out of the jungle and into the open spaces, fills this somewhat inconsistent tale with some of the most delightful comedy the screen has held in a long time. Even if you rebel in spots, you'll care for this picture in a big way, in spite of yourself, for it has great gusto and paprika.

Joan is loose on a Montana ranch, this time, with Johnny Mack Brown doing yeoman service as an ignorant foreman of cow-gentlemen. And Joan does a tango with Ricardo Cortez that you'll like. In addition, Metro-Goldwyn-Mayer turned loose its comic force in full, and Benny Rubin, Karl Dane and Cliff Edwards are funny. Bubbling Joan is back where she belongs, in a light and frolicsome picture, and her fans will welcome the change of style.

"MONTANA MOON" — M-G-M. — From the story by Sylvia Thalberg and Frank Butler. Continuity by Sylvia Thalberg and Frank Butler. Directed by Malcolm St. Clair. The cast: *Joan*, Joan Crawford; *Larry*, John Mack Brown; *Elizabeth*, Dorothy Sebastian; *Jeff*, Ricardo Cortez; *"The Doctor,"* Benny Rubin; *Froggy*, Cliff Edwards; *Hank*, Karl Dane; *Mr. Prescott*, Lloyd Ingraham.

APR.

SO LONG LETTY—Warners

TWO discontented husbands swap wives. That's the story. But Charlotte Greenwood as *Letty* is the whole show. Just to look at her boisterous antics is to laugh. You'll recognize the theme song, "So Long Letty." Bert Roach, Patsy Ruth Miller, Grant Withers and Claude Gillingwater add to the fun.

"SO LONG LETTY"—WARNERS.—From the play by Oliver Morosco and Elmar Harris. Adapted by Robert Lord and Arthur Caesar. Directed by Lloyd Bacon. The cast: *Letty Robbins*, Charlotte Greenwood; *Tommy Robbins*, Bert Roach; *Grace Miller*, Patsy Ruth Miller; *Harry Miller*, Grant Withers; *Claude Davis*, Claude Gillingwater; *Ruth Davis*, Marion Byron; *Sally Davis*, Helen Foster; *Clarence De Brie*, Hallam Cooley; *Joe Casey*, Harry Gribbon; *Judge*, Lloyd Ingraham.

APR.

☆ *SONG O' MY HEART—Fox*

IN a contest conducted by PHOTOPLAY there were more requests for John McCormack to sing "Little Boy Blue" and "I Hear You Calling Me" than any other numbers. These are the hit pieces, and when he sings 'em you break down and tell your right name. Does that Irishman touch the old heart strings? The romance concerns one *Sean O'Carolan* who loves the girl who married another. And, although McCormack isn't expected to do any heavy acting, his is a pleasing personality. The settings are gorgeous. Most of it was filmed, you know, in the Land of the Shamrock.

With much publicity ballyhoo, Maureen O'Sullivan was brought to this country from Dublin to carry the heart interest. She doesn't make the grade, but Tommy Clifford, the eleven-year-old kid, playing her brother, is a sensation. Maureen will undoubtedly go back to the old fireside, but Tommy can park his Irish brogue in Hollywood as long as he likes. John Garrick is again charming as a young lover, Joe Kerrigan and Farrell MacDonald bring in a lot of laughs, and Alice Joyce plays McCormack's sweetheart without much success.

But who cares about the other actors or the story or anything when there stands McCormack right before your very eyes, singing with all the tenderness and beauty for which his voice is famed? You find yourself reaching for the dry handkerchief. See it by all means.

"SONG O' MY HEART"—Fox.—From the story by Tom Barry. Continuity by Sonya Levien. Directed by Frank Borzage. The cast: *Sean O'Carolan*, John McCormack; *Mary O'Brien*, Alice Joyce; *Fergus O'Donnell*, John Garrick; *Peter Conlon*, J. M. Kerrigan; *Joe Rafferty*, Farrell MacDonald; *Eileen O'Brien*, Maureen O'Sullivan; *Tad O'Brien*, Tommy Clifford; *Mona*, Effie Ellsler; *Elizabeth*, Emily Fitzroy; *Vincent Glennon*, Edwin Schneider.

APR.

A happy group under the California sun. John McCormack, his wife, his daughter Gwendolyn and Charlie Farrell at Fox-Movietone City, where McCormack has just finished his first film. Charlie and Gwendolyn were often together

APR.

BE YOURSELF—United Artists

THAT old "My Man" plot gets dusted off for another Fanny Brice picture. Fanny is the little self-sacrificer who stakes her heart and money on a boxer who repays her by falling for a gold-digger. Just another movie.

"BE YOURSELF"—UNITED ARTISTS.—From the story by Joseph Jackson. Adapted by Thornton Freeland and Max Marcin. Directed by Thornton Freeland. The cast: *Fannie Field*, Fanny Brice; *Jerry Moore*, Robert Armstrong; *Harry Field*, Harry Green; *McCloskey*, G. Pat Collins; *Step*, Budd Fine; *Lillian*, Gertrude Astor; *Lola*, Marjorie "Babe" Kane; *Jessica*, Rita Flynn.

APR.

LITTLE JOHNNY JONES—First National

THIS would have been just another race track yarn but for two things. One is Eddie Buzzell, a musical comedy star who can sing and act, too. The other is the famous George M. Cohan music. Alice Day, as the Jockey's sweetheart, gives a sincere show.

"LITTLE JOHNNY JONES"—FIRST NATIONAL.—From the comedy by George M. Cohan. Directed by Mervyn LeRoy. The cast: *Johnny Jones*, Eddie Buzzell; *Mary Baker*, Alice Day; *Vivian Dale*, Edna Murphy; *Ed Baker*, Robert Edeson; *Wyman*, Wheeler Oakman; *Carbon*, Raymond Turner; *Ramon*, Donald Reed.

APR.

LORD BYRON OF BROADWAY—M-G-M

LIFE, for *Roy*, is just one theme song after another. He's a song writer who gets (a) swell-head, (b) deflated, (c) a happy ending. The story's strong enough to be festooned with Technicolored girls, ballets, songs and effects without breaking down. One good revue scene. Charles Kaley and Cliff Edwards sing; Benny Rubin wisecracks; Ethelind Terry acts; Marion Shilling is pretty. You'll like this.

"LORD BYRON OF BROADWAY"—M-G-M.—From the story by Nell Martin. Continuity by Crane Wilbur and Willard Mack. Directed by William Nigh and Harry Beaumont. The cast: *Roy*, Charles Kaley; *Ardis*, Ethelind Terry; *Nancy*, Marion Shilling; *Joe*, Cliff Edwards; *Bessie*, Gwen Lee; *Phil*, Benny Rubin; *Edwards*, Drew Demorest; *Mr. Millaire*, John Byron; *Red Head*, Rita Flynn; *Blondie*, Hazel Craven; *Riccardi*, Gino Corrado; *Marie*, Paulette Paquet.

APR.

PUTTIN' ON THE RITZ—United Artists

HARRY RICHMAN'S first talkie is another backstage story with a new twist or two. Harry and Jimmy Gleason play two actors, and their feminine partners are Joan Bennett (at her best and loveliest) and Lilyan Tashman, furnishing many of the laughs. There is some good Irving Berlin music, particularly "Alice in Wonderland." Harry shows little in looks or acting, but you'll like his warbling.

"PUTTIN' ON THE RITZ"—UNITED ARTISTS.—From the story by John W. Considine, Jr. Directed by Edward Sloman. The cast: *Harry Raymond*, Harry Richman; *Dolores Fenton*, Joan Bennett; *James Tierney*, James Gleason; *Mrs. Teddy Van Renssler*, Aileen Pringle; *Goldie Devere*, Lilyan Tashman; *George Barnes*, Purnell Pratt; *Fenway Brooks*, Richard Tucker; *Bob Wagner*, Eddie Kane; *Dr. Blair*, George Irving; *Schmidt*, Sidney Franklin.

APR.

THE BIG PARTY—Fox

A SUE CAROL picture, starring Dixie Lee! Dixie doesn't steal it—they hand it to her on a red-hot platter. She's sensational. A roaring comedy, built around the adventures of three shop girls—principally Dixie. True love and villainy chase each other, with laughs winning. Fine work by Frank Albertson, Richard Keene and Douglas Gilmore (ssss!), and comedians Walter Catlett and Charles Judels.

"BIG PARTY, THE"—Fox.—From the story by Harlan Thompson. Directed by John Blystone. The cast: *Flo Jenkins*, Sue Carol; *Kitty Collins*, Dixie Lee; *Jack Hunter*, Frank Albertson; *Goldfarb*, Walter Catlett; *Eddie Perkins*, Richard Keene; *Billy Greer*, Whispering Jack Smith; *Allen Wetherby*, Douglas Gilmore; *Dupuy*, Charles Judels; *Mrs. Dupuy*, Ilka Chase; *Mrs. Goldfarb*, Elizabeth Patterson; *Virginia Gates*, Dorothy Brown.

APR.

HONEY—Paramount

REMEMBER when Ruth Chatterton played "Come Out of the Kitchen" on the stage, and Marguerite Clark did it in pictures? The same story is now a phonoplay bearing the title "Honey." It stars Nancy Carroll (although she hasn't a lot to do) and boasts an excellent cast, among whom is that amazing kid, Mitzi Green. The comedy is light and the songs are pleasant.

"HONEY"—Paramount.—From the play "Come Out of the Kitchen" by Alice Duer Miller. Adapted by Herman J. Mankiewicz. Directed by Wesley Ruggles. The cast: *Olivia Dangerfield*, Nancy Carroll; *Burton Crane*, Stanley Smith; *Charles Dangerfield*, Skeets Gallagher; *Cora Falkner*, Lillian Roth; *Hellon*, Harry Green; *Doris*, Mitzi Green; *Mayme*, ZaSu Pitts; *Mrs. Falkner*, Jobyna Howland; *Randolph Weeks*, Charles Sellon.

APR.

PEACOCK ALLEY—Tiffany Productions, Inc.

HERE'S happy Mae Murray doing a talking version of that once glorious picture "Peacock Alley." It's a sorry affair now, with Miss Murray more affected and more bee-stung of mouth than ever. You'll laugh at the drama and weep over the comedy, for the story concerns a stage star who wants marriage and will accept no substitutes. Mae dances, sings and emotes. She dances well.

"PEACOCK ALLEY"—Tiffany Productions, Inc.—From the story by Carey Wilson. Continuity by Frances Hyland. Directed by Marcel De Sano. The cast: *Claire Tree*, Mae Murray; *Stoddard Clayton*, George Barraud; *Jim Bradbury*, Jason Robards; *Martin Saunders*, Richard Tucker; *Dugan*, W. L. Thorne; *Bonner*, Phillips Smalley; *Paul*, E. H. Calvert; *Crosby*, Arthur Hoyt; *Walter*, Billy Bevan.

FOX
MOVIETONE
Follies of 1930
The most thrilling musical entertainment ever put on the screen! Better than the record-breaking Fox Follies of 1929! One hundred of Hollywood's most glorious girls and a dozen principals—among them El Brendel, the world's funniest Swede; William Collier, Jr.; Marjorie White, song and dance imp; Miriam Seegar and Noel Francis—gorgeous golden-voiced prima donnas. *And* a brilliant story, by Owen Davis, dean of American playwrights and Pulitzer prize dramatist.
Presented by WILLIAM FOX
Directed by Benjamin Stoloff

WORLD'S GREATEST MUSICAL COMEDY!

Here is sheer delight from first to last—a gorgeous, glittering, star-studded screen musical comedy with song hits galore, including "Sweeping the Clouds Away" and "Any Time's the Time to Fall in Love," hilarious comedy bits, flashing dance numbers, dazzling Technicolor scenes . . . Paramount, with 18 years of supremacy, is proud to name it "PARAMOUNT ON PARADE" and send it to you as the world's greatest musical comedy!

CREAM OF SCREEN AND STAGE STARS

(Listed in alphabetical order. Read the entire list!)

RICHARD ARLEN ✯ JEAN ARTHUR WILLIAM AUSTIN ✯ GEORGE BANCROFT CLARA BOW ✯ EVELYN BRENT ✯ MARY BRIAN ✯ CLIVE BROOK ✯ VIRGINIA BRUCE ✯ NANCY CARROLL ✯ RUTH CHATTERTON ✯ MAURICE CHEVALIER GARY COOPER ✯ LEON ERROL ✯ STUART ERWIN ✯ STANLEY FIELDS ✯ KAY FRANCIS ✯ SKEETS GALLAGHER HARRY GREEN ✯ MITZI GREEN ✯ JAMES HALL ✯ PHILLIPS HOLMES ✯ HELEN KANE ✯ DENNIS KING ✯ ABE LYMAN and his BAND ✯ FREDRIC MARCH NINO MARTINI ✯ DAVID NEWELL JACK OAKIE ✯ WARNER OLAND ZELMA O'NEAL ✯ EUGENE PALLETTE JOAN PEERS ✯ WILLIAM POWELL CHARLES "BUDDY" ROGERS ✯ LILLIAN ROTH ✯ STANLEY SMITH ✯ FAY WRAY

Supervised by Elsie Janis

Dances and ensembles directed by David Bennett

✯ ✯ ✯ ✯ ✯ ✯ ✯ ✯ ✯ ✯

PARAMOUNT PUBLIX CORPORATION
ADOLPH ZUKOR, PRES., PARAMOUNT BLDG., N. Y. C.

Paramount

"If it's a Paramount Picture it's the best show in town!"

Pictures

Autrey

Janet Gaynor was born Oct. 6, 1906, in Philadelphia. She is five feet tall; has auburn hair and brown eyes; weighs 96 pounds. Married Lydell Peck last fall

TIME, change and talkies cannot dim the sweet and appealing charm of little Janet Gaynor. The tiny sprite of the Fox lot got a hatful of hallelujahs for her quaint singing in "Sunny Side Up," and since then her bosses have given her many good jobs, including the latest big one, "Playmates"

Arthur Loves Two Women—Ma And Sis

ARTHUR LAKE is a veteran trouper. He'll never have a second childhood—because he'll never get over his first. He's that way. He is back in California from his first trip to New York, where he broke three engagements to be sure of a ride on the subway before he had to leave. He's crazy about football and lying on the beach. And flying, even though his mama bawls him out for it. And dogs—he cried bitter tears when his dog "Bummer" died last Christmas.

He's careful about his "good side" and his "bad side" and if he's not more careful driving his car he'll smash both sides into hamburger.

Women?—surrounded by battalions of 'em, in Hollywood, and in love with two of 'em. One's his mother; the other's his sister, Florence.

Papa and mama—the family name is Silverlake—toured the South in variety and repertoire. Soon as the kid could toddle he worked, too. So did Florence. Ma Silverlake taught them first.

By fourth grade time, they went to Detroit to live, and schooled there, and later in California. He was a "Fox Kiddies" star, but vaudeville was the family meat until they inherited from a grandpa and settled down in Nashville. After Dad Silverlake died, the youngsters and their mother went back to the stage.

They joined a car show in one-night stands until the car burned up. Then they tent-showed. Arthur's work was easy. All he had to do was play the drum, take tickets at the door, sell candy, do specialties in intermissions and play kid parts.

FLORENCE got a picture job and they went to California. Arthur got a job in a cleaning and pressing shop until she found him a part at Universal.

He puppy-loved so well that he got a five-year contract. When it expired, he and Universal couldn't agree. Now he's with Radio. Remember "Tanned Legs" and "Dance Hall"? "Tommy" is his next.

He's six feet and a half inch tall. He loves to eat on dining cars and wears the cutest red and green feather in his hat.

From Chorus Girl To Prima Donna

WHAT if she does temperamentally wham a tiny foot down now and then?—and utter exclamation points? Who cares, as long as Jeanette MacDonald remains as screen-audibly satisfying as she's been in "The Love Parade" and "The Vagabond King" and "Let's Go Native"?

Whoever or whatever predetermines that "this one shall be plain, this one ugly, this one beautiful," must have been in an ambitious state of mind when Jeanette was up for planning.

Jeanette was one of the first Broadway draftees in the War to Make the Microphone Safe for the Films. With her training in stagecraft, what wonder she clicks?

Ever since she was in knee dresses, she's been studying singing and dancing. Then old marster Ned Wayburn showed her how when she was in his Capitol Theater revues.

JEANETTE took the up-from-the-ranks route. Chorus cutie in "Night Boat," small part in "Irene," better part in "'Tangerine." Then a break—a leading rôle in "Fantastic Fricassee," which is what the Greenwich Village Theater WOULD call a production.

There Henry Savage saw and liked her work, and when the fricassee was scraped into the pail, he placed her under contract and gave her the lead in support of Mitzi in "The Magic Ring."

After that, it was just one musical comedy leading rôle after another on Broadway until Paramount got the idea of making "Nothing But the Truth" as a Richard Dix talkie, and needed a leading lady. Since Jeanette was singing the lead in "Yes, Yes, Yvette"—which is the musicomedy version of the N-But-the-T thing—they gave her a test. The test was awfully good to her.

Then Paramount changed a mind or two and the golden-haired, green-eyed Jeanette found herself in the lead opposite Maurice Chevalier in "The Love Parade," hey hey . . .! "The Vagabond King" followed and then "Let's Go Native."

Not that it's awfully important, but she's a native of Philadelphia.

(EDITOR'S NOTE to Mr. R. R., millionaire broker, New York City. Dear Sir: Yes, she says she'll marry you just as soon as some stratagem is devised to overcome that awkward matter of the 3,000-odd miles between Hollywood and New York. Anyway, she's wild about you. Aren't telephone tolls and airplane hire high?)

By
Katherine Albert

Why everyone with the price belongs to a beach club in Southern California. Lillian Roth, the singing girl, takes a huge drink of seashore sunshine

She Raised *the* Roof

THE scene was the glittering Ziegfeld Roof, that after-theater resort on top of the New Amsterdam Theater where it costs about four dollars to stare at the head waiter.

At a ringside table sat Mr. Jesse L. Lasky, overlord of Paramount production.

He was there to feast his eyes and ears on the star of the show, M. Maurice Chevalier, the French hullabaloo already under contract to Mr. Lasky's outfit. But ho!

Forth came a shapely little minx, with snapping eyes and a mop of wild black hair.

Out of her throat came a deep, resonant voice, singing a blues song in a way that raised the fur along Mr. Lasky's spine.

"A bet!" thought Mr. Lasky, mentally figuring contracts. "A bet!"

And that's how young Lillian Roth, nineteen and full of hoopla, came to Hollywood to delight you in "The Love Parade" and make you her devoted slave in "The Vagabond King."

She's as natural as three and seven on a pair of dice. She has all the girlish charm and zippo that was Clara Bow's when the redhead first hit Hollywood. She wouldn't know an affected mannerism if one came up to her riding a duck. And she's aces up at Paramount.

'Twas not always thus.

Lillian Roth began tinkering around the theater when she was six. At that advanced age she made her début in a play called "The Inner Man."

Then, in her earliest teens, she went into vaudeville. She had to do dramatic impersonations because the Gerry Society wouldn't let her sing and dance. This slowed her up.

But you can't keep a good blues singer down—not for long.

THE time arrived for the peppery young Lillian to make her first hit—and it was in Chicago that it happened.

There she caught on with a Shubert "Artists and Models" revue, and the Windy Citizens sat up on the end of their spines as that voice came out of the pretty little girl.

Broadway began to hear rumors—then reports—of a little singer named Lillian Roth who was knocking Chicagoans into Lake Michigan with her warbling. *(continued on next page)*

Lillian Roth was a vaudeville trouper when she was eight. Here she is shown with little sister Ann, five. The team of tiny tots sang and danced wherever the Gerry Society would let them get away with it. Lillian is now an ace Paramount songstress in "The Vagabond King"

MAY

CHASING RAINBOWS—M-G-M

JUST one too many carbon copies of "The Broadway Melody" have been made, and this pleasant little singie is it. Charles King and Bessie Love again play tangled lovers behind the scenes, and the good old tale holds very little interest. But that pleasing team, Polly Moran, Marie Dressler, together with George K. Arthur dig out some laughs, and because of their labors and the leads' charm, the film entertains.

"CHASING RAINBOWS"—M-G-M.—From the story by Bess Meredyth. Adapted by Wells Root. Directed by Charles F. Riesner. The cast: *Carlie,* Bessie Love; *Terry,* Charles King; *Eddie,* Jack Benny; *Lester,* George K. Arthur; *Polly,* Polly Moran; *Peggy,* Gwen Lee; *Daphne,* Nita Martan; *Cordova,* Eddie Phillips; *Donnie,* Marie Dressler; *Lanning,* Youcca Troubetzkoy.

MAY

CHILDREN OF PLEASURE—M-G-M

IF you don't know what a song writer's heart is like, see this picture. If you don't care, that's your business. Lawrence Gray—remember how grand he was in "Marianne"?—is the sharps-and-flats gentleman. "The Whole Darned Thing's for You" and "Leave It That Way" are hit numbers. There are two leading ladies—one of whom, Wynne Gibson, has everything it takes. You'll be seeing more of this kid.

"CHILDREN OF PLEASURE"—M-G-M.—From the play "The Song Writer" by Crane Wilbur. Scenario by Richard Schayer. Directed by Harry Beaumont. The cast: *Danny Regan,* Lawrence Gray; *Emma Gray,* Wynne Gibson; *Pat Thayer,* Helen Johnson; *Rod Peck,* Kenneth Thomson; *Bernie,* Lee Kolmar; *Fanny Kaye,* May Boley; *Andy Little,* Benny Rubin.

(continued from preceding page)

At fifteen she was a feature in vaudeville—sparkling, laughing, and forever singing.

It was a thousand to one shot that Broadway would get her, and it wasn't long! Winnie Lightner stepped out of a sickly show called "Delmar's Revels," and in pranced Lil! Weakling though the show was, and all run down with box-office anaemia, the Roth kid stood out like a boil on teacher's nose, and it wasn't long till she was snapped up by the big leagues of the show world.

Well, then it was easy.

Earl Carroll signed her for his "Vanities." The opera opened on a sticky night in August, and even then Lillian stuck out.

She got wonderful notices in all the papers, and when that show struck out for the tall and uncut, Miss Roth went up ten or twelve flights and joined Mr. Ziegfeld's roof show, where not even the star-spangled Chevalier dimmed the glory of her chest tones.

And then, children, Mr. Lasky got psychic, packed her off to Hollywood and gave her to us in long lengths of sizzling celluloid.

The rest you almost know. Playing opposite Lupino Lane, she was one of the gay spots of "The Love Parade."

Again the path of the merry little singing girl paralleled that of the great French revue star!

She moved into "The Vagabond King," playing a dramatic rôle, and playing it all over the screen.

In addition, she has one of the great numbers of that tuneful Friml show, and how she sings it is our business!

And there'll be many other good parts, and songs to sing, before Hollywood sees and hears the last of this sunny child.

Of course, she's in "Honey"—in fact, she's a lot of "Honey."

LILLIAN photographs older than she looks, and a good deal taller. Out West she lives with her mother and sister—works hard, and has a good time.

Oh yes, there's a boy-friend lurking.

He's a broker, not connected with the industry.

He may be some day—that is, by marriage!

Free warning to Ireland—look out, or you'll lose one of your favorite sons. Big John McCormack is so happy in California that he's bought an estate there at least half the size of Connaught

A colleen and a couple of spalpeens. John McCormack, Tommy Clifford and Maureen O'Sullivan in a scene from "Song O' My Heart." The two youngsters were brought over from Ireland for this picture

John *Goes* California

By
Harriet Parsons

IRELAND is a bit worried. Park Avenue, New York, raises its lorgnette and tilts up its nose.

For John McCormack—John of the golden throat—has gone California! That's what the talkies have done to a good man.

The Little Green Isle, of course, will always be his first love. His summers will still be spent at Moore Abbey, his huge estate in the County Kildare. But his winters will be spent under the California sun.

Yes, in his forties, with a glorious concert career behind him and millions in his jeans, McCormack has found two new loves.

One is the California climate and scene.

The other is the new medium of the talking, singing screen. And he expected neither!

He admits that he took a chance when he signed with William Fox to make a talking picture. Of course, the financial end was just great. But there were working conditions to consider, and always the great picture-going public in the offing. Would he be happy? Would the people like him?

Well, he has his answer now! No Pollyanna ever came skipping back from Hollywood with a gayer song of cheer than that sung by the great McCormack.

After filming much of "Song O' My Heart" in Ireland, he went West. He was king of the Fox lot the minute he stepped aboard it. They had built him a thatch-covered cottage—see picture elsewhere in this issue—for a studio and dressing room—piano and all, and for all I know, a couple of pigs and a potato patch in the back yard.

Working conditions? Just dandy! The people? Interesting and cordial!

But California? Here the handsome McCormack face breaks into a smile that would soften the heart of a traffic cop.

He likes the sun, the outdoor life, the opportunities for tennis and golf. He is so mad about the whole works that before you could say "synchronization," he stepped out and bought a huge estate just ten minutes walk from Hollywood Boulevard.

There he'll make his headquarters from now on, under the California sun—with summers at his Irish home.

As for the Park Avenue apartment he leased for five years before hopping West—it's just too bad. McCormack tells me he's giving it up entirely.

That means that all his precious paintings and other works of art—worth at least a million dollars—will be shipped to Hollywood, to be enshrined in the new home.

"Just a shack on a hill," McCormack calls it.

Don't hint that the great John has gone Hollywood! He's apt to say "The back of me hand to ye," and perhaps fetch you a clout.

He doesn't know a Hollywoodian, or what such a creature is, unless it is a Californian who lives in picture town. He says that the idea of a particular and peculiar race living in Hollywood is all bosh and blather. He thinks there's very little jealousy out there, professional or personal.

AS for the talkies, oh me and oh my! McCormack is enthusiastic.

They'll play a great part in the future of music, he's sure.

"Think of posterity not only being able to hear, but to see, the great musical artists of our time," says he, his eyes snapping.

"If I could only see and hear Mario and Patti as our grandchildren will be able to see and hear the great artists of today!"

He wants to make more pictures—though, as the old song says, "It all depends on you!"

The hours on the big sound stages are not heavy, and he is fascinated by the technique of the talkies.

McCormack had been working hard on his picture for fifteen straight days. At last Director Frank Borzage called time out.

"Go and play some golf." *(continued on next page)*

(continued from preceding page)

Borzage told the star, "We won't need you at all tomorrow. Get a rest and some sunshine."

Did he?

At eleven the next morning, McCormack was on the set. He couldn't stay away—just wanted to watch the company act up. That's what the talkies have done to one of the world's greatest concert tenors—certainly its leading tugger-at-the-heartstrings.

Does he want to make more pictures? And, as Aunt Maggie used to say, how!

Now, at the height of his career McCormack is a handsome dog, with a fine head, hair waving back from a high forehead, clear cut features—and a fascinating smile. His brogue—and what a brogue!—is rich and musical.

Here's a grand man, with the whole world his playground, going California, for all the world like the first tourist from Iowa who went out there accompanied by his rheumatism and remained to play polo!

BUT we can't close on this hysterical note, much as we'd like to for the sake of the International Pollyanna League.

Was there *NOTHING* that he didn't like?

Oh yes—one thing!

He detests the long, 200-foot kisses of the pictures' silent days. He says he'd have been a bit riled if anything like that had gone on, as such matters are the exclusive prerogative of the boudoir.

But McCormack was spared that, and it is as well, for his figure is, well, impressive.

That's the only tiny discord in the McCormack symphony of happiness, and it doesn't spoil the tune.

As for the rest—sunshine, roses, and the birdies tweeting. The talkies are great. And, asks the great McCormack, will the public like him and want more of his sweet singing?

He certainly hopes so. For John McCormack has gone Holly—no, California!—in a huge and happy way!

MAY

THE MELODY MAN—Columbia

COLUMBIA has turned out a pleasant sentimental picture about the conflict between youth and old age. Though the film stars William Collier, Jr., and Alice Day, the better work is done by John Sainpolis. There is a pretty song, "Broken Dreams," which young Collier sings, and even a Technicolor sequence.

"MELODY MAN, THE"—Columbia.—Continuity by Howard J. Green. Directed by R. William Neil. The cast: *Al Tyler,* William Collier, Jr.; *Elsa,* Alice Day; *Von Kemper,* John Sainpolis; *Joe Yates,* Johnny Walker; *Martha,* Mildred Harris; *Prince Freierich,* Albert Conti; *Gustav,* Tenen Holtz; *Adolph,* Lee Kohlmer; *Von Bader,* Bertram Marburgh; *Franz José,* Anton Veverka; *Bachman,* Major Nichols.

MAY

SONG OF THE WEST—Warners

OWING to a mediocre script and uninspired direction, what might have been a magnificent outdoor operetta, all-Technicolor, is pretty feeble. "The Song" is faint, in spite of excellent singing by John Boles and a vigorous tragi-comic performance by Joe E. Brown. Some of the Vincent Youmans music is gorgeous, but unexploited. Ambitious but dull.

"SONG OF THE WEST"—Warners.—From the operetta "Rainbow" by Laurence Stallings and Oscar Hammerstein II. Screen play by Harvey Thew. Directed by Ray Enright. The cast: *Stanton,* John Boles; *Virginia,* Vivienne Segal; *Hasty,* Joe E. Brown; *Lotta,* Marie Wells; *Davolo,* Sam Hardy; *Penny,* Marion Byron; *Sergeant Major,* Eddie Gribbon; *Colonel,* Ed Martindel; *Singleton,* Rudolph Cameron.

MAY

SHE COULDN'T SAY NO—Warners

WINNIE LIGHTNER *should* have said NO when Warners tried to star her as a dramatic actress. Winnie's a grand entertainer—but as a broken-hearted night club hostess—no! The picture isn't bad entertainment—but you've seen it all before. Chester Morris is fine in the same rôle he's been playing ever since "Alibi." Sally Eilers shows promise.

"SHE COULDN'T SAY NO"—Warners.—From the story by Benjamin M. Kaye. Adapted by Robert Lord and Arthur Caesar. Directed by Lloyd Bacon. The cast: *Winnie Harper,* Winnie Lightner; *Jerry Casey,* Chester Morris; *Iris,* Sally Eilers; *Tommy Blake,* Johnny Arthur; *Big John,* Tully Marshall; *Cora,* Louise Beavers.

MAY

One of the largest and most exciting picture sets in the history of the films, devised and erected by Metro-Goldwyn-Mayer on the lot at Culver City. Officials say it is the highest so far built. On the stage, Austin Young and the Dodge Sisters are leading a number for the big picture tentatively titled "The March of Time," while to the rear guards and pretty convicts are doing a lock-step dance planned by Sammy Lee. Note the enormous battery of lights needed for the scene

NEWS ITEM—"Lawrence Tibbett sings from the time he gets up in the morning until he goes to bed at night"

MAY

Can you blame poor old Buddy Rogers for looking panicky and nervous? The kid is surrounded by the five high-powered pippins who support him in "Safety in Numbers." They are—Carol Lombard, Kathryn Crawford, Josephine Dunn, Virginia Bruce and Geneva Mitchell. Safe?

MAY

☆ *PARAMOUNT ON PARADE—Paramount*

AND now Paramount goes revue!

No story, and who cares? But color that thrills; singing that challenges Tibbettan heights; comedy that goes from chuckles to hawhaws; sugar-coated romance, sophisticated satire and slapstick burlesque; beauty in scene, sound and girls! Let's go! Chevalier, Chatterton, Oakie and—well, AND!!!! Sounds perfect, doesn't it? Glorified vaudeville that brings in virtually everybody on the Paramount lot. Oakie, Skeets Gallagher and Leon Errol are masters of unceremony. Chevalier swaggers off with the lion's share, but everybody gets a chance. Unceasing speed, beauty of sound and picture—these are outstanding characteristics.

Song hits: "Anytime's the Time to Fall in Love," "All I Want Is This One Girl," "Sweeping the Clouds Away."

"PARAMOUNT ON PARADE"—PARAMOUNT.—Directed by Dorothy Arzner, Otto Brower, Edmund Goulding, Victor Heerman, Edwin Knopf, Rowland V. Lee, Ernst Lubitsch, Lothar Mendes, Victor Schertzinger, Edward Sutherland, Frank Tuttle. The cast: Richard Arlen, Jean Arthur, William Austin, George Bancroft, Clara Bow, Evelyn Brent, Mary Brian, Clive Brook, Virginia Bruce, Nancy Carroll, Ruth Chatterton, Maurice Chevalier, Gary Cooper, Leon Errol, Stuart Erwin, Kay Francis, Skeets Gallagher, Harry Green, Mitzi Green, James Hall, Phillips Holmes, Helen Kane, Dennis King, Abe Lyman and his band, Frederic March, Nino Martini, David Newell, Jack Oakie, Warner Oland, Zelma O'Neal, Eugene Pallette, Joan Peers, William Powell, Charles Rogers, Lillian Roth, Stanley Smith and Fay Wray.

MAY

THE GREAT DIVIDE—First National

A LOT of things went wrong with this talkie version of "The Great Divide," the grand old play of years ago. Dorothy Mackaill overdoes in her attempt to be a flip society girl, and Ian Keith is more than a little hammy as the big he-person who tries to make her sensible. There are some nice Mexican fiesta scenes, but, as a whole, this is hard to take.

"GREAT DIVIDE, THE"—FIRST NATIONAL.—From the play by William Vaughan Moody. Screen play by Fred Myton. Directed by Reginald Barker. The cast: *Ruth Jordan*, Dorothy Mackaill; *Stephen Ghent*, Ian Keith; *Texas Tommy*, Lucien Littlefield; *Dutch Romeo*, Ben Hendricks; *Manuella*, Myrna Loy; *Wong*, Frank Tang; *Edgar*, Creighton Hale; *MacGregor*, George Fawcett; *Verna*, Jean Laverty; *Amesbury*, Claude Gillingwater; *Joe Morgan*, Roy Stewart; *Ruth's friend*, James Ford; *Polly*, Jean Lorraine; *Ruth's friend*, Gordon Elliott.

MAY

Looking down into the lighted well of a talkie set from the light gallery. Under the battery of arcs, far below, Jack Oakie and Zelma O'Neal are singing "I'm in Training for You" in "Paramount on Parade"

MAY

☆ ***THE VAGABOND KING—Paramount***

WITH the flash and clang of sword play and the thunder of stirring choruses, "The Vagabond King" forges into the lead of phonoplay operettas.

Once this story of Francois Villon, Paris poet-vagabond who was king of France for a day, was a book. Then it was a play, and still later a stage operetta. Now, thanks to the genius and daring of Director Ludwig Berger, it is a startling example of what sound and rich color, added to a dashing story, can do for the screen. Berger does astonishing things with his all-Technicolor work—keeping his cameras on the move through palace and den, playing all sorts of tricks with light and shade.

Dennis King, who starred in the operetta on the stage, sings the lead for the screen with enormous gusto and some permissibly operatic acting. He's handsome, and can sing. Jeanette MacDonald is a beautiful but rather colorless princess. The acting star is O. P. Heggie, who gives a remarkable performance as sleazy *King Louis*. And Lillian Roth is a little better than good in a sympathetic rôle. And she gets the beautiful "Huguette Waltz" to sing—a prize! Warner Oland is more villainous than ever.

Magnificent color work, gorgeous Friml music and some first-rate acting and singing make "The Vagabond King" memorable in the life of a picture-goer. You'll be thrilled.

"VAGABOND KING, THE"—PARAMOUNT.—From the novel by Justin Huntley McCarthy. Screen adaptation by Herman J. Mankiewicz. Directed by Ludwig Berger. The cast: *Francois Villon*, Dennis King; *Katherine*, Jeanette MacDonald; *Louis XI*, O. P. Heggie; *Huguette*, Lillian Roth; *Thibault*, Warner Oland; *Olivier*, Arthur Stone; *Astrologer*, Thomas Ricketts.

MAY

☆ ***HAPPY DAYS—Fox***

"HAPPY DAYS" is Fox's latest in the big parade of phonoplay revues. It wears a minstrel suit and carries a huge red banner. A bunch of entertainers band to help an old showman save his troupe. And what an entertainment! Fox throws all its actors and all the resources of the studio into play—McLaglen and Eddie Lowe, who sing a number; El Brendel, Charlie Farrell, Janet Gaynor, Will Rogers, Walter Catlett and dozens more. Marjorie White again is a sensation. Dick Keene and Frank Albertson play rivals for her hand. Some bright tunes. The Gaynor-Farrell number is a little unfortunate. They have to sing a sentimental song—and are so swell in romantic drama! Good, speedy entertainment. "Happy Days" was shown at the Roxy, New York, on the new wide Grandeur screen, and made everybody gasp.

"HAPPY DAYS"—FOX.—From the story by Sidney Lanfield. Directed by Benjamin Stoloff. The cast: *Col. Billy Batcher*, Charles E. Evans; *Margie*, Marjorie White; *Dick*, Richard Keene; *Jig*, Stuart Erwin; *Nancy Lee*, Martha Lee Sparks; *Sheriff Benton*, Clifford Dempsey. Minstrel Ensemble: Janet Gaynor, Charles Farrell, Victor McLaglen, El Brendel, Edmund Lowe, William Collier, Tom Patricola, Dixie Lee, George Jessel, Sharon Lynn, Will Rogers, Walter Catlett, Warner Baxter, Ann Pennington, David Rollins, Nick Stuart, Frank Albertson, Rex Bell; George MacFarlane and James J. Corbett (Interlocutors).

MAY

GAY MADRID—M-G-M

COLLEGE whoopee in Spain is, according to this picture, no different from college whoopee any other place. With one grand exception. In Spain they fight duels and play guitars. But it doesn't matter when Ramon Novarro, past master of charm, swashbuckles and sings. There are roistering student songs and tender love ditties. Dorothy Jordan is again the heroine. It's pretty good!

"GAY MADRID"—M-G-M.—From the story by Alejandro Perez Lugin. Continuity by Bess Meredyth and Salisbury Field. Directed by Robert Leonard. The cast: *Ricardo*, Ramon Novarro; *Carmina*, Dorothy Jordan; *La Panterita*, Lottice Howell; *Marques*, Claude King; *Donna Generosa*, Eugenie Besserer; *Rivas*, William V. Mong; *Dona Concha*, Beryl Mercer; *Jacinta*, Nanci Price; *Octavio*, Herbert Clark; *Ernesto*, David Scott; *Enrique*, George Chandler; *Corpulento*, Bruce Coleman.

MAY

LET'S GO PLACES—Fox

WELL, if here isn't our old friend, Mistaken Identity Plot, out for an evening's fun! And the fun materializes! The big and only idea in making this film was to make folks laugh. It does. Charles Judels and Eddie Kane, going into tantrums as two temperamental Frenchmen take comedy honors. And there are at least two songs that will make a lively bid for popularity.

"LET'S GO PLACES"—Fox.—From the story by William K. Wells. Directed by Frank Strayer. The cast: *Paul Adams*, Joseph Wagstaff; *Marjorie Lorraine*, Lola Lane; *Virginia Gordon*, Sharon Lynn; *J. Speed Quinn*, Frank Richardson; *Rex Wardell*, Walter Catlett; *Dixie*, Dixie Lee; *Du Bonnet*, Charles Judels; *Mrs. Du Bonnet*, Ilka Chase; *Ben King*, Larry Steers.

MAY

THE GOLDEN CALF—Fox

SUE CAROL is the efficient but homely secretary of a famous artist. Behind her spectacles flash eyes of love, so she makes herself over, poses as a Southern belle and becomes his model. (It's a wonder optometrists don't lose business through pictures like this.) The only things that save this from mediocrity are Sue Carol's work, the best she's done in many a day, and El Brendel's comedy.

"GOLDEN CALF, THE"—Fox.—From the story by Aaron Davis. Continuity by Marion Orth. Directed by Millard Webb. The cast: *Marybell Cobb*, Sue Carol; *Philip Homer*, Jack Mulhall; *Knute Olson*, El Brendel; *Alice*, Marjorie White; *Tommie*, Richard Keene; *Edwards*, Paul Page; *Master of Ceremonies*, Walter Catlett; *Comedienne*, Ilka Chase.

MAY

These New Faces

Watch for This Each Month

EDDIE BUZZELL ("Little Johnny Jones," First National) came from the musical comedy stage, where for a good many years he has been a featured comic, with singing and dancing thrown in. His last venture in that line was "Lady Fingers," which he also helped write. He is the husband of Ona Munson, one of the prettiest and best musical show dancers.

NOEL FRANCIS ("The Girl Who Wasn't Wanted," Fox) is a real Ziegfeld girl captured by talking pictures. Not only is her beauty up to the best Ziegfeld tradition—she can sing and dance elegantly and has a nice speaking voice. Fox discovered her on the New York stage, gave her a test, immediately signed her on the dotted line, and shipped her West.

ETHELIND TERRY ("Lord Byron of Broadway," M-G-M) has for some years been one of the noted beauties and best prima donnas on the New York music stage. She came to notice in the first "Music Box Revue," and her last big assignment on the Great White Way was the prima donna rôle in "Rio Rita," sung on the screen so notably by Bebe Daniels.

WALTER CATLETT ("Happy Days," Fox) comes to pictures with a brilliant stage career behind him, as one of the theater's leading comedians. He came to nation-wide note in "Sally," in support of Marilyn Miller—the Ziegfeld smash which ran for years, and has since been seen in innumerable musical shows. He made good with a bang at Fox.

MAY

 *FREE AND EASY—M-G-M*

BUSTER KEATON'S first big talkie is in the bag—on ice—over the top with a large, vociferous bang. Little Frosty Face makes his audible début in a whizzing comedy that has everything—from earthquaking laughter to a lot of interesting peeks beyond the watchman on the sound stages.

Keaton plays the manager of a beauty contest winner who brings his belle to Hollywood to crash pictures. Their adventures fill the film with screams and howls of joy.

Wandering around the studio you'll see, for the same admission price, Lionel Barrymore, Cecil De Mille, Gwen Lee, Fred Niblo and lots of others of note at Metro-Goldwyn-Mayer. Anita Page is the girl, and Robert Montgomery is excellent as the romantic leading man. Keaton Kops, or No Busts for Buster!

"FREE AND EASY"—M-G-M.—From the story by Richard Schayer. Adapted by Paul Dickey. Directed by Edward Sedgwick. The cast: *Elmer,* Buster Keaton; *Elvira,* Anita Page; *Ma,* Trixie Friganza; *Larry,* Robert Montgomery; *Director Niblo,* Fred Niblo; *Officer,* Edgar Dearing; *Bedroom Scene,* Gwen Lee, John Miljan, Lionel Barrymore; *A Guest,* William Haines; *Master of Ceremonies,* William Collier, Sr.; *Cave Scene,* Dorothy Sebastian, Karl Dane; *Director Burton,* David Burton.

JUN.

Marilyn Miller is wearing a "hostess negligee" from Bergdorf Goodman. It is of soft blue satin, with a draped bodice and neckline. The long, irregular pleated skirt is a distinct novelty

JUN.

Lawrence Gray wasn't going so hot, there for a time. But the romantic lead in "Marianne" with Marion fell into his lap, and since then he has been handed all sorts of nice jobs

Hurrell

THE latest sister team to send Hollywood dancing mad, and to practise on our sensibilities from the talking screen. Meet the Dodge Sisters, two beautiful and talented young ladies who came to pictures from the Broadway musical comedy stage, after serving a term in the *Folies Bergere* of Paris. Their names are Beth and Betty, and they will be seen in Metro's old-timers' revue

VITAPHONE
JOINS TWO JOYOUS STARS IN ONE GREAT COMEDY SPECIAL
Funniest thing on four feet—Joe E. Brown and Winnie Lightner . . .
Teaming for the first time, in a picture teeming with laughs!
"HOLD EVERYTHING" held all hilarity records in its one-year run on Broadway . . .
Now here it is on the talking screen, with every riotous roar retained by Vitaphone.
"'Hold Everything' is a riot . . . rich and rare" . . . "full of the best 'gags' ever developed"—say famous newspaper experts who have seen it.
But don't take their word for it.—See for yourself!
Use the Vitaphone sign as a guide to the best of good times. It appears only on pictures produced by Warner Bros. and First National Pictures. "Vitaphone" is the registered trademark of The Vitaphone Corporation.
WARNER BROS. present
HOLD EVERYTHING
ALL IN TECHNICOLOR with
JOE E. BROWN ★ WINNIE LIGHTNER
Georges Carpentier ★ Sally O'Neil ★ Dorothy Revier
Abe Lyman and His Band
A WARNER BROS. & VITAPHONE TALKING & SINGING PICTURE

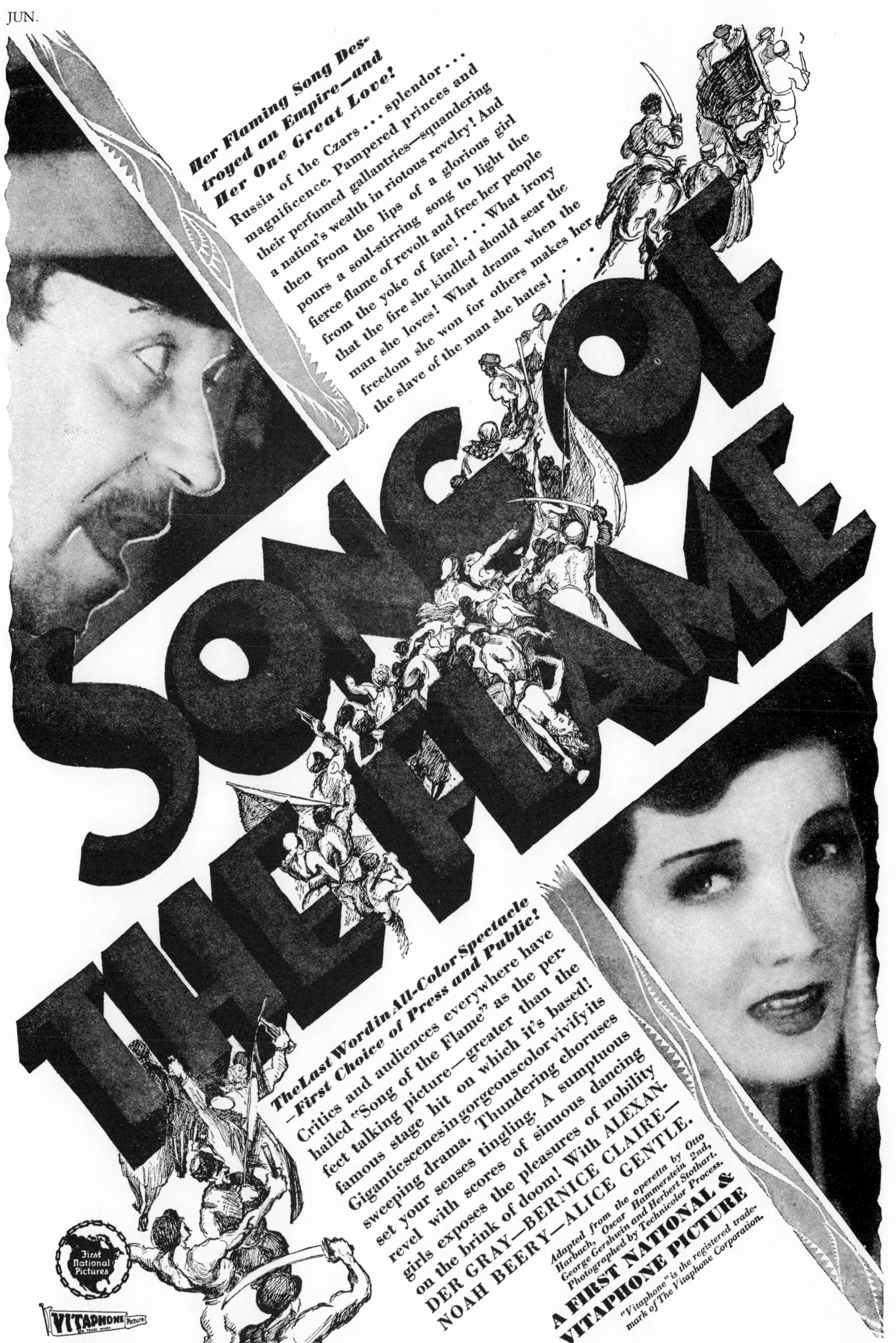
Her Flaming Song Destroyed an Empire—and Her One Great Love!
Russia of the Czars . . . splendor . . . magnificence. Pampered princes and their perfumed gallantries—squandering a nation's wealth in riotous revelry! And then from the lips of a glorious girl pours a soul-stirring song to light the fierce flame of revolt and free her people from the yoke of fate! . . . What irony that the fire she kindled should sear the man she loves! What drama when the freedom she won for others makes her the slave of the man she hates! . . .
SONG OF
THE FLAME
The Last Word in All-Color Spectacle—First Choice of Press and Public!
Critics and audiences everywhere have hailed "Song of the Flame" as the perfect talking picture—greater than the famous stage hit on which it's based! Gigantic scenes in gorgeous color vivify its sweeping drama. Thundering choruses set your senses tingling. A sumptuous revel with scores of sinuous dancing girls exposes the pleasures of nobility on the brink of doom! With ALEXANDER GRAY—BERNICE CLAIRE—NOAH BEERY—ALICE GENTLE.
Adapted from the operetta by Otto Harbach, Oscar Hammerstein 2nd, George Gershwin and Herbert Stothart. Photographed by Technicolor Process.
A FIRST NATIONAL & VITAPHONE PICTURE
"Vitaphone" is the registered trademark of The Vitaphone Corporation.
First National Pictures
VITAPHONE Picture

JUN.

Lawrence Tibbett, still in boots and coachman's coat from "The Rogue Song," glowers, in a deep baritone way, at his rival across the page

JUN.

"IN my opinion, no picture except an operetta should have more than four songs, but these four should be sung often. Even a musical comedy shouldn't have more than four, or at the most, five, songs, of which two are almost certain to become hits."—Irving Berlin, song writer.

JUN.

"CECIL B. DE MILLE says he doesn't believe television will keep people from the theater. . . . No, sir, it will probably take another thousand or so versions of 'Broadway' to turn the trick!"—The Toledo Blade.

JUN.

THE first Jewish talking pictures have made their bow.

Judea Films, Inc., are making a series of twenty-six two-reelers in Jewish. Two were released in early spring, with notables of the Jewish theater in the casts.

The first was a musical comedy called "Style and Class," featuring Marty Baratz and Goldie Eisman, well known in New York's East Side theaters.

Later on, Judea Films will make a feature film on Zion's history.

JUN.

"THE Queen" is dead. Long live Gloria Swanson!

Old "Queen Kelly," the $800,000 beauty begun by Eric von Stroheim and finished by general decay, has been finally thrown away. It was to have been Swanson's first talkie.

There was some talk of making an operetta out of it, but no good came of that. Somewhere are many, many film cans. They hold all that is mortal of eight hundred thousand good American dollars tossed into a movie that turned sour, and could never be made sweet again.

JUN.

THERE'S a brand new wrinkle in th Gloria Swanson productions, and it isn't in one of Gloria's Hollywood frocks either.

For the first time in the history of the motion picture business, a film has been "shot" in dress rehearsal form. Gloria's forthcoming comedy, "What a Widow!" was shot in three days. Of course, the public will never see this film. Scenes were made on partially dressed stages, and the cast in many sequences wore street clothes. But the play itself was complete.

THIS novel experiment is the idea of Joseph P. Kennedy, in general charge of Gloria's productions. He believes it will save time and money in the long run. Before the actual film destined for release is made, the cast, director and technicians can view the complete dress rehearsal, rectify mistakes and allow adequate spacing for comedy lines in the correct places instead of taking wide chances.

After the rehearsal film was completed, the actual shooting was expected to take just ten days, or thirteen days in all on a thirty-five-day shooting schedule. Not one scene was expected to be made that could not be used in the finished product after the visual rehearsal. The cost of the dress rehearsal did not exceed by more than $10,000 the carrying on of actual rehearsals with the full cast.

It is a daring experiment in Hollywood, but after all, the public will be more interested in Gloria's twenty-one new gowns.

JUN.

Just about the prettiest picture of a pretty girl we could find among several thousand samples submitted by the glib press agents. This is little Helen Twelvetrees as she looks in Pathe's musical circus picture, "Swing High"

JUN.

JUN. GOSSIP hounds of Hollywood are rubbing their hands in uncontrolled glee and preparing to spend a lot of merry hours on the "Follow Thru" set.

Nancy Carroll is in the picture. So is Zelma O'Neal. Both are red heads. The picture is in Technicolor. Nancy's hair photographs red. Zelma's doesn't. Or it didn't until Zelma went and had it dyed so that it would be just the right color. And there's an unwritten law in Hollywood that one red head to a picture is the absolute limit. Heigh-ho! There'll be some temperamental days and hectic nights on that little fillum.

Maurice Chevalier, in the spangles of "The Love Parade," gives Monsieur Tibbett one of those grins— nice, but more than a little naughty

Mannatt

"SWINGIN' IN THE LANE," as sung and swung by Marion Davies and Lawrence Gray in a scene from her new picture, "The Florodora Girl." Seated on a cluster of arcs you will see Mr. Harry Beaumont, the director. He represents The Thirsty Thirties, we suppose. Note that the mike swings with them

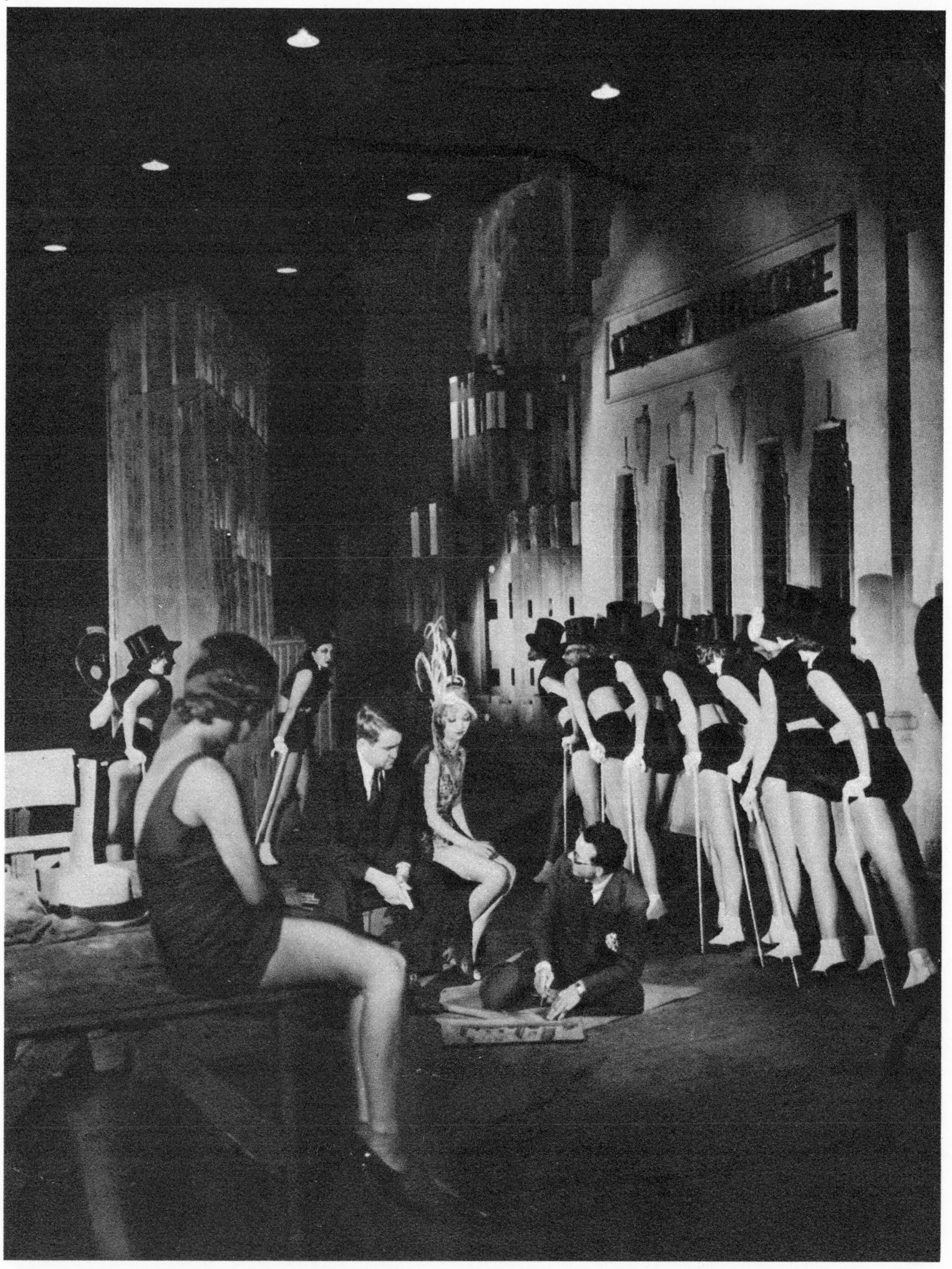

YOU would be surprised at how much technical preparation is required by camera-and-microphone revues. Every step must be carefully planned. Here's Director Cline and his dance director telling Alice White just where to move when the camera and orchestra start on "Sweet Mama," which, from the looks of things, will not be exactly a Chautauqua affair

He has The Girls Gasping!

By

Miriam Hughes

Hollywood's belles are tinkling about Walter Pidgeon, who charms as well as he sings

WHAT causes those loud huzzahs I hear echoing up and down Hollywood Boulevard?

Did you notice that not-so-well suppressed excitement over the luncheon tables at the Embassy Club?

What is that rustling noise? Why, that's all the powder puffs in the film capital scurrying over all the ladies' noses.

Why are all the feminine heads together and all the feminine tongues clacking?

Don't you know? Haven't you heard? There's a gentleman in town! An eligible one! An unattached one! In the city that has been called (and rightly, too!) a manless town, such a phenomenon is the event of the more or less social season.

In the hamlet that harbors the aloof Mr. Colman, the inaccessible Mr. Powell and the much-married Mr. Gilbert, Walter Pidgeon has created a sensation.

Name sounds vaguely familiar, doesn't it? Saw him in a couple of silents some years ago, didn't you? Or was it two other handsome men?

He was, like John Boles, neglected by the silent "drama." He has just come into his own along with the microphone. He's the toast of the film colony. Directors of musical films cry for him. Just a few short months ago he couldn't get a job. Now he has more than he can do.

Wait until you see him and hear him in "Bride of the Regiment." Now he's doing the lead in "Mlle. Modiste," and pretty soon he begins work in "Sweet Kitty Bellairs."

However, it is not alone his professional activities that interest us (and you, too, madame). I know you won't believe me when I tell you about it so if you'll send a self-addressed, stamped envelope I'll furnish signed affidavits to the effect that:

He is tall—six feet something or other—remarkably handsome and always well-tailored.

HE is consistently gallant, is never at a loss for a *Beau Brummel* phrase, but in no way suggests the smart-cracker.

His home is one of the most perfectly appointed and smoothly managed in the hills of the Beverlys.

His wines are excellent although he, himself, has never tasted them.

He is as natural as the key of C, and as charming as a Barrie hero.

Walter has the finest head of hair of any man on the screen. And here's his secret—he never washes it!

He keeps his scalp clean and in the pink of condition by brushing it several times a day. He uses an extra large brush with bristles of whalebone, about an inch and a half long. And he has been doing this for years.

He is still young, thirty-two or three, I should say, but is quite past the bounding juvenile stage (I'm sure that even at seventeen he was not a juvenile).

He is always master of himself in any situation whatsoever. (continued on next page)

Walter Pidgeon, like John Boles, is a singer who gave up his voice to be a nonentity in silent pictures. Then, again like John, the microphone gave him his big shot. Now he's a hit in singies, and a social lion!

(continued from preceding page)

I realize that all this sounds like Elinor Glyn in her most vibratory mood and I shed a tear for our good old pal, Cal York, who'll be laid up with writer's cramp from rumoring Walter's engagements. (No less than eight charming damosels have confided a secret crush and have offered me huge sums of money for an introduction.)

But Walter is a bit too suave, a bit too sure of himself to let the world in on his affairs of the heart. And surely he'll never talk about them. But he is, without doubt, the most attractive man who has graced these wan shores in many a California sun.

It is not snap judgment (at which, I must admit, I'm never any good, anyhow) that makes me go on like this. The first time I saw him was at the studio. He had been held up by a fencing lesson, and the studio commissary was crowded when we arrived. The only small table was occupied by a solitary and very grumpy looking gentleman.

"I'm afraid we'll have to sit at this big table," I said.

"Nonsense," said Pidgeon. "No such thing." He strode across the room to the man at the small table. What he said I don't know. I expected to see frowns and black looks cast in my direction. On the contrary, I watched Walter move the man—coffee cup, sandwich and all—to the big table while we took the small one. And the man smiled and bowed and seemed pleased that he had been allowed the privilege of moving.

A FEW evenings later we dined at Pidgeon's home. There were six of us (Walter seldom entertains a larger group). He opened the door himself.

"I haven't a butler," he said, "but I rather like doing the job myself."

The drawing room to which we were admitted is charming, with no hint of bizarre Hollywood in its dull drapes, its soft, rich rug and the excellent collection of books that line the walls.

At dinner (a perfect meal, sturdy and a bit English, for Walter was born in Canada) he managed the roast and the conversation with equal grace and facility.

Coffee and cigarettes were served in the living room.

And very good talk, not brilliant, not high-flown but just nice and comfortable.

The whole evening was touched, magically, by charm.

There was music later. Walter at the piano thumbing through various scores and singing whatever bits were called for. Wagner's "Dreams," Brahms' "Sapphic Ode," Schumann, Shubert, "Duna" and a Negro spiritual or two.

He insisted that we were leaving much too early when he took us to our cars.

It is difficult to set down such things on paper. Grace and charm don't behave very well on a typewriter, but as we left, one of the gentlemen who is inclined to grow a bit pedantic at times, said, "Now, that boy is a credit to the motion picture industry."

The phrase will suffice until there is a better one.

But he is more than that. He is one of Hollywood's most delightful young men.

His background is rather what you might expect. He went to war, served in the trenches and languished in a French hospital for eighteen months after the Armistice. When he was well enough to be up and about he came to the United States and put what money he had inherited into a brokerage firm in Boston. But music interested him more than bonds and he made annual trips to Europe to keep up his studies.

It was at this time that he married a non-professional girl who bore him one child, a girl, and died at the baby's birth.

IMMEDIATELY afterwards a financial crash wiped him out and ill health claimed him. But he isn't a quitter, and he went on with his music until he at last found an opportunity of going on concert tour with Elsie Janis. Later, he went into vaudeville with her and played in musical comedies and revues.

Several years ago when he came to Hollywood Walter was granted an interview with Louis B. Mayer.

"You're not an American, are you?" Mayer asked.

"No, I'm from Canada," said Walter.

"What part?"

"New Brunswick."

"What town?"

"St. Johns."

Mayer frowned. "Who told you to say that?"

Walter was puzzled. "I don't know what you mean."

"That's my home town," said Mayer. "I left when I was sixteen but I love the place. I thought maybe somebody tipped you off about it. But I see they didn't. Let's have lunch and talk about all the old friends."

But Walter's accomplishments were not appreciated in the studios.

With the coming of the sound film, however, his success was assured.

He is not only, as our friend said, a credit to the motion picture industry. In a town devoted to manners it is refreshing to find one person, at least, with manner!

JUN.

Short Subjects of the Month

THIS month PHOTOPLAY inaugurates its newest department, designed to make your talkie shopping easier and happier.

Each month we shall review outstanding short subjects of the hour. The coming of talkies has brought astounding advances in the field of short pictures, particularly in the comedy line.

This month we review the first comedy made with Mack Sennett's own natural-color process.

RADIO KISSES

Sennett-Educational

Not only is this Master Mack's first comedy made with his own Sennett-Color process, but he turns composer and writes its theme song, "Radio Kisses." The color is soft-toned. About a radio love-adviser who gets her own man.

HELLO, THAR!

Warner Vitaphone Variety

Eddie Buzzell, the little singing comedian, is the star of this two-reel satire on the Yukon's gold-rush days. It has a bit of a story, tied together with Eddie's well-told gags, old and new. Eddie even stops satirizing long enough to sing a song. Above average.

THE DRESDEN DOLLS

Paramount

The old collector's figurines come to life and cut up high jinks at midnight. "Gamby," toe dancer, formerly of Roxy's gang, a duo of comical eccentric dancers, and a bit of melody make this a bright one-reeler.

MARTINELLI

Warner-Vitaphone

While this is just ten minutes of "Faust" music by one of the leading tenors of the Metropolitan, it is worthy of note because it is another of the excellent and very popular Martinelli numbers. The tenor here is supported by two other singers as *Marguerite* and *Mephisto*.

JUN.

He Didn't Know How!

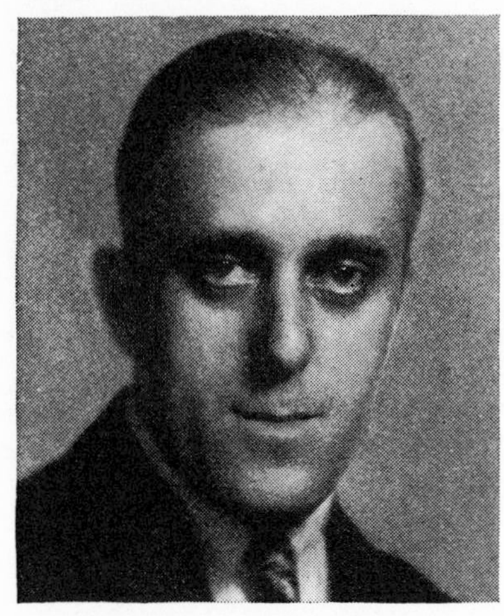

John Murray Anderson, who directed "King of Jazz"

But John Murray Anderson taught old movie dogs new tricks in making "King of Jazz"

By

Harry Lang

Paul Whiteman, big star of Universal's big revue

FIVE months ago he knew absolutely nothing about making moving pictures.

Then they came to him and said:

"See here, you. We want to make a picture that will make everybody in and out of moviedom sit up and yell for more. We want to do things with color and cameras and sound that have never been done before. We want to spend a million or two on it. We want *you* to direct it!"

Sounds crazy, doesn't it?—just like walking up to a paper-hanger and saying to him: "Say, we're going to produce a grand opera and we want you to be the star."

But it wasn't like that, exactly. You see, the man to whom the amazing proposal was made was John Murray Anderson—though a tyro in movies, one of the outstanding stage revue producers of the age.

Anderson was flabbergasted at the proposition. He knew his ignorance of movie-making.

"Well," he finally said, "you're taking an awful gamble on me. I don't know a thing about pictures. If you want to be that crazy, though, I'll go. But I've got to have absolute charge of the picture!"

"O. K.," said Universal. And so, strange as it is, they gave outright command of making a two-million-dollar movie to a man who didn't know any more about it than an Eskimo knows about sausage-grinding in Bavaria.

And *what* a picture John Murray Anderson has just finished! You probably know about it by now—the Paul Whiteman "King of Jazz" revue. It takes sound-screen revues by the scruff of the neck and yanks them leagues forward in progress.

This story is about some of the things John Murray Anderson has accomplished in "King of Jazz"—and his own explanations, reasons, ideas and philosophy. For while it's conceivable, though hardly probable, that you won't like the picture, it's nevertheless certain that you'll be amazed at it. And you ought to know about them.

In the first place, the "tricks"... ! Camera tricks, sound tricks, doubling tricks.

Anderson doesn't believe in this Hollywood hush about that sort of thing. He believes that the picture fan is intelligent enough to realize that if a picture is great, it's great no matter what was done in the studio to make it so. He doesn't "shush" everybody who tries to tell how this or that effect was produced. He tells you himself, and then tells you how it made the picture better.

And so he tells you that every musical number in "King of Jazz" is "ghosted." Another word for it is "dubbed." That is to say, the sound and the picture were shot at different times. When you see and hear Whiteman's band playing from the screen, or the *Rhythm Boys* hot-voicing it, you may as well know right now that the music or song you are hearing was recorded at an entirely different time and place than the picture in which you see them producing it!

Why?

"For two reasons," Anderson tells you. "In the first place, Whiteman, master of modern jazz music, felt that all sound recording should be done under the most perfect possible sound conditions. You can't get perfect sound conditions yet on a stage while you're shooting a big scene. There are poor acoustics, extraneous noises, the bad effect on the musicians produced by the watching off-stage workers.

"AND so when we made the sound-tracks we made them separately from the picture, just as we'd make phonograph records. We concentrated on making as perfect a record as possible. And we got sound results that will be evident to any hearer instantly.

"After we had the sound we shot the scene. With the sort of rhythm music in this picture, it was comparatively easy to get perfect synchronization. I defy anybody to detect, when 'King of Jazz' is seen, that sound and sight were *not* shot simultaneously.

"Another thing—the fact that the sound was already recorded when we made the picture gave me, as director, the same latitude the old-time silent picture director had. Though I was directing a sound film, I could nevertheless talk as much as I wanted to during shooting of the picture. Stage workers could make as much noise as they needed to; cameramen, technicians could all work undisturbed by the cramping necessity for silence. We were unhampered—and the result, I believe, shows as definitely in the excellence of the picture as in the perfection of the sound."

Anderson tells you about camera tricks.. *(continued on next page)*

THE Paul Whiteman picture, "King of Jazz," almost turned out to be another "Hell's Angels" for cost.

Universal hired Paul and his band before they had a story. Then they tried to write a love story around big Whiteman. Hollywood roared. Thousands of dollars dribbled out, and still no picture.

Then they hired John Murray Anderson, stage revue producer, who knew nothing about pictures.

Well, the "film ignoramus" has finished "King of Jazz." It cost $2,000,000, but Universal says they'll get their money back.

Read this story of John Murray Anderson and his $2,000,000 beauty!

(continued from preceding page)

"The film is full of them," he says, blandly, while horrified press-agents stand by aghast. "I've tried to crowd as many camera tricks in as I could—not for the sake of doing tricks, but only because I wanted to get effects that make the picture more entertaining."

For instance, here are some of the stunts—

AT Whiteman's first entrance, he carries a suitcase. He opens the suitcase—and his famous band steps out and plays for you.

In the "Rhapsody in Blue" number, the scene opens with a pianist playing the Gershwin gem.

The piano grows and grows and grows, until finally it's so big that the top opens up and out pops Paul and his band and a flock of chorus girls who dance the tune on the keys.

That for tricks.

Now here's another thing for which Anderson deserves approbation:

For the first time he has made extensive use of projected color in Technicolor photography. Let's explain that.

Heretofore, they have photographed colored costumes and sets under white light. But Anderson snapped his fingers and said: "Why can't we shoot colored lights?"—the same as the spotlights and floodlights on the stage, to which he had been accustomed.

So they tried it.

"—and I want to say right here," Anderson interpolates, "that in all these new things I had the whole-hearted cooperation of our technicians. When I suggested trying something that hadn't been done in pictures before, they didn't yell 'It can't be done!' Instead, they did it!"

So in "King of Jazz," you'll see the use of colored lights—green, and red, and blue. You'll see iridescent effects that are startling. You'll see colors changing—colors of costumes, of sets; colors on players' faces.

A DANCER, his body painted brilliant black, like patent leather, dances atop a huge drum. From one side, a red light is focused on him; from the other, a green glare; from in front, a white ray.

And, as a result, on the background behind the dancer will appear three dancing shadows—one black, one red, and one green.

It is the old "multiple shadow" effect—a thing that has bothered directors before and caused more light-moving to get rid of it than a little. But Anderson, instead of trying to get away from the multiple shadows, used them!

Of course, Anderson has used things that were not new to the pictures—but how he has used them! In the Whiteman picture, there are the "Gold Set" in which the beautiful "Melting Pot" sequence is played; the "Rhapsody in Blue" set, in which a gigantic blue piano is set on a mirror-like floor, backgrounded against a glittering silver drop, and trick sets in which things move and change until you wonder how they do it.

NOW, let Anderson explain how he feels about it all. A lifetime in the theater has trained him in stage ideas. Yet he's not what you would expect to find. He's a quiet-spoken man who thinks. He looks ahead. He anticipates, and he prophesies. He sees a dying theater, and a new art that will arise out of what the screen is now going through.

"The theater," he says, "is fading into insignificance. When we get stereoscopic film, together with the improved sound that is coming, and the new color achievements that are inevitable, things will be possible to the camera to which the stage could never hope to aspire.

"The man who doesn't realize the importance of the screen now is just a fool. The theater man who comes to the screen and tries to bring the limited teachings of the stage with him is also foolish.

"A new type of entertainment is springing up. The actor or actress trained in stage artificiality is doomed. Singers will arise who could never get anywhere on the stage, for in the sound pictures, volume is not necessary; the recording provides that artificially. Quality of voice will rule, not quantity. I, if I make more pictures, will cast not from the stage, but from players who know the screen.

"Color will make the screen become to the director like the canvas to the artist. Subtleties of color which are barely approximated on the stage will be used to the utmost on the screen.

"And the legitimate stage, except in New York, will die. For who in the world will pay five or six dollars to see a revue done on the stage with shoddy scenery, second-rate actors and second-rate musicians, when for less than a dollar they can see a show like 'The Rogue Song'—and greater ones in the future? The stage will die because it simply won't be able to compete.

"WHEN I came here, ignorant of pictures but trained in everything of the stage, I cast all that aside. I started with no idea of making a stage revue, but I did have a definite idea of doing things not possible on the stage. To try to bring the artificiality of the theater to the screen is drivel. In a stage revue, the story is merely stupidity on which one hangs the numbers; but on the screen, you've got to have a story—a real story—in addition to the numbers.

"What the screen will bring in the future—pictures, colors, sound—is unimaginable. We can only guess at it. Already, I have some ideas for another picture which would now, if I told them, sound like impossible imaginings. But wait . . ."

JUN.

These New Faces

Watch for This Each Month

RICHARD KEENE ("Happy Days," Fox) is another young song and dance man lured from the Broadway stage by the singies. Dick appeared in innumerable musical shows in New York, but Fox snared him and put him under contract. He made his picture début in "Big Time," and since that big time has played in "Why Leave Home," "The Big Party" and "The Golden Calf."

"GINGER" ROGERS ("Young Man of Manhattan," Paramount) is an Independence, Mo., girl who was discovered by Paul Ash, and was a sensation singing in Publix presentations. Then she went into "Top Speed," a Broadway musical show, and scored again. Paramount, who found Helen Kane the same way, lost no time in getting "Ginger" on the dotted line.

HARRY RICHMAN ("Puttin' on the Ritz," United Artists) has been in the headlines for months as the "fiance" of Clara Bow. Harry got his start in New York singing in night clubs, several years ago. Then for two seasons he scored heavily singing the hit songs in George White's "Scandals." Now he has his own night spot, "The Club Richman."

ALLAN PRIOR ("Bride of the Regiment," First National) has for some years been one of the leading lights in American operetta, notably those produced by the Messrs. Shubert during the recent operetta vogue. He did his best singing in "The Song of Love," done five years ago. With the present musical craze in pictures, it was certain Allan would be heard.

JOBYNA HOWLAND ("Honey," Paramount) is one of the best known comediennes on the comedy stage. Over six feet tall, she was first famous for her work in Belasco's stage production of "The Gold Diggers," with Ina Claire. Later, she went to London for the same rôle. She played in the Eddie Cantor show, "Kid Boots," for three entire seasons.

JUN.

☆ *KING OF JAZZ—Universal*

HERE'S that Paul Whiteman revue at last—and when fans fight over which revue is best, this will have heavy backing! Two factors greaten it—Whiteman's music, and the daring innovations wrought for the screen by Stage Director John Murray Anderson. In color, lighting, spectacle and photography he has opened new fields.

Items: Gershwin's "Rhapsody in Blue" is tremendously played and pictured. How John Boles and male chorus sing that "Song of the Dawn"! Gorgeous beauty in the Wedding Veil sequence. For sheer spectacle, the Melting Pot finale can't be beaten. Jeanette Loff blondely lovely; John Boles lustily vocal; William Kent freshly comic. Whiteman's Band *is* great!—and those Rhythm Boys . . . !

If you like revues—oh boy!

"KING OF JAZZ"—UNIVERSAL.—Scenario by Edward T. Lowe. Dialogue by Charles McArthur. Directed by John Murray Anderson. The cast: Paul Whiteman and his band, John Boles, Jeanette Loff, Laura La Plante, Charlie Murray, George Sidney, Glenn Tryon, Merna Kennedy, Billy Kent, Grace Hayes, Jeanie Lang, The Sisters G, Charles Giles, Frank Leslie, The Brox Sisters, Charles Irwin, Al Norman, Paul Howard, Stanley Smith, Jacques Cartier, Paul Whiteman Rhythm Boys, Marian Statler and Don Rose; The Tommy Atkins Sextette, Kathryn Crawford, and The Russell Markert Dancers.

JUN.

HOLD EVERYTHING—Warners

THIS is a patchwork quilt, interesting only in spots. Joe E. Brown is swell as the slug-nutty prize fighter, Winnie Lightner has some snappy songs, and Georges Carpentier looks good in the boxing ring. Otherwise it lacks whatever made it a hit on Broadway when it was a show. It was filmed several months ago, and you'll be shocked to see the girls in knee dresses.

"HOLD EVERYTHING"—WARNERS.—From the play by B. G. De Sylva and John McGowan. Adapted by Robert Lord. Directed by Roy Del Ruth. The cast: *Gink Schiner*, Joe E. Brown; *Toots Breen*, Winnie Lightner; *Georges La Verne*, Georges Carpentier; *Sue Burke*, Sally O'Neil; *Pop O'Keefe*, Edmund Breese; *Nosey Bartlett*, Bert Roach; *Norine Lloyd*, Dorothy Revier; *Murph Levy*, Jack Curtis; *Bob Morgan*, Tony Stabenau; *Dan Larkin*, Lew Harvey; *The Kicker*, Jimmie Quinn.

JUN.

SHOW GIRL IN HOLLYWOOD—First National

ALICE WHITE'S best talkie, without a quibble! McEvoy's story of the adventures of a little New York show girl in movieland fits this cute child to perfection, and she plays it grandly. A lot of interesting back-set stuff, with plenty of laughs in the satire on studio ways. Some magnificent Technicolor, and a song or so. This is first-rate entertainment, in spite of a soggy spot or two.

"SHOW GIRL IN HOLLYWOOD"—FIRST NATIONAL.—From the story by J. P. McEvoy. Adapted by Harvey Thew. Directed by Mervyn LeRoy. The cast: *Dixie Dugan*, Alice White; *Jimmy Doyle*, Jack Mulhall; *Sam Otis, producer*, Ford Sterling; *Donna Harris*, Blanche Sweet; *Frank Buelow, director*, John Miljan; *Nebbick's secretary*, Virginia Sale; *Office Boy*, Spec O'Donnell; *Kramer*, Lee Shumway; *Bing*, Herman Bing.

JUN.

SAFETY IN NUMBERS—Paramount

PEACHES-AN'-CREAM for the Buddy Rogers fans. The other three or four people in America will probably like it, too. Buddy plays a $25,000,000 heir who's put by his worldly-wise uncle in care of three good little "Follies" girls for an education. He gets it, and one of the girls for good measure. Buddy sings a half dozen songs. One number is headed for a hit. It is called "The Pick-Up."

"SAFETY IN NUMBERS"—PARAMOUNT.—From the story by George Marion, Jr. and Percy Heath. Scenario by Marion Dix. Directed by Victor Schertzinger. The cast: *William Butler Reynolds*, Charles "Buddy" Rogers; *Jacqueline*, Kathryn Crawford; *Maxine*, Josephine Dunn; *Pauline*, Carol Lombard; *Cleo Carewe*, Geneva Mitchell; *Bertram Shipiro*, Roscoe Karns; *Phil Kempton*, Francis MacDonald; *Alma McGregor*, Virginia Bruce; *F. Carstair Reynolds*, Richard Tucker; *Jules*, Raoul Paoli; *Commodore Brinker*, Lawrence Grant; *Messaline*, Louise Beavers.

JUN.

THE CUCKOOS—Radio Pictures

CHECK your critical goggles and roar at this nonsensical musical comedy. It features Bert Wheeler and Robert Woolsey, who hit a screen high in "Rio Rita." It's a big show, too, with all the trimmings, including some elegant playing by Dorothy Lee and Jobyna Howland. You'll take home one fine tune, "I Love You So Much." But oh, what laughs! Great for spring fever.

"CUCKOOS, THE"—RADIO PICTURES.—From the musical comedy "The Ramblers" by Guy Bolton, Harry Ruby and Bert Kalmar. Adapted by Cy Woods. Directed by Paul Sloane. The cast: *Sparrow*, Bert Wheeler; *Professor Bird*, Robert Woolsey; *Ruth*, June Clyde; *Billy*, Hugh Trevor; *Anita*, Dorothy Lee; *The Baron*, Ivan Lebedeff; *Gypsy Queen*, Marguerita Padula; *Julius*, Mitchell Lewis; *Fannie Hurst*, Jobyna Howland.

JUN.

MAMMY—Warners

AGAIN Al Jolson, one of the world's greatest entertainers, rises above his story to make an entertaining movie, singing good Irving Berlin songs. "Mammy" is a minstrel piece, with good performances by Lois Moran, Lowell Sherman and Louise Dresser backing up the star. Louise is the mammy. A good spot of Technicolor, and some tunes that leave the theater with you. Good Jolson!

"MAMMY"—WARNERS.—Brom the story by Irving Berlin. Adapted by L. G. Rigby. Directed by Michael Curtiz. The cast: *Al Fuller*, Al Jolson; *Nora Meadows*, Lois Moran; *Mrs. Fuller*, Louise Dresser; *Westy*, Lowell Sherman; *Meadows*, Hobart Bosworth; *Slats*, Tully Marshall; *Tambo*, Mitchell Lewis; *Sheriff*, Jack Curtis; *Pig Eyes*, Stanley Fields; *Props*, Ray Cooke.

JUN.

SPRING IS HERE—First National

AT last Ford Sterling gets a chance to do his stuff in a very big way, and Louise Fazenda gives a priceless characterization as the hen-pecked wife. Beyond this, the picture is an average musical comedy. The featured players are Bernice Claire and Alexander Gray. Both these people have lovely voices, and all the music of the original show is retained and well recorded. Excellent entertainment.

"SPRING IS HERE"—FIRST NATIONAL.—From the musical play by Owen Davis. Adapted by James A. Starr. Directed by John Francis Dillon. The cast: *Steve Alden*, Lawrence Gray; *Terry Clayton*, Alexander Gray; *Betty Braley*, Bernice Claire; *Emily Braley*, Louise Fazenda; *Peter Braley*, Ford Sterling; *Rita Clayton*, Natalie Moorehead; *Mary Jane Braley*, Inez Courtney; *Stacy Hayden*, Frank Albertson.

JUN.

CAPTAIN OF THE GUARD—Universal

THEY went and spoiled a thrilling and massive picture of the birth of the *Marseillaise* with some trite, gooey bits, and a jumbled story. But its thundering mobs race the pulse, and John Boles sings superbly and acts well. Laura La Plante does what she can with a part that doesn't fit. Charles Wakefield Cadman supplies some good tunes. Stunning in spots, but it might have been great.

"CAPTAIN OF THE GUARD"—UNIVERSAL.—From the story by Houston Branch. Adapted by Arthur Ripley. Directed by John S. Robertson. The cast: *Marie Marnay*, Laura La Plante; *Rouget de L'Isle*, John Boles; *Bazin*, Sam De Grasse; *Marnay*, James Marcus; *Colonel of Hussars*, Lionel Belmore; *Louis XVI*, Stuart Holmes; *Marie Antoinette*, Evelyn Hall; *Magistrate*, Claude Fleming; *Piette*, Murdock MacQuarrie; *Danton*, Richard Cramer; *Materoun*, Harry Burkhardt; *Robespierre*, George Hackathorne; *Priest*, De Witt Jennings.

JUN.

ROUGH ROMANCE—Fox

"ROUGH ROMANCE" is a good title for this. The edges are rough too. It's all about the goings on of lumberjacks in the Oregon forest. Scenery is grand but nature gets the credit for that. George O'Brien's chest is seen to good advantage and Helen Chandler goes Gish. Poor Antonio Moreno is lost as the rough villain. Time is taken for a few chorus routines. Boop-a-doop. It doesn't help a bit.

"ROUGH ROMANCE"—Fox.—From the story by Kenneth B. Clarke. Scenario by Elliott Lester. Directed by A. F. Erickson. The cast: *Billy West*, George O'Brien; *Marna Reynolds*, Helen Chandler; *Loup LaTour*, Antonio Moreno; *Sheriff Milt Powers*, Roy Stewart; *Chick Carson*, Harry Cording; *Dad Reynolds*, David Hartford; *Laramie*, Eddie Borden; *Flossie*, Noel Francis; *Pop Nichols*, Frank Lanning.

JUN.

A composer goes wild. Director Allan Dwan and Gloria Swanson don't seem to care for the tunes pounded out by Vincent Youmans, who is doing the music for her new film, "What a Widow"

JUN.

SUNNY SKIES—Tiffany Productions

MOVIE college students are at it again. Drinking and loving and making touchdowns in the last minute of play. You can almost bear it until Benny Rubin starts getting pathetic and his pal gives him a blood transfusion. Then you've just got to get away from it all. Couple of good tunes are "Wanna Find a Boy" and "Must Be Love."

"SUNNY SKIES"—TIFFANY PRODUCTIONS.—From the story by A. P. Younger. Continuity by Earl Snell. Directed by Norman Taurog. The cast: *Benny Krantz*, Benny Rubin; *Mary Norris*, Marceline Day; *Jim Grant*, Rex Lease; *Doris*, Marjorie Kane; *Isadore Krantz*, Harry Lee; *College Widow*, Greta Granstedt; *Stubble*, Wesley Barry; *Dave*, Robert Randall; *Smith*, James Wilcox.

JUN.

Amos 'n' Andy, in the flesh and without the burnt cork. The famous radio team has just signed to make a feature comedy for Radio Pictures, for plenty money. Their real names, as pictured, are Freeman F. Gosden (Amos), of Richmond, Va., and Charles J. Correll (Andy), of Peoria, Ill. A year ago they were getting $100 a week

JUL.

THE Girls and the Big Bull Fiddle—one of the remarkable chorus numbers in Metro-Goldwyn-Mayer's old-timers' revue called, during its production, "The March of Time." With the dancing girls on the bridge in the center, and the violin chorus below, it's a thrilling bit of music in motion

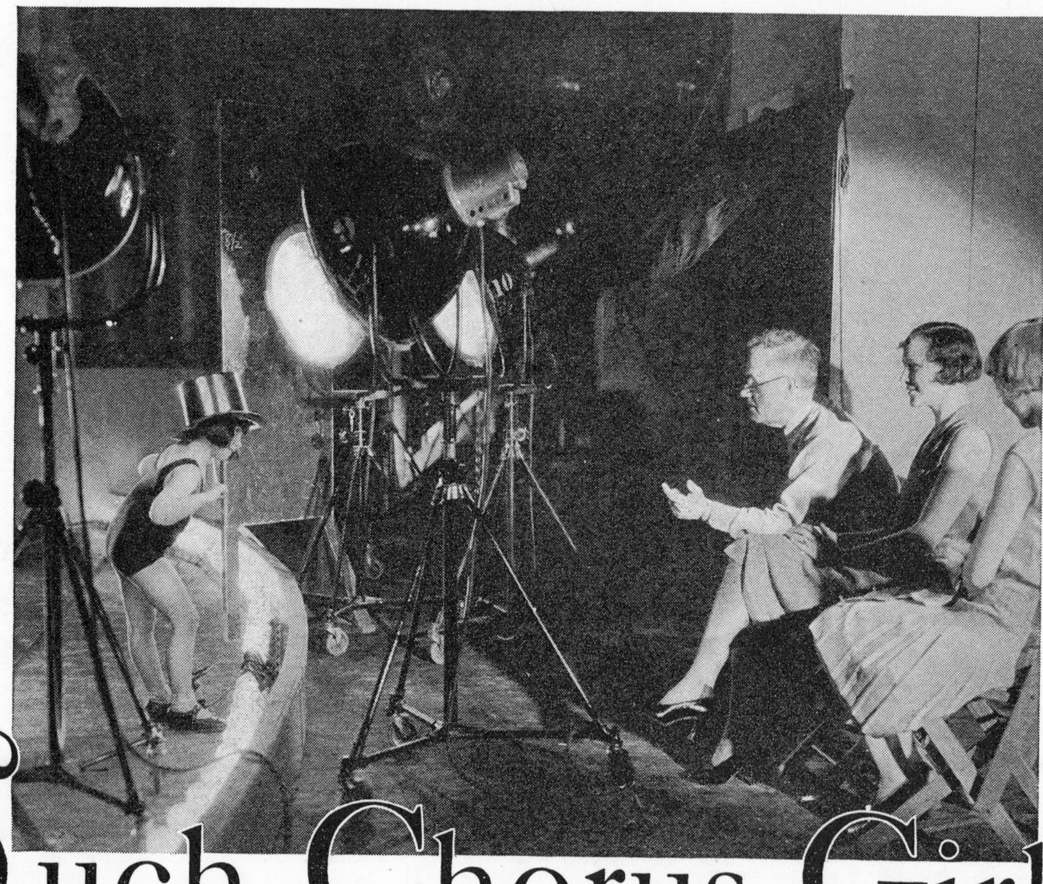

Such Chorus Girls!

When the ice cream wagon comes around they all quit work

THERE are three hundred chorus girls in Hollywood who:

—never appear in public without their mothers

—have never smoked a cigarette

—have never all their lives known the taste of liquor or gone to wild parties

—are in bed every night at eight-thirty or even before that

—have never been inside a night club or a speakeasy

—have never had their pictures in the Sunday supplements

—wouldn't know a butter and egg man even if they saw one

—have never been mixed up in any sort of nasty scandal

And, what's more, they're all young and beautiful!

Ah-ha, you doubt it! Very well, you old cynic! These little paragons of virtue are the Meglin Kiddies, who turn out dancing and singing revues. The babes have already made three two-reelers, "The Big Revue," "Kiddie Kabaret," and "Hello, Sunshine." They're going to make a lot more, for they sing, they dance, they play musical instruments and they even master the ceremonies.

Ethel Meglin started it some years ago by sending out kid vaudeville acts, and a few months ago Jules Burnstein saw the possibility of film material and signed them all up.

No child is over twelve. The youngest ones are four, and in that line of capering kids there are, no doubt, many stars of the future.

WHEN there are two hundred children on the set there are twenty teachers who instruct them in the more prosaic reading, writing and arithmetic between waltz clogs and flip flops. They would work until they dropped—these kids—but they're only allowed to dance for four hours at a time. Then they must rest for two. If you think they can't do anything the grown-ups can do, you should see the way they dash off cart-wheels and nip-ups.

Because it is everybody's aim to keep them as natural and unspoiled as possible they are allowed the liberty of the lot. But when Director Dallas Fitzgerald wants them together he has the orchestra start playing their numbers. They come quickly enough then. They're afraid of missing something.

The other day, right in the midst of a scene, they heard the tinkle of an ice cream wagon. Two seconds later the set was deserted and until every chocolate and strawberry cone was finished they could not be persuaded to return. Real chorus girls are lured by *pâté de foie gras* and Lobster Newburgh. A nice gumdrop will work havoc with the Meglin kiddies.

Director Fitzgerald says: "I never want to direct another grown-up. These kids are so easy to handle. They don't get moody or cross, and I've only had one case of temperament. We took two kids out and gave them a specialty. They thought they were prima donnas and didn't want to work in the line. But we fixed that up all right. You can't spank a temperamental adult star, you see.

"I keep the kids from being spoiled by keeping them at their distance, by not making too much of them. Kids are smarter than you think and they're quick to catch on. They know just by a look in my eye when they're getting too fresh."

MRS. MEGLIN declares that it takes about three months to get a youngster who is bright and quick ready for the most difficult chorus work. In two weeks she can tell whether or not the child has ability.

The mothers are not allowed in the rehearsal hall, but they flock on the set to watch their offspring go through their paces. The mamas are as appreciative of talent as the old-fashioned bald-headed row at the "Follies."

And these babies can do anything, from the most difficult toe work to the peppiest jazz numbers.

Here are the potential Garbos, the Chattertons, the Bows of 1940 and 1950. Their dancing feet can't get too far off the ground with Director Fitzgerald to keep them in place. But their bright eyes are already focused on the stars—and they mean to be numbered among them, someday when they, too, are grown-up ladies.

SHE came to light in "The Marriage Playground." She was a hit in "Honey," with her grand clowning. And in "Paramount on Parade" she brings houses tumbling down with her Chevalier impersonation. And here is Mitzi Green, just nine, in her own Hollywood garden

Inside the Monitor Room

By
Elaine
Ogden

Here he sits, fussing with his gadgets high above the set—the all-powerful Man in the Monitor Room, who sees that the voices of the players come out of the horn just as sweetly as they went into the microphone. He is the uncrowned ruler of the studios, these talkie days

IN a little room perched high above the sound stage, away from the temperament and excitement and petty chatter of the set, overlooking the beauty and glamour of the studio world, sits a solitary man anxiously toying with what appear to be four or five radio dials.

Technically, he is known as a "mixer."

They call him God around the studios and a god indeed he is, since he controls the destinies of the famous ones of filmdom. All the strange and beautiful favorites who delight you are in his power. He is the *Jove* of Hollywood, the *Wotan* of the screen world. He sits high above the stars and looks down upon them.

This little room, which contains only him and a loud speaker, is called a monitor room. It is, really, Mount Olympus and Valhalla. He sits before his row of dials. He turns one ever so slightly. He turns another. The voices from the stage below thunder out at him. He can make or break the stars.

I don't pretend to know how it's done, but I do know that that little room is more dramatic and exciting than the satin-draped dressing rooms of the stars, or the mahogany-paneled conference chambers of the executives. Fate and the mixer enact their rôles.

THIS mixer fellow is the man of the moment.

I can't go into technicalities. The effort I made to understand and untangle the maze of such scientific phrases as "high and low frequency," "controls," "re-recording" and the rest would give me a worse headache than Hollywood gin. I can't tell you why the mixer controls the voice fate of the stars. And, although the sound engineers are very fussy about having their deeds reported correctly, I can make no attempt at it.

I know only this, that I've sat breathless in that little monitor room (approached by a flight of steep stairs, barren except for the loud speaker) and felt as if I were in the presence of Fate.

When you're down on the set below you may glance up and see the mixer sitting there, an ordinary enough looking worker behind his double plate glass window. But when you're there with him, looking down upon that same set, hearing the voices of the great ones below, you realize the power, drama and strange beauty—beautiful because of its very force—of the monitor room. You know that by a touch the mixer can make them. By another touch he can break them. He has more power than the camera man ever had.

Meet the new god of the studios. We unlock the door of the mystery room of the talkie stages and show you the man inside —the magician who can make or break the voices of the stars

For the voice is more important than the face in these trying days. Time was when the stars brought large red apples daily to their favorite cameraman. He was master then. Little extra girls begged for his advice about make-up and angles. Great actresses sought him out for consultations.

For he—this cameraman—could photograph a mediocre face and make it look like an angel's. By a simple twist of the lights he could turn the divine profile of a Helen of Troy into a hateful caricature.

The cameraman still has his place, of course, but the voice has superseded the face. It is that little man who photographs the voice, the mixer, who is the big shot at the studios now.

In the old days the stars used to insist on their favorite cameraman. Now they struggle for the best mixer. Ramon Novarro has Ralph Shugart mix all his talking pictures. He will have no other. And, because Ramon is a technician as well as an artist, he works hand and hand with his mixer, and seeks him out for his words of wisdom.

Like the once all-powerful cameraman, the mixer has no illusions. He knows what he can and can't do with the voices in his power. He knows all the little speech foibles and vanities of the stars. He knows that he controls their destinies and could, if he chose, ruin any scene for them.

HE'S a hard-boiled guy, this god of the high places.

With very few exceptions, the mixer likes a natural voice. Maybe you've welcomed the horde of new stage folk with open arms. As a rule they are, to the mixer, just another monkey wrench in the machinery.

These "legit" people are always talking to that slightly deaf old gentleman in the last row of the gallery. They have been taught for years to throw their voices, to give volume. That's bad on the sensitive ears of the microphone. The mixer will give them all the volume they need if they'll let him. That's his little job.

As a rule, the stage people are arbitrary. They feel that they have nothing to learn. And, as a matter of fact, they have more to overcome than the screen folk. They must forget entirely the old technique. The sons and daughters of Hollywood are natural. They don't go tossing their voices all over the place.

The great stage stars, the ones who have carved their particular niches in celluloid, are the ones who have worked with the mixers and have taken their sound advice (no pun, either, there you!).

Paul Neil was the recording man on Lawrence Tibbett's "The Rogue Song." The volume of the baritone's notes shattered many a sensitive tube. Nothing, apparently, could be done about it, until at last Neil hit upon this simple and efficacious method.

"I PLACED my microphones as best I could," he said. "I put the dials at what I thought the proper place. Then I went to the other side of the room, stopped up my ears and trusted to God. That's all you can do with Tibbett." And that you may take with a grain of salt, because Neil did a careful and superb job with "The Rogue Song."

Franklin Hansen, now head mixer at Paramount, who was responsible for the sound in "The Vagabond King," had like trouble with Dennis King. King is, by far, the most dramatic actor on the lot. Sometimes in just one scene his voice ranges from the lowest whisper to the highest shout, and if he were held down, if he were told to be more careful, the beauty and dramatic power of his performance would be gone. So it is the mixer's job to follow him and record him properly. The mixer must catch the low whisper as well as the high notes.

During rehearsals the mixer saw about what was expected and worked the dials accordingly, but King is an artist, an emotional artist, and he never did the scene twice alike. The mixer had to be just one jump ahead of him and try to figure out his next vocal move.

Maurice Chevalier, too, was difficult. He spoke his lines very low and quietly. He sang his songs loudly. But Ernst Lubitsch, who directed "The Love Parade," is a careful workman. He demanded absolute perfection. He insisted that every word be sharp and distinct and nothing was too difficult for him to attempt. *(continued on next page)*

(continued from preceding page)

Greta Garbo has an almost perfect microphone voice—if there is such a thing. Her pitch is low, her diction clear. The mixer on her set has a Roman holiday. She speaks slowly, too, which is a great help.

IN fact, the bit players and extras with a line to read give more trouble than the stars. These folk are usually nervous and tense, eager to make a good impression on the director. They speak too loudly, they hurry over their lines. The great emotional actors and actresses—those volatile, intense ones—are also difficult.

Although Renee Adoree's voice, in the last picture she did before she went to the sanitarium, is clear and distinct, she is such an *artiste*, she throws herself so completely into her rôle, that she forgets the mike, and the mixer must be continually on the alert to record her correctly. But many little tricks can be done. In a small way you've done them yourself on your own radio. You know how you can increase and decrease the volume and tune out other sounds. That is the mixer's job.

Ruth Chatterton came to the studio one day with a bad cold. She could hardly speak above a whisper. It was the mixer's task to give her the volume she lacked. He did.

When Billy Haines began to talk on the screen it was discovered that his voice recorded a couple of tones lower than it actually was. The mixer had to bring that up.

When Buster Keaton worked in a Spanish version sometimes his accent was not perfect, so the mixer slurred it a trifle, as a cameraman soft focuses a wrinkled face and makes it look beautiful.

Clara Bow, by the way, gives the mixers very little trouble, as she speaks plainly and naturally.

You might imagine that the people who have good radio voices also have fine screen tones. Not necessarily! At the radio station you talk directly into the microphone. At the studio the little instrument of torture is many feet away. Morton Downey, who has a leading rôle in Eddie Goulding's picture, "The Devil's Holiday," came through much better when his mouth was directly in front of the mike than when it was farther away, but since he must be photographed as well as heard, the microphone had to be in its proper place.

Helen Kane, the boop-oop-a-doop girl, suffered in like fashion. Her voice is not loud and her radio and phonograph recording training did not help her on the sound stages.

The mixer, or, as some studios call him, the recordist (he's still just a mixer to you) must please a much more discriminating audience than the cameraman. After all, the public is sound-wise. You know a good tone when you get it on your radio. You've been educated up to recording, whereas, with the exception of a few amateur photographers, the public does not pay a lot of attention to good and bad camera work.

As a rule, any voice that is pleasing to the ear is pleasing to the microphone. A very bad voice will record badly no matter how skilled the mixer may be. The god of the high place is not a wizard after all. He can only ruin a good voice or make an ordinary one better. Several famous actors and actresses have failed before the microphone, just as many beautiful women will not photograph. One voice of a beautiful blonde star could not be helped with any amount of skilful mixing.

The position of the mike on the set is of utmost importance, as is the volume control.

Well, then, from whence come these lords of destiny? What are their requirements? How do they get like that? Theirs must be a combination of many talents.

First of all, they must have a basic knowledge of sound technique, and after that they must have good taste and a knowledge of dramatics. They must know the lines and the music of a film as well as the players do, for it is their duty to follow every word and to pick up every cue from the various microphones placed about the set. And they must also give life and color to the recording.

A man's voice is deeper than a woman's. If a mixer recorded the two the same, the effect would be wrong. It is his job to know what is expected from each scene.

SOME mixers have worked up from other studio jobs. You'll find among them ex-cameramen, "still" men and actors. But, for the most part, they have been connected with radio broadcasting. This is good training if they bring along artistic ability.

So all those boxes of candy in the stars' dressing rooms and all those Christmas ties are little gifts to be taken to the gods. The cameraman is still on the set, but his nose is out of joint.

The red apples, these days, are for the mixer man who sits above the set all day long and listens to the voices of the great.

JUL.

Short Subjects *of the* Month

HUMANETTES, NO. 1

Radio Pictures

A decided novelty. A glorified puppet-show, with your favorite's head on the puppet's neck. The first one has Benny Rubin as star of a sort of revue, with a row of snappy black-outs. Benny is a dancing doll, and June Clyde and Raymond Maurel, singer, are in it. These should click.

THE REDHEADS

Pathe

A musical comedy squeezed into two reels. Nat Carr is the leading comic and Charles Kaley the handsome juvenile, and a chorus of pretty girls disport leggily. It moves fast, has a pretty song or two, and a few laughs. Just an in-and-outer.

ARIA FROM AIDA

Warners—Vitaphone

This short operatic number is reviewed here because it is the eleventh recorded by the great Martinelli of the Metropolitan! It was Martinelli who made the "Pagliacci" short which was on the first Vitaphone program ever shown. And the new "Aida" aria is grand.

JUL.

WAR broke out between two famous comedians not long ago. So far no peace treaty has been signed, and a smack on the nose may come any day.

One of the most noted low comics on the New York stage is Mr. Bert Lahr. This year he is a riot in a musical comedy, "Flying High." Last season he mowed down the yeomanry in "Hold Everything" on the stage.

Comes Mr. Joe E. Brown playing the same part in the talkie version of the same show. Mr. Lahr charges, with some show of justice, that Mr. Brown has lifted many of his mannerisms, "unique expressions" and bits of business. This imperils, says Mr. Lahr, his future in the talkies, as film fans who do not yet know would say, after seeing "Hold Everything" on the screen, that he is just copying the methods of Mr. Brown.

So there's a big mad on, and I'd like to be around when they meet. Mr. Lahr is one of the funniest men in America. And I have a hunch he is in strict training for his meeting up with Mr. Brown.

JUL.

June Clyde and Arthur Lake, supported by a clever chorus, prove how appropriate is the title of that sparkling Radio Picture, "Tanned Legs"

JUL.

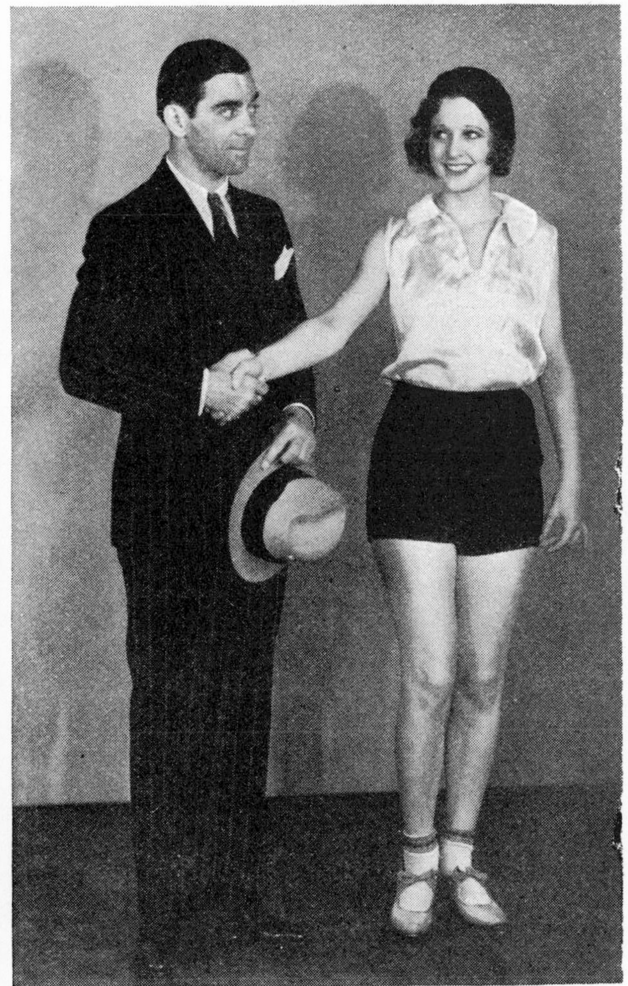

The famous Eddie Cantor with a very lucky girl. This is Eleanor Hunt, the red-headed lady of the ensemble who was taken from the chorus to play the ingénue lead in the Ziegfeld-Goldwyn-Cantor film "Whoopee"

JUL.

WOMEN EVERYWHERE—Fox

J. HAROLD MURRAY has a voice that can't fail to charm you. This story deals with him as a Yankee sailor, rescued from death for gun-running by a French girl singer, Fifi Dorsay. Scenes are laid in North Africa. Murray is worth going to see and hear and Fifi is always entertaining.

"WOMEN EVERYWHERE"—Fox.—From the story by George Grossmith and Zolton Korda. Continuity by Harlan Thompson and Lajos Biro. Directed by Alexander Korda. The cast: *Charles Jackson*, J. Harold Murray; *Lili LaFleur*, Fifi Dorsay; *Aristide Brown*, George Grossmith; *Zephyrine*, Rose Dione; *Sam Jones*, Clyde Cook; *Michel Kopulos*, Ralph Kellard.

BORN to SING!

By
Marquis
Busby

Alexander Gray and Bernice Claire playing a scene together. Talk of a romance between them is very trying, they say

Alexander Gray gave up the gadgets of engineering for the High C's

ALEXANDER GRAY comes from a long line of Pennsylvania Scotch Presbyterians, pretty stern, uncompromising folk.

But by every right Alexander Gray should be a confirmed fatalist. Fate has ruled his professional career, first on the stage and now in Hollywood.

It has been a long chain of circumstances that has brought him to Hollywood, each one linked to the other, and every one related.

Marilyn Miller, the graceful little prima donna of the Ziegfeld pageants of pulchritude, liked Alexander Gray better than any of her leading men. When she came West to make the Vitaphone production of "Sally" she requested that Gray sing opposite her. He had appeared with her in the stage production.

Gray made his test in New York, and because he didn't want to work alone, he persuaded Bernice Claire to appear with him. Bernice and he had appeared together as *Margot* and the *Red Shadow* in "The Desert Song." Bernice had no thoughts of a picture career, but she won a contract on the strength of her appearance in Gray's test.

Now, because they do not have many friends in Hollywood, Bernice and he are occasionally seen together. Not in the night clubs and theaters, but at quiet restaurants. Accordingly, Hollywood, running true to time-hallowed tradition, has begun to scent a romance. Some of the hardier have even rumored an engagement.

Gray is not particularly pleased with the gossip that links their names.

"Bernice is my friend, one of my best friends," he said. "Fate threw us together at a very trying time for both of us. She came into the cast of 'The Desert Song' while we were playing on the road. It was her first important stage appearance, and she was facing a terrific test. The rest of the cast had been playing together for many months, and they weren't anxious to rehearse with a newcomer. I tried to help her. I knew what she was up against. I went into the production of 'Sally' under the same circumstances. I don't mean that my assistance meant much to Bernice. She worked things out for herself.

"Bernice, her brother, my wife and I became very good friends. After a long engagement in Chicago, the company was going on to Pittsburgh for a run. My wife decided to drive my car East. Bernice and I had to travel with the troupe. I persuaded her brother to accompany my wife and relieve her at the wheel.

"One afternoon, as we finished a matinée, word came of the terrible accident in a little Ohio town. My wife had been killed. Bernice's brother was very badly injured. We left in a few hours in a taxicab for Ohio, the only transportation we could get. It was a ghastly ride. I knew what was ahead of me. Bernice didn't know whether she would find her brother alive or not.

"People who are together at times like that usually become close friends. There is a bond of sympathy and understanding. We have worked together in 'No, No, Nanette' out here. Sometimes we go out together. Never to dancing places. I used to like to dance, but not since my wife has gone.

"I'm not particularly pleased that people are suggesting that I could have another romance so soon—it has only been a little more than a year. I don't believe that I shall ever marry again. I suppose that these rumors of an engagement do not actually harm either of us, but we don't like them."

Gray is not the easiest person to *(continued on next page)*

(continued from preceding page)

become friendly with. He is a quiet, extremely reserved person. There is tragedy still in his serious, blue eyes. His natural reserve is augmented by shyness.

He will not forget in a hurry a scene he had to play in "Viennese Nights," his forthcoming operetta with Vivienne Segal. He had to walk into a crowded cafe, down a long flight of stairs, with a woman of the streets. He had to act very drunken and make a spectacle of himself before the woman he loves.

"When we rehearsed the scene I had to go through it with the set crowded with extras, property men and visitors. At first I didn't think I could do it, but I gritted my teeth and started in. I'm glad that I didn't ask everybody to leave. It was good experience for me, and it was easier when it came to filming the scene."

Again that Scotch Presbyterian training was the shadow in the background. As a child he had seen little demonstrative affection in his home. His father and mother were ideally happy, but the affectionate display of many families was missing. He grew up to hide his own feelings.

In "Viennese Nights" he is wearing a blond, curly wig. The blond hair is more becoming to him than his own darker brown shade, but he feels very foolish about it.

"Why don't you adopt blond hair permanently?" someone asked him. "Women never hesitate to take the shade of hair that is most becoming to them. Why shouldn't a man do the same?"

"I'm afraid that I spent too many years as an engineer," he answered.

And, after all, engineering may not be the best experience in the world as preparation for singing tender love ballads in the shell-pink ear of a prima donna.

HE never thought of the stage when he enrolled in Penn State College. During his first year he tended furnaces and waited on tables to pay his expenses. In his second year he joined Delta Upsilon fraternity. It immediately became apparent that a fraternity man would have to adopt some more dignified labor than nursing furnaces and passing the boarding house hash. So he sold aluminum ware.

"How I hated it," he confessed. "I was terribly bashful to begin with, and it almost killed me to have some indignant housewife slam the door in my face."

That part of Pennsylvania must be full of indignant housewives who are paying good money to see Alexander Gray on the screen, never dreaming that they once slammed their own doors in his face.

He began to sing in college. He joined the glee club, and took part in musical shows. He never had a vocal lesson until after he had gone in business. In Chicago he worked for several years as an advertising man for motor trucks.

Then in his spare time he began to train his voice.

AT first there was little thought of the stage. He wanted to do concert work. He took up the stage as a last resort because it offered him a living, and time to continue his study of music.

His first work of any importance was in Ziegfeld shows. He was at first merely a singer, never having any lines to speak. He came to serious attention in "Sally," and won his greatest popularity during the several seasons he sang the lead rôle in "The Desert Song."

JUL.

These New Faces

Watch for This Each Month

GRACE MOORE (Metro-Goldwyn-Mayer) is the screen's great loan from the grand opera stage. Born in Jellico, Tenn., Miss Moore sang in church choirs in her home state. Entering musical comedy, she scored tremendous successes in the great "Music Box Revues" of Irving Berlin. In 1928 she made her début at the Metropolitan as *Mimi* in "La Boheme."

JILLIAN SAND ("Are You There?" Fox) is a young English girl who was brought over with the idea that she would go into a Will Rogers picture, but was sent into the Bee Lillie film instead. She played on the stage in London, and made several pictures in England. Her real name is Gillian Sandlands, and she was born Feb. 22, 1908.

PERT KELTON ("Sally," First National) began in show business as one of the Four Keltons, a family vaudeville turn. A natural comic and mimic, Manager Charles Dillingham picked her out and gave her a big rôle in "Sunny," in which she scored. Then she was featured in "The Five O'Clock Girl." And now she seems certain of much screen success.

JUL.

FOX MOVIETONE FOLLIES OF 1930—Fox

BY 1930 the Fox Follies is just another revue. Good enough as such things go, but there have been so many. However, if you like revues you'll enjoy this. Some fair songs; plenty of high-light comedy by Marjorie White and El Brendel; some love story provided by William Collier, Jr., and Miriam Seegar, and a series of big spectacular scenes.

"FOX MOVIETONE FOLLIES OF 1930"—Fox.—From the story by William K. Wells. Directed by Benjamin Stoloff. The cast: *Axel Svenson,* El Brendel; *Vera Fontaine,* Marjorie White; *George Randall,* Frank Richardson; *Gloria De Witt,* Noel Francis; *Conrad Sterling,* William Collier, Jr.; *Mary Mason,* Miriam Seegar; *Marvin Kingsley,* Huntly Gordon; *Lee Hubert,* Paul Nicholson; *Maid,* Yola D'Avril.

JUL.

YOUNG MAN OF MANHATTAN—Paramount

THE human side of newspaper business—a young sports writer and his movie-critic bride struggling with everything that besets young folks—love, liquor, misunderstanding, ambition defeated by laziness. Well directed by Monta Bell, and with beautiful performances by Claudette Colbert and Norman Foster, with a few laughs from Charlie Ruggles.

"YOUNG MAN OF MANHATTAN"—Paramount.—From the novel by Katharine Brush. Adapted by Robert Presnell. Directed by Monta Bell. The cast: *Ann Vaughn,* Claudette Colbert; *Toby McLean,* Norman Foster; *Puff Randolph,* Ginger Rogers; *Shorty Ross,* Charles Ruggles; *Dwight Knowles,* Leslie Austin; *Sherman Sisters,* Four Aalbu Sisters; *Doctor,* H. Dudley Hawley.

The Girl *on the* Cover

JEANETTE MacDONALD says she has an Irish temper, Scotch thrift, and is as absent-minded as the professor that kissed the cat good night and put his wife out the front door!

Most beautiful stars will admit they have the dispositions of angels. Maybe, oh, just maybe, they will confess to an "eentsie-teentsie" bit of temperament—just *ze grande artiste* coming to the surface, you know.

But Jeanette, of the red-gold hair and the sea-green eyes, has an indestructible sense of humor and she knows she isn't an Elsie Dinsmore.

All of the lucky stars in the skies must have been clustered directly over her during the making of "The Love Parade," her début in the talkies. She was guided through the first intricacies of the cinema by no less a master than Ernst Lubitsch.

"The Vagabond King" followed. "Let's Go Native," and "Bride 66," the Hammerstein production for United Artists, claimed her talents in rapid succession.

Now she is working with Lubitsch again in another light opera. Jack Buchanan, the English stage star, is her leading man. You saw him on the screen with Irene Bordoni in "Paris."

JEANETTE was born in Philadelphia, of Scotch, Irish and English ancestry. She thinks there is no thrill in the world like returning to the home town, important and successful.

She began her stage career in the chorus. She is proud of beginning there, for she knows now just how necessary each minor member of a big troupe can be. She "crashed" the footlights during the last, fading days of the statuesque "lady of the ensemble," the tall but attractive girls who could not dance, but could wear clothes beautifully and drove down Riverside Drive in their own Rolls Royces.

Jeanette says she will never forget her embarrassment at displaying her own humble undergarments in the dressing room before these gilded lilies. Bloomers and cotton vests were all she could afford, and she always explained to the girls that she had just rushed over from her gymnasium class!

With her first salary check she bought some grand silk underwear, and undressed with a flourish!

In her very first show she understudied the prima donna, and used to pray every night that the lady would come down with a bad cold—nothing serious like pneumonia, just bad enough to keep her out of the theater for a few nights! But the star was healthy, and never missed a performance.

Confesses Her Faults and Laughs at Her Own Shortcomings

JUL.

DANCING SWEETIES—Warners

WINNING a dancing cup, and then marrying the prettiest girl in town, may be some accomplishment, but it's nothing compared to learning how to meet the problems of the first year of married life. *Bill Cleaver*, played by Grant Withers, had to be hit pretty hard before he could see. Sue Carol, as the wife, even had to present him with twins. Edna Murphy and Eddie Phillips play the other couple.

"DANCING SWEETIES" — WARNERS. — From the story "Three Flights Up" by Harry Fried. Adapted by Gordon Rigby and Joseph A. Jackson. Directed by Ray Enright. The cast: *Bill Cleaver*, Grant Withers; *Molly O'Neill*, Sue Carol; *Jazzbo Gans*, Edna Murphy; *Mr. Cleaver*, Tully Marshall; *Mrs. Cleaver*, Kate Price; *Emma O'Neill*, Adamae Vaughn; *"Needles" Thompson*, Eddie Phillips.

JUL.

CHEER UP AND SMILE—Fox

THE heartaches and love affairs of youth are beautifully portrayed by Arthur Lake and Dixie Lee in this comedy drama. There are a number of unexpected twists to the story and young people will adore it. Baclanova returns as an alluring vamp, trying to steal Arthur away from that blonde cutie, Dixie. It's lucky Arthur lost no more than his voice, but you will lose a pound laughing at him.

"CHEER UP AND SMILE"—Fox.—From the story by Richard Connell. Adapted by Howard J. Green. Directed by Sidney Lanfield. The cast: *Margie*, Dixie Lee; *Eddie Fripp*, Arthur Lake; *Yvonne*, Olga Baclanova; *"Whispering Jack" Smith*, Himself; *Andy*, Johnny Arthur; *Pierre*, Charles Judels; *Tom*, John Darrow; *Paul*, Sumner Getchell; *Professor*, Franklin Pangborn; *Donald*, Buddy Messinger.

"I used to think that I would have one of those overnight successes if I only got my chance," she said. "It was lucky for me that the chance never arrived. I was still in my 'teens, and the star rôle was that of a sophisticated married woman. I would have looked too ridiculous."

BUT the driving ambition, the grim determination to "get somewhere," was never dampened through her early, lean stage days. She had reached stardom on Broadway when she was lured to Hollywood with a lucrative picture contract. She had appeared in a long succession of musical stage hits—among them "Marjolaine," "Oh, Kay," "Tip-Toes," "Boom-Boom," and "Yes, Yes, Yvette."

Now that she has become a motion picture star she is not content to coast along, but she plans to win new laurels.

Jeanette believes that a star, to remain successful in talkies, should know at least two foreign languages. Spanish is particularly advisable, she thinks, since there are so many theaters wired for sound in the Latin Americas and Spain. So she is diligently studying Spanish.

BUT, returning to the faults—and the faults of a beautiful lady are always more interesting than her virtues—she tells an amusing story about her forgetfulness.

One of the boys from the set told her that she would have to work late that night. Jeanette, just coming from the projection room where she had been listening to playbacks, nodded. Her mind was on the playbacks and not on the boy.

That night she was furious when she was reminded that she would have to return to the studio. It was outrageous, she said, that she should have to work late without any notice. Things reached a deadlock. The boy swore that he had told her, and Jeanette was just as positive that he hadn't. No one on the set could figure which one was doing the fibbing!

And she holds grudges! She admits she can't help but gloat over the very grand stage actress who ritzed her consistently during her early days in the theater—and who is now, in Hollywood, glad to play any kind of rôle.

But her faults, which are not so heinous after all, are more than counterbalanced by a gorgeous sense of humor.

JEANETTE is unmarried, and lives with her mother. But there is a fiance, very much in the picture.

She vows she will not "go Hollywood."

JUL.

HIGH SOCIETY BLUES—Fox

THE personal popularity of Janet Gaynor and Charlie Farrell carries this little musical romance to what success and worth it achieves. They look adoringly at each other, and do some more of what is so naively and hopefully labeled singing. Plot—Charlie's folks try to chisel into high society, meaning the old Boston Gaynors. Some laughs, some songs, and even a little acting.

"HIGH SOCIETY BLUES"—Fox.—From the story by Dana Burnet. Adapted by Howard J. Green. Directed by David Butler. The cast: *Eleanor Divine,* Janet Gaynor; *Eddie Granger,* Charles Farrell; *Horace Divine,* William Collier, Sr.; *Mrs. Divine,* Hedda Hopper; *Pearl Granger,* Joyce Compton; *Eli Granger,* Lucien Littlefield; *Mrs. Granger,* Louise Fazenda; *Jowles,* Brandon Hurst; *Count Prunier,* Gregory Gaye.

JUL.

LET'S GO NATIVE—Paramount

THIS is madness—weird, wonderful madness! Every gag in history turns up somewhere in this insane hash of song, dance and story. There's a wonderful burlesque of the old shipwreck, desert island theme. Skeets Gallagher is king of the isle, and Jack Oakie, Jeanette MacDonald, James Hall, Kay Francis and William Austin are the castaways. Terrific nonsense—and how you'll scream!

"LET'S GO NATIVE"—PARAMOUNT. — From the story by George Marion, Jr., and Percy Heath. Directed by Leo McCarey. The cast: *Joan Wood,* Jeanette MacDonald; *Voltaire McGinnis,* Jack Oakie; *Wally Wendell,* James Hall; *Jerry,* Skeets Gallagher; *Basil Pistol,* William Austin; *Constance Cooke,* Kay Francis; *Chief Officer Williams,* David Newell; *Wallace Wendell,* Charles Sellon; *Creditor's Man,* Eugene Pallette.

JUL.

SONG OF THE FLAME—First National

AN operetta version of the Russian Revolution. Russia was freed by Bernice Claire, soprano, and Noah Beery, who sings a bass solo surprisingly! All-Technicolor, with some beautiful and stirring music, some very ham acting, some able singing and a few fine scenes. A large and elaborate picture, but it does get boring, for most of the music is familiar, and comic-opera bolshevists are silly.

"SONG OF THE FLAME"—FIRST NATIONAL.—From the operetta by Otto Harbach, Oscar Hammerstein, II, George Gershwin and Herbert Stothart. Adapted by Gordon Rigby. Directed by Alan Crosland. The cast: *Aniuta, the Flame,* Bernice Claire; *Prince Volodya,* Alexander Gray; *Konstantin,* Noah Beery; *Natasha,* Alice Gentle; *Grusha,* Inez Courtney; *Count Boris,* Shep Camp; *Henchman,* Ivan Linow.

JUL.

SWING HIGH—Pathe

PLEASANT entertainment, this story of love and intrigue among the players in an old time wagon circus. Director Santley hasn't overlooked chances for color and action. Fred Scott sings a couple of numbers that seem headed for popular hits, while a negro chorus offers a rollicking song, "Chasing the Hoodoo Away." Helen Twelvetrees is quite Gish-like as the heroine who saves her lover from the vamp.

"SWING HIGH"—PATHE.—From the story by Joseph Santley and James Seymour. Adapted by James Seymour. Directed by Joseph Santley. The cast: *Maryan,* Helen Twelvetrees; *Garry,* Fred Scott; *Trixie,* Dorothy Burgess; *Doc May,* John Sheehan; *Mrs. May,* Daphne Pollard; *Pop Garner,* George Fawcett; *Ringmaster,* Bryant Washburn; *Billy,* Nick Stuart; *Ruth,* Sally Starr; *Major Tiny,* Little Billy; *Babe,* William Langan; *Sam,* Stepin Fetchit; *Sheriff,* Chester Conklin; *Bartender,* Ben Turpin; *Doctor,* Robert Edeson; *Mickey,* Mickey Bennett.

That MULLIGAN Spirit!

By

Robert Cranford

It lured and drove Lola Lane from Indianola, Iowa, to the threshold of film stardom

Dot Mulligan found that she wasn't getting anywhere in particular in her home town of Indianola, Ia. So she bustled her way to the screen as Lola Lane. See that old Mulligan spirit in her eyes?

DEAR SALLY:
—or Jenny, or Louise, or whatever your name is:

Did you ever feel like getting out in front of the congregation and dancing a Charleston, just in sheer rebellion?

And do you ever feel like taking your seventeen-dollar-a-week job and throwing it in the manager's face, because you felt it wasn't getting you anywhere, and never would?

In short, don't you feel like being yourself instead of what people or circumstances want to make you be?

Well, then, read the fable of Dot Mulligan, the Small-Town Girl who was herself, and, as a result, is getting many dollars a month and a growing spot in the Hollywood limelight!

* * *

DOROTHY MULLIGAN began by being born in a town called Indianola, which is in Iowa, and has about three thousand inhabitants. Lots of other girls were born there, and are still there—not so much because they want to be, thinks Dorothy Mulligan, but because they just didn't have the courage to cash out.

Dorothy decided early in life, although she couldn't have expressed it so succinctly then, to be her own woman.

Maybe that's why it was that she scandalized the town one Sunday by waiting until church was letting out—and getting out in front of the horrified townspeople and dancing a particularly violent Charleston (which was what they were dancing at the time this happened).

"There's that Mulligan kid again," they said. "She'll never amount to anything." (As a matter of fact, Dorothy Mulligan is going back to Indianola this summer—and the townspeople are going to pay the unheard-of sum of five dollars apiece to see and compliment her. But that's later on in the story.)

In her early 'teens, the Mulligan kid knew she wanted to be something besides maybe a nice Indianola housewife and sewing circle member, or maybe a farmer's wife. She didn't know just what she wanted to be, but she didn't want to be what her mama and her townsfolk thought a properly-raised Indianola girl ought to be.

So she got a job in the movie house, playing the piano. For seven dollars a week. "So the Mulligan girl has settled down," they said. "Now maybe she'll marry a nice Indianola boy, and she could give piano lessons, too."

But in a little while, Dorothy Mulligan knew this was not what she wanted.

"Isn't it foolish to sit here ten or eleven hours a day, thumping piano keys for seven dollars a week, when right before me I see girls on the screen who are making much more?" she said to herself.

So she went to the manager and quit! Quit a good job for no reason that anybody could understand—except herself, who knew that she wasn't being herself staying there.

"I don't want to be a small-town girl," said Dorothy to herself.

So her mother let her go to Des Moines, which was a big town to her. "I didn't know what I wanted to do," says the girl who was that Dorothy Mulligan, now, "but I knew I didn't want to stay in Indianola."

She went to an employment agency and sat down. The manager bawled: "Who wants a job in an ice-cream factory?" Everybody jumped up, but Dorothy Mulligan jumped the fastest. She got the job.

Fifteen a week. Here was success!—she learned how to make ice cream and cardboard boxes, and to sweep floors.

But she knew darned well that this wasn't what she wanted. Maybe some other girl might have stuck there, and become the Ice-Cream Queen of the country, with a chain of ice-cream factories or something. But it wasn't Dorothy's field. So she quit, with only forty cents in her pocket. She spent twenty-five of it for a sundae, and went back to the employment agency.

THIS time she got a job in a little notions store. It paid her seventeen dollars a week. Maybe, said Dorothy to herself, this was the beginning of a great commercial career. Who could tell? She would try it. She did—for four weeks. At the end of that time, she had saved enough to buy a new pair of shoes; had decided that commerce was not her *metier*, and had made up her mind to stay a couple of weeks longer before quitting, in order to save enough for a pair of stockings.

But the owner of the store came to her and said he had to let her go.

"Why?" demanded Dorothy.

"My wife," said the owner. "She is jealous of you. For four weeks she has been looking *(continued on next page)*

The Story of a Girl Who Just Wouldn't Settle Down!

(continued from preceding page)

through a hole in the back wall of the store, thinking there was something between us."

"Oh ho!" said Dorothy. "Then I quit." Dot Mulligan had discovered, anyway, that she wasn't cut out to be a business woman.

Then came the first ray of light. She met a woman through whom she got a chance to go on the Chautauqua circuit singing and playing piano. She liked it! Here was something in her line, it seemed.

Dorothy Mulligan was beginning to find herself. And besides, there was the queenly salary of forty dollars a week!

But week after week of the Chautauqua, and Dorothy Mulligan once again felt the walls of limitation.

Again she quit! Quit a job she really liked, because she knew she couldn't be herself by staying in it forever. Call it ambition, call it determination, call it whatever you wish, but Dorothy Mulligan quit the Chautauqua job to be herself.

Her mother insisted that she come back home and finish college. Dorothy knew that she didn't want to be a college girl above all, but one ought to please one's mother. So she found a compromise—

"I went back home with the determination to show mother that I didn't want to be a college girl."

She went to school late. She raised heck in the dorms. She cut classes and got other girls to do the same. She calculated ways to be called onto the carpet before the principal for a bawling out. And finally she was expelled.

"Oh, how I loved it," she says.

Now she made up her mind that there must be something for her in New York. She began to have an idea that stage life was her field. She wrote to Gus Edwards, a perfect stranger, and told him that he had to see her! Then she borrowed two hundred dollars and went to New York and to Gus Edwards' house.

She must have had talent. For she became one of Gus Edwards' protégées! On the stage, Dorothy knew that now she had found what she wanted to be!

And when a four hundred and fifty dollar a week vaudeville contract came along, she was more than ever sure of it. But the vaudeville tour took her to California—and in Los Angeles she was offered a screen test.

"The moment I saw the inside of the studio, I knew that that was what I wanted."

From that moment on, Dorothy was unhappy on the stage. She wasn't being herself, once again. She had her eye always on the pictures. And at last, the break came—they needed a leading lady for "Speakeasy," and Ben Stoloff was in New York making talkie tests of actresses there.

One day, the manager of the show in which Dorothy Mulligan was playing stepped into her dressing room and said—

"There's a big movie director downstairs."

That was all he had to say. Dorothy Mulligan was herself on the instant—by rushing to meet the big movie director. Stoloff gave her a test—and she made good. Since then—

WELL, you know who Lola Lane is! The star of James Cruze's "The Big Fight," and the girl who is headed for one of the foremost places in filmdom, if the unanimous opinion of executives, directors and critics is any criterion.

Well, Lola Lane is Dorothy Mulligan.

She believes that every girl who has any spark of talent at all can only develop it by being herself everlastingly and always. When she goes back to Indianola this summer, to be the big attraction at a church bazaar for which they're going to charge the unprecedented admission of five dollars a person, she's going to advise any Indianola girl who asks her how to succeed, to be herself.

"If being yourself is being happily married to a farmer boy, then be yourself that way," Lola Lane Mulligan will tell her. "If you feel that being yourself is something else, then don't marry him. Try always to be yourself, no matter what the cost in courage to do it."

Lola Lane wants to tell every girl—not alone the girls back in Indianola, but the girls in all the Indianolas in the country, and in all the New Yorks and Chicagos and other places, too—to be themselves!

JUL.

☆ THE FLORODORA GIRL—M-G-M

MAKING this picture could NEVER have been work. With all those "gay nineties" gags, Marion and Lawrence and the other boys and girls must have had more fun!

It's a rollicking tale of the love tribulations of one of the original Florodora girls and a gay young blood. Marion Davies as the tomboyish chorus girl and Larry Gray as the youth whose flirtation develops into love, are delightful.

What makes the picture extra-delicious is the atmospheric stuff evolved. The bathing beach, the horseless carriage ride, the leg-o'-mutton sleeves and the rest of the gad-awful fashions for ladies, are too precious!

And of course, the Florodora number, done in Technicolor, is the beauty high-light. If you take mama and papa, don't be surprised if they break into their reminiscences.

"FLORODORA GIRL, THE"—M-G-M.—From the story by Gene Markey. Directed by Harry Beaumont. The cast: *Daisy,* Marion Davies; *Jack,* Lawrence Gray; *DeBoer,* Walter Catlett; *Hemingway,* Louis John Bartles; *Fanny,* Ilka Chase; *Maud,* Vivian Oakland; *Old Man Dell,* Jed Prouty; *Rumblesham,* Claud Allister; *Fontaine,* Sam Hardy; *Mrs. Vibart,* Nance O'Neil; *Commodore,* Robert Bolder; *Constance,* Jane Keithly; *Mrs. Caraway,* Maude Turner Gordon; *Georgie Smith,* George Chandler; *Vibart Children,* Anita Louise; Mary Jane Irving.

JUL.

☆ THE BIG POND—Paramount

CHEVALIER clicks again! This time, in a new field—straight romantic comedy, with just a dash of song.

"The Big Pond" tells the story of a flashing but empty-pocketed young Frenchman who makes good in the American chewing gum business so that he can marry the daughter of his boss. It has pace and humor, and Maurice gets several chances to sing. Listen for "You Brought a New Kind of Love to Me."

A Broadway cast, new to pictures, helps out well. You already know Claudette Colbert, opposite the star. She's fine. Another medal for Director Hobart Henley.

Paramount is mixing them up well for their new ace, the romantic panic. This is a pleasant change from the costume things. Still another slant on the fascinating Parisian.

"BIG POND, THE"—PARAMOUNT.—From the play by George Middleton and A. E. Thomas. Adapted by Robert Presnell and Garrett Fort. Directed by Hobart Henley. The cast: *Pierre,* Maurice Chevalier; *Barbara Billings,* Claudette Colbert; *Ronnie,* Frank Lyon; *Mr. Billings,* George Barbier; *Mrs. Billings,* Marion Ballou; *Pat O'Day,* Nat Pendleton; *Toinette,* Andree Corday; *Jennie,* Elaine Koch.

The smile that won the screen world's heart! The million candle-power, full-faced, infectious grin that lights up the face of Maurice Chevalier and makes every beholder feel good all over. The best cure for That Down Feeling!

Being the Romantic and Exciting Life Story of Maurice Chevalier—Man, Soldier, Artist

Part I

IN the crowded lunchroom of the New York Paramount Studios, a group of men—obviously hard-headed customers, to whom the wonderland of millions was only a place where they earned their living—sat at a table near the cashier's desk over their coffee and cigars.

The door opened to admit a smooth-haired man, a little over medium height, one hand thrust deep into his trousers pocket, his eyes startlingly blue in a dark-skinned face that was rather stern in repose. But, catching sight of an acquaintance, he flashed him a sudden grin that was like a glimpse of the sun after a forty-day deluge!

One of the men at the table looked after him, shifted his cigar to a corner of his mouth and out of the other corner pronounced judgment: "*Shevally!*" he informed his companions. "'S a regalar guy!"

It is an opinion shared by all Maurice Chevalier's associates, from Jesse L. Lasky, who hired him, to the cameramen who shoot his scenes. "Say, there's nothin' high-hat about that feller," one of them revealed in a burst of confidence, "like a lot o' these ninnies in pictures. Why, we was shootin' fer two days in the chewin' gum factory, an' this bird hobnobs with them workin' men, not like he was snootin' 'em, y'understand, but like he likes 'em. An' believe me, sister, they like him too. An' fer a fact," he concluded thoughtfully, "I like him myself."

"He's a good sport," said a publicity man. "A society of French War Veterans wanted to present him with a testimonial, and I dragged him down to City Hall for the ceremony. He was tired out from the French and English versions of 'The Big Pond,' and he was leaving for Hollywood next day.

"HE'D been making trailers for me all morning, and he had plenty of other things to do, but he shifted his arrangements when I said it was important, and came.

"Well, when we got there we found that someone had gummed the works, and the Mayor wasn't there, and the whole thing was off. I wouldn't have blamed him if he'd lit into me. But when I got into the taxi with him, feeling like a prize jackass, all he said was:

"'Don't worry about it—it's just one of those things that can't be helped. When I get back from California, you arrange the details yourself and we'll get it done!'"

These tributes will surprise no one even casually acquainted with the temperament and career of this Frenchman who, presented to American audiences for the first time in as soppy a picture as ever came out of Hollywood, rose superior to its trumpery story, took the hearts of American fandom by storm, hung up box-office records all over the country, and magnificently justified Jesse Lasky's faith in him—all through the sheer pull of a vital and engaging personality.

THERE may be many reasons why Maurice Chevalier has neither a high hat nor a swelled head, and the principal one is probably that he was born that way.

He is naturally simple and genuine, blessed with humor and common sense, with a knowledge of his own value both as man and entertainer, but no exaggerated ideas of his own importance.

In addition, the circumstances of his life have been such as to keep his feet on the ground. His has been no overnight triumph, no sudden bewildering leap into fame and fortune.

Step by step, since he was twelve, he has fought to the top.

A Chevalier of FRANCE!

By

Ida Zeitlin

He has struggled against poverty, family opposition, public indifference; against the havoc of war in his private and professional life; against the ill health produced by a shrapnel bullet in his lung. He has overcome all these handicaps and achieved such success in his work as comes to few.

All France adores him and America bids fair to follow in her wake. But Chevalier's eyes are not dazzled and his head is not turned. He is pleased by the warmth of his reception, as who wouldn't be?

But he doesn't bask in the sunlight of his own admiration. He is proud of his success, and humble at the same time.

He knows that popular favor is fickle and that he can hold the heights he has scaled only by the same persistent, intelligent effort that got him there.

SO, whether he is doing it for the first time or the tenth, he puts into every scene he plays, into every song he sings, the same energy and abandon that drew the delighted applause of his first audience when he appeared before them, an eager, green youngster of twelve, in a Parisian music hall on amateur night.

It is perhaps the same sense of responsibility—toward his family, toward his employers, toward his work and his fellow-workers, toward all his obligations, whatever their nature—that is the cornerstone of Maurice Chevalier's character.

It was laid early. He came of a family of laborers, which may partly account for his interest in the chewing gum workers. He was born, the youngest of three sons, in Menilmontant, one of the poorer and rowdier outlying districts of Paris—"a bit of an Apache neighborhood," as he himself describes it.

His father died when he was ten, and when his brothers were fifteen and twenty-four respectively.

The eldest was earning a tradesman's wage of less than two dollars a day, the second was still an apprentice, and Maurice was at school. He finished his schooling, like all French boys of the laboring classes in those days, at twelve, when he,

(continued on next page)

A family group worthy of the genius of a Whistler. Chevalier, his wife and his mother—the little Madame Chevalier of Menilmontant who encouraged her young son in his earliest stage efforts when the rest of his family wanted the boy to learn a good trade. It is one of Maurice's greatest sorrows that she passed away before his American triumphs

(continued from preceding page)

Chevalier—from the music hall amateur to the pet of Paris!

too, was apprenticed to a carpenter. But his soul was elsewhere.

It is true that life was no bed of roses for Maurice, but he enjoyed it, nevertheless, as children do. He played with his own gang, and avoided the others whose activities didn't appeal to him. He has been blessed with a merry heart, and two treasures besides.

One of them was his mother. He does not say, like so many stars, that he owes all he is today to his mother. He knows very well that he owes most of it to his own talent, ambition and toil. But everything that a mother can give her son in the way of sympathy, support and morale, his mother gave him.

She fought for him against his eldest brother's opposition to his stage career. She worked at night in a lace-making establishment to eke out the family income, for by the time Maurice was earning a tiny wage, one brother was married, and by the time he was making a dollar a day, he and his mother were alone.

SHE beamed over his small triumphs and comforted him when things went badly. Never once, during those dark days when they didn't know where tomorrow's food was coming from, did she utter a sound of complaint or reproach.

The habit that she formed, during the lean years, of waiting up for him at night to hear what had happened at the theater, she kept during the years of plenty; and she was never happier than when Maurice and his friends were filling the house with their clamor.

She had the joy of living to see her son hailed as the idol of the Parisian stage; and he had the joy of providing rest for her toilworn hands and peace for her anxious heart. She died while he was making his first picture in America.

"It will always be a great sorrow to me," he said simply, "that she couldn't know about all this that is happening now."

Young Maurice's second treasure was a dream—a dream in which he lived constantly and which was nourished and renewed every Sunday night, when he went with his mother or brother to the suburban music hall near their home. He longed for Sunday night as a sculptor might long for the feel of clay under his fingers. It turned mere living into a thrilling adventure.

ALL the color and wonder of existence were for him concentrated on the stage of that shabby music hall. The acrobats and singers were gods, and the world they lived in was a fairy tale.

It is no wonder, then, that he mooned on his bench at the carpenter's shop, and when he was sent on an errand, forgot to come back. For the carpenter and all his works were shadows to him, and his real life was going on inside his head, where he was tumbling with the jugglers and singing over and over the comic songs of the current music hall favorite.

From doing them in his head, it didn't take long before he was doing them in earnest, and one day he went into solemn conference with his seventeen-year-old brother.

THEY decided to put on an acrobatic brother-act. Somewhere they found an appropriate poster, at the top of which they pasted in large letters the words, CHEVALIER BROS.—because all good acrobats were English, and all good acrobats advertised themselves as "BROS." Once that important detail was attended to, they began practising.

There is no doubt that Maurice went into acrobatics with his characteristic fervor. So vigorously did he practice that it wasn't long before he fell and hurt his leg badly enough to keep him in bed for a week.

Madame Chevalier, who up to then had watched her sons' antics with indulgent amusement, grew a little uneasy. But Maurice reassured her. "Just a little accident, *maman*. It might happen to anyone, even a very good acrobat. But it won't happen to me again."

Fortunately — for how could even the prince of acrobats compete with the singing Chevalier?—it did happen again. "Instead," he says, "of turning one somersault, I turned one-and-a-half, and instead of landing on my feet, I landed on my face." It didn't need his mother's frightened protests, when she saw his green and purple countenance, to tell him that his tumbling career was at an end. He faced the fact that he wasn't cut out for an acrobat.

But he wasted no time in lamentation. If one road was barred to him, he could concentrate all his energies on the other. He followed the whole show on Sunday night with his usual absorbed attention, but he kept his eyes and ears glued on the singer, drinking in his songs, eating up his pantomime, and going home to imitate them to his appreciative audience of two.

At last he felt he was ready to present himself at one of the Saturday night tryouts for amateurs. He tied around his middle a pair of trousers many times too large for him; he whitened his face and reddened his nose and pushed his cap down from behind to a devilish angle. With eyes blazing and heart pounding with excitement, he walked out on the stage.

Evidently the wine is just terrible. At any rate, Maurice Chevalier, aged twelve and a half, is making faces at it. This picture was taken during one of his first professional appearances

WHEN they saw him, they laughed and applauded. The boy was so small and the make-up was so grotesque! He was enchanted with the applause. He grinned at them—the same whole-souled grin through his make-up that warms the hearts of his audiences today. The applause grew louder.

Still smiling, he launched into a song. It was a rowdy song, whose double meanings were apparently not very clear to the singer. This tickled his hearers, to begin with. Besides, he sang it with such gusto and good-will, with such smiles and gestures, with such a thrill of excited happiness quivering through all his body that it communicated itself to the whole house.

When he had finished, they *(continued on next page)*

(continued from preceding page)

thundered their approval and shouted for more. It didn't matter that his voice wasn't good and that he couldn't keep the pitch. It didn't matter that he couldn't follow the piano and that the piano had to follow him. He swept them away on the wave of his own joyous friendliness, and they laughed at everything, especially his mistakes.

IT was his first big night, and when it was over, Heaven opened before him. The manager asked him to come back. Of course he couldn't pay him anything, but he generously offered Maurice the freedom of his stage, where someone was bound to see him eventually and give him an engagement.

Which was exactly what happened. It was a small-time artist who saw him and his possibilities, and talked to him after the show and said he thought he could get him work. Maurice ran home to his mother with the news.

By that time he had been thrown out of several trades by various disgusted employers, whose time he had wasted and whose tools he couldn't handle. He told his mother that the man had said he could make twelve francs a week (about $2.50). That was more than he could earn as an apprentice, even if he succeeded in sticking to a job, which was doubtful.

It was a serious decision he was asking his mother to make. Madame Chevalier called into consultation her eldest son, who stood in a father's place to the little family. Without an instant's hesitation, he said no!

Who had ever heard of an actor in the family? They had all earned their bread with their hands, and Maurice could do the same. Did his mother know what it meant to be an actor? It meant a wicked life—it meant keeping company with a set of good-for-nothing loafers who had neither money nor morals, who were a disgrace to any self-respecting family. Let Maurice put that folly out of his head and buckle down to work like the rest of them!

Madame Chevalier looked from the stormy face of her big son into the pleading eyes of her little one. It must have been as difficult to resist his appeal then as it is now. Womanlike, having sought advice, she decided not to take it.

"He's a good boy," she said. "Let him try it, since his heart is set on it. If he fails, he always has time to be a carpenter." (It may be interesting to note in passing that before many years had gone by, this same stern brother's proudest boast was: "I am the brother of Chevalier!")

So Maurice tried it. It would be pleasant to record that his success was immediate and startling. It was neither. In his clownish make-up he scored a small hit, but the sensation of his amateur night was not repeated. However, there was no more talk of returning to a trade. It was understood between him and his mother that he was to be an actor, and that whatever difficulties had to be faced would be faced together.

HE went from one small engagement to another. There were weeks when he worked and weeks when he didn't. But, little by little, the two-and-a-half dollars grew to four-and-a-half, and one day he went over so big with the patrons of a certain music hall that its manager not only offered him a weekly salary of seven dollars, but billed him week after week in response to the demands of his admirers.

It was then that his second brother, whose earnings had helped support the household, married, so that even the fine sum of seven dollars was hardly enough to keep Madame Chevalier from lace-making or their minds from worry. And though the seven-dollar engagement was a long one, running for several months, it came to an end at last.

There followed the most miserable period of Chevalier's existence. It was a hot summer and work was scarce. Day after day he tramped baking streets, tired and disheartened, hunting in vain for a job—any job. The depths of his wretchedness may be measured by the fact that he was ready to take what offered, even if it landed him in a carpenter's shop. The stage had been his vision of Paradise, but as between his vision and his mother, the vision would have to go.

FOR himself, it wouldn't have mattered. He could have lived happily on hot dogs and beer, and a man can always find a place to sleep. It might even have been rather romantic, a picturesque chapter in an actor's career. But what would have been fun for himself alone, was less than fun for himself and his mother together. His heart ached over her very cheerfulness in the face of privation. If she had grumbled, he would probably have borne it better.

During those days he vowed a private vow that he never broke. Whatever money he earned in the future, no matter how little, no matter how much, he would live on half of it. The other half he would put aside, so that he could be safe in the knowledge that his dependents would have something to depend upon.

The time came when there was no money in the house, and he did something that to this day he hates to talk or think about. He asked permission of a café owner to sing in the café and to pass the hat. Though he was still hardly more than a child, and was doing out of desperate necessity what many boys of his age might have done as a lark, the experience so wounded his self-respect as to leave a scar that never disappeared.

But he had lived through his darkest hour. At the end of the summer he was engaged as a sort of chorus boy for a big musical show called *La Parisiana*. His special talents soon became apparent to the manager, who decided to experiment with him. That was how it happened that young Maurice, in the same buffoon's rig that had been so popular with his less sophisticated audiences, appeared one night on the stage of a fashionable Parisian theater, and sang and gave his imitations of well-known stars with such success that his salary was promptly raised to fourteen dollars a week.

He had the satisfaction of knowing that he was earning more money at his "disreputable" calling than either of his big brothers at their highly respectable ones.

HE was then sixteen. "I think the next few years of my life are not so interesting for people to read about; though," he adds with a reminiscent smile, "they were very interesting for me to live. I did not have much trouble to secure engagements. I played in Paris and also in the provinces, and since there was not the great worry about money, I worried instead about my work.

"Not worried exactly either, you understand—but I tried always to think how I could make the people out there like me more. I was never one to run after flattery when I left the theater." He spoke with the simplicity that carries conviction. "It seemed to me always a waste of time and emotion. But as an actor, I did all in my power to please them.

"I tried to think what I would enjoy if I were sitting in the audience and the other fellow was on the stage. I wanted them to feel that I was one of them—not from a different world because the footlights came between us—but just an ordinary fellow, trying to make them laugh and have a good time."

One of the things he did to "make the people out there like him more" was to add dancing to his repertoire. In those days there was no such thing on the Parisian stage as a song-and-dance-man. If you were a singer, you sang, and that was the end of it.

But there came to Paris at about this time an American, who charmed the French theater-going public by executing intricate dance steps with his songs, and jigging to the music as skilfully as he sang to it. He became the rage, and like all rages was soon being imitated in every corner of the city.

ONE of his most successful imitators was the young *comique*, Chevalier, who was beginning to be a drawing card and whom the big producers were watching speculatively. To see him in his baggy trousers and red nose tripping elegantly—with just an inspired touch of exaggeration—through the graceful measures that the American had popularized, was to see something more than an imitation. It was a kind of animated caricature, a funny picture come to life, and it brought down the house.

Once again Chevalier knew the thrill of his first night, once again the audience rose to its feet and shouted till the rafters rang, and refused to be quieted. And this time the fruits of his success were prompt and glorious. He was offered an engagement in what was then the smartest, gayest, most extravagant revue in town—the goal of all music hall artists—the *Folies Bergères*.

During that engagement he underwent a transformation. He suddenly decided, one evening, to play a scene straight, without his ludicrous makeup. He was doubtful about the wisdom of such a step, for he had won his popularity as a clown, and that was how his public knew and liked him. Still, once the idea had occurred to him, he wanted to try. After all, what great harm could it do? If they didn't like it, he had only to run back to his dressing room to turn clown again.

SO he removed the false face and the rest of his disguise, donned dress clothes and stuck a straw hat down over one eye at the angle he had long since made his own, and breezed out onto the stage. He felt queer, he felt unnatural, he felt just a little naked. He would have liked to dash back, but it was too late.

The ominous silence that greeted him made him feel queerer still. So he'd been right! They didn't like him. Well, the only thing left for him to do was to sing his song and get out of their sight as fast as he could. At the first sound of his voice, at the first glimpse of his smile, there was a little stir and murmur of amazement. Why, this was Maurice Chevalier!

They hadn't realized it—they hadn't recognized the zany they knew in this handsome, well-groomed youth whose smile was more dazzling than ever, now that the disfiguring mask had been removed, and whose humor and charm leaped like a living thing across the footlights, as if some veil between them had been withdrawn. It was a revelation! They must have felt that someone had been holding out on them. Their astonishment changed to delight, and their delight burst forth at the end of his song in the most frantic applause that had ever greeted him.

They wouldn't let him go back to being a clown! They wanted him as he was, with his youth and his pleasant face and his debonair manner, in his dress clothes and straw hat, singing the sprightly songs that the French know so well how to concoct!

When he saw that his work no longer needed the artificial props of costume and make-up, but could stand unsupported on its own feet, he was ready to oblige them. He would sing an occasional song in character, but for the major part of his program he gave his admirers what they wanted—Chevalier straight!

(continued on next page)

(continued from preceding page)

HE had gone to the *Folies Bergères*, more or less on trial, as a funny man. He emerged, a handsome young juvenile, the acknowledged male favorite of the French music hall stage, runner up to such blazing luminaries as Mistinguette and Gaby Deslys, his place in the sun assured.

It had often been rough going as he climbed, but now, looking back, it seemed almost a miracle that he could have traveled so far and so fast. He was actually doing what it is given few lucky mortals to do—living his dream—and all of life stretched smooth and golden ahead of him.

It was true that the time had come when his work must be interrupted by military service. He wasn't exactly elated at the prospect, but neither was he downcast. He would do the job that every son of France was asked to do, and then come back. He was so firmly entrenched in public favor that he knew he would be as impatiently waited for as he himself would be impatient to return.

So he began his term of service as a soldier and so, like all other years, the tragic year of 1914 dawned!

[In the next installment Chevalier tells Miss Zeitlin of his war service, his severe wound, his capture by the Germans, his life in a prison camp. It's as exciting as the most thrilling war novel. Read it in the August issue of PHOTOPLAY.]

(Part 2 begins on the next page)

JUL.

They aren't going to make a type player of Gloria Swanson—not if she knows it. In her new picture, "What a Widow!" she's right back in an almost slapstick rôle. The young man tempting her with the cocktails is Lew Cody. It's good to see him back, after his long illness

PART 2

Chevalier—giving the world both barrels of his tremendous personality, his zest, his charm! This is the straw-hatted Maurice who stormed and took America, also New York

MAURICE CHEVALIER was born in Menilmontant, the youngest of three sons in a family of laborers. His father died when he was ten, and when he had finished his schooling at twelve, he was apprenticed to a carpenter.

But his heart was elsewhere—on the stage of a small music hall of his neighborhood. There, at twelve, he made his début as an amateur! Soon he was a poorly paid comedian, touring the halls. A few years later he adopted the conventional dress and the straw hat that mark his stage work today—and almost overnight became the toast of the Folies Bergères and the pet of Paris. Then, as success dawned, he entered the service of France as a common soldier.

It was the tragic war year—1914!

AUGUST, 1914. War burst over a horrified world and the boys who were making ready to embark on the adventure of life took arms and went forth on the great adventure of death, instead.

To Maurice Chevalier the call came while he was serving the regular period of military duty required of all young citizens of France.

The German tide rolled Southward—mighty, irresistible. To stem it, France's standing army was rushed to the North, there to fight as long as might be while other classes were called to the colors and the full military might of the Republic was marshalled.

Much has been written of Britain's little army of "Contemptibles," whose dogged, fighting retreat from Mons kept the German army from the Channel ports. The army of France was larger, and it, too, fought an equally courageous, though losing fight, stretched far across the Motherland from Belgium to the Swiss border.

We have not heard quite so much of these gallant *poilus*, in the pitiful blue coats and red trousers of peace time, who stood against the field-gray masses until Papa Joffre could rally his strengthened forces and roll the enemy back from the Marne.

But a young war poet wrote well of this first French army—the flower of the nation's youth, who first met the enemy horde and made their country like a castle—

"Their breasts the bulwark, and their blood the moat."

In this first army, that melted away like the snow of spring, Chevalier served as a private in a regiment of infantry.

In those fearful, tragic early weeks of war there were no set engagements, with names that now have a place in history. It was one long battle—never ending, day and night. The French army fought, and then retreated, still fighting—hurled backward by the might of the great gray war machine from the North.

In one of those nameless battles of 1914 Chevalier fell, wounded in the chest by shrapnel. His right lung was pierced. The wound might well have been mortal.

In the days of that terrible retreat warfare was still open—the retiring French had not even a protecting shadow between their bodies and the terror of the shells. When Chevalier's company found a roadside ditch in their path, it was as though God's arms had opened to receive them.

Dizzy and sick, Maurice managed to pick himself up and tumble into the poor shelter with his comrades, dimly realizing

(continued on next page)

(continued from preceding page)

that later he might drag himself to the dressing station farther back.

But he soon saw that his presence with his friends was only a hindrance. He stumbled and fell in agony. Anything, he thought, would be better than this torture.

DELIRIOUS, he climbed from the ditch and started back—fell, rose again, wavered a few steps, fell unconscious. He did not know that bayonets were flashing in the shelter he had just left, and that his comrades were killing and being killed as the German wave rolled over them.

He lay like one dead, on that pitiful battlefield, his life saved by the same freak of fate that had taken his fellow soldiers' lives.

When Chevalier recovered consciousness, he was in the field dressing station he had been trying so desperately to reach.

But he didn't stay there long. Within a few hours it was captured by the Germans, ana the wounded were placed on hospital trains and sent, as prisoners of war, to the hospital in the city of Magdeburg.

So ended Maurice Chevalier's active service for France in the Great War.

No "hero," in the abused sense of the word, this smiling fellow. He was a soldier of his country when the call came. He faced the enemy bravely, interposing his body between the Northern host and his country's heart. In the heat of battle, he fell, gravely wounded. Could any man do more?

A brave man and a good soldier. Those two titles belong to Maurice, and no man can ask for better.

The German shrapnel that entered Chevalier's lung more than fifteen years ago is still there—sometimes stationary, sometimes roving. Sometimes troublesome, more often not.

The doctors at Magdeburg decided it would be less dangerous to leave it where it was than to operate. When questioned as to whether he thinks they were right, Chevalier shrugs his shoulders.

Shrapnel in the lung is no unmixed blessing, but it might very well have been worse if they'd tried to remove it. It no longer bothers him actively. He is conscious of it on rainy days, and it prevents him from dancing as energetically as he once did.

BUT what he probably regrets most is that it put an end to his boxing activities. He had been one of the best amateur boxers in France, and had kept in trim by sparring so vigorously with professionals that he sometimes had trouble repairing his damaged face sufficiently to present it to his audiences.

He is still an ardent fan, and may frequently be seen at boxing matches, accompanied by a slim, dainty young woman, whose glowing, dark eyes follow an exciting bout with the intelligence of a *connoisseur* and an enthusiasm hardly less than her husband's.

In connection with his boxing prowess, a story is told, too good to be omitted here. It happened in wartime, after his return to Paris, when the well-known piratical tendencies of Parisian taxi-drivers were uncontrolled. The particular robber, who had taken Chevalier and the lady he was escorting to a popular café in the heart of an Apache section, demanded something so grotesque in the way of fare that his passenger—never a man to be bamboozled even by a taxi-driver—laughed in his face and offered him what he considered a reasonable fee.

The taximan eyed it, spat with great deliberation, and delivered himself of a stream of crackling language intended to convey his excessively low opinion not only of Chevalier and all his ancestors, but of the lady with him, who, he stated, was, in point of fact, no lady.

Chevalier knocked him down, and an unsympathetic crowd

(continued on next page)

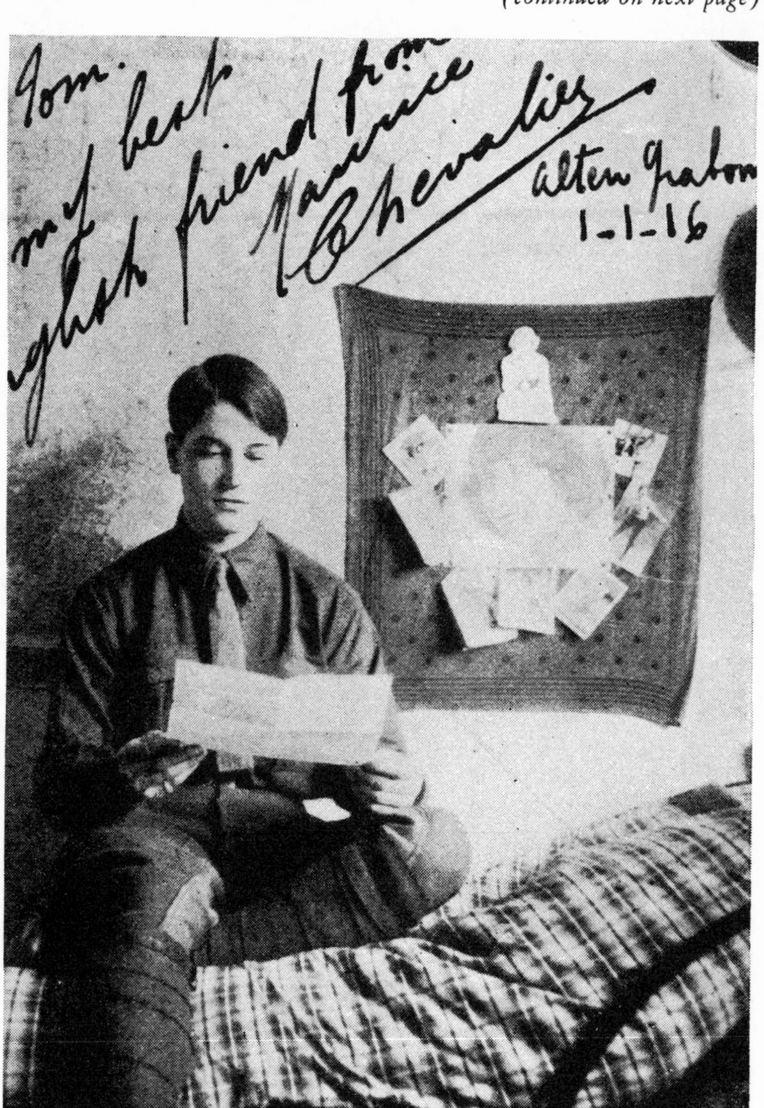

The young prisoner of war. Chevalier at the German prison camp of Alten Grabow in 1916, after he had been wounded and captured in one of the 1914 battles

King of the Paris music halls! Chevalier during his early fame in the French capital, when he was as much one of the city's great sights as Montmartre and the Eiffel Tower

(continued from preceding page)

gathered—the taximan was one of their own, and the stranger was far too well dressed to take their fancy. As he tried to force a lane through the jeering throng, there loomed in his path a vaguely familiar and unattractive face which he suddenly recognized as that of a notorious bad man who went by the appealing name of *Zuzu des Batignolles*.

Beginning at his patent leather shoes and traveling upward to his top hat, Zuzu took Chevalier in, while the crowd held its breath in gleeful expectancy. At last his narrowed eyes met those of his enemy. "So you're the guy," he croaked, "that eats everybody."

"No," answered Chevalier, "I don't. But neither do I allow anyone to insult a lady under my protection."

But Zuzu wasn't going to have his big scene ruined. "So you're the guy—" this time he bellowed it, crouching a little and thrusting his ugly jaw under Chevalier's nose, "—that *eats* everybody!"

A moment earlier, searching vainly out of the tail of his eye for a policeman, Chevalier hadn't the faintest notion how he was going to get his companion and himself out of this mess. Now he stopped thinking, and acted almost automatically. To a boxer that jutting chin was a thing of beauty, "a gift," as he himself described it later, "dropped straight from heaven."

His elbow jerked back, his fist shot forward, and the next second Zuzu lay sprawling in the gutter among his stupefied admirers, while an elegant young gentleman and his girl went sprinting down the street as fast as their legs would carry them.

WHILE Chevalier lay in the hospital at Magdeburg, too sick to know or care what was going on about him, the military authorities reported him as missing. For three months his mother had no word from him—for three months Paris hummed with conflicting rumors of his fate—he had been killed, he had been captured, he had lost his sight, his arms or his legs had been amputated.

At the end of three months a letter to his mother got through, putting an end to conjecture and relieving her heart of its blackest dread. And now, as never before, her son might rejoice in that early resolve of his to save half of whatever money he might earn—for it was thanks to that resolve that his mother was spared the misery of want while he was gone.

From the hospital he was sent to a prison camp where, with fifteen or twenty thousand fellow prisoners— *(continued on next page)*

Monsieur and Madame Chevalier sitting before one of the mammoth posters which heralded the appearance of the star at the far-famed *Casino de Paris*

(continued from preceding page)

English, Russian and French—he was destined to spend twenty-six long, disheartening months. The discipline was rigid. Despite his discharge from the hospital, he felt weak and unsteady most of the time, and his physical state aggravated the natural depression induced by the months of dreary prison routine. But his captivity yielded him one priceless boon—the best piece of good fortune, he says, that ever came his way. That piece of good fortune was a British prisoner who happened to be a school teacher. He and the French actor agreed to exchange lessons in their respective languages, but Chevalier maintains that it was a one-sided bargain.

"That fellow, he could *teach!*" he declares admiringly. "Me—I told him the French word—this is a table—this is a chair—this is a music hall singer—but he could have found it as well in the book without me."

THOSE lessons, providing him with a regular task and giving his mind something to chew upon, did more than anything else to bolster his drooping spirits, and by the time he was released he could speak and write English correctly and easily—a knowledge that proved invaluable in his brilliant post-war career.

Apart from his family, the one person from whom he heard regularly during those months was an English performer named Tom Hearn, whose *Lazy Juggler* act had placed him at the head of his profession, not only in England and on the continent, but in America as well. Their friendship had been born of a curious accident. For no good reason but simply because he liked the sound of it, Hearn's brother had adopted the name of Chevalier for professional purposes, and Hearn was interested to see that a man with the same name was booked to play at the *Folies Bergères* while he was playing there.

He made a point of looking the man up to tell him of the coincidence, and they soon found they had many things in common, among them a love of sport and a distaste for hard drinking. Hearn would go home with Maurice after the show, to share the suppers that his mother delighted in preparing for them, and before long the two had formed a fast friendship.

During the war, Hearn joined the air service, and after eight weeks in France, was shot down in his plane. Lying flat on a hospital cot for six months, he still found the means of sending to the German prison camp letters of encouragement and packages of food and cigarettes.

THE friendship, formed in lightheartedness and strengthened by adversity, endured through all the years during which the Frenchman rose to fame and the *Lazy Juggler* gave up his juggling to become a producer. So that when Chevalier needed a manager for his American undertaking, it was to Tom Hearn he turned, the drawling, genial English-Irishman who now receives so kindly the ever-growing mob of promoters, song-writers, interviewers, unrecognized geniuses and ordinary pests camping on Chevalier's trail, and turns them away so courteously that it takes them a minute or two to realize that they haven't got what they came for.

The war dragged on, the months stretched into years, and the gray monotony of prison life—unrelieved by a hint of what was going on outside—made each year a century. Chevalier suddenly resolved on a desperate scheme. There was to be an exchange between France and Germany of imprisoned Red Cross workers, and he decided to pose as one of them.

He was taking a long chance. He would have to falsify his papers in the first place, and then he would have to pass an examination in something that he knew nothing whatever about. If his trick was discovered, the life he had led hitherto would be paradise compared with what would follow. Nevertheless, he sent in his application. Nothing happened. For weeks he waited in dread, not knowing whether the next day would find him before a court martial or in solitary confinement, when suddenly there came the news that Red Cross applicants for repatriation would be examined the following morning. And on the list Chevalier's name appeared.

That night he didn't sleep. In twenty-four hours he tried to stuff his head with as much as it would hold of wounds and dressings, of the position of the heart and the function of the liver, with the natural result that when he faced the German officer next morning his mind was so confused that if his life had depended on it, he couldn't have told whether his lungs were for breathing and his stomach for digesting, or vice versa. He stood in line in the same fatalistic mood in which he had climbed out of the ditch, and steeled himself to meet what the Lord would send.

The German examiner threw him a sharp glance. This face was familiar to him as the face of a man who sang for the prisoners at Sunday night concerts. He turned to the French doctor standing beside him, who knew exactly what Chevalier was trying to do.

"BUT this one isn't a Red Cross man!" said the German, while the actor's dramatic talents deserted him, and he turned red and white and red again, and wondered how long his trembling legs would hold him.

The French doctor eyed him inscrutably. "Oh, yes," he answered, "he *is* a Red Cross man. He's been in the prison hospital and I know him well."

The German slowly nodded his head, but what the nod was intended to convey it would have been impossible to guess. He examined his list of questions, selected one and opened his mouth to put it to the stony-faced applicant who was praying for the earth to open and swallow him up. What happened was hardly less amazing. Whether there was something in Chevalier's expression that stirred his sympathy, whether the Sunday night performances had inspired in him that benevolent glow that it is Chevalier's peculiar gift to inspire or whether he was acting on a moment's impulse, is a matter for conjecture. The fact remains that, with his mouth open to ask the question, the officer suddenly changed his mind cried: "Applicant passed! Next!" and waved his hand in a gesture that sent a shaky but happy young man back to his own country.

Arrived in France, Chevalier was given three months' leave in which to recuperate. There were two things he was bent on discovering—the truth about his physical condition and the possibility of continuing his professional career.

The French doctors could give him little satisfaction—to operate now would be a ticklish business—"better let it sleep while it sleeps," they advised him. His loss of appetite and vitality, his constant fatigue and his fits of dizziness might be due to the wound, or they might as readily be due to the long confinement and the nervous strain he had undergone. Time alone would show.

HE accepted an engagement. Hardly had he opened his mouth to sing when he was overwhelmed by such a wave of giddiness that he had to stop. He made a fresh start, but couldn't get any air into his lungs, and his voice sounded choked and smothered, as if it were struggling vainly to force its way beyond the barrier of his own throat. Shaking uncontrollably, somehow he got to the end of the song and walked off the stage and didn't go back again.

As far as the theater was concerned, it looked as though he were through. As far as the war was concerned, he undoubtedly was. When his leave was over and he reported for duty, he was awarded the *Croix de Guerre* and discharged from the army as unfit for military service.

He traveled on the advice of one doctor, and rested on the advice of another. He tried mountain climates and he tried mineral baths, he forced himself to eat, though all food tasted like a dish of wooden shavings, but nothing helped. He returned to Paris where he met a wise man who said to him: "Go back to the theater. Never mind if you're rotten—never mind if they give you the razz. Make a fool of yourself once, twice, a dozen times if necessary—but the only way you'll ever find out if you *can* get back is to go back—and the sooner you go, the sooner you'll find out."

He followed his friend's advice literally. He went back to the theater and he was rotten. He went through his paces without enthusiasm and he was received without enthusiasm. But he stuck it out. Little by little, he improved. His voice began to grow stronger and surer, and with his voice came returning hope and returning confidence.

ONE day he noticed that something he ate had the taste of food again instead of sawdust, and it is that day that he marks as the turning point in his illness. Still it took him two years to regain what he had lost, and it was his newly acquired command of English that helped him more than anything else to regain it.

Paris was crowded just then with English and American soldiers and war workers, and Chevalier conceived the idea that it would be a friendly gesture as well as a stroke of good business to include in his repertoire songs they would understand. His war audiences were sympathetically disposed to begin with, for in the program appeared a straightforward little note to the effect that Mr. Chevalier had been a soldier, had been wounded and honorably discharged, and that if he was playing while they were fighting, it was because he had done his job.

And when he stood before them and, with his endearing grin, his captivating accent, his radiant friendliness and sly humor, sang to those homesick boys that war classic: "How're you goin' to keep 'em down on the farm?" the ensuing riot was something to listen to. The word was passed along, and among the few indispensable forms of entertainment that marked the Parisian sojourns of Tommy and doughboy were the songs of Maurice Chevalier.

At first he played in revues with Mistinguette—that perennially youthful lady whose illustrious legs still twinkle for the delight of Parisian theater goers. To her Chevalier feels he owes a debt of deep gratitude. Open-handed and open-hearted, with a man's forthrightness and a man's loyalty, she is affectionately known to the entire stage fraternity as the "best of good sports," and to Chevalier she proved herself a staunch friend.

WHILE he was making his laborious climb to favor before the war, she was riding the crest of the wave, and her recognition of his unusual talents and her choice of him as her dancing partner were in those days like a royal seal of ratification upon his career.

When he returned, a very tired man, from captivity, she not only helped him with advice and encouragement but, as soon as he was ready, made a place for him in her revue.

(continued on next page)

(continued from preceding page)

lending him the support of her prestige until he should feel steadier and surer of himself. It was only after Chevalier's drawing power grew too great for co-starring that this famous theatrical partnership was terminated.

The success of his English songs turned his thoughts, once the war was over, to America. An American triumph is to a European performer the crown of his career. It surrounds him with the kind of glamour he can acquire in no other way, by stamping him as an entertainer of international quality. But to fail in America is, by the same reckoning, a calamity. However popular you may be in your own country, the stigma can never quite be lived down.

SO, though he dreamed of trying for the prize, Chevalier was frankly afraid to take the chance—especially after playing a London engagement with Elsie Janis in 1919. Not that the Londoners didn't respond to him—they did. But he didn't respond to them. He didn't, to use a graphic expression of his own, "feel in his shoes." For once his work was really work instead of fun and he wasn't happy doing it. Suppose, with much more at stake, he should feel the same way in America!

He turned down the numerous offers made him to stay in England, and when he went back to Paris, it was with the idea of giving up his more ambitious plans and contenting himself with the plaudits of his countrymen.

He still made occasional tours of the provinces, and there is a story of one of these tours that he likes to tell on himself. His brother—the one who had formed the other half of the acrobatic partnership of CHEVALIER BROS.—was ambitious to follow in Maurice's footsteps, and though his brief career trailed no clouds of glory, he did manage to get some engagements, largely—one may be excused for suspecting—on the strength of the relationship.

It happened that the brothers were once playing the same town, and it also happened that Maurice was lying one morning in a barber's chair, lathered beyond recognition, while two citizens, awaiting their turn, discussed the affairs of the day. Having exhausted the weightier topics, one inquired of the other: "Have you seen this fellow Chevalier that they're all raving about?"

"Yes," answered his neighbor, "I've seen him. And what's more, I've seen his brother—the one that's playing in the little theater at the end of town—and it's my opinion that they're all crazy. The other's worth a dozen of this one—sings better, acts better, dances better. This Maurice has a reputation and that's *all* he's got! Mark my words, friend"—and he wagged an emphatic finger under his companion's nose—"that bird won't last a year."

THERE was nothing left for that bird to do but gather up the shreds of his self-esteem and sidle out of the shop to avoid the severe gaze of his brother's admirer.

Among the applicants for the 1923 Chevalier revue was a shy little dancer, with magnificent dark eyes, named Yvonne Vallée. She had begun dancing at the age of eight, not with the idea of making it her profession, but because she had been a frail child and the doctor had told her mother it would do her good. But her talent had been so apparent that she had been encouraged to study for the stage—with happy results. Not only was she engaged for Chevalier's show, but her dancing pleased him so well that he chose her as his partner for an important number.

The choice proved a popular one—she was so tiny beside his height and so demure that she gave the effect of a small charming bird fluttering about him—and she danced like a fairy and she had a sense of comedy that supplemented his own.

The following season she became his official dancing partner, and the comradeship between them developed into something warmer. They might have married long before they were, except that they had a feeling against combining the personal with the professional, and Yvonne wasn't ready to give up her work. For two more seasons they danced and played together, and then Chevalier's dancing partner disappeared to make way for Chevalier's wife.

Her charm, quieter than his, is equally unmistakable. She combines a woman's graciousness with a child's appeal, and her fine eyes look out on the world with a child's friendliness, eager and reserved at the same time.

Beneath the gravity of her expression, as she talks to a stranger, lurks a hint of that sparkling vitality that is characteristically French, and every now and then one corner of her mouth quirks upward in an enchanting smile. She apologizes for her English and promises earnestly that she will soon improve. She thinks America is a wonderland and gasps in dismay at the thought of what she would have missed if she hadn't come here.

She would like to dance on the stage again if a favorable opportunity offered—since, she hastens to add, Maurice has no objection—but that's a matter that will have to take care of itself. Her husband's career interests her far more than her own, and she is his unofficial but respected adviser in all things that concern him. Except for the demands of his work, all their time is spent together and it is only necessary to see them, unobtrusively but serenely happy in each other's company, to understand why their marriage has been called one of the most successful in the theatrical world.

WHEN Mary Pickford and Douglas Fairbanks made their first trip to Paris together, they went to see Chevalier's show, and were so impressed that they made it their business to meet the star and urge upon him the advisability of a visit to the United States. They took to each other at once, and became, as Chevalier says, such "big friends" that when he and his wife took their first trip to Hollywood, their natural stopping place was *Pickfair*.

On their return from France, Fairbanks told Charles Dillingham, the producer, what he thought of Chevalier, with the result that Dillingham sent an agent to Paris to sign him up, sight unseen. Chevalier, still timid, but encouraged by his friends' enthusiasm, signed a contract to appear in New York the following fall in *Dédé*—his current revue that had then been running in Paris for two years.

That summer he went to New York for a three weeks' visit. He attended American revues, listened to American songs, watched American singers, and each day his heart sank lower. Each day he grew more and more firmly convinced that Paris couldn't compete with New York, and that Maurice Chevalier wasn't good enough to cut any real figure among the outstanding Broadway favorites. He thought their songs were catchier, he knew their voices were better, he even, by some strange reasoning, came to the conclusion that their humor was funnier than his. Having signed a contract, he'd have to go through with it, but he could already taste on his tongue the bitterness of defeat.

Returning to Paris to wind up his season there, he was stricken with appendicitis and intestinal trouble, and the run of *Dédé* had to be brought to an abrupt close. He came successfully through his operation, but whatever fighting spirit he had managed to hang on to up to then was left behind in the hospital. He makes no bones about it—he was plainly and simply frightened—far too frightened to face even the thought of a New York appearance and the possible disaster in which it might end. He asked Mr. Dillingham to release him, and he has never forgotten the prompt generosity of Mr. Dillingham's response. "If you won't be happy," he cabled, "don't come."

IN April of this year Chevalier played a phenomenally successful New York engagement under Dillingham's management in partial fulfilment of that old contract, and he has made the statement that Dillingham will always have the first call on his services for any future appearances, not only because he was the first producer to invite him to this country, but because he is the kind of gentleman with whom business relations are a pleasure.

The following year Mary Pickford asked him to play the male lead in one of her pictures—an invitation he was obliged regretfully to decline because of his French contracts. He was now emerging as France's bright particular star, and mounting steadily to a pinnacle occupied by no one before him.

It isn't enough to say that he was the popular favorite—the people loved him, highbrow and lowbrow alike. He had his own show, and so long as he was in it, it didn't much matter what was left out. He had his own theater, the *Casino de Paris*—or at least people called it his, because to them its only reason for existence was Maurice Chevalier—and it became the Mecca for natives and foreigners in search of the most piquant and ingratiating dish the French stage had to offer. He was doing the thing he had been born to do, and in creating pleasure for others, he was creating the maximum amount for himself.

"If by some impossible chance," said one of his friends, "it should happen that Maurice couldn't *make* money doing his stuff, he'd probably pay everything he has to be *allowed* to do it. Else life wouldn't be worth living."

And so things might have continued indefinitely if the talkies hadn't come to change the whole face of the motion picture industry, and sent its leaders scurrying through Europe in search of new material for the new art. That was how it happened that after the performance one night a callboy knocked at Chevalier's dressing-room door to announce Mr. and Mrs. Irving Thalberg of Hollywood!

(In Part III, to appear in the September issue of PHOTOPLAY, Miss Zeitlin tells of Chevalier's conquest of the new world, and his swift climb to the height he now occupies in the interest and affection of America.)

(Part 3 begins on the next page)

A Chevalier *of* France

By Ida Zeitlin

PART 3

His first view of a new world to win! Maurice Chevalier, on the deck of the liner that brought him to America, peers at the towering peaks of the Manhattan skyline. Fearful of his reception in this country, within a few short weeks Chevalier had captured the fancy of Americans

MISS ZEITLIN, in preceding installments, has told of the humble birth of Maurice Chevalier in a Paris suburb, and of his early struggles to attain eminence in the French theater.

Last month you read of his brief and tragic war service, and of his post-war triumph as the most beloved music hall comedian in France. As last month's story closed, a knock had come at his dressing room door. The caller was Mr. Irving Thalberg, of Metro-Goldwyn-Mayer.

Soon his conquest of America was to come!

IT would be difficult to find words more graphic than Chevalier's own to describe the interview that took place between him and Irving Thalberg in his dressing room that night. As he spoke of it, there was frank apology for himself in his opening words.

"In France," he said, "there are two worlds of the theater. One is the little world—not great as here—of the cinema. The other is the world of the stage, and the people of those two worlds do not meet. Each of us knows, of course, the important names in the other, but—" with an expressive shrug, "nothing more. Of American names I knew only the big stars. Irving Thalberg—I am sorry—meant nothing to me—Norma Shearer, yes—but I had not seen her on the screen, and I did not know Mr. Thalberg's wife, pretty lady though she was, to be Miss Norma Shearer.

" 'We have seen your show,' said Mr. Thalberg to me, 'and we think you have great possibilities for the pictures. I am an American producer and I would like to make a test of you.'

"At once came memories of a test they had made of me in London a few years ago—in the open—without lights—with silly songs. And I didn't want that thing to happen again. So I said, 'No—thank you, Mr. Thalberg. I think you come too late. I had a test made in London several years ago and nothing turned out of it. And now that I have become a star in Paris, I do not want to feel that I have done something not good enough to be taken seriously. I have passed the state of making tests and all that. If you want to engage me, engage me. If not,—' " and he finished the speech with eloquent hands and eyebrows.

"I was very unreasonable, *hein?*" he went on. "But Mr. Thalberg was not. He was kind. 'It is not a question of talent,' he said, 'but of knowing if your personality will come out of the screen. What tests did they make of you in London? Did they have good lights for you? Did they help you?'

" 'NO—there were no lights at all. It was only in the street.'

" 'But I have an American cameraman with me, and our tests would be made with all the American knowledge of how to light the personality and make it come out.'

"He was very friendly—very charming—but still I did not find myself excited. If it turned out badly the second time, I would feel—how do you say—not insulted—but cheap inside of myself, knowing that I wasn't good enough. I was happy in my work on the stage—why should I risk all that trying to do something which perhaps I had not the talent to do? I said, 'I will think it over,' but in my heart I said, 'Goodbye, Mr. Thalberg.'

"When he went out, someone asked me, 'Do you know who is this fellow?'

" 'Yes—he said he is in a picture firm in America.'

" 'Well, he is one of the heads of Metro-Goldwyn-Mayer

Armed Only with His Infectious Grin, Maurice Chevalier Marches on America, and Conquers!

—a very young man but a very clever and important one. You have not been wise. Even the very best actor must submit to a screen test.'

"I think of what my friend has told me and I see he is right—I have not been wise. So I ask Mr. Thalberg to come again to see me. 'Excuse me,' I say, 'if I did not know you before. We in France live in another world. Now I have been told exactly who you are, and if you wish I will make this test tomorrow. But on one condition—that you give me also a copy of that test. I do not wish to be left here, while you return to America, without a sign of what I have done. I want to see for myself if I am good or not—I want to judge for myself if I have a chance—and if not—well, I will stay in my own country and that's all.' "

SO it was agreed. Chevalier made the test the following day, and the Thalbergs left for Baden Baden. The verdict came from there two weeks later. "Seen your test. Think you have wonderful possibilities. Writing." And this was followed by an enthusiastic letter of confirmation, in which for the first time the important question of terms was broached.

Chevalier was gratified, but he wanted to see his test before he made any decisions. "And when I received it and had it run off," he said, nodding his head like a pleased child, "I liked it. I saw at once that I am not the romantic hero type—but I feel there is something—

The irresistible Maurice in the picture that brought him to the summit of his early American fame—"The Love Parade." It was this swaggish, romantic story, inimitably directed by Ernst Lubitsch, that made Maurice's reputation here secure

It was in "Innocents of Paris," with little David Durand, that Maurice Chevalier overcame a sugary story to subdue American audiences with the sheer force of his astonishing personality

a kind of sunshine that comes out of the screen. So I ask Douglas Fairbanks, who is in Paris, if he will look at it and tell me without kidding"—pronounced *keeding*—"what he thinks."

So Fairbanks looked at the test and pronounced it, without "keeding," one hundred per cent perfect. "Stop worrying," he said. "There's nothing to worry about. Stop thinking you're not good enough. You're good! You're fine! Sign your contract and get over there! They'll eat you up!"

Thus encouraged, Chevalier took up with Thalberg the question of terms. He was *(continued on next page)*

(continued from preceding page)

getting at the *Casino de Paris* what was for France—but not for Hollywood—an enormous salary. Mr. Thalberg offered him on behalf of Metro-Goldwyn exactly fifty per cent of that sum.

"But listen—" Chevalier protested, "—you understand I cannot leave Paris, have my house running here and all that, and go to California to get half of what I am getting in France."

"BUT we can't possibly pay you anything like what you're getting here," the other explained. "No star in Hollywood ever received such a salary without first proving himself a box-office attraction."

"Then—I thank you for your kindness—but I will stay where I am. I will go to America at the salary I am getting here, or I will not go at all. I beg you to understand it as I mean it—I do not bargain with you—I do not try to lift your price—but I tell you simply that I cannot afford, with more expense to myself, to take less money from you than I now earn. If you cannot afford to give it to me—well—we will part friends."

Cables began flying across the Atlantic between Irving Thalberg and his associates, and Thalberg was finally authorized to offer the French star a salary that came within $500 of the sum he asked. Chevalier refused it.

"Very well," said Thalberg, "I'll go back to Hollywood and fight for you there. I'm sure to convince them and you'll hear from me very soon."

He returned to Hollywood, but Chevalier didn't hear. The Frenchman's cables remained unanswered. He flashed them a final signal of distress. "Please wire yes or no must make plans for next season." Came nothing.

So when, not many weeks later, he was told at the theater that Mr. Lasky was out front, he didn't quiver an eyelash. "I lost my faith," he says. "I told myself, if the other one thinks I am not worth even the same salary that I get in France, why should this one think some other thing?" He went out and sang his songs with his customary verve and sparkle—not for Mr. Lasky or Hollywood—but for his friends in the audience whom he never disappointed and who never disappointed him.

APPARENTLY it was good enough for Mr. Lasky. Hardly was the act over when he knocked at the star's door.

"I like the way you sing American songs," he said. "Will you come and talk to me tomorrow about the pictures? I am here for only three days."

"Yes, Mr. Lasky," said Chevalier, "I will come. And—" with a grin, "I will do more. I will save you the money and the trouble to make a test. I will show you the test that was made of me two months ago."

"That," he mused, "was the funny side of it. Two hours after he saw the test, Mr. Lasky signed me for Paramount at the same salary I was getting in Paris. And that," he concluded, "is the story of how I came to America to work in the pictures."

Chevalier is very grateful to Mr. Lasky—grateful for his faith and for his generosity. He is one of the five people whom the Frenchman recognizes as having exerted a crucial influence on his career.

They make an interesting list. J. W. Jackson, who taught him how to dance; Norman French, who brought a new type of dancing comedy to Paris and whom Chevalier imitated with such success; Mistinguette, who made him her partner before the war and after his return from the prison camp; Ronald Kennedy, the British schoolmaster who taught him English when he was a war prisoner at Alten Grabow; and Jesse L. Lasky, who brought him to America and who has reaped the reward of his good judgment.

There have been other kind and helpful friends, but these five provided the stepping stones that enabled him to display his talents to the best advantage, and thus attain his present eminence.

If the truth must be told, there were no loud outcries of joy from Paramount when they learned he was coming. So many European hopes had been transplanted to Hollywood amid a fanfare of expensive ballyhoo—and where were they now? Wilted, apparently, by some blight in the California atmosphere, collapsed and carted quietly away—the ballyhoo packed in camphor until the next time.

He was introduced to them and to the newspaper men at a press luncheon. It was his first American crowd, and he did to them what he has done to every American crowd he has met since. He talked to them and captured their attention, he sang to them and warmed their hearts, he grinned at them and they were his. They set to work with every ounce of energy they owned to put him over—not alone because it was their job, but because they felt that here was an investment certain to repay tenfold whatever effort they might spend on it.

THE French star went to Hollywood to make "Innocents of Paris." The shooting began, the first rushes were shown and Paramount immediately took up his option for one year at a small increase in salary. That was fine, but still it represented only the reaction of his employers who believed in him, and who wanted to believe in him. What about that terrifying unknown quantity, the American public, who had no knowledge of him, no interest in him, financial, sentimental or otherwise, in whose hands lay the final judgment? Would it be thumbs up or thumbs down?

Chevalier went to the preview with moist hands and a sinking sensation in the pit of his stomach. He was about to present himself at the bar of American public opinion and hear the verdict pronounced that would bestow or withhold the final crown.

The theater was filled with a regulation movie crowd, Paramount officials scattered here and there among them. Chevalier sat alone—too nervous to tolerate anyone near him—his friends in another part of the house.

"It was a kind of first night," he said, "without the possibility of being myself on the stage to feel how it goes, and maybe change a little here, a little there. It is all fixed, finished. I can look, listen, but I must sit still in my chair and do nothing. That is a terrible thing!" And he wiped the perspiration from his hands at the very thought of it.

His name appeared on the screen:

Maurice Chevalier
in
"Innocents of Paris"

Then came a brief, humorous introduction of the star by himself. "When my face came on," said Chevalier, "nothing happened—of course. They didn't know me, they had never heard of me. And they didn't see a very handsome man—just the face of a fellow. But after a minute I begin to feel some response—a little smile, a little laugh. And when I tell the story of '*Comment? Qui est-ce? Papa?*' they laugh very much and even applaud. I begin to think, it goes. I even smile myself, because—if you will understand me well—I responded also to that fellow I was seeing. I thought, if that fellow was not Maurice Chevalier, I would like him all right. Then suddenly I hear from behind me one word—" here he twisted his mouth upward in perfect imitation of a hard-boiled young tough, and out of that twisted corner of his mouth he spat the word, "terrible!"

"It is like a cold shower on my head. I look around and there sits a third-class American fellow with his girl, and he is scowling as if he is my worst enemy. My hopes go down—I think, maybe the audience is nice because they know I am a stranger and in their kindness wish to make me feel good—but in their hearts they think, like this man, that it is 'terrible!'

"THEN the picture begins. Soon there is a laugh—another. They laugh in all the right places—I can see it takes hold of them. Their faces are changed, interested—their eyes are bright—and when I sing to the little crying boy, '*Dites moi, ma mère*,' they clap so hard that the end of the song is drowned. Someone near me is clapping very loud, indeed and when I turn to look—well, what do you think—it is my 'terrible' friend from before. That is good, *hein?* But certainly," shaking his head at the recollection, "he was a very hard egg at first.

"Well, you would say it is enough to prove to me that all will be well. But no—I am still nervous—so nervous that I cannot wait for the end. I run from the theater before the picture is finished, and later I meet my friends and they tell me it is a great success. Next day the papers tell me also the same. They are all wonderfully kind, because they take me out of the picture and they say I have got what you call in America the stuff."

Most people who have seen "Innocents of Paris" will probably concede that Chevalier's first starring vehicle had a weak and sloppily sentimental story. It was a picture doomed under ordinary conditions, if not to failure, then certainly to a common-place career.

But the star refused to take either himself or the picture too seriously and, through the leaven of his humor and personality, transformed it from melodrama to sparkling comedy, to a picture hailed by press and public, by layman and professional, as one of the outstanding hits of 1929. No wonder the "hard egg" cracked!

It wasn't long after that Chevalier happened to meet one of the Metro-Goldwyn officials. "Do you know Mr. Chevalier?" asked the friend who introduced them.

"Yes, I know Mr. Chevalier," said the official as he shook hands and drew a handkerchief out of his pocket. "I know Mr. Chevalier, and it's a sad, sad story."

Still more important than the choice of his first was the choice of his second picture, since it involved the problem of crystallizing the popularity he had won.

Lubitsch, who had watched with delight his performance in "Innocents of Paris" came to him and said: "I have a good part for you in my next pixture, 'The Love Parade.' Will you play with me?"

"I WOULD be only too proud to play with you, "was the answer. "What is that part?"

But when he learned that it was the part of a queen's husband, and that it meant wearing stiff uniforms, he shook his head. "I cannot do that prince stuff," he said. "I cannot wear uniforms and make elegant gestures. Thank you very much for the compliment, but I must refuse."

"I was myself very disappointed," he went on, "because nothing would have pleased me more than to play with Lubitsch. But—I am not the lady-killer type. I think women like me because I make them smile, but they do not say—" here he dropped his chin into his palm and rolled his eyes heavenward—"oh, that Chevalier!"

(An impression, by the way, that he seems to retain despite everything the ladies of our broad land can do to persuade him to the contrary.)

"When the big dramatic scene comes I do not feel in my shoes. I try to play it naturally—as I feel it—as it would happen in life—with a little humor, if possible—because, though all my life has not been so funny, I find there is a funny side in many serious things. But still I do not like these romantic rôles. I like best to play the part of a plain fellow that women understand and that men understand, too."

Lubitsch, however, was not content to accept

(continued on next page)

(continued from preceding page)

Chevalier's decision. He returned a few days later and asked whether he might outline the story. Listening, Chevalier grew interested. "I see," he said, "that although that fellow is a prince, it is a story that might happen also to working people—a woman who wants to wear the trousers—a fight between a husband and a wife. So I say, 'Listen, Lubitsch! I like that story. But I don't like the big palace and the grand wedding and the uniforms and all that. I think I am too much of the people to look like something in a uniform.

"'But I'll tell you what I'll do. I'll have a photo taken in a uniform. I'll see how I look. And if I look possible, I'll play the part for the human interest there is in it, although—' he concluded sadly, 'it is a prince and I don't like princes.'"

THE photos were taken and Lubitsch "got crazy" over them. "You must do the part, Maurice," he cried. "I will have no one else." And even Maurice had to concede that he didn't look as stiff as he had expected. To prove it, little Madame Chevalier, who had been sitting quietly in a corner, tiptoed over at this juncture, to display a drawing made of her husband in that same uniform—tall Hussar's hat at a jaunty angle, tight collar, famous smile—a picture that has since grinned profitably down from the billboards of every city in America.

What happened when "The Love Parade" was released is motion picture history—a press that poured forth columns of glowing praise, a public enchanted by a smile and the personality behind it, record runs all over the country and a thirteen weeks' showing to capacity audiences on Broadway, a blazing new star in the talkie firmament who in two pictures had shot his way to the zenith where there were few, if any, to dispute his domain—and in the offices of Paramount a contract destroyed and a new one signed for four pictures at a huge increase in salary.

The first of those four was "The Big Pond"—the second is to be "The Little Café," now in rehearsal under the direction of Ludwig Berger, who directed "The Vagabond King." It's a kind of little *entente internationale* on the Paramount lot—Berger, the German war veteran, directing first Dennis King, the ex-Tommy, then Chevalier, the *ex-poilu*, who by the way will have his heart's desire in the new picture, since he plays in it the rôle of a very "plain fellow" indeed—a singing waiter in a Parisian café.

As might have been expected, Chevalier has had certain difficulties to overcome in adjusting himself to the American scene. Actor though he has been all his life, yet acting in the studios of Hollywood is an experience so far removed from acting on the stages of France that it might almost be regarded as another profession.

"I DO not think," he says, "that I am temperamental, though I believe every artist must be allowed his little nervous moment now and then. It is not so easy always to be calm, when he must play the same scene over and over again, giving it each time all his heart and strength, knowing it will go through the whole world to speak for him, knowing, once it is finished, he can do nothing to change it.

"But everyone—electricians, cameramen, actors, directors—they have been very kind to me—and I think—it may be I am wrong—but I think they feel I do always my best to be reasonable—they do not take me for one of those fellows who tries to blow out his chest and show he is the star."

An incident that occurred during the filming of "The Love Parade" proves Chevalier right. He had caught his hand somehow on a wire that was protruding in a place where it shouldn't have been, and inflicted a painful wound. In the midst of the commotion that followed, one mechanic was heard muttering to another: "Say, it shoulda happened to one o' these black-eyed-susans bouncin' around the lot insteada this guy! Then we'da had a laugh!"

The feature of his work that probably troubled Chevalier most at first had to do with publicity. He was totally unprepared for American publicity methods, which are unknown in France, and the Paramount people found they had their job cut out for them to persuade this potential gold mine that he must play with them if they were to put over certain stunts that seemed to them desirable. He couldn't understand why it should be necessary—he believed that his work ought to stand on its own feet, and even after they had convinced him that he must lend himself to their schemes, he felt he was doing so at the sacrifice of a certain amount of personal dignity. But there was one occasion, at least, when he put down his foot.

"The Love Parade" had been enjoying a long run at a San Francisco theater and when the attendance began to fall off, the manager conceived the idea of stimulating business by means of an essay contest among the feminine patrons of the theater on the subject of, "Why I Like Chevalier," the winner to receive a prize.

LEARNING that Chevalier was to be in San Francisco for the Motor Show, he suggested that if the Frenchman would agree to present the prize, he could probably keep the show running forever. But when the idea was tactfully broached to Chevalier, he exploded. "How can I do that thing?" he cried. "How can I make of myself such an imbecile to stand up in front of those women and say, 'Here, madame, is a prize for liking me!'"

It has been said of Chevalier often and with truth that he is a good business man. It has also been said, with overtones of disapproval, that he is a "shrewd article" and a hard driver of bargains. He himself makes no secret of his desire—which he shares with most of his fellowmen—to earn as much money as he can. He sets what he considers a proper value on his services, and if you don't agree with him, that is your privilege. But he refuses to haggle. He prefers not to take a job at all than to take it at a figure below the one he has set. And though he may be a hard bargainer, he is also a fair one, as the following story indicates.

A REPRESENTATIVE of the automobile industry was sent to New York, where Chevalier was making "The Big Pond," to negotiate for his services as master of ceremonies at the Motor Show. The Committee on the Coast, waiting impatiently for a decision, were unable to get from their agent any satisfactory response to their wires. "This man doesn't know how to talk business," was the gist of his replies. At length came a testy telegram from California. "Stop stalling. Get an answer one way or the other or come on home." The agent took the plunge. "Chevalier will come for twenty-five thousand, not a penny less."

Chevalier was engaged, but the affair may have rankled a little in the Chairman's bosom. For when he introduced his expensive master of ceremonies at the official dinner preceding the opening of the Show, he told the story of that telegraphic interchange and wound up with the remark: "For a man that can't talk business, I predict that this lad will go far."

Chevalier rose to reply. After a good-humored acknowledgment of the thrust, he went on: "It is quite right," he said, "that $25,000 is a great deal of money for the work of one week. Too much money, you think now perhaps. I hope you will not think so later. But if you do—if you find that the Motor Show is not a big success—if you find that I have not earned my money when the week is over — then we will tear up my contract and make new terms."

In spite of the stock market crash, in spite of the fact that the motor industry had been prepared for reduced sales, the Show at which Chevalier presided broke the previous year's record by eighty per cent and all existing motor show records by twenty-five per cent. There were no further wise-cracks offered on the subject of his $25,000 fee.

CHEVALIER has been criticised, too, for his refusal to appear in charity benefits, but his critics apparently overlook the fact that he stages charity benefits of his own. In New York last winter one of the town's swankier hostesses succeeded in getting him to a party—no mean feat in itself. He was there as a guest, not as an entertainer. Before long, however, his hostess floated up to coo: "Oh, Mr. Chevalier, we're all dying to hear some of those fascinating songs of yours. Won't you be an angel and sing for us?"

There was a moment's awkward pause, then a sigh of relief as Chevalier bowed and said: "With pleasure, Madame." But the relief was short-lived. "My fee," he added, "is $1,000." Cornered, the lady accepted the situation as gracefully as she could, and Chevalier sang. But when the time for payment came, he asked that the check be made out to the *Dispensaire Maurice Chevalier*.

The *Dispensaire Maurice Chevalier* is a hospital recently established in Paris for the care of theatrical people who can't afford to pay little or nothing for medical treatment. When the idea was conceived, a committee waited upon Chevalier with the request that he lend the hospital the prestige of his name. He agreed, and though it was understood that he should assume no obligation, moral or financial, toward the undertaking, he has since given at least one performance annually for its benefit.

During the first three months of this year, a sum close to $10,000 was received by the hospital as a result of his activities, and when he made a personal appearance in Los Angeles not long ago, the first night's receipts were divided between American charities and the *Dispensaire Maurice Chevalier*—the former in acknowledgment of what he feels to be his obligation to the American public, the latter in discharge of a voluntary debt to his own people.

His appeal seems to be universal. Hairy-chested he-men, to whom the average movie actor is a severe pain in the neck, fall for Chevalier. "He makes me feel good," says one. "He don't act like he loves himself," says another.

A gunman, shackled to a detective, was traveling prisonward on an ugly charge in the same train that was taking Chevalier to Hollywood. He gazed sullenly into space, as the Frenchman talked to his guard, but suddenly something attracted his interest and he looked up. Chevalier grinned at him. Before long they were deep in conversation—with "the frog" doing most of the talking and the gunman most of the listening.

CHEVALIER was telling him of his own childhood—of the young gangsters of Menilmontant among whom he had grown up, of how he had gradually come to realize that association with them would be likely to land him in jail. "And since I was sure," he said, "that I didn't want to go to jail, I stayed away from them. You have all great courage," he went on, "you have courage to do things which other men have not. It seems to me a great pity to waste that courage by fighting the law."

A little later, after Chevalier had returned to his compartment, a message was delivered to Tom Hearn, his friend and manager who was traveling with him. Hearn stuck his head through the door of the compartment. "Your friend in the handcuffs wants an autographed photo," he reported. (P.S. He got the photo.)

(continued from preceding page)

What is there about this man that has won for him in a few brief months the heart of a whole country? What is it that makes level-headed critics bubble over with extravagant adjectives in his praise? Why is it that people who "couldn't be dragged to the talkies" can't be dragged away from Chevalier's pictures? Why is it that his appearance and his appearance alone in a revue crowded with popular favorites is greeted by frantic applause?

What made it possible for him to fill a New York theater night after night with audiences willing to pay top prices for a half hour of his songs?

Why are cold-blooded captains of industry ready to give him what seem fantastic sums in exchange for a little of his time and his talent?

THE answer cannot be told in two words. But if you could have seen him, as I did, on the Paramount lot, singing a sly French song for the French version of "The Big Pond"—and if you could have seen the effect of that song on the people who listened, though they didn't understand a single word of it—if you could have watched their broadly beaming faces as he writhed and glared in mock anguish over it didn't matter what—if you could have felt the sense of exhilaration that lifted their hearts and made them brothers as he flung out his arms and his voice and his radiant smile in a last joyous burst of triumph—

And if, when the song was over, you could have seen them, shifting scenery, adjusting cameras, applying make-up, their eyes still alight, their bodies still lilting to the rhythm of the song, humming, whistling, grinning—if you could have basked in the atmosphere of gayety and good cheer and human warmth created by one man—then you would know why Maurice Chevalier has been called the king of entertainers and the best box-office bet that Paramount or any other company has ever had the good luck to sign!

AUG.

The costume ball of the future, or Cecil de Mille seein' things again! This mechanical marvel is the fancy dress ball held on board a Zeppelin in the old Plumbing-Master's new picture, "Madame Satan." Yes, sir—looks like a genuine old-time de Mille orgy!

AUG.

TOP SPEED—First National

A MUSICAL comedy, with emphasis on the comedy. Jack Whiting, of the stage, is a personable hero and Bernice Claire sings like the proverbial lark. But to us the whole thing is simply a framework for the antics of Joe E. Brown and Frank McHugh. The highlight is a thrilling speed-boat race.

"TOP SPEED"—FIRST NATIONAL.—Musical comedy by Harry Ruby, Bert Kalmar and Guy Bolton. Adaptation and dialogue by Humphrey Pearson and Henry McCarty. Directed by Mervyn LeRoy. Photography by Sid Hickox. The cast: *Elmer Peters*, Joe E. Brown; *Virginia Rollins*, Bernice Claire; *Gerald Brooks*, Jack Whiting; *Tad Jordan*, Frank McHugh; *Babs Green*, Laura Lee; *Daisy*, Rita Flynn; *Spencer Colgate*, Edmund Breese; *The Sheriff*, Wade Boteler; *Vincent Colgate*, Cyril King; *J. W. Rollins*, Edwin Maxwell.

AUG.

BRIDE OF THE REGIMENT—First National

THIS is another of First National's gorgeously dressed, sumptuously mounted and very slow-paced operettas taken from the theater. It positively glitters, and some of its Technicolor is grand, but it is a ponderous piece of business. Vivienne Segal, Walter Pidgeon, Allan Prior and Myrna Loy sing the leads, and Louise Fazenda and Ford Sterling try hard for laughs. But the pace is funereal.

"BRIDE OF THE REGIMENT"—FIRST NATIONAL.—From the operetta "The Lady in Ermine" by Rudolph Schanzer and Ernest Welisch. Screen play by Humphrey Pearson and Ray Harris. Directed by John Francis Dillon. The cast: *Countess Anna-Marie*, Vivienne Segal; *Count Adrian Beltrami*, Allan Prior; *Colonel Vultow*, Walter Pidgeon; *Teresa, the Maid*, Louise Fazenda; *Sophie*, Myrna Loy; *Sprotti, Ballet Master*, Lupino Lane; *Tangy, Silhouette-cutter*, Ford Sterling; *Sgt. Dostal*, Harry Cording; *Capt. Stogan*, Claude Fleming; *The Prince*, Herbert Clark.

A Hundred Million Eager Hearts Await Their Coming To The Screen!

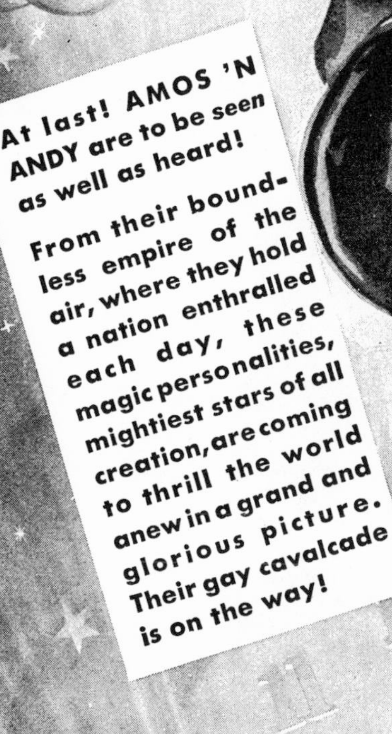

Watch for RADIO PICTURES This Year!

The **Radio** trade-mark will be your best assurance of fine entertainment, for millions of dollars and the genius of the greatest creative minds are going into **Radio** Pictures. **AMOS 'N ANDY** is but one of the treats in store. There's **"CIMARRON,"** Edna Ferber's great epic of empire, to look forward to; RICHARD DIX plays the coveted role of Yancey Cravat. **"DIXIANA,"** glamorous romance of Mardi Gras, brings BEBE DANIELS, EVERETT MARSHALL, Metropolitan Opera Star; Bert Wheeler, Robert Woolsey and a thousand others. Victor Herbert's **"BABES IN TOYLAND"** is coming in lavish extravaganza. There are many others of equal interest, including Rex Beach's **"THE SILVER HORDE"** and John Galsworthy's **"ESCAPE."**

Naturally you will want to see them all! The manager of your favorite theatre is now arranging his season's bookings and will appreciate it if you let him know your wishes in entertainment. He is anxious to please you. **Tell him you want to see these great RADIO PICTURES** at his house.

R. K. O. DISTRIBUTING CORPORATION
(Subsidiary of Radio Corporation of America)
1560 Broadway, New York City

Radio PICTURES

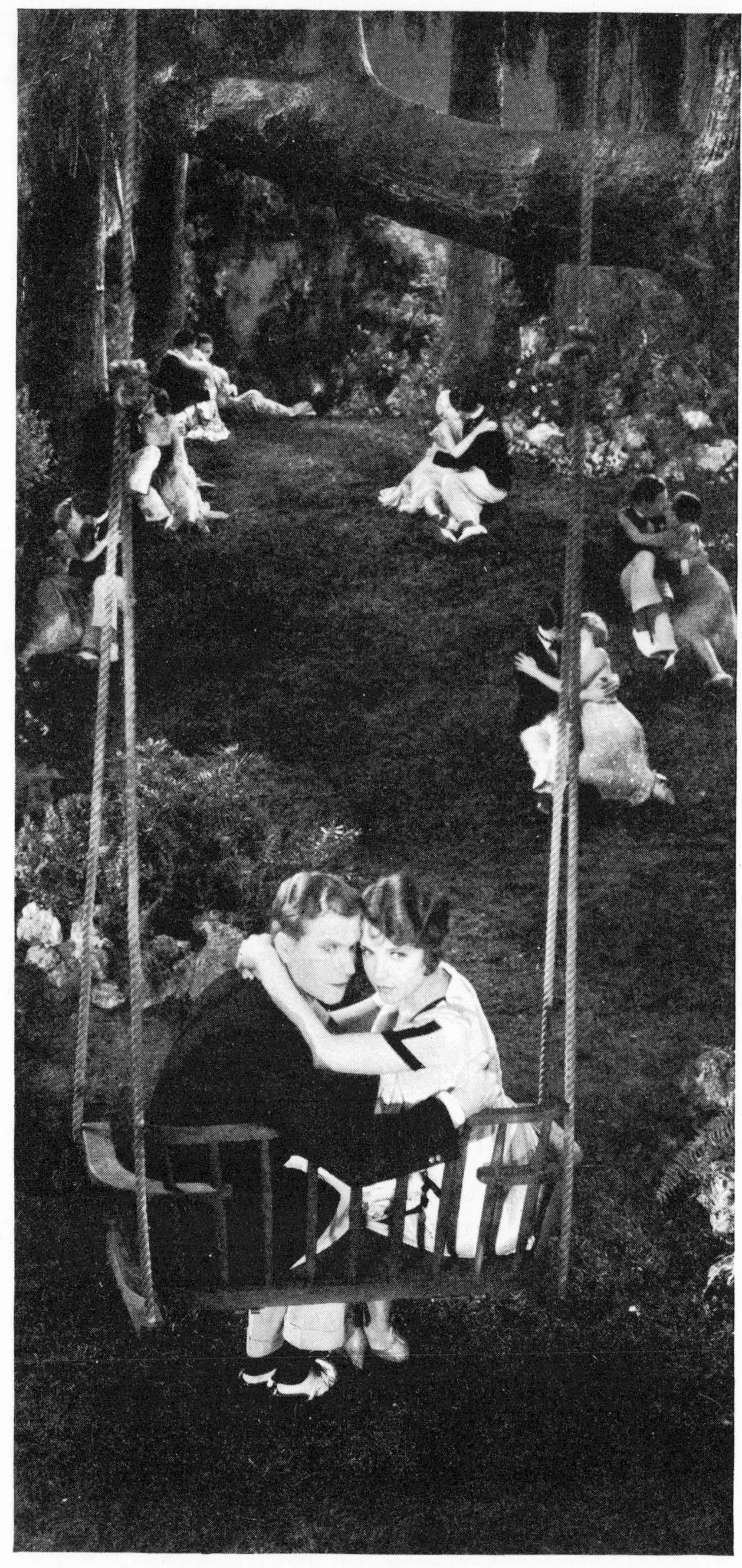

While Bernice Claire and Jack Whiting are busy facing the still camera, the extra boys and girls in the background seize the moment for a little innocent canoodling—as we called love-making in our neck of the woods. And it's a studio forest, too. A scene from "Top Speed." Bernice has been in great demand since her smashing success in First National's "No, No, Nanette"

AUG.

THE TOAST OF THE LEGION—First National

AFTER twenty-five years of vigorous life, "Mlle. Modiste," Victor Herbert's famous operetta, comes to the singing screen under this name. The great "Kiss Me Again" show is a beauty in the new medium, all in Technicolor, with good voices singing the pretty tunes. Bernice Claire scores heavily in the Fritzi Scheff rôle, and others are Walter Pidgeon, June Collyer and Edward Everett Horton.

"TOAST OF THE LEGION, THE"—FIRST NATIONAL.—From the operetta "Mlle. Modiste" by Victor Herbert. Adapted by Julian Josephson and Paul Perez. Directed by William A. Seiter. The cast: *Mlle. Fifi*, Bernice Claire; *Paul de St. Cyr*, Walter Pidgeon; *Rene*, Edward Everett Horton; *Count de St. Cyr*, Claude Gillingwater; *Francois*, Frank McHugh; *Mme. Cecile*, Judith Vosselli; *Marie*, June Collyer; *General de Villafrance*, Albert Gran; *Specialty Dancers*, Sisters "G."

AUG.

GOOD NEWS—M-G-M

THIS one, like the pardon from the governor, came too late. "Good News" has been stolen so many times that now it's no longer news. But it is done in a sprightly manner and if you haven't seen the Varsity Drag so often that you're bored, you'll love it. It is college run rampant, with Bessie Love, Stanley Smith, Mary Lawlor, Lola Lane and Ukelele Ike helping it run.

"GOOD NEWS"—M-G-M.—From the play by Lawrence Schwab, Lew Brown, Frank Mandel, B. G. DeSylva and Ray Henderson. Scenario by Frances Marion. Directed by Nick Grinde and Edgar J. McGregor. The cast: *Connie*, Mary Lawlor; *Tom*, Stanley Smith; *Babe*, Bessie Love; *Kearney*, Cliff Edwards; *Robbie*, Gus Shy; *Bat*, Lola Lane; *Coach*, Thomas Jackson; *Beef*, Delmer Daves; *Freshman*, Billy Taft; *Professor Kenyon*, Frank McGlynn; *Flo*, Dorothy McNulty; *Girls*, Helyn Virgil, Vera Marsh and Abe Lyman and his band.

AUG.

DIXIANA—Radio Pictures

THIS screen operetta, for which Harry Tierney has written delightful music, is a grand spectacle. And it doesn't stop at that. Everett Marshall, of Metropolitan fame, makes his screen début, and proves he has both voice and personality. And Bebe Daniels is at her best as a circus girl of old New Orleans. With Mardi Gras in Technicolor and negro spirituals, you will be charmed by this.

"DIXIANA"—RADIO PICTURES.—From the story by Anne Caldwell. Adapted by Luther Reed. Directed by Luther Reed. The cast: *Dixiana*, Bebe Daniels; *Carl Van Horn*, Everett Marshall; *Peewee*, Bert Wheeler; *Ginger*, Robert Woolsey; *Cornelius Van Horn*, Joseph Cawthorn; *Mrs. Van Horn*, Jobyna Howland; *Poppy*, Dorothy Lee; *Royal Montague*, Ralf Harolde; *Blondell*, Edward Chandler; *The Contortionist*, George Herman; *Cayetano*, Raymond Maurel; *Colonel Porter*, Bruce Covington; *Specialty Dancer*, Bill Robinson; *Cupid*, Eugene Jackson.

AUG.

QUEEN HIGH—Paramount

AN ace musical comedy—lots of laughs, plenty of pretty girls and some nice tunes. This sort of thing is the screen's hope in the light musical line. Charlie Ruggles and Frank Morgan are responsible for the chuckles, and Ginger Rogers' youth and charm are swell. Others who make this an unusually happy film are Stanley Smith, Nina Olivette and Helen Carrington.

"QUEEN HIGH"—PARAMOUNT.—From the play "A Pair of Sixes" by Edward Peple. Adapted from the musical comedy by Lawrence Schwab, Lewis Gensler and B. G. DeSylva. Directed by Fred Newmeyer. The cast: *T. Boggs Johns*, Charles Ruggles; *Mr. Nettleton*, Frank Morgan; *Polly Rockwell*, Ginger Rogers; *Dick Johns*, Stanley Smith; *Mrs. Nettleton*, Helen Carrington; *Cyrus Vanderholt*, Rudy Cameron; *Florence Cole*, Betty Garde; *Mrs. Rockwell*, Theresa Maxwell Conover; *Coddles*, Nina Olivette; *Jimmy*, Tom Brown.

AUG.

These New Faces

Watch for This Each Month

INEZ COURTNEY (First National) peeped from the screen in a tiny rôle in "Song of the Flame," and was immediately liked. She has had and is to have more and better parts. Inez has long been known as one of the very best of Broadway's dancing comediennes. She did two comedy dances with Gus Shy in "Good News" that were famous. Pictures were sure to get her.

FRED SCOTT ("Swing High," Pathe) is a newcomer who'll go far, with his fine tenor voice. While he was studying with Bebe Daniels' singing teacher, Bebe liked his voice and got him a small part in "Rio Rita." On the strength of that, and tests, he got the lead opposite Helen Twelvetrees in Pathe's big circus film. A good contract was his reward for *that*.

MARY LAWLOR ("Good News," M-G-M) is another Broadway musical comedy lead to strike out for the Gold Coast to catch some of the talkie money. She has for some time been in great demand for girly plays in New York, and created the "Good News" lead she is now playing on the screen. You'll like Mary—she is one of the stage's prettiest and very best.

ROBERT WOOLSEY ("The Cuckoos," Radio Pictures) has been teamed with Bert Wheeler in all his Radio Picture appearances. They clicked in "Rio Rita," did "The Cuckoos," and will next be seen in "Dixiana." Bobby, like his partner, Bert, is a veteran young comic of the Broadway stage. He has appeared in innumerable musicals, last with Wheeler in "Rio Rita."

IRENE DUNNE (Radio Pictures) is slated for big parts at this studio. She is mentioned for the feminine singing lead in "Babes in Toyland" and "Present Arms." Irene is another of New York's favorite musical comedy prima donnas. Golden haired and blue eyed, she has had many Broadway successes. One of her first hits was in "Sweetheart Time."

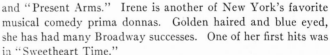

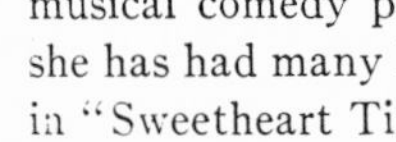

GUS SHY ("Good News," M-G-M) is another graduate of the stage production of "Good News." This seems to be their month in this department. Gus has been clowning around for a long time, but he scored sensationally in this success, and followed it with another wow in the comedy rôle in "New Moon," the beautiful operetta. Then films nabbed him.

AUG.

BRIGHT LIGHTS—First National

NOW we know why Dorothy Mackaill spent so much time in Honolulu. It was so she might out-hula the best of them. And she does it in "Bright Lights." This musical extravaganza, with original music, is entirely Technicolor, and gives both Dorothy and Frank Fay a fine opportunity. The result is delightful. Even though Dorothy broke a rib in making this, we think it is worth it.

"BRIGHT LIGHTS"—FIRST NATIONAL.—From the story by Humphrey Pearson. Adapted by Humphrey Pearson and Henry McCarty. Directed by Michael Curtiz. The cast: *Louanne*, Dorothy Mackaill; *Wally Dean*, Frank Fay; *Miguel Parada*, Noah Beery; *"Windy" Jones*, Eddie Nugent; *Peggy North*, Inez Courtney; *Mame Avery*, Daphne Pollard; *Tom Avery*, Tom Dugan; *Connie Lamont*, James Murray; *Violet Van Dam*, Jean Bary; *Harris*, Edmund Breese.

AUG.

Short Subjects *of the* Month

A BATTERY OF SONGS

Warners-Vitaphone

This is interesting because of its two personalities—Waite Hoyt, the Detroit baseball pitcher, singing—J. Fred Coots, composer of many popular song hits at the piano. And in the short is one Miss Questelle, a boop-a-dooper who won a prize imitating Helen Kane.

THE STILL ALARM

Warners-Vitaphone

This howling short was made from the best comedy scene in the famous "Little Show," Broadway revue, and has the original leading comedians, Fred Allen and Clifton Webb. It's a silly piece of business, with all being nonchalant while the building burns. You'll enjoy it.

SEPT.

JACK OAKIE **JEANETTE MacDONALD**

in

"LET'S GO NATIVE"

A mad, merry musical farce with a hand picked cast of Hollywood fun makers including Skeets Gallagher, James Hall, Kay Francis, Eugene Pallette, William Austin. By George Marion, Jr., author of "Sweetie" and "Safety in Numbers" and Percy Heath. Directed by Leo McCarey. Music by Richard A. Whiting. Lyrics by George Marion, Jr.

SEPT.

THINGS happen in mad, weird, wonderful Hollywood that authors could never dream for their story books.

There's the tale of Jeanie Lang, for instance.

Before "King of Jazz" was publicly shown, it was previewed for the press. Reporters wrote their reviews in advance, to be released the morning after the public premiére.

A little unknown girl named Jeanie Lang sang one song. Reviewers felt they had discovered a new, fresh and sparkling talent. Their pieces for the papers carried raves about Jeanie.

But before the public first night, the film was cut again—Jeanie and her song were eliminated entirely—became a girl and a tune on the cutting room floor.

When the reviews appeared, there was consternation! A great hullabaloo over Jeanie—and she wasn't even in the film as it was being shown.

Hurried re-patching, and Jeanie's restoration in the big Universal revue!

And in Los Angeles, advertisements appeared. "Jeanie Lang New Cinema Sensation," they read.

The breaks. It could only happen in Hollywood, where incredible things are believed every day, and impossible things come true!

Radiant Youth . . .
Passionate Love and
Rollicking Comedy . . . A
stirring romance glorified
by the golden voice of the
world's greatest tenor . . .
SONG O' MY HEART
A PICTURE THAT WILL BRING HAPPINESS TO MILLIONS
with
JOHN McCORMACK
MAUREEN O'SULLIVAN • ALICE JOYCE
JOHN GARRICK • J. FARRELL MacDONALD
JOSEPH KERRIGAN • TOMMY CLIFFORD
Directed by FRANK BORZAGE
FOX

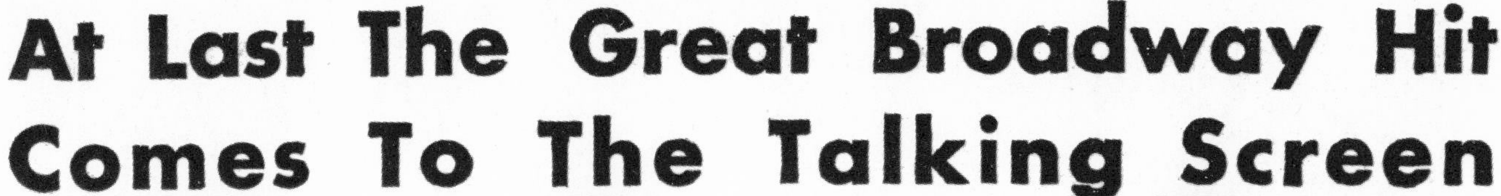

GOOD NEWS

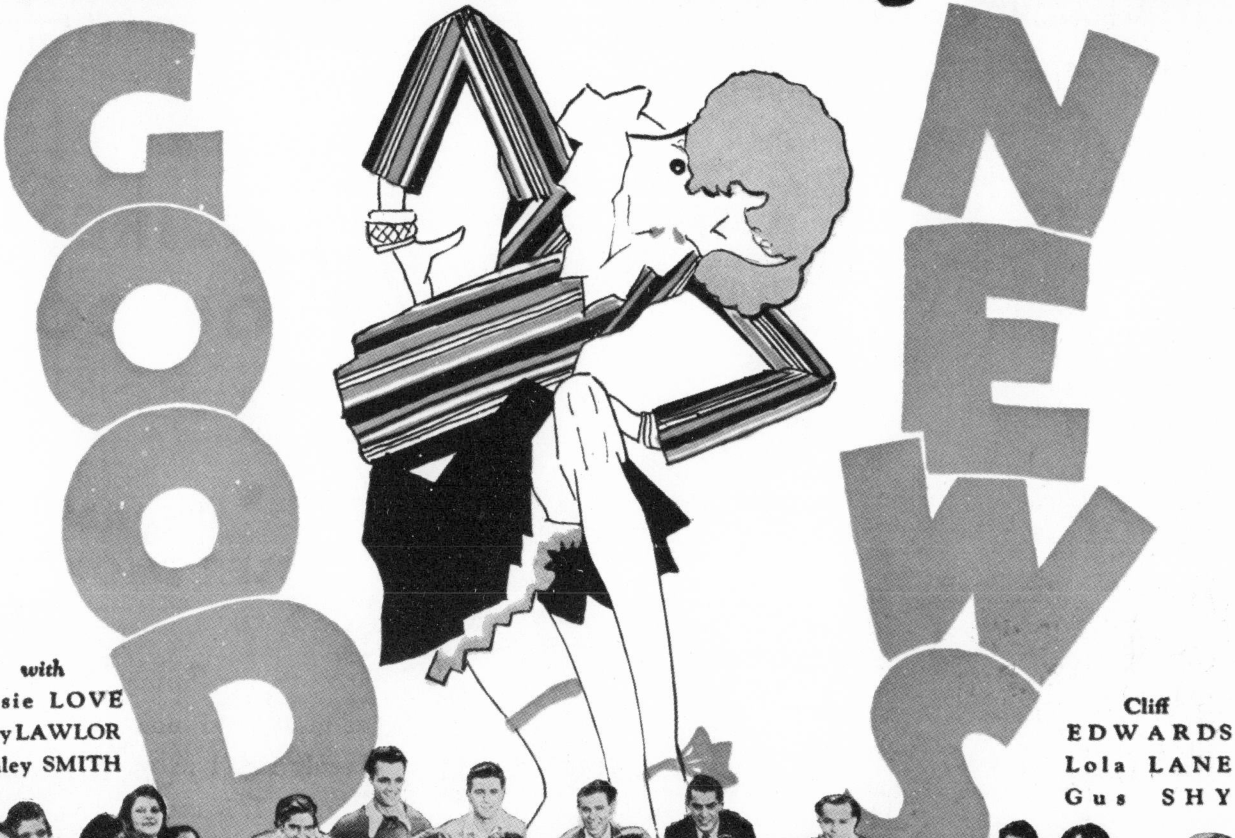

with
Bessie LOVE
Mary LAWLOR
Stanley SMITH

Cliff
EDWARDS
Lola LANE
Gus SHY

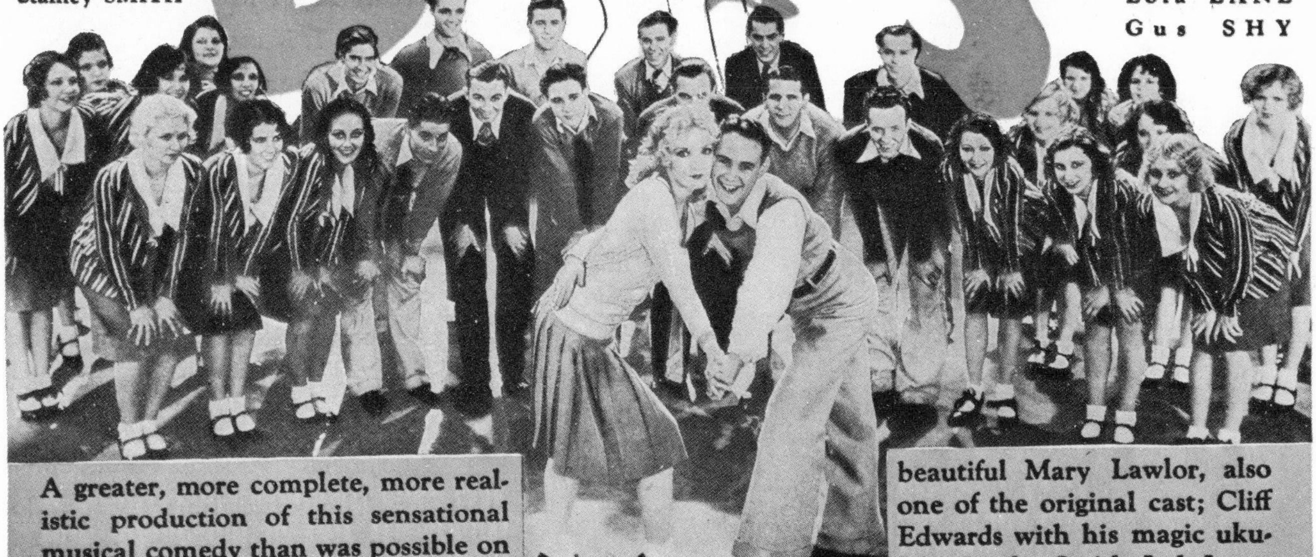

A greater, more complete, more realistic production of this sensational musical comedy than was possible on the stage. "GOOD NEWS" brings you the soul of college life—its swift rhythm, its pulsing youth, its songs, its pep, its loves, its laughter—crowded into one never-to-be-forgotten picture. A cocktail of hilarious, riotous entertainment!

What a cast! Bessie Love, of "BROADWAY MELODY" fame; Gus Shy, who starred in the Schwab & Mandel Broadway presentation; beautiful Mary Lawlor, also one of the original cast; Cliff Edwards with his magic ukulele; Stanley Smith, Lola Lane, Dorothy McNulty and a campus-full of cute co-eds and capering collegiates.

Marvelous music by De Sylva, Brown & Henderson. *"The Best Things in Life are Free"*, *"The Varsity Drag"* and others. Mirth! Melody! Speed! That's "GOOD NEWS"!

Scenario by Frances Marion—Dialogue by Joe Farnham
Directed by Edgar J. MacGregor and Nick Grinde

METRO-GOLDWYN-MAYER

THE METRO GOLDWYN MAYER LION — THE GREATEST STAR ON THE SCREEN

"More Stars Than There Are in Heaven"

TEN-MINUTE THRILLS..

that will add 100 Hours a Year to your Talking Picture Entertainment!

FAMOUS BANDS

OPERA

RIPLEY'S "BELIEVE IT OR NOT"

"LOONEY TUNES"

VAUDEVILLE HEADLINERS

CONCERT STARS

AND COLOR

Now you'll like the "SHORT SUBJECTS", too!

Why not enjoy ALL the time you spend at the Talking Movies?

You will if you'll make sure that the one and two-reel pictures on the bill are VITAPHONE VARIETIES.

VITAPHONE VARIETIES have raised "short subjects" for the first time to the quality level of the finest feature pictures.

All the vast resources that back VITAPHONE full-length pictures have been marshalled for the making of this new series of "Ten-Minute Thrills"!

Look and ask for VITAPHONE VARIETIES. They will add many hours of real enjoyment to your evenings at the theatre.

WARNER BROS. & VITAPHONE VARIETIES

"Vitaphone" is the registered trademark of The Vitaphone Corporation

Imagine Seeing Stars and Novelties like these as "Extra Attractions!"

Only by patronizing theatres that advertise VITAPHONE VARIETIES will you be sure to see—

RIPLEY drawing and describing his world-famous "BELIEVE IT OR NOT" oddities.

"LOONEY TUNES"—the funniest animated cartoon series ever devised.

CAPSULE MUSICAL COMEDIES in all the glory of Full Natural COLOR.

And such famous stars as—LEW FIELDS—ANN PENNINGTON—FRED ALLEN—BERT LAHR—EDDIE BUZZELL—RUTH ETTING—CHESTER CONKLIN—HENRY HULL—SPENCER TRACY—MARTINELLI

WARNER BROS. & VITAPHONE VARIETIES

Color scenes photographed by the Technicolor Process

VITAPHONE VARIETIES

MINIATURE MASTERPIECES OF THE TALKING-SINGING SCREEN

Quick success at 21; a sudden swoop downward toward failure at 22; and a hard-won place near the top again at 23. That's Sue Carol's motion picture history.

As Evelyn Lederer she went to Hollywood from Chicago for a visit a few years ago and crashed the movies without even half-trying. She made a hit in "Soft Cushions" with Douglas MacLean in 1927, later signing with Fox.

Then Sue and Nick Stuart, who played young lovers in Fox pictures, were married, secretly for a time. Maybe their fans lost interest when the reported romance was known to have terminated in commonplace matrimony. The Fox company, at any rate, lost interest in Sue as a box office bet. They gave her a part secondary to Dixie Lee in "The Big Party," followed by six months of poor stories.

And then, her darkest hour right at hand, her contract with Fox completed, Radio Pictures cast her opposite Arthur Lake in a picture that just suited her. Their faith justified, they signed her to a long-term contract.

Sue's climbing to more substantial success. Good luck to a good trouper!

(picture from Sept., text from Nov.)

Marilyn Points Her Toe!

A LOVELY girl who has brought dreams of youth and beauty into the dusty hearts of millions since she first burst upon us in "The Passing Show of 1914"—Marilyn Miller. And she's still as lithe and young and beautiful!

SUNNY SALLY

Smiling Marilyn, now intent on following her big "Sally" film with an equally splendiferous "Sunny"

This and That About a Girl of Genuine Charm— Marilyn Miller

By Michael Woodward

MARILYN MILLER can't, for one thing, sleep with light striking her eyelids, and it dawns at the unreasonable hour of about five, these Hollywood mornings. So Marilyn has a folded black silk handkerchief on the table by her bedside.

When dawnlight wakes her, she simply reaches over, lays the hankie across her eyes, and goes back to sleep until she's darned good and ready to get up.

ANOTHER thing—she simply can't sleep in a messy room. It's got to be as neat as a cat's idea of Paradise. She says it's because she hates to wake up in the morning to be greeted with a sight of disorder to begin the new day. So she folds her clothes and puts them away as she undresses. And her dressing table has to be all prettied and tidied up before she goes to bed.

And she doesn't like pajamas for sleeping. They're all right for lounging, and she has dozens of pairs of 'em for that. But for sleeping, give Marilyn a good old nightie, please. And she has to have her sleep, too. She lets nothing interfere with getting her full quota, and that's one reason she's the beauty she is, even though she's thirty-two. She's about the only thirty-two-year-old beauty in Hollywood who says she's thirty-two. The others try to reverse the digits.

AND now let's get out of her bedroom and consider breakfast—although, matter of fact, she takes it in bed. And she likes, above any other breakfast dish, chicken hash in cream!

She's fond of chicken in almost any fashion—particularly fried, with hot biscuits on the side. No, girls, she doesn't have to worry about her figure; dancing keeps it like it is.

SHE pours heavy cream over her baked potatoes, too, although she doesn't like milk, which, to her, is only food for calves.

Her favorite dinner is a pot roast, with dumplings and hot biscuits, cooked by her ma. With old fashioned strawberry shortcake—the biscuit-and-cream kind—to top it off. She doesn't go much for ritzy dishes with fancy French names, but does like salad, mixed in a bowl at the table.

AND she loves to ride through Central Park, in New York, eating a hot dog.

She's superstitious. Hates parrots because she thinks they're bad luck, and belongs to the theatrical clan who believe whistling in a dressing room is worse than the seven-years' plague. She always makes a wish when she sees a load of hay, knocks wood according to the best etiquette of superstition, and insists on hooking little fingers and making a wish whenever she and someone else say the same thing at the same time.

SHE declines to learn card games because she doesn't think cards are interesting. Besides, she's seen too many arguments at the bridge table, and says it isn't worth fighting over, so she doesn't want to play. She can't play the piano, either, but wishes she could, so she always talks about learning to do it. But doesn't. The only instrument she can play is the zither, and she can play only one tune on that. She had to learn it for "Sunny." She's a wow with the drums, though. At informal home dances, she not infrequently leaves the floor, ousts the drummer from his place and takes the sticks and traps.

She likes swimming, and splashes about the pool of her Beverly Hills home every day. She takes sunbaths, too, but not *à la* Garbo!—she wears a bathing suit. The Beverly Hills house she lives in is the one Lita Grey Chaplin owns. Marilyn calls it her Lita Grey Home in the West!

SHE loves wisecracking, too. Her idea of a grand time is not playing bridge, but having a houseful of smart people and indulging in fast repartee. She likes people with a sense of humor, and has a grand one of her own. She can see a joke even when it's on herself. She's a great mimic—her imitations of Eddie Cantor and Evelyn Laye are Hollywood classics. She's great fun on a party.

She has two maids, a butler, a chauffeur, a gardener, a secretary and a cook, and she likes to scramble eggs for her guests herself. She runs her own house but not her cars, although she has three—a Rolls-Royce town car, a Chrysler sports roadster and the inevitable Ford.

SHE'S a good horsewoman and likes to ride, but can't take the risk. She might be thrown or crushed and her legs be ruined—which would be as bad for Marilyn as it would be for Paderewski if he hit his thumb while hanging pictures. Her adept legs, however, make her a first-rate tennis and badminton player.

(continued on next page)

(continued from preceding page)

By the way, she can dance for an hour without tiring, and loves it.

She is one of the few great dancers who have not permitted their calves to be ruined by bulging muscles. The answer is that she always bathes them in ice cold water after a hard session.

HER greatest hobbies are her work and her family. She spends two to three hours a day practicing and devising dance steps, and another hour daily vocalizing, for she keeps her voice as fit as her legs. She likes to sing, and doesn't mind a bit when she's asked to sing at parties.

She loves to be complimented. She gets as great a kick out of being told a nice thing the millionth time as she did the first time she heard it.

And she's quite sure she can distinguish between sincerity and flattery.

It's not hard to sincerely compliment her. Her hair is natural gold, and her eyes are green, not blue. Her smile is famous. She is a genuine beauty. Her hair is bobbed, but she doesn't like it that way. She can't let it grow because her rôles all call for short locks. She used to wear curls to her shoulders before she joined "The Passing Show" in 1914, and she wishes she could wear curls now. She never gives way to temper, and her sweet disposition is 18 karat genuine.

She likes parties, but prefers them small and select—the selection to be confined to smart people. She doesn't care for people with a set "line."

And much as she likes parties, she ditches them regularly when she's in production, because she's so interested in her work that she devotes all her time to it.

She's a good business woman and transacts all her own business in person. She's one of the few actresses who have no business manager or agent.

She gets $200,000 a picture. She's always ahead of time for her business appointments, and almost always late for her social engagements.

She likes people and has many friends, but they're almost all men. She doesn't get on half as well with women as with men. She's been married twice—Frank Carter, her first, whom she married while yet a kid, was killed in an auto accident before their first anniversary, and Jack Pickford was her second — she divorced him because Hollywood and Broadway didn't mix. Now she's supposed to be engaged to Michael Farmer, a rich automobile man of Paris, who telephones her very often across the Atlantic and the United States, and damn the cost! They plan to marry this fall. Maybe.

THE fourth man in her life was Ben Lyon. They are still good friends.

Marilyn was a guest at Ben's marriage to Bebe Daniels, and the three of them are a clubby little set.

Marilyn likes smiling faces and can't stand doleful ones. Once a new butler—a colored man—was hired while Marilyn was away. The maid explained to the new man that Miss Miller wanted cheerful faces about her. When Marilyn returned, the new butler took it so seriously that he laughed out loud. Marilyn liked it.

SHE likes solid colors in clothes and has dozens and dozens of outfits, of course, including many elaborate dressing gowns. Yet she almost always uses an old pongee kimono that she's had for years, and that no chorus girl would want to be found dead in! She's worn it when receiving such dignitaries as the Prince of Rome and the Prince of Wales. And her face was all smeared up with cold cream when she met the latter. It was in her dressing room in New York.

She kept the cold cream and the ancient kimono on with charming unconcern while she chatted with the prince.

The walls of her dressing room are covered with autographed photos of stage and screen stars, and her dressing mirror looks as though she'd gotten it for two bits in a second-rate second-hand shop. It's cracked straight across; she's had it for years; and won't have any other.

She adores jewelry and has a great collection of it. One piece—a cross of diamonds—she wears almost always. She never goes out, either, without pinning somewhere inside her clothing—a little bunch of religious medals. She believes they bring her good luck. They went through the war on an American soldier and although she has lost them several times, they've always been returned to her.

She loves oriental objects—and oriental mystery stories, too. But her preference in reading is the biographies of famous persons of history.

SHE collects elephants and has nearly a hundred of every kind and size. One set from India consists of dozens of tiny elephants, each carved from a different kind of wood; another set is made of various kinds of semi-precious stones.

She loves cats and has a Siamese in her New York home, but none in Hollywood. In Hollywood her pet is "Sunny"—one of those underslung Scotty dogs.

She hasn't gotten used to movie fame yet and it embarrasses her to be stared at by fan crowds. She doesn't like to be pointed out as "there goes Sally." She insists that she's not beautiful—expresses it with: "There are so many people prettier than I!" But she knows she has perfect lips.

She is not in the least affected or self-conscious.

Once, for a gag, she signed a note to a friend only by kissing the paper with heavily rouged lips.

The friend recognized it at once.

It was a male friend.

SEPT.

DANGEROUS NAN McGREW—Paramount

THIS picture should teach us all a lesson. When we want to make a talkie, we'd better get a story. This is a very bad picture because it has no story at all. Some cute people try to make it stand up—Helen Kane, Stuart Erwin, Victor Moore and Frank Morgan—but it doesn't hold us for more than a minute at a time. Helen and Victor run a medicine show up North. Feeble.

"DANGEROUS NAN McGREW"—PARAMOUNT.—From the story by Charles Beahan, Garrett Fort, Paul Gerard Smith and Pierre Collings. Directed by Malcolm St. Clair. The cast: *Nan McGrew,* Helen Kane; *Doc Foster,* Victor Moore; *Bob Dawes,* James Hall; *Eustace Macy,* Stuart Erwin; *Muldoon,* Frank Morgan; *Mrs. Benson,* Louise Closser Hale; *Clara Benson,* Roberta Benson; *Godfrey,* Allen Forrest.

SEPT.

OH SAILOR, BEHAVE!—Warners

IF you manage to sit through the second reel of this you'll discover that Lowell Sherman makes a swell comedy prince. But a few more like this and song writers and song birds will be going back to Broadway. There are mean old generals, scheming adventuresses, Johnson and Olsen, and Charlie King as a singing reporter. Lotti Loder, heralded as a find, proves she can roll her eyes.

"OH SAILOR, BEHAVE!"—WARNERS.—From the play "Nancy From Naples" by Elmer Rice. Screen play by Joseph Jackson. Directed by Archie Mayo. The cast: *Nanett Dodge,* Irene Delroy; *Charlie Carroll,* Charles King; *Prince Kosoff,* Lowell Sherman; *Roumanian General,* Noah Beery; *Simon,* Ole Olsen; *Peter,* Chick Johnson; *Louisa,* Lotti Loder; *Kuni,* Vivian Oakland; *De Medici,* Charles Judles; *Mitzi,* Elise Bartlett; *Von Klaus,* Lawrence Grant; *Stepan,* Gino Corrodo.

SEPT.

LOVE AMONG THE MILLIONAIRES—Paramount

IS there a plot afoot to keep Clara Bow off the screen? If her personal peccadillos don't do it, bad stories will. This one, a musical comedy, concerns the railroad lunch counter waitress, the son of the president of the road who poses as a brakeman, and the attempt on the girl's part to disillusion the boy about her for his own good. It's pretty discouraging, and Clara gets much too cute.

"LOVE AMONG THE MILLIONAIRES"—PARAMOUNT.—From the story by Keene Thompson. Adapted by Grover Jones and William Conselman. Directed by Frank Tuttle. The cast: *Pepper,* Clara Bow; *Jerry Hamilton,* Stanley Smith; *Clicker,* Stuart Erwin; *Roots,* Skeets Gallagher; *Penelope,* Mitzi Green; *Pop,* Charles Sellon; *Jordan,* Theodore Von Eltz; *Mr. Hamilton,* Claude King; *Virginia,* Barbara Bennett.

SEPT.

BIG BOY—Warners

HERE'S Al Jolson's stage thriller about race-track intrigue, done into high comedy talkie. Al is blackface throughout except for a short afterpiece, cracks some old gags and some fast new ones, and sings about eight numbers, than which could any Jolson fan beg more? It's all done in a grand air of rollicking levity that adds to the fun. Go, and get a nightful of laughs.

"BIG BOY"—WARNERS.—From the play by Harold Attridge. Adapted by William K. Wells and Perry Vekroff. Directed by Alan Crosland. The cast: *Gus,* Al Jolson; *Annabel Bedford,* Claudia Dell; *Mrs. Bedford,* Louise Closser Hale; *Jack Bedford,* Lloyd Hughes; *Coley Reed,* Eddie Phillips; *Doc Wilbur,* Lew Harvey; *Jim,* Franklin Batie; *Joe,* John Harron.

SEPT.

FOLLOW THRU—Paramount

THE stage's best golf musical comedy has come to the screen as a beautiful, peppy singie-talkie-dancie-golfie, with Buddy Rogers and Nancy Carroll as pert co-stars and Jack Haley, Zelma O'Neal and Eugene Pallette to furnish the laughs. This is as entertaining as they come. This boy Haley is a fine picture bet. It's all Technicolor, and all good, fast entertainment!

"FOLLOW THRU"—PARAMOUNT.—From the play by Schwab and Mandel. Directed by Lawrence Schwab and Lloyd Corrigan. The cast: *Jerry Downs,* Charles "Buddy" Rogers; *Lora Moore,* Nancy Carroll; *Angie Howard,* Zelma O'Neal; *Jack Martin,* Jack Haley; *J. C. Effingham,* Eugene Pallette; *Ruth Van Horn,* Thelma Todd; *Mac Moore,* Claude King; *Mrs. Bascomb,* Kathryn Givney; *Babs Bascomb,* Margaret Lee; *Dinty Moore,* Don Tomkins; *Martin Bascomb,* Albert Gran.

SEPT.

☆ *THE SINGER OF SEVILLE—M-G-M*

RAMON NOVARRO'S new talkie popularity will be strengthened and extended by this romantic story tailored to his talents. As a devil-may-care dancer of Seville, embarked indifferently on an operatic career, Ramon is charming. Dorothy Jordan, opposite the star once more, is delightful. This is the last picture Renee Adoree appeared in before her present illness. And it's a delightful one.

"SINGER OF SEVILLE, THE"—M-G-M.—From the story by Dorothy Farnum. Directed by Charles Brabin. The cast: *Juan,* Ramon Novarro; *Maria* Dorothy Jordan; *Esteban,* Ernest Torrence; *Mother Superior,* Nance O'Neil; *Lola,* Renee Adoree; *La Rumbarita,* Mathilde Comont; *Enrique,* Russell Hopton.

SEPT.

Short Subjects *of the* Month

COCK-EYED NEWS

Paramount

This is a whale of an idea, this burlesquing the newsreels, but they'll have to be a little funnier. Here Eddie Cantor introduces it, and sings a song. Then are shown a series of straight captions introducing kidding pictures. Sample—Title, "Tag Day in Scotland." Scene, empty street.

MANHATTAN SERENADE

Metro-Goldwyn-Mayer

This is one of the prettiest and most distinctive musical comedy shorts of the month—if not THE most. Mary Doran and Raymond Hackett introduce people. The three Brox Sisters sing, and there is some elegant hot dancing by principals and chorus. Much of the film's in color.

THE ROYAL FOUR-FLUSHER

Warner Vitaphone Variety

A travesty on medieval royalty, starring that droll little fellow, Eddie Buzzell, who sings two songs. Most of it is knockabout comedy, stretched thin over two reels. Eddie carries on a comic intrigue with the court dressmaker, Doris Dawson. Mild.

SEPT.

MAN TROUBLE—Fox

AN underworld "king" befriends a discouraged girl. But she doesn't repay him with her love. That goes to a romantic young newspaper columnist. All of which makes a thrilling picture of life as it's supposed to be lived in New York speakeasies. Milton Sills is sensational as the popular notion of a fearless gangster. Dorothy Mackaill's lovely mouth can sing—throbbingly. She rates second honors.

"MAN TROUBLE"—Fox.—From the story by Ben Ames Williams. Adapted by George Manker Watters and Marion Orth. Directed by Berthold Viertel. The cast: *Joan,* Dorothy Mackaill; *Mac,* Milton Sills; *Graham,* Kenneth MacKenna; *Trixie,* Sharon Lynn; *Scott,* Roscoe Karns; *Eddie,* Oscar Apfel; *Goofy,* James Bradbury, Jr.; *Chris,* Lew Harvey; *Uncle Joe,* Harvey Clark; *Aunt Maggie,* Edythe Chapman.

SEPT.

These New Faces

Watch for This Each Month

JOE COOK ("Rain or Shine," Columbia) really needs little introduction to anybody. For years he was a vaudeville juggler, with a tremendous flow of conversation, utterly insane, that soon made him a featured comedian in many Broadway shows. His last Broadway offering was "Rain or Shine," which he has now turned into a talkie for Columbia. Should be a panic.

FRANK MORGAN ("Dangerous Nan McGrew," Paramount) is one of the most able and distinguished actors on the American stage, and a brother of Ralph Morgan. While making two films at the Paramount Eastern studio, Morgan was playing the featured rôle in "Topaze," a delightful French comedy, on Broadway. He was featured in "The Firebrand" several seasons ago.

DOROTHY LEE ("The Cuckoos," Radio Pictures) is a little dancer who has come far very fast. She was appearing in vaudeville with Fred Waring's Pennsylvanians, and worked with that band in its picture, "Syncopation." Dorothy made such an impression that Radio Pictures hired her, and she was immediately successful in the ingénue rôle in "Rio Rita."

VICTOR MOORE ("Dangerous Nan McGrew," Paramount) has been a leading comedian in America for over thirty-five years. Fifteen years ago he made several silent comedies. He appeared in vaudeville for many years with his wife, Emma Littlefield. Recently he has been featured in many Broadway musical comedy hits. And now he faces cameras that hear!

OCT.

Studio Rambles

By Harriet Parsons

How about the M-G-M studio? Always something doing there. Right! Off to Culver City. If we're good maybe Owens will let us drive the Ford onto the lot. Owens is the amiable tyrant who guards the gate. Try to get in!

What have we here? Must be the hallway of an old Southern home, for there are Mammy and old Uncle George looking expectantly up the great stairway. Joan Crawford descends it, looking charming in a blue tailored sports coat and tam-like hat.

The picture is "Great Day," a musical comedy laid in the South. Joan plays a fourteen-year-old girl at the start of the story. We saw her taking a test the other day in a blue-checked gingham dress and socks, looking young enough to be in "Our Gang."

Between shots, Joan and Cliff Edwards and John Miljan gather around a miniature piano. Joan sings "More Than You Know" in a low, pleasing voice. Her eyes have a far-away look. Probably thinking about that good-looking husband of hers. Cliff sings, too, and clowns.

Before we go let's drop in on the "Jenny Lind" set. Maybe we can hear Grace Moore sing. What? She's not singing today—they're just shooting the final love scenes. Too bad.

What a charming little Swedish cottage—so quaint and cosy. Look at that funny old-fashioned china dog on the shelf. There's Grace's voice offstage—and here she comes down the stairs in a high-waisted frock with an enormous full skirt. She doesn't look like the usual buxom opera star.

By the way, wasn't Jenny Lind a coloratura soprano? And Grace Moore is a mezzo. How on earth can she sing those pyrotechnical coloratura arias that the "Swedish Nightingale" was famous for? Ah, well—stranger things have happened in the movies!

Guess we're getting too curious. Better go home before we're thrown out for asking impertinent questions.

SEPT.

The poor lady at the upper end of this tremendous train is poor Bebe Daniels, with Everett Marshall in "Dixiana." If she didn't have the help of eight chorus girls, she'd fall down those stairs and break her neck. And we can't have Bebe's neck broken just now—nor can Ben Lyon!

OCT.

THE LOTTERY BRIDE—United Artists

THE thrill of this one is Jeanette MacDonald, who goes in for histrionics in a big way. You knew she could sing and look beautiful. Here she acts. The story, your old favorite "Bride 66," is powerful in a melo sort of way and the music is grand. Some big spectacle stuff and lots of snow and ice.

"LOTTERY BRIDE, THE"—United Artists.—An Arthur Hammerstein Production. From the story by Herbert Stothart. Adapted by Horace Jackson. Directed by Paul L. Stein. The cast: *Jenny*, Jeanette MacDonald; *Chris*, John Garrick; *Hoke*, Joe E. Brown; *Hilda*, ZaSu Pitts; *Olaf*, Robert Chisholm; *Alberto*, Joseph Macaulay; *Boris*, Harry Gribbon; *Nels*, Carroll Nye.

OCT.

ONE MAD KISS—Fox

BUT for the glorious voice of Don Jose Mojica, young tenor from the Chicago Opera Company, we should advise passing this. But Mojica plays a romantic Spanish outlaw that will steal the female hearts. Mona Maris, pleasing to look upon, is too good an actress to be compelled to sing, but these two afford entertainment for a satisfactory evening.

"ONE MAD KISS"—Fox.—From the story by Adolf Paul. Directed by James Tinling. The cast: *Jose Savedra*, Don Jose Mojica; *Rosario*, Mona Maris; *Don Estrada*, Antonio Moreno; *Paco*, Tom Patricola.

OCT.

KATHLEEN MAVOURNEEN—Tiffany Productions

A WEAK-KNEED Irish story, built from the ancient play by Dion Boucicault. Sally O'Neil plays a little colleen who comes from Ireland to marry the sweetheart of her youth, only to have the ward boss fall in love with her after all. But she finally marries the plumber! Charles Delaney and Robert Elliott play plumber and boss, respectively.

"KATHLEEN MAVOURNEEN" — Tiffany Productions.—From the play by Dion Boucicault. Continuity by Frances Hyland. Directed by Albert Ray. The cast: *Kathleen*, Sally O'Neil; *Terry*, Charles Delaney; *Dan Moriarity*, Robert Elliott; *Aunt Nora Shannon*, Aggie Herring; *Uncle Mike Shannon*, Walter Perry; *Butler*, Francis Ford.

OCT.

MAYBE IT'S LOVE—Warners

MAYBE it's love, but it isn't college, with Joan Bennett wandering at will into men's dormitories and football training quarters. The gridiron scenes are good. They should be with eleven of the outstanding stars of the country playing on the field and acting in the picture. Joe E. Brown provides snickers, and James Hall is the handsome hero. That Bennett beauty sings well.

"MAYBE IT'S LOVE"—Warners.—From the story by Mark Canfield. Adapted by Joseph Jackson. Directed by William Wellman. The cast: *Nan Sheffield*, Joan Bennett; *Speed Hansen*, Joe E. Brown; *Tommy Nelson*, James Hall; *Betty*, Laura Lee; *Mr. Nelson*, Anders Randolf; *Whiskers*, Sumner Getchell; *President Sheffield*, George Irving; *Professor*, George Bickel; *Coach Bob Brown*, Howard Jones; *Bill*, Bill Banker; *"Racehorse" Russell*, Russell Saunders; *Tim*, Tom Moynihan; *Schoony*, W. K. Schoonover; *Elmer*, E. N. Sleight; *George*, George Gibson; *Ray*, Ray Montgomery; *Otto*, Otto Pommerening; *Ken*, Kenneth Haycraft; *Howard*, Howard Harpster; *Paul*, Paul Scull; *Brown of Harvard*, Stuart Erwin.

OCT.

LEATHERNECKING—Radio Pictures

IN spite of a lot of things, they're still making musical romances. This is one of them, but Allah be praised, the curse is taken off by some top-hole comedy in which a rare cast of funsters collaborate hilariously. You'll roll with laughter while Benny and Louise and Ned and the rest of them do their funny stuff, and that makes up for all the singing and dancing.

"LEATHERNECKING"— Radio Pictures. — From the play by Herbert Fields, Richard Rogers and Lorenz Hart. Adapted by Alfred Jackson. Directed by Eddie Cline. The cast: *Delphine*, Irene Dunne; *Frank*, Ken Murray; *Hortense*, Louise Fazenda; *Ned Sparks*, Ned Sparks; *Edna*, Lilyan Tashman; *Chick*, Eddie Foy, Jr.; *Stein*, Benny Rubin; *Fortune Teller*, Rita LaRoy; *Douglas*, Fred Santley; *Richter*, Baron von Brinken; *The Colonel*, Carl Gerrard; *Richter songs*, Werther and Wolfgang.

OCT.

GOLDEN DAWN—Warners

IF you're tired of players who break into song and dance without much provocation, this won't help a bit. Noah Beery dons blackface and plays an African native, enamored of the girl, *Dawn*, played by Vivienne Segal. Walter Woolf is the upstanding British officer who loves her. In spite of all-Technicolor mounting it's pretty dull.

"GOLDEN DAWN" — Warners. — From the story by Oscar Hammerstein II. From the play by Otto Harbach. Directed by Ray Enright. The cast: *Tom Allen*, Walter Woolf; *Dawn*, Vivienne Segal; *Shep Keyes*, Noah Beery; *Blink*, Lee Moran; *Joanna*, Marion Byron; *Sister Hedwig*, Julanne Johnston; *Maid in Waiting*, Nena Quartaro; *Mooda*, Alice Gentle; *Napoli*, Nick de Ruiz; *Captain Eric*, Otto Matiesen; *African Piper*, Sojin; *Fan Boy*, Harold Clarke; *Anzac*, Frank Dunn; *Dancing Instructor*, Eduardo Cansino; *British Officer*, Carlie Taylor; *Hasmali*, Nigel de Bruilier; *Col. Judson*, Ivan Simpson.

WOMAN'S LOVE ... MAN'S HATE ... BLAZING ROMANCE
IN A CITY AFLAME WITH CARNIVAL PLEASURES!
DIXIANA
In staggering magnificence . . . in thundering emotions comes "DIXIANA" to hold the world spellbound! ALL THAT IS LIFE HAS BEEN ENGULFED IN THIS AMAZING PRODUCTION! Romance . . . Fiery Drama . . . Bouncing Comedy . . . Revelry . . . Stupendous Spectacle! The story of Two Men . . . and a Woman who set men's hearts aflame . . . amid the Mad Abandon and Fevered Passions of Mardi Gras!
with
BEBE DANIELS
Glamorous star of song and great emotions.
EVERETT MARSHALL
Famous star of Metropolitan Opera Company.
BERT WHEELER
AND
ROBERT WOOLSEY
DOROTHY LEE
JOSEPH CAWTHORN
RALF HAROLDE
JOBYNA HOWLAND and
BILL ROBINSON
World's Greatest Tap Dancer)
Music by Harry Tierney, Book by Anne Caldwell
Directed by LUTHER REED . . . Supervised by WM. LE BARON
SCENES IN GLORIOUS TECHNICOLOR
TUNE IN EVERY
TUESDAY EVENING
and
THURSDAY AFTERNOON
for the great
RKO HOUR
over N.B.C. Network
Famous stars . . favorite entertainers, news of Hollywood and coming productions.
COMING WITH A RUSH! AMOS 'N' ANDY in their first talking picture, Edna Ferber's "CIMARRON", John Galsworthy's "ESCAPE", "BABES IN TOYLAND", "LEATHER NECKING" and "HALF SHOT AT SUNRISE" with Bert Wheeler and Robert Woolsey . . . not to mention a grand and gorgeous galaxy of other great attractions in THE NEW PAGEANT OF THE TITANS!
Radio PICTURES
RKO DISTRIBUTING CORPORATION
(Subsidiary of Radio Corp. of America)
1560 BROADWAY, NEW YORK CITY

A QUEEN of German films begins her career in America! The beautiful Marlene Dietrich with the spangles on, as she appears in the leading feminine rôle of "Morocco," in which Gary Cooper and Adolphe Menjou labor. This gorgeous girl with the slumbrous eyes was discovered in Berlin by Director Josef von Sternberg. She is hallmarked for big things in talkies!

Marlene Dietrich was born in Germany, the daughter of an army officer. She has red-gold hair and blue eyes. She is married and has a little daughter, who is in Germany

OCT.

☆ *WHOOPEE—United Artists*

ON the stage the Indian reservation scene was a colorful backdrop. In the picture, the entire cast was able to move to Arizona and shoot the sequences on the spot. On the stage the white expanse of desert was a scene painter's idea. In the picture, it's the real thing and that is partly what makes the film, "Whoopee," better than the original.

It's Sam Goldwyn at his best, Flo Ziegfeld at his best. You can't beat a team like that.

Don't say you're fed up on musical comedies. Go to see "Whoopee" instead. The million and a half spent on it is justified. Ziegfeld brought his most beautiful show girls with him and Hollywood gave its very best.

The result, all in Technicolor, is enough to make you catch the first train to the Gold Coast. The girls, led by such dancers as Jacques Cartier and Joyzelle, are accompanied by George Olsen's fifty-piece orchestra. Dorothy Knapp leads the ultra show girls.

But besides all the lavishness there is Eddie Cantor as the chief high comic. He is one of the funniest men ever seen on the screen and pulls a gag a minute.

This is the new type of screen musical. There is no attempt at realism. It's simply a rollicking, roistering, beautiful production that will make you forget Hoover's advice to sit tight because better times are coming. Heck! They are here!

"WHOOPEE" — UNITED ARTISTS. — From the musical comedy by William Anthony McGuire. From the play "The Nervous Wreck" by Owen Davis. From the story "The Wreck" by E. J. Rath. Directed by Thornton Freeland. The cast: *Henry Williams*, Eddie Cantor; *Sally Morgan*, Eleanor Hunt; *Wanenis*, Paul Gregory; *Sheriff Bob Wells*, John Rutherford; *Mary Custer*, Ethel Shutta; *Jerome Underwood*, Spencer Charters; *Black Eagle*, Chief Caupolican; *Chester Underwood*, Albert Hackett; *Andy McNabb*, Will H. Philbrick; *Judd Morgan*, Walter Law; *Harriett Underwood*, Marilyn Morgan; *Show Girls*, Jeanne Morgan, Virginia Bruce, Muriel Finley, Ernestine Mahoney, Christine Maple, Jane Keithley, Mary Ashcraft, Georgia Lerch and Betty Stockton.

OCT.

DOUGH BOYS—M-G-M

THAT sad-faced little comedian, Buster Keaton, wanders through some of the funniest gags that have ever been pulled on the screen. In many ways this is reminiscent of Chaplin's immortal "Shoulder Arms." It's a war comedy, but in excellent taste. Sally Eilers looks beautiful and Cliff Edwards (Ukelele Ike) gives Keaton a run for his comedy money in many of the best scenes.

"DOUGH BOYS"—M-G-M.—From the story by Al Boasberg and Sidney Lazarus. Adapted by Richard Schayer. Directed by Edward Sedgwick. The cast: *Elmer*, Buster Keaton; *Mary*, Sally Eilers; *Nescopeck*, Cliff Edwards; *Sergeant Brophy*, Edward Brophy; *Svendenburg*, Victor Potel; *Gustave*, Arnold Korff; *Captain Scott*, Frank Mayo; *Abie Cohn*, Pitzy Katz; *Lieutenant Randolph*, William Steele.

OCT.

LOVE IN THE ROUGH—M-G-M

ROMANCE, buffoonery, golf, slapstick, music, dancing—here's a hodge-podge that emerges as a welcome dose of laugh-antidote for that blah feeling you get from seeing too many sentimental things. Bobby Montgomery and Dorothy Jordan supply the love interest, while Benny Rubin and co-comickers run off with the film. You'll like it if you don't take it seriously.

"LOVE IN THE ROUGH"—M-G-M.—From the play "Spring Fever" by Vincent Lawrence. Adapted by Sarah Y. Mason. Directed by Charles Reisner. The cast: *Kelly*, Robert Montgomery; *Marilyn*, Dorothy Jordan; *Benny*, Benny Rubin; *Waters*, J. C. Nugent; *Virgie*, Dorothy McNulty; *Tewksbury*, Tyrrell Davis; *Gardner*, Harry Burns; *Johnson*, Allan Lane; *Martha*, Catherine Moylan; *Williams*, Edward Davis; *Proprietor*, Rosco Ates; *Brown*, Clarence Wilson.

OCT.

WHAT A WIDOW!—
United Artists

GLORIA SWANSON bit her polished finger nails to the quick when she was trying to find a vehicle as grand as "The Trespasser." She didn't do it in this broad comedy, with good old Sennett moments. Gloria goes slapstick but manages to be entertaining in light farce. Anyhow, the clothes are swell, and Lew Cody deserves three rousing cheers and a couple of huzzahs for his come back.

"WHAT A WIDOW"—UNITED ARTISTS.—From the story by Josephine Lovett. Directed by Allan Dwan. The cast: *Tamarind,* Gloria Swanson; *Gerry,* Owen Moore; *Victor,* Lew Cody; *Valli,* Margaret Livingston; *Mr. Lodge,* Wm. Holden; *Jose Alvarada,* Herbert Braggiotti; *Bastikoff,* Gregory Gaye; *Paulette,* Adrienne D'Ambricourt; *Marquise,* Nella Walker; *Masseuse,* Daphne Pollard.

OCT.

ANIMAL CRACKERS—
Paramount

THE Four Marx Brothers, who scored in "The Cocoanuts," turn another of their musical shows into a talkie comedy, and click again. One song for Lillian Roth—this, with a couple of choruses, is all the music. One, two, or all of the Marx boys are on the screen all the time, and the howls are continuous. Strictly a laughing matter, although there is the usual silly music show plot.

"ANIMAL CRACKERS"—PARAMOUNT.—From the play by George S. Kaufman and Morris Ryskind. Adapted by Morris Ryskind and Pierre Collings. Directed by Victor Heerman. The cast: *Captain Jeffrey Spaulding,* Groucho Marx; *The Professor,* Harpo Marx; *Signor Emanuel Ravelli,* Chico Marx; *Horatio Jamison,* Zeppo Marx; *Arabella Rittenhouse,* Lillian Roth; *Mrs. Rittenhouse,* Margaret Dumont; *Roscoe Chandler,* Louis Sorin; *John Parker,* Hal Thompson; *Mrs. Whitehead,* Margaret Irving; *Grace Carpenter,* Kathryn Reece; *Hives,* Robert Greig; *Hennessey,* Edward Metcalf; *Six Footmen,* The Music Masters.

OCT.

One of the remarkable pictures that will come to you within the next few months is to be called "Just Imagine." The action takes place fifty years hence. This shot from the production shows an operating room in 1980. The doctor, played by Wilfred Lucas, is reviving a man who died in December, 1930. The story is full of whimsy. The guy they are reviving is El Brendel. We don't know the reason

OCT.

☆ MONTE CARLO—Paramount

HERE'S another Lubitsch operetta—witty, sophisticated, full of charm. An impoverished countess runs away to Monte Carlo on the eve of her wedding to a wealthy baron. A young count poses as a hairdresser to gain admittance to the countess' rooms. He wins the job—and her love.

That's all the plot — but how brilliantly it's done! Lubitsch seems able to imbue actors with his own piquant sense of comedy. You'll adore Jeanette MacDonald as the *Countess*—she's beautiful, she's deliciously amusing and she sings gloriously. Jack Buchanan is equally delightful. What a hairdresser! What a man! Then there are Claud Allister and ZaSu Pitts as the deserted baron and the countess' maid, respectively. And some grand songs.

Ah, zat Lubitsch! What a director! What a picture!

"MONTE CARLO"—PARAMOUNT.—From the story by Ernest Vajda. Directed by Ernst Lubitsch. The cast: *Count Rudolph Falliere*, Jack Buchanan; *Countess Vera von Conti*, Jeanette MacDonald; *Maria*, ZaSu Pitts; *Armand*, Tyler Brook; *Prince Otto von Seibenheim*, Claud Allister; *Duke Gustavo von Seibenheim*, Edgar Norton; *Paul*, John Roche; *Master of Ceremony*, Albert Conti; *Lady Mary*, Helen Garden; *Monsieur Beaucaire*, Donald Novis; *Horald*, David Percy; *Lord Windorset*, Erik Bey.

OCT.

☆ MADAM SATAN—M-G-M

DON'T try to believe it. Just accept it for what it's worth, the most amazing, lavish, gorgeous De Mille spectacle ever put on the screen. With true De Millian inconsistency, a dull wife, in order to win back her husband, acquires a French accent and *risqué* clothes, thereby succeeding. Ask your husband what he thinks about it.

However, Kay Johnson is swell and as convincing as possible under the circumstances. Reginald Denny is a real contribution—dashing, fascinating and what a baritone!

The Zeppelin sequence is De Mille at his most spectacular. Ladies running around in costumes that only a madman could conceive, smart dialogue fairly crackling, orgies right before your very eyes and everybody jumping out of the airship in parachutes. Vivid entertainment!

"MADAM SATAN"—M-G-M.—From the story by Jeanie Macpherson. Dialogue by Gladys Unger and Elsie Janis. Directed by Cecil B. De Mille. The cast: *Angela Brooks*, Kay Johnson; *Bob Brooks*, Reginald Denny; *Trixie*, Lillian Roth; *Jimmy Wade*, Roland Young; *Martha*, Elsa Petersen; *Captain*, Boyd Irwin; *First Mate*, Wallace MacDonald; *A Roman Senator*, Wilfred Lucas; *Romeo*, Tyler Brooke; *Eve*, Lotus Thompson; *Call of the Wild*, Vera Marsh; *Fish Girl*, Martha Sleeper; *Water*, Doris McMahon; *Confusion*, Marie Valli; *Miss Conning Tower*, Julanne Johnston; *Empire Officer*, Albert Conti; *Pirate*, Earl Askam; *Little Rolls Riding Hood*, Betty Francisco; *Babo*, Ynez Seabury; *Spain*, Countess De Liguoro; *Spider Girl*, Katherine Irving; *Victory*, Aileen Ransom; *Electricity* (*Ballet Mechanique*), Theodore Kosloff; *Herman*, Jack King; *Biff*, Edward Prinz; and Abe Lyman and his band.

OCT.

Short Subjects *of the* Month

THE SONG PLUGGER

Warners-Vitaphone Variety

Joe Frisco is the cigar-smoking jazz dancer whose first short, "The Benefit," was very successful. His imitation of Helen Morgan made it so. Here he plays an employee of a music publishing house. He sings a little, hoofs a little and tells a long yarn about his first wife.

OCT.

RAIN OR SHINE—Columbia

JOE COOK, the noted vaudeville clown and musical show star, makes his talkie début in "Rain or Shine," one of his song shows with all the music taken out. If you like Joe's fast, nutty chatter you'll probably like this. His laughs are supplemented by the clowning of Tom Howard and Dave Chasen, from the stage. A circus story, with the big top burning down for the punch finish.

"RAIN OR SHINE"—COLUMBIA.—From the play "Rain or Shine" by James Gleason. Directed by Frank Capra. The cast: *Smiley*, Joe Cook; *Frankie*, Louise Fazenda; *Mary*, Joan Peers; *Bud*, Wm. Collier, Jr.; *Amos*, Tom Howard; *Dave*, David Chasen; *Dalton*, Alan Roscoe; *Foltz*, Adolph Milar; *Nero*, Clarence Muse; *Mr. Conway*, Ed Martindale; *Grace Conway*, Nora Lane; *Lord Gwynne*, Tyrrell Davis.

OCT.

These New Faces

Watch for This Each Month

EVELYN LAYE ("Lilli," Goldwyn-United Artists) will soon break upon our view as the latest British contribution to the screen's blonde beauties. An ornament of English musical comedy for some years, the dainty Evelyn scored a triumph in New York last winter in the Noel Coward operette, "Bitter-Sweet." After that, Hollywood was a sure shot.

CLAUDIA DELL ("Big Boy," Warners) is one of Ziegfeld's loveliest graduates. Claudia (real last name Smith, of the San Antone Smiths) is a tall, lovely blonde in the true "Follies" tradition. After her musical comedy experience, she went West to seek her fortune in pictures, and Warners signed her for five years. She débuted in "Sweet Kitty Bellairs."

JACK HALEY ("Follow Thru," Paramount) began, as so many do, in vaudeville. He was a member of the well-known team of Crafts and Haley. You've seen 'em. Jack broke upon Broadway in a very large manner as the comedy lead in the stage production of "Follow Thru," the golf musical show, and Paramount naturally picked him for the picture version.

From a Broadway music store to the swankiest hotel in Havana . . . Winnie Lightner and Irene Delroy as amateur gold diggers . . . leaving a trail of roaring laughs behind them.
With the most gorgeous gowns ever seen in one picture, the funniest horse race ever run on any turf, and FULL COLOR to add zest and sparkle to this greatest of all laugh pictures, THE LIFE OF THE PARTY hits the high spot record for all time entertainment.
"Vitaphone" is the registered trademark of The Vitaphone Corporation. Color scenes by the Technicolor Process.
WARNER BROTHERS Present
"THE LIFE of the PARTY"
with
WINNIE LIGHTNER
IRENE DELROY
JACK WHITING
CHARLES BUTTERWORTH
CHARLES JUDELS
BASED ON THE ORIGINAL STORY by MELVILLE CROSSMAN
DIALOGUE and ADAPTATION by ARTHUR CAESAR
DIRECTED by ROY DEL RUTH
A WARNER BROS. & VITAPHONE PICTURE

New York *in* 1980!

BUILDINGS 250 stories high! . . . Traffic on nine levels . . . Rockets that shoot from star to star . . . Airplanes that land on the roofs of buildings . . . A whole meal in a capsule that can be swallowed at one gulp . . . No—this isn't a Jules Verne dream induced by a welsh rarebit . . . It's New York in 1980, as foretold in the new Fox picture, "Just Imagine!" . . . A picture of the great set showing the metropolis fifty years hence—the most intricate setting ever created for pictures . . . It took 205 engineers and craftsmen five months to build it, at a cost of $168,000 . . . It was designed after long conferences with noted artists and scientists who dare peer far into the future . . . The set stands in a balloon hangar at a former Army flying field twenty miles from Hollywood. . . . Seventy-four 5,000,000 candle power sun arcs light the set from above . . . Fifteen thousand electric light bulbs illuminate its buildings and streets . . . DeSylva, Brown and Henderson, the trio responsible for "Sunny Side Up," conceived "Just Imagine!" . . . The leads are played by John Garrick, Maureen O'Sullivan, El Brendel and Kenneth Thomson . . . In 1980—people have serial numbers, not names . . . Marriages are all arranged by the courts . . . Prohibition is still an issue . . . Men's clothes have but one pocket. That's on the hip . . . But there's still love! . . . Don't laugh! Our granddaddies laughed at the thought that men might fly! Fantastic? Certainly—but stranger things have come to pass than those which have been portrayed in this dream New York of A. D. 1980!

NOV.

Otto Dyar

PROBABLY an adoring flapper would say Stan came sweet from "Sweetie." But Stanley Smith probably wouldn't like that. He's only twenty-three, but six years of rich stage experience preceded his film début in 1929. His work in "Sweetie" set countless maids to mooning and moaning

Stanley Smith was born in Kansas City, Mo., Jan. 6, 1907. He is 5 feet, 11; weighs 160, has blond hair, blue eyes. Educated at Hollywood High School

NOV.

(Scene from "Check and Double Check," Radio Picture)

"How does you like the change to this picture propolition, Amos?"

"Change, Andy? Ain't no change 'tall. Seems like you do all the settin' and I does all the workin', same as in the radio and tooth-paste business!"

NOV.

Here's a cute dodge for the benefit of those who spot their hankies with lipstick. Dorothy McNulty, of Metro, shows a handkerchief with a square of red hemstitched in one corner. Lipstick's there, but no can see

NOV.

ARE YOU THERE?—Fox

IMAGINE Beatrice Lillie as a lady detective whose disguises range from adagio dancer to big game hunter! It ought to be funny—yet this never quite clicks. It's too scrambled—and for all her brilliant comedy and undeniable good looks the irrepressible Lillie doesn't get across on the screen. The supporting cast includes Baclanova, George Grossmith, John Garrick and Jillian Sand a promising newcomer.

"ARE YOU THERE?"—Fox.—From the story by Harlan Thompson. Directed by Hamilton MacFadden. The cast: *Shirley Travis*, Beatrice Lillie; *Geoffry*, John Garrick; *Countess Helenka*, Olga Baclanova; *Duke of St. Pancras*, George Grossmith; *Barbara Blythe*, Jillian Sand; *Hostler*, Lloyd Hamilton; *Barber*, Roger Davis; *International Crooks*, Gustav Von Seyffertitz, Nicholas Soussanin, Richard Alexander, Henry Victor; *Page*, Paula Langlen.

NOV.

One of the Fairest "Follies"

"SWEET Kitty Bellairs" set a new star on the screen and brought a five-year contract to Miss Claudia Dell. She is Warner Brothers' newest, most promising prima donna. And she never actually had planned a theatrical career.

Claudia Dell was merely Claudia Dell Smith, of San Antonio, Texas, who came to New York to visit her aunt, vaudeville's Claudia Coleman. Aunt Claudia suggested she try the stage, just to see whether or not she liked it. And having nothing better to do, Claudia tried it. She didn't have to try very hard, either. Ziegfeld looked at that beautiful blonde with a show-girl figure and put her in the "Follies."

She had nothing to do but be ornamental in the revue, and she never took being a Ziegfeld beauty seriously. Her chance to use that thrilling voice came later, when she was sent to London to play Marilyn Miller's rôle in "Rosalie."

Claudia took her mother with her to London. She always has lived with some member of the family, even as a "Follies" girl, though "Follies" girls generally are presumed to lead a gaudy life.

In Hollywood, Claudia lives with mother, aunt and grandma. She lives simply, in an apartment in the non-professional district, driving a modest coupe to and from the studio. She dresses conservatively, dines in tea rooms and goes to the picture show.

She modestly insists it was luck which made her a movie star. Luck, without a single bow to such potent factors as a thrilling voice, graceful figure, bewitching smile, charm and beauty.

"It just happened to me. I've just been unbelievably lucky," says Claudia, whose latest good fortune has been to win the leading rôle in Warner's most ambitious musical production, "Fifty Million Frenchmen."

NOV.

. . . "Dancing with Tears in My Eyes" was yanked out of "Dancing Sweeties" because they didn't think it was a good enough song to stay in, and "Dancing with Tears in My Eyes" is one of the biggest-selling popular song hits in recent years . . .

NOV.

He Is Frank and Earnest, Too

SOMEBODY saw him clowning about the Hollywood High school and gave him a chance at a few days' extra work. From that moment Frank Albertson was an actor. The unfortunate thing was that nobody could be convinced of it. Young, cocky, fresh, he quit school and haunted the casting office. Haunted it so blithely and so unsuccessfully that his mother had to call him into conference.

She had been working for a small salary in an apartment house office and trying to increase the family income by handling Ken Maynard's mail for fifteen dollars a week. Frank had to be made to understand responsibility and advised to settle down.

This generous mother gave him three months to find a job—and keep it. Frank went right over to Fox to get a prop boy's job. In six weeks Director Dave Butler had made a test of him and had him signed to a long-term contract.

He's scheduled for stardom. After "Men Without Women" and "Wild Company," he was chosen for the juvenile lead in "Just Imagine," one of the most pretentious productions on this year's program.

Frank has arrived with Hollywood's youngest set. His great friends are Johnny Darrow and Billy Bakewell. He enjoys living and clowning and is convinced that this is the best of all possible worlds.

NOV.

That Little Radio Lee Girl

HER name isn't Dorothy. And it isn't Lee. The pert and peppy little comedy whirlwind of Radio Pictures is Marjorie Millsap, who lived right around the corner from the old FBO studios all her life and always wanted to break into pictures. Marjorie Millsap didn't mean a thing to the movies. But she consoled herself with athletics and became a ninety-six pound lacrosse star, ball pitcher, high jumper and better scrapper than any boy in the neighborhood.

Three years ago the ninety-six-pound strong woman marched into the Fanchon and Marco offices with the grim intent of going on the stage. Her size, her peppiness, her sauciness amused the producers. They watched her athletic stunts, saw her dance, heard her sing, and signed her.

She borrowed the name "Lee" from grandmother and adopted "Dorothy" because it seemed to go with "Lee." As Dorothy Lee she went on tour with a Fanchon-Marco unit and finally landed in the Broadway show, "Hello, Yourself," with Waring's Pennsylvanians. She was the hit of the show.

When Waring's Pennsylvanians played in "Syncopation," along went Dorothy to sing "Do Do Something." She sang herself into a Radio Pictures contract. "Rio Rita" and her zestful clowning with Wheeler and Woolsey established her.

Dorothy gives Fred Waring credit for her success. He advised her on management. And told her to buy bonds.

Dorothy still lives with her mother in the same house to which they moved when she was four years old, way back in 1915. She hasn't changed much since then, nor has the house.

Pint-sized, wide-eyed, saucy-nosed, nineteen, Dorothy already has three hits on her scoreboard, "Rio Rita," "The Cuckoos," "Dixiana." Her latest is the Bert Wheeler-Robert Woolsey musical farce, "Half Shot at Sunrise."

NOV.

☆ *HALF SHOT AT SUNRISE—Radio Pictures*

PEEVISH after a tough day? Anything wrong? Well then, park the grouch and toddle to wherever they're showing "Half Shot at Sunrise." It's one of the most absurdly ridiculous, nonsensical messpots of assorted comedy that ever was cooked up from celluloid.

It's virtually all Wheeler and Woolsey. These crack-brains play two A. E. F. privates madly A. W. O. L. in Paris. How they get away with it is the story, embellished with some of the funniest lines and situations ever devised.

Incidentally, while it's not a musical, there are a few good song numbers. Leni Stengel as the Paris vamp, cuddlesome Dorothy Lee as the colonel's daughter, and George MacFarlane as the colonel take whatever honors Wheeler and Woolsey don't gobble up.

"HALF SHOT AT SUNRISE"—RADIO PICTURES.—From the story by James A. Creelman, Jr. Directed by Paul Sloane. The cast: *Tommy*, Bert Wheeler; *Gilbert*, Robert Woolsey; *M. P. Sergeant*, John Rutherford; *Colonel Marshall*, George MacFarlane; *Eileen*, Roberta Robinson; *Olga*, Leni Stengel; *Annette*, Dorothy Lee; *Lieut. Jim Reed*, Hugh Trevor; *Mrs. Marshall*, Edna May Oliver; *Military Policeman*, Eddie de Lange; *General Hale*, E. H. Calvert; *Capt. Jones*, Alan Roscoe.

NOV.

VIENNESE NIGHTS—Warners

THE best operetta of recent months—a thing of beauty, with lilting music by Sigmund Romberg (oh, what waltzes!) and excellent singing and acting by a strong cast. Vivienne Segal and Alexander Gray outdo themselves in the romantic leads, aided by Bert Roach, Walter Pidgeon, Louise Fazenda and Jean Hersholt. If you are weary of just plain talk, you'll enjoy this to the full.

"VIENNESE NIGHTS"—WARNERS.—From the story by Oscar Hammerstein II. Symphony composed by Sigmund Romberg. Directed by Alan Crosland. The cast: *Otto*, Alexander Gray; *Elsa*, Vivienne Segal; *Hocher*, Jean Hersholt; *Franz*, Walter Pidgeon; *Grell*, Louise Fazenda; *Barbara*, Alice Day; *Gus*, Bert Roach; *Mary*, June Purcell; *Bill*, Milton Douglas.

NOV.

PLAYBOY OF PARIS—Paramount

CHEVALIER deserves better pictures than this. Although this light farce is exceedingly entertaining in spots and has some amusing situations it is sometimes very dull. And no Chevalier picture has any excuse for being that. Chevalier fans will be disappointed, for the irresistible Maurice sings only two songs. Frances Dee, a newcomer, is refreshingly lovely and Stuart Erwin contributes some grand comedy.

"PLAYBOY OF PARIS"—PARAMOUNT.—From the play "The Little Cafe" by Tristan Bernard. Adapted by Percy Heath. Directed by Ludwig Berger. The cast: *Albert*, Maurice Chevalier; *Yvonne*, Frances Dee; *Philibert*, O. P. Heggie; *Paul*, Stuart Erwin; *Pierre*, Eugene Pallette; *Mlle. Berengere*, Dorothy Christy; *Mlle. Hedwige*, Cecil Cunningham; *Cadeaux*, Tyler Brooke; *M. Jabert*, Frank Elliott; *M. Bannock*, William Davidson; *Gastonet*, Charles Giblyn; *Jacqueline*, Erin LaBissoniere; *Plouvier*, Fred Lee; *The General*, Edmund Breese; *The Doctor*, Olaf Hytten; *Manager of Night Club*, Edward Lynch; *Street-cleaner*, Guy Oliver; *Waiter*, William O'Brien.

NOV.

SWEET KITTY BELLAIRS—Warners ★

AS dainty a bit of fantasy as you'll find—this beautifully Technicolored operetta of the gallant days in Merrie England. Claudia Dell, a Dresden doll of a girl, and a coming star. Lovely music. Walter Pidgeon in knee breeches and fine baritone. Pretty June Collyer, Ernest Torrence's clever comedy. You'd better not miss this one. It has romance, beauty, grand laughs. And Claudia! Watch her!

"SWEET KITTY BELLAIRS"—WARNERS.—From the book by Egerton Castle. From the play by David Belasco. Adapted by J. Grubb Alexander. Directed by Alfred E. Green. The cast: *Sweet Kitty Bellairs*, Claudia Dell; *Sir Jasper Standish*, Ernest Torrence; *Lord Verney*, Walter Pidgeon; *Captain O'Hara*, Perry Askam; *Julia Standish*, June Collyer; *Colonel Villiers*, Lionel Belmore; *Captain Spicer*, Arthur Edmund Carew; *Old Dame*, Flora Finch; *Thomas Stafford*, Douglas Gerrard; *Lydia*, Christiane Yves; *Lord Markham*, Edgar Norton; *Verney's Valet*, Bertram Johns; *Innkeeper*, Albert Hart; *Megrim*, Tina Marshall; *Lord Northmore*, Geoffrey McDonell.

NOV.

SWEETHEARTS ON PARADE—
Columbia

ANOTHER nice little girl from the country goes to the big city. Another suave millionaire, with more money than morals, lures the little girl to his yacht. Another poor but honest hero saves her. And another movie is born. Alice White, pert and peppy, is the nice girl. Marie Prevost, who looks as young as your kid sister, proves that they can come back.

"SWEETHEARTS ON PARADE"—COLUMBIA.—From the story by Al Cohn and James Starr. Continuity by Colin Clements. Directed by Marshall Neilan. The cast: *Helen*, Alice White; *Bill*, Lloyd Hughes; *Nita*, Marie Prevost; *Hendricks*, Kenneth Thomson; *Hank*, Ray Cooke; *Parker*, Wilbur Mack; *Denham*, Ernest Wood; *Department Store Manager*, Max Asher.

NOV.

COLLEGE LOVERS—First National

THIS begins the annual fall production of football pictures. And it's just another football picture and don't get excited. Even the fact that it snaps its fingers at tradition by NOT having the hero make a touchdown for old Alma Mater in the last three seconds of play doesn't make it hot. Jack Whiting and Marian Nixon play the leading rôles. Ho, hum!

"COLLEGE LOVERS"—FIRST NATIONAL.—From the story by Earl Baldwin. Adapted by Douglas Doty. Directed by John Adolfi. The cast: *Frank Taylor*, Jack Whiting; *Madge Hutton*, Marian Nixon; *Al "Tiny" Courtley*, Guinn Williams; *Eddie Smith*, Russell Hopton; *Coach Donovan*, Wade Boteler; *"Speed" Haskins*, Frank McHugh; *Josephine*, Phyllis Crane; *Gene Hutton*, Richard Tucker.

NOV.

Short Subjects *of the* Month

THE LEGACY
Warners-Vitaphone Variety

This is Betty Compton's début in the talkies, Betty being one of New York's favorite singing and dancing ingénues. Her beauty and dancing ability show up here, though it is a rather conventional tiny musical short. She is supported by John Hundley, Jack White and others.

NOV.

These New Faces

Watch for This Each Month

IRENE DELROY (Warner Brothers) is one of the latest Broadway beauties of musical comedy to desert the main stem for Hollywood. One of her earliest jobs in show business was Tom Patricola's partner in a vaudeville act. As singing and dancing leading woman, her most recent stage jobs were in "Top Speed," "Follow Thru" and "Here's How."

PAUL GREGORY ("Whoopee," United Artists) is a Broadway musical comedy favorite who appeared in the same musical comedy on the stage. Before coming to Flo Ziegfeld, Gregory sang leading rôles in "Rose-Marie," "Song of the Flame," and "Golden Dawn," all lavish musical shows presented by Arthur Hammerstein. "Whoopee" is Paul's first motion picture fling.

ELEANOR HUNT ("Whoopee," United Artists) jumped into the feminine lead in this big Eddie Cantor musical picture just twelve months after her début as a chorus girl. She played in "Whoopee" and "Animal Crackers" on the stage, and was selected for the picture lead over dozens of more experienced girls. Eleanor is a New York girl and was educated there.

DEC.

Another pretty blonde Cinderella happens in Hollywood. Meet June McCloy, musical comedy girl from Broadway, who was "discovered" and given a big rôle in "Reaching for the Moon," the Irving Berlin singie

NOV.

The Old Master of Revue Producing watches his most famous star. A great dancing master looks at his most famous pupil. At the left, Marilyn Miller rehearses a scene for "Sunny." The man in the Russian blouse is Theodore Kosloff, her ballet master. Next is William Seiter, directing her. Next, holding the Panama and leaning on the camera, is Jack Warner, her boss. At the right is Flo Ziegfeld, in whose great musical shows Miss Miller came to her greatest fame

DEC.

FOLLOW THE LEADER—Paramount

ED WYNN, no howl in silent pictures, is a scream in this, now that the talkies give us his apologetic, squeaking voice. It's a good transcription of his former musical comedy hit. He's been given grand support—Ginger Rogers, Stanley Smith, Lou Holtz, Bobby Watson and others. Why must musicals be going out, when some are like this?

"FOLLOW THE LEADER"—PARAMOUNT.—From the play by William K. Wells, George White and DeSylva, Brown and Henderson. Screen play by Gertrude Purcell and Sid Silvers. Directed by Norman Taurog. The cast: *Crickets*, Ed Wynn; *Mary Brennan*, Ginger Rogers; *Jimmie Moore*, Stanley Smith; *Sam Platz*, Lou Holtz; *Ma Brennan*, Lida Kane; *Helen King*, Ethel Merman; *George White*, Bobby Watson; *R. C. Black*, Donald Kirke; *Bob Sterling*, William Halligan; *Fritzie Devere*, Holly Hall; *Two-Gun Terry*, Preston Foster; *Mickie*, James C. Morton.

DEC.

BROADWAY'S two favorite singing comics came back to the main stem—in the flesh—the same week.

Al Jolson calmly accepted $20,000 and a cut of the gross over $80,000—if any—for a week of personal appearances at the Capitol Theater, New York.

And Eddie Cantor did his stuff at the Broadway première of "Whoopee." Eddie, after singing a song, launched into a spirited defense of Hollywood, and pictures in general. But he topped it cutely by saying, "Well, of course, if anything goes wrong with my next picture, I'll tell you the truth!"

AND Cantor told a gag that rolled the stuffed shirts in the aisles. Just to illustrate the maturing, sophisticating Hollywood influence.

Eddie said he overheard one of his little daughters talking with two neighbor girls out on the front stoop of the Cantor mansion.

One of the youngsters said she thought she might like a drink, and a glass of spirits was forthcoming.

The first child sniffed it. "Scotch," she remarked.

The second took it. "You're wrong," she said. "It's rye."

It was the little Cantor's turn.

"I'm sorry, girls," she said, "you're both wrong. It's gin—and it's been cut."

NOV.

What a big screen wedding looks like from the light gallery! This is the 'board-ship wedding procession for Marilyn Miller's new "Sunny." In the center, foreground, you will recognize Marilyn on the arm of Joe Donahue

DEC.

EVERYBODY who knows Samuel Goldwyn and Florenz Ziegfeld looked for a clash of temperaments when they combined their efforts to make "Whoopee."

Will Rogers said the dialogue rights for a dictagraph record of their conferences during the production would be worth five thousand dollars.

The clash occurred when it came to costuming the Ziegfeld show girls in the Indian reservation scene. The Broadway squaws were all dolled up with feathers and not much else.

GOLDWYN'S costume designers ordered ten thousand goose feathers. When Ziegfeld heard of this he hit a new high, and rushed into Goldwyn's office.

"Indians don't wear goose feathers," he cried, "and I won't stand for it. I want real eagle feathers."

"But they'll look just as good on the screen," said Goldwyn. "And besides there aren't enough eagle feathers in existence."

"Nevertheless I want eagle feathers. You're not going to make geese out of my girls."

Ziegfeld won. They searched two weeks and bought all the eagle feathers west of the Mississippi. They cost only twenty-five thousand dollars.

DEC.

THE HOT HEIRESS—First National

LAUGH-CRAMMED picturization of the theory that the female is deadlier than the male—especially when it's a millionaire's daughter on the make for a poor but virile steel riveter. She gets her man and you get swell entertainment. Ben Lyon as the riveter is a punch; Ona Munson as the girl has what it takes. Inez Courtney and Tom Dugan are great.

"HOT HEIRESS, THE"—FIRST NATIONAL.—From the story by Herbert Fields. Directed by Clarence Badger. The cast: *Juliette Hunter*, Ona Munson; *Hap Harrigan*, Ben Lyon; *Bill Dugan*, Tom Dugan; *Olly*, Walter Pidgeon; *Margie*, Inez Courtney; *Lola*, Thelma Todd; *Irene*, Elise Bartlett; *Mr. Hunter*, Holmes Herbert; *Mrs. Hunter*, Nella Walker; *The Doctor*, George Irving.

DEC.

HEADS UP—Paramount

A PLEASANT little musical comedy picture, with the smiling Mr. Charles Ex-Buddy Rogers playing a gallant young coast-guardsman, Victor Moore and Helen Kane contributing laughs and things. The real news of the whole matter is that in this picture the impeccable Mr. Rogers actually smokes a cigarette! Fie! A well-made singie that isn't good enough to be outstanding.

"HEADS UP"—PARAMOUNT.—From the play by John McGowan, Paul Gerard Smith, Richard Rodgers and Lorenz Hart. Adapted by Jack Kirkland. Directed by Victor Schertzinger. The cast: *Jack Mason*, Charles Rogers; *Betty Trumbull*, Helen Kane; *Skippy Dugan*, Victor Moore; *Mary Trumbull*, Margaret Breen; *Mrs. Martha Trumbull*, Helen Carrington; *Rex Cutting*, Gene Gowing; *Georgie Martin*, Billy Taylor; *Captain Denny*, Harry Shannon; *Larry White*, C. Anthony Hughes; *Captain Whitney*, John Hamilton; *Naval Officer*, Stanley Jessup; *Blake*, Preston Foster.

DEC.

Short Subjects *of the* Month

ROSELAND

Warners-Vitaphone Variety

One of the very best of song shorts, made by Ruth Etting, that excellent singer of musical comedy and vaudeville fame. As a background for her typical "torch songs," Miss Etting has been given a little story about a dance hall girl. The story idea is a good notion.

WHEN you see Warners' new Technicolored comedy, "Fifty Million Frenchmen," you'll see Claudia Dell and William Gaxton having tender moments in a taxi-cab. But this is the way it's done—as private as Times Square at theater hour!

A LUSCIOUS morsel of youthful prettiness which has been adorning the Metro-Goldwyn-Mayer lot of recent months—and, it is fair to suppose, is inducing a lot of eye-strain! She's Harriet Lake, who tore herself from Broadway to light up some Metro talkies. Ah, when such as Harriet are at large, it must be terrible to be blind in Hollywood!

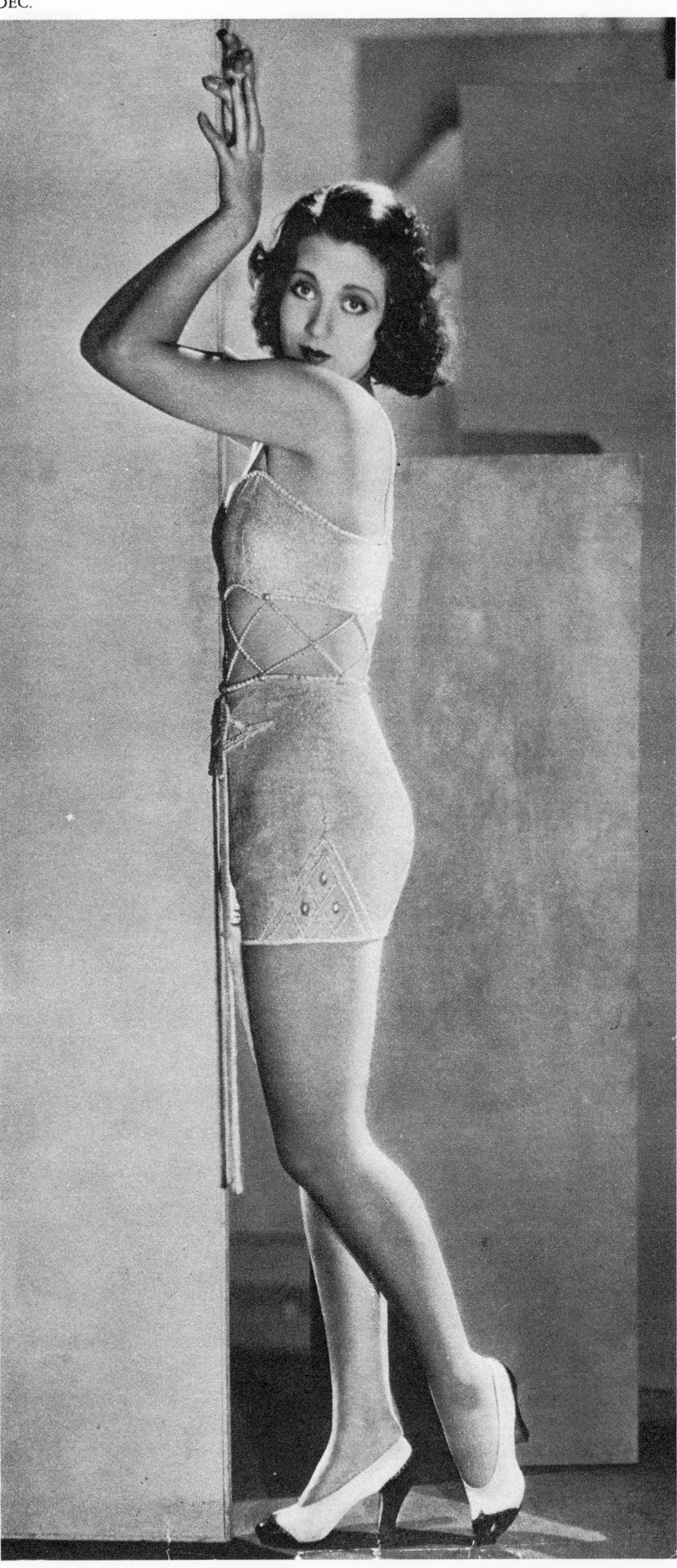

Harriet Lake, up to the time of joining the M-G-M forces, was one of the little girls of the merry-merry who brighten the early evenings of Broadway's Blase Business Men

Clarence Sinclair Bull

Why I'm On *the*

New York is all cluttered up with stars and near-stars who have had a movie fling and are now daring the footlights

NEW YORK has become so cluttered with ex-movie stars the street-cleaners are complaining about the awful number of ermine-tails they are required to sweep from Broadway every rosy dawning.

Trailing their inevitable ermine evening wraps, exuding the inevitable odor of special blend musk and ambergris, the glittering sorority swoops down upon every first night, opens every new supper club, views every new fashion showing, lunches on the East Side, larks on the West Side. And it's all so jolly. What a relief from Hollywood and the grind of being a picture star!

At least that's what they say when some chatter writer, hard pressed on Monday morning for a hot celebrity to interview, remembers that Miss Kissy Fadeout is around town.

Illusion is the business of a movie star, so they may be permitted to harbor a few of their own. But reality peeps through the pretty tulle ruffle of pretense. New York wouldn't seem quite so gay were Hollywood to insert one tiny notice in the most obscure metropolitan agony column:

"Kissy, come home. All is forgiven. Contract waits.
Mama Movies."

Trains would be so crowded the exquisite orchids of the screen would be riding in baggage cars with their orchidaceous griffons.

THE stars in New York are the stars on the outside. Waning popularity. Too many box-office flops. Overbuilding. There are as many reasons why certain stars are on the outside as there are alibis to evade them. Of course, many of them WILL come back. But at present they work while they wait.

The most popular alibi is: "I wanted some stage experience." This one is pulled by stars who have landed jobs in legitimate, vaudeville, road shows, and picture house presentations.

"Hollywood is terrible. It's killing to live there." This is pulled by stars who went out to the Coast on six-month options, flopped, came back.

"I needed a change. Hollywood staleness was getting me." This is pulled by stars who haven't yet decided whether to sail for Europe or open a miniature golf course.

And they all harbor a little secret yen to try a come-back as they peep wistfully over the studio fence. One day many of them will jump over again. But not just now.

Let's crash a Broadway first night. It must be a pretentious one. Legitimate. Heavens, not movie!

Who's that exquisite blonde with the dashing Latin cavalier down in the second row? Vilma! Yes, and it's Rod La Rocque. Rod and Vilma are to be co-starred this season in a Hungarian comedy—one in which Vilma's accent won't be grotesque. Vilma's position in the movies became dubious with the dissolution of the Colman-Banky team. Then talk. Then the accent. Vilma's a stage star now.

And the smart brunette in the next row? Can that sophisticated looking young woman be the gamin Colleen Moore? Sure enough. She, too, is rehearsing a play for Broadway.

Colleen's divorce from the movies was long predicted, but still spectacular. With no stage training and little movie experience, Colleen skyrocketed to the top as a type. She was the greatest box-office star, the darling of the exhibitors, until the advent of the Bow. Dethroned by Clara, Colleen nevertheless held her own and, under the shrewd managership of husband John McCormick, commanded one of the biggest salaries ever paid a film star.

She gamely tried to talk. First an Irish accent. Then a French. But a Polynesian accent wouldn't have forestalled what was in the cards. Miss Moore finished her contract with First National. Negotiations with other companies came to zero. Incompatibility stepped in. Colleen divorced her husband-manager. The movies divorced Colleen. She's harvesting experience on the legitimate stage.

COLLEEN and Virginia Valli have taken a pent-house apartment—with a lease. Virginia is another decorative member of New York's interesting ex-movie star colony.

There's Lina Basquette over there. Lina is going to dance again. Convinced that sinister influences were at work against her in Hollywood, depriving her of her child, thwarting her career, Lina is back on the Broadway from which she started. Her movie career was tragic. She'll begin all over again as the dancing star of one of the most popular supper clubs. Harry Richman's to be exact. He's a Clara Bow boy friend.

There's Dennis King. Why, it's hardly a year since he went into the movies. Back so soon! Never such a hoopla was raised over a screen acquisition as Paramount optimistically built for Dennis. Thousands were spent to exploit a new matinée idol. Carloads of critics were imported from key cities to attend the Broadway opening of "The Vagabond King." Raves were carefully mixed and baked in Paramount's hottest

Outside Lookin' In

By

Paul Jarvis

good-will ovens. Hundreds of corks popped. But so did Dennis!

Dennis isn't the only King dethroned from the movies. Charlie, over there, is back on Broadway. And a year ago he was M-G-M's pet of song-and-dance films. Broadway hooted when Charlie King went West to break into movies. Charlie was no chicken. But when "The Broadway Melody" broke loose, presenting a King who looked no older than Charles ex-"Buddy" Rogers, the laugh was not on Charlie. He was aces—for a few months.

Then song-and-dance films went out. And song-and-dance men with them. The King had had his day.

THE decline of musical movies tossed plenty of stars over the fence. See Bernice Claire over there? What a build-up Miss Claire got. First National was so convinced she was a potential box-office queen, they put her in straight drama, "Numbered Men," when the tide turned back from color and music. But Bernice never quite clicked. Now she and Alexander Gray are working out their contract in vaudeville, in the same act—and the same boat.

Tom Patricola's back in vaudeville, too. He and El Brendel were snatched away from the halls at about the same time. Brendel went over. Tom, whose specialty was eccentric song-and-dancing, went over the fence.

The Spanish looking gentleman over there is Paul Muni, erstwhile Muni Weisenfreund of the Yiddish Art Theater. He's back on Broadway for a different reason. Muni was let out because he was too young to be a character star and too good to be a pretty-boy juvenile. A critics' actor. The critics raved. But the fans didn't want realism. They wanted romance. Over the fence went the distinguished Mr. Muni.

The girl with her hat down over her eyes, so timid about being recognized? Why, our old friend Lillian Gish. Lillian listened to the advice of her friend, Mary Pickford, and tried a come-back. "One Romantic Night" was a poor picture. Miss Gish was presumed to have "outgrown" the movies, anyhow. She has the desire to do "artistic and worth while" things in the theater, *à la* Eva Le Gallienne.

Dorothy, too, is turning to the stage, while husband James Rennie sports a brand new First National contract to become a movie star.

The big-eyed brunette in the next row? You remember Lya de Putti, of "Variety." Everybody remembers "Variety" and tries to forget Lya's disastrous career as an American star under the guidance of American directors. Lya came to America with all the fanfare which attended the Negri advent. But nothing happened. The fans said, "No, thank you," and Lya was outside.

Yes, that's Greta Nissen. Greta is frank about her ambition to crash the movies again. If Garbo, from Sweden, can speak English and make good, Greta, from Norway, can try. She has been in vaudeville and stage plays for two years. If some producer doesn't give her a chance to come back, she'll be on Broadway another year more.

LILLIAN ROTH, over there? You'd never believe that Lillian was on the wrong side of the fence. They say it was temperament and mama-management, but Lillian is just working out her contract in submerged rôles like the ingénue lead of "Animal Crackers." Then back to vaudeville. An ex-movie star.

Olive Borden, sure enough! A vaudeville sketch for Olive. Last year it looked as though she finally were going to make good. Radio Pictures got Olive as a souvenir with FBO. They tried everything, even dyeing her hair. But she was still Olive Borden. A tepid box-office star.

Yes, the blonde in blue is Dorothy Mackaill. But you needn't worry about Dorothy. A few weeks ago she was slated for the discard. Her contract had expired. Her fans had gone cold. Then along came "The Office Wife." A box-office picture with Dorothy Mackaill! New impetus! If First National didn't re-sign Dorothy, a competitor would. So First National re-signed, at more money, and with the sensational stipulation that the star might have something to say about her stories.

The Mackaill case was unique in the movies. Never before has any player landed solidly as a star with what was to have been the final picture!

Dorothy's contrasting experience is eloquent. The box-office said "Yes" on Mackaill. It had said "No" on the others. The omnipotent fans have given back to Broadway the most glittering army of erstwhile and almost-movie stars which ever have ornamented the poor old stage.

WHAT happens to our movie friends when contracts expire, talkies menace or they are otherwise smitten by fate? They go on the stage! Two years ago stage actors were hustling to Hollywood for the infant talkies. Now the big parade is marching the other way. Favorites of the silent days fill Broadway, hoping and working for new success and popularity in the theater.

DEC.

☆ *SUNNY—First National*

WHO said singies were through? A gem of a picture like this makes us wonder. The radiant personality of Marilyn Miller smashes over this gay and tasteful film version of the stage hit in which she starred. To rave about her dancing would be to gild the lily. Excellent support is given by Lawrence Gray, Inez Courtney and Joe Donahue, brother of the late Jack. Swell!

"SUNNY"—FIRST NATIONAL.—From the play by Otto Harbach and Oscar Hammerstein II. Music by Jerome Kern. Adapted by Humphrey Pearson and Henry McCarty. Directed by William A. Seiter. The cast: *Sunny*, Marilyn Miller; *Tom Warren*, Lawrence Gray; *Jim Deming*, Joe Donahue; *Wendell-Wendell*, Mackenzie Ward; *Peters*, O. P. Heggie; *"Weenie,"* Inez Courtney; *Marcia Manners*, Barbara Bedford; *Sue*, Judith Vosselli; *Sam*, Clyde Cook; *The Barker*, Harry Allen; *First Officer*, William Davidson; *Second Officer*, Ben Hendricks, Jr.

DEC.

☆ *JUST IMAGINE—Fox*

IT must be terrible to be the sort of person who can't get a kick out of this sort of thing! There may be a few such, and they're to be pitied! "Just Imagine" is delightful buffoonery, backgrounded by an ironical, fantastic conception of life in 1980. You shouldn't and can't take a second of it seriously—which makes it top entertainment.

Imagination explodes everywhere—especially in your funny-bone. There are colossal miniatures—what a paradox! Every-day life, food and drink, marriage, prohibition—all depicted as of a half-century hence. There are beautiful songs, romance enough, and a wealth of beauty. El Brendel runs off with the cast honors. John Garrick and Maureen O'Sullivan are young lovers, and Frank Albertson and Marjorie White hilariously lampoon young passion.

"JUST IMAGINE"—Fox.—From the story by DeSylva, Brown and Henderson. Music by DeSylva, Brown and Henderson. Directed by David Butler. The cast: *Single O*, El Brendel; *LN-18*, Maureen O'Sullivan; *J-21*, John Garrick; *D-6*, Marjorie White; *RT-42*, Frank Albertson; *Z-4*, Hobart Bosworth; *MT-3*, Kenneth Thomson; *X-10*, Wilfred Lucas; *B-36*, Mischa Auer; *AK-44*, Sidney De Gray; *Commander*, Joseph Girard; *Looloo*, *Booboo*, Joyzelle; *Loko*, *Boko*, Ivan Linow.

DEC.

☆ *THE QUEEN OF SCANDAL—United Artists*

ANOTHER musical hit, even if they do burst into melody at weird moments. Evelyn Laye, a beauty from England with a Broadway stopover, is charming, and John Boles is in grand voice and looks. Louis Bromfield wrote the story. Lilyan Tashman plays a bad beauty from Budapest, and Leon Errol's accordion legs gather their laughs, as usual. The thing is beautifully produced. Call it a sound success!

"QUEEN OF SCANDAL, THE"—UNITED ARTISTS.—From the story by Louis Bromfield. Adapted by Sidney Howard. Directed by George Fitzmaurice. The cast: *Lilli*, Evelyn Laye; *Mirko*, John Boles; *Otto*, Leon Errol; *Fritzie*, Lilyan Tashman; *Janos*, Hugh Cameron; *Liska*, Marion Lord; *Zagon*, Lionel Belmore; *Papa Lorenc*, George Bickel; *Egan*, Vincent Barnett; *Almady*, Henry Victor.

DEC.

MOROCCO—Paramount

THIS picture introduces Marlene Dietrich, Paramount's new sensation from Germany, to the American screen. She's like Garbo, like Jeanne Eagels, but most like Marlene. A vivid, fascinating woman, bound to stir up storms of talk. Gary Cooper, starred, is grand as a woman-chasing Foreign Legionnaire. And Director Von Sternberg introduced a thrilling new talkie technique. Hot stuff, this. Don't miss.

"MOROCCO"—PARAMOUNT.—From the play "Amy Jolly" by Benno Vigny. Adapted by Jules Furthman. Directed by Josef Von Sternberg. The cast: *Tom Brown,* Gary Cooper; *Amy Jolly,* Marlene Dietrich; *LaBissiere,* Adolphe Menjou; *Adjutant Caesar,* Ullrich Haupt; *Anna Dolores,* Juliette Compton; *Corporal Tatoche,* Francis MacDonald; *Col. Quinnevieres,* Albert Conti; *Mme. Caesar,* Eve Southern; *Barratire,* Michael Visaroff; *Lo Tinto,* Paul Porcasi.

DEC.

☆ ***CHECK AND DOUBLE CHECK—Radio Pictures***

FIFTY million Amos 'n' Andy fans are going to mob the theaters to see their idols for the first time. And they will not be disappointed. Big, hulking *Andy* and brow-beaten, but rebellious, *Amos,* materialize on the screen without losing the quality that made them famous as voices. In many ways, their first picture is a brilliant job. Situations and dialogue are hilariously funny, and there are two or three gags that are masterpieces.

You'll see the famous Fresh Air Taxi, the pompous *Kingfish,* and a classic meeting of the Mystic Knights of the Sea. True, *Ruby Taylor* and *Madame Queen* do not appear, although they figure in the story. There's lots of *Amos* (Freeman Gosden) and *Andy* (Charles Correll)! Sue Carol, Irene Rich and others are in it. Great entertainment.

"CHECK AND DOUBLE CHECK"—RADIO PICTURES.—From the story by Bert Kalmer and Harry Ruby. Adapted by J. Walter Ruben. Directed by Melville Brown. The cast: *Amos,* Freeman F. Gosden; *Andy,* Charles J. Correll; *Jean Blair,* Sue Carol; *Richard Williams,* Charles Morton; *Ralph Crawford,* Ralf Harolde; *John Blair,* Edward Martindel; *Mrs. Blair,* Irene Rich; *Elinor Crawford,* Rita LaRoy; *Kingfish,* Russell Powell.

DEC.

A LADY'S MORALS—M-G-M

INTRODUCING Grace Moore, young and beautiful prima donna of the Metropolitan Opera, to pictures. And what a voice! The story is based on incidents in the life of the famous Jenny Lind, and Miss Moore sings several lovely numbers, notably one written especially for the picture by Carrie Jacobs Bond. Reginald Denny is fine opposite the star. This will surely please you.

"LADY'S MORALS, A"—M-G-M.—From the story by Hans Kraly and Claudine West. Directed by Sidney Franklin. The cast: *Jenny Lind,* Grace Moore; *Paul Brandt,* Reginald Denny; *Barnum,* Wallace Beery; *Olaf,* Gus Shy; *Josephine,* Jobyna Howland; *Broughm,* Gilbert Emery; *Innkeeper,* George F. Marion; *Maretti,* Paul Porcasi; *Zergo,* Giovanni Martino; *Innkeeper's Wife,* Bodil Rosing; *Louise,* Joan Standing; *Selma,* Mavis Villiers; *Rosatti,* Judith Vosselli.

DEC.

These New Faces

Watch for This Each Month

JOE DONAHUE ("Sunny," First National) is just ten years younger than his late lamented brother, Jack, who was the star of "Sons o' Guns," musical comedy hit. The Donahue boys were both born in Boston, and for several years Joe has been acting as general pinch-hitter for Jack. Marilyn Miller decided Joe was just the lad for "Sunny," so here he is!

PERRY ASKAM ("Sweet Kitty Bellairs," Warners) is a Seattle, Wash., boy who made good in Coast productions of famous operettas such as "The Desert Song," and "The New Moon." He is six feet, two, and tips the beam at 185. He made his stage début in "The Passing Show of 1921," and since then has been busy with big singing rôles on the stage.

LENI STENGEL ("Half Shot at Sunrise," Radio Pictures) is the result of Radio's search for a siren lady with an excellent soprano voice. Miss Stengel has appeared in drama and operetta both here and abroad. She is an accomplished linguist, an excellent actress and a remarkably beautiful girl. What more does the screen require?

KEN MURRAY ("Leathernecking," Radio Pictures) is one of vaudeville's peppier graduates. Ken scored a sensational hit as comedian and master of ceremonies in RKO vaudeville two or three years ago, and since then has been a standby of the big time. His transfer to Radio Pictures means he will play the same houses—from the screen!

1931

WHEN THE YEAR BEGAN, several musicals produced late in 1930 were still being released. Most of these were doomed however to play to half-empty houses, as the public's hostility toward musicals became widespread.

It is curious that in this time of economic Depression the public did not choose to find a welcome escape in as artificial a form as the musical, but it simply did not. Perhaps musicals seemed too frivolous, too lavishly self-indulgent. Whatever the reason, only a handful of musicals were made in 1931, and of these only Eddie Cantor's *Palmy Days* found an enthusiastic general public. Because of his personal appeal and stirring baritone, Lawrence Tibbett's two vehicles, *The Prodigal* and *The Cuban Love Song,* also found admirers. The sophisticates applauded Lubitsch's *The Smiling Lieutenant* with Chevalier. But this list is a minute fraction of the number of musical hits of the two previous years.

One of the great curiosities of the year was the film version of Cole Porter's popular Broadway hit, *Fifty Million Frenchmen.* The show had been produced in 1929 at the height of the musical fever and was the first stage production ever backed entirely by a Hollywood studio (Warners) in order to secure film rights. By the time the show closed and Warners by contract was obliged to shoot it in Technicolor, the craze for musicals had passed. So *Fifty Million Frenchmen* went before the cameras in 1931 with William Gaxton and Helen Broderick of its stage cast, but with its entire Cole Porter score vocally eliminated. The musical themes are heard simply as background accompaniment. The film has been included in this book because of its unusual relationship to the genre.

Because of economic difficulties and a lack of suitable subjects, the industry stopped shooting in color. These were the grim days of the Depression, unrelieved by song or dance.

M. K.

WARNER BROS. presents
VIENNESE NIGHTS
THE GREATEST LOVE STORY EVER TOLD!
Old Vienna—gay, charming—capital of glorious romance; the inspiration of artists and the home of love and youth! Through its eventful years echoes the story of a great love that enriches each generation with its enduring beauty. Old times, rich with remembrance... mirrored again in the new life of today. Beauty that never dies; love that lives on forever, each growing more beautiful as the long years pass.
"Viennese Nights" is the original creation of Sigmund Romberg and Oscar Hammerstein II. It was written especially for the Vitaphone and is filmed entirely in Technicolor.
A WARNER BROS. & VITAPHONE TALKING PICTURE
"Vitaphone" is the registered trademark of The Vitaphone Corporation
A WARNER BROS. & VITAPHONE Picture

JUST IMAGINE
New laws for love...the sky swarming with 'planes... a giant rocket shot to Mars... El Brendel a riotous stowaway... LooLoo, Queen of Mars, throwing a sky party for the rocketeers. JUST IMAGINE Broadway in
1980
New York gone futuristic... a towering tangle of pinnacles, viaducts, bridges... and what fashions in dress... JUST IMAGINE an amazing spectacular musical production with story and song by those masters of marvelous entertainment,
De SYLVA, BROWN AND HENDERSON
and an extraordinary cast, including
EL BRENDEL
MAUREEN O'SULLIVAN
JOHN GARRICK
MARJORIE WHITE
FRANK ALBERTSON
Dances staged by Seymour Felix
Directed by DAVID BUTLER
FOX

A scene from "Check and Double Check," *Amos 'n' Andy's* first picture for Radio. *Kingfish*, in the person of Russell Powell, seems to be laying down the law to the boys. They, as is their wont, are taking it calmly

JAN.

Short Subjects *of the* Month

LONELY GIGOLO
Warners-Vitaphone Variety

Nine minutes of Technicolor in which Lotti Loder, the little Viennese of whom Warners expected much, sings two numbers. She also does a couple of not too startling dance routines. The tiny girl is surrounded by a group of tall chorines. This is not an especially thrilling short.

WHILE THE CAPTAIN WAITS
Paramount

A little one-reel musical piece which features Armida, the little Mexican girl. The scene is aboard an ocean liner. While the hoity-toity ship's concert is on, Armida entertains the steerage with her songs and dances. Armida here dances better than she sings. Mild entertainment.

FLOWER GARDEN
Metro-Goldwyn-Mayer

An opulent and expensive short remindful of the talkies' early days. A lavish flash act in color, with Cliff Edwards, Lottice Howell, some dancers and a chorus of thirty. Cliff sells a couple of songs for a hit, and the short can be rated as pleasant. But not worth the outlay.

JAN.

IRVING BERLIN'S music has always been popular. Yet four out of five of the songs he wrote for a forthcoming United Artists picture were cut out because "The public is tired of songs and singing in pictures."

Gentlemen, gentlemen. The public is not tired of songs and singing.

They're just fed up with the musical noises and senseless lyrics that come forth from Hollywood with all the lilting cadence and ecstasy of a sausage machine transforming little porkers into hot dogs. If you don't think so, go and watch the audience while they listen to Grace Moore in "A Lady's Morals." *There* is a picture in exquisite good taste, and there, my friends, is song and singing.

"SUNNY" is just the word for this sparkling girl, who pirouettes from triumph to triumph on stage and screen with everlasting grace and charm. If you feel you need to regain lightness of heart, we prescribe a copious dose of Marilyn Miller in her new "Sunny"!

Marilyn Miller (Marilyn Reynolds) was born in Evansville, Ind., Sept. 1, 1900. She is 5 feet, 3; weighs 100 pounds, has blonde hair, green eyes. Has been married twice

JAN.

☆ *NEW MOON—M-G-M*

THIS melodious, dramatic operetta brings one of the greatest combinations in screen history to the fore—Lawrence Tibbett and Grace Moore, both Metropolitan Opera song-birds. It was a smash on the stage, and it is a beauty bright on the screen. It's now Russian, with Miss Moore making a gorgeous princess and Tibbett playing a dashing lieutenant. It's full of color and drama, and you may think you've heard "Lover Come Back to Me" sung—but you haven't until you've heard this brilliant pair.

There is some new music in the score, but "Stout Hearted Men," the baritone's big moment, has been retained for Larry. Music-drama of the first rate. As long as companies can make song pictures like this, there will always be room for them on any screen in the world.

"NEW MOON"—M-G-M.—Book and lyrics by Oscar Hammerstein 2nd, Frank Mandel and Laurence Schwab. Adapted by Sylvia Thalberg and Frank Butler. Directed by Jack Conway. The cast: *Lieutenant Michael Petroff*, Lawrence Tibbett; *Princess Tanya Strogoff*, Grace Moore; *Governor Boris Brusiloff*, Adolphe Menjou; *Count Strogoff*, Roland Young; *Potkin*, Gus Shy; *Countess Anastasia Strogoff*, Emily Fitzroy.

JAN.

ZWEI HERZEN IM 3-4 TAKT— (Two Hearts in Waltz Time)— *Associated Cinemas*

BY all odds the most charming sound picture yet to come from Germany. It is so gay and light-hearted and tuneful that it simply steals the heart, this sprightly little operetta in the Viennese manner. It ran for several weeks to packed houses at a little New York theater. The names of the cast mean nothing to American audiences, but they are all deft, smart players. All-German talk.

"ZWEI HERZEN IM 3-4 TAKT"(Two Hearts in Waltz Time)—ASSOCIATED CINEMAS.—Scenario by Walter Reich and Fritz Schulz. Directed by Geza Von Bolvary. The cast: *Tom Hofer*, Walter Janssen; *Nicky Mahler*, Oscar Karlweiss; *Vicky Mahler*, Willy Forst; *Hedi*, Gret Theimer; *Anni Lohmeier*, Irene Eisinger; *Theater Director*, Szoeke Szakall; *Cashier Schlesinger*, Karl Etlinger; *The Notary*, Paul Morgan; *a cab driver*, Paul Hoerbiger; *Hofer's Butler*, August Vockau.

JAN.

UNDER SUSPICION—Fox

HERE'S a grand travelogue of the gorgeous Northwest, and even though you may not care very much what happens to the hero and the villain, you'll get your money's worth out of the scenery. The title sounds like the usual crook stuff, but it's really something sentimental about the Royal Northwest Mounted Police. Lois Moran does exceptionally fine work.

"UNDER SUSPICION"—Fox.—From the story by Tom Barry. Directed by A. F. Erickson. The cast: *John Smith*, J. Harold Murray; *Alice Freil*, Lois Moran; *Doyle*, J. M. Kerrigan; *Darby*, Erwin Connelly; *Freil*, Lumsden Hare; *Inspector Turner*, George Brent; *Suzanne*, Marie Saxon; *Marie*, Rhoda Cross; *Major Manners*, Herbert Bunston; *Ellen*, Vera Gerald.

JAN.

OH, FOR A MAN!—Fox

ONE of the month's brightest, without a doubt—the story of a grand opera star who marries a burglar. A farcical notion which comes off because of its excellent treatment by Director Hamilton McFadden and the merry acting of Jeanette MacDonald and Reginald Denny, in the leads. Nice work also by Warren Hymer, Marjorie White and Alison Skipworth. A worthy winner.

"OH, FOR A MAN!"—Fox.—From the story by Mary F. Watkins. Screen play by Philip Klein and Lynn Starling. Directed by Hamilton MacFadden. The cast: *Carlotta Manson*, Jeanette MacDonald; *Barney McGann*, Reginald Denny; *Totsy Franklin*, Marjorie White; *Pug Morini*, Warren Hymer; *Laura*, Alison Skipworth; *Peck, Carlotta's Manager*, Albert Conti; *Frescatti*, Bela Lugosi; *Costello*, Andre Cheron; *Kerry Stokes*, William Davidson.

JAN.

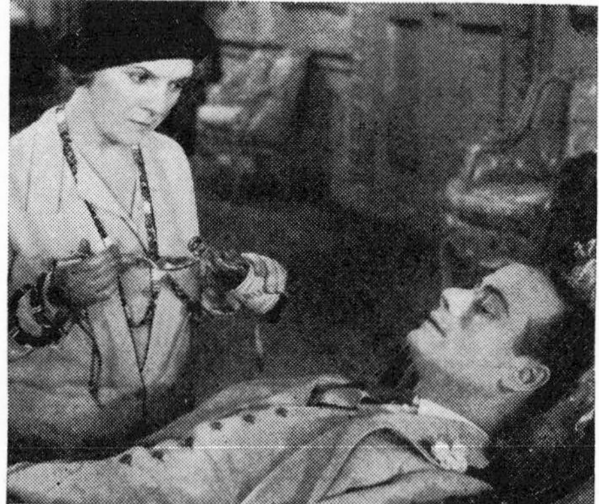

THE LIFE OF THE PARTY —Warners

WHAT laughs! Winnie Lightner, Charles Butterworth and Charles Judels simply pour out rough, loud fun. The story is about the adventures of two feminine song pluggers who make a splurge in Havana's speedier drinking and racing set. All-Technicolor, of the better grade. Irene Delroy and Jack Whiting, the love interest, mean little. But Winnie and the boys are great.

"LIFE OF THE PARTY, THE"—WARNERS.—From the story by Melville Crossman. Adapted by Arthur Caesar. Directed by Roy Del Ruth. The cast: *Flo*, Winnie Lightner; *Dot*, Irene Delroy; *A. J. Smith*, Jack Whiting; *Col. Joy*, Charles Butterworth; *M. Le Maire*, Charles Judels; *Mr. Smith*, John Davidson; *Secretary*, Arthur Hoyt.

JAN.

These New Faces

Watch for This Each Month

GENEVA MITCHELL ("Her Wedding Night," Paramount) is still another who began as a chorister in Ziegfeld's girl opera. Later she became a specialty dancer, and still later was Leon Errol's leading woman in "Louie the Fourteenth" on tour. She made her picture début with Charles Rogers in "Safety in Numbers"—playing one of the numbers.

JAMES CAGNEY ("The Doorway to Hell," Warners) is another New York stage product who shows definite talent in talkies. When Cagney finished at Columbia University he went into the theater, appearing in musical comedy and later "Outside Looking In," "Women Go On Forever," and "Maggie the Magnificent." Whereupon Warners took him for pictures.

JAN.

AND who'd ever have thought that Douglas Fairbanks, Sr., would play comedy under Charlie Chaplin's direction?

It's true—in one scene, anyway. That'll be in "Reaching for the Moon," wherein Fairbanks and Bebe Daniels are co-starred, with Edmund Goulding directing.

It so happened that on the day Charlie visited the United Artists studio recently, Fairbanks and Bebe were working in a farce cocktail-drinking scene.

Charlie stepped on the stage and watched. After a while he shook his head.

"The tempo," he said, "is all wrong."

"How?" they asked.

"Watch," said Charlie. Then, without the trick shoes, moustache, cane or hat, Charlie did the scene in pantomime—playing each part—Fairbanks', Bebe's and even Edward Everett Horton's.

"There," said he, "that's the way it SHOULD be."

"Do it that way," ordered Goulding.

Fairbanks, Bebe and Horton did. And Chaplin directed while Goulding stood by and watched.

JAN.

—A girl named Wilma Wyatt was married to a fellow named Bing Crosby, and it wasn't until several days later that the public learned that Wilma is really Dixie Lee, the blonde heating element of Fox films, and Bing is one of Paul Whiteman's Rhythm Boys.

JAN.

International

The inmates of what Eddie calls "The Cantor Home for Girls." Eddie Cantor, the missus and their five daughters on the lawn of their Beverly Hills home. Left to right, Marilyn, Edna, Eddie, Natalie, Janet, Mrs. Cantor and Marjorie. The big and happy family have become California fans. And now Eddie wants a boy!

Doug's New Picture—

Doug Fairbanks' idea of a busy executive with a few telephones. We suppose the idea is that there's bound to be an unbusy number on at least one of them. Douglas, with Jack Mulhall and Helen Jerome Eddy, in a scene from "Reaching for the Moon," written by Irving Berlin. It's the first film in years Doug hasn't made on his own

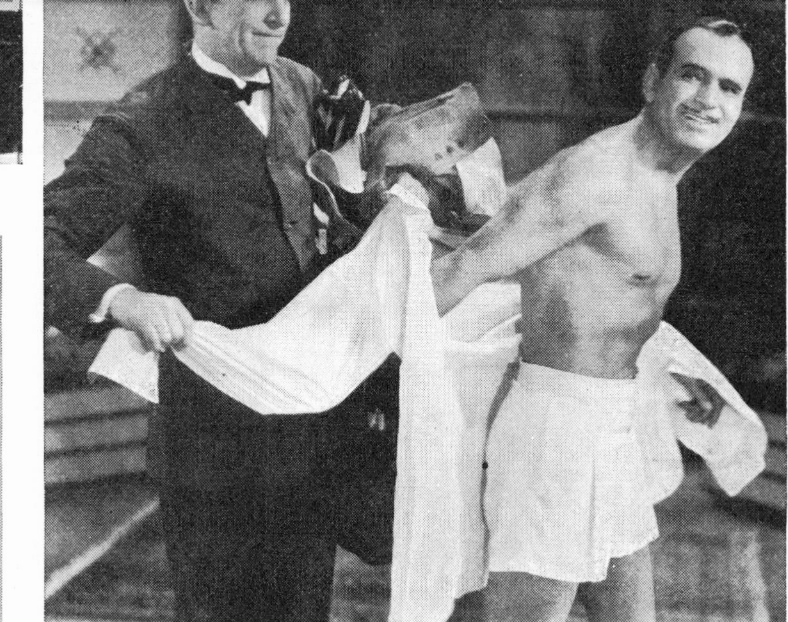

Just to let you know that the flitting years have had no ill effects on Doug's magnificent physical equipment. A scene from "Reaching for the Moon" in which Edward Everett Horton also figures

Behold Hollywood's newest blonde! Bebe Daniels, Doug's leading woman in "Reaching for the Moon," will startle us with light hair, after all these years

IMAGINE THEM TOGETHER IN ONE PICTURE! *The most amazing combination of world famous stars ever brought to the screen!*

Lawrence

TIBBETT

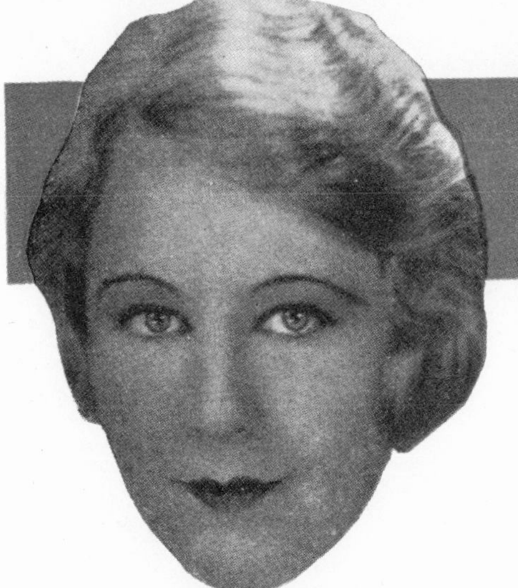

and Grace

MOORE

IN THE YEAR'S TOWERING TALKIE ACHIEVEMENT

"NEW MOON"

with

ADOLPH MENJOU and Roland Young

Every producer in motion pictures tried to get this prize stage sensation. M-G-M brings it to you with all the thrills that made it Broadway's wonder show for more than a year. Great stars — dramatic story — superb action — soul stirring love scenes — glorious voices. Don't miss it!

Book and Lyrics by OSCAR HAMMERSTEIN, 2nd, FRANK MANDEL *and* LAURENCE SCHWAB. *Music by* SIGMUND ROMBERG. *Directed by* JACK CONWAY.

METRO-GOLDWYN-MAYER

"More Stars Than There Are in Heaven"

SHE was a pretty musical comedy prima donna, singing the conventional "I Love You" songs, and praying the show would be a hit. It seldom was, somehow. Then she went to Hollywood, and under the magic wand of Old Master Lubitsch became one of the best comediennes in pictures. Read Jeanette MacDonald's story across the way

The Prima Donna *and* "*the Old Man*"

How a great director made a fine comedienne of a golden girl from musical comedy

By Leonard Hall

THIS is the story of how The Old Man made a Red-Headed Prima Donna into one of the best comediennes on the American screen.

For human interest, the yarn has few equals—even in the dizzy, fizzing Hollywood of the talkie era.

Of course, The Old Man isn't really old. As a matter of fact, he's just nudging forty—gently. But Hollywood, where he has scattered his cinematic genius for nearly a decade, is apt to call anyone old who has left the Torrid Twenties for the Thirsty Thirties. And, too, the Prima Donna's hair is as gold as it is red. But we'll let the overture stand.

Jeanette MacDonald—for that indeed, reader, is our heroine's name!—had brought to Broadway youth, beauty and a pleasant soprano voice. All these commodities are common on Cuckoo Canyon. As fast as they are expended, fresh trainloads arrive from Dodge City and Wapakoneta, and the show goes on.

Moreover, Jeanette's story was quite the usual one. She had been the cutest, prettiest tot on the block. She had sung "'Come, little leaves,' said the Wind, one day," for the neighbors when she was three or four. She took singing lessons, and maybe "elocution." I suspect that she even sang in a choir. This could lead only to one thing. She packed her youth, loveliness and other hat in her first valise and set out to conquer the theater with her face, figure and voice.

AFTER the usual ups, downs and dead levels, she became a Broadway prima donna. That is to say, she was hired to sing duets with the leading tenor in various musical comedies—songs about "I loved you in Junetime—now it is croontime," and so on. She made musical comedy love—losing the boy friend at the end of the first act, and getting him back at the close of the second.

These things are as solidly patterned as so many sewing machines. Jeanette was competent, but she got nowhere in particular, save from road to New York and back again.

I myself sat under her soothing ministrations several times. There were "Yes, Yes, Yvette," and "Sunny Days," to name two. But her shows had a habit of dying under her. Whenever a prima donna "friend' tumbled into a success, she took pains to meet Jeanette and purr, "My dear, I *do* wish you could get a hit!" Good old kitty-kitty Broadway!

AND Jeanette smiled prettily. This could have gone on forever, or until Jeanette's youth and beauty were gone. Then a new shipment would have arrived from Tulsa, and the girl with the red-gold hair would be hopelessly climbing the managers' stairs—and steep they are.

At this moment Fate, Kismet, Providence, Luck, Monkey-Business—you name it!—stepped into the life and times of our heroine.

Electrical engineers, fooling around with their mysterious gadgets, had rigged up the talkies. The great gold rush from Broadway to Hollywood was on!

La Belle MacDonald, as did a couple of hundred other singing girls, had a test made. It was then stuck up on a shelf behind a jar of pickled peaches, and the show went on.

And so enters our hero, The Old Man—a short, stocky, Germanic gentleman with a shrewd eye, a shrewder head and a large brown cigar. In short, Ernst Lubitsch—director extraordinary, tamer of Pola Negri, a very giant among the Lilliputians and Singer Midgets of Hollywood.

THE Old *Meister* was in a quandary, and have you ever been in a good, deep, muddy quandary? It's no fun—I'd almost rather be on the horns of a dilemma, and I do hate a dilemma horn.

Herr Lubitsch was looking for a leading woman for this French meteor, Chevalier. The picture was to be a gay, frothy, phony-kingdom business, "The Love Parade." He'd tried girl after girl, and it was no dice.

At last, eye-weary, he hurled himself into the offices of Paramount.

"Show me some old tests," he groaned, "*und* then I'll *mein* head blow off!"

Jeanette MacDonald's test was taken from the shelf, dusted, and shown to The Old Man. That's how it began.

(continued on next page)

The Prima Donna and "The Old Man" play a tune. Jeanette MacDonald and Ernst Lubitsch between scenes of "The Love Parade"

(continued from preceding page)

Lubitsch saw something in the singing, talking shadow of the beautiful girl with the red-gold hair. His smart showman's sense told him he could add to it—oh, gayety, *finesse*, and most important of all, glamour! Perhaps he saw here perfect, malleable clay for his master-potter's hand. Maybe he didn't.

At any rate, Ernst Lubitsch played a perfect *Pygmalion* to Jeanette MacDonald's *Galatea*.

THE pretty, conventional statue came alive at the command of his intelligence and will. Her dormant humor, her sense of fun that had lain in the bud while she trilled "I Love You," burst into bloom.

To me, the rebirth of Jeanette MacDonald at the touch and under the training of Lubitsch is one of the little miracles of the talkie times.

For born again she was—more beautiful, more glamorous as a woman, and as an entirely new and fascinating artist in the matter of alluring and sexy comedy.

Some things he taught her. Other talents which had lain in her unused, he brought out. Her promise in "The Love Parade" came to full flower in "Monte Carlo," that charming bit of fluff that became something hugely delightful at the magic touch of The Old Man.

How did the little miracle happen? I had a long talk with Jeanette over a tomato omelette and a smidgin of toast. And I think I know.

For one thing, they found, early in their professional association, that their senses of humor jibe. They, a little like *Mike* and *Ike*, laugh alike. If Lubitsch thought of a laugh plum to stick in the picture, Jeanette giggled, and it wasn't just politeness.

The Old *Meister*, sensing that he had pliable material and fertile ground, suggested, taught, instructed and hinted. MacDonald, being a smart girl and a good trouper, picked up every Lubitsch cue.

In a sense, they were teammates. As a matter of fact, Jeanette remarks that the studio always said that she and Lubitsch "did an act." That is to say, The Old Man and the Prima Donna had a pretty elaborate ritual of daily jokes, politenesses and comments. It made for ease and it made for good work.

And daily The Old Man saw *Galatea* begin to breathe—then act, with grace and charm.

What is more important than mere liking, MacDonald had, and has, tremendous respect for the talents of Herr Ernst. She knew that *he* knew, and no fooling! She was anxious to learn from an acknowledged master of his trade—which was three-fourths of the battle. And learn she did!

In all their association through two long and tricky pictures, they had but one serious scrap.

"I had come late three days hand-running," says Jeanette. "The last time I was just five minutes behind time. But Mr. Lubitsch had finally lost all patience and more temper.

"He was in a rage. 'Who do you think you are?' he roared. 'Do you know who I am? You aren't big enough to do this to me!'

"The upshot was that I had hysterics and he stormed into the front office—while a company waited an hour instead of five minutes. But before noon we had made it up, and our friendship and professional understanding were stronger than ever."

And so the team of Lubitsch and MacDonald laughed and toiled successfully through two of the finest sophisticated comedies ever made for the screen. At this writing, her Paramount term over, Jeanette MacDonald is on the Fox lot. But she isn't the conventional prima donna any more. She's a trained and tricky comedienne, taught by a master.

JEANETTE'S a smart girl. She won't forget what teacher taught. She admires and respects him as a master, likes him as a friend. If the Fox directors are smart, they will cash in on this beautiful girl, and all get rich and famous together.

Her first, under the new contract, is to be "All Women Are Bad," with Eddie Lowe opposite and the able William K. Howard holding the reins. And we will see what we shall see—and hear. Boy, there's true romance in the story of The Old Man and The red-haired Prima Donna! It's a little miracle-play, done under the Hollywood arc lights.

Lucky Jeanette, a pretty Broadway girl, whom fortune favored with months of association with a real master! Lucky Paramount, who had her beauty and developed talents in two first-rate comedies! Lucky Fox, crafty enough to sign her for more! Yes, and lucky Lubitsch, too! What greater fortune—or satisfaction—can come to a great moulder of human talents than to see a still, white statue come alive at the touch of his genius?

FEB.

REACHING FOR THE MOON—United Artists

IF anybody but Doug Fairbanks played in this, you might not like it. But Doug, with the vitality of a kid, leaps merrily through a dizzy hodge-podge of gags good and bad, old and new. He plays a mad, bounding Babbitt who makes and loses fortunes between reels. Bebe Daniels, gone beautiful and blonde, is opposite, and Edward Everett Horton and Claude Allister hand laughs. Written by Irving Berlin, but no songs.

"REACHING FOR THE MOON"—UNITED ARTISTS.—From the story by Edmund Goulding. Additional dialogue by Elsie Janis. Directed by Edmund Goulding. The cast: *Larry Day*, Douglas Fairbanks; *Vivian Benton*, Bebe Daniels; *Rogers*, Edward Everett Horton; *Jim Carrington*, Jack Mulhall; *Sir Horace Partington Chelmsford*, Claud Allister; *James Benton*, Walter Walker; *Kitty*, June MacCloy; *Secretary*, Helen Jerome Eddy.

FEB.

A NEW singing team headlined at New York's famous Palace not so long ago.

The billing read, "Bernice Claire and Alexander Gray."

Big shots in Hollywood singies less than a year ago. Then the producers thumbed down the musical stuff. Bernice and Alex sing their songs for the two a day, and doing all right, thanks.

Heigho! Build 'em up—knock 'em down.

FEB.

SOUS LES TOITS DE PARIS—Tobis

EVEN if your French is limited, you'll enjoy this, because it relies more upon pantomime than dialogue, which is in French. Director Clair has caught the picturesque Parisian slum atmosphere. Albert Prejean, reminding one of Chevalier, and Pola Illery, who manages to say a lot with a look, get acting honors. Inconsequential, slow story, but you'll be humming two of the songs.

"SOUS LES TOITS DE PARIS" ("UNDER THE ROOFS OF PARIS")—TOBIS.—From the story by M. Clair. Directed by M. Clair. The cast: *Albert*, Albert Prejean; *Pola*, Pola Illery; *Louis*, Edmund Greville; *Fred*, Gaston Modot; *Bill*, Bill Bockett; *A Customer*, Paul Ollivier.

FEB.

☆ ***THE BLUE ANGEL—UFA-Paramount***

IT'S Emil Jannings first talkie in English. It is the picture that brought Marlene Dietrich to the fans of the world. It was directed by the able Josef Von Sternberg. And it's a knockout!

It's the simple story of a pompous German high school professor who falls in love with a beautiful, bad singer in a low cabaret, and sinks first to degradation, and then to death. Plenty of types and atmosphere, and one sweet tune.

Jannings plays all his old parts again—plays them magnificently, as only Jannings can. He doesn't talk much, and then very heavily. Dietrich is beautiful and fine, and looks only like Dietrich. A sombre story, badly recorded in Germany—but a picture that will fascinate you—by the sheer power and glory of its two leads.

"BLUE ANGEL, THE"—UFA-PARAMOUNT.—From a novel by Heinrich Mann. Adapted by Robert Liebmann. Directed by Josef Von Sternberg. The cast: *Prof. Immanuel Rath*, Emil Jannings; *Lola Frohlich*, Marlene Dietrich; *Kiepert*, Kurt Gerron; *Guste*, Rosa Valetti; *Mazeppa*, Hans Albers; *Director of the School*, Eduard V. Winterstein; *The Clown*, Reinhold Bernt; *The Beadle*, Hans Roth; *Angst*, Rolf Muller; *Lohmann*, Rolant Varno; *Ertzum*, Karl Balhaus; *Goldstaub*, Robert Klein-Lork; *The Publican*, Karl Huszar-Puffy; *The Captain*, Wilhelm Diegelmann; *The Policeman*, Gerhard Bienert; *Publican's Wife*, Ilse Furstenberg.

MAR.

☆ ***THE SOUTHERNER—M-G-M***

THIS gay picture has charm, excellent comedy—and Lawrence Tibbett. It's mighty entertaining.

"The Southerner" also brings back Esther Ralston to the screen, and she proves her right to an important place in talking pictures by her work here. And she seems more beautiful than ever, if that's possible.

Tibbett plays the singing black sheep of a wealthy Southern family, who tramps for five years and then comes home to Esther. And the picture is aided tremendously by the sterling comedy of Roland Young, Cliff Edwards and Stepin Fetchit.

You'll see Tibbett out of uniform for the first time. But, even in the rags of a tramp, the man has glamour. And how he sings!

"SOUTHERNER, THE"—M-G-M.—From the story by Bess Meredyth and Wells Root. Directed by Harry Pollard. The cast: *Jeffry*, Lawrence Tibbett; *Antonia*, Esther Ralston; *Doc*, Roland Young; *Snipe*, Cliff Edwards; *Rodman*, Purnell B. Pratt; *Christine*, Hedda Hopper; *Mrs. Farraday*, Emma Dunn; *Hokey*, Stepin Fetchit; *George*, Louis John Bartels; *Carter Jerome*, Theodore Von Eltz; *Peter*, Wally Albright, Jr.; *Elsbeth*, Suzanne Ransome; *Naomi*, Gertrude Howard; *Jackson*, John Larkin.

MAR.

Short Subjects *of the* Month

WE, WE, MARIE

Universal

Universal is still using the "All Quiet" sets for this funny number in the series of Slim Summerville-Eddie Gribbon comedies. Laughter here comes from action and not dialogue, and there's plenty of funny action. You'll enjoy seeing little Pauline Garon as *Marie*.

GIOVANNI MARTINELLI

Warners—Vitaphone Variety

Martinelli made one of the first Vitaphone shorts, and is still a prominent figure on the Warner list of short subjects. Here, instead of appearing in a scene from an opera, the tenor sings two semi-popular numbers, "Love's Garden of Roses" and "Because."

JUST a bunch of kiddies spending a tranquil story hour at a tin-can tourist camp. Oh yes? Unfortunately for the kiddies' peace, it's all on the set where they are shooting a scene for "Children of Dreams," a new Warner musical. The place is filled with a huge orchestra, scads of bosses and a lot of interested parents. Just a quiet studio day!

A Quiet Day *in the* Country!

MAR.

These New Faces

Watch for This Each Month

JUNE MacCLOY ("Reaching for the Moon," United Artists) came to Hollywood via the popular musical show route—"Scandals," to be exact. June was born in Sturgis, Mich., and went to school at Ursuline Academy, Toledo, O. Well liked in the Fairbanks film, she's now under contract to Paramount. June is twenty-one, blonde and blue-eyed.

MAR.

FIFTY MILLION FRENCHMEN —Warners

THIS *is* a comedy. It moves so fast you're weak when you leave the theater. No songs, no dances—just one gag right after the other and good gags, too. It's all in Technicolor. Olsen and Johnson walk away with honors. There's everything in it but the kitchen sink and you wouldn't be surprised to see that. It concerns American tourists in Paris. Be sure to see it.

"FIFTY MILLION FRENCHMEN"—WARNERS.—From the play by Herbert Fields. Adapted by Joseph Jackson, Al Boasberg and Eddie Welch. Directed by Lloyd Bacon. The cast: *Jack*, William Gaxton; *Simon and Peter*, Olsen and Johnson; *Violet*, Helen Broderick; *Baxter*, Lester Crawford; *Michael*, John Halliday; *Pernasse*, Charles Judels; *Looloo*, Claudia Dell; *Joyce*, Evalyn Knapp; *Marcelle*, Carmelita Geraghty; *Mrs. Carroll*, Daisy Belmore; *Mrs. Rosen*, Vera Gordon; *Mr. Rosen*, Nat Carr; *Fakir*, Bela Lugosi.

APR.

JUNE MOON —Paramount

AS the dumb oaf from the electric works, who thinks he's a song writer, Jackie Oakie is a swell excuse for a lot of laughs. Most of the wisecracking lines in this are by Ring Lardner, excellently sustaining the current allegation that he's an ace humorist. A fine supporting cast helps Oakie put this over, with Harry Akst almost stealing the show. You're going to like this one.

"JUNE MOON"—PARAMOUNT.—From the play by Ring Lardner and George S. Kaufman. Adapted by Keene Thompson. Directed by Edward Sutherland. The cast: *Fred Stevens*, Jack Oakie; *Edna Baker*, Frances Dee; *Lucille Sears*, Wynne Gibson; *Maxie Schwartz*, Harry Akst; *Eileen Fletcher*, June MacCloy; *Paul Sears*, Ernest Wood; *Young Goebel*, Harold Waldridge; *Mr. Hart*, Sam Hardy; *Goldie*, Ethel Sutherland; *Window Cleaner*, Frank Darien; *Miss Rixey*, Jean Bary; *Joe McCloskey*, Eddie Dunn.

APR.

These New Faces

Watch for This Each Month

WILLIAM GAXTON ("Fifty Million Frenchmen," Warners) has long been prominent in musical comedy and vaudeville on Broadway. A San Francisco boy, he came East and appeared with great success in "The Music Box Revue," "Connecticut Yankee" and "Fifty Million Frenchmen." He is married to Madeline Cameron, musical comedy actress.

HELEN BRODERICK ("Fifty Million Frenchmen," Warners) was long one of vaudeville's favorite comediennes, with her husband and partner, Lester Crawford. In addition, she appeared in many musical comedies, among them "Fifty Million Frenchmen." She plays the same rôle in the film. She was one of the late Jeanne Eagels' best friends.

FIFTY MILLION FRENCHMEN
The $7.70 Show that Thrilled Broadway for Two Seasons
Now Bigger, Grander, Funnier on the Vitaphone Screen
—and most of the original Broadway Stars are in it!
Why do Americans go to Paris? To taste the wine? To meet the girls? To see the shows? Perhaps—but especially to find out just what it is that fifty million Frenchmen can't be wrong about! Here's your chance to learn the secrets of la vie Parisien without crossing the ocean and getting your feet wet. » » » »
FIFTY MILLION FRENCHMEN
is based on the play by Herbert Fields
The screen adaptation was made by
Joseph Jackson, Al Boasberg and
Eddie Welch
Photographed by Technicolor
Directed by LLOYD BACON
CLAUDIA DELL
WILLIAM GAXTON
HELEN BRODERICK
JOHN HALLIDAY
OLSEN AND JOHNSON
A WARNER BROS. & VITAPHONE TALKING PICTURE
"Vitaphone" is the registered trademark of The Vitaphone Corporation
A WARNER BROS. & VITAPHONE PICTURE

APR.

THE LITTLE CAFE (LE PETIT CAFE) —Paramount

THIS is the French version, Hollywood-made, of Maurice Chevalier's American picture, "The Playboy of Paris." And it's a beauty. Maurice, of course, expands in his native French, and more songs are included. Yvonne Vallée (Mme. Chevalier) is gay and sprightly opposite her husband. Frances Dee played the part in English. A very blithe and charming picture. If you get a chance, give your French a workout on it.

"LITTLE CAFE, THE" (LE PETIT CAFE)—PARAMOUNT.—From the play by Tristan Bernard. Adapted by Vincent Lawrence and Bataille-Henri. Directed by Ludwig Berger. The cast: *Albert Lorifian,* Maurice Chevalier; *Yvonne Philibert,* Yvonne Vallee; *Mlle. Berengere,* Tania Fedor; *Pieree Bourdin,* Andre Berley; *Philibert,* Emile Chautard; *Mlle. Edwige,* Francoise Rosay; *Paul Michel,* George Davis; *M. Cadaeux,* Jaques Jou-Jerville.

APR.

CHILDREN OF DREAMS—Warners

ANOTHER reason why the box-office turned thumbs down on musicals. Sigmund Romberg and Oscar Hammerstein, II, are responsible for the tale, which has fruit-pickers (accompanied by an orchestra) singing through orchards, and a hero tenor warbling to the girl friend "And Every Morning at Seven A. M. We'll Climb a Tree." The cast works hard.

"CHILDREN OF DREAMS"—WARNERS.—From the story by Oscar Hammerstein II. Directed by Alan Crosland. The cast: *Molly Standing,* Margaret Schilling; *Tommy Melville, Jr.,* Paul Gregory; *Gus Schultz,* Tom Patricola; *Hubert Standing,* Bruce Winston; *Dr. Joe Thompson,* Charles Winninger; *Gertie,* Marion Byron.

MAY

The famous composer of "Rhapsody in Blue" takes off his coat and concocts some music for the talkies. George Gershwin at his piano on the Fox lot. Beside him is his brother Ira, who writes lyrics. On the piano, Guy Bolton, librettist

MAY

PAGLIACCI—Audio Cinema Production

BAD grand opera poorly transferred to the screen. The well-worn Leoncavallo song-story of the clown with the breaking heart is sung by members of the San Carlo Grand Opera Co., with Fernando Bertini as *Canio.* This pioneer opera-film is crudely made, and acted in the sticky operatic manner.

"PAGLIACCI"—AUDIO CINEMA PRODUCTION in association with FORTUNE GALLO.—From the opera by Ruggiero Leoncavallo. Directed by Joe W. Coffman. The cast: *Nedda,* Alba Novella; *Canio,* Fernando Bertini; *Tonio,* Mario Valle; *Silvio,* Giuseppe Interranti; *Beppe,* Francesco Curci.

A Studio Ramble

By

Frances Kish

The irrepressible Maurice trying to "break up" Miriam Hopkins in a studio still picture for which they are posing. You can see her working hard not to give in and laugh

SUCH a pretty blue and silver boudoir. Or it would be, if it had a ceiling and if the walls weren't cut off at the top in a jagged line. But it doesn't matter, because that won't show in the picture.

It's a scene in "The Smiling Lieutenant," the latest Chevalier film. Maurice strides on the set, his step taking its cue from the martial and resplendent uniform he wears. Someone picks up a spur from the floor and wisecracks about "the spur of the moment." Maurice registers the famous Chevalier grin and fastens the spur to his boot.

From his chair next to a camera a short, heavy-set man rises, his dark eyes alive under an untidy lock of black hair which hangs across his forehead. It is Ernst Lubitsch, director of that other Chevalier hit, "The Love Parade."

"All right, Maurice," he says. "Let's do somesing now." He turns to Miriam Hopkins, the Princess of this picture. (You probably remember her in "Fast and Loose.") "All right, Mariam," he says, mispronouncing her name and making her like it. "Rehearsal," he orders. "Everyone quiet."

Three bells ring as the signal for silence all through the big Paramount Eastern Studios. Chevalier opens a door in the torn-off wall and waits on the other side for his cue to come on the set.

"Action, Mariam," instructs Mr. Lubitsch.

Chevalier comes through the door, quietly closes it after him, hesitates a moment and goes to the side of his bride. But an amazing thing has happened. There are, suddenly, two Princesses—the slender Miriam and the short, dark-eyed man on the sidelines.

EVERY expression on Miriam's face is duplicated in Mr. Lubitsch's. That startled look, when she hears the door close behind the man she has just married. Her astonishment when he stands beside her and says, "Good-night, dear." Her uncomprehending shyness. All these are duplicated and intensified on the face of the man who peers from beneath the camera.

"What an actor!" you want to shout.

Fascinated, you watch the same scene rehearsed half a dozen times, the same double acting of girl and director. Then a brief rest. Chevalier autographs a photograph of himself for an admirer. Miriam and Mr. Lubitsch go over part of her scene, smoothing out the action, and giggling like a couple of school children at recess. Hammers pound on the floor above, where sets for "Tarnished Lady," Tallulah Bankhead's talkie bow, are being torn down to make way for the new Nancy Carroll-Fredric March picture.

On the Lubitsch set lights are shifted and cameras adjusted. The "dolly," a rubber-tired truck on which a camera is mounted, is carefully placed and its course marked by white chalk lines to be followed as the camera advances for close-ups.

Make-up is freshened. A prop boy rushes forward to adjust the train of Miriam's lace wedding dress—a lovely, square-necked gown with long, tight sleeves. Her long veil trails behind her like a white cloud.

"Zis is a take," says Mr. Lubitsch. The bells signal silence. It's just like a rehearsal, except for a tenseness that communicates itself to everyone. Suddenly Mr. Lubitsch growls "Cut." His alert ear has caught the sound of a hammer pounding on another set, a sound that would be magnified to the proportions of a thunder storm by the sensitive microphones. Someone has disregarded orders. A messenger is sent to investigate.

THEY start again. All goes well, until Chevalier gets a "frog" in his throat. "Are you not my wife?" he asks the puzzled Princess. "Am I not your—" and try as he will, the word "husband" will not come out of his mouth. Everybody laughs, and the scene starts again. This time it goes well. But Mr. Lubitsch sees a chance for improvement. They do it again. They do it another time, and another time. Mr. Lubitsch says, "Now, Miriam, try that line wissout the 'Oh.'"

Finally, he is satisfied. "Cut," he orders. "Zis is okay for me," he says. "How about sound?"

"Okay for sound," comes the report from the monitor room.

"Perfect timing in that scene," exults the director.

Another rest, for everyone but Miriam Hopkins. The scene is to be repeated for the French version, and Miriam is feverishly rehearsing her lines, parrot-like. Mr. Lubitsch has wisely selected a cast equally at home in English and French—Chevalier, Claudette Colbert, George Barbier—but Miriam's French appears to be somewhat uncertain.

But, on the first take, it is Chevalier's French that strikes a snag. He mixes it with a little English, with amusing results. What a howl goes up from the others! Maurice joins in the general laugh and says with his funny little rising inflection after each word: "It's a great thing, is eet not, to talk two langua-a-ges. Not ev-ery-body can talk two langua-a-ges so pair-fect, *n'est-ce pas?*"

"And," laments Miriam, "just when I was getting along so swimmingly with my part of it!"

The next time it goes all right. "Hooray!" shouts Chevalier. And, "Da-a-rn good!" is his final comment.

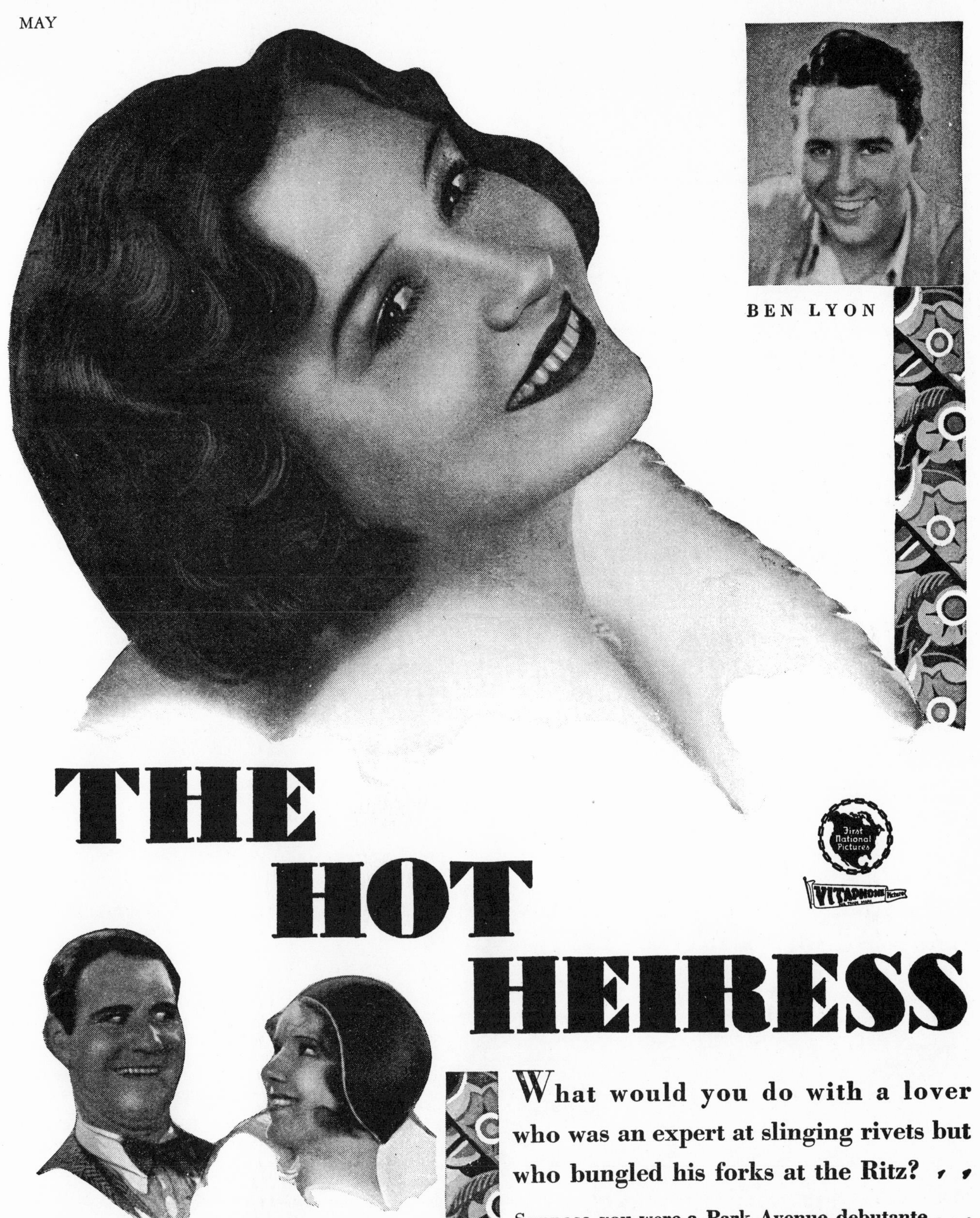

What would you do with a lover who was an expert at slinging rivets but who bungled his forks at the Ritz?

Suppose you were a Park Avenue debutante . . . and some husky brute of an ironworker was mean enough to spoil your beauty sleep by pounding rivets right outside your bedroom window . . . and then you saw he was big and strong and handsome . . . and Oh! look out—he's falling—falling in love with you!

See what charming Ona Munson does when Park and Third Avenues meet! It's her newest, biggest part and you're going to like this rising young star.

BEN LYON
ONA MUNSON
WALTER PIDGEON
TOM DUGAN, INEZ COURTNEY

Original Story by Herbert Fields

Music and Lyrics by Richard Rodgers and Lorenz Hart

Directed by CLARENCE BADGER

"Vitaphone" is the registered trademark of The Vitaphone Corp.

A FIRST NATIONAL & VITAPHONE PICTURE

JUN.

INDISCREET
—United Artists

IF your requirement of a picture is entertainment—this is a good picture. There are only two songs in the picture, sung beautifully by Gloria Swanson. Not quite as good as "The Trespasser," it is materially better than "What A Widow!" There is comedy good for many laughs. Ben Lyon is delightful; Arthur Lake unusually good. Gloria keeps her come-back lead. Well worth your time.

"INDISCREET"—UNITED ARTISTS.—From the story "Obey That Impulse" by DeSylva, Brown & Henderson. Directed by Leo McCarey. The cast: *Jerry (Geraldine Trent)*, Gloria Swanson; *Tony Blake*, Ben Lyon; *Jim Woodward*, Monroe Owsley; *Joan Trent*, Barbara Kent; *Buster Collins*, Arthur Lake; *Aunt Kate*, Maude Eburne; *Mr. Woodward*, Henry Kolker; *Mrs. Woodward*, Nella Walker.

JUN.

Short Subjects *of the* Month

SKY HIGH

Vitaphone Variety

There is a definite place in the short subject field for little musical pieces, and this is a good one. It contains singing, dancing and a little comedy—it features a beautiful Broadway hot-song singer named Janet Reade (she's a platinum blonde) and it pleases the folks.

JUN.

Is the famous Chevalier smile a little forced here? Yours would be if you were in his spot. It seems that the slaps Miriam Hopkins and Claudette Colbert exchange in "The Smiling Lieutenant" are a bit too lusty! Tut, tut ladies—not jealous?

JUN.

NO matter what way you may look at it, it's still a funny business—this movie-making.

For instance, John Boles was originally put on contract by Universal because of not so much his good looks as his good voice. So they had him sing and sing.

Then musicals "went out," as Hollywood believes, and they put John Boles, the singer, into the leading rôle in "Seed," wherein he doesn't sing a note.

And now they're talking about "bringing musicals back!"

Is there NO reason?

Indiscreet

Through one indiscretion – a woman with a future became a woman with a past

A new ***year***..... A new ***life*****.....**

So Jerry Trent (Gloria Swanson) made her New Year's ***resolution***....Her past was a closed book ....Her ***romance*** with Jim Woodward was forgotten ....On fresh, clean pages she'd write the story of a new and greater ***love***...But the winds of ***fate*** blew... Love demanded a ***sacrifice***...

Joseph M. Schenck presents
A DeSYLVA, BROWN and HENDERSON
Production

GLORIA SWANSON
in
"INDISCREET"
with
Ben Lyon Arthur Lake

Directed by Leo McCarey

A UNITED ARTISTS PICTURE
"UNITED FOR YOUR ENTERTAINMENT"

JUL.

WITH Herr Lubitsch leading him by the hand, back comes Chevalier in one of the breeziest and most tuneful pieces of entertainment that we have seen in a long time. And what a relief this is, too, from some of the current types of pictures!

Here is Chevalier at his best, as an Austrian lieutenant in love with a girl orchestra leader (Claudette Colbert) but forced into marrying a princess of one of those George Barr McCutcheon kingdoms. It's really an educational film for girls who are inclined to be a little too old-fashioned!

If we must have man-and-woman and triangle stories in films, please let Mr. Lubitsch do them. He can put over a red-hot love affair and dare the censors to say it is anything but a game of checkers. The audience just grins and chuckles and laughs throughout. It's a cure for these depression blues.

The music is so generally good that there is hardly any outstanding hit. Miriam Hopkins is great as the princess, Claudette Colbert is lovely, and you will scream with laughter at George Barbier, as the king of the hokum kingdom. And, girls, just between us, notice how those actresses sock each other! *Ja wohl,* Herr Lubitsch.

 ***THE SMILING LIEUTENANT—Paramount***

"SMILING LIEUTENANT, THE"—PARAMOUNT.—From the story by Felix Dorman and Hans Muller. Adapted by Ernst Vajda and Samson Raphaelson. Directed by Ernst Lubitsch. The cast: *Niki,* Maurice Chevalier; *Franzi,* Claudette Colbert; *Anne,* Miriam Hopkins; *King,* George Barbier; *Orderly,* Hugh O'Connell; *Max,* Charlie Ruggles; *Adjutant Von Rockoff,* Robert Strange; *Lily,* Janet Reade; *Emperor,* Con MacSunday; *Baroness Von Schwedel,* Elizabeth Patterson; *Count Von Halden, Master-Ceremonies,* Harry Bradley; *Joseph,* Werner Saxtorph; *Master Ceremonies (Austrian),* Karl Stall; *Bill Collector,* Granville Bates.

JUL.

Short Subjects *of the* Month

MOTHER GOOSE MELODIES
Columbia

A Walt Disney Silly Symphony that is the perfect short for the kiddies and grown-ups, too. With King Cole as the central character, most of the other Mother Goose characters come to life to a fetching variety of tunes. Expertly and cleverly done.

BETTY CO-ED
Paramount

A good melodious short, with plenty of college atmosphere. Rudy Vallée and his Connecticut Yankees furnish the musical accompaniment. Rudy also delivers a solo with the dancing ball keeping time for the audience to join in. The young folks will like this one.

JUL.

"Oh, Animal Crackers!" disrespectfully shout three little Marx boys as they line up in front of Papa Samuel Marx—Harpo, that silent fourth, just snaps his suspenders. This family group was shot at Paramount where Harpo, Groucho, Chico and Zeppo are making "Monkey Business" for Paramount

JUL.

Ruth Etting puts across one of those low, so blue, croons for the benefit of the mike. You will hear this expression in Vitaphone's "Freshman Love"

"THE SMILING LIEUTENANT"

a Paramount 20th Birthday JUBILEE Triumph

Based upon "The Waltz Dream" by Leopold Jacobson and Felix Dormann, and the novel, "Nux Der Prinz-gemahl" by Hans Muller

CLAUDETTE COLBERT

CHARLIE RUGGLES MIRIAM HOPKINS

Music by OSCAR STRAUS

Irresistible! Gay Maurice, debonair as ever, laughing his way in and out of love as beautiful Claudette Colbert and Miriam Hopkins play at hearts with him. Produced by Ernst Lubitsch, whose sure deft touch and surprise situations make his pictures such a delight. You'll go out of the theatre feeling happy as a lark, a sparkle in your eyes, a song in your heart. It's *that* kind of picture—don't miss it! *"If it's a Paramount Picture it's the best show in town!"*

PARAMOUNT PUBLIX CORP., ADOLPH ZUKOR, PRES., PARAMOUNT BLDG., N. Y.

AUG.

LE MILLION —Tobis Soundfilm

YOU don't have to understand French to get all the fun and flavor out of this French musical farce, a gorgeous burlesque on all other musical farces, but adept and hilarious in its own right. Two English-speaking players are ingeniously woven into the story to explain the action. Please bring Rene Clair, the director, to America to teach some of our directors. This should open their eyes.

"LE MILLION"—TOBIS PRODUCTION.—From the play by G. Berr and M. Guillemaud. Scenario and direction by Rene Clair. The cast: *Beatrice*, Annabella; *Michel*, Rene Lefebure; *Prosper*, Louis Allibert; *Crochard*, Paul Ollivier; *Vanda*, Vanda Greville; *Sopranelli*, Constantin Stroesco; *The Singer*, Odette Talazac.

SEPT.

HONEYMOON LANE— Sono Art

NOT a great picture, but a thoroughly delightful one. No sex, no gang murders, but plenty of laughs and chuckles and entertainment. Eddie Dowling and June Collyer team up for romantic delight, while amazing Ray Dooley will tie you up in laugh-knots. The story is negligible, but the handling of it is charming—and there's a song number by Dowling which proves music has its place on the screen.

"HONEYMOON LANE"—SONO ART.—From the story by Eddie Dowling. Directed by William J. Craft. The cast: *Tim Dugan*, Eddie Dowling; *Mary Baggott*, June Collyer; *"Dynamite,"* Raymond Hatton; *Gerty Murphy*, Ray Dooley; *Tom Baggott*, Noah Beery; *Mother Murphy*, Mary Carr; *King of Bulgravia*, Adolphe Milar; *Paulino, Major Domo*, Gene Lewis; *Col. Gustave*, Lloyd Whitlock; *"Noisy,"* George Kotsonaros; *Betty Royce*, Corliss Palmer.

SEPT.

Short Subjects *of the* Month

Bing Crosby's crooning is getting to be infectious and his popularity is mounting steadily. The series of shorts he is making for Educational not only get over the Crosby voice, but the Crosby personality, which seems to be quite sumpin'. His latest release is reviewed below

I SURRENDER, DEAR

Sennett-Educational

Bing Crosby, crooning Bing Crosbyishly, makes this highly entertaining. Bing's work, plus the usual array of good Sennett gags and a not-too-involved romantic plot, provide a half hour's fun.

THE GOOFY GOAT

Eshbough-Weingart

Here's the first of a new company's series of comic cartoons in color. The central character, apparently out after some of Mickey Mouse's pickings, is (or have you guessed it?) a goofy goat. In this, he's good. Let's see more.

SEPT.

MEN OF THE SKY—First National

ANOTHER in that group of war pictures which gave Marlene Dietrich and Doug. Fairbanks, Jr., such excellent vehicles, but which is too flimsy and miscast to come up to the standard set by these two. If you can imagine Bramwell Fletcher, an English actor with a decided English accent, playing a German officer, yours is a vivid imagination, indeed. Irene Delroy and Jack Whiting belong in musical comedy, not drama.

"MEN OF THE SKY"—FIRST NATIONAL.—From the story by Jerome Kern and Otto Harbach. Directed by Alfred E. Green. The cast: *Madeleine*, Irene Delroy; *Jack Ames*, Jack Whiting; *Eric Von Coburg*, Bramwell Fletcher; *Madeleine's Father*, John Sainpolis; *Oscar*, Frank McHugh.

SEPT.

THE MERRY WIVES OF VIENNA— Super Film Prod.

WHEN foreign-made films are sober, few of ours compare with their gloom. But when they're gay, like this one, where are others so sparkling? Even if you no speak *Deutsch*, you'll enjoy this. You'll love the music, especially the rippling waltz songs.

"MERRY WIVES OF VIENNA, THE"—SUPER FILM.—From the scenario by Walter Reich. Directed by Geza von Bolvary. The cast: *Augustin Tuschinger*, Willy Forst; *Anselme Leitner, Commissioner of Monuments*, Paul Hoerbiger; *Alois Stanigi*, Ernst Wurmser; *Grell*, Lee Parry; *His Excellency, Waldmueller*, Oskar Sima; *Therese Zelenka, known as Flotte Motte*, Cordy Millowitsch.

The MARX BROTHERS

Stars of "THE COCOANUTS" and "ANIMAL CRACKERS"

Directed by Norman McLeod

in "MONKEY BUSINESS"

Celebrate Paramount's 20th Birthday Jubilee!

•

Paramount is celebrating 20 years of leadership with the greatest pictures in its history! Watch for "24 HOURS," "A FAREWELL TO ARMS," "NO ONE MAN," "LIVES OF A BENGAL LANCER." And such stars as HAROLD LLOYD, GEORGE BANCROFT, MARLENE DIETRICH, RUTH CHATTERTON and others in the greatest pictures of their careers!

PARAMOUNT PUBLIX CORPORATION
ADOLPH ZUKOR, PRES., PARAMOUNT BLDG., N.Y.

LAUGHING days are here again! With that famous frenzied foursome, The Marx Brothers, in a new madhouse of merriment—"MONKEY BUSINESS." It's the first of the great pictures in Paramount Jubilee Month—September—when leading theatres everywhere will feature Paramount Pictures. Watch for announcements. *"If it's a Paramount Picture it's the best show in town!"*

OCT.

☆ *PALMY DAYS—United Artists*

TEN-TO-ONE, this will bring back film musicals in a veritable inundation. It's *that* good!

"Palmy Days" is a typical Cantor-and-nonsense show. What plot there is becomes merely the skeleton on which the comedy, the gags, the songs, the dances, the beauty, the action of this film have been hung.

It moves with zip from start to finish, with never a dull moment.

It's mostly Eddie Cantor, of course. He's never been funnier than as the sap in the trick bakery—an amazing cruller factory that's run entirely by gorgeous girls who wear as little as possible whenever possible. Ah, me . . .!

Cantor's gags are hilarious, whether old or new. Charlotte Greenwood is another grand funster.

Barbara Weeks, lovely and snappy, makes a sensational screen début.

There are several songs, at least one of which—"Yes, Yes"—may prove a big hit. Eddie and Charlotte revive the chiropractor gag, and if that sequence doesn't tie audiences in knots, then nothing's funny. And in spite of the fact that the girls present extensive epidermic displays, the fun always manages to remain clean.

If they can make musicals like this, then there's no reason at all why they shouldn't come back.

"PALMY DAYS"—UNITED ARTISTS.—From the story by Eddie Cantor, Morrie Ryskind and David Freedman. Continuity by Keene Thompson. Directed by Edward Sutherland. The cast: *Eddie Simpson*, Eddie Cantor; *Helen Martin*, Charlotte Greenwood; *Joan Clark*, Barbara Weeks; *Mr. Clark*, Spencer Charters; *Steve*, Paul Page; *Yolando*, Charles Middleton; *Cake Eater*, Walter Catlett; *Plug Moynihan*, Harry Woods; *Joe*, George Raft.

OCT.

MONKEY BUSINESS—Paramount

MESSRS. Marx, Marx, Marx & Marx in another outbreak of assorted lunacy. It has no beginning and no end, as far as any real plot is concerned—but if you're of that group who like gorgeous nonsense, then by all means split your sides over the latest Marxian antics as herein manifested. Groucho's absurdities rattle off his tongue; Harpo is silent but mad; the other two are Marxes, too.

"MONKEY BUSINESS"—PARAMOUNT.—From the story by S. J. Perleman and Will B. Johnstone. Directed by Norman McLeod. The cast: *Groucho*, Groucho Marx; *Harpo*, Harpo Marx; *Chico*, Chico Marx; *Zeppo*, Zeppo Marx; *Lucille*, Thelma Todd; *Gibson, the First Mate*, Tom Kennedy; *Mary Helton*, Ruth Hall; *Joe Helton*, Rockliffe Fellows; *Capt. Corcoran*, Ben Taggart; *Second Mate*, Otto Fries; *Manicurist*, Evelyn Pierce; *Opera Singer*, Maxine Castle; *Briggs*, Harry Woods.

OCT.

Short Subjects *of the* Month

OLD SONGS FOR NEW
Welshay

A one-reeler in color; fast comedy of the gay nineties. A miniature revue, with swell music by Georgie Stoll's band, reminiscent of the "good old days." There are plenty of good laughs, too.

NOV.

Short Subjects *of the* Month

Anything for a laugh—and Tom Patricola comes up singing. Good comedies like "The Tamale Vendor," reviewed below, will cure your blues

THE TAMALE VENDOR

Educational-Ideal

Just enough story to provide a background for Tom Patricola's bag of tricks, his nimble dancing, pleasing singing and strumming accompaniment. Some laughs, a couple of pretty girls, and a hilarious gag situation at the finish.

NOV.

A STUDENT'S SONG OF HEIDELBERG (EIN BURSCHENLIED AUS HEIDELBERG)—UFA

WHETHER or not you understand German this is a grand picture, with rollicking students, rollicking tunes and rollicking acting. The extras are all real Heidelberg boys and the cameras did their grinding on the old Heidelberg campus, or whatever they call it over there. There's a story, with very good actors, but the scenery and the songs are what make it worthwhile.

"STUDENT'S SONG OF HEIDELBERG, A" (EIN BURSCHENLIED AUS HEIDELBERG)—UFA.—From the story by Ernst Neubach and Hans Wilhelm. Directed by Karl Hartl. The cast: *John Miller,* Ernst Stahl-Nachbaur; *Elinor Miller,* Betty Bird; *Robert Dahlberg,* Willi Forst; *Bornemann sen,* Albert Paulig; *Bornemann junr,* Hans Brausewetter; *Sam Mayer,* Hermann Blass; *The Landlady,* Ida Wuest.

HOT-CHA-CHA and whoopee! Lupe and Larry—and are they a team? The maddest, gayest set on the M-G-M lot. Lupe Velez and Lawrence Tibbett are playing together in "The Cuban," with old "Trader" Van Dyke, who took a troupe into darkest Africa, directing

Stagg

LUPE is the dancing and singing girl in a Havana cabaret and Larry is a big marine who casts that sort of eyes her way. Jimmy Durante is also in it. What a picture it should be! Music, romance, comedy. Everything's hot on this set—even the camera!

"Ginsburg!"

Maurice Chevalier and one of his fiddler boy friends sneak up on the microphone and make a record that sparkles with pep

By Ida Zeitlin

THE time is 10:15 of a pleasant morning. The place is the recording studio of the Victor Company—a huge, windowless room, artificially lighted and ventilated, and equipped with an assortment of musical instruments of so many shapes and varieties that you would probably have trouble naming half of them.

Yet so vast is this room that, despite its paraphernalia, despite the twenty people, the piano, the platform and the score of chairs held comfortably within its middle region, it creates an impression of emptiness. You notice at once that the floor you walk on, the ceiling over your head, the walls around you, are different from the floors and the walls and the ceilings of your every-day existence; and upon inquiring, you are informed that, for technical reasons, all these surfaces have undergone some special and mysterious process of treatment.

The chairs are occupied by musicians, mostly young. On a dais facing them, close to a microphone, stands the conductor—a curly-haired, pleasant-faced youth whose manner is friendly and free of any trace of bumptious authority. Yet make no mistake. This amiable young man, who works in shirt-sleeved brotherhood with his orchestra and addresses them for the most part as "chiselers," is no less surely the boss of his outfit than Toscanini standing in glory on the stage of Carnegie Hall.

There is a sense of expectancy in the air—that feeling which pervades a theater just before the curtain goes up. The orchestra is rehearsing an unfamiliar melody, at the same time keeping its eyes cocked toward the door that leads into the street. The prevailing spirit of good humor is catching. It even manages, somehow, to sneak its way into the dreamy notes of the waltz they're playing, that sounds as if it were destined to become one of the season's favorite dance tunes.

There seems to be some confusion as they near the end. The conductor sends an inquiring eyebrow toward the piano. "Say, Len!" comes a plaintive voice from that direction, "these four bars at the end don't mean nothin'!"

Maurice Chevalier, the boy who breaks records, also makes them. Now read how!

"Len"—otherwise Mr. Leonard Joy, whose name seems singularly appropriate to the genial atmosphere he creates—joins the pianist. Their knitted brows and rhythmic fingers are bent above the score. The others relax. One of them eyes me speculatively; then, taking the plunge, calls in a confidential whisper, "You gunna write us up?"

But the whisper isn't confidential enough. "Hey, fellas, look what wants a write-up!" chortles his neighbor. "It ain't us she's gunna write up, nitwit!" he adds severely. "It's the French egg!"

THIS releases a flood of contributions.

"What a guy that is!"

"Does that bird know his business!"

"Takes him an hour 'n' a half to do his stuff where it takes the rest of 'em double."

"An' that's no buggy-ride!"

"Say, lady, watch him talk to the mike. It's a laugh!"

"All right, boys, let's go!" calls the leader. "We'll take it with the second ending."

Once, twice, three times they play the song—play it until each note emerges, clear and round, and the melody seems to assume an airy shape of its own that floats charmingly about the room on its dancing feet.

The last quiver of sound dies away. "Ginsburg!" comes a deep-throated chorus from the players who look rather pleased with themselves as they lower their instruments. Ginsburg? Well, it certainly sounded like Ginsburg, unless my ears are playing me some fancy trick. Mr. Joy takes pity on my mystified face and explains.

"It's a gag," he says. "One of the fellows brought it back from a picture studio where he worked. Every time the director shot a scene he'd say to his head yes-man, 'It's good, Ginsburg!' So they started

(continued on next page)

(continued from preceding page)
yelling it here whenever they liked themselves—and after a while it came to be just 'Ginsburg!' Means—" he concluded with a deprecating grin, "it's swell!"

It is past ten-thirty—the hour at which the French singer for whom they are waiting is scheduled to arrive. He had, to be sure, stepped off the Hollywood train only that morning. Tardiness under such conditions might be considered excusable.

Yet when, at promptly ten-forty, a man of average height, in a gray suit and a fedora hat, with warm blue eyes and a slightly protruding lower lip, makes his appearance—producing, incidentally, on the occupants of the room the effect of a slight and stimulating electric shock that stiffens their backs and brings a sparkle into their eyes—there is apparent on the newcomer's agreeable face a look of genuine distress.

"I am late," he says, turning to Joy, and the voice and the accent are those that within the brief space of three years have grown to be a familiar delight in every corner of the world. But the still more famous smile is missing. In repose Maurice Chevalier's face is unexpectedly grave, even stern—reflecting, perhaps, the sternness of the poverty-haunted years of his early youth. "I am late, but I think it is not my fault. No one told me I must come here, so I went first to 44th Street. I am terribly sorry."

THEY get down promptly to business. Mr. Joy raises his baton and the notes of the waltz they have just been rehearsing drift once more through the room. Chevalier, having removed his collar and lighted a cigarette, hums the air as he listens. The first violinist, a boy with great dark eyes who looks about eighteen, smiles up at him and Chevalier smiles back. Impossible to analyze that smile, still more impossible to resist it. It seems to hold the essence of all the friendliness and kindly warmth that one human being may feel for his fellows.

Chevalier nods his approval, hangs his coat and vest over the back of a chair, and, hands in pockets, takes his place at the microphone. The god of the control room, where the technical equipment is housed, emerges, makes some adjustment in the combination radio-Victrola that stands against the wall, and disappears.

A second's pause is followed by a long, wavering buzz, which is the signal for silence. Another buzz, long and steady. Two flutes in the back stand up. A third buzz, repeated, short and sharp, and the music floats out.

Chevalier begins to sing. Gone is the serious mask, gone the preoccupied air. His face lights up, his hands move easily from gesture to gesture, and wherever he puts them is the place where they should be; his shoulders talk, his eyebrows are more eloquent than most people's tongues. His whole body is the sensitive instrument through every inch of which he conveys, far more vividly than in words, the spirit of his song.

FINISHING the first chorus, he steps away from the mike to make room for the dark-eyed, long-lashed boy who, looking more childish than ever with his grave face bent above the violin, plays a brief solo into the microphone. As he in his turn steps back from the instrument, Chevalier makes him a low bow which he as ceremoniously returns.

It's a love ditty that he's singing, written by the authors of "Louise," that popular ballad of his first picture. Its words contain none of the humor, none of the sophistication of the French favorites with which he earned his European reputation. It is a purely American product, boasting a purely American flavor. "Will I ever find the girl in my mind, the girl who is my ideal?"

Yet, those of you who saw "Innocents of Paris," who saw Chevalier standing by a flower-covered wall in the moonlight singing to the wistful girl above him, who remember the half-tender, half-mischievous smile with which he seemed to mock the sentimentality of the words as he sang them, who realized how by the deftness and grace of his touch he lifted that scene out of the commonplace, and transmitted it into a genuine emotional expression of the beauty and pathos of young love, will understand how he worked a similar miracle with this one.

The first test is finished. Everyone gathers about the radio-Victrola to listen with professional concern to the reproduction. There's something a little eerie about this instantaneous mechanical repetition of the sounds that a moment before were being made by .... human hands and a human throat. "Although she may be late, I trust in fate and so I wait for my ideal." Mr. Joy looks to Chevalier for his verdict, Chevalier looks to Mr. Joy. They shake their heads simultaneously. It may sound perfect to your ears or to mine, but their trained senses have detected a flaw. The whole thing has to be done over again.

ONCE more the signals sound, once more Chevalier sings and the young violinist plays his solo between choruses, once more a judiciary group forms about the machine. Chevalier sits with lowered head, his hands hanging between his knees. This time he makes no comment when the song is ended. "Does that sound better?" the conductor asks him anxiously. Gravely he raises his head, gravely he looks Mr. Leonard Joy in the eye.

Then, with a comic effect impossible to convey, his polite Parisian voice solemnly pronounces the single word "Geenzborgh!" which wise-crack is greeted with roars of delight from his audience, and is enjoyed by no one more hugely than the perpetrator himself.

The test having been found good, the master-records may now be made—three in all, from which the best will be chosen for ultimate use. The procedure is the same, except that the song does not come back through the Victrola; but the mechanical reception is different, and it is the engineer in the control room who passes judgment on these final recordings.

And still Chevalier hasn't done his duty by "My Ideal." There remains the French version to be sung for the clamorous and profitable French market, for his American triumphs have multiplied a hundredfold his popularity in his own country. Whereas formerly he sang to perhaps two thousand people a night in Paris and was hardly more than a name to the great majority of his compatriots, he has now through his pictures become a beloved figure in every town and hamlet that boasts a cinema, and "*notre* Maurice" bids fair to achieve a place that has hitherto been reserved for *Charlot* (Charlie Chaplin) alone.

So smoothly does the machinery of this studio run, so well do the leader, the orchestra and the singer understand their business and one another, so intelligently and considerately do they work together, that this whole laborious process of tests and master-records, English and French, involving some dozen repetitions of the same song, which must—and does—sound as fresh and lively the dozenth time as the first—all this has been completed in something less than an hour. A well-earned respite of five minutes is announced, and the "chiselers" repair to the corridor to stretch their legs and smoke a cigarette, while Chevalier in his courteous fashion sits down to entertain the visitor.

"THESE fellows," he tells me, "are really wonderful." The appreciation of good craftsmen for one another. "I like always to come here and work with them. It cannot perhaps be seen by one who is not a singer, but usually it takes hours to rehearse such a song. Yet here they know the music already before I have come, and when I have sung it with them once, it is—" interlocking his fingers, "like this!"

He comments on the tunefulness of the air he has just been singing, and I ask him about the next song.

"Ah—the next! The next is a gay bird! That is how it should be—eh? First a sweet one, then a merry one. It goes like this—" and he hums a few bars. " 'It's a great life if you don't weaken; you're a great guy if you won't weaken.' When we were making the picture in Hollywood and someone on the set looked—how do you say?—with the mouth down, then I sang him this song, and at once he felt much better. Or so they told me. It may be—" and his smile flashes "—it may be they were just keeding me."

The musicians are returning to their places and Chevalier goes into consultation with Mr. Joy. A moment later the first sprightly strains of the "gay bird" strike the air. The effect is instantaneous. Feet begin beating time, shoulders lift, heads sway, eyes brighten.

Chevalier is at the microphone. "If you don't lose heart, the hardest part is the first hundred years." And the microphone is suddenly transformed under your very nose from an instrument of wood and steel into a human being of flesh and bone—a human being with his "mouth down," whom Chevalier is trying to cajole out of the blues as he cajoled the people on the Hollywood set.

"YES, a great world with a kick to it!" He laughs exultantly, yet sobers down at once, seeing that the man he's facing remains unconvinced. He reasons with him, his hands plead, his eyebrows go up into his hair. "*If* you let him *biff* you, Mr. Gloom will knock you cold!" The words don't matter—you hear only the serio-comic coaxing in the voice, you see only the solicitous pucker of the brows that is belied by the quizzical glint in the eye. Any second now he's likely to throw an encouraging arm around the microphone's neck.

Mr. Joy, glancing up from his score, catches that fugitive look, and grins helplessly across at me. We are bound by a moment's fellowship in laughter—and it is just here perhaps that Chevalier's greatest charm lies—in the warmth that kindles an answering warmth in his audience, that makes strangers turn to one another and laugh together as if they were old friends.

He's coming dangerously close to the end. His arguments are exhausted, and this is a tough customer. He pins his faith to repetition and emphasis. "It's a great life if you don't weaken," he chuckles, nodding his head vigorously and beaming his most radiant. "You're a great guy if you won't weaken!" Maybe he can flatter this fellow into a good humor. "If you do—ah, well—" Tolerance is also a virtue. "It's *still* a great life!" he shouts defiantly, flinging out both his arms as if he would embrace not only the Melancholy Mike but all the world as well.

"*Ginsburg!*" comes in thunderous acclaim from a score of lusty throats. And heartily you respond, Amen.

Our Guest Page

Every month PHOTOPLAY will have a guest writer. We didn't pay Eddie for this and if you read it you'll know just why—The Editor

By Eddie Cantor

I HAVE been asked by more than a dozen important minds in this country, including the Editor of PHOTOPLAY, to say something about the Depression. Oh, you must have heard of it! The mere mention of the word makes a lot of business men see "red." Let's get away from this depression business for a minute.

In "Palmy Days," you will find for the first time that beautiful girls have been properly photographed. Dozens of 'em, not just one or two. The critics all over the country have raved about these gals. They were selected with the same care that leading ladies are picked. Just because "Palmy Days" happens to be a musical comedy picture is no reason why the producer should send out a call for a bushel of pretty girls. No sir! They were hand-picked and they look it.

Personally, and with all due modesty, I have never been funnier in my life than in this picture. There are two dances in it, and I venture to say that the staging of them will never be duplicated. True, the story has no great weight, but if you find yourself laughing and applauding for an hour and a half, brothers and sisters, you have been entertained. "Palmy Days" is a swell picture. I am in it.

NOW back to the Depression. If you heard my Sunday night broadcast on the Chase & Sanborn hour, you probably have wondered why I've been doing it. When Jimmy Wallington said to me last Sunday, "Eddie, you ought not to talk about the depression so much—maybe there's no depression," and I answered, "Well, if there ain't no depression, Jimmy, this is the smallest boom we have had in years," I just knew people all over the country enjoyed it.

After each broadcast, for a full week, they wrap me in cellophane to retain my freshness. For instance, in the book "Yoo Hoo Prosperity," which is sold at most book stores and railroad stations at $1.00 per copy, I've explained the why's and wherefore's of the depression and the Five Year Plan for bringing back prosperity. If you haven't read the book I think you're a sucker. If you have read it, I know you are.

At any rate, in the Five Year Plan, I speak of doing away with unemployment. How? Listen. You've never heard of my doubling up system. In baseball, why should there be only nine men on each side? Why not eighteen men per team? Instead of three umpires, let's have six. Instead of having two fighters in a ring, why not have four on each side? Then maybe there would be a fight. Instead of one referee, let's have three.

Take the races, for instance. Why should there be only one little jockey on a horse? For the smallest horse could take care of at least two jockies. This is just a rough idea. I can go on with this indefinitely. But is PHOTOPLAY paying me? Don't be silly.

Now regarding this topic of Depression. Before I left for New York, I signed a nice contract with Samuel Goldwyn to make one picture a year for the next five years. Why one? Well, we figured it would be better to make one good one than three not so good. Good?

I OPENED at the Palace Theater in New York City on October 31 for a run. If you happen to be in New York, drop in and see me. Also, speaking of Depression, I've a piece of property at Great Neck, Long Island, that I would like to sell at a bargain. Write me about it.

So you see, the way to write about any subject is to tear it apart and make it clear to your readers. If you think what I've written is sound, one of us is crazy.

I wonder how much I'll get paid for this.

Eddie Cantor is known in private life as the logical successor to Rudolph Valentino. That's because of his Latin impetuosity. Here he is in one of his most passionate moments in "Palmy Days." A true lover's gesture. The clinging vine is Charlotte Greenwood

DEC.

☆ *THE CUBAN LOVE SONG—M-G-M*

WHEN you put Lawrence Tibbett's glorious singing and splendid acting, Lupe Velez' entrancing lovemaking, and Jimmy Durante's darn foolishness all together in one film—you've got a picture. This is the best Tibbett opus since "The Rogue Song," and they'll be starring Durante soon. He's great.

It tells the yarn of a trio of marines—Tibbett, called *Terry* in the story, Durante and Ernest Torrence—in Cuba. Although Tibbett has a patrician sweetheart in the States, he falls in love with a concentrated bundle of heat named *Nenita*, a peanut vendor, who is, of course, Lupe. There follows a love sequence that is idyllic in its sweetness—and then comes the war, and the marine goes to battle. Ten years later, married to his American sweetheart, he hears in a café the peanut vendor song and it recalls *Nenita*. In a hilarious jag he finds his ex-buddies and goes back to Cuba—only to discover his *Nenita* married and mother of three children. But the eldest is named *Terry*.

How sweetly it's told you won't know until you see it. And when Tibbett sings, you forget you're in a theater. There's no hesitancy in recommending this because it has everything—romance, comedy, music!

"CUBAN LOVE SONG, THE"—M-G-M.—From the screen play by G. Gardiner Sullivan and Bess Meredyth. Directed by W. S. Van Dyke. The cast: *Terry*, Lawrence Tibbett; *Nenita*, Lupe Velez; *Romance*, Ernest Torrence; *O. O. Jones*, Jimmy Durante; *Crystal*, Karen Morley; *Elvira*, Louise Fazenda; *John*, Hale Hamilton; *Aunt Rosa*, Mathilda Comont; *Terry, Jr.*, Phillip Cooper.

DEC.

Short Subjects of the Month

OLD KING COTTON

Paramount

George Dewey Washington, negro singer, dashes off some grand tunes in this dramatic little short about a young darkie who leaves the plantation for Harlem, only to discover that old scenes are best. You'll like it.

DEC.

The nose that has launched a thousand laughs

ON February 10, 1893, Mrs. Barthelmo Durante became, at the Durante flat at 90 Catherine Street, New York, the mother of a 7-pound, 9-ounce baby boy. Three and a half pounds of that weight, they saw, was the baby's nose. He still has it, and that's why they call him "Schnozzle" instead of his given name of James, or Jimmy.

Early in life, Jimmy realized, like *Cyrano de Bergerac* before him, that nobody'd ever take him seriously with a nose like that. So he became one of the greatest comedians there is. Papa Durante wanted Jimmy to follow in the barbering trade, and had him lather customers' faces. But they laughed so hard at Jimmy's beak that papa cut them here and there, so Jimmy went out into the world. He still hates to shave. And now he makes as much in one week as seventeen barbers in a row of months.

He loves parties. Let him loose in one, and he steals the show.

Cornflakes with milk is his favorite dish! Give him a box of flakes, a bottle of milk, and he's happy. He even entertains, now and then, at cornflake dinners.

He's as nervous as a cat; does everything jerkily and quickly. Walks that way and with a slight stoop to his shoulders. Doesn't care what he wears. When he gets up he puts on the first things he lays his hands on, regardless of color combinations or appearance. Smokes cigars constantly.

When he was ten, his mother started him on piano lessons at a dollar apiece. Jimmy learned that half the time he could spend the dollar on ice cream and things and make up the lesson by practicing at home. He did, and can play anything from opera to jazz on the keys. Once, in his early days, he was accompanist to a singing waiter named Eddie Cantor, in a Coney Island cafe.

He never sleeps more than five hours a night and is an early riser.

His wife is Jean Olsen. He met her when he was "Ragtime Jimmy" at Coney Island. Her first remark to him was, "You're the worst piano player I ever heard." That started a romance that's still hot fourteen years later.

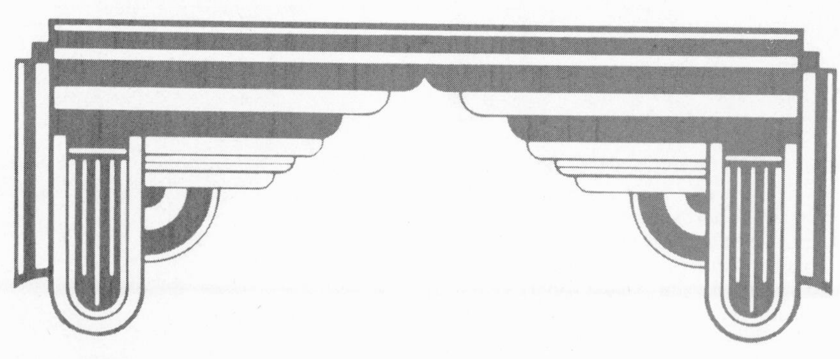

1932

THE MUSICAL MORATORIUM CONTINUED throughout 1932. Ironically, it was in this year that Paramount, easily the most creative studio during this period, produced two of the finest and most innovative musicals of all times, *Love Me Tonight* and *One Hour with You,* and three others of considerable inventiveness, *The Big Broadcast, The Phantom President,* and *This Is the Night.* Eddie Cantor's *The Kid from Spain* proved the only traditional musical to find audience favor in 1932.

M. K.

JANET GAYNOR CHARLES FARRELL

in

delicious

It's well-named...this most entrancing of Gaynor-Farrell romances. Here Janet is a Scotch lass...very close to your heart. A handsome American (Charlie Farrell to you) falls madly in love with her, a romantic Russian adores her, a Swede befriends her and a burly Irish detective pursues her!

You've never seen such a comedy of errors, so gay a tangle of laughter and romance. A love story *deliciously* different!

Six sparkling musical hits by world-renowned George Gershwin, composer of "Rhapsody in Blue," are woven into the story. You'll enjoy Gershwin's new and brilliant "Second Rhapsody."

Ask the manager of your favorite theatre when they're playing DELICIOUS. And keep an eye out for other superb attractions soon to come: *Elissa Landi* and *Lionel Barrymore* in THE YELLOW TICKET, *Will Rogers* in AMBASSADOR BILL, *James Dunn, Sally Eilers* and *Mae Marsh* in OVER THE HILL.

FOX

JAN.

HER MAJESTY, LOVE— First National

IF all barmaids were as lovely as Marilyn Miller, Volstead wouldn't have a chance. But she's one of the musical comedy variety that never existed—tossing off songs between every glass of beer. Her dancing is okay, too. Ben Lyon is the heavy love interest and some of the best comedians in Hollywood make you chuckle. This is light but pleasantly entertaining.

"HER MAJESTY, LOVE"—First National.—From the story by R. Bernauer and R. Oesterreicher. Scenario by Robert Lord and Arthur Caesar. Directed by William Dieterle. The cast: *Lia Toerrek*, Marilyn Miller; *Fred von Wellingen*, Ben Lyon; *Lia's Father*, W. C. Fields; *Otmar*, Ford Sterling; *Baron von Schwarzdorf*, Leon Errol; *Emil*, Chester Conklin; *Hanneman*, Harry Stubbs; *Aunt Harriette*, Maude Eburne; *Reisenfeld*, Harry Holman; *Factory Secretary*, Ruth Hall; *The "Third" Man*, Wm. Irving; *Fred's Sister, Elli*, Mae Madison.

JAN.

☆

FLYING HIGH— M-G-M

THIS snappy picture proves that producers have learned how to use music—sparingly and appropriately—and they haven't allowed dancing and vocal numbers to interfere with an otherwise rapid-fire, knock-'em down and drag-'em out comedy plot. Bert Lahr and lanky Charlotte Greenwood are a comedy team second to none in talkies. The fast and furious chorus numbers are presented from weird angles.

"FLYING HIGH"—M-G-M.—From the musical comedy by DeSylva, Brown and Henderson and John McGowan. Screen play by A. P. Younger. Directed by Charles F. Reisner. The cast: *Rusty*, Bert Lahr; *Pansy*, Charlotte Greenwood; *Sport*, Pat O'Brien; *Eileen*, Kathryn Crawford; *Doctor Brown*, Charles Winninger; *Mrs. Smith*, Hedda Hopper; *Mr. Smith*, Guy Kibbee; *Gordon*, Herbert Braggioti; Gus Arnheim and his orchestra.

JAN.

PEACH O'RENO— Radio Pictures

THOSE nut comedians—Bert Wheeler and Robert Woolsey—are at it again. This time they do all their funny business in Reno's fashionable divorce colony. It's an absurd plot concoction and although the story is weak on romance it's long on laughs. Peppy Zelma O'Neal comes close to stealing the picture from right under Woolsey's cigar. Dorothy Lee is as cute and pretty as ever.

"PEACH O'RENO"—Radio Pictures.—From the story by Tim Whelan. Adapted by Ralph Spence. Directed by William Seiter. The cast: *Wattles*, Bert Wheeler; *Swift*, Robert Woolsey; *Prudence*, Dorothy Lee; *Joe Bruno*, Joseph Cawthorn; *Aggie Bruno*, Cora Witherspoon; *Pansy*, Zelma O'Neal; *Judge Jackson*, Sam Hardy; *Crosby*, Mitchell Harris; *The Secretary*, Arthur Hoyt.

FEB.

DELICIOUS— Fox

ANY picture with Janet Gaynor and Charlie Farrell is of interest, and this is specially recommended because it is clean. Without Gaynor and Farrell you wouldn't walk two blocks to see it. But you will like the musical score by George Gershwin. Janet is a Scotch waif who tries to elude immigration officials. Charlie is the wealthy American. Encourage this clean picture by attending it.

"DELICIOUS"—Fox.—From the story by Guy Bolton. Adapted by Guy Bolton and Sonya Levien. Directed by David Butler. The cast: *Heather Gordon*, Janet Gaynor; *Larry Beaumont*, Charles Farrell; *Jansen*, El Brendel; *Sasha*, Raul Roulien; *O'Flynn*, Lawrence O'Sullivan; *Olga*, Manya Roberti; *Diana*, Virginia Cherrill; *Mrs. Van Bergh*, Olive Tell; *Mischa*, Mischa Auer; *Tosha*, Marvine Maazel; *Momotschka*, Jeanette Gegna.

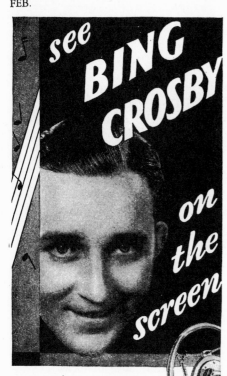

FEB.

MAR.

THERE are several songs in "Delicious," the principal one being such an unutterably banal ditty that I must print its opening line: "You're so delicious (pronounced delic-i-ous). "And so capricious (pronounced capric-i-ous)" etc. Well, it's probably malic-i-ous of me to print these lyrics out, but they are really so stupid that I am certain that they will be popular.—*John S. Cohen, Jr., in the New York Sun.*

MAR.

Short Subjects of the Month

CLOSE HARMONY
Paramount

The Boswell sisters, whom you've been hearing on the radio for quite a spell, show their faces to the camera. They are nice faces, too. The idea of this amusing sketch is that the girls sing in the barnyard and inspire the chickens and the cows to better efforts.

DREAM HOUSE
Educational-Sennett

This is another one of the comedies featuring the famous radio crooner, Bing Crosby. Bing seems more at ease in this quite amusing skit than in previous ones. You'll like his songs.

MAR.

One picture rôle (in "Delicious") made Raul Roulien a favorite

And here's a surprise! Raul Roulien scored second in the mail bag. Some of you don't know him, but after you've seen "Delicious" you will want to know all about him.

Raul is a newcomer. He was born in Rio de Janeiro, Brazil, South America, on October 12, 1905. His father, before his death, was the director of the National Musical Institute of Rio de Janeiro. Raul made his first stage appearance at the age of five. From then until he was twelve he travelled all over Brazil with various companies. Then he returned to school.

After he finished school he resumed his pursuit of a stage career. He formed his own musical comedy company and travelled all over the world. He composed the song, "Adios Mis Farras," the sale of which ran up to 1,700,000 on records and 386,000 printed sheets in seventy days. He wrote and staged more than twenty plays, such as "The Irresistible Robert," "Miss Charleston," "Heart," "Petals," and others. In addition to his achievements as song writer, playwright and composer, he has an architect's degree. His next picture will be "Widow's Might."

This Giant Camera Crane

HERE is a complete trip through a studio, on two pages. Study this picture carefully and you'll find everything there is to be seen on a sound stage. And some things that have never been used before.

See those two fellows sitting in the nest of the giant camera crane? They are an assistant director and a cameraman and while the brisk action for Paramount's "Dancers in the Dark" goes on, on the floor of the stage, these two men enact a little drama of their own.

Long-shots and close-ups are being taken simultaneously. The floor camera takes the long-shots while the men and apparatus in the crane are silently projected, winging like some giant bird, up and out and down, picking up whatever bit of business looks interesting, swooping from the orchestra at the back to Miriam Hopkins and William Collier, Jr., in the foreground. The crane is manipulated as easily as a child's toy.

Every extra girl is acutely aware of the camera of fate which hangs above her head. No matter how far in the background she may be, that crane can find her. Therefore, she must continually keep in the mood of the character she is playing for the camera may be fifteen feet away from her one second and taking a close-up of her the next. Every girl knows the legend of Hollywood—that one striking close-up might make her a star, and every girl is prepared for the time when her chance at fame will come. But only once in a movie moon does such a thing happen.

May Pick Out A New Star

Photo by Stagg

To the left is the microphone. It, too, is projected forward on a small crane of its own and follows the camera, as you see it doing in the picture, so that both sound and action may be caught at the same moment.

The men working the microphone apparatus must be as alert as the men on the crane. The mike must hang just above the head of the person being photographed.

In the foreground you'll discover, besides Miriam Hopkins putting on the hot cha-cha for William Collier, Jr., a little platinum dizzy called Lyda Roberti. (She is wearing the ostrich trimmed dress.)

The director whispers that she is knocking out a swell performance.

Off to the right, behind the floor camera, is Al Hall, cutter; director David Burton (with hat on), assistant director Russel Mathews (in sweater, crouching), Slavko Vorkapic, another assistant director; Karl Struss, head cameraman and Howard Kelley, head electrician. Every detail of the scene is watched by these men. Each is a specialist in his own line, each divides the scene to suit his own particular **interest.**

If you can find an incorrect detail, your eyes are better than six pairs of the sharpest in the business.

When you see the film there will be flashes of the long-shots, interspersed by close-ups.

And now that we've let you in on the secret, you'll know exactly how the effect was achieved.

Otto Dyar

ALL right, you music lovers and you lovers of whimsical light comedy—here's the answer to your prayers. It won't be long until you'll be hearing Jeanette MacDonald and Maurice Chevalier warbling together again. Look out for the film. It's called "One Hour With You." It's splendid and it is reviewed in this issue of PHOTOPLAY

APR.

☆ *ONE HOUR WITH YOU—Paramount*

IT has Chevalier. Oh, how it has Chevalier—this gay, naughty, sizzling little farce. And, too, it has Jeanette MacDonald, and behind it all, is Lubitsch. Ernst himself. Need more be said?

It races and patters along its risqué, saucy way to snappy, lingering music by Oscar Straus and Richard Whiting. And every once in a while, Maurice steps right out of the picture, walks down front, and takes us into his confidence.

Maurice, a doctor (oh doctor, my operation), married to Jeanette, is happy and peaceful until along comes his wife's friend *Mitzi*. Played too Mitzyish for words by Genevieve Tobin. *Mitzi* sets out to get Doctor Maurice. And poor Maurice hesitates, weakens, and alas, succumbs.

But *Mitzi's* husband, played by Roland Young, and how he plays it, sets out to divorce *Mitzi* and names the philandering Chevalier as co-respondent.

Charlie Ruggles, as a would-be lover, is a howl.

"One Hour With You," as the musical version of "The Marriage Circle," is even better than the silent version. George Cukor, the director, with Lubitsch as supervisor, turned out a picture a bit naughty, but oh, so "nize."

"ONE HOUR WITH YOU"—PARAMOUNT.—From the play by Lothar Schmidt. Screen play by Samson Raphaelson. Directed by Ernst Lubitsch. The cast: *Dr. Andre Bertier*, Maurice Chevalier; *Colette Bertier*, Jeanette MacDonald; *Mitzi Olivier*, Genevieve Tobin; *Adolph*, Charlie Ruggles; *Prof. Olivier*, Roland Young; *Police Commissioner*, George Barbier; *Mlle. Martel*, Josephine Dunn; *Detective*, Richard Carle; *Policeman*, Charles Judels; *Mitzi's Maid*, Barbara Leonard.

APR.

Folks, meet Betty Boop (right). You'll be seeing a lot of her because she is the new animated cartoon character who is trying to cut in on Mickey Mouse's popularity. Does she look familiar to you? Now look at little boop-a-dooper Helen Kane. Helen was the cartoonist's inspiration for Betty, the first time a real life character has been used for the popular jumping comics

Hollywood's

By Sara Hamilton

HE'S GOT a lower lip like Chevalier. One medium good eye, slightly blue. Twelve hairs on the top of his head. All violently curly. A nose like a rootin' wart hog. And he's the big sheik daddy of Hollywood. They're crazy about him, these ladies of Hollywood. Why, Jimmy Durante is the biggest sensation since Valentino. Bigger even, for you see Rudy didn't have Jimmy's nose. He's a panic. That's what he is. A downright panic. One of these Eyetalian lovers. That's "Schnozzle."

The fans can have their Gables and their Chevaliers. Hollywood has taken itself a boy friend.

What do they do, these Hollywood beauties? Why, they ups and gives parties for him. In the Embassy. The very day he's worn the same "shoit" for three days. And do they care about the "shoit"? Huh! They ups to him, anyhow. And what do they do at this Embassy thing? Here he is, mind you, one man and twelve lovely women and they, every one, bring him gifts.

Gigolo Durante.

But I ask you, do they ever come bearing gifts and glad tidings to Gable? Naw, you know they don't. Or Montgomery either. But Jimmy. Well, and here's the "woist" of it. They bring him everything, see, in one color. Handkerchiefs, socks, ties, all one color. A gorgeous, luscious shade of pansy.

How mortifyin'.

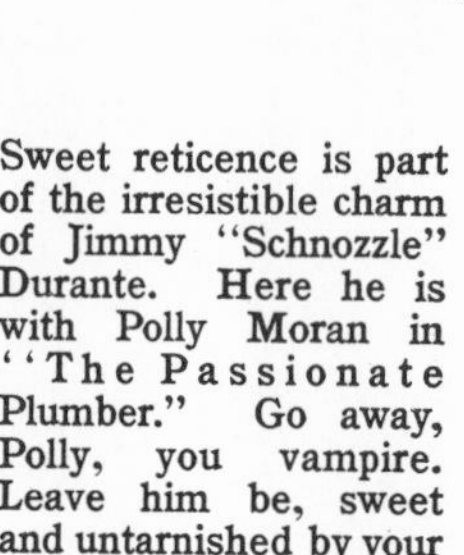

Sweet reticence is part of the irresistible charm of Jimmy "Schnozzle" Durante. Here he is with Polly Moran in "The Passionate Plumber." Go away, Polly, you vampire. Leave him be, sweet and untarnished by your wicked Hollywood wiles

"It's the Eyetalian lure," Jimmy explains. "Haaaaaaaaah."

But the comic part is, Jimmy never knows who anybody is. He couldn't remember his own grandmother. He wouldn't know Mary Pickford if she walked right up and said, "Good afternoon, Mr. Durante." He wouldn't know Garbo from Polly Moran. But he greets everyone like a thirsty buffalo that's just found a waterhole. "Hi, there." And all the time they're tickled to death at Jimmy's enthusiasm, he's whispering out of the side of his mouth, "Quick who is that? Slip it to me."

Several weeks after he arrived in Hollywood a man stopped him on the M-G-M lot and said, "Listen, Jimmy, how come you never come up to my office to see me? You've been to all the other offices and, after all, I knew you first. Besides, I'm the fellow that hands out the checks and I should think you'd come to see me first."

"Oh, dat's all right, pal," Jimmy said with a hearty slap on the back. "I'll be up one of dese days when I need some dough, eh? I'll be seeing you den," and with another wallop on the back, Jimmy strolled away.

That night he attended a large party at the home of Louis B. Mayer, one of the heads of M-G-M Studios, and over by the door he noticed the same man all dressed up in evening clothes, bowing and shaking hands with all the notables.

"Cheeze," Jimmy said to a friend. "Look, there's de bookkeeper we seen this afternoon. For a bookkeeper he mus' be some guy to be asked to a party like dis."

"Where's a bookkeeper?" the friend asked.

"Over by the door. The guy wit de glasses," Jimmy said.

The friend looked wild. "My gosh, Jimmy," he whispered, "that ain't no bookkeeper. That's your host. That's Louie B. Mayer."

How mortifyin'.

Friends that know of Jimmy's complete lack of memory will bring up perfect strangers.

"Jimmy, here's an old friend you'll remember for sure."

"Oh, sure," Jimmy enthuses, "I remember him. Now don't tell me the name. I got it now. Don't tell me. Don't tell me."

And do they laugh.

Why, one time in New York he actually parked his new car on a side street and for two days he tried to remember what had become of it.

And is he a stickler on clothes, this Durante guy? Say, Jimmy don't care any more for clothes than Gandhi. They cover him, so what? Day after day, he'll grab the same thing he took off the night before, until his wife or friends will say, "For heavens sake, Jimmy, haven't you had on that suit long enough? And how about another shirt?"

Imagine Ivan Lebedeff's disgust.

And jewelry. He's had more watches with the name Jimmy

New Lover

The picture stars, to a girl, have a crush on the new cotillion leader of the Cinema Smart Set

"It's my Eyetalian lure," says the new Latin bonfire from the lower East Side

Durante engraved on or worked out in jewels, and rings and whatnots, handed out to him than any other two men. And he gives it all away. Usually to his brother who is a policeman on the New York force. For himself he carries a three dollar watch he's had for years. That seldom, if ever, runs.

He'd just as leave wear a pair of light brown shoes with a tuxedo as not. And usually removes his tuxedo to reveal a dress shirt with the sleeves cut off above the elbow.

One night Jimmy was asked to the home of Mr. Chrysler, the millionaire, to do a little "So I Ups to Him" for the guests. And here he was at the last minute without a dress shirt. So Jimmy stopped at the laundry on the way out and picks up a clean dress shirt. And changing it in the taxi what do you think happens? He ups and tears the button hole. Imagine. So Jimmy takes out his knife and stabs a hole at random. It lands somewhere around the side of his neckband so that when Jimmy puts on his collar, the bow tie hits him somewhere under the left ear. And his shirt studs were somewhere in the vicinity of his right bosom. And was Jimmy bothered? Why say, he just kept yanking the tie over and singing "Ups to Him" and yanking and "Upsing" and yanking until it was a riot. And, as usual, all the ladies of the social élite thought Jimmy just too fascinating for words. And him with a tie under his ear. So you see how it is. There's no explaining it. They all go for him.

Right from the lower (you can't get really lower) East Side of New York comes Jimmy Durante. An Italian with a mad, hysterical sense of humor and an ear for music. Playing the piano in cheap little cafes. Liked by everyone. Bums and all. The same glad hand for a Bowery waiter as he hands out to shining celebrities.

"Jimmy, why gee, he hasn't changed none," his friends tell you.

Somewhere on his way up he picked up Lou Clayton and Eddie Jackson. The three went on to vaudeville where Jimmy's famous "I Ups to Him" (written while Jimmy was in the hospital) was introduced. Then on to their own night club. And boy what a club. They clubbed the orchestra, *(continued on next page)*

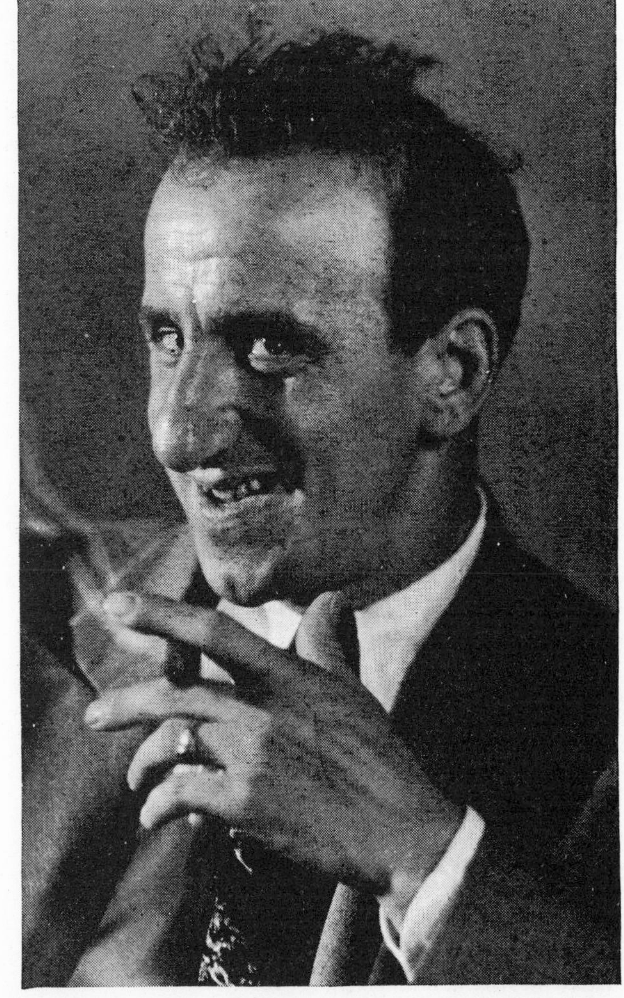

(continued from preceding page)

clubbed the customers, clubbed each other. It was grand.

On to big shows. "Show Girl," "The New Yorkers," where Donald Ogden Stewart, Percy Hammond, Chevalier and others gathered weekly to enjoy the earthquake. Then on to Hollywood and "Get-Rich-Quick-Wallingford," "The Cuban" and "The Passionate Plumber"!

AND clumsy! Schnozzle is just as dainty as a rhinoceros on the loose. It keeps Jimmy's right hand man paying the damage bills as they go along.

On the road, when Jimmy was through with a piano, the piano stayed through.

It was wrecked. The piano stool was a mere shadow of its former self. Props mashed. Bass drums punctured. Just like an ostrich stepping out.

No grace at all. No style or charm. And still they fall for him. What do you make of it?

He'll attend the swankiest of luncheons at the Ritz or Waldorf and order ham and eggs every time.

And he goes in for pie crust in a big way. He'll eat everyone's pie crust for tables and tables around him.

For the first time in twenty-five years Jimmy found himself out of a cafe on last New Year's Eve. "And where was I?" Jimmy asks. "Where was I? On a desert. On a desert, mind you. Sure, they got a big desert down at a place called Palm Springs and I was on it. And was it unexcitin'? Cheeze. Nuttin' doin', see, and all them swells and stars and things and everybody actin' sedate 'n' everyting, so I start a little playin' and singin' and say, in fifteen minutes they wuz all playin' Farmer in the Dell and grabbin' hands and goin' around in circles, and then everyone wanted to sing and play and the place was a riot. De manager come over and wit tears in his eyes he said, 'Jimmy, you've saved the day. The place is yours. Any time you care to come.' "

AND did the beauties flock around Jimmy with, "Oh, please, Mr. Durante, won't you dance with me next? Please do."

"You see," Jimmy confides, "it's just because they wuz seein' me in pusson."

James!

We sat across the luncheon table from Jimmy at the M-G-M commissary the other day. About us sat all the handsome heroes of the screen, Gable, Montgomery, John Barrymore and others.

Suddenly, in the doorway stood a vision of blonde loveliness. Young and beautiful. Every eye was on her. Her lips parted in greeting.

Every eye smiled in return. Every masculine face beamed welcome.

Jimmy went right on eating his apple puddin'. With ice cream.

SUDDENLY, the young woman darted forward. The men, almost as one, half rose to their feet.

"Jimmy," she cried, and made straight for him. "You lamb," she cooed and kissed him smack on the top of his head before Jimmy even knew she was there.

To this day he's trying to figure out who she is.

You see, half the time he doesn't even see them. And they go for him just the same.

I told you. He's the biggest sensation in years. Jimmy, he goes his way and they go his way.

He might, this Durante person, "do wit out Hollywood, but could Hollywood do wit out Jimmy?"

How mortifyin'.

MAY

Short Subjects *of the* Month

MAY

☆

DANCERS IN THE DARK—Paramount

AS a dime-a-dance girl, in a cheap dance palace, Miriam Hopkins retains the laurel crown she won for past performances. But Jack Oakie, the orchestra leader who tries to quash the romance between his pal, Buster Collier, and Miriam, almost tucks the picture into his megaphone and strolls away with it. George Raft, the sleek bad man of the picture, is a real find.

"DANCERS IN THE DARK"—PARAMOUNT.—From the story by James Ashmore Creelman. Adapted by Brian Marlow and Howard Emmett Rogers. Directed by David Burton. The cast: *Gloria,* Miriam Hopkins; *Duke,* Jack Oakie; *Floyd,* William Collier, Jr.; *Gus,* Eugene Pallette; *Fanny,* Lyda Roberti; *Louis,* George Raft; *Max,* Maurice Black; *McGroady,* DeWitt Jennings; *Benny,* Paul Fix; *Spiegel,* George Bickel; *Ruby,* Frances Moffett.

THAT RASCAL
Vanity-Educational

Introducing another male torch singer; Harry Barris, a rival to Bing Crosby. This young man is a composer, pianist, radio star, and what have you. But he can't count acting as one of his accomplishments. You'll enjoy his songs, but find his comedy dull

MAY

GIRL CRAZY—Radio Pictures

IF you don't go to see this picture you will miss a lot of your favorites—Bert Wheeler, Robert Woolsey, Dorothy Lee, clever Mitzi Green, Eddie Quillan, debonair Ivan Lebedeff, Arlene Judge and many more. And Mitzi Green does her famous imitations of George Arliss, Marlene Dietrich and Edna May Oliver.

"GIRL CRAZY"—RADIO PICTURES.—From the story by John McGowan and Guy Bolton. Adapted by Herman Mankiewicz. Directed by William Seiter. The cast: *Jimmy Deegan,* Bert Wheeler; *Slick Foster,* Robert Woolsey; *Danny Churchill,* Eddie Quillan; *Patsy,* Dorothy Lee; *Tessie Deegan,* Mitzi Green; *Kate Foster,* Kitty Kelly; *Molly Gray,* Arlene Judge; *Ivan Borloff,* Brooks Benedict; *Lank Sanders,* Stanley Fields; *Mary,* Lita Chevret; *Pete,* Chris Pin Martin.

JUN.

WHEN Ernst Lubitsch saw what a good picture "One Hour With You" had turned out to be he wanted his name on the title sheet as director.

As a matter of fact, he had supervised the picture and George Cukor had done the actual directing. However, Lubitsch had been on the set all the time.

So everybody quarreled and at last credit was divided like this. "Directed by Ernst Lubitsch, assisted by George Cukor."

All of which seems ridiculously childish to folks who don't give a gosh darn who does the directing just so long as the picture is good.

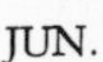

☆ *THIS IS THE NIGHT—Paramount*

HAD this picture been less good than it is, we would still have had to include it among the best of the month. In the midst of excellent but heavy dramatic films, here is the light and farcical interlude that movie-goers long for. Three clever tunes, "Madame Has Lost Her Dress," "This Is the Night," and "Tonight Is All a Dream," are introduced in an unusual way. Roland Young and Charles Ruggles are marvelous comedians. When they're on the screen it's never dull, and they're on practically all the time. Lily Damita is charming, and Thelma Todd shows those gorgeous legs. In fact, that's an important part of the plot! Sophisticated and highly spiced. Junior and Sister should stay home and get their laughs from Eddie Cantor's new book.

"THIS IS THE NIGHT"—PARAMOUNT.—From the play by Avery Hopwood. Adapted by George Marion, Jr. Directed by Frank Tuttle. The cast: *Germaine*, Lily Damita; *Bunny West*, Charlie Ruggles; *Gerald Grey*, Roland Young; *Claire*, Thelma Todd; *Stepan*, Cary Grant; *Jacques*, Irving Bacon; *Chou-Chou*, Claire Dodd.

JUN.

CONGRESS DANCES—UFA-United Artists

A PLEASING picture, made in Germany, with English dialogue. Good performances by Lilian Harvey, Lil Dagover and Conrad Veidt, but the theme of kidding royal pomp and ceremony has been used so many times. You'll be crooning two lilting Viennese waltz songs, "Live, Love and Laugh," and "Just Once For All Time."

"CONGRESS DANCES"—UFA-UNITED ARTISTS.—From the story by Norbert Falk and Robert Liebmann. Directed by Eric Charell. The cast: *Christel*, Lilian Harvey; *Prince Metternich*, Conrad Veidt; *The Countess*, Lil Dagover; *Czar Alexander of Russia*, Henry Garat; *Uralsky*, Henry Garat; *Bibikoff, the Czar's Adjutant*, Gibb McLaughlin; *Pepi, His Secretary*, Reginald Purdell; *Ambassador of Saxony*, Eugen Rex; *Ambassador of France*, Jean Dax; *The Princess*, Helen Haye; *The Duchess*, Olga Engel; *The Finance Minister*, Spencer Trevor; *The Mayor of Vienna*, Thomas Weguelin; *The Cafe Singer*, Tarquini d'Or.

JUN.

There were screen musical composers before the days of the microphone. Griffith was the first to score his films. The music was pounded out on a tin pan piano by a girl who chewed gum and missed her cues. Here's Griffith composing his own music—with Carli Elinor

JUN.

MAYBE you saw a very amusing little animated cartoon called "Peg Leg Pete," in which cats, dogs and mice banded together on board ship and sang together in the most highly acceptable Gilbert and Sullivan light operatic manner.

Of course, even I knew that it wasn't those drawings doing that high class warbling. And I got out my pet pack of bloodhounds to investigate.

I discovered a very earnest, very perspiring group of musicians who put the sound in the Terry-Toon Cartoons. There is a quartette of very serious gentlemen, all slightly bald and all wearing glasses, and a young lady with a high soprano. But they are splendid singers and the music, written by Philip Scheib, is really very lovely, high class stuff.

But when you hear it upon the screen that little man, the one with the least hair of all, will be the leader of the mice throng who will bear down upon the cat king. The maddened cat king is a sweet looking little man in a dark blue suit and pince-nez. And they all work so hard.

OVER in a corner sits a gentleman with a heavy black moustache who does nothing but flash a light on and off in time with the music. He, it seems, is called a "beater" and in some mysterious way that flashing light makes it possible for the cartoonist to fit action to the synchronization. The music is recorded first.

The short they were making the day I watched will be called "The Mad King" and I bet it will be swell. But I wonder what those singers think when they hear their voices—such nice voices, too—coming out of the mouths of pen and ink cats and mice.

Ann Dvorak, who is Hollywood's sensational newcomer, and her mother

By Ruth Biery

"THE other generation"—that's what Ann Dvorak calls her mother and her mother's contemporaries.

Ann's mother sacrificed a brilliant career for marriage.

Ann took a solemn oath that she would never do that, no matter how much she loved a man. Then Ann married Leslie Fenton. How could she reconcile this gesture to her earlier vow? The times—along with modes and manners—had changed. Ann knows that marriage and a career can march along hand in hand now. But I'm getting ahead of my story.

Anna Lehr, Ann's mother, was one of the most promising emotional actresses of the early films. When the editor of PHOTOPLAY visited Hollywood in 1914, he met her and the one-year-old baby. It was his first trip to the motion picture colony. But he predicted that this beautiful young mother would carve out a place for herself in celluloid. Anna was making the first version of "Ramona" at the time.

Above, Ann Dvorak, the girl who determined that neither love nor marriage should ruin her career and then decided that—but read the story to find out. She inherited much from her mother, Anna Lehr (right) who, when this old still was made in 1914, was one of the most promising emotional actresses of the screen. Below is a different Ann, with Paul Muni in the sensational gangster film "Scarface." Here Ann is the serious dramatic actress and they say her performance is one of those things that you will never forget

Miss Lehr returned to the stage soon after the editor's visit, but came back to Hollywood, when baby Ann was six, to fulfill her earlier promise. "Parentage," "Child for Sale" and other dramatic pictures gave her a place in the front starring lines.

But to the women of that day—those whom Ann Dvorak calls "the other generation"—romance meant more than anything else. Careers were secondary. As for combining the two—well, that was a difficult task then.

Besides, Anna Lehr had tried that. She had married Edward McKim. Ann was born when the mother was just sixteen. The effort to have both career and marriage failed and a divorce was the result.

SO when Anna Lehr fell in love again with a handsome young Californian named Arthur Pearson, she chucked ambition, fame and success for romance and marriage, and devoted herself to making a home for her husband.

Baby Ann was in boarding school, where she remained until she was graduated from high school and went out "on her own." In fact, she was "on her own"—independent of her stepfather—before graduation. She worked her way through high school by teaching French, washing dishes and waiting on tables.

You'll see Ann in "Scarface," Howard Hughes' spectacular gangster picture, which the censors of New York made famous before its release by refusing to okay it. You'll also find her giving James Cagney a race for *(continued on next page)*

(continued from preceding page)

rst honors in "The Crowd Roars." She re-used to accept star billing in "The Strange ove of Molly Louvain." With just one day etween pictures she commenced work on Love Is a Racket" with Douglas Fairbanks, r.

Ann is one of two people under contract to Ioward Hughes. Jean Harlow is the other. 'irst National made frantic efforts to buy Ann's contract. When they failed, they rented er for six months, and are rushing her from ne picture to another to get the most of her alent possible for their money.

SO much for Ann's career. It's quite an amazing one for a girl who was unknown just a few months ago. But Ann believes that the eason she was able to accomplish what she has s because she is an individualist and did not hange her theories to suit "the other generation."

Ann cherishes the thought that her straight backbone, her determined chin, her ambition o live her life as she wills, are not inherited.

But she's wrong. Anna Lehr was feminine nough to give up a career for marriage, in a day when one had to make the choice, but her will was as strong and her chin as determined s Ann's.

Anna Lehr was one of eight children. Her ather was a tailor, an Austrian who could hardly speak English. He worked at a tailoring shop until he was seventy, fighting for bread and butter, shoes and mittens for his amily. As soon as the children were able to earn as much as a penny, they had to help out.

Anna Lehr danced in music halls at an age when Ann was in a convent. She fought for ame and success and money with the same spirit that Ann is fighting now. Her back was just as straight, her will just as firm, and when she married and left the screen she passed on her gifts to Ann with a heart that cried, "Take them; go on and complete what I have started."

"I will," said Ann. "But I won't give up my success and marry. I've fought too hard for that success."

Her mother smiled.

Ann did fight.

She got a job with a small stock company in a suburb of Los Angeles when she was fifteen. The company folded in a week.

She then answered an ad for dancing girls at the Pom Pom Café.

"Can you dance?" the manager asked.

"Yes," said Ann.

"Show me." He nodded to the orchestra and Ann suddenly found herself dancing to some fast jazz tune. She had never done a solo dance before.

"Okay," said the manager. "Do you object to wearing scanty costumes?"

Ann's chin went a little higher. "No."

"And as for my salary—I pay the girls $25 a week."

"I got $80 for my last engagement," Ann lied.

AND the girl who never danced before, but who was the daughter of a mother who had supported seven little brothers and sisters when she, herself, was only a child, walked out of the place with a $65 a week contract.

But it was after that job ended and Ann went to apply for a place in M-G-M's musical, "The Hollywood Revue," that she showed what she had inherited.

A long line of dancing girls, of which Ann was one, were being put through test routines. The director told those he didn't want to step out of line. Ann was the first one out.

She walked up to the director. "Are you running this show?"

He nodded.

"Well, I'm as good as the ones you chose. Why didn't you pick me? I'm going to get somewhere. I'm sincere. I work. I have ambition."

When supervisor Harry Rapf came out to look over the two dozen chosen ones he asked what Ann was doing among them.

"She's a substitute," he was told. "If somebody sprains an ankle. . . ."

Somebody did, the first day. Ann took the girl's place and practiced routines all night long at home and during her noon hours on the set, and in six months dance director Sammy Lee persuaded the studio to sign her up as his assistant. She worked with Joan Crawford on Joan's routines for "Dance Fools, Dance." She, with another girl, originated "The Hoosier Hop" for the Duncan Sisters. What she did for M-G-M's stars along the dancing line would make another story.

She also wrote music, poked her nose into the story department and made suggestions —until they told her to go back to her high kicking.

AND then Karen Morley, her friend, took her to Howard Hughes.

Hughes had a hunch, made a test, and gave her her chance.

Ann was now well established.

All during this time her mother was with her, dividing her time between her husband and her child. And Anna Lehr revelled in the success her daughter had earned.

She is still young and beautiful, is Anna, and she looked at her daughter with eyes that said, "What one generation started, the other finishes."

So that's how it was, and everybody in Hollywood said, "That Dvorak girl is one who won't be getting silly ideas about love and romance. That kid is all for a career."

Then she met Leslie Fenton, a suave man of the world over whom women raved, but who kept himself aloof from them all. Almost before Hollywood knew what was happening, the papers announced their marriage.

Anna Lehr talked to her daughter. "You said, Ann, that there was no place for marriage in your life. I thought it was only success you were after—and independence." The mother smiled.

"It is success I'm after—but it's different now. I'm after two kinds of success. The other generation couldn't manage it. My generation can. I can make a go of my work and my marriage, too. You had to give up one for the other, mother. I don't. You just watch and see if I can't have both!"

Anna Lehr believes Ann Dvorak can!

JUL.

"Give us more pictures with George Raft," the fans implore. And no wonder! George brought a fascinating new type of villain to the screen in "Dancers in the Dark," with Miriam Hopkins

MOVIE-GOERS continue to like their heroes rough and ready. The chap who topped the "question" list this month is George Raft, who hails from Tent' Avenoo and Forty-foist Street, New York City. George was born in the toughest part of the town, known as "Hell's Kitchen." He is 5 feet, 11 inches tall, weighs 160 pounds and has black hair and brown eyes.

Folks who see him on the screen as the bad, bold villain never suspect that Georgie once tripped the light fantastic in one of New York's dance palaces for a dime a spin. For several years he hoofed with Texas Guinan's Gang. He was a good hoofer, too. He also appeared on the stage in "City Chap," "Gay Paree," "Manhatters," and Ziegfeld's "Palm Beach Nights." A European tour followed, during which he met the Prince of Wales and taught him the Charleston.

George's screen career, which began in April, 1931, boasts of such pictures as "Quick Millions," "Hush Money," "Palmy Days," "Dancers in the Dark," and "Scarface." He was recently given a long-term contract by Paramount.

George was married to a nurse in a New York dentist's office. She once gave him a bracelet inscribed "To My Gigolo."

The Nuttiest Quartette in the World

By Sara Hamilton

Zeppo Harpo Groucho Chico

The "Mad Marx Brothers," who act just as goofy off the screen as they do on

THERE are some people who swear the Four Marx Brothers were pulled out of a silk hat along with two white rabbits and a soiled dove. For their grandpappy, as a magician, toured Europe for fifty years in a covered wagon that carried his wife, innumerable children, together with his scenery and a harp.

He could just as easily have been a sewing machine agent for all the magic he knew. But he got by. For each night at the end of a dubious performance, grandpappy very generously offered to cut off anyone's head and put it back on again.

So you see the Marx madness began with grandpa who lived to be one hundred and one, and thought nothing at the age of ninety-five of snitching a cold potato from the ice box, in the middle of the night, and eating it.

For several reasons no one ever hastened to take up grandpa's offer of a head amputation.

So his standing as a worker of magic, stood. Doubted of course, but still stood.

Until one eventful night when a huge German yokel decided grandpa knew his business and volunteered.

Grandpa was flabbergasted. He produced an ax. Hoping the victim would back out. He never flinched. Deciding the ax was too easy, he came on with a saw. Rusty around the edges. The yokel thought he saw a big improvement. He was for it one hundred per cent. Grandpa was stumped. Finally he came on carrying a basin and towel. And the yokel loved it. Actually grew impatient for the proceedings to begin.

So grandpa stepped quietly out the back door and somewhere else, his career as a magician considerably damaged in places.

But one of the little girls beneath the cover of that wagon, felt the call, the lure of the theater even after she grew up, came to America, and married Sammy Marx, the tailor.

Hence the Four Marx Brothers on an American stage and screen.

They have caught the spirit of grandpa's gay blufferino and they carry on.

As a matter of fact the *way* they carry on is the stock-in-trade of the four Marxes.

Theirs is an indefinable, gay, swirling, sweeping madness that's beyond description. Or understanding. Or explaining.

There is nothing of the practical joker about them. Or crudeness. Or maliciousness. As a matter of fact, beneath it all lies a smattering of common sense, which makes it all the more confusing.

LIKE the tea party in "Alice" when the March Hare, sadly dipping his broken watch up and down in the tea, remarked to the Mad Hatter he didn't think he should have put the butter in the watch as the Hatter suggested, as now it wouldn't go at all. Whereupon the Mad Hatter shrugged and answered, "Well, it was the best butter."

Which, of course, silenced the Hare, who nevertheless felt somewhere, something was wrong. But what?

So it is with the Marxes.

For instance, here comes *Herr* Lubitsch across the lot. The inevitable big cigar in his mouth. A genius. An artist to whom Hollywood serenely bows. Out of their dressing-room step the Marxes. Without a word, without an instant's planning, or a moment's hesitation, Harpo will seize *Herr* Ernst and into a wrestling bout they'll go. In broad daylight. For no reason. The other three standing by. Seriously contemplating the twirling two.

And Lubitsch, completely *(continued on next page)*

(continued from preceding page)

bewildered, will wrestle for his life. Without knowing why. Tug. Pull. Roll. Toss. The cigar still clenched in his teeth. Not a smile. Everything very serious.

Suddenly, Harpo unwraps himself from the wrestling Lubitsch and off he trots. Without a word. While *Herr* Lubitsch stands in stunned amazement at what has just happened. Looking after him. Bewildered. Still unable to believe that he had openly participated in a wrestling match. For no reason.

LADY interviewers, no matter how sedate, never look quite the same after a Marx interview. At lunch in the commissary they'll wrap their legs about the interviewer's feet. Lay their ridiculous heads in her unsuspecting lap or decide, as a whole, that what she really needs is a good chiropractic treatment and, before the entire dining-room, proceed to rub the lady's back into a blister. Limping home with bruised ankles, skinned back, torn teddy straps, the lady calmly considers the whole thing, sits herself down on the nearest curb and laughs herself sick.

It's so silly.

They're absolutely unawed by anyone. They have as much fun with a carpenter on the set as with the Duke of Manchester in a palace. And this, of course, to a snobbish Hollywood, is beyond complete understanding.

A high and, ah me, how important executive, immaculate in blue coat and white flannels, came across the lot the other day. Mere writers and directors stepped reverently out of the way.

Then out from their dressing-room stepped the Marxes. Suddenly, as one, they spied the executive. And with no word spoken they were at it. They unbuttoned his coat. Tugged at his belt. Loosened his tie. And with both hands clutching his fast slipping trousers, the executive ran for shelter. While three newspaper reporters lay yowling and kicking in hysterical mirth, on the grass.

Groucho it was who, in New York, approached Adolph Zukor, president of Paramount Pictures, and very politely offered him the use of the upper berth in Groucho's drawing-room.

"Of course," he explained, "you'll be in the way a bit and no end of a nuisance but it will save you a little money and give you a place to sleep."

TO this day Zukor still wonders.

They are the least socially ambitious people imaginable.

They are invited to many swanky parties of the New York 400. If they are sure of an amusing time, they go. If not, regardless of Mrs. Astorbilt's pearl necklace, they stay at home. And play poker.

'Tis said Groucho (Julius), the wall-eyed professor with the comic mustache, has the quickest, keenest wit of any man in America. It works with a lightning-like speed that leaves one breathless. He's two sentences ahead of anyone. The complete joke is uttered before one ever gets half way to it.

Little as it's suspected, Groucho Marx is shy. He developed his rapid delivery so that if one joke died a quick and horrible death, he'd have another ready to fill in. He'll omit old jokes in a show and substitute new ones in a flash. There is no half-way station about Groucho. He's either extremely serious, grave or depressed, or extremely mad.

A friend will call on Groucho one night and find him dancing up and down stairs on his hands, and the next night deeply concerned over a coal miner's fate in England or a Chinaman's fate in burning Shanghai.

He's a father with a mother's fierce, maternal love. Groucho adores his Stephen, aged eleven, and his Marion, just four. At gay, hilarious beach parties at Malibu, you'll find Groucho with Stephen, yards up the beach hunting shells by themselves. In the slush and thaw of a spring at Great Neck, New York, they'll come traipsing in from a two-handed ball game, both caked and drenched with slush and mud. But happy. "Don't put Marion to bed for another fifteen minutes," I've heard him phone from the set. And a bit later, "Mama, we were held up again, couldn't she stay up a little longer? I want to say goodnight."

Apart from Stephen, from mama, from Marion, is the other Groucho who recently gave a birthday party to his dad and placed a pistol beside each of his brother's places and came in wearing a gun and holster. All prepared for a family fight!

Chico (Leo) who performs on a piano as no self-respecting piano was ever performed on before, is the oldest, and business manager. He it is who negotiates contracts and walks out on twelve-thousand-dollar-a-week offers with the nonchalance of a man turning down two dollars a month. His little daughter, Maxine, adores her daddy, laughs at all his jokes, and thinks he's much funnier than her uncles.

"On the set at nine, Chico," the director said recently. "Oh, I can't," Chico replied. "Why not?" the surprised director asked. "Oh, I'll be oversleeping tomorrow," he shrugged and strolled off.

If one is late on the set, the others rag him unmercifully.

They criticise one another's work while the director looks helplessly on. "More action here, Chico," Groucho will say. "More pep." And Chico does it again. With more pep.

Harpo (Arthur), the dumb one with the floor-mop wig, inherited the love of the harp in grandpa's covered wagon. Harpo, with his utter simplicity and lack of pretense, is the pet of the New York intelligentsia. A close friend of Alexander Woollcott. A man whom even Bernard Shaw traveled to see in London. And laughed uproariously when Harpo sprang out of his swimming pool, to greet him, entirely in the nude. The only bachelor, he lives at the beach with a cook and man servant. Thrust by his mother onto a stage in an ill-fitting yachting suit and exactly two and one half minutes notice, with nothing to say, so he said it. And has remained dumb ever since. And spends most of his time, on and off the screen, chasing blondes.

Harpo is an authority on bridge, backgammon and badminton. He will bet on anything.

SO well does a certain New York producer think of Harpo's talent, he recently offered him a serious play of a Theater Guild quality, that even John Barrymore would have leaped at. Instead, Harpo went swimming.

He may look dumb, and act dumb. But you ask someone sometime.

Zeppo (Herbert), the good-looking youngest one, is the least understood. Next to Harpo. Forced by necessity of plot, to be just a handsome juvenile, few know that Zeppo has, next to Groucho, the keenest, quickest wit of any ten thousand men.

Young, handsome, married, Zeppo it is who goes in for swankiness. Rolls-Royces and town houses. While the others live in extreme modesty. He plays the piano, the saxophone and a swell game of bridge.

Many a radio contract as a "crooner" has young Zeppo Marx turned down. His voice is astonishing.

And it's noticeable, too, that at a gathering it's Zeppo at whom they laugh most. His quick wit surprising those who expect this Zeppo to be as unfunny off the screen as on.

THEIR father, seventy years old, who looks fifty and acts thirty, calls them all "darling." He'll visit his darlings on the set.

In snappy spats. Cane. Boutonnière.

The boys call him "Frenchy." Occasionally the boys would take Frenchy with them to view the day's rushes. But Frenchy immediately went into such hysterics at his darlings' antics, that one of the darlings had to lead him out. So he doesn't go any more.

On the last trip out to California, the engineer, conductor and numerous passengers

(continued on next page)

SEPT.

DID you ever wonder, girls, as you sat there listening to the husky tones of Bing Crosby's voice just how he picked up that name "Bing"?

Well, it seems Harry Crosby was one of those little boys the girls all picked on. Which is a pretty sure sign a little miss is interested.

At any rate, one of his tormentors went a bit too far one day and Harry chased her all the way home.

She dashed inside the house and leaning out a window called, "You look just like Bingo in the funny papers." And that was enough. They shortened it to "Bing" and "Bing" it's been ever since.

And now he's in Hollywood, girls, making "The Big Broadcast" for Paramount, and soon you'll hear those husky tones from the screen. In case you're interested.

(continued from preceding page)

alighted from the train, complete nervous wrecks. With Harry Ruby, who writes shows, and insists upon wearing a baseball cap and playing ball, they alighted at every station and immediately began playing ball. The engineer would whistle, their wives would plead, the conductor would beg, and still they played. Running bases. Striking out. Until the train finally pulled out. Then it was a chase and a scramble to get on. At Albuquerque, the word of the four Marxes' arrival had gone ahead. Even Indians, by the hundreds, had gathered. Chico stood on the back platform and made the address. In broken Italian. While old Indian squaws looked at Indian chiefs, in puzzlement.

Zeppo accidentally dropped a glove and there was an immediate scramble for it, so he tossed off the other one as the train pulled out. Immediately, Chico seized the bell cord, stopped the train, ran back to his berth, grabbed out a suitcase, scattered pajamas, socks, handkerchiefs until he found what he wanted. Then back through the coaches he tore and with a flourish threw out his gloves.

A WEALTHY young friend on the train had arranged for his plane to meet him at Indio, Calif., and he invited the four Marxes to fly on to Hollywood with him.

The studio, all dressed up and ready to meet the train at four o'clock, received their first wire at one-thirty. "The Marx Brothers arrive at four P.M." At two o'clock came, "The Marx Brothers will arrive by plane." At two-thirty, "The Marx Brothers will arrive by train." At three o'clock, "The Marx Brothers won't arrive by train." And at three-fifteen, "I doubt if the Marx Brothers ever arrive."

Deciding to accept the friend's generous offer to go by plane, they left the train at Indio.

Then it was found the combined weight of the Marxes with the plane owner and the pilot was too much for the plane. So without a moment's hesitation, the Marxes calmly removed the owner of the plane and waving farewell to an astonished friend on a large and sandy desert, they flew away.

Halfway there, they discovered they had forgotten to eat lunch, so forcing the pilot to return they alighted for lunch and a bit of baseball.

AND after the train had arrived in Los Angeles the Marx Brothers flew into sight at Clover Field. Exactly two hours and forty-five minutes behind the train.

A Marx Brothers conference is something that defies description. Writers, gag men, Marxes, supervisors, director and producers assemble themselves to discuss the story. The supervisor holds the script. "Who thought up this line?" he asks. And maybe he had never heard it before but up will go Groucho's hand. "And this one?" Up goes the hand. "This one?" And up it goes until long after he's through asking and has launched into a discourse, Groucho's hand keeps bobbing up until the supervisor looks helplessly around and gives up.

Harpo, who carries about a miniature harp for practice, will suddenly pull out the harp and begin to practice. Suddenly, for no reason, Groucho and Chico are wrestling about on the floor. Zeppo, as referee, hops about. Zipping off a writer's shirttail for a towel. Harpo plays on.

Now the boys are out of their corners and at it again. The supervisor sits in a corner, wiping huge beads of perspiration from his brow. He glances around wildly. Harpo plays on.

"Now here, fellows," a writer screams above the din, "let's get this straight. We've got all the entrances fixed but what about the exits?"

"Oh, exits?" the four Marxes yell and grabbing up harps and themselves from the floor, they dash for the door. "Well," they say, "speaking of exits."

And the four, mad Marx Brothers exit.

AUG.

☆ ***BLESSED EVENT—Warners***

ANOTHER entry in the great columnist-picture sweepstakes, and a pippin! A real picture, with Lee Tracy, that chronic movie newspaper man, hilariously funny as the boy who prints news of Blessed Events before they occur. The dialogue is great, and good performances abound. This is the sort of red-hot and moonstruck madness that talkies do well—and a credit to all! Good old Lee!

"BLESSED EVENT"—WARNERS.—From the play by Manuel Seff and Forrest Wilson. Adapted by Howard Green. Directed by Roy Del Ruth. The cast: *Alvin*, Lee Tracy; *Gladys*, Mary Brian; *Frankie*, Allen Jenkins; *Miss Stevens*, Ruth Donnelly; *Moxley*, Ned Sparks; *Bunny Harmon*, Dick Powell; *Moskowitz*, Milton Wallace; *Gobel*, Edwin Maxwell; *Alvin's Mother*, Emma Dunn; *Miller*, Walter Walker; *Office Boy*, Bobby Gordon; *Dorothy Lane*, Isabel Jewel; *Miss Bauman*, Ruth Hall; *Hanson*, George Chandler; *Reilly*, Frank McHugh; *Cooper*, Tom Dugan; *Boldt*, Walter Miller; *Flint*, William Halligan; *Church*, George Meeker; *Shapiro*, Jess DeVorska; *Bell Boy*, Harold Waldridge; *Emil*, Herman Bing; *Kane*, Charles Levinson; *Louis De Marco*, Jack LaRue; *Joe*, Lew Harvey.

AUG.

And how would you like to be awakened in the morning by a camera on a giant camera crane swinging over your bed? Although she smiles and smiles and smiles, Jeanette MacDonald wishes the cameraman would swing just a little to the right. It would make her feel more comfortable. This is a shot for "Love Me Tonight"—and what's a Maurice Chevalier picture without a scene showing the gorgeous Jeanette in bed?

SEPT.

Sound your A, crooner! All those actresses who have been emoting to Bing Crosby's phonograph and radio singing gave him a big welcome when he arrived in Hollywood to work in "The Big Broadcast." That's wifey, Dixie Lee, with him

SEPT.

When Marlene Dietrich made "Shanghai Express" she didn't show even so much as a dainty ankle. And did the movie-goers howl! "Okay," said Marlene in a throaty guttural, "if they want legs—I'll give 'em legs." And this is the way she got herself decked out for "The Blonde Venus." If you can waste your time looking at the lady's wig, you will discover that it's so very, very blonde and exotic

Don English

AUG.

"One Hour With You" was another triumph for Jeanette MacDonald. But it brought Genevieve Tobin out in a new type of rôle. Proving herself a deft comedienne, she and Jeanette ran a very close race for the feminine honors

THERE are a lot of arguments this month about whether Jeanette MacDonald or Genevieve Tobin had the main lead in "One Hour With You." Well, I'll be the referee. Jeanette was Chevalier's leading lady but Genevieve certainly gave her a good chase for first place and almost stole the picture from her.

And now, to satisfy hundreds of questioners, here is a short sketch of each girl's history:

Jeanette was born in Philadelphia, Penna., on June 18, 1907. She is 5 feet, 5 inches tall, weighs 125 pounds and has red-gold hair and green eyes. She was a favorite in musical comedy, appearing in "Irene," "Tip Toes," "Yes, Yes, Yvette," and "Sunny Days." She got her first break in pictures in August, 1929, when she was given the lead opposite Chevalier in "The Love Parade." Among the pictures that followed were, "Her Wedding Night," "The Lottery Bride," "Oh, for a Man," "Monte Carlo," and "The Affairs of Annabelle." Her next will be "Love Me Tonight," in which she again appears opposite Chevalier.

Genevieve is a native of New York where she was born on November 29, 1904. She is 5 feet, 3 inches tall, weighs 109 pounds and has blonde hair and gray eyes. Appeared on the stage in "The Trial of Mary Dugan," "Fifty Million Frenchmen," "Little Old New York," and "Murray Hill." She made several silent pictures way back in 1924, then deserted pictures for the stage and returned to the screen in 1930 in "A Lady Surrenders." Since then she has appeared in "Seed," "Up for Murder," "The Gay Diplomat," and others. Her next will be "Hollywood Speaks," with Pat O'Brien.

Both Jeanette and Genevieve are still single, but Jeanette is engaged to Rob Ritchie, who is her manager.

SEPT.

Short Subjects of the Month

Here are the funny little fellows who enliven that very bright animated cartoon, "The Mad King," which is reviewed below. The music is really first-class and you will thoroughly enjoy this gay piece

THE MAD KING

Educational-Paul Terry-Toons

Don't miss this gay, foolish bit of animated cartoon nonsense. It's very Gilbert and Sullivanish with rollicking tunes and a fair damsel in distress. It's actually a grand parody of "The Vagabond King."

A REGULAR TROUPER

Vitaphone

Ruth Etting is the star of this and, in spite of the fact that the brief story doesn't give her much to do, she does manage to get in two songs. The yarn has a backstage atmosphere.

HATTA MARRI

Educational-Mack Sennett

In spite of the title, this isn't a real burlesque of the Garbo picture. Harry Gribbon bursts into song every few scenes or so. The plot, if you can call it that, is a hodge-podge. Dorothy Granger is *Hatta Marri*. Fairly funny.

AUG.

Longworth

WHEN you see it on the screen, Maurice Chevalier will be putting across a song all by himself. So what you might not know is that it took several dozen people behind the acting lines to make the apache number a success in Paramount's "Love Me Tonight." Besides the general set workers, there is a huge orchestra, only part of which is shown here

Paramount LEADS THE WAY TO GREATER ENTERTAINMENT *with*

Marlene
DIETRICH
in
BLONDE VENUS

with HERBERT MARSHALL CARY GRANT

A JOSEF VON STERNBERG PRODUCTION

The amazing Dietrich! Her past performances seem perfection—until her newest picture appears! Here her beauty, her glamour, her charm will thrill you in a brand new way!

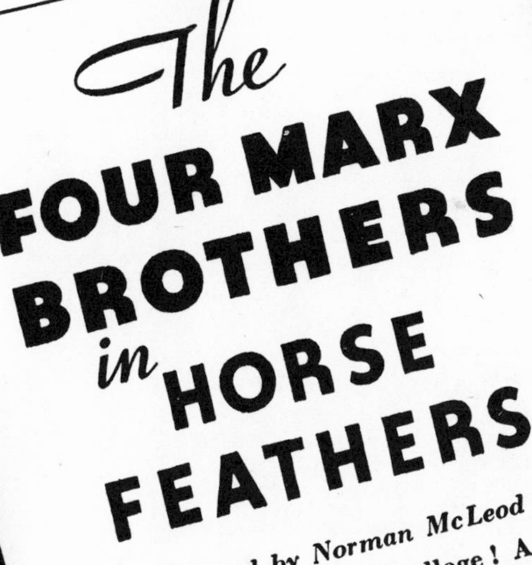

The
FOUR MARX BROTHERS
in
HORSE FEATHERS

Directed by Norman McLeod

The Marx Brothers in college! A riot of laughs that'll make you ache all over! A frolic of fun that'll make you go back to see it all over!

Paramount Pictures

PARAMOUNT PUBLIX CORP., ADOLPH ZUKOR, PRES.
PARAMOUNT BUILDING, NEW YORK, N.Y.

AND WATCH FOR—

"The Big Broadcast" with Bing Crosby, Stuart Erwin, Burns & Allen, Boswell Sisters, Cab Calloway, Mills Brothers, Arthur Tracy (The Street Singer). Maurice Chevalier in "Love Me Tonight" with Jeanette MacDonald, Charlie Ruggles, Charles Butterworth and Myrna Loy. Harold Lloyd in "Movie Crazy". "A Farewell To Arms" with Helen Hayes, Gary Cooper and Adolph Menjou. "The Phantom President" with Geo. M. Cohan, Claudette Colbert, Jimmy Durante, Gene Raymond, Frances Dee. And more to be announced later.

Here it is! The scandalous comedy of a scandal columnist who rose FROM A KEYHOLE TO A NATIONAL INSTITUTION

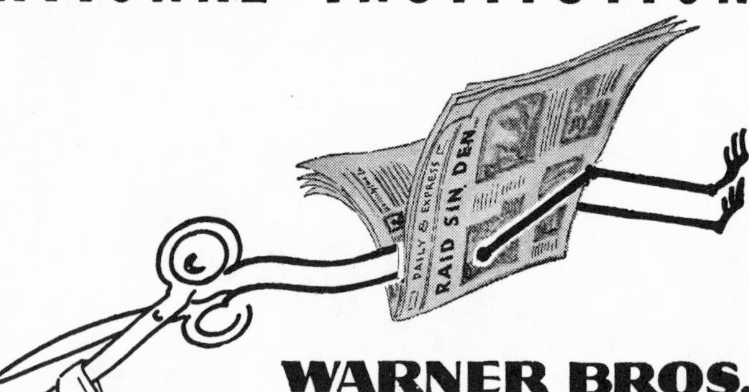

WARNER BROS.
set another new style in picture production by bringing you the sensational New York stage success

"BLESSED EVENT"

with **LEE TRACY . . . MARY BRIAN**
DICK POWELL
Directed by ROY DEL RUTH

The famous Longacre Theatre where New York crowded to pay $3.30 a seat to see "Blessed Event"

The private life of the man who abolished privacy...The lowdown on the Gossip King whose name bounced from Broadway 'round the world!...Take the *Los Angeles Times'* word for it—"it's the best screen entertainment seen in many a day"...By all means watch for your theatre's announcement of this great hit.

WARNER BROS. will bring you the new season's biggest thrills!

He has bedroom eyes—and a nose for news...

Predicts babies like the weather bureau predicts the weather . . .

Sells scandal by the square inch—and cleans up in the shock market . . .

Sees all—knows all—and tells everything!

OCT.

☆ *LOVE ME TONIGHT—Paramount*

WHAT a picture! First, you have Chevalier (and last, you have Chevalier, and all through this riot of entertainment you have Chevalier)—zat Maurice who captures you with his risqué songs, his magnetic smile and his rakish straw hat. And, adding her beauty and lovely voice, you have that delightful Jeanette MacDonald. And those two ridiculous Charlies—Ruggles and Butterworth. And C. Aubrey Smith, who plays a doughty old duke and puts over a solo as inimitably as Maurice. Then there is Myrna Loy. And others equally good. The story? About a lowly tailor who woos a princess. The music? Woven through the whole picture like a brilliant symphony, accented with some of the catchiest tunes of the season. You'll surely be humming, "Isn't It Romantic?" or we miss our guess.

"LOVE ME TONIGHT"—PARAMOUNT.—From the play by Leopold Marchand and Paul Armont. Screen play by Samuel Hoffenstein, Waldemar Young and George Marion, Jr. Directed by Rouben Mamoulian. The cast: *Maurice Courtelin*, Maurice Chevalier; *Princess Jeanette*, Jeanette MacDonald; *Vicomte*, Charlie Ruggles; *Count de Savignac*, Charles E. Butterworth; *Countess Valentine*, Myrna Loy; *The Duke*, C. Aubrey Smith; *First Aunt*, Elizabeth Patterson; *Second Aunt*, Ethel Griffies; *Third Aunt*, Blanche Frederici; *The Doctor*, Joseph Cawthorn; *Dressmaker*, Ethel Wales.

OCT.

☆ *HORSE FEATHERS—Paramount*

IT'S full of Marx Brothers. The four, mad, hysterical Marxes. It has horse feathers and horse laughs. Nonsense and no sense. If you want to forget your troubles and you yearn for a long laugh, a howl and a yelp, see Groucho as maniacal professor, Harpo as a dog-catcher and Chico as a combination bootlegger and ice man.

Through nine long reels and Thelma Todd's bedroom they race and tear, dripping wisecracks as they go.

Zeppo, the youngest, is Groucho's son, in love with the college widow. Groucho sets out in overshoes and carrying an umbrella to break up the romance, only to succumb himself. The football game is a scream. You won't know at all what it's all about. But then neither do the Marx Brothers. Who cares? It's that funny.

"HORSE FEATHERS" — PARAMOUNT. — From the screen play by Harry Ruby, Bert Kalmar and S. J. Perelman. Directed by Norman McLeod. The cast: *Professor Wagstaff*, Groucho Marx; *Harpo*, Harpo Marx; *Chico*, Chico Marx; *Zeppo*, Zeppo Marx; *Connie Bailey*, Thelma Todd; *Jennings*, David Landau; *Peggy Carrington*, Florine McKinney; *Mullens*, James Pierce; *McCarthy*, Nat Pendleton; *President of Huxley*, Reginald Barlow; *Professor Hornsvogel*, Robert Greig.

OCT.

The great Lubitsch and his cigar, with George Cukor. These two guided Maurice Chevalier through "One Hour With You"

OCT.

Hot-cha-chaaaaaaa! We can't fool you. Right away quick you know that the gentleman in the stove pipe lid is Jimmy Durante, but who's the lad in all that burnt cork? Yep, it's flag-waving George M. Cohan, much, much farther away from Broadway than forty-five minutes. He and Jimmy are making a picture together—"The Phantom President"—out in Hollywood

OCT.

CROONER—
First National

CROONERS are would-be singers that girls go for in a big way and men would like to choke, according to this picture. It hands a loud but quite amusing razz to all such radio performers. It took courage for good looking David Manners to play a college lad who becomes one of these ridiculed crooners. Ken Murray and Ann Dvorak help to make this bright and entertaining.

"CROONER" — FIRST NATIONAL. — From the novel by Rian James. Adapted by Charles Kenyon. Directed by Lloyd Bacon. The cast: *Teddy*, David Manners; *Judy*, Ann Dvorak; *Peter*, Ken Murray; *Hat Check Girl*, Sheila Terry; *Pat*, William Janney; *Henry*, Eddie Nugent; *Meyers*, J. Carroll Naish; *His Secretary*, Betty Gillette; *The Drunk*, Guy Kibbee; *Theater Manager*, William Halligan; *Mack*, Teddy Joyce; *Boy*, Sumner Getchell; *Tom*, Clarence Norstrum; *Ralph*, Allen Vincent; *Head Waiter*, William Ricciardi; *Constance*, Claire Dodd; *Band Boys*, William Morgan, Johnny Harron, Sumner Getchell.

OCT.

BLONDIE OF THE FOLLIES—
_M-G-M_

A SPRIGHTLY, well-framed story with brilliant backstage atmosphere, thrills, suspense and some very tender moments. Marion Davies is charming as the little Eastside girl who makes a success in the Follies, and Billie Dove has never been more lovely. The high point comes when Marion and Jimmy Durante do a burlesque of "Grand Hotel." Bob Montgomery plays the lead.

"BLONDIE OF THE FOLLIES"—M-G-M.—From the story by Frances Marion. Directed by Edmund Goulding. The cast: *Blondie*, Marion Davies; *Larry*, Robert Montgomery; *Lottie*, Billie Dove; *Jimmy*, Jimmy Durante; *Pa McClune*, James Gleason; *Gertie*, ZaSu Pitts; *Pete*, Sidney Toler; *Murchenson*, Douglas Dumbrille; *Ma McClune*, Sarah Padden; *Ma Callahan*, Louise Carter; *Dancer*, Clyde Cook; *Rocky Twins*, By Themselves.

OCT.

Musical films like "The Desert Song" linger in the memory, according to many letters. "Give us good pictures with gay songs and pleasing singers, and we'll give them our support at the box-office," one man writes

OCT.

SHE SIGHS FOR THE "SINGIES"

Just because producers gave singing actors poor pictures that the public didn't patronize, must we be deprived of hearing our favorite stars sing in good pictures? Please let us have more singing from Ramon Novarro and John Boles, in pictures as good as "The Pagan," "Desert Song," and "Rio Rita."

BETTINA BONNELL.

NOV.

"LOVE ME TONIGHT"

Maurice Chevalier in "Love Me Tonight" is the best entertainment the movies have offered since that other charming musical Paramount picture, "This Is The Night." I hope producers will give us more of this type of picture, for the light musical and, yes, even the spiced touch in these films make them a great relief from some of the overdone and heavy dramatic stuff.

BOB ADAMS, Northeast Harbor, Me.

OCT.

Hurrell

Come, come, Billie Dove, do you think it's fair to give Marlene Dietrich so much competition? But you've got to admit that the Dove has never looked so lovely as she does in this —ahem—may one call it costume? that she wears in Marion Davies' new picture, "Blondie of the Follies"

NOV.

Jeanette MacDonald and Maurice Chevalier in "Love Me Tonight" brought down the house with their music and charm. But many readers begged Maurice to stick to the *double entendre*, if he must, but to be less frankly naughty. Director Mamoulian got high praise for his work

NOV.

GEORGE M. COHAN has gone back to Broadway. His Paramount picture, "The Phantom President," completed, he lost no time in shaking the Hollywood dust from his shoes. "If I stay in Hollywood," a friend quotes him, "I fear for my sense of humor. Maybe I'll laugh about what has happened to me when I go home. But I can't laugh here."

NOV.

IS George M. Cohan a regular fellow, or "just another actor" from Broadway? Don't ask Hollywood, which, in spite of its reputation for garrulity, can refrain from critical comment of the departed guest; and don't ask George, either; for he has already spoken his little piece.

Here's what happened: When George was invited by Paramount to come out to Hollywood and make a picture, everyone was happy over it, and the studio welcomed him as one whose reputation as an actor entitled him to the greatest respect.

But the man who made the Stars and Stripes famous twenty-five years ago by running up and down the stage yelling "It's a grand old flag," accepted Hollywood's hospitality complacently, if not graciously, and then proceeded to show everybody how they ought to run the business.

On the third day on the set he had a unique idea—this idea usually comes about that time—he began to show the director how to direct.

SAID George in effect: "This is the way we do it on the stage; that's the way we do it in New York," and it took all the California hospitality the director possessed to refrain from retorting: "And these are the ways we're not going to do it in this picture!"

Anyhow, George finally went on his way, proclaiming to the press that picture dialogue was silly and that he would be ashamed of his children if they should write anything so poor.

Well, some people "go Hollywood," and some "go Broadway"; only, the latter malady seems to be incurable.

When Eddie Lang plunks his guitar and Bing Crosby begins his rhapsodizing about "the blue ovver eyes" and "the gold ovver hair," all the brunettes sigh and reach for a bleach

Oh, for the life of a crooner! Nothing to do, says Bing, but get up at seven in the morning, to bed by twelve, with song recordings, stage shows and a couple of broadcasts in between

"I Surrender, Dear"

IT'S almost time. The hour hand points to seven. The minute hand is creeping slowly but surely, slowly but surely. There is an air of hushed expectancy in the house. A hush. A tenseness. Dad looks up suddenly from his tapioca pudding to discover the table deserted. He sits alone. He and his shadow and his little dish of tapioca. Startled, he glances quickly around. Over the top of his glasses. Yes, there they are. Ma and the three girls and Mrs. Watkins from next door, who hasn't a radio. Sitting still and tense and quiet.

Now it's seven. The clock in the hall strikes the hour. A few mumbled words. Twenty. Count them. No more. No less. *And then.* A voice. A whistle. Something about the "Blue ovver eyes" and the "gold ovver hair." And then dad. "Good heavens, is that Crosby guy on the air again?"

It is. It's Bing.

And "We Surrender, Dear."

Bing's mother didn't raise her boy to be a crooner. When little Harry Crosby (nicknamed "Bingo" by the neighborhood kids, and later shortened to "Bing") went galloping on a broomstick up in Spokane, Washington, there were no crooners. Only bogey-mans. And mamas would have thought any "bogey-mans" living, sane and sensible compared with a grown man who stood nightly before a little round black thing, and, with no one near and for no reason that anyone could see with the naked eye, made funny noises about "surrendering, dear." It didn't make sense.

But learning to be a lawyer, there was some sense to that, they thought. So the Crosbys sent "Bing" off to Gonzaga College to be one. The kind that stood before judges and argued like anything.

But, dear me, they should have known. When Bing would walk out on any *habeas corpus* proceedings to practice on the trap drums, they should have known. They should have been warned. And were.

So the Crosbys have been prepared for anything that followed. And it did follow. Bing organized a seven-piece orchestra and began playing for all the college dances. Having sung in the college glee club, he saw no reason why he shouldn't go on singing with his orchestra. And he did. So you see from innocent little acts like that, even great crooners are born.

A LOCAL theater manager heard Bing and his boys and booked them for a vaudeville tour. And all thoughts of law were forever forgotten.

Bing was on his way.

Whiteman (Paul the Great) heard Bing and his friend, Al Rinker, sing in Los Angeles, and lo and behold, with the addition of Harry Barris to the duet, the famous "rhythm boys" came into being. And went rhythming about the country with Paul and his band.

But when Whiteman came to Hollywood to make "King of Jazz," Bing liked Hollywood so well he stayed behind and tortured a microphone nightly at the Cocoanut Grove.

The fellow who could leap-frog over three notes to a note that wasn't in the

By Lois Shirley

(continued on next page)

(continued from preceding page)

song in the first place, that could slur three little notes together that hadn't even been on speaking terms before, that could stop in the middle of a word, gulp twice and catch up two lines later, was growing famous.

He made records, that begged sobbingly in many a famous star's dressing-room and many a family living-room for "Just One More Chance."

HE made movies for Mack Sennett that always ended by Bing proving he was really Bing by slowly fading out of the picture chirping about the "blue ovver eyes" (whistle, whistle, whistle) and "I surrender (gulp twice) dear."

And so he came to the Columbia Broadcasting and to thousands of homes.

A famous crooner. Or singer. Or whatsoever he may be.

And the feminine world thrilled and quivered, and wondered at the romantic idol whose husky voice promises so much "when the blue (whistle) ovthenight, meets (gulp) the gold ovtheday, da dum doodee doo."

While behind the cold little microphone stands a stocky blue-eyed boy of twenty-eight, who has to watch his diet and isn't concerned about his too-large ears. Who must remember to tell his wife about that early rehearsal and, gosh, do these shoes hurt his feet, and at the same time advise a thousand palpitating hearts to "Wrap their troubles in dreams and dream your troubles away," or however it goes. And him with his feet hurting and all.

The life of a radio singer-movie star, record-maker, stage star is anything but a song. It's a foot race, a trapeze act and endurance contest all in one.

For instance, Bing is up at seven. At eight he's ready for the day's work. Songs are to be gone over and tried out. Publishers submit a number of songs for his approval. Not being able to read a single note or play chop-sticks, even on the piano, he has an accompanist who plays all the tunes submitted over and over and over, while Bing listens. If one takes his fancy, they read over the words. The words play an important part, he thinks.

"Wouldn't I get the razz if I began chirping about 'honey bunchy' and 'ducky wucky'?" he asks.

So if there are no "ducky wuckys" in the tune they like, it's held for further consideration.

In this way they choose about three numbers. A sentimental ballad, a hot song and a lively ballad. With these they "fool around," as Bing says, and get the feel of them. He never has any set way of singing a song. One day he may sing it, "Wrap your troubles in do dum dee day and do dum ee day them away" or for a big surprise to mama and the girls the very next night he may suggest that they "Wrap their do dum ee days in dreams and dream their do dums away."

AND that, he thinks, is exactly what keeps up the excitement. A body never knows from one night to another just where he will be "do dumming" or why.

The songs that get the biggest reaction are the ones they repeat. And that's how simple that is.

Now it's ten-thirty or eleven o'clock. And no records made this morning. So they rush down to the recording studio and "Just One More Chance" is canned for a thousand more homes.

And look at the time. Twelve o'clock and no mail answered. Rush home where a secretary is pacing up and down looking thunder storms at every one.

The form letters have been answered. Only the personal or really intelligent requests (usually begging for just one chance and not one more) await answering.

If, for instance, you write Mr. Crosby that you would like to meet him, the secretary immediately snatches out form letter number one, which says something about Mr. Crosby will be glad to sing "Too Many Tears" next week. Or if you write you would like very much to have a picture of your idol, they immediately snatch out form letter number two, which says something about Mr. Crosby not being in the market for any more songs just now. And strange as it may seem, the autographed picture is included.

Letters from jealous husbands have them completely stumped.

"Dear Mr. Crosby, you are breaking up my home," they read. "My wife feeds me sardines at five o'clock in the afternoon so she can hear you make a noise at seven. What are you going to do about it?"

Bing never has the slightest idea what to do about it. There is no form letter to cover a situation like that.

Two girls write from California. "Dear Mr. Crosby, what are we going to do? Our dad is terribly mad at us because we won't let him eat celery at dinner, for he always makes so much noise with the celery, we can't hear your thrilling songs. And dad says unless we let him eat his celery in peace, we can't go to the club dance on Saturday night. Dear Mr. Crosby, won't you tell us what to do, as we are simply cuhrazy about you and yet we can't miss the ducky club dance. And remember Mr. Crosby (Bing), we 'surrender, dear.' "

And there is no form whatsoever to cover a situation like that, either.

THEN there's the letter received from a colored boy "down South."

"Dear Mr. Croz bee," he wrote, "I declare, times is gettin' that good I jus' naturally can't get over it. My gal, she jus' keeps in such a good humor all the time wif your singin' and all, that we ain't had no fights fer a long time. That's a fact, Mr. Croz bee, and what's more, used to be I could walk down the street and I wouldn't fin' more than one good cigar butt for ten blocks, but since you been singin' on that cigar program why, honest, Mr. Croz bee, wif no trouble a tall, I can pick up twenty of them good cigar butts, only half smoked, to every block. I'm tellin' you, I got myself a backache jus' pickin' 'em up. And my girl she's jus' no trouble to me a tall anymore and hoping you are the same, I certainly do thank you, Mr. Croz bee."

And try to find a form letter to answer that one!

And then some one glances at the clock—twelve forty-five and he's due for his first appearance at the Paramount Theater at one. It's a mad dash in a taxi, horns honking, a rush, a scramble and just as the orchestra is playing the final chords of the tune that says "the gold of her hair crowns the blue of her eyes," Bing Crosby steps out to wild applause.

A snatch of lunch and another performance later in the afternoon and then to the broadcasting station on the run for a bit of rehearsal and Eastern broadcast at seven. Another wild taxi ride back for more shows at the theater and, if he is making a Western broadcast, another dash back to the broadcasting station at eleven.

Sometimes, with traffic congestion, he'll arrive just as the orchestra has played the last note of his song and he'll begin his "surrendering, dear" almost at the door.

And several times they've shoved the printed words of his song in his hand as he entered and half way through "Too Many Tears" he'd feel unsure of a word, glance down at the pages and discover to his horror he was holding the words of "I'll Be Glad When You're Dead, You Rascal, You."

Or, in his rush, he'd find himself with a frog in his throat with no time to clear it and go through the entire song of "Paradise" expecting to get as far as "she takes me to——" and then croak like a frog or leap like a toad. It's awful.

THERE are no night clubs or gay times for a busy crooner.

He must keep fit.

In bed at twelve, he's awake at seven ready for another day of singing and rushing and singing and rushing.

The three days on the train to Hollywood with no "surrendering" to do were like heaven. And then back into the rush of making two shorts for Mack Sennett in two weeks.

And immediately afterward, at work on the feature picture, "The Big Broadcast," for Paramount.

He's the "Hi, there, boy" of the Paramount lot.

A glad hand from everyone.

Posing for pictures with everyone. Eager and willing.

As interested in this strange world of Hollywood as a kid. "Look," he'll say, "here comes Von Sternberg into the dining-room without Dietrich. Gee, hope those two aren't spatting again."

And he thinks Jackie Cooper a simply swell actor.

He licks the butterscotch off his spoon like a kid and opens his package of cigarettes with his teeth. And gazes wistfully at a passing tray of roast beef and potatoes.

But motion picture actors must keep slender. So Bing eats lettuce. And never surrenders, dear.

The little waitress comes coyly over with a note. Bing opens it and his face lights up with a grin. "Look. It says there's another fellow in this studio dining-room with big ears, too. Gosh, I'll bet it's Gable. He's over here at Paramount making a picture." And like a kid, he's up gaping around for Clark.

"Never knew there was anything the matter with my ears till I made this picture. And now look. All stuck back to my head with goo," he grins.

The minute "The Big Broadcast" was finished, he took himself off deep sea fishing with Lew Ayres. And was like a kid playing hookey.

And now movies and vacations are over for another spell for Bing. It's back to radio, to personal appearances, record-making, rushing, singing.

It's nearing seven in the family living-room again. This time dad sits alone in the next room with his prune whip and vanilla wafer.

MUSIC. A few words. And then a voice. Husky. Imploring. A you-chase-me-and-I'll-chase-you voice. Begging for "One Hour With You."

While Mary and Alice and Edna sit tense and thrilled. Wondering and dreaming about their dream-idol of the radio and movies. Their superman hero.

While behind the little black microphone stands a nice, ordinary young fellow like Jack Smith across the street. Not too bright or geniusy. But nice. And bewildered at what has happened.

Just twenty-eight, and on the top. With no place left to go. Knowing that tomorrow may bring another idol. Will, in fact. And for him—?

But that's another day. Today he sings.

And thousands of feminine hearts beat wildly.

And surrender, dear.

Whooie! Here

By Sara Hamilton

ILLUSTRATED BY VAN ARSDALE

HIS mother watched him from the porch as he trudged up the street on sturdy little legs.

"Joey," she called to him, "have you got a clean handkerchief?"

Joe E. Brown laid down the neatly wrapped bundle that held a pair of patched underdrawers (handed down from three brothers ahead) and an extra shirt.

"Yes, ma," he yelled and every house in Toledo, Ohio, swayed gently on its foundations as the echo of that call reverberated through the town.

"All right," she said, "and don't get your feet wet or get stepped on by an elephant, for heaven's sake."

And he was gone. Around a corner of Toledo and the corner of a young life.

Walking, not running, mind you, away to join a circus. A little nine-year-old boy with twinkly blue eyes, a nose that looked for all the world like a stubby little engine emerging from the open tunnel of a mouth beneath.

One actually waited any moment for the whistle to blow and the passengers to alight.

But just the same, Joe E. was on his way.

He was now one of the Five Marvelous Ashtons, though none of them were really marvelous and, for that matter, none of them were Ashtons. But Joe was that little ball that flew madly from Papa Ashton to Cousin Ashton from a trapeze fifty feet in the air. And often as not never completed the journey from papa to cousin and landed in a net below. And broke a jaw or something.

It was a life. He had all the strength, heart, life and soul beat and pommeled out of him, but doggedly kept on. Going back every winter to Toledo for school and never breathing to his ma what he endured in circuses during the summer. He knew he'd never get to go back if he did.

It grew pretty bad. Even when Joe joined a tumbling troupe and was hurled to the stage because of a mistake and broke a leg. Zowie! Just like that.

Then Joe picked up the pieces that remained after five years of circus life and took himself off to join a vaudeville act. And was he terrible? In several villages (they wouldn't let him in the towns) the citizens actually called a town meeting to know what could be done with the gosh-darned drought that "wuz a ruinin' the crops and that there pesky vaudeville team that kept on playin' when no one wanted to see 'em."

And then came one of the tragedies of Joe's young life (soft music, please). They reached a village with several other acts and proceeded to put on a show in the combination fire house, hoosegow and barber shop. They stretched up a canvas in a four by six space and the women dressed on one side and the men dressed on the fire truck. Hanging their clothes all over the thing.

Joe, in his tights (and *there* was a picture!), stood in the wings watching a heartrending and soul-stirring act, according to the bill boards, and everything was sad and very quiet. Si Perkins had durned near wept his goatee off when suddenly there was a loud clang over their heads. THE FIREBELL! Ding dong, ding dong.

In an instant every last ninety-four citizens of that village were in a turmoil and the fire engine half way to Centerville before Joe could open that mouth of his and yell. It was on its way to a fire with Joe's pants hanging on the side. And for three hours he shivered and shook until the fire engine returned with a pair of wet, bedraggled pants. With the seat and one leg missing.

THEN on to San Francisco. Joe was a big boy of fifteen now and old already in the ways of show business. That night they completed their act that grew mustier as the years wore on and Joe went home and went to bed. But suddenly he was out of bed again with the bed flatter than a pancake and the whole city doing a shimmy.

The great earthquake was on. Joe rushed outdoors. "Save my things," the landlady screamed as the fire broke out over the city. So Joe rushed in, seized a grandfather's clock, dragged it for two blocks and a half and fell exhausted before the open door of a delicates-

Comes Joe E.

sen shop. The inside looked inviting, so Joe filled his pockets with cheese and crackers and seized what he thought was a case of soda water. Piling his case on the clock he made for the nearest hill.

Never, he thought, had he heard soda make such a disturbance when opened. It went *pop!* And after the second *pop* he was waving his champagne bottle, still thinking it was soda water, in the air, two-stepping and admiring the fireworks. "Suza good show. Swell lil' city to put on this show (hiccup) for a fella."

AND then he made it. The end of every actor's rainbow of dreams. Broadway. Yes sir, he was on it. Good old Broadway. He had come a long, heartbreaking way and here he was. He was to substitute that night for the leading man in "Listen, Lester."

At five o'clock in the afternoon he was in the dressing-room, made up. Six o'clock came, then seven, and years later it was eight. Joe had fumed and fussed until his make-up had worn off and he had to put on more. Finally, the overture. And then it was played again, and by the time they began playing it the third time, Joe was wild with nerves. Then came the manager.

"No show, Joe," he said.

Joe could only stand and open and shut that mouth. Not a word came out.

"Equity just called a strike," the manager explained. So Joe took off the make-up and wandered aimlessly, and completely stunned, up Broadway. No show, no money, one wife, two babies, a sore back, his father had just died and well, you just name anything sad. It was Joe's.

The police force of Beverly Hills planted their heavy feet on the velvet carpet and charged upon the dreadful, house-rocking sound with all the intrepid gallantry of a battalion of troops

But strikes don't keep on striking and Joe was back again on Broadway in "Jim Jam Jems," "Listen, Lester" and "Greenwich Village Follies." And then one day his name was ready to go up in lights.

It was just six o'clock in the morning in New York City. A funny, little guy paced up and down, up and down before a theater. Several hours later a workman on the roof looked down and said to another workman, "Say, look at that guy down there. He walks past here and then he runs. Then he trots up and down like a kangaroo. What's the matter with him?"

"Aw, he's nuts," the other said and went on with his work.

But he wasn't nuts. It was *(continued on next page)*

(continued from preceding page)

just Joe E. walking past that huge sign up there that said JOE E. BROWN on the front of the theater and trying to see if it were visible from all angles, to anyone whether trotting, hopping or just walking past.

Between shows he tried baseball. The thing he loves next to acting. He actually belonged at one time to the New York Giants. But didn't get far for, you see, when Joe got up to bat and opened his mouth to grin, the pitcher refused to throw the ball.

"What's the matter?" the umpire asked.

"Look at that," the pitcher said. "I can't throw a ball at that. He'll swallow it. And we're short on balls."

And there was the time the bases were full and two men had struck out. There was a moment of tense silence as the third man came to bat.

Now. The pitcher threw the ball. The batter swung. He hit it and made for second base, when suddenly Joe let out that "call of the wild" yell of his and in two seconds the pitcher had tramped the catcher silly trying to get out, the batter was still running two blocks away, the umpire lay in a dead swoon and the stadium had completely emptied.

So Joe kind of gave up baseball. He has his own ball team out in Hollywood that even belongs to a league. And they do splendidly until Joe expands the "wide open spaces" and lets go that yell in the wrong places.

He claims he acquired that famous yell one summer at a lakeside camp. When the rest of the boys were a mile or so off shore fishing and Joe wanted to call them in for breakfast, he would go down to the shore, open up his mouth, begin a sound down in the region of the larynx and finally let go that water buffalo shout that not only brought in the fishermen but all the trading boats on Lake Erie as well. And Joe's been using that war whoop ever since.

And his mouth, strange as it may seem, isn't too noticeably large in every day life. Unless Joe wants it to be and opens it accordingly. Otherwise it's just a slightly unusual opening in a very pleasant countenance.

He has a tremendous following, officially ranking among the first ten in box-office pull. And he's really considerate and thoughtful of his fans.

His is one of the few contracts that definitely state every fan letter must be taken care of with no expense to the fan. And do they write!

From San Francisco comes a letter from a judge. "Well, Joe," he writes, "I was on my way to a doctor last night when I passed a movie with your mug out front. I never did care for doctors so I decided to postpone the ordeal an hour or two and see my friend Joe again. Why, say, you shook every ill and pain out of me. I never did see that doctor, you rascal, you!"

From Bombay, India: "Dear Sahib Brown: I never fail to miss one of your pictures when it comes here."

And Joe is still scratching his head over that one.

ALSO, there was the time Joe was having lunch at a fashionable hotel in Washington, D. C. About him sat the city's best.

Presently a beautiful young lady, neatly dressed, came over to Joe's table.

"Mr. Brown," she said a little confused. "I have a favor to ask of you."

"Why, what is it?" Joe asked in surprise.

"May I touch you?" she blushingly asked.

"Why certainly," Joe grinned sheepishly.

She laid a dainty finger on his sleeve.

"Now I have a favor to ask you," Joe said.

"Oh, what?" she asked breathlessly.

"May I touch you?"

And he laid a finger on her sleeve.

And then as though it were the most natural thing in the world, they bowed, shook hands and departed.

He's a home body, Joe is. In love with his wife, two boys and baby girl. And despite the fact he's a rather serious minded and decidedly unfunny person off the screen, his two boys, fourteen and twelve, think he's a card. And much funnier than the four Marx Brothers. Much. Everything he says is a scream to the boys.

For instance, if Mr. Brown remarks to Mrs. Brown at the dinner table that the situation in China looks bad, the boys know immediately Daddy must be clowning and go into such hysterics they have to leave the table. Isn't he the funny one, their dad, though?

Then there's that recent high excitement out in the exclusive suburb of Beverly Hills.

Strange, ghostly noises were issuing nightly from a grand mansion on one of the very quiet streets.

It went on for a week. With the sounds growing more and more terrifying.

Finally, the neighbors, in feverish excitement, but loathe to bring in vulgar outsiders, were unable to control themselves further, and summoned the cops.

Aforesaid cops were awed as they crowded past several butlers and footmen. Up the tastefully carpeted stairs their big feet tore to where the sounds issued from a front room.

As one, they made a dash for the door only to have two sedate and composed French maids open the door.

In the center of the room stood madam looking at them in astonishment. They stared back at her in equal astonishment.

"WHAT," she demanded, in icy, cultured tones, "is the meaning of this?"

She raised a gold lorgnette and peered at them haughtily.

"Why,—that is, lady," Officer Reilly stammered, "we heard a terrible noise and came to investigate."

"The idea," the dowager sniffed. "Can't a lady practice yelling like Joe E. Brown without the entire police force interrupting?"

And they carefully tiptoed downstairs and outside.

While upstairs a great social light went on with her practicing of yelling like Joe E. Brown. Whoowowwwie!

NOV.

BLONDE VENUS—Paramount

THIS picture attempts to de-glamourize Marlene Dietrich. She is a down-to-earth person and is exotic only in a few sequences. But her exotic scenes remain the best and you are not quite convinced by her other type of work. It is a mother love story, and besides smooth direction, there is the unforgettable Herbert Marshall as the soul-torn husband, and charming little Dickie Moore.

"BLONDE VENUS"—PARAMOUNT.—From the story by S. K. Lauren and Jules Furthman. Directed by Josef von Sternberg. The cast: *Helen Faraday,* Marlene Dietrich; *Edward Faraday,* Herbert Marshall; *Nick Townsend,* Cary Grant; *Johnny Faraday,* Dickie Moore; *Charlie Blaine,* Francis Sayles; *Dan O'Connor,* Robert Emmett O'Connor; *Ben Smith,* Gene Morgan; *Taxi Belle Hooper,* Rita La Roy; *Detective Wilson,* Sidney Toler; *Iola,* Evelyn Preer; *Otto,* Jerry Tucker; *Norfolk Woman,* Cecil Cunningham; *Henry,* Ferdinand Schumann-Heink; *Bob,* Charles Morton.

NOV.

BOB, WASHINGTON, D. C.—The Four Mad Marxes were all born in New York City. Chico, who plays the piano, was born on March 22, 1891. Harpo, the red-wigged silent one was born on November 21, 1893. Groucho, with the black moustache and glasses was born on October 2, 1895, and Zeppo, the youngest, on February 25, 1901. Their real names are Leonard, Arthur, Julius and Herbert, respectively. There is still another brother, Milton, who is in the dress business. His nickname is Gummo.

NOV.

THE GIRL FROM CALGARY—First Division-Monogram

ANOTHER little girl from the wide open spaces wins an Atlantic City (is that all they do in that town?) beauty contest, gets a coveted spot in the Follies, falls into the naughty hands of a designing millionaire, but is saved by her honest press-agent. Fifi Dorsay is cute and plump as the girl. Paul Kelly, making a comeback, plays opposite. Interesting, despite the aged plot.

"GIRL FROM CALGARY, THE"—FIRST DIVISION-MONOGRAM. — From the screen play by Sig Schlager and Leon D'Usseau. Directed by Phil Whitman and Leon D'Usseau. The cast: *Fifi Follette,* Fifi Dorsay; *Larry Boyd,* Paul Kelly; *Mazie Williams,* Astrid Allwyn; *Bill Webster,* Robert Warwick; *Monte Cooper,* Edward Fetherstone; *Earl Darrell,* Edwin Maxwell.

NOV.

Short Subjects of the Month

MICKEY'S REVUE
Walt Disney-Columbia

Mickey's giving a small town musical revue this time—and don't miss it! Musical instruments range from ash cans to wash tubs—and the syncopation, is it hot! We don't have to tell you that it's fun.

NIAGARA FALLS
RKO-Pathe

June McCloy's nice, huskily sung ditties save this from being just another comedy. The good old plot of three girls trying to evade the irate landlady while they find work, is dusted off again. Gertrude Short and Marion Shilling complete the trio. Only mildly amusing.

NOV.

☆ ***PHANTOM PRESIDENT—Paramount***

IF you're laugh-hungry, don't miss this riot of political farce, which introduces George M. (flag waving) Cohan to the talking screen. George is a scream in a dual rôle that allows him to play both a stodgy bank president—a presidential candidate—and his double who thinks this country needs more pep and personality in politics.

Jimmy Durante—laughing already? Well, Jimmy is the double's pal who crashes the convention hall and causes a riot. His songs are great, done in the inimitable Durante manner. Claudette Colbert, who hasn't much to do, adds a touch of beauty to the production.

Singing and dancing only add to the sparkle of this film. It's utter nonsense, of course, and just the sort of thing to give you one swell evening's entertainment. Don't miss it.

"PHANTOM PRESIDENT, THE"—PARAMOUNT.—From the novel by George F. Worts. Screen play by Walter DeLeon and Harlan Thompson. Directed by Norman Taurog. The cast: *Theodore K. Blair, Peter Varney*, George M. Cohan; *Felicia Hammond*, Claudette Colbert; *Curly Cooney*, Jimmy Durante; *Jim Ronkton*, George Barbier; *Professor Aikenhead*, Sidney Toler; *Senator Sarah Scranton*, Louise Mackintosh; *Jerrido*, Jameson Thomas; *Senator Melrose*, Julius McVicker.

NOV.

He Orders Ham And Eggs

HE played himself in his first picture, "Blessed Event," as combination orchestra leader, crooner and master of ceremonies. For that's exactly what Dick Powell is. Directly from the Stanley Theater in Pittsburgh comes Dick after three and a half years as master of ceremonies. And still he smiles. And thinks life dandy.

Born in a little town in Arkansas, his family finally moved into the big city of Little Rock and Dick's career was on. In the daytime he worked for the telephone company. At nights he sang in church choirs.

Then he received an offer to sing and play a banjo with an orchestra in Indianapolis. There was only one slight drawback to the offer. He couldn't play a banjo. A horn, a saxophone or a piccolo, yes. But not a banjo. But he wanted to go, so he rushed out, bought a banjo and practiced until every man, woman and child was glad to see him bound for Indianapolis, with his banjo under his arm.

From there he went to the Smoky City, where he did a Gable with the girls. In fact, for three years the whole town was Dick Powell conscious.

He's boyish, has a lot of charm, wavy hair and a cute smile. He's a regular he-man.

His hands are large; he loves ham and eggs; plays a good game of golf and can fly a plane anywhere.

Began flying lessons early one morning and had made his first solo flight before dark.

He reads popular magazines, and spends most of his spare time rehearsing.

Has a five-year contract with Warners with a twelve-week vacation clause each year.

Was borrowed by Fox to play the boy in Will Rogers' picture, "Jubilo," because the boy had to sing. Then they cut out all the songs and left Dick high and dry with a straight part for the first time in his life.

He lives with his father and mother in Hollywood and if the movie thing doesn't turn out well, he's sure of one thing.

He can always go back to Pittsburgh.

DEC.

"I'm glad George M. Cohan made 'The Phantom President' before he got mad at Hollywood," says a reader. "A grand picture—and wasn't Claudette Colbert lovely?" All right—we'll answer. She was!

DEC.

FOGS and rain descended on "The Kid From Spain" set when the bull fight was only half completed. And the overhead was mounting.

Sam Goldwyn walked down to the set to talk it over with Eddie Cantor and Director Leo McCarey.

"It's terrible," Sam groaned. "This thing is costing too much. Something will have to be done. I'm worried sick."

"You do look a bit drawn," Eddie sympathized.

"Drawn?" the Irish director said. "Why, Sam, you actually look overdrawn."

And even Goldwyn laughed.

DEC.

WITH Al Jolson saying she won't and George Jessel saying she will, Norma Talmadge's friends are wondering if she really will return to the screen in "Wunderbar."

Jessel insists he has the screen rights to the piece and Jolson says he hasn't.

The feud between Jessel and Jolson, if it could be called a feud, dates from, "The Jazz Singer."

That was Jessel's outstanding stage hit, but when Warners planned to make it into a picture, he demanded so much money that Jolson was put in the rôle as a sort of second choice.

HE'S STARTING SOMETHING DEC.

Here is a nice big bouquet (including all his favorite flowers) for Director Rouben Mamoulian. After seeing "Love Me Tonight," I realize more than ever how important expert direction is. Close cooperation between writer, director and star (I've placed them in order of their importance in my opinion. Now I'm waiting for brickbats to fly from ardent star fans after they read that) will soon raise the level of pictures to the height they belong.

L. NISSMAN, Philadelphia, Penna.

DEC.

A débutante and her escort. Shirley Temple is the lady, and Eugene Butler the young man in the case. They are playing in the Educational comedy, "Glad Rags to Riches"

DEC.

A pair whose voices and sheer nonsense have won a big place in the hearts of all radio listeners—George Burns and Gracie Allen. They've made personal appearances, but everybody can see them now in Paramount's "The Big Broadcast"

MARLENE DIETRICH

as the "Blonde Venus"

Dietrich the glamorous — Exotic beauty of "Morocco"—Tragic heroine of "Dishonored"—Lovely derelict of "Shanghai Express"— Now more entrancing—more gloriously luscious—as a girl who played with love. Only Dietrich can give such beauty, such dignity, such allure to the scarlet letter!

MARLENE DIETRICH *in* "BLONDE VENUS"

with HERBERT MARSHALL
CARY GRANT · DICKIE MOORE

Directed by JOSEPH VON STERNBERG

PARAMOUNT PUBLIX CORPORATION, ADOLPH ZUKOR PRES., PARAMOUNT BLDG., NEW YORK

Up the Ladder *with* Jeanette

She sneaked into the chorus back row. That was the first rung to fame

"Can you dance—can you sing?" they asked Jeanette MacDonald. "Certainly," she answered—and then proceeded to learn how

SHE wanted to go on the stage. She could dance a little, sing a little and act a little. And she wanted to be an actress. So does everybody, well, nearly everybody, else.

But Jeanette MacDonald wanted to be a big star. A famous, beautiful woman.

And so does everybody, well, nearly everybody, else.

Only Jeanette did. With plenty of odds against her, she did. After ten long, hard years, Jeanette became a famous woman. On a moving picture screen.

And if you're anxious to profit by Jeanette's experience, to avoid the pitfalls, and can take some good solid advice from a red-headed woman who knows, we'll tell you about the rise from a scrawny little Philadelphia High School kid to the recipient of Maurice Chevalier's screen attentions. And isn't that something!

She borrowed her older sister's fur coat and started out. She looked like something that had roamed down out of the mountains in search of food, but no difference.

She thought she was the last word as she waddled (the heavy coat kept getting under her feet) into Ned Wayburn's office and asked for a job. She kept going back and going back until Mr. Wayburn felt there must be some talent beneath the fur robe, and gave her a job. The last row in the chorus.

So the family moved to New York and the career was on. Or off, mostly.

Near the close of the show (note, please, that Jeanette didn't wait until the show was over) she decided to call upon Mr. Dillingham, the great theatrical producer.

She was told he was out of town. It didn't phase her. She inquired at the box-office how to get to Mr. Dillingham's office and the boy was so overcome at such nerve, he told her. Only, he called after her, Mr. Dillingham was out of town.

She climbed the steps and sat in the reception room. He may be in Algiers, but no one could say, in her old age, that she hadn't tried to see Mr. Dillingham. The office boy gave her a black look, but still she sat. After all, it took but two or three weeks to get back from Algiers and she didn't have anything in particular to do, in the daytime, anyway. So, she decided, she'd sit right there. And she sat.

Presently the office boy disappeared and Jeanette tiptoed quietly about. She found a door and turned a knob. It opened. A handsome, gray-haired man sat behind the desk. It was Mr. Dillingham, no place but right there in New York. He sat very still and quiet. And appeared worried.

Jeanette went in. So sorry to be rude, she told him, but she'd been waiting such a long time and after all she had something to sell and he wanted to buy and dear me, did she lay it on thick. She went into detail about how good she was and what she could do and well, really, she wasn't the least bit backward.

AND the producer smiled and seemed amused as Jeanette went on to say she merely wanted a feature part with the agreement she was to understudy the star. And that was every last thing she wanted.

"Could she dance?" he asked. Now mind, could she dance. And could she sing, he wanted to know. And Jeanette nearly dropped dead at the suggestion she wasn't the world's best.

"Well," he smiled, "would she accept a place in the chorus of 'Nightboat,' playing in Rochester." We-ll yes, she would. After one-half second's deliberation, yes, she would. Only that morning he'd had a wire wanting a girl to fill a vacancy and had been sitting there, worrying over whom to send.

So you see. Fools rush in where angels wouldn't be caught. But be foolish every so often. It pays. So off to Rochester dashed our heroine, only to *(continued on next page)*

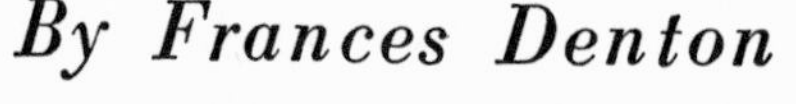

By Frances Denton

(continued from preceding page)

discover there was no vacancy. The girl had decided to stay. Here was a fine how-to-do. But (and jot this down in your notebook, you aspiring young artists) Jeanette stayed and henpecked and tortured everyone until she got a job right in "Nightboat." And while Ernest Torrence, Willie Collier, Sr., Hal Skelly and the White sisters spoke the lines, Jeanette romped in the chorus.

AND then a certain gentleman connected with Mr. Dillingham's office took a great interest in Jeanette. She rehearsed whole plays for him. Took to her singing in earnest and worked diligently. And then one night he suddenly seized her in his arms. He pressed his mouth on hers and held her tightly while he promised much. She struggled free. And knew she must make a decision quickly.

She made it. And it cost her her job in "Nightboat." And it was exactly eight months before she got another bit of work to do.

Jeanette MacDonald thinks it wouldn't be fair to talk about her ten long, weary years of struggle without mentioning that unfortunate episode. She managed to succeed on her own. Her success belongs to herself. And she wouldn't trade that knowledge for five years of life. Now mind, the going was rougher. And slower. But if you think success can't come by being true to oneself, look at Jeanette. In fact, she wants you to. And to know. And she isn't preaching, either.

Days of weary tramping. Weeks of haunting stuffy offices. Trudging, tramping streets. But behind her stood a loyal dad and mother. And now a word to these other mothers and fathers of young world-beaters. If you could know, Jeanette claims, how much it means to have someone believe in you. To stand behind you. When feet are weary and heart is sore, to have someone steal into one's room at night and whisper, "It's all right, honey, I know you're good. I believe in you." It helps.

And then came a chance to try out for Mr. Savage in a show starring Mitzi Hajos, the little Hungarian actress. She rolled her music under her arm, pulled on her galoshes and went. The music was a little high and she asked the accompanist to play it an octave lower. So they began. He playing it exactly as it was written. She stood there alone on the stage and sang. And suddenly she came to the high note and she couldn't make it. She froze in horror. Her voice cracked.

She looked down at Mr. Savage. "Why, I always could take that note," she said. "Well, never mind," he said, "let's see you dance." So Jeanette removed her galoshes and went into her dance. Halfway through she sprawled flat on her face. Slowly she gathered herself up. "I—I think you make me nervous," she said, and went home. The next day he sent for her. She had the part.

AND then Jeanette's father died. And everything depended on her. Somehow her shows kept folding up under her. And then there would be months and months of more tramping.

It was tragic. So often the golden apple was held out, only to be snatched away. She never managed to find herself in a hit.

She took a test for Warner Brothers that was a darb. She looked exactly like old aunt Dinah.

For some reason she had photographed a dark brunette.

She was down to the last dollar of her savings when the chance came to play in "Yes, Yes, Yvette." Jeanette isn't sure whether she was the Yes, Yes, or just Yvette and even if it wasn't the biggest hit in the world her name went up in lights and Maurice Chevalier came to America. Two great events in her life.

Lubitsch was hunting a leading lady for "The Love Parade." He'd seen every one in New York.

And then he came back to Hollywood and began looking at old tests. And there was one Paramount had made of Jeanette and forgotten about.

Her show was in Chicago. He went to see her. "You are too thin," he told her. "You must gain fifteen pounds at least." So Jeanette set about gaining fifteen pounds by worrying herself silly and not sleeping nights. She ate potatoes during the day and then worried away two pounds for fear she wouldn't gain fifteen.

So she left the show and went to a milk farm. She would gain weight or die. And she nearly died.

Appendicitis overcame her and when the once vivacious Miss MacDonald stepped from the train in Hollywood some few weeks later, Herr Lubitsch took one look and gasped, "Mein Gott, I'm ruined," for she weighed exactly twenty-five pounds less than she had in the beginning.

But she drank milk on the set and ate candy. And as the picture progressed she grew rounder. In fact, life as a queen agreed with her. By the end of the picture she was just right.

But something happened during the making of the picture that, she feels, may have hindered her success. Just a little thing, of course, but little things count. So if you do reach the top as Jeanette finally did, watch for them.

The vogue for false eyelashes had just reached Hollywood. And no matter how long or thick one's own lashes might be, false ones had to be worn. No one knew exactly why, but they did. So Jeanette was handed a pair of lashes and put them on. They didn't want her to see the daily rushes. But after several days of suspense she sneaked in, and the sight of herself in those lashes about finished her. They did something strange to her eyes. So without saying a word to anyone, she appeared the next day with her own lashes.

No one noticed a thing. But a day or so later Lubitsch came over and peered at her closely. "Have you done anything to yourself?" he demanded. "You look different." "Why, no," Jeanette assured him, she hadn't.

AGAIN he peered at her closely. "Open your mouth," he commanded. He peered anxiously down her throat. "Huh," he exclaimed, "everything seems to be there."

"Maybe it's the eyelashes," Jeanette ventured. And he hit the ceiling with a bang. She had ruined his picture. But Jeanette knew in her heart the lashes, for her, were wrong. They viewed the rushes together that night and agreed. Be sure you know what is right, and stick to it. But be sure, first.

Now, many an actress has come to the screen from the musical comedy stage and flopped. One or two pictures, and their career on the screen was over. Grace Moore, of the exquisite voice, is an example. Marilyn Miller, another. But Jeanette has gone on to bigger and better pictures. She holds a unique place on the screen. And guards it carefully. It isn't enough to have arrived, you know. A place at the top must be held and fought for, if necessary. And with her far-seeing manager, Bob Richie, Jeanette MacDonald has waged a beautiful battle.

For instance, she has no contract. And won't accept one. And fancy that, in a contract-grabbing land. But her bitter taste of mediocre pictures that followed "The Love Parade" showed her the pitfalls that await young actresses from the musical stage. So she picks and chooses and does a good job of it, if you ask Hollywood. "Monte Carlo," "One Hour With You," and "Love Me Tonight" were hits.

She turned down the lead in "Back Street." It wasn't for her, she felt. Someone could do better than she in the part. And she was right. Irene Dunne was perfect as *Ray Schmidt*.

BENEATH that red-gold hair is a lot of hard, common sense. She has builded this beautiful, glamorous woman from material that was not one bit richer than yours. It's the truth, I promise you.

As a kid she was known as "broomstick legs." "Hey, hey," the kids taunted, "there goes broomstick legs." And instead of Jeanette sticking out a tongue of scorn or weeping crocodile tears, she did something about it. For one thing she took a good long look at her legs in the glass and realized those kids spoke the truth. Her legs were thin and shapeless. From this point she went on. Exercising her legs. Piling up her arithmetic and speller on the floor and practised stepping up and down. Up and down.

Hour after hour she kept after it while the neighborhood kids played hopscotch and had all kinds of fun.

And oh, those legs now.

In the show, "Nightboat," she was actually and truthfully known as the ugly duckling. Gorgeous, golden Jeanette. And again she wasted no tears but did things about it. She learned to walk properly, to do things with her hands. She studied her complexion, her hair.

After her first picture, "The Love Parade," a New York critic wrote he liked the work of this Miss MacDonald, but her buck teeth, long neck and jutting jaw left him cold. Naturally, Jeanette has none of the defects, but instead of flying into a tantrum or simply saying, "Why, the man's crazy," and dismissing it, she thought it over calmly and sanely and went again to see the picture through his eye. And saw exactly why he might reach such comical conclusions.

She hadn't used the proper make-up on her neck and she experimented and thought until she discovered a darker shade of powder on her jaw made it less full.

And again she profited and learned. And thanks him for it.

SHE claims we all look at ourselves with eyes of love. Blind to our defects: That's why Mrs. Brown looks ridiculous in that new hat and never suspects. And why we are apt to look just as comical and imagine we're the last word. View yourself critically, Jeanette says, and not through eyes of self-love.

A famous theatrical producer once told Jeanette a secret of success that works. She's passing it on to you.

"Go to your room and shut the door," he told her. "Stand before the glass and say very earnestly and sincerely to yourself, 'I will be a successful and beautiful woman. I will.' Say it over and over and watch the confidence and poise and assurance that comes stealing over you."

So while the other girls rushed off to the good times Jeanette MacDonald sat by herself in a dingy little dressing-room saying over and over and over, "I will be a beautiful and successful woman." And worked for it.

And so she is.

Eddie goes Spanish

An Irish director, a Brooklyn matador, bulls and beauty and *the* Cantor himself. Wow!

By

Sara Hamilton

WE'RE Spanish. Carramba, Septemba, Octoba. We're Spanish! And try to stop us. We have bulls, big and black, that mean business. And bull fighters? You should see those side-burns. Those apple-green pants with the Christmas tree trimmings, and those pink socks. That's how Spanish we are.

Over on the United Artists lot in Hollywood, Sam Goldwyn is making "The Kid From Spain" with Eddie Cantor as the *Kid*, and even the bulls are flabbergasted. And wait till Spain sees it!

The director is Irish, the cameraman is French, his assistant is Japanese, the still man is German, one villain is Dalmatian, the other is Irish, the comedienne is Polish and the "Kid" himself is Jewish. The bulls came from Mexico and the matador from Brooklyn. And still we go Spanish.

They began with girls. Beautiful senoritas—from Iowa. Out of eighty-five hundred girls they chose a few dozen hot tamales, sewed them up in open-work lace and the business man rush was on. Every man in Hollywood remembered, very suddenly, he had an appointment on the United Artists lot. Good old Sam Goldwyn. Must see Sammy.

Wives phoned stenographers, "Where's my husband? It's seven-thirty and the steak is cold."

"Sorry, Mrs. Brown, he remembered some business on the United Artists lot."

So one thousand steaks grew cold as one thousand papas grew warmer. Such a climate.

They paraded languidly, these beauties in their sewed on lace, up and down staircases, holding little "Eddie Cantor" dolls before them. Their glances lingered and their legs twinkled. Two gentlemen were carried out feet first, one of the villains kept his eye glued on his baby's picture, Bob Young was seized with the heaves (his youth was against him) and Eddie Cantor dictated a letter to his ever-present secretary, "Will take five thousand dollars and not a cent less, Yours truly, Eddie Cantor."

In barged Goldwyn. The parade was still on. "Stop," he screamed. "So. I get the most beautiful Spanish girls ever born in America and what? You cover them with dolls. Dolls. Bah. Here, throw those dolls in the river."

SO the parade continued without the dolls. And six men were removed unconscious. And Eddie Cantor dictated a letter, "Five thousand dollars. Not a cent less. Very truly yours, Eddie Cantor."

Three hours later the prop boy rushed in. Exhausted. A lather of perspiration. "Mr. Goldwyn," he gasped, "Mr. Goldwyn."

"What is it?" he answered. "Quick. Tell me at once."

"I can't do what you asked. I tried but I can't."

"Can't do what?" Goldwyn shrieked. "Don't keep me in suspense."

"I couldn't throw the dolls in the river. There was no water in it." So they paid him thirty dollars a week to stay home. And were in money.

They took off John Miljan's own mustache. And that made him Spanish. They put one on Bob Young. And that made him Spanish. They dressed Eddie in green pants and pink socks.

THEN came Eddie's big scene. The two Spanish villains were to chase Eddie in and out doors, through patios and over balconies. The cameras were set, the doors were marked and the chase was on. Eddie tore and leaped and ran. Five minutes later, he bounded through a door and two carpenters in the room each swallowed four ten-penny nails, in surprise. "Get out of here," Eddie screamed. "You're spoiling my scene."

"What's the matter with you, young fella?" they said.

"Why, I'm making a movie," Eddie replied, suddenly looking around. "Say, where am I?"

"Why, you're on the back lot, in Mary Pickford's prop room," they said. And ten minutes later a weary and sheepish *Kid* found his way back to his set. Where a surprised company waited.

"Where in heaven's name have you been?" the director asked.

"Oh, just up to Pickfair and over to Malibu for a swim," he groaned. And did they kid Eddie?

Ronald Colman and Kay Francis were making "I Have Been Faithful" on the same lot. A feud grew up between this company and Eddie's. For, no sooner did a man from the Colman company put his nose on the "Kid From Spain" set, for a peek

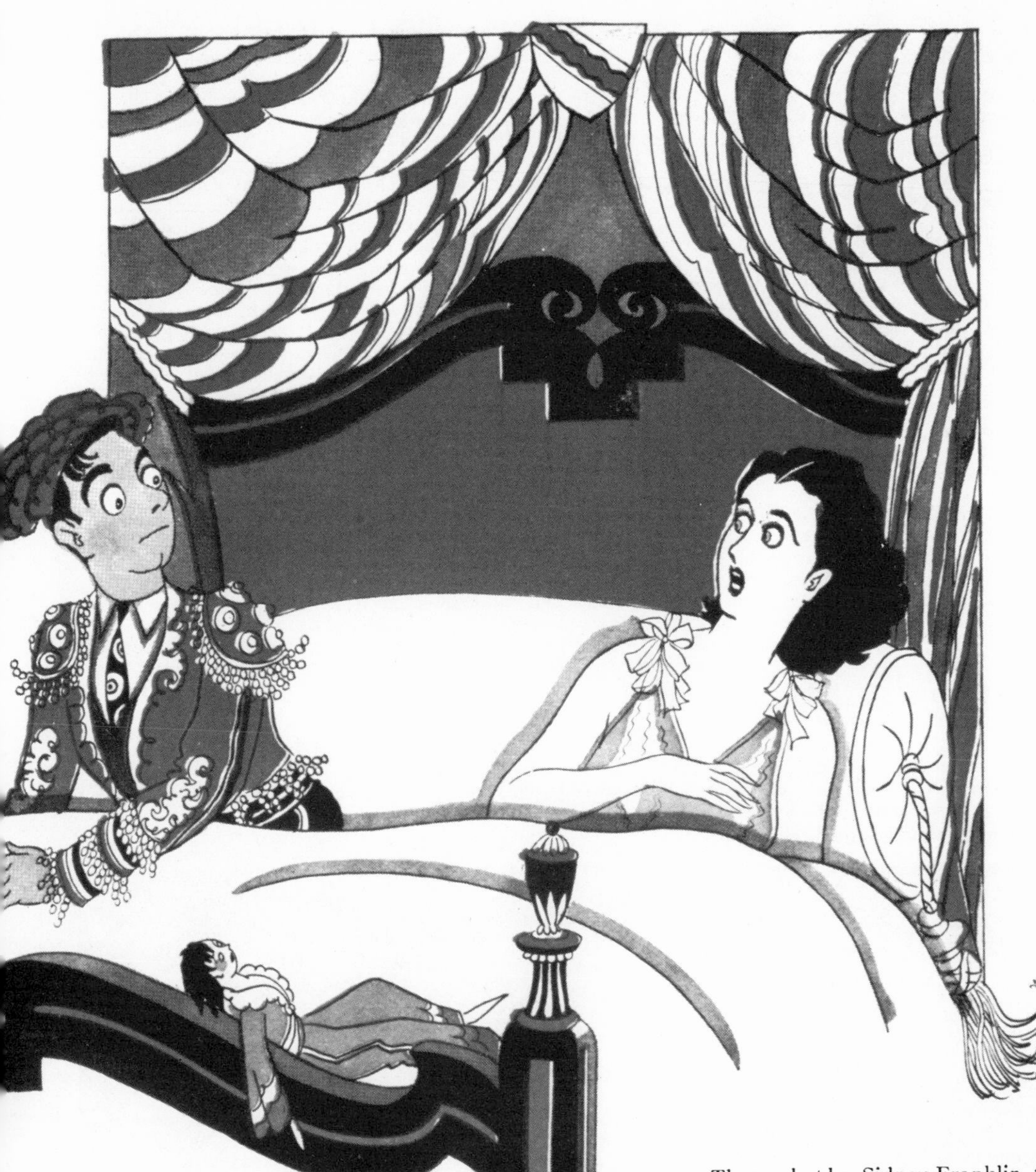

Eddie was gazing bug-eyed at Kay Francis. The stage door opened and there entered Mrs. Cantor and the five Cantor girls. "Papa," the girls screamed. "My heavens look at papa"

ILLUSTRATED BY
VAN ARSDALE

at those girls, than the electricians and cameramen were at him with a rush. And off he went. Usually on his ear. Eddie was vaguely conscious that people were being thrown out, but who or why, he hadn't the least idea. So, during an idle moment, he decided to visit the other set. Serenely he entered the stage door and almost as one they were at him. The director's chair was upturned, lights were overturned, and without knowing why Eddie ran for his life.

Out of the corner of his eye, he spied a bed on the set and made one leap under the covers. Instantly there was a scream. A yell. And there was Eddie gazing bug-eyed at Kay Francis. In the same bed. And to cap the climax, like the third act of a play, the stage door opened and there was Mrs. Cantor and the five Cantor girls.

"Papa," screamed the girls. "My heavens look at papa."

And papa fell back in a swoon.

ALL the time the "Idkay from Ainspay" romped over the lot, and the beautiful Spanish "goils" pranced up and down staircases, they were constantly aware of the menace that did some high-class lurking on the rear lot. Five black Muira bulls. Glaring, red-eyed and snorting. Awaiting the bull-fighting scenes. While outside their pen sat a huge Mexican on guard, with two guns, and a can of "Flit." And no one could decide which glared the fiercest. The Mexican or the bulls.

Visitors were escorted quietly and in awe to a platform, high above the pen, where they looked down upon this mass of horned man-haters. And all left shaking with fear, and duly impressed.

Then, what ho, Sidney Franklin, the famous American matador from Brooklyn, was summoned to Hollywood to add some real color to the affair. The hero of many a bull-fight in Spain, he arrived at ten-thirty in the morning and by two in the afternoon, had gone actor with a bang. He fussed with photographers and make-up men. He worried over his eyebrows and his hair. He had no objection to being slightly gored in places, but he was going to look hot-cha while it was going on. And who could stop him? Practically nobody.

THE director, Leo McCarey, had thought bull, dreamed bull and planned bull, until he couldn't sleep. His nerves were wrecked and torn. Everywhere he looked, there were bulls, snorting, raring, goring. It was awful. He arose from his bed one night and determined to walk until exhausted. He walked as far as the corner and, suddenly, his wife heard a scream. She ran to him. And there he was. Throwing stones and shrieking curses at a "Bull Durham" sign on the other side of the street. While a large bull glared down at him. He ran a fever for days.

Then Franklin was taken to see his future playmates, the bulls. All the cast, as well as writers, reporters and publicity men, went along to get his reaction.

Franklin walked up to the gate keeper, spoke a few words in Spanish and, without a moment's hesitation, entered the pen. Two writers fell off the other side of the platform, Lyda Roberti let out a shriek, Eddie swallowed his huge wad of gum and could only gurgle noises, a publicity man ran for Goldwyn, a reporter lost his balance and fell toward the pen when lo, a nail caught him firmly by the pants and there he hung, directly over the bulls. Someone called the fire department. It was awful. A panic, nothing short.

While, down in the pen, *(continued on next page)*

(continued from preceding page)

Franklin paused to gaze at his eyebrows in a pocket mirror (he was sure they wouldn't photograph well) and uttering a low wail of "toom, toom, toom, toom," for all the world like a jungle drum, stood in the pen completely surrounded by bulls. "Toom, toom, toom, toom," the low cry went on and, suddenly, the fiercest bull was advancing. Head down. Coming slowly at him. "Toom, toom, toom, toom," he was coming.

He lowered his head, the deadly horns sweeping from side to side. He reached Franklin and leaned over tenderly while Sidney gently scratched his back.

The sun shone down brightly the next day, as Eddie and Lyda Roberti stood on an old Spanish balcony and made violent love. Eddie had kissed until he was purple in the face. And still the director wasn't satisfied. Over and over, he took the giggling Roberti in his Spanish arms and made Spanish love that would surprise any Spaniard living. And suddenly he saw them down there below. Two of his daughters. Gazing, pop-eyed and open-mouthed, at papa.

He leaned over the balcony, and called to them softly. "Listen, children," he said, "don't tell mama. Papa's got to work for his living, you know."

THE next scene called for Eddie to be tied on a pole, with wires, and swung directly over the bulls' pen. Everything was set. The lights were set, the camera placed and the director called, "Cameras, go," when Eddie called, "Stop, I forgot something." His secretary came running. "Listen," said Eddie, still hanging to the pole, "did I say five thousand dollars in that letter or five hundred? Put it five thousand comma and not a cent less, yours very truly, Eddie Cantor."

And the shooting continued.

Finally the day of days arrived. The big bull-fight where Eddie fight-a-de-bull-a. He arrived in a suit completely covered with Christmas tree trimmings. Eddie's youngest took one look and ran home to hang up her stocking. You could almost hear Santa and his reindeer in the distance. Two Spanish clad attendants stood at the gates that opened to the bull pen. And, inside the arena, waiting for friend bull, stood Eddie. His cape ready. His banjo-eyes fairly popping.

THE grandstand was crowded with spectators, senoritas in lace mantillas and Spanish lads in tight pant-illas. The place was a riot of color, while beneath the surface ran a tremor of fear. After all, a bull is a bull. Even in Hollywood.

And now, everything was ready. The cameras were placed within a strong stockade at one end of the arena. On top, just out of reach, sat the director.

The signal was given. The gates were opened. The sound of beating hoofs could be heard. The bull was coming. And then. There he was. Through the open gates he plunged. Eddie feebly waved his cape and turned a bilious green. On came the bull. Suddenly it stopped and took one look at Eddie. And never budged another inch. No sir, move he wouldn't. The sight of Eddie had completely licked him.

Sidney Franklin, the brave matador, stood outside the fence and poked him with a pole. Still he stood. Then Franklin, the hero of Spain, stood outside the arena and calmly shot pebbles at the bull, with a sling shot. Oh, if Spain could only have seen that. And still the bull was either too overcome or paralyzed at the sight, to move. So they led him away.

A new bull was tried. The plunging hoofs sounded harder this time. And then, there he was. In the arena. A huge tuft of red hair, like a grotesque wig, grew out from between his horns. Eddie took one look. "My Gawd," he screamed, "it's Harpo Marx." And ran for his life, with Harpo after him.

Through the safety, he tore. And through the safety, the bull tore. Snorting and bellowing. Now, he was out of the arena. People were screaming. The assistant director took one look and made for the Hollywood hills. He isn't back yet. Someone ran for Goldwyn. Castro, a brave little Mexican matador, waved his cape. The bull plunged. And missed him by an inch. And then it spotted Eddie half way over the fence and straight for the rear of Eddie, he made. There was a loud roar. And the "Kid from Spain" suddenly took an unexpected and unplanned journey through the air and landed, over the fence, in the fat Spanish lap of an extra woman in the top row.

THE gate boy ran screaming to the director. "Say, a bull just now checked out the front gate. Shall I mark him off the payroll?"

While Eddie lay gasping and gurgling, in the grandstand. Dictating a letter. "Ten thousand or nothing. Yours truly, Eddie Cantor."

And thus we go Spanish. Castoroila, Hunkadoria, Adios!

DEC.

☆ ***THE BIG BROADCAST—Paramount***

DIAL in on this one for an evening of fun, with radio stars who go movie in a big way.

Stuart Erwin, as an oil man from Texas, and Bing Crosby, as himself, are two despondent Romeos who decide to end it all, only to be rescued by a girl, Leila Hyams. Stu buys a defunct broadcasting station and arranges the big broadcast with the Boswell Sisters, Kate (the moon comes over the mountain) Smith, the Vincent Lopez band, Donald Novis, Arthur Tracy, the Mills Brothers, Cab Calloway with his "Minnie, the Moocher," and finally Bing.

Sharon Lynne is grand as the fickle dancer, and if you don't grow hysterical at Burns and Allen, you're hopeless. The story's pretty weak, but the music's grand. Are you listenin'?

"BIG BROADCAST, THE"—PARAMOUNT.—From the story "Wild Waves" by William Ford Manley. Screen play by George Marion, Jr. Directed by Frank Tuttle. The cast: *Leslie McWhinney*, Stuart Erwin; *Bing Hornsby*, Bing Crosby; *Anita Rogers*, Leila Hyams; *Mona Lowe*, Sharon Lynne; *Clapsaddle*, George Barbier; and the stars of the radio: Burns and Allen; Kate Smith; The Mills Brothers; The Boswell Sisters; Arthur Tracy (The Street Singer); Vincent Lopez and his orchestra; Cab Calloway and his orchestra; Donald Novis.

DEC.

Salesmanship love. George M. Cohan puts over a big idea with Claudette Colbert in "The Phantom President." "How's it for a little ride in the country, baby?" asks George with a slight leer

DEC.

RACKETY RAX—Fox

HERE is Victor McLaglen again in the kind of roughneck comedy that made him famous. It's an utterly nonsensical plot, about a big shot racketeer who buys a college so he can have his own football team and cut in on the football racket. There are some good dance numbers by a chorus of cuties and some sprightly tunes. Good for a lot of laughs on a dull winter's evening.

"RACKETY RAX"—Fox.—From the story by Joel Sayre. Screen play by Ben Markson and Lou Breslow. Directed by Alfred Werker. The cast: *Knucks McGloin*, Victor McLaglen; *Voine*, Greta Nissen; *Doris*, Nell O'Day; *Speed Kendall*, Arthur Pierson; *Counsellor Sultsfeldt*, Alan Dinehart; *Mike Dumphy*, Allen Jenkins; *Dutch*, Vincent Barnett; *Mrs. McGloin*, Marjorie Beebe; *Sister Carrie*, Esther Howard; *Tonsilitis*, Ivan Linow; *Gilotti*, Stanley Fields; *Brick Gilligan*, Ward Bond; *Dr. Vanderveer*, Eric Mayne; *McGloin's Bodyguards*, Joe Brown, John Keyes; *Coaches*, Alonzo P. Stagg, Howard Jones; also famous football players.

1933

JUST AS A BACKSTAGE MUSICAL, *The Broadway Melody,* had initiated the first craze for this film genre in 1929, *42nd Street* opened the floodgates for a torrent of musicals that splashed across America's screens during the 1930's. By the end of 1933, RKO had teamed Fred Astaire and Ginger Rogers in *Flying down to Rio;* Paramount starred Mae West in two saucy comedies-with-song, *She Done Him Wrong* and *I'm No Angel;* and Nelson Eddy made an obscure screen debut in MGM's first post-moratorium musical, *Broadway to Hollywood.* Bing Crosby, who had impressed movie audiences in 1932's *The Big Broadcast,* was raised by Paramount to top stardom in *College Humor* and *Too Much Harmony.* The Depression blues were soon being whistled and danced away by myriad stars whose skill and charms still delight audiences today: Shirley Temple, Alice Faye, Grace Moore, Irene Dunne, Eleanor Powell, Ray Bolger, and Judy Garland among them.

M. K.

JAN.

☆ ***THE KID FROM SPAIN—Goldwyn-United Artists***

LAVISH, nonsensical—with the loveliest chorus of girls Hollywood has produced—and topped by an utterly ridiculous fight between Eddie Cantor and a bull, "The Kid From Spain" is the culmination of musicals on the screen.

From the point of sheer beauty it makes Producer Sam Goldwyn the Florenz Ziegfeld of the movies.

There's a typical musical comedy plot. Eddie, after being implicated in a bank robbery, is forced to flee the country and is introduced as *Don Sebástian the Second*, the greatest bull-fighter of all time, so he has to make good on his title. From the opening scenes in the girls' dormitory to the last mad shots in the bull-ring, Eddie is always in trouble and always triumphs. He was never funnier nor more peppy, and his songs are a riot.

Second to Eddie is Lyda Roberti as a senorita. She's a grand comedienne. The rest of the cast—Robert Young, Ruth Hall, John Miljan and a dozen others—help along the fun while each new and madder adventure awaits Eddie. Sidney Franklin, the American bull-fighter, furnishes a few thrilling scenes as the film's only serious note, a genuine bull-fight. Leo McCarey did a grand job of directing.

Here is the season's opportunity to laugh your head off.

"KID FROM SPAIN, THE"—GOLDWYN-UNITED ARTISTS.—From the story by William Anthony McGuire, Bert Kalmar and Harry Ruby. Directed by Leo McCarey. The cast: *Eddie*, Eddie Cantor; *Rosalie*, Lyda Roberti; *Ricardo*, Robert Young; *Anita*, Ruth Hall; *Pancho*, John Miljan; *Alonzo Gomez*, Noah Beery; *Pedro*, J. Carroll Naish; *Crawford*, Robert Emmett O'Connor; *Jose*, Stanley Fields; *Gonzales*, Paul Porcasi; *Dalmores*, Julian Rivero; *Martha Oliver*, Theresa Maxwell Conover; *Dean*, Walter Walker; *Red*, Ben Hendricks, Jr.; *Sidney Franklin*, Sidney Franklin.

JAN.

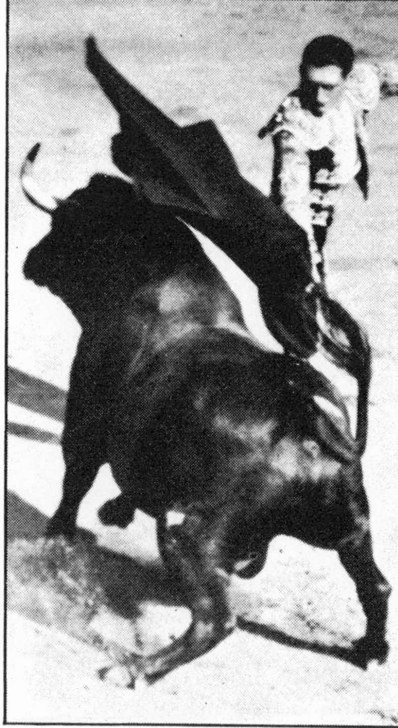

That serious bull-fight scene in "The Kid From Spain" is the real McCoy. Sidney Franklin, one of the world's great bull-fighters, visited his friend Eddie Cantor in Hollywood and stayed to make a thrilling sequence in Eddie's uproarious new picture

JAN.

The three girls who appeared at the switchboard in "The Big Broadcast" (can you imagine having operators hmmmmm in your ear like that?) were not the Boswell Sisters. They are singers known to radio listeners as "Major, Sharp and Minor." Their real names as Josephine Riley, Anita Nieto and Barbara Johnstone.

JAN.

M. P. S., WEST POINT, NEB.—The three lads who were known as "The Rhythm Boys" in Paul Whiteman's picture, "King of Jazz," were Crosby, Renker and Barris. Yes, our own Bing Crosby made his singing début in that picture. What a long way he has come since then. Joan Crawford, James Murray, House Peters and Creighton Hale had the main leads in "Rose Marie."

JAN.

A. T., BROOKLYN, N. Y.—Oh, yes, Fifi Dorsay has gone back into pictures after a successful vaudeville tour. Her latest picture is "The Girl from Calgary." It's the story of a girl from the wide open spaces, who, with the aid of a good press-agent, lands on the Great White Way. I won't tell you any more. See it for yourself. And does Fifi sing in it? Oo-la-la! How she puts over those tunes, "Misbehaving Feet," "Comme ca va" and "Maybe, Perhaps."

JAN.

A triple treat is the pet comedy, "The Big Broadcast," with screen, stage and radio names. Bing Crosby is song bird and lover romancing with Leila Hyams. Stuart Erwin also clicks. In its array of "air" stars the picture makes the networks look sad and steals a march on television

Inaugurating a NEW DEAL in ENTERTAINMENT! . . . .
WARNER BROS. set the pace with the ENTERTAINMENT MIRACLE of 1933—"42nd Street"... Super-drama—super-spectacle! Two mighty shows in one!...Gripping story of playgirls and payboys... Packed with love-thrills and wonderful music... Gorgeous pageant of beauty pulsating with passionate rhythm... Filled with surprises!... The Greatest Show of 1933!
42ND STREET
14 STARS
WARNER BAXTER
BEBE DANIELS
GEORGE BRENT
RUBY KEELER
UNA MERKEL
DICK POWELL
GINGER ROGERS
GUY KIBBEE
NED SPARKS
GEORGE E. STONE
EDDIE NUGENT
ALLEN JENKINS
ROBERT McWADE
H. B. WALTHALL
and
200 GIRLS
Directed by LLOYD BACON
WARNER BROS'. Sensational Musical Hit!
Coming to your theatre soon... Don't miss it—it's going to be the most talked-about picture of the year

The Lure of New York Stage

HERE is something that, it is said, has never appeared upon the screen before. It will be shown in Warner Brothers' production of back stage theatrical life—"42nd Street."

The new feature you will see in this picture is a series of three revolving stages, each of which is really a large disc, turning in opposite directions. The cameras are mounted on the outer disc and, of course, travel with it.

As the dancers go through their movements, the effect is dizzying and breath-taking—one finds himself gripping the seat ahead for support.

Above we see one of the big dance numbers of the show.

Life Set to Music and Drama

Photo by Stagg

Those two cute girls with the lights turned full upon them are Ginger Rogers and Una Merkel, whose parts call for a place in the chorus.

This is one of those scenes in the production for which highly technical knowledge is necessary.

So directors stand back while a dance expert—the man with out-pointed finger—puts the hoofers through special dance steps.

And looming over all are the figures of Dick Powell, Warner Baxter, Ginger Rogers, Bebe Daniels and George Brent—the major characters in the rhythm, the laughter, the music and the heartaches of "42nd Street."

MAR.

42ND STREET —Warners

RUBY KEELER'S début as a picture personality—and, make no mistake about it, a new star is born. As the country girl who comes to Broadway and steps in at the last minute for a musical queen, she makes good in a big way. Almost an out-and-out musical, with one number at least sufficient to stop any show. Excellent performances by Warner Baxter, Guy Kibbee, George Brent, Bebe Daniels, and Ginger Rogers.

"42ND STREET"—WARNERS.—From the novel by Bradford Ropes. Screen play by Rian James and James Seymour. Directed by Lloyd Bacon. The cast: *Dorothy Brock*, Bebe Daniels; *Julian Marsh*, Warner Baxter; *Pat Denning*, George Brent; *Lorraine Fleming*, Una Merkel; *Peggy*, Ruby Keeler; *Abner Dillon*, Guy Kibbee; *Barry*, Ned Sparks; *Billy Lawler*, Dick Powell; *Waring*, Lyle Talbot; *Ann*, Ginger Rogers; *Mac Elroy*, Allen Jenkins; *The Actor*, Henry B. Walthall; *Terry*, Edward J. Nugent; *Jerry*, Harry Akst; *Leading Man*, Clarence Nordstrom; *Jones*, Robert McWade; *Andy Lee*, George E. Stone; *Al Dubin*, Al Dubin; *Harry Warren*, Harry Warren.

JUN.

HAIL, "42ND STREET"!

"42nd Street" with its abundance of entertaining glamour, fairly picked me up out of my seat and knocked me down for the "count."

I was so utterly thrilled with its beautiful settings and clever routines that I stayed to see it twice. After the picture came to a dramatic close for the second time, I was brought back to earth by the realization that there were gnawing pains of hunger inside. How happy I'd have been if I could have nibbled upon the top of the seat in front of me and then, appeased, lose myself in the glory of a third performance! Cheers for "42nd Street!" Let's have more like it.

ETHELDREDA MCDONOUGH, Pittsburgh, Pa.

Just recently I saw "42nd Street" and did I enjoy it! There's a picture fast moving and entertaining. When you watched that chorus backstage you could readily see that those acting the parts had done some heavy rehearsing themselves. Warner Baxter made a director who will make some girls hesitate before they decide on being chorines. I never dreamed of how hard such a life could be. My eyes are opened now, thanks to Warner Bros.

IDA J. AUER, Chicago, Ill.

A new picture personality, a new star born and does she twinkle? Verily, from her scintillating eyes, to the tips of her dance mad feet—*she twinkles.* Ruby Keeler in "42nd Street." We don't wonder that Al Jolson sings *like that*, with Ruby for an inspiration. Hail Queen Ruby!

MRS. MARVIN M. GRAY, Palmyra, Mo.

MAY

International

If the gods had descended on Manhattan, there couldn't have been more excitement than when the "42nd Street" Special pulled into Grand Central Station. Seated, left to right, some of the famous cargo: Eleanor Holm, former Olympic swim champ; Joe E. Brown; Leo Carrillo; Bette Davis; Tom Mix (of course his equine pal came along, too); Laura La Plante. Those lasses in white in the back-ground, are chorines. And since no party is complete without a stowaway, Doris McMahon (behind Tom Mix) was found hiding in the baggage car after the train left San Bernardino. They let her stay on. Wouldn't you?

In "42nd Street," Ruby Keeler, who heads this line under George Stone's coaching, plays a chorus girl who crashes through to fame in one show. "42nd Street" was Ruby's first film—and what a hit! She went over those movie barriers like the British fliers over Mt. Everest

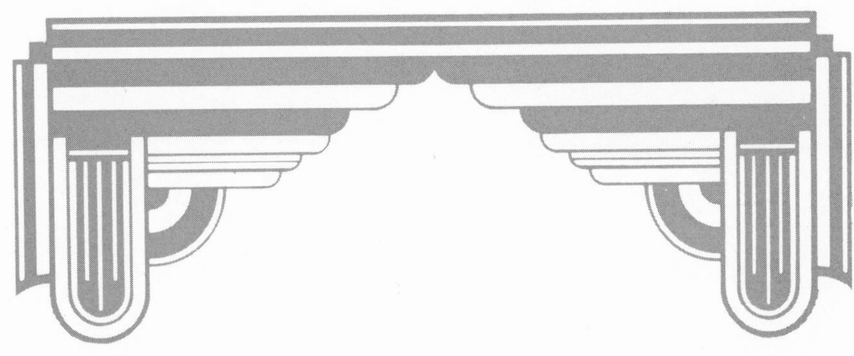

UNTIL THE BIRTH OF TALKIES, America's better popular songs almost invariably emanated from Broadway. Because of the restrictions of long-distance travel in those days, however, only a small portion of the American public had the opportunity to hear a song being introduced by its creator in New York, or perhaps in a later road tour. By the late 1920's, most songs were first heard by the mass public on the radio or phonograph records, with the sale of sheet music a widespread practice as well.

With the advent of talkies the entire situation was dramatically altered, for within weeks audiences throughout the nation had the common experience of witnessing the same star introduce a song in precisely the same mounting, and performed in a movie palace of unrestrained opulence and comfort.

With over seventy musical films produced in 1929 alone and isolated songs interpolated into the action of numerous nonmusicals, the industry's search for new and better songs was insatiable. Having guarantees of easy working conditions and fat salaries, the composers began a westward trek that resulted in a shift of origin of the nation's hit tunes from the east to the west coast, all within one year.

Suddenly the market blossomed for the purchase of movie-originated records, and to guide its readers, PHOTOPLAY introduced in its October, 1929, issue a review of some of the latest discs (and often piano rolls) from films. This historically important feature lasted for a year, until the public decided it had had enough songs in its pictures. With the rise of the musical moratorium in 1930, the column was abandoned. As an interesting feature we have grouped all the record reviews into one final chapter.

M. K.

Music of the Films

Photoplay's Record Review Department

NOW that the day of the theme song is upon us, now that Tin Pan Alley has taken up its residence in Hollywood, there is a new angle of pictures to be considered, studied and reported on.

Fans all over the country are dancing to tunes from "Fox Movietone Follies," "On With the Show," and "Hollywood Revue of 1929.' Out in Gering, Nebraska, and up in Thetford, Vermont, they are singing "Hang on to Me" from "Marianne"—and other numbers from other talkie hits.

Daily, the makers of phonograph records and piano rolls are adding more numbers from current talking pictures to their bulletins. Daily, movie-goers—and non-movie-goers for that matter—are demanding their favorite songs from the talkies recorded for their phonographs and player pianos.

As a matter of service to readers, PHOTOPLAY *will from now on review all such records and music rolls. Just as we try each month to give you a complete and fair estimate of all pictures which have been released to date, we will try to give you a summary of all recorded versions of tunes from these pictures.*

We want this department to serve as a guide—to enable you more easily to find melodies which you like, played and sung by artists who please you.

When you want to know whether your favorite dance tune has been recorded by Victor or Brunswick or Columbia, or whether Ampico or Duo-Art has included your pet sentimental ditty among its newest numbers, turn to the Record Review Department of PHOTOPLAY.

Brunswick 4445. Fox trot

"Am I Blue" from "On with the Show"

This is one of the most popular numbers yet produced by the talkies. Libby Holman sings it and—well—this reviewer confesses to an unconquerable weakness for Miss Holman's particular vocal idiosyncrasies! We're "that way" about Miss Holman's voice, that's all.

The other side of the record presents "Moanin' Low," another of Libby Holman's torrid tunes—and not to be sniffed at either.

Columbia 194091 and 148569

"Just You, Just Me," from "Marianne"

Cliff Edwards proves that he can discard his bag of vocal tricks and still be a headliner. Except for one brief passage where he outmoans the saxophone, Ukulele Ike sings this "straight" in a sweet and insinuating tenor. You'll want to play this one often.

"Hang on to Me" from "Marianne"

A clever number with a patter chorus that is going to be sung with innovations wherever three or four of the brothers and sisters get together. This is a more typical Ukulele Ike number, and Cliff romps through it in great style. No one knows better than Mrs. Edwards' boy, Cliff, just how and when to take liberties with the rhythm of a song.

Columbia 148788 and 148789

"Am I Blue" from "On with the Show"

Played by Ben Selvin and his orchestra this makes a verra, verra warm dance number.

(continued on next page)

Herb Nacio Brown and Anita Page are "Singin' in the Rain" in M.-G.-M.'s "Hollywood Revue." Herb can sing in the bathtub or any place else that suits his fancy and there'll be no complaints—for he authored "Wedding of the Painted Doll" the smash hit from "The Broadway Melody," and "Singin' in the Rain" from the "Hollywood Revue"

(continued from preceding page)

There is some mean saxophone and brass work which raises it out of the average dance record class. A vocal refrain by a gentleman with nice diction but not much temperature.

"My Song of the Nile" from "Drag"

Not much could be done with this song, anyway. It's one of those one-two-three waltzes that simply won't be jogged out of the even tempo of its ways. Ben Selvin does his best with an undistinguished tune—and the vocal soloist enunciates even more clearly—but all to no avail. Incidentally, it comes as a shock to be able to understand the words of a song without putting one's head inside the machine and repeating the record three times.

Columbia 148672 and 148673
"Do I Know What I'm Doing" from "Why Bring That Up"

This is not a Waters song—there's not a blush in the whole thing—but it's a tuneful ditty with a come-hither rhythm. Anyway, Ethel Waters could sing the "Pilgrims' Chorus" and make it sound hotter than "Shake That Thing" if she took a notion. Besides Ethel, there's a tricky accompaniment which, alone, would put this on the prize list.

"Sho - Sho - Bogie - Boo" from "Why Bring That Up"

This is in the coon-shouter idiom and right up Waters' alley. And there's a saxophone break that shakes your shoulders and prickles your scalp.

Ampico 70213F
"Fox Movietone Follies": Selections: Fox trot

Featuring the four best numbers from the Fox Follies: "That's You, Baby," "Breakaway," "Walking With Susie," "Big City Blues." A well-arranged medley played by those two exceedingly popular young men, Victor Arden and Adam Carroll. You can dance to this.

Ampico 211941E. Fox trot
"Do Something" from "Nothing But the Truth"

Helen Kane's first talkie number, divorced from Helen and recorded for the Ampico by Harry Shipman and Victor Lane. There is not enough variety in the Lane and Shipman piano recording and it registers as decidedly monotonous after the snappy Fox Follies medley

Duo-Art 0655. Waltz
"I'll Always Be In Love With You" from "Syncopation"

A number with a swinging rhythm and a catchy melody, played with nice shading by Frank Milne. It's a good dance and song roll and will make both the hoofers and the crooners of the family happy.

Duo-Art 104335. Song roll with words
"Pagan Love Song" from "The Pagan"

Watch out—we're going to get excited! This reviewer listened to a Duo-Art organ recording of the overworked waltz ballad from "The Pagan"—and almost bought an organ just for this one number. But we couldn't fool the Duo-Art people into accepting cigar coupons for new bills. Lew White plays it—and in our opinion Lew can lick both the Jesse Crawfords with one hand tied behind his back.

Duo-Art 0654. Fox trot
"Breakaway" from "Fox Movietone Follies"

This fast-rhythm fox trot is played by Gene Kerwin in a snappy manner with plenty of variety. If you like the piece you'll like this recording.

Duo-Art 104355. Song roll with words
"Walkin' with Susie" from "Fox Movietone Follies"

One of those slow, lazy fox trots for the boys and girls who like to take their dancing easy. Gene Waldron gets some novel effects, including a nice change of key in the last chorus.

Duo-Art 0656. Fox trot
"That's You, Baby" from "Fox Movietone Follies"

To our mind, this is the catchiest of the three Fox Follies numbers recorded by Duo-Art. It has more lilt than the others. As played by Ralph Addison it makes a danceable dance and a singable song—and that's about as much as you can ask of a music roll. Addison pounds a mean piano and knows his Broadway idiom.

Duo-Art 104365. Ballad
"Little Pal" from "Little Pal"

A typical Jolson heartbreaker and "Sonny Boy's" successor. Gene Waldron does well by this ballad—but to us a Jolson song without Jolson is just so much misguided emotion.

Duo-Art 104375. Ballad
"Why Can't You?" from "Little Pal"

This recording by Thompson Kerr is not quite up to the preceding one—it rather drags in spots. However, there is a nice variation in tempo, which helps. We liked especially the parts where Kerr double-times.

Duo-Art 0659. Fox trot
"Do Something" from "Nothing But the Truth"

A corking arrangement and a snappy rendition by Frank Milne. Milne gets the most out of the rhythm of the piece and adds a little of his own. There are some swell breaks. Nothing we like so much as a good break, rhythmical or otherwise—but most good little breaks—rhythmical or otherwise—have gone to Hollywood.

Victor 22041-A and 22041-B
"Low-Down Rhythm" from "Hollywood Revue of 1929"

This is not so low-down. In fact it rates as one of the best canned tunes made in Hollywood so far. It's one of those irresistible fast-time fox trots with a mad and misbehaving rhythm. Played by the High Hatters who are about as hot a jazz factory as you can find anywhere. We liked the saxophone, banjo, piano and Mr. Frank Luther, who bursts into song.

"Got a Feelin' for You" from "Hollywood Revue of 1929"

Another prize number from M.-G.-M.'s super-revue snappily recorded by the High Hatters and Frank Luther. There's more of that banjo in this one, and a muted saxophone. Waiter, bring me a muted saxophone—double portion.

Victor 22057-A and 22057-B
"Orange Blossom Time" from "Hollywood Revue of 1929"

Sung by Johnny Marvin, with a saxophone solo by Andy Sannella. The combination of Marvin's voice and Sannella's sax (sax, we said) deserves a better vehicle than this sickly sweet melody.

"Singin' in the Rain" from "Hollywood Revue of 1929"

Marvin is interrupted this time by the Frohne Sisters Quartet.

Whether it's the piece, which is pretty tin-panny or the Sisters Frohne themselves, we don't know, but they reminded us a lot of the old man who used to cry "Ragsoliron" up and down the street in piercing and monotonous tones.

The BIRTH *of the* Theme Song

A musician tells how music came to the films and what it did for the shadows on the screen

By

Maurice Fenton

THE Theme Song has arrived. Further, it looks as though it intends to stay awhile. Why not? The mystery is: Why so late in the day?

The Theme Song is described as a special melody designed to breathe the feeling of a particular picture.

In other words, we are given to understand that from now on "seeing" and "hearing" are hooked up.

If this is so we ask, "What of it?" for under the circumstances it was high time the Theme Song was recognized and given a name. For when Dolores del Rio had made "Ramona," and nobody was too wild about it, Emil Hensen, the publicity man responsible, scratched his thatch in an endeavor to stir up inspiration.

The idea of a special song struck him. What he wanted was a special melody, to special words, titled after the picture, dedicated to Dolores and to be used with the showing in such a way as to become part of it. He 'phoned a music publishing house to send around a man to take his order.

The end of that was Wayne and Gilbert's song, "Ramona," which gets much of the credit for the million and a half brought in by the picture.

Of "Ramona," they say that it was the first of the Theme Songs, that it started the intimate combination of music from the orchestra pit and action in the story. As a matter of fact it was the forerunner of a new phase of something as old as the stage itself.

When the light operas of Vienna centered themselves around a waltz theme it was the same thing, and as soon as the first flickering comedies were shown, it was to the accompaniment of music supplied by pianists.

AS the theaters were enlarged the orchestras did little more than broaden the idea of the pianists. As early as "The Wrecker" of Rex Beach, deliberate attempts to harmonize accompaniment and drama were made.

When the special score came into vogue, with Dr. Hugo Reisenfeld in the front rank, movie fans, who scorned the idea of sitting through an opera, were becoming familiar with operatic excerpts without knowing it.

An early production of "Tosca" used as much of Puccini's music as could be fitted to its length. Each of the characters in "Way Down East" had a musical line intended to be typical of it.

When the movies threatened to start talking there were rattlings throughout the world. First came the shorts. Opera singers and musical comedy stars did their turns. Then Warners stepped out with "The Jazz Singer," George Jessel in the middle of it. Plans were held up. Four songs were required and Jessel could not see his way clear to put these in. So it was decided to approach Al Jolson—Mammy singer par excellence. Jolson could do what contracts forbade Jessel to undertake and the effect was instantaneous.

BY that time the lesson had been learned. Music and action were inseparable. If there was a scarcity of material on the open market, the songs must be specially made.

So three Mammy-makers signed contracts. In Hollywood they found themselves caged up. They chewed their nails, solved innumerable cross word puzzles and punched their private time clock. But not a song came out.

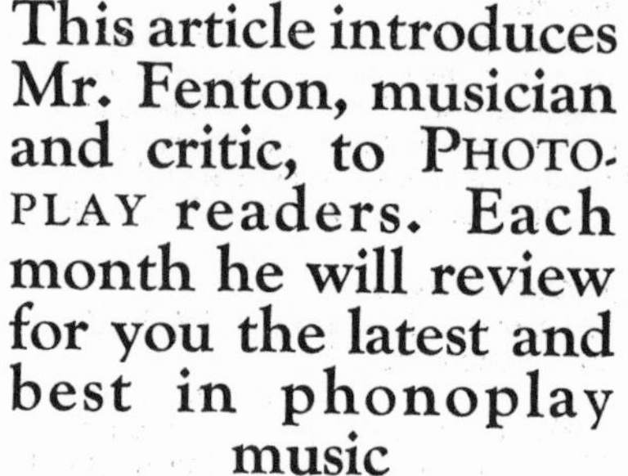

This article introduces Mr. Fenton, musician and critic, to PHOTOPLAY readers. Each month he will review for you the latest and best in phonoplay music

"They'll soon settle down," producers said.

They seemed to be settling, but not a melody was turned in. Then occurred the scandal. One fine morning the birds-who-wouldn't-sing failed to check in. The next morning they were still A. W. O. L. And the next.

THEN headquarters received a clue and sleuths mounted to the upper story of a hotel. Through a closed door issued snatches of song. The door was forced.

One was at, and another on the piano. The third was scribbling at a table. Over piles of cigarette butts the invaders demanded an explanation. They got it . . . A couple of sure-fire song hits and a cartload of ideas!

(continued on next page)

(continued from preceding page)

With the selling of composers down the river other questions came up. It is all very well to have a song, but what to do with it once it is being sung. What about the fans who would want to try it over on their pianos?

RADIO! If politicians and toothpaste mixers found it worth while broadcasting their stuff, why not have the made-to-order songs flung far and wide—by getting into the broadcasting business?

So, among others, Warners acquire Witmark's and Paramount get half of the Columbia Broadcasting System—and the movement is only beginning.

Naturally, *contretemps* arises. Music publishers have quaint attachments to bearded old ditties. "My Rosary." "Silver Threads Among the Gold." "When You Come to the End of a Perfect Day." . . . They love these veterans because they are the backbone of their business. But the new masters have new notions. "Scrap everything composed before last Wednesday!"

Which seems to have brought us to the point we have been trying to reach. The fatherly interest which is growing in the breasts of the gentlemen in charge of the canned music factories.

"If these are go-getter songs, we'll get them."

And they have.

NOW no talking machine company dreams of issuing a monthly list without its section devoted to the songs made by and for the Movies. Coming eastward, after finishing a picture, actors take time to visit the laboratories. There experts run them up against a familiar looking mike and bid them yodel. The stars are beginning to twinkle orthophonically. What next?

So far as we are concerned, just this: Without malice aforethought, we propose to survey this output.

Here Are a Few of the Records Available from Recent and Current Hits

THE BROADWAY MELODY

The Broadway Melody	**Ben Selvin and Orchestra**	**Columbia 1738-D**
	Charles King	**Victor 21964**
The Wedding of the Painted Doll	**Harold Lambert**	**Brunswick 4380**
	Leo Reisman	**Columbia 1780-D**
	Charles King	**Victor 21964**

Should be familiar by this time. The advantage here is that you get both for the price of one from Victor.

COQUETTE

Coquette	**Paul Oliver**	**Victor 21898**
	Pete Woolery	**Columbia 1805-D**

Could never make out exactly what this had to do with the show but it goes over well and the records are about equal.

CHRISTINA

Christina	**The Columbians**	**Columbia 1817-D**
	Lewis James	**Victor 21962**

"Make my dreams come true, Darling I love you" type of innocuous waltz. When waltzes are used for this purpose they must be pretty good ones. Christina has a long way to go, poor girl.

DRAG

My Song of the Nile	**Melody Three**	**Victor 22028**
	The Columbians	**Columbia 1817-D**

A waltz again. One up on the last, however. Both well played.

THE DESERT SONG

One Alone	**Richard Crooks**	**Victor 1370**
	Don Voorhees	**Columbia 1824-D**

Lasted almost a lifetime on Broadway and probably deserved it. Crooks does it to perfection.

EVANGELINE

Evangeline	**Andy Senella**	**Columbia 1846-D**
	Paul Oliver	**Victor 22011**
	Harold Lambert	**Brunswick 4369**

From this we will pass on, without further ado, to:

INNOCENTS OF PARIS

Louise	**Dick Robertson**	**Brunswick 4367**
	Maurice Chevalier	**Victor 21918**
	Paul Whiteman	**Columbia 1819-D**

Felt as if we were handling stolen goods when we played with these. Where have we heard something like it before?

IS EVERYBODY HAPPY?

I'm the Medicine Man for the Blues / Wouldn't It Be Wonderful	**Ted Lewis and His Band**	**Columbia 1882-D**

Typical Ted Lewis moaning and well recorded.

ON WITH THE SHOW

Am I Blue?	**Ethel Waters**	**Columbia 1837-D**
	Shilkret and Orchestra	**Victor 22004**
Birmingham Bertha	**Waters**	**Columbia 1837-D**

Blues stuff. The Ethel Waters, original screen artist, one are the best if only for that reason—and you get them both on one Columbia.

THE PAGAN

Pagan Love Song	**James Melton**	**Columbia 1853-D**
	Harold Lambert	**Brunswick 4369**
	Franklyn Baur	**Victor 21992**

Nothing very pagan about this boy. The usual waltz with the usual limitations. Plenty of sentiment but nothing like a cave-man here.

DO-RE-MI-FA-SOL!

By Maurice Fenton

PHOTOPLAY'S Tune Critic Tells You All About the New Movie Music

SOPHIE TUCKER seems to have been having some home-coming weeks. She doesn't have to go very far to celebrate one of these things, for Soph seems to be equally at home in these U. S. and London, in musical comedy, vaude, revue, the talkies or on records. For without a doubt her voice has "IT," which is proved when you listen to it over the old musical box without her inviting grin behind it. In other words, the voice with the smile of its own.

Her "Honky Tonk" numbers, recorded by Victor, are the best signs current for the continuation of this column—but more of that lower down the page. **"He's a Good Man to Have Around"** and **"I'm Doing What I'm Doing for Love"** are the more characteristic items. In the same series comes, **"I'm Feathering a Nest for a Little Bluebird."**

While on the subject of Sophie, which, after all, is quite a large one, another release of hers might as well be noted. When she chants, **"I Don't Want to Get Thin,"** we entirely agree with her and are even willing to join in the chorus. But don't expect too much for your boodle here. On the back she informs us, to a second rate tune, **"That's What I Call Sweet Music."** Sweetish, maybe, but not so hot.

FROM down near the bottom of the drawer we have dug up four Columbia records which are going to have a run before the end of the year. There never is a real back number, and Moran and Mack are due for a few extra dividends on an investment made over two years ago.

When these were first unloaded on the market the publicity department labeled them "the funniest series ever recorded." With "Why Bring That Up?" doing what it is, the **"Two Black Crows"** discs, eight sides of twelve inches, are going to be brought up again to paralyze the fans. They were made by the new electrical method, and as most of the stuff these two black faces pulled in vaudeville has been crammed into their first talkie, they are thoroughly up to date. Which proves that you might as well keep those bonds in the safe—you never know when they'll come back.

ALL the recording companies have tried kicking in on "The Dance of Life." That is, they have recorded two of the numbers and omitted the one which is any good at all.

"True Blue Lou" needs Hal Skelly and the "Pagliacci" situation to mean anything at all. Coming all by itself down the unromantic funnel of a machine, it matches the title of its companion—**"The Flippity Flop."** This other is a good, whole hearted accompaniment for a soft shoe prance, but will get on your nerves if you have not got plenty of others to play between repetitions. Seeing the picture, we got the idea that the best part of it was **"Ladies of the Dance"**—musically, at least. No one, to date, has bothered to put it on record. We should like to hear it in cold blood and see if we were right. We probably shall.

THE more Helen Kane sticks to talkie material, the better for business. This time we have **"He's So Unusual,"** from "Sweetie," and it stands out like a work of art—which, of course, it is in its own sweet way. A beau has to be something out of the ordinary to catch Helen's eye, apparently, and this sheik was that way. And behind it all is a distinctly pleasant little *too-toodleoo-too-too* melody which deserves to be heard a little better. Perhaps the pick of the bundle this time.

Perhaps the pick, because the numbers we have talked about so far are not strictly Theme Songs. In fact, if there are not some signs of bullishness in this market before long, the bottom will fall out of it. Try this trick: Hypnotize yourself into thinking you had composed some of this month's offerings yourself and then see if you feel proud. There must have been some blushing composers hiding in the shadows of projection rooms recently.

HERE are some of the incidental crop:

"How Am I To Know?" out of "Dynamite." Put out by all the recording houses in various forms, but though all the orchestras do their darndest they cannot make a silk purse out of a whateveritis. The catch in the thing is supposed to be, "Lyrics by Dorothy Parker." Not the best Dottie ever wrote by a long stretch, but still worthy of more trouble from the music department.

"After the Clouds Roll By" from "Half Marriage." The idea seems to have been that half a marriage only deserves half a tune. If so, the management have succeeded. Saxophones *doodle-doodle-doo-doo* in no particular direction but (it's a ten incher) actually do get to an end somehow.

"Waiting at the End of the Road" from "Hallelujah." Stand by for Opus Umpteen of Irving Berlin, and then doubt your ears. It was a long road that was being waited on, and the interval was extraordinarily like any other—at a couple of moments in it we thought of other tunes we had heard somewhere else.

"Lovable and Sweet" from "Street Girl." This is more like it. If you must have a theme song, and apparently you must, why not have it molded to match your theme? This one does to some extent, and consequently does not disappoint. More than that, it might actually set you dancing. Sydney Clare and Oscar Levant, who put this together, are our best bets in the business, at present.

"When They Sing the Wearin' o' the Green" from "Lucky in Love" and **"Smiling Irish Eyes"** from "Smiling Irish Eyes," are recommended as sure things. You can twist any series of Irish musical phrases into any conceivable shape and display the result as a winner—or so we are told by someone who is living on the proceeds of just such a trick. Further, these are—if nobody is getting tired of our theme—Theme Songs. They mean what they say and provide the required atmosphere for the screen story.

HOWEVER, we are not giving up all hope. Rumors from the studios have almost got us het up over what we are to hear during the next few weeks. The Theme Song business is still at its experimental stage, with everyone clinging to the back of the wagon for dear life, whether they deserve to be there or not.

SIGNING off with a complaint recently heard from a distinguished Indian moviehouse owner, who visited these hospitable shores in search of reels to show his dusky audiences.

He was in despair about the talkies and felt he was on his journey over the hill to the county farm. "My audiences are Gujerati, Hindustani, Bengali, Urdu, Telegu and Hindi. How can they understand American voices or listen to American music when they cannot understand each other?" The "American—American" part was touching from a man who is loyal to the British.

So we asked about the possibilities of his troubles being settled by the English. "Not for years, twenty-five, maybe. So far they have been unable to make pictures for themselves. What hopes for us?"

In this monthly service department Mr. Fenton will help you fill the old family record album by scouting the newest phonoplay discs

DO-RE-MI-FA-SOL!

By Maurice Fenton

PHOTOPLAY'S Tune Critic Tells You All About the New Movie Music

THE do-deo-do department is still more or less on its ear—the old cabbage being close to the ground in hopes of picking up something worth reporting.

There is little change in the market, but from rumors and gossip that have leaked out to us the better days are just around the corner —as usual. Theme Songs still persist in being top-heavy, bullish on Theme but short on the Song side. Is a picture supposed to support its music or is the yodelling designed to bolster up the picture?

We were tucked up in the corner of a plush orchestra seat the other evening watching the thrilling adventures of True Blue Somebody and having our hairs stood on end in military regularity. Just as the strain reached a pitch too strenuous to stand, a beauty-boy trotted down a flight of stairs, a hidden orchestra leaped into action and the spell was broken. Out of the darkness about us came hoarse, cutting whispers:

"Theme Song! Ugh! . . . Now for the Theme Song. . . ." etc.

Before the singer had got to the exciting part of his bit something that sounded very like snores rose to the ceiling. The tune did not do its job. It sounded as if it had been bought across the counter of a five-and-ten at the last moment.

WHICH brings us to the kick of the month about records. If a talkie number looks at all good, all the companies pounce on it and turn it out in two or three forms. You can have it as a solo played "as is." You can pick it up as a straight waltz or fox trot or whatever and use it for dancing purposes.

In this latter variety is the "vocal refrain" stunt necessary? Does a vocal refrain help a dance record, or are we right? It's all very well in a night club or a dance hall where one can see the excruciatingly funny faces of the singers and watch their comic stuff, but in the great silences of the ancestral mansion the only noticeable thing about the orchestral warblers is that they should be taking a few elementary lessons in vocal culture. The majority of the boys trying to do it for the discs this year are on the light side.

Our bet is that, even as you and I, some of the great world are due for the bump of their short lives when they get around to hearing Gloria's first records. La Swanson, incidentally, made the grand tour in connection with "The Trespasser," blazing the trail that all the stars will have to follow very shortly.

Having made the picture she skipped to Europe to be mobbed on the night of the première in London. Back again, then, to land up at Camden, N. J., to make a couple of records, both from the picture. Off, after that, to the N. B. C. Studios to broadcast the same programme on the night before Victor released the discs, and then a period of rest until Moran and Mack made way for her at the Rialto by fading off that bill.

And it seems to be worth while. The records she made stand out of the mass.

On one side or the other of the Swansoniana comes the four sides that Brunswick has been turning out by the old reliable Jolson from "Say It With Songs." Al made some of the records we bought with our first musical box in the dark ages so he knows his stuff from both sides. In consequence the old slogan about "if you liked the picture you'll go wild over these" is half the story. The bits are better than anything that happened in the picture itself.

Victor also gets a bite out of the same picture. Paul Oliver seldom, if ever, appears in public, but the odds are that through his records and broadcasting he is better known than if he did. He has made **"One Sweet Kiss"** from the Warner opus and sings it like a lark—if you have ever listened to a tenor lark you will understand what we mean. Recommended.

Class A selections close with mention of a couple of sides that we itched to hear. How would Bebe Daniels record? Now we know. She takes a couple of numbers from "Rio Rita"—**"If You're in Love You'll Waltz"** and **"You're Always in My Arms"**—and more or less twists them round her little fingers. This against difficulties.

Here are some new ones:

MARRIED IN HOLLYWOOD

Once Upon a Time
Dance Away the Night
Peasant Love Song

Our money is on No. 2. At the pace it goes it promises to be a long and not very eventful evening, but it is just enough out of the run to be worth it.

OUR MODERN MAIDENS

I've Waited a Lifetime for You

At the end of which period, one gathers, the boy is a bit too tired to do anything about it. Melodious and well accompanied.

PARIS

Miss Wonderful

Earns our *grand prix* for taking liberties with rhyme. May we bore you with some specimens?

You've got a style so beautiful,
You've got a smile so cutiful. . . .

You're just the right age,
Stay-out-at-night age,

You're a wow,
And how. . . .

I can't resist you,
Think if I kissed you,
That I would fall,
Beautiful dawl (doll for short)

We hope he got all that was coming to him. And even with those handicaps, or encouragements, the composer has plunged in and produced a fair job.

ILLUSION

When the Real Thing Comes Your Way
Revolutionary Rhythm

Look out for the composer of the second bit. He's going to do something one of these days.

SUNNY SIDE UP

Turn on the Heat
Pickin' Petals o' Daisies
If I Had a Talking Picture of You
Sunny Side Up
Aren't We All

The Daisies get our vote here. It starts as if it was really going to be something, gets half way and stays at that level, which after all is far above the present average.

GIRL FROM HAVANA

Time Will Tell

Quite right. What it will tell is another matter. Think this will last until February.

WORDS AND MUSIC

Steppin' Along

We liked this one and so did the neighbors.

HALLELUJAH

Swanee Shuffle

Probably at the head of all these extras.

And an apology to finish off. Our cracks at **"True Blue Lou"** of last month are hereby revoked. No, we haven't met the composer. Someone put it on one of those repeater gadgets and after the third playing we found that it falls into the top shelf.

The Best Music of the New Pictures

Some of the tunes that will haunt your dreams and set your feet to dancing

By
Maurice Fenton

ONE of the great ideas behind conducting a column seems to be to start an argument. Here we are with a trifling one on our hands already.

Do you prefer selections with vocal effects, or does your taste run to straight orchestras? Some of the fans asked to be warned in order that they can give the "go-by" to discs with a snatch of yodeling in the middle of them. Others asked to be notified of the same thing because that's exactly what they want.

Our own preference has been forcibly set down long since and still stands. The trick comedian of the Oowah Boys may have the knack of tying us up in knots when we watch him in the flesh, but on a record there is nothing but his voice to recommend him, and we have found that he is seldom anything in the way of a Caruso.

For those who want to know, there is not a single piece of silent picture music this time, unless you include the waltz piece from "Deja" which, strictly speaking, does not belong. It comes from a French picture, and evidently the people on this side did not have time to translate the words.

Now to the other side of the fence. Records made by the original performers always seem to have an extra kick to them. Which is the reason we open with special reference to some vocals. For instance, this time we have the two Helens (Kane and Morgan) each with a double-sider, and there is also Irene Bordoni doing her own stunt from "Show of Shows."

Helen Kane has been shot at before in this column. We have noticed, however, that whenever we grab off a bunch of discs with one of hers in it, that it invariably finds its way to the top of the pile. Just as the crowd starts slipping into overcoats and the rush for the door begins, somebody ups and says: "What about putting on Helen Kane—just once more?" That's what we regard as public opinion, and pass it along. We only hope she never grows up.

BUT the old family music box hasn't helped Helen Morgan in her phonoplay work. On the back of her **"Applause"** number is **"More Than You Know"** from **"Great Day"** which is a cut above the other, and on Victor No. 22199 you will find two songs from **"Sweet Adeline"** which make up for any other mistakes. **"Great Day"** and **"Sweet Adeline"** are legitimate stage offerings. Can it be that the talkie fare is not robust enough for her?

But Bordoni is Bordoni. If you are one of those who don't know a thing about music, but do know what you like, here's a chance to test your taste. As for us, thumbs way up.

Before moving along to the orchestras, we want to mention another disc which lays claim to being a phonoplay by-product. On one side the Happiness Boys go terribly tough and sing something they think should have been put into "The Cock Eyed World." As *Sergeants Flagg* and *Quirt* they give noisy impersonations of the boys who won the war for L. Stallings, and sum up everything in "What Price Glory" and its sequel in three verses, with incidental dialogue and sound effects. If for no other reason, this should be put into the archives to serve as a lasting souvenir of the hit of hits before the last but one, or was it the one before that?—these marvels flash by so quickly.

On the reverse side the same boys are a month or two out of date. **"I Can't Sleep in the Movies Anymore"** has not been a current complaint for at least three weeks. Even in Australia they are getting used to the surprising bass bellowings of the hitherto silent starettes.

From the orchestras, the first sign of anything startling comes from "The Great Gabbo." These two numbers, in the same strain, have much in common with the picture to which they belong—one feels they should be so much better than they are. In any case, they make A-1 dance numbers and will help to keep the family warm during the next few blizzards.

RUDY VALLÉE'S **"Vagabond Lover"** selections seem to settle the question about singing with an orchestra. If they taught him nothing else at Yale, this distinguished graduate certainly knows how to temper his vocal chords to the storm in such a way that his chanting is quite unobtrusive and yet improves the general effect. The affair about the little kiss each morning and evening is an opus of Harry Woods. There's a big place waiting for him.

"Lady Luck" from "Show of Shows," done by Ted Lewis, should command the usual respect. We also recommend the Ben Bernie disc which, besides giving **"Lady Luck"** on one side and **"Singin' in the Bathtub,"** from the same phonoplay, on the other, is an excellent specimen of the young maestro's work at its best.

Columbia does the better job with **"You're Responsible"** from "Tanned Legs." It appears that the tan was artificial after all. The trouble with the other version lies entirely with Johnny Johnson's soloist, who ought to go back to his bassoon or whatever he plays.

The rather plaintive waltz that Nat Shilkret has picked from "Deja" is out of the ordinary in that it contains a moving little change of mood in the middle. It is all very French, if you know what we mean by that, and perhaps we should blush when advising it. There's no accounting for tastes.

POINTED HEELS		
Ain'tcha I Have to Have You	Helen Kane	Victor
SHOW OF SHOWS		
Just an Hour of Love	Irene Bordoni	Columbia
Lady Luck	Ted Lewis and Orchestra	Columbia
	Dick Robertson	Brunswick
	Ben Bernie	Brunswick
Singin' in the Bathtub	Eddie Walters	Columbia
	Dick Robertson	Brunswick
	Ben Bernie	Brunswick
APPLAUSE		
What Wouldn't I Do for That Man?	Helen Morgan	Victor
	Charleston Chasers	Columbia
THE GREAT GABBO		
I'm in Love with You	Ben Selvin and Orchestra	Columbia
The Web of Love	High Hatters	Victor
THE VAGABOND LOVER		
A Little Kiss Each Morning	Hal Kemp and Orchestra	Brunswick
	Guy Lombardo and Royal Canadians	Columbia
	Rudy Vallée and Connecticut Yankees	Victor
I'll Be Reminded of You	Rudy Vallée and Connecticut Yankees	Victor
I Love You, Believe Me, I Love You	Hal Kemp and Orchestra	Brunswick
SKIN DEEP		
I Came to You	Henry Busse and Orchestra	Victor
	Oscar Grogan	Columbia
TANNED LEGS		
You're Responsible	Johnny Johnson and Statler Pennsylvanians	Victor
	Merle Johnson and Ceco Couriers	Columbia
LORD BYRON OF BROADWAY		
The Woman and the Shoe Only Love Is Real	Ben Selvin and Orchestra	Columbia
DEJA		
Love Me	Nat Shilkret	Victor
NOT CLASSIFIED		
Sergeant Flagg and Sergeant Quirt I Can't Sleep in the Movies Anymore	Happiness Boys	Victor

The Best Music of the New Pictures

Some of the tunes that will haunt your dreams and set your feet to dancing

By
Maurice Fenton

A LETTER recently addressed to this column asks: "Can you tell me what songs from 'The Love Parade' are on records? Are any of them by Maurice Chevalier?"

Before we had sat through half of the picture mentioned we had reached the conclusion that it was made of the very stuff which is our particular meat. To our best recollection it contained the following numbers, upon which the very light threads of a typical pre-war musical comedy were hung:

"My Love Parade." Presumably the Theme Song. A light and airy bit of sophistication, with words and music well balanced.

"Dream Lover." A trapeze for the soprano to exercise her vocal cords to the sentimental satisfaction of all concerned.

"Paris" and **"Nobody's Using It Now."** A couple of character bits for the leading man—more about them later.

"Let's Be Common." For the comedians (male and female). Enough in the words for a run of laughs, and enough in the music for some eccentric dancing.

Something that evidently was supposed to be the National Anthem of Sylvania, in which the soprano tried to sing against the male chorus, with disastrous results to all concerned. A number quite unworthy of the rest of the show.

With the exception of the National Anthem thing, all of it was well above the present average. Which is why we are making all this fuss about it.

As far as we can discover, only two of these numbers have been recorded. After "The Innocents of Paris," Victor turned out a Chevalier record, so there is hope that **"Nobody's Using It Now"** will yet see the light of our living room. When it does we will celebrate in a worthy manner..

TWO new versions of numbers which have been previously mentioned have turned up in the interval. One carries a couple of Rudy Vallée performances and makes us feel glad that we said something about him once before. If there must be vocal accompaniments, this is the boy to do them without annoying. But you know all about the way in which he exploits a voice which practically amounts to nothing at all, and at the same time runs a pretty snappy band.

These two are other bits from his own "Vagabond Lover," not out in time to catch last month's issue. **"I Love You, Believe Me, I Love You"** is infinitely better than its title would make one think. And the other side, **"If You Were the Only Girl,"** should be popular if only for the fact that it has been going strong for nearly fifteen years. We first heard it, with the same words, about 1915.

"The Show of Shows" repertoire also receives additions. **"Singin' in the Bath Tub"** is about as good as this month can do anywhere. Except for the first few yodels, which do not fit the music box, Frank Luther's vocal accompaniment comes across in great style. It has lots of life to it. On the back is another **"Lady Luck,"** but long since we thumbs-downed anything in this class of waltz.

THIS is the welcome of the column to Welcome Lewis, who should have been heard from before. **"Look What You've Done to Me"** from "Why Leave Home?" is more or less what the name suggests, but Miss Lewis has what is getting to be known as a Radio technique, putting all the required meaning and significance into a voice which is hardly raised above her upper lip so that it does not strain the old sound box.

"Chasing Rainbows" contained more musical sob stuff than any other picture we have seen in months. Two of the worst have been done and we have duly washed the veneer off the machine giving them a chance. **"Lucky Me—Lovable You"** sounded promising until we found that the singer did not seem to really appreciate his luck but went steadily on whining to the end. **"Love Ain't Nothin' but the Blues"** advertises itself. As "Blues"—which it claims to be, after all—it is all there, but we long to be cheered up a bit these days. But not in the way **"Happy Days Are Here Again"** tries to do it. Evidently the composers thought the other two numbers were rather tragic, so they cleared the atmosphere with a sure-fire hit based on "School Days." But that is a matter for the individual to decide.

Out of the remaining pile we have selected three other double sides as being at least average, and beg to report that in our opinion the average is slightly higher than it was two months ago. On this score we were duly tickled when Serge Rachmaninoff, returning for a concert tour, supported our ideas as expressed lately. The present state of supply is due to growing pains. Give them a little time and the tin-panners will surprise us with what they turn out.

THE NEW HITS
Right Off the Records

LOVE PARADE		
Dream Lover	Tom Gerun Nat Shilkret	Brunswick Victor
My Love Parade	Tom Gerun	Brunswick
SNAP INTO IT		
Lonesome Little Doll	Al Goodman Nat Shilkret	Brunswick Victor
VAGABOND LOVER		
I Love You, Believe Me, I Love You	Rudy Vallée	Victor
If You Were the Only Girl	Rudy Vallée	Victor
SHOW OF SHOWS		
Singin' in the Bath Tub	High Hatters	Victor
Lady Luck	High Hatters	Victor
DEVIL MAY CARE		
Shepherd's Serenade	Abe Lyman	Brunswick
If He Cared	Abe Lyman	Brunswick
CHASING RAINBOWS		
Lucky Me—	Leo Reisman	Victor
Lovable You	Abe Lyman	Brunswick
Happy Days Are Here Again	Leo Reisman	Victor
Love Ain't Nothin' but the Blues	Abe Lyman	Brunswick
WHY LEAVE HOME?		
Look What You've Done to Me	Welcome Lewis	Victor
SONG OF THE WEST		
West Wind	Ben Bernie	Brunswick
The One Girl	Ben Bernie	Brunswick
SALLY		
Sally	Wayne King	Victoı
If I'm Dreaming	Wayne King	Victor

As far as Rudy Vallée's new music in "The Vagabond Lover" is concerned, latest reports prove that it has furnished the blond crooner one enormous hit—**"A Little Kiss Each Morning, A Little Kiss Each Night."**

All the dance bands are playing it, the air is full of it, it wails from every stage. Three tunes have made and kept the boy noted. **"Deep Night"** brought him to fortune, **"I'm Just a Vagabond Lover"** held him there, and now **"A Little Kiss"** will increase his pull with the sentimental.

The Best Records from New Pictures

By Maurice Fenton

THE BEST SELLERS

"A Little Kiss Each Morning" from "The Vagabond Lover." "Singin' in the Bathtub" from the "Show of Shows." "If I Had a Talking Picture of You" from "Sunny Side Up."

AS this is tapped off, New York is 100 per cent agog over Lawrence Tibbett's singing in "The Rogue Song."

The great Metropolitan Opera baritone, destined to be one of pictures' outstanding stars, sings the familiar music from Lehar's "Gypsy Love," plus a sentimental interpolated number by Herbert Stothart.

Six records from this picture are on the stands.

The White Dove	**Lawrence Tibbett**	**Victor**
When I'm Looking at You	**Lawrence Tibbett**	**Victor**
Narrative	**Lawrence Tibbett**	**Victor**
The Rogue Song	**Lawrence Tibbett**	**Victor**
The Rogue Song	**Shilkret Orchestra**	**Victor**
The Rogue Song	**Columbia Photo Players**	**Columbia**

Get the Tibbett records! They're marvelous!

DEVIL MAY CARE

Charming	**Frank Munn**	**Brunswick**
	Ben Selvin	**Columbia**
	Leo Reisman	**Victor**
Shepherd's Serenade	**Ben Selvin**	**Columbia**
	Leo Reisman	**Victor**
	Frank Munn	**Brunswick**
March of the Old Guard	**Frank Munn**	**Brunswick**

The music from the Ramon Novarro picture is pretty thin stuff. "Charming" is a nice enough piece, but ordinary.

SWEETIE

Alma Mammy	**Waring's Pennsylvanians**	**Victor**
My Sweeter Than Sweet	**The Ipana Troubadours**	**Columbia**

These two numbers from "Sweetie" are both aces. "Alma Mammy," which Jack Oakie warbled on the screen, is dazzlingly played by the excellent Waring boys from Tyrone, Pa. As for "My Sweeter Than Sweet," it is now a best-seller, and Rudy Vallée breathes it on the radio as one of his best numbers. This recording is good. It is probable that Vallée will get it on a disc, and then watch out!

IT'S A GREAT LIFE

Hoosier Hop	**The Duncan Sisters**	**Victor**
I'm Following You	**The Duncan Sisters**	**Victor**

One of the prize discs. The Duncans, stars of this picture, record two of its hits for Victor in fine, harmonizing style. A good buy for any album.

THE LOVE PARADE

Nobody's Using It Now	**Marion Harris**	**Brunswick**
March of the Grenadiers	**Jeanette MacDonald**	**Victor**

The excellent and foot-teasing tunes from the uproarious Maurice Chevalier phonoplay strike the wax far too slowly.

Marion Harris, one of the best of the "hot" singers, does the Chevalier ace number well, but it's essentially a piece for a man. The leading lady of the film, the fair Jeanette, does well by the stirring march song, but it's nothing to get goose-flesh over.

The companies still overlook a bet in "Let's Be Common."

HALLELUJAH

Waiting at the End of the Road	**Paul Whiteman**	**Columbia**
	The Revellers	**Victor**

This fine song, sung so beautifully by Daniel Haynes in the King Vidor picture, is a real winner. And we have two exceptional recordings of it. Whiteman's band gives it all stops and shadings, while the close-harmony Revellers give it superlative treatment on the Victor platter.

UNTAMED

Chant of the Jungle	**The Revellers**	**Victor**
	Paul Specht	**Columbia**

Joan Crawford's stirring number from the picture "Untamed" has both vocal and instrumental hearings here. The Revellers bear down in their accustomed manner, while Maestro Paul Specht turns his band loose on it with good results.

SONG OF LOVE

I'll Still Go on Wanting You	**Welcome Lewis**	**Victor**
	James Melton	**Columbia**

This is a sentimental ballad from Belle Baker's Columbia picture. Welcome Lewis is really welcome. She is a lady who puts just the right number of tears into such a thing. The Melton boy is a melting tenor.

The Best Records *from* New Pictures

By Maurice Fenton

Dennis King, whose recording of "The Vagabond King" music is reviewed here this month

DENNIS KING'S singing in "The Vagabond King," Paramount's big all-Technicolor operetta, is interesting the screen fans and the record-players just now.

These are the new "Vagabond King" discs available—

If I Were King	**Dennis King**	**Victor**
Only a Rose	**Richard Crooks**	**Victor**

On the other side of the first, King sings "Nichavo," from "Paramount on Parade." The Crooks record is excellent. He is a tenor.

However, if you want some good "Vagabond King" recording, have your dealer dig out a double-faced record made by Victor several years ago, when the operetta was the stage rage.

On one side, Dennis King and chorus sing "The Song of the Vagabonds," on the other Carolyn Thomson, of the stage production, sings "Only a Rose." A big seventy-five cents' worth—if you can get it.

THE LOVE PARADE

Paris, Stay the Same		
You've Got That Thing (from "Fifty Million Frenchmen")		
Nobody's Using It Now	**Maurice Chevalier**	
My Love Parade	**Maurice Chevalier**	**Victor**

At last the magnetic Chevalier hits the wax—four times, and hard. These records are well worth your time and money.

SPRING IS HERE

Have a Little Faith in Me	**Waring's Pennsylvanians**	**Victor**
	Lombardo's Canadians	**Columbia**
Cryin' for the Carolines	**Waring's Pennsylvanians**	**Victor**
	Ruth Etting (vocal)	**Columbia**

Good, light numbers, particularly "Cryin' for the Carolines," which is one of the biggest hits of the spring.

PUTTIN' ON THE RITZ

Singing a Vagabond Song	**Irving Kaufman (vocal)**	**Columbia**
	Shilkret's Orchestra	**Victor**
With You	**Johnny Marvin (vocal)**	**Victor**
	Lombardo's Canadians	**Columbia**
There's Danger in Your Eyes, Cherie	**Irving Kaufman (vocal)**	**Columbia**
	Lombardo's Canadians	**Victor**

These are grand pieces by Irving Berlin for the first talkie to star Harry Richman, who will no doubt get around to recording his own music soon. One of the best numbers, "Puttin' on the Ritz," is not yet represented.

SONG OF THE WEST

The One Girl	**John Boles**	**Victor**
West Wind	**John Boles**	**Victor**

This is John Boles' first record of his movie music, and the fans will hop to it! His tenor records well, and he'll do better when he gets used to the wax. The numbers are from his latest screen operetta. The first, particularly, is a beauty.

BE YOURSELF

When a Woman Loves a Man	**Fanny Brice**	
Cooking Breakfast for the One I Love	**Fanny Brice**	

Fanny, the great comedienne, is certainly welcome back to the records. These two excellent numbers are from her latest United Artists picture, and are sung as only she can sing them.

POINTED HEELS

I Have to Have You	**Helen Kane**	**Victor**
	Sunshine Boys	**Columbia**
Ain'tcha	**Helen Kane**	**Victor**

The Boop-a-doop girl again, doing two songs from her latest Paramount singie. If you are a Kane addict you will need this for your album.

LOVE COMES ALONG

Until Love Comes Along	**Nat Shilkret's Band**	**Victor**
	Lee Morse and Band	**Columbia**

This is the hit number from the latest Bebe Daniels picture. The Victor platter has Shilkret's well known band, while Miss Lee Morse croons the other, accompanied by her Blue Grass Boys. A Victor Herbertian waltz.

HIT THE DECK

Keepin' Myself for You	**Paul Specht's Band**	**Columbia**
	Belle Mann and Hi-Hatters	**Victor**

This is one of the numbers interpolated into the Youmans' score of "Hit the Deck," filmed by Radio with Jack Oakie featured. Both are dance records, with Belle Mann recording a patter refrain on the Victor disc.

JUN. 1930

The Best Records from New Pictures

By Maurice Fenton

John McCormack Records Four Songs

THE BEST SELLERS

"The One Girl," from "Song of the West." "Cryin' for the Carolines," from "Spring Is Here." "Nobody's Sweetheart," from "The Vagabond Lover."

THE big news of this month is that John McCormack has newly recorded, on Victor Red Seal records, four of his numbers in "Song o' My Heart." They are:

The Rose of Tralee
Ireland, Mother Ireland
I Feel You Near Me
A Pair of Blue Eyes

The four numbers are on two double-faced discs. They are as good as any records John has ever made, and Victor has a tremendous list of them, exclusively.

LOVE COMES ALONG

Until Love Comes Along	**Bebe Daniels**	**Victor**
	Lee Morse and her Blue Grass Boys	
Night Winds	**Bebe Daniels**	**Victor**

Bebe is getting better, disc by disc. These two numbers from her musical picture are beautifully sung.

MAMMY

To My Mammy	**Gene Austin, tenor**	**Victor**
Let Me Sing, I'm Happy	**Gene Austin, tenor**	**Victor**
	Waring's Pennsylvanians	**Victor**
Looking at You	**Gene Austin, tenor**	**Victor**
	Waring's Pennsylvanians	**Victor**

While we are waiting for Al Jolson to put his latest movie music on the wax, these numbers, sung by Gene Austin and played by Fred Waring's band, will do nicely.

They are all Irving Berlin's songs, from the score of Al's latest singie, and are all in the old master's best popular manner. And that's plenty good.

PARAMOUNT ON PARADE

Sweepin' the Clouds Away	**Coon-Sanders Orchestra**	**Victor**
	The Photoplayers	**Columbia**
Anytime's the Time to Fall in Love	**Phil Spitalny's Orchestra**	**Victor**

Last month we told of the arrival of a Dennis King record of "Nichavo," one of the songs from the big Paramount revue.

Here are two more hits therefrom, done by dance bands. Phil's effort is particularly fine, he having a smart band and being a smart boy. More records from "Paramount on Parade," one of the Spring's really big pictures, are on the way.

HONEY

In My Little Hope Chest	**High Hatters**	**Victor**
	Photoplayers	**Columbia**
Sing, You Singers	**Photoplayers**	**Columbia**
	Charleston Chasers	**Columbia**

Two of the frothy, light numbers from Nancy Carroll's latest picture—"Sweetie's" successor. The first is a ballad—the second, a chorus piece. The Columbia Photoplayers get better with each record.

PUTTIN' ON THE RITZ

Puttin' on the Ritz	**All by Brunswick**
There's Danger in Your Eyes, Cherie	
Singing a Vagabond Song	
With You	

Well, here you are—Harry Richman himself singing the hit songs of his United Artists picture for the wax.

Richman sings mighty well. And you'll be interested in hearing Clara Bow's boy-friend (ex?) singing the numbers he does on the screen. Burtnett's band accompanies him.

HOT FOR PARIS

Sweet Nothings of Love	**Merle Johnson and his Columbia Ceco Couriers**

A piping hot number played with the lid off by Johnson and his blistering band. Hot like the McLaglen talkie.

THE GRAND PARADE

Molly	**Charles Lawman, tenor**	**Columbia**
	Ipana Troubadours, band	**Columbia**
	Huntley's Orchestra	**Brunswick**

A nice Irish number, in waltz time. A smooth, easy and pretty piece, getting very popular. From Pathe's minstrel picture.

The Best Records *from* New Pictures

By Maurice Fenton

Buddy Rogers Sings for the Records!

A DISC of the month that is bound to attract picture fans is Buddy Rogers' own recording of "Any Time's The Time to Fall in Love," his song hit sung with Lillian Roth in "Paramount on Parade." On the other side he sings the Chevalier flash finale song.

Beside the Rogers record, a slew of other excellent numbers from that picture have hit the wax, including two by the great Chevalier. The "Paramount on Parade" list follows:

Any Time's The Time to Fall in Love	**Buddy Rogers**	**Columbia**
Up On Top of a Rainbow	**Maurice Chevalier**	**Victor**
	Colonial Club Orchestra	**Brunswick**
	Buddy Rogers	**Columbia**
All I Want is Just One	**Maurice Chevalier**	**Victor**
	Gus Arnheim Orchestra	**Victor**
Dancing to Save Your Sole	**Gus Arnheim Orchestra**	**Victor**

KING OF JAZZ

Paul Whiteman and his famous band, stars of this glamorous Universal revue, play all six of the numbers here listed, in addition to recordings by the others mentioned. The "King" lineup—

Bench in the Park	**By Whiteman only.**	**All Whiteman records are by Columbia**
Ragamuffin Romeo		
I Like to Do Things for You	**Reisman's Orchestra**	**Victor**
	Grace Hayes	**Victor**
It Happened in Monterey	**Lambert's Orchestra**	**Brunswick**
	Olsen's Orchestra	**Victor**
Song of the Dawn	**Olsen's Orchestra**	**Victor**
Happy Feet	**Reisman's Orchestra**	**Victor**

CAPTAIN OF THE GUARD

Here's a John Boles record for you that's the best yet. This fine screen tenor improves his recording month by month.

You, You Alone For You	**John Boles**	**Victor**

MONTANA MOON

The Joan Crawford starring picture gives forth two tunes. "The Moon is Low," likely hit, is particularly well sung by Cliff "Ukulele Ike" Edwards.

The Moon is Low	**Ukulele Ike, vocal**	**Columbia**
	Frank Luther, vocal	**Victor**
	Olsen's Orchestra	**Victor**
Montana Call	**Olsen's Orchestra**	**Victor**

FOR JOLSON FANS

Here's a treat for those of you who go for Al's records. He sings the six numbers here listed—all for Brunswick. Most of the numbers are Irving Berlin hits from Jolson's latest, "Mammy." Other recordings are listed here. But remember that Jolson also does the lot on Brunswick wax, accompanied by Abe Lyman's fine band.

Let Me Sing and I'm Happy	**Selvin's Orchestra**	**Columbia**
	Waring's Orchestra	**Victor**
	Gene Austin, tenor	**Victor**
	Ruth Etting	**Columbia**
Across the Breakfast Table	**Selvin's Orchestra**	**Columbia**
	Waring's Orchestra	**Victor**
	Irving Kaufman, vocal	**Columbia**
To My Mammy	**Gene Austin, tenor**	**Victor**
	Irving Kaufman	**Columbia**
Dirty Hands, Dirty Face	**only by Jolson**	**Brunswick**
My Mammy		

FROM HOLD EVERYTHING

When the Little Red Roses Get the Blues for You	**Al Jolson**	**Brunswick**

THE CUCKOOS

The Bert Wheeler-Bobby Woolsey farce lets forth its first record. Bound to be more. These two are fox trots.

I Love You So Much	**Ohman-Arden and Orchestra**	**Victor**
Dancing the Devil Away		

The Best Records from New Pictures

By

Maurice Fenton

The Best Sellers of the Month: "It Happened in Monterey," from "The King of Jazz," "Sweepin' the Clouds Away," from "Paramount on Parade," and "The Moon is Low," from "Montana Moon."

HELEN KANE fans will be glad to know that the pouting baby singer has crashed through with another double-faced record for their delight.

Both songs are from Helen's new picture—

DANGEROUS NAN McGREW

Dangerous Nan McGrew	Helen Kane	Victor
I Owe You	Helen Kane	Victor

Those who like to hear Buddy Rogers' young voice give off a song or so—and those who are just Rogers crushes and like a record of his for company—can get two new ones.

This time America's Boy Friend records two of his songs from the picture—

SAFETY IN NUMBERS

I'd Like to Be (A Bee in Your Boudoir)	Buddy Rogers	Columbia
My Future Just Passed	Buddy Rogers	Columbia

THAT "HONEY" SONG

Two new recordings have been made of "Sing, You Sinners," that sensationally effective spiritual that Lillian Roth gave off in "Honey."

The records are

Sing, You Sinners	The Revellers	Victor
	Belle Baker	Columbia

The Revellers' recording is especially fine.

THE KING OF JAZZ

It Happened in Monterey	Jesse Crawford Organ	Victor
	Regent Club Orchestra	Brunswick
Song of the Dawn	Burnett's Biltmore Orchestra	Brunswick
Ragamuffin Romeo	Paul Whiteman and Band	Columbia
I Like to Do Things for You	Paul Whiteman and Band	Columbia

Here are some excellent recordings from the Whiteman-Universal picture. Particularly those by the old master himself—who begins where all other modern bandmasters leave off in the matter of arrangements.

UNDER A TEXAS MOON

Under a Texas Moon	Gene Austin (vocal)	Victor
	Nawahi's Hawaiians	Columbia

This record marks the first use of Hawaiian instruments in recording motion picture music as we know it at present—via the talkies.

Helen Kane Records Two More!

And it's very effective. The number, of course, is the very sweet piece used all the way through Frank Fay's first starring picture.

THE BIG POND

You Brought a New Kind of Love to Me	Ben Bernie's Band	Brunswick
	The High Hatters	Victor
	Belle Baker (Vocal)	Brunswick
	Paul Whiteman's Band	Columbia
Livin' in the Sunlight	Ben Bernie's Band	Brunswick
Lovin' in the Moonlight	Paul Whiteman's Band	Columbia
	Bernie Cummins' New Yorker Orchestra	Victor

How the companies rush to get the Maurice Chevalier song hits on the wax! They just can't wait. All these recordings are orchestral fox trots with the exception of Belle Baker's warbling. Maurice's recordings will probably be along by next month.

IN GAY MADRID

Into My Heart	Nat Shilkret's Orchestra	Victor
	Paul Specht's Orchestra	Columbia
Santiago	Paul Specht's Orchestra	Columbia
Dark Night	Nat Shilkret's Orchestra	Victor

The boys hop right after Ramon Novarro numbers, too. They remember the enormous success of "Pagan Love Song," one of the great early theme song hits.

These three are from the latest Novarro romance, played by two big-league recording bands. Maybe Ramon will sing for us soon.

The Best Records *from* New Pictures

By Maurice Fenton

THE recording companies who go heavily for picture hits and picture voices have fallen down on us this month.

They've given us a thin list. The one number, as we arpeggio to press, which has given the most satisfaction among the new group is another John McCormack recording of the "Song o' My Heart" batch.

This is the famous "Little Boy Blue" song, based on Eugene Field's everlasting little lyric. It has been recorded before in the pre-electrical days, but in the new recording it has been tremendously popular, and I recommend this as one of the most touching of the new discs.

However, I am going to step away from pictures for a second to present one record made by a lad who made but one full-length movie, and yet is being talked about and listened to by picture fans everywhere.

That, of course, is Rudy Vallée. The titles are pretty hard to take, and the songs themselves are not too hot, but for the thousands who like the crooner they are acceptable.

Here's the record—

A Song Without A Name	**Rudy Vallée**	**Victor**
My Heart Belongs to the Girl Whose Heart Belongs to Somebody Else	**Rudy Vallée**	**Victor**

SWING HIGH

With My Guitar and You	**Ben Selvin's Orchestra**	**Columbia**
	Don Azpiazu's Havana Orchestra	**Victor**
There's Happiness Over the Hill	**George Olsen's Music**	**Victor**
Shoo the Hoodoo Away	**George Olsen's Music**	**Victor**

Some of the gay numbers from this big Pathe circus picture here make their appearance. Let me recommend the Cuban boys' recording as being of particular interest. Full of dash, and an unusually smart arrangement. Watch for more from this singie! Its songs are its best bet.

FROM here on, owing to the lassitude of the recorders, I am going to list some songs from well-known current films, in their new recordings. They require little or no comment. If you liked a song in a certain picture, you may find a record of it here.

FLORODORA GIRL

My Kind of Man	**Ethel Waters**	**Columbia**

You know Ethel Waters' brand of hot singing if you're a record fan. This is it. 'Nuff sed.

CHEER UP AND SMILE

Where Can You Be?	**Jack Smith**	**Victor**
You May Not Like It	**Jack Smith**	**Victor**

He Records Two New Songs

"The Whispering Baritone" is back on the wax after a long absence, this time in a Fox picture. The vaudeville and movie house and record favorite is still whispering in his famous confidential style. He doesn't accompany himself any more, but bears down on his whispering.

As you remember, this fellow was a recording sensation five years ago.

He's still there, using numbers from his film début.

MOVIETONE FOLLIES OF 1930

Here Comes Emily Brown	**Charleston Chasers**	**Columbia**

GOOD NEWS

If You're Not Kissing Me	**Nat Shilkret's Orchestra**	**Victor**

Shilkret is at his best in a number from this musical hit, and Shilkret's best is plenty good.

QUEEN HIGH

Seems to Me	**Lee Morse**	**Columbia**

This Paramount picture gives this number, with Lee, the famous girl crooner, bearing down.

HIGH SOCIETY BLUES

I'm In the Market for You	**Johnny Marvin, tenor**	**Victor**
	Haring's Orchestra	**Brunswick**
Just Like a Story Book	**Haring's Orchestra**	**Brunswick**

If you liked the Farrell-Gaynor film, you'll like these.

The Best Records *from* New Pictures

By

Maurice Fenton

THOSE of you who saw and heard "Song of the Flame" know that Noah Beery sings a far meaner and deeper bass than many a basso who devotes himself exclusively to warbling for a living.

So successful was Father Noah's singing in that picture that he has recorded two songs on Brunswick wax.

They are the "One Little Drink" number from the above-mentioned operetta, and "The Whip," from "Golden Dawn," another First National singie.

"Dixiana," Bebe Daniels' new Radio Picture, comes to the records in a large way.

Everett Marshall, her leading man, sings two of his own songs from the film. They are "Goodbye, Old Pals," and "Mr. and Mrs. Sippi." Nat Shilkret and his Victor Orchestra record the latter, and on the other side is a "Dixiana" fox-trot made up of themes from the whole Harry Tierney score. These are all Victors.

One of the month's very best sellers comes in three forms.

It is "Singing a Song to the Stars," from "Way Out West," which is Willie Haines' new picture.

Lewis James tenors it for Victor. "Ukelele Ike" Edwards ukes and sings it for Columbia. Earl Burtnett's Los Angeles Biltmore Orchestra plays it for dancing.

These recorders can smell a hit afar off. This is one.

And then there's Helen Kane.

This month she does two on a record for Victor. They are "I've Got It," from "Young Man of Manhattan," and "My Man Is on the Make" from "Heads Up."

Aileen Stanley, that ace of stage and record singers, has put "I Love You So Much" on wax, with a Victor label.

It's the hit song from "The Cuckoos."

The California Ramblers also record it as a dance number under the Columbia brand.

J. Harold Murray, the operetta singer working for Fox films, sings two of his songs from "Women Everywhere" for the records.

They are "Smile, Legionnaire" and "Beware of Love."

Now follows a list of general picture music. Reach in and take your pick!

LET'S GO NATIVE

I've Gotta Yen for You	**Gus Arnheim's Orchestra**	**Victor**
It Must Be Spring	**Waring's Pennsylvanians**	**Victor**

CALL OF THE FLESH

Lonely	**Ben Selvin's Orchestra**	**Columbia**

Noah Beery Records His Bass Songs!

IN GAY MADRID

Dark Night	**Roger Wolfe Kahn's Orchestra**	**Brunswick**
Into My Heart	**Roger Wolfe Kahn's Orchestra**	**Brunswick**

GOOD NEWS

If You're Not Kissing Me	**Nat Shilkret's Orchestra**	**Victor**

THE SEA BAT

Lo-Lo	**Green Brothers Marimba Band**	**Victor**
	Ben Selvin's Orchestra	**Columbia**

SUNNY SKIES

You for Me	**The High Hatters**	**Victor**
	Tom Cline's Music	**Brunswick**
Must Be Love	**Eddie Walters (vocal)**	**Columbia**

DANCING SWEETIES

The Kiss Waltz	**Ben Bernie's Orchestra**	**Brunswick**

BRIGHT LIGHTS

Nobody Cares If I'm Blue	**Miss Lee Morse (vocal)**	**Columbia**
	Marion Harris	**Brunswick**

Two of filmland's favorite warblers are represented this month by two new double-faced discs. Both the boys have been toilers in the Metro-Goldwyn vineyard. The singers and their songs are:

CHARLES KING

Leave a Little Smile	**Brunswick**
Here Comes the Sun	**Brunswick**

CLIFF "UKELELE IKE" EDWARDS

Sing a Song to the Stars	**Columbia**
Sing a Pretty Little Thing	**Columbia**

INDEX OF FILMS

WHEN A PAGE NUMBER is followed by an R, the review of the film will be found on that page (many of the reviews are accompanied by stills). When a page number is followed by an A, an advertisement for the film will be found on that page. When a page number is followed by an asterisk, there is a still or production shot on that page. When a page number is printed in *italics,* there is a major article about the film on that page. All errors in the original material, typographical or otherwise, that have come to our attention have been tacitly corrected in this index.

WHEN A PAGE NUMBER is followed by an asterisk, there is a picture of the performer on that page. When a page number is printed in *italics* there is a major article about the performer on that page (always accompanied by a portrait). All errors in the original material, typographical or otherwise, that have come to our attention have been tacitly corrected in this index.